D0072752

DISCARDED

PRUITT CAMPUS LIBRARY
Indian River State College

DISCARDED

RETHINKING MANAGEMENT
INFORMATION SYSTEMS

RETHINKING MANAGEMENT INFORMATION SYSTEMS

An Interdisciplinary Perspective

edited by

WENDY CURRIE AND BOB GALLIERS

OXFORD
UNIVERSITY PRESS

Oxford University Press, Great Clarendon Street, Oxford OX2 6DP

Oxford New York

Athens Auckland Bangkok Bogotá Buenos Aires Calcutta
Cape Town Chennai Dar es Salaam Delhi Florence Hong Kong Istanbul
Karachi Kuala Lumpur Madrid Melbourne Mexico City Mumbai
Nairobi Paris São Paulo Singapore Taipei Tokyo Toronto Warsaw

and associated companies in Berlin Ibadan

Oxford is a registered trade mark of Oxford University Press

Published in the United States
by Oxford University Press Inc., New York

© the various contributors 1999

The moral rights of the authors have been asserted

First published 1999

All rights reserved. No part of this publication may be reproduced,
stored in a retrieval system, or transmitted, in any form or by any means,
without the prior permission in writing of Oxford University Press.
Within the UK, exceptions are allowed in respect of any fair dealing for the
purpose of research or private study, or criticism or review, as permitted
under the Copyright, Designs and Patents Act 1988, or in the case of
reprographic reproduction in accordance with the terms of the licences
issued by the Copyright Licensing Agency. Enquiries concerning
reproduction outside these terms and in other countries should be
sent to the Rights Department, Oxford University Press,
at the address above

This book is sold subject to the condition that it shall not, by way
of trade or otherwise, be lent, re-sold, hired out or otherwise circulated
without the publisher's prior consent in any form of binding or cover
other than that in which it is published and without a similar condition
including this condition being imposed on the subsequent purchaser

British Library Cataloguing in Publication Data

Data available

Library of Congress Cataloguing in Publication Data
Rethinking management information systems : an interdisciplinary
perspective / edited by Wendy Currie and Bob Galliers.
p. cm.
Includes bibliographical references and index.
1. Management information systems. I. Currie, Wendy, 1960– .
II. Galliers, Robert, 1947– .
HD30.213.R47 1998
658.4'038'011—dc21   98-44182

ISBN 0-19-877533-4 (Hbk)
ISBN 0-19-877532-6 (Pbk)

1 3 5 7 9 10 8 6 4 2

Typeset in 10/12 pt Baskerville
by Graphicraft Limited, Hong Kong
Printed in Great Britain
on acid-free paper by Bookcraft Ltd,
Midsomer Norton, Somerset

PREFACE

OVER the last few decades a number of books and articles have been published which debate a range of issues principally concerned with management information systems and technology (IS/IT).[1] Important themes arising from this literature are strategy formulation and implementation, project management methodologies and techniques, performance measurement and benchmarking, developing capabilities and skills, managing networks, outsourcing, IT-enabled business process re-engineering (BPR), cross-cultural comparisons, the management of knowledge workers, and the organisational and human impacts of managing change. Within the business and management area, broadly conceived, much of the literature on the above themes is classified under the subject areas of accounting and finance, management science, organisational analysis/behaviour (OA/OB), human resource management (HRM), strategic management/corporate strategy, and international business. The subjects management information systems (MIS), information management (IM), and information systems (IS) are often viewed by many business and management schools and departments as outside the mainstream of *core subjects* and are therefore treated as subareas or subdisciplines.

So what exactly are MIS, IM, and IS,[2] and should they be treated as one or even three distinct areas within business and management education? The interpretations and meanings attached to these three subject areas vary widely within the international academic and business communities overall. This is probably because of the relative 'newness' of the subject matter in each area. Since there are few coherent definitions available about the nature and scope of MIS, IM, and IS, respectively, there continues to be much disagreement and confusion among observers of and practitioners and researchers in this topic area. If we consider a narrow definition of the three areas, it would appear that the soft (behavioural) issues become somewhat eclipsed by the hard (technical) aspects. First, the acronym MIS

[1] Although many writers do not make a distinction between the areas of management information systems (MIS) and the management *of* IS/IT, the literature may be divided into harder and softer perspectives. The 'harder' MIS literature is usually located within computer sciences in the subject areas of information systems, information technology, database management, and programming. The 'softer' management *of* IS/IT literature is found within the subject areas of managing innovation, technology management, management of change, information management, quality management, corporate strategy, organisation behaviour, accounting and finance, and human resource management. In recent years, the harder and softer approaches have become more integrated, particularly with the development and expansion of the business and management schools internationally.

[2] Alongside the terms MIS, IM, and IS, there are others such as strategic information systems (SIS), strategic management information systems (SMIS), and strategic information management (SIM). At present, there is no consensus among the academic community about the definitions of all these terms.

would suggest that the subject matter focuses on information systems rather than behavioural (managerial) issues. In other words, the information systems used by, or on behalf of, management. Second, IM suggests that it is concerned with the management *of* information. Once again, this would suggest that the focus is more on information than on (behavioural) managerial issues. Third, IS is a *catch-all* term and may imply that the focus is on the hardware of technology and not on the behavioural or people issues. To this end, MIS, IM, and IS attract many different interpretations based upon a manipulation of the words *management, information,* and *systems.*

In reviewing the literature in these areas, it would appear that the earlier (pre-1990) work tended to emphasise the harder side of the subject. More recently, however, there has been a definite shift towards the softer, behavioural aspects. This is largely because of the growing interest within business schools in understanding the *management* of information systems. In this context, an overview of the MIS, IM, and IS *literature*[3] shows it is polarised into two, often conflicting, approaches which serve the interests of two audiences—practitioners and academics. To begin with, there is the prescriptive, consultancy-based literature which tends to offer 'quickfix' panaceas to organisations. This work is largely practitioner focused and seeks practical solutions to resolve a host of IS/IT-related problems (e.g. lack of alignment between corporate and IS strategy; poor project management; computer failures; worker resistance to new technology; business process re-engineering, etc.). These offerings are frequently criticised for their glib and over-simple interpretation of inherently complex systemic, processual, and political conditions within organisations. However, within business and management education *per se,* this work has largely been of interest to students on MBA and other post-experience courses and to practitioners in general.

At the other end of the spectrum there is the theoretical and interpretative literature which addresses many of the criticisms levelled at the former approach, yet frequently fails to demonstrate any *relevance* in a practical organisational and managerial context. To some extent, many of the more academic (scholarly) and theoretical contributions from MIS, IM, and IS are derivative of research work arising from other (more established) areas within business and management (i.e. accounting, corporate strategy, organisational behaviour, and HRM) and from the so-called *reference disciplines* (i.e. economics, sociology, philosophy, history). This is both an advantage and a disadvantage for MIS, IM, and IS. It is an advantage because academics working within departments or using these titles can demonstrate that the historical and contemporary issues and debates in this area are

---

[3] The editors recognise the inherent problems in defining MIS, IM, and IS literature. Suffice to say that there is now a whole range of books and journals, many of which are written by academics from business and management, computer science, information and library studies, etc., which use these subject classifications.

interdisciplinary, multifaceted, complex, and relevant as a research and teaching area in its own right. Indeed, the development and diffusion of new technology has been described as a 'revolution' within society and there are now thousands of books and articles on the subject.

Yet it is a disadvantage in that other *quasi-disciplines* within business and management equally lay claim to much of the subject matter of MIS, IM, and IS. It has therefore become increasingly difficult for MIS, IM, and IS to become established as a mainstream area or distinctive body of knowledge within business and management education. Moreover, academics who describe their research and teaching as falling within the area of MIS, IM, and IS may find themselves competitively disadvantaged in their own institutions compared with their colleagues from other, more established subject areas. There is some evidence of this as management science has often been disbanded or incorporated into other subject areas within business and management schools and departments.

This raises two important questions. Does the treatment of MIS, IM, and IS as subareas or subdisciplines within business and management matter? and, what is the future of MIS, IM, and IS as important research and teaching areas in business and management schools internationally? The first question is provocative and is likely to generate much disagreement and debate given that research and teaching under the subject classifications of MIS, IM, and IS is established unevenly throughout universities, colleges, and schools worldwide. Whereas some institutions have departments in the name of one or more of these areas, others do not recognise them as distinctive fields of investigation and so incorporate these subareas or subdisciplines into others. This is perhaps unsurprising when we consider that the research offerings on the management of information systems originate from other fields,[4] thus blurring the intellectual and subject boundaries within business and management. This is not simply an issue for MIS, IM, and IS, but for *all subject areas* in the business and management fields. So perhaps the question is not whether these subareas or subdisciplines should be brought into the mainstream of business and management, but whether the subject boundaries which have been built up over time should be dismantled altogether. Subjects could then be delineated according to designated research themes. This issue has been, and continues to be, debated in many business and management departments in all regions of the Western world. But while a change in the way research and teaching is classified may be attractive from an intellectual position, there are, undoubtedly, many vested political and practical interests which are likely to prevent this from happening.

---

[4] Since MIS, IM, and IS are relatively *new* subjects within business and management, much of the research and teaching has hitherto come under other headings (see n. 1). However, much of the subject matter has its roots in economics, sociology, philosophy, psychology, and history.

At one level, the delineation of business and management into distinct subject classifications (or *disciplines* as some would describe them) is likely to stifle creativity and innovation in research by imposing intellectual and practical constraints. For example, should research into IS/IT strategy formulation fall within the domain of corporate strategy, organisational behaviour, accounting and finance, human resources, or all or none of these areas? Or should it be a subject in its own right which is distinct from others within business and management? It is certainly the case that academics embarking upon rigorous research into MIS will soon find that important issues and debates from the wider business and management field are also relevant. The same may be said for all other serious research enquiry. To this end, the issue of whether MIS, IM, and IS should be treated as a mainstream (core) discipline or as a subarea/subdiscipline within business and management becomes somewhat irrelevant and *academic!* But the same may be equally true for other subjects in our domain.

The answer to the question posed about the future of MIS, IM, and IS is therefore displaced in the light of the above discussion. At the present time, these subjects are not, by and large, fully integrated as *core disciplines* within business and management in quite the same way as those of corporate strategy and HRM, for example. However, the body of literature which has developed over time on issues relating to management information systems suggests that it is indeed central to mainstream business and management.

The rationale for this book originated from a discussion between the editors about the future of the related areas of MIS, IM, and IS within business and management education. Recognising that the subject is interdisciplinary and is highly relevant for understanding historical and contemporary organisational change involving information systems (i.e. process innovation, the networked organisation, re-engineering, electronic commerce, emerging markets, the Internet, competitive benchmarking of IS/IT, and many other areas), questions arose about the status and position of other business and management subjects in relation to MIS, IM, and IS. In conjunction, many of these questions were being posed by the recently formed UK Academy for Information Systems (UKAIS)[5] which stressed that, 'In order to try to obtain appropriate recognition for our subject in the Research Assessment Exercise (RAE),[6] we attempted to define the subject and describe its scope to the Higher Education Funding Council (HEFCE)'.[7] This publication by UKAIS defines the academic subject of information systems as follows: 'The study of information systems and their development is a multi-disciplinary subject and addresses the range of strategic, managerial

[5] The American Association of Information Systems (AIS) also poses these questions.
[6] The Higher Education Funding Council for England (HEFCE) and its counterparts in other countries within the United Kingdom have undertaken a four-yearly review of university research—the Research Assessment Exercise (RAE)—since the late 1980s.
[7] The United Kingdom Academy for Information Systems, *Newsletter*, 1, 3 (Sep. 1995).

and operational activities involved in the gathering, processing, storing, distributing and use of information, and its associated technologies, in society and organisations.' Against the background of the creation of the AIS and the UKAIS, coupled with a desire to demonstrate that research and teaching within the fields of MIS, IM, and IS is interdisciplinary, the editors believe that a book which incorporates a variety of theoretical and practical contributions on a range of topics is both relevant and timely. Whether or not we accept the existing definitions of MIS, IM, and IS is not our main concern here. What is important is to recognise the historical and contemporary relevance of MIS research and teaching within international business and management education. In so doing, it is hoped that a greater understanding will emerge about the range of philosophical, epistemological, and methodological issues underpinning the subject.

Moreover, it is also important that information systems should not be treated simply as a 'black box' within the business and management field. All too often, research on the management of information systems either ignores the influence of technology in the management of change (thus treating technology as a 'black box') or adopts a technologically deterministic position (suggesting that technology drives organisational change). This volume presents a range of contributions on the diffusion, adoption, and management of information systems and argues that it remains one of the most significant and fertile research areas within business and management education.

This book brings together a collection of research and discussion papers by established academics from across the globe. It is divided into four broad themes: theories and perspectives; strategic management and evaluation; developing and implementing change programmes; and organisation and management issues. The important objective here is not to lay claim that all these subjects fall within MIS, IM, or IS, but rather to stress the interdisciplinary nature of the MIS field. Whereas some of the chapters place information systems at centre stage of the discussion, others are more concerned to explore theoretical positions which are relevant to the management of information systems in contemporary organisations. Readers are therefore encouraged to consider the range of philosophical, historical, economic, sociological, and political issues and debates surrounding the subject, rather than merely to enter into a sterile debate about whether a particular contribution should or should not be included in this volume!

One of the more disheartening observations of some of the literature in journals relating to MIS, IM, and IS is a failure of some writers to recognise the relevance of key issues and debates emerging from other fields within business and management,[8] broadly conceived. Put simply, MIS is

---

[8] This tendency is not peculiar to MIS, IM, and IS but one that is widespread throughout the business and management field.

not only about the *hardware* of information systems, as HRM does not only address *people issues.* However, academic researchers who pursue a narrow research agenda may be in danger of adopting a *tunnel vision perspective.* In other words, they ignore the research offerings emanating from subject areas they perceive to be outside or peripheral to their own. Such a perspective is both dangerous and inappropriate and does little to broaden our intellectual horizons. So, in agreement with M. Gibbons,[9] we argue that, as we enter the twenty-first century, much new knowledge can be gained from an interdisciplinary or transdisciplinary approach. In other words, an approach which does not ignore the relevance and contribution to knowledge of different methodological and epistemological positions.

To this end, the editors invited contributions on a broad spectrum of 'soft' and 'hard' issues within MIS.[10] Some examine the development and influence of past and present theoretical perspectives. Others are empirically based and are likely to be of greater interest to the practitioner community. In presenting a volume comprised of contributions from competing epistemological and methodological standpoints, it is hoped that a deeper analysis of the field of MIS will ensue. To some extent, this may avoid the pervading managerialist tendency to produce yet another offering which simply evaluates the merits and pitfalls of emerging new ideas in management education (notably BPR and process innovation, etc.). Whilst we recognise the significance of new ideas, and how they may influence, and be influenced by, past and present theory and practice, we also urge caution against the ever present tendency to *reinvent the wheel.*[11]

Given the growing complexity of the subject of MIS, particularly in the light of rapid technological changes, the subject seems to be approaching its golden anniversary. The relatively simple, one-dimensional world of the early MIS practitioners and researchers seems long gone. It is now timely to rethink, or take stock of the field of MIS, broadly conceived, so we may develop the subject for future audiences. Finally, we believe that an interdisciplinary approach to the study of MIS is the only worthwhile way forward if it is to have any relevance, not just to the business and management field but to the wider academic community generally.

W.L.C.
R.D.G.

November 1997

[9] M. Gibbons (1994), *The New Production of Knowledge: The Dynamics of Science and Research in Contemporary Society* (London: Sage).

[10] The editors are conscious that this volume excludes some theoretical contributions they believe are relevant to the field of MIS. However, due to space limitations as well as a lack of consensus about what constitutes the subject matter, this was unavoidable.

[11] One observation of the field of business and management is a common tendency of writers to 'reinvent the wheel' by offering new ideas which, in essence, are a modification of past ideas. Indeed, the roots of many new 'management fads' can be traced to earlier contributions often emanating from the field of industrial sociology.

CONTENTS

LIST OF FIGURES

LIST OF TABLES

LIST OF CONTRIBUTORS

David E. Avison is Professor of Information Systems in the Department of Management, University of Southampton.

Richard J. Boland, Jr., is Professor in Information Systems and Professor in Accountancy at the Weatherhead School of Management, Case Western Reserve University, Cleveland.

Peter Checkland is a professor in the Department of Management Science, University of Lancaster.

Claudio U. Ciborra is a professor at the Institut Theseus, Sophia Antipolis, France.

Wendy L. Currie is Professor in Strategic Informations Systems at Brunel University.

Michael J. Earl is Director of the Centre for Research in Information Management and Anderson Consulting Professor of Information Management, London Business School.

Barbara Farbey is a Research Fellow at the School of Management, University of Bath.

David F. Feeny is Director of the Oxford Institute of Information Management, Templeton College, Oxford.

Guy Fitzgerald is Professor of Information Systems at Brunel University.

Bob Galliers is Professor in Information Systems at Warwick Business School, University of Warwick.

Ian A. Glover is Lecturer in Management at the University of Stirling.

Rudy Hirschheim is a professor at the College of Business Administration, University of Houston.

Juhani Iivari is a professor in the Department of Information Processing, University of Oulu.

Matthew Jones is a lecturer at the Judge Institute for Management Studies, University of Cambridge.

Mary C. Lacity is Professor in Management Information Systems at the University of Missouri, St Louis; and Visiting Fellow at Oxford Institute of Information Management, Templeton College, Oxford.

Frank Land is Visiting Professor at the University of Bath, London School of Economics.

Allen S. Lee is a professor in the Faculty of Management, McGill University Montreal.

Kalle Lyytinen is a professor at the University of Jyvaskyla.

M. Lynne Markus is a Professor at the Claremont Graduate School, Claremont, Calif.

Enid Mumford is Emeritus Professor of Organizational Behaviour at Manchester Business School.

Chris Sauer is Senior Research Fellow at the Australian Graduate School of Management, University of New South Wales.

Harry Scarbrough is Professor of Organizational Analysis at the University of Leicester.

Jacky Swan is Senior Lecturer in Organisational Behaviour, Industrial Relations and Organisational Behaviour Group, Warwick Business School, University of Warwick.

David Targett is Professor in Information Management at Imperial College, London.

Robert I. Tricker is Honorary Professor of Warwick Business School, University of Warwick, and the Director of the International Corporate Policy Group.

Leslie P. Willcocks is a Fellow in Information Management at the Oxford Institute of Information Management, Templeton College, Oxford.

PART I

Theoretical and Methodological Perspectives

Introduction

This section discusses theoretical and methodological perspectives which have influenced thinking on the management of information systems within organisations. One important question which is always at the forefront of any research enquiry is: what is the theoretical foundation of and methodological approach to the study? Whilst it is outside the scope of this volume to enter into a philosophical debate on this subject, it is recognised that, for a research enquiry to have validity, it should be underpinned by theoretical and methodological approaches which are relevant and applicable. This is irrespective of whether the researcher adopts a unitary or pluralist research perspective. Moreover, a failure to address these important theoretical, epistemological, and methodological questions may result in a research offering which may be of interest to practitioners, but lacks intellectual credibility within the academic community.

One of the common criticisms about management research is the tendency of some researchers to commence a research project without first thinking through the theoretical and methodological issues. Research should not occur in an intellectual vacuum, devoid of any theoretical, epistemological, or methodological association. Important questions which are sometimes not addressed by researchers are, for example, 'Can quantitative and qualitative techniques be used together? What are the philosophical objections to adopting a phenomenological as opposed to a positivist approach?', 'How can the preconceptions and biases of the researchers be addressed?', 'Is it possible to adopt a multi-paradigm research methodology for the same research project?', 'What are the key aims and objectives of this research enquiry?'

Although these questions and concerns are difficult to resolve in any research enquiry, no matter how interesting the research problem may be, they should at least be given more than just lip-service by researchers. This is because, all too often, the results of a research study presented at an academic conference or in the form of a journal article frequently confuse *fact* with *interpretation*. In other words, ideology, interpretation, and speculation is often presented as 'objective reality'. This sometimes occurs when researchers present quantitative data on individual attitudes to specific social phenomena as *proof* of objective reality. Conversely, these researchers often seek to dismiss *interpretative* accounts of reality as 'mere speculation', even though their own use of statistics is based upon representing people's views in the form of numerical information about factors they themselves have chosen to measure and on a scale of their choice.

Whereas some researchers recognise the inherent epistemological and methodological difficulties of undertaking social science research, others dismiss these important issues altogether. The latter results in the tendency to produce mediocre research studies which fail to stand up to any rigorous academic or intellectual scrutiny. So it is just as well to remind ourselves of the key differences of undertaking research in the *natural* as opposed to the *social* sciences. This is aptly summed up by Ryan, writing more than twenty-five years ago:

the logical requirements of adequate explanation can be met in the social sciences, although the differences between the subject-matters of the natural and social sciences make important practical differences, and will, of course, make a great deal of difference to the content of the explanations.[1]

Although we do not intend to enter into a deep philosophical debate about competing research paradigms in the social sciences, it is useful to consider the difference between so called *first-order* (factual) questions and *second-order* (conceptual) questions. As Ryan eloquently points out, a first-order question is essentially designed to elicit factual information about social phenomena. Examples of this type of question are: 'How many people use personal computers in company *x* as opposed to company *y*?', or, 'What are the three largest outsourcing deals in the world?' Whilst the answers to these questions are interesting in themselves and are relevant in a social and organisational context, they do not address philosophical or conceptual issues. Second-order questions are therefore about philosophical enquiry. As Ryan claims, 'Philosophy is a second-order enquiry, devoted to clarifying and subjecting to rational analysis the procedures involved, and the results achieved, in our first-order, factual investigations' (ibid. 24).

In the social sciences, the second-order questions may arise from understanding the answers to first-order or factual questions. In respect of our question on outsourcing, above, we may pose a number of second-order questions. Thus, 'Does the PC give a company a competitive advantage?', 'Can we align IT with the corporate strategy?', 'What do people understand by the concept of outsourcing?', 'Does outsourcing mean the same to people as contracting out?', 'Does outsourcing change people's behaviour within organisations?' As we can see, these questions require a significant amount of interpretation on the part of the social science researcher. But to interpret each question, we must first attach meaning to the phenomena

[1] A. Ryan (1970), *The Philosophy of the Social Sciences* (London: Macmillan Press): 22.

under scrutiny. What do we mean by *outsourcing*? Equally, terms like *corporate strategy, alignment of IT, competitive advantage* may also present problems as they may mean different things to different people. This is very likely to occur in cross-national comparisons where respondents from different countries interpret research questions differently.

In Part I, we present six contributions on theoretical and methodological perspectives peculiar to social science research. Since one of the central debates within the MIS field concerns research methodology, we believe the following contributions are a firm foundation on which to build this volume. As we can see from the eclectic offerings, methodological and theoretical unity is absent. For example, whereas some writers advocate methodological pluralism[2] (i.e. the desire to use different methodological approaches) for research enquiry, others reject this view by claiming they are incommensurable research paradigms.[3]

Our first chapter is by Alan Lee who offers a thought-provoking discussion of MIS research where he examines the concept of *instanciation* and how this relates to information systems and their organisational context; each having transformational effects on the other. He poses the question, 'What is research?' and discusses both positivist and interpretative research paradigms and how they are applied in MIS research. In his chapter, he asserts that researchers in the MIS field ought to adopt a different approach which he labels: critical social theory (CST).

The next three chapters analyse key theoretical contributions within social science and, more specifically, the MIS field. Enid Mumford, in her discussion of the origins of socio-technical theory, relates the work of the Tavistock Institute to the more recent development of business process re-engineering (BPR). Unlike the more enduring ideas emanating from socio-technical theory, the future of BPR as a significant contribution to theory and practice looks doubtful. Even the architects of BPR make this point by claiming that implementation of BPR initiatives has often proven unsuccessful in practice. Further critical reflection on BPR, this time utilising the organisational literatures associated with IS implementation and technology diffusion, is provided by Jacky Swan and Bob Galliers in Chapter 15. In Chapter 3, Peter Checkland discusses the contribution of systems thinking in four parts: the origins of systems thinking; the core ideas behind the concept 'system'; the varieties of systems thinking; and the implications of this for the MIS field. Systems thinking has been very influential in the MIS field and more widely in the business and management literature. Indeed, many recent offerings use these ideas as the foundation for research on innovation and technology management.

---

[2] Positivism, interpretativism, phenomenology, and ethnography are examples of different methodological approaches.
[3] The view that different research paradigms cannot be used in the same research enquiry, hence, they are incommensurable.

In Chapter 4, Juhani Iivari and Kalle Lyytinen present a comprehensive analysis of information systems research in Scandinavia. These writers argue that the Scandinavian contribution to the IS field has been significant. Their evidence for this statement is reinforced by the profusion of information systems development (ISD) approaches characterised by a plurality of theories, research methodologies, and subjects under investigation. This chapter is therefore appropriately placed to conclude this section, since it draws together a number of competing theoretical, epistemological, and methodological research paradigms relevant to the field of IS.

In Chapter 5, Matthew Jones discusses the significant contribution of structuration theory to more recent work in our field. In particular, he analyses the development of structuration theory within European sociology in the late 1970s. The considerable contribution of Anthony Giddens is comprehensively examined to demonstrate the relevance of structuration theory to the IS field.

Finally, Claudio Ciborra discusses a theory of IS based upon the concept of improvisation. He criticises current systems design principles and proposes new design strategies based on what he calls 'smart or competent improvisation'. One of the central themes of the discussion is how to align IT to smart improvisation given its contradictory features, i.e. being 'simultaneously rational and unpredictable; planned but emergent; purposeful but opaque; effective but irreflexive; discernible after the fact, but spontaneous in its manifestation'.

Part I considers multi-paradigm research which demonstrates the interdisciplinary nature within IS, broadly conceived. Whilst some of the chapters tend to focus more on the theoretical underpinnings of MIS, others examine important epistemological and methodological issues. The contribution of Part I is to build on the literature that already exists by revisiting some of the more established traditions while introducing more recent thinking into various topics currently being debated.

1

Researching MIS

ALLEN S. LEE

Introduction

What constitutes the activity of 'researching MIS'? What ought to constitute the activity of 'researching MIS'? In this chapter I will venture some answers to these two questions.

The answers to these questions will depend, in turn, on the answers to some related questions: What is MIS? What is research? What forms does 'researching MIS' currently take? What forms *should* 'researching MIS' take in the future? Certainly, there would be differences in how different MIS researchers answer these questions—and the differences themselves would all be significant to any effort aimed at empirically establishing what 'researching MIS' is. The following discussion contributes to such an effort where I offer some answers to these questions.

What is MIS?

An answer to the question, 'What constitutes "researching MIS"?,' depends on what we mean by 'MIS' in the first place. And what we mean by 'MIS' is, in turn, a non-trivial matter because its empirical referent is itself always in a state of change.

MIS begins where computer science ends (Lee, 1991*a*). Computer scientists deserve accolades for developing and delivering ever more advanced forms of information technology: hardware technology; software technology; and network technology. Yet because no technology implements itself, there is more to MIS than just information technology. In a sense, an information system is an *instantiation* of information technology, where the same information technology can be instantiated in different ways. One dimension of MIS, therefore, is that it involves not just information technology, but also its instantiation. There are the rich organisational and political processes whereby a given set of information technology is instantiated and there are the rich organisational and political processes pertaining to the continual managing, maintaining, and changing of the information technology so as to sustain the instantiation.

Robert Zmud, editor in chief of *MIS Quarterly*, refers to another commonly accepted dimension of MIS in his description of *MIS Quarterly's* Theory and Research section. He describes MIS research, at least as published in *MIS Quarterly*, as 'either enhancing existing theory or building new theory regarding the management of information systems in organisations' (1995: p. v). A significant element in his characterisation is that (unlike computer science) MIS involves the information system *and* the organisation. I take this a step further. An information system and its organisational context each have transformational effects on the other. They are more like the reagents that react to and change each other's properties in a chemical compound than the inert elements that retain their respective properties in a chemical mixture. The reactive process is what leads some MIS researchers to describe MIS phenomena as 'emergent' (Markus and Robey, 1988). In the same spirit, socio-technical systems theory makes the claim that separate efforts to optimise the technical system alone and the social system alone will not only lead to a global suboptimum, but can even be unfeasible in the first place. Equally, the same information system can be a success in one organisation but a failure in another, while the same organisation can experience success with one information system but failure with another. Hence, the information system and the organisational context must be studied, understood, and managed together, not separately. So another dimension of MIS is that it involves, as reactive and inextricable elements, both an information system and its organisational context.

A subset of the previous dimension is so significant that it deserves its own classification as a separate dimension. It derives from information technology's being an *intellectual* technology, as opposed to an *industrial* technology (Curley and Pyburn, 1982). The latter, like a drill press or a steam engine, typically has a fixed set of functionalities. The former, however, has functionalities that are not fixed at the outset, but can be innovated endlessly, depending on its interaction with the intellect of the human beings who implement and use it. Information technology is an intellectual technology. In the process of its instantiation into one or another information system, a given set of information technology becomes subject to the shaping influence of the intellects of its implementors and users, who can end up creating an information system that the inventors of the supporting information technology never had in mind. Even more important, the information technology, once instantiated, can react with and extend the intellects of its implementors and users. They can then turn their transformed intellect towards innovating even additional functionalities for the information technology that, once instantiated, can again react with and extend the intellect of its implementors and users, who can then . . .

Implicit across the three dimensions above, but worthy of being made explicit, is that no MIS researcher is or even should be an objective, disinterested scientist. MIS researchers seek to contribute to the documentation, innovation, or illumination of better ways in which people in organisational contexts can use, manage, and maintain (or, in short, 'instantiate') information technology. Unlike some behavioural scientists who seek to avoid Hawthorne effects, MIS researchers *want* Hawthorne effects (Jönsson, 1991); we *want* our observations and theories ultimately to make a difference, in good ways, to what it is that we are observing. MIS involves what our own research subjects themselves consider to be a profession and corporate function. Unlike the situation for most behavioural scientists, the relationship between MIS researchers and their research subjects is that the latter are constituents to whom the former are responsible and whom, to some extent, they must serve. Without MIS as a profession or corporate function, there would be no *raison d'être* for MIS research.

The four interrelated dimensions of MIS are as follows: (1) MIS involves not just information technology, but also its instantiation; (2) MIS involves, as reactive and inextricable elements, both an information system and its organisational context; (3) MIS involves information technology as a form of intellectual technology; and (4) MIS involves the activities of a profession or corporate function which are integral to the essence of what 'MIS' is. Clearly, the four dimensions mentioned here differentiate MIS from, and move it beyond, the empirical domains traditionally and appropriately researched by computer science, organisational behaviour and theory, economics, operations research, and other so-called 'reference disciplines'. (Indeed, because of this, I no longer view them as reference disciplines, but instead, at best, as 'contributing disciplines'.) As for what form 'researching MIS' currently takes and what form it ought to take, especially with regard to the four dimensions—I may appropriately venture an answer only after attending to another antecedent question.

What is Research?

In this section of the chapter, I shall momentarily suspend discussion of MIS and focus instead on research. Numerous research traditions were already in existence long before MIS ever came into being and certainly before MIS researchers began to draw upon them. A discussion of research traditions is therefore appropriate.

Typically, definitions of research refer to formal procedures, such as those of statistical inference, interviewing, construct validation, and so forth. Research certainly involves these procedures, but a point requiring emphasis is that *all research is socially constructed* (Berger and Luckmann, 1967). To plunge us into what I mean by 'social construction', I begin by discussing the work of the philosopher and sociologist Alfred Schutz concerned with 'multiple realities' (Schutz, 1973: 207), in which he refers also to the work of the psychologist William James:

there are several, probably an infinite number of various orders of reality, each with its own special and separate style of existence. James calls them 'sub-universes' and mentions as examples the world of sense or physical things (as the paramount reality), the world of science, the world of ideal relations, the world of 'idols of the tribe', the various supernatural worlds of mythology and religion, the various worlds of individual opinion, the worlds of sheer madness and vagary. The popular mind conceives of all these sub-worlds more or less disconnectedly, and when dealing with one of them forgets for the time being its relation to the rest. But every object we think of is at last referred to one of these subworlds. 'Each world whilst it is attended to is real after its own fashion; only the reality lapses with the attention.'

Certainly, *research* would include the world of science and the world of ideal relations, though it is not restricted to these two worlds. However, before I add to the list of worlds and subworlds that 'research' includes, it would be instructive to examine one such world in detail so as to illuminate what I mean by 'social construction'.

I have argued that Euclidean geometry (which is a subworld of the world of ideal relations, mentioned above) is a socially constructed reality (Lee, 1994). The world of Euclidean geometry does not exist in the physical world of nature. It is, strictly speaking, a fiction; it is something that people have constructed. Furthermore, the people who carry knowledge of it, including its originators, can come and go, but the object that we call Euclidean geometry persists. Like a physical object, the world of Euclidean geometry can retain the same form across the different individuals who encounter it. In this sense, the world of Euclidean geometry is objective, not subjective. It is an objective, socially constructed reality.

Moreover, suppose I am reading a Euclidean research paper. Its meaning is not restricted to the Euclidean argument that its author is making, but also involves the entire socially constructed apparatus that comprises Euclidean geometry—its axioms, theorems, symbols, and logic, all of which transcend what is in the research paper and all of which were in existence prior to the author's writing of the research paper. The research paper itself is just one possible instantiation of this apparatus. Upon grasping this socially constructed reality, I become Euclidean myself and I become able to identify any inconsistencies and suggest improvements in the research paper, thereby even transcending the author's own understanding. This means not only that I can appropriate the research paper or what the author had in mind, but also that the research paper and the socially constructed world behind it (here, the world of Euclidean geometry) can appropriate *me*. Upon this appropriation, I am no longer an independent individual exercising free will (if indeed I ever was), but I become an agent of the socially constructed world of Euclidean geometry. Other individuals, placed in the same situation as me, would be likewise appropriated and transformed. We could then (and only then) engage one another in a dialogue about this Euclidean research paper, collectively enact some meanings for it, and—after some time, effort, and perhaps struggle—reach a shared understanding of it. Moreover, rather than being agents under the total control of the socially constructed Euclidean world that has appropriated and transformed us, we could still, as a group, eventually render change in this world, perhaps by contributing to its collection of theorems or by offering resolutions to any logical inconsistencies or gaps that we identify in it.

Note that, in the above discussion, we can substitute *physics, mathematics, experimental* and *quasi-experimental design, sociology, economics, anthropology,* etc., for *Euclidean geometry,* and the argument would be the same. The point is that every research world—both the product of research (a body of knowledge) and the process of research (individual and group activities that involve application of research procedures)—is socially constructed. No research procedure (which I see as a form of technology) applies itself, but necessarily involves individuals, their activities, and their institutions in its instantiation. (There are additional parallels between research procedures and information technology to which I will return in the essay's concluding section.) A person appropriates a research world while the research world appropriates the person, with the result that the person becomes an agent of the research world while the research world becomes susceptible to advancement by those who have appropriated it. Research, therefore, is not an entity that has an existence independent of knowing subjects; research (even research in the natural sciences) is a human creation and social activity.

With regard to the natural sciences, I reject the notion that the laws of nature govern nature. I believe that the *laws of nature* have no existence independent of human beings, but instead are constructed and continually revised by human beings so that, as human-made fictions, the *laws of nature* end up conforming to nature, rather than vice versa. Because of the fictional status, the term 'theory' is more appropriate than 'law'. I believe that this argument is no less true for the social sciences. It is the behaviour of society (which includes people, groups, and organisations) that governs the human-made fictions known as the theories of social science; it is hardly the case that there are any 'laws' or even theories of social science that govern the behaviour of society. Research, in my view, consists of individual and group activity aimed at the construction of theories, whether they are theories about nature or theories about individuals, groups, organisations, and society. As such, theories are only theories: they are fictions; they are social constructions. They are not already 'there', waiting to be discovered; rather, we invent them. Researchers interested in investigating MIS phenomena have drawn primarily from just two already existing worlds of research. They are the research worlds of positivism and interpretativism.

The World of Positivism

Among social scientists, positivism is often known as the 'natural science model' of research. A social scientist who appropriates the world of positivism proceeds to implement, in his or her own research, an image (as held by followers of positivism) of how research proceeds in physics, biology, and other natural sciences. Descriptions of the world of positivist research sometimes use the terms 'ontology' and 'epistemology' (and also 'methodology', as distinct from 'method'); these terms are from the philosophy of science, which itself originated and advanced positivism as a model or an account of what science is. However, I will avoid these terms in this essay. In my experience, most researchers who do positivist research do not know what these terms mean, nor do their actions suggest that they are putting into use the concepts underlying these terms. Furthermore, the positivist model of what science is, at least as articulated by positivist philosophers of science, has been shown to be unfeasible and thereby been discredited.[1] (In this light, it is ironic that positivism remains the predominant world of research among scholars not only in academic departments of MIS, but other fields of management studies and social science research as well.) Therefore, in my characterisation of the world of positivism, I will refer more to *positivism-in-practice* than to the *formulation of positivism* by the philosophy of science.

In practice, positivism's natural science model of social science research involves three interrelated sets of logic: the rules of formal logic, the rules of experimental and quasi-experimental design, and the rules of hypothetico-deductive logic. The natural science model maintains that natural science research complies with all three sets of rules. Social science research, in complying with the same three sets of rules, would be following the natural science model.

Rules of formal logic

In the natural science model, mathematics is the ideal form in which a researcher may express a theory. A researcher may use the rules of mathematics (the rules of algebra provide an excellent illustration here) not

---

[1] Schön (1983) quotes Bernstein (1976: 207): 'There is not a single major thesis advanced by either nineteenth century Positivists or the Vienna Circle that has not been devastatingly criticized when measured by the Positivists' own standards for philosophical argument. The original formulations of the analytic-synthetic dichotomy and the verifiability criterion of meaning have been abandoned. It has been effectively shown that the Positivists' understanding of the natural sciences and the formal disciplines is grossly oversimplified. Whatever one's final judgment about the current disputes in the post-empiricist philosophy and history of science . . . there is rational agreement about the inadequacy of the original Positivist understanding of science, knowledge and meaning.'

only to relate different propositions to one another in her construction of a theory, but also to derive new theoretical propositions from existing ones. Expressing a theory in mathematical form thereby facilitates a researcher's efforts to bring about the internal logical consistency of the theory. A researcher could also apply the rules of mathematics for the purpose of checking the validity of the derivations and other operations already performed. Where a researcher expresses a theory in words rather than in mathematics, the researcher may still use the rules of formal logic (of which the rules of mathematics are a subset) for the same purpose. This is exemplified in syllogistic logic (e.g. 'All men are mortal,' 'Socrates is a man,' 'Socrates is mortal').

Whereas theoretical propositions can be expressed verbally, theoretical propositions expressed mathematically are more easily managed, if only for the reason that researchers are more likely to be already familiar with the rules of mathematics (particularly algebra) than with the rules of formal logic in general. The use of mathematics as a tool for rendering logical consistency in a theory is a likely reason why academic journals in management and other social science disciplines can give the impression, to practising managers and other non-academic researchers, of being journals of applied mathematics.

Logical consistency, while a necessary quality of a theory, is not enough to make a theory. Consider that systems of non-Euclidean geometry and systems of imaginary numbers are logically consistent, but do not (and need not) have any empirical referents. In addition to being logical, a theory must also be empirical.

Rules of experimental and quasi-experimental design

Overall, this second set of rules pertains not so much to how a researcher may properly relate the propositions of a theory to one another (which still needs to be accomplished for the theory to be logical), but to how a researcher may properly relate the propositions of a theory to the *real-world* or empirical referent that the researcher is crafting the propositions to explain (so that the theory may also be empirical).

In the world of positivism, researchers often express theories in terms of independent and dependent variables. A theory could posit that as an independent variable X (say, user friendliness of an information system) increases, the dependent variable Y (say, system usage) increases. Of course, this raises the issue of how to 'operationalise' a measure in the first place (for instance, how might a researcher establish that his or her way of measuring X is indeed a good measure of the user friendliness of an information system?)—an issue for which Straub (1989) provides an excellent treatment. Still, when a researcher empirically tests the theory and observes that, when X increases, Y does too, how can the researcher (and her colleagues) be sure that this was not simply a coincidence? Perhaps sometimes Y will increase even when X does not; perhaps, over time, Y increases by itself anyway, regardless of whatever changes do or do not take place in X. Or perhaps X does not always increase when Y does, but only when an increase in Y is accompanied by the presence of another factor, Z. Indeed, perhaps the researcher should posit that it is changes in Z, rather than changes in Y, that are associated with changes in X. In short, when empirically testing for relationships theorized to exist among different factors, a researcher working in the world of positivism must somehow remove, control, or otherwise account for the potentially confounding influences of all other factors. Laboratory experiments (ideally, involving a researcher's varying of just one factor in a 'treatment group', while also involving the researcher's holding constant of other factors in a 'control group'), statistical experiments (involving 'statistical treatments' and 'statistical controls' implemented through such multivariate tools as regression, LISREL, and PLS), and natural experiments (involving a researcher's identification, in the field, of factors that are naturally held constant while other factors naturally vary) all exist for this purpose. Whatever form of experimentation, the rules of experimental and quasi-experimental design (Campbell and Stanley, 1963; Cook and Campbell, 1979; Nagel, 1979) help the researcher to ensure that an empirical test of a relationship theorized between particular variables is indeed an empirical test of just this relationship and no other.

The need to make theories empirical, and not just logical, is the reason why the research published in academic journals in management and other social science disciplines routinely employs statistical experiments and laboratory experiments. Statistical experiments are common also for the reason that they obviously involve mathematics, hence facilitating the positivist requirement of logical consistency in a theory. Furthermore, the popularity of statistical experiments is also explained, in part, by the popularity of surveys and questionnaires, which readily supply the data needed to conduct statistical experiments.

The rules of hypothetico-deductive logic

In the world of positivist research, does a researcher test a theory through induction or deduction? I argue that it is the latter. Using induction, a researcher would generalize across n observations in order to arrive at a theory. Proponents of induction maintain that the greater n is, the more general or 'generalisable' the resulting theory. As commonsensical as this inductive procedure may appear, it is flawed. The flaw is that induction itself is not empirically justifiable. Any attempt to establish the empirical validity of induction ultimately applies induction itself, thereby leading to an infinite regress in reasoning (Popper, 1968, citing Hume). In particular, is the proposition 'inductive inference leads to valid theories' itself empirically valid? To justify it, we would marshal *n* examples in which inductive inference leads to valid theories. However, this would create a new problem: we would be applying inductive inference to justify itself. Then, to justify this application as valid, we would marshal *n* examples of such applications. Hence, whereas induction may be useful for generating a theory, it cannot contribute to the testing or justification of the theory. Even the discipline of statistical inference has distanced itself from the notion of induction. For instance, students in introductory statistics courses learn that the action of increasing a sample size does *not* increase the probability that a statistically inferred proposition (such as a confidence interval) is correct; instead, increasing a sample size would only have the effect of increasing what statisticians call the 'level of confidence' that they place in their sampling procedure.

I have argued (1989) that the logic of research in the natural science model is not inductive, but deductive. In his classic text, Copi describes the hypothetico-deductive logic in use by the natural sciences (1986: 483): 'Few propositions of science are *directly* verifiable as true . . . For the most part they concern *unobservable* entities, such as molecules and atoms, electrons and protons, chromosomes and genes.' As a result, justification in natural science research is indirect rather than direct. 'The pattern of indirect testing or indirect verification consists of two parts. First, one deduces from the proposition to be tested [the proposition being the theory] one or more other propositions capable of being tested directly [these later propositions being the predictions]' (p. 486). In the terminology of logic, a theory's predictions are its conclusions. 'Then these conclusions are tested and are found to be either true or false.' The researcher then compares what the theory predicts and what she actually observes. 'If the conclusions are false, any proposition that implies them [namely the theory] must be false also. On the other hand, if the conclusions are true, that provides evidence for the truth of the proposition being tested, which is thus confirmed indirectly' (p. 486). Note, however, that when the conclusions or predictions turn out to be true, the truth of the theory (from which the prediction originated) is *not* proven, but is only 'corroborated', 'supported', or 'confirmed' in the instance of this single test. A different instance, involving a different set of conditions in another experiment, would result in yet additional predictions, which would open up the same theory to yet another opportunity for its falsification. Thus, in positivism's natural science model, the ever-present possibility for contradictory evidence to surface in a subsequent test requires that a theory always be considered *falsifiable*. I regard the widespread characterisation of theories, even in the social sciences, as *falsifiable, testable, refutable,* or *disconfirmable* as an indication of the widespread extent to which the deductive testing of theories is practised.

In a hypothetico-deductive framework, a researcher can achieve generalisability in a theory not so much by increasing the number of observations or data points, but by increasing the variety of the experimental tests to which he or she subjects the theory. The more varied the sets of experimental conditions in which the theory can predict correctly, the more generalizable the theory. It is the greater range in experimental conditions, rather than the greater number of observations *per se*, that leads to greater generalisability in a theory.

Summary

Positivism is, in practice, a socially constructed world, populated with social science researchers whose shared beliefs include what I have portrayed and described, above, as the three sets of interrelated logic. A researcher who studies and appropriates what the three sets of logic refer to would, in turn, be appropriated by the world of positivism and thereby become its instrument or agent. The result is that this researcher, and others who likewise experience the appropriation, end up inventing theories that conform to positivism's natural science model of social science research.

The World of Interpretativism

With Ojelanki Ngwenyama, I have argued (Ngwenyama and Lee, 1996) that, whereas the world of positivism has shaped much social science research, its allegiance to natural science research as the normative model for social science research has limited its applicability. A dimension of the subject matter that social scientists examine, but not the subject matter that natural scientists examine, is what the field of phenomenology calls the 'life world', which refers to, among other things, the world of consciousness and humanly created meanings. 'Unlike atoms, molecules, and electrons, people create and attach their own meanings to the world around them and to the behavior that they manifest in that world' (Lee, 1991*b*: 347, referring to Schutz, 1973). Atoms, molecules, electrons, and other objects of natural science enquiry do not 'mean' anything to each other (Schutz, 1973). However, people, who are integral to the subject matter of the social sciences, *do* mean something to each other. In this way, the world of humanly created meanings, however 'subjective' they may be, is an integral part of the subject matter that the social scientist is studying. Because of this, 'the social scientist must collect facts and data describing not only the purely objective, publicly observable aspects of human behavior', which constitutes a subject matter which the procedures of positivism's natural science model are indeed well suited to studying, 'but also the subjective meaning this behavior has for the human subjects themselves', which constitutes a different subject matter whose study requires procedures that have no counterparts among those of the natural sciences (Lee, 1991*b*: 347). In contrast to the world of positivism, the world of interpretativism gives explicit recognition to the 'life world'. Not originating in the natural sciences, interpretativism involves research procedures such as those associated with ethnography (from anthropology), participant observation (from sociology), history, and hermeneutics, all of which give explicit recognition to the world of consciousness and humanly created meanings. In most interpretative approaches, a central idea is 'mutual understanding'—the phenomenon of a person understanding (i.e. 'interpreting') what another person means —whether it is a person engaged in everyday life taking a *natural attitude* to understanding another person in everyday life, or it is a person engaged in scientific research taking a calculated *scientific attitude* to understanding everyday people in their everyday lives.

Unlike in the world of positivism, a researcher in the world of interpretativism avows that the researcher herself is the instrument of observation. Sanday writes (1979: 528): 'Fieldworkers learn to use themselves as the principle and most reliable instrument of observation, selection, coordination, and interpretation. Ethnography as Metraux . . . says, "depends on this highly trained ability to respond—and to respect that response— *as a whole person*"' (emphasis added). In the world of positivism, researchers typically write their papers in the third person or the passive voice, as if their knowledge could exist independently of knowing subjects; in the world of interpretativism, researchers more often write their papers in the first person, making no pretence that their interpretative knowledge is inextricably linked to themselves as the human instruments of observation. Indeed, to the extent that a researcher seeks a mutual understanding of another person, the researcher may, of course, do so only as a person; in other words, the researcher must use himself as an instrument of observation.

Of the different interpretative approaches, I am most familiar with hermeneutics. I will turn to hermeneutics in this discussion to bring out some concepts that I believe are common across different interpretative approaches.

Hermeneutics originally referred to the interpretation of ancient texts, such as the Bible. Today, interpretative scholars take a hermeneutic approach to the interpretation of human and organisational behaviour. The motivating idea behind hermeneutics is that *reading a text* provides the model for *reading human behaviour*. In other words, the process of achieving an understanding of a text can provide insights to the process of achieving a mutual understanding with another person. In this model, people and organisations are a text, which we 'read'.

To illustrate this model, consider the set of ten words in Fig. 1.1. In the first sentence, the ten words mean one thing. In the second sentence, the same ten words mean another thing. And in the third sentence, the ten

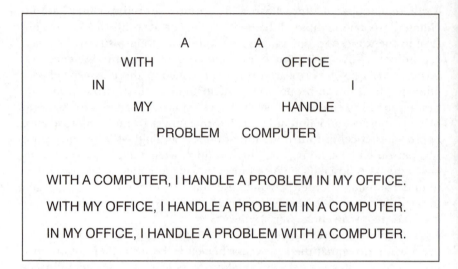

FIG. 1.1. *Reading a text as a model for reading human behaviour*

words mean something else entirely. The same word and even the same set of words can end up meaning different things. The meaning of an individual word and the meaning of the sentence as a whole are mutually dependent and, as a reader, I form my understanding of both simultaneously.

I apply the same model to human behaviour. The same publicly observable behaviour can have different meanings in different organisational arrangements. The meaning of an individual action and the meaning of the organisational setting as a whole are mutually dependent and, as an interpretative researcher, I form my understanding of both simultaneously.

Modelling interpretation on reading is useful for bringing out three points. First, interpretation, like reading, is not a mysterious, esoteric activity (Boland, 1985). This model promises the following: if we can read, we can interpret. Second, based on our experience in reading, we are already familiar with some of the basic elements involved in interpretation: meaning; its expression by one person; its understanding by another. Most important of all, our everyday practice of reading is, in itself, a demonstrative proof that interpretation works. Interpretation is 'do-able', no less than reading is 'do-able'.

I have encountered at least twelve different, serious definitions of hermeneutics.[2] I will present just one hermeneutic approach that I derive from the work of the historian of science Thomas Kuhn. Consider the situation where I have a text whose author, and the audience for whom the author

---

[2] See Palmer (1979: 33) for six definitions. See Tice and Slavens (1983: 297) for another six definitions.

wrote, are from a time and culture far removed from my own. I have a dictionary and I know the grammar. How do I proceed? Kuhn offers the following advice (quoted in Bernstein, 1983: 132): 'When reading the works of an important thinker, look first for the *apparent absurdities* in the text and ask yourself how a sensible person could have written them. When you find an answer . . . when those passages make sense, then you may find that more central passages, ones you previously thought you understood, have changed their meaning.'

Accordingly, when I encounter a passage that I find absurd or irrational, I have a choice to make. Either I may draw a conclusion *about the author*— that she thinks in a way that she herself would consider absurd—or I may draw a conclusion *about myself*—that *I* have not succeeded yet in figuring out what the author meant. When doing a hermeneutic interpretation, I choose the conclusion about myself. A basic premiss in this hermeneutic approach is that *the author knows what she's talking about.*

The same premiss applies when I am reading human behaviour. Suppose I observe a systems developer who professes the value of persuading managers to use information technology, even though I see that he is resistant to using CASE tools in his own work. Either I could draw a conclusion about the subject—namely, that this person is acting in a way that *he himself* would consider absurd and irrational—or I could draw a conclusion about myself—namely, that *I* have not succeeded yet in figuring out what the subject himself means by his own behaviour. Whether taking a hermeneutic approach in particular or an interpretative approach in general, I choose the conclusion about myself. A premiss in hermeneutic and other forms of interpretation is that *people know what they're doing.* Rosabeth Moss Kanter has expressed this more elegantly: 'With Michel Crozier, I wanted to demonstrate that everyone is rational, that everyone within an organisation, no matter how absurd or irrational their behavior seemed, was reacting to what their situation made available, in such a way as to preserve dignity, control, and recognition from others' (Kanter, 1977: 291). What initially appears to me, in my role as an interpretative researcher, as irrational behaviour therefore might not be irrational at all; it could instead be a rational response by rational people to the irrational conditions of their situation. In such cases, the task of the interpretative researcher is to discern, if not the rationality, then at least the *rationale*, behind apparently irrational behaviour.

Returning to the situation where I have encountered a passage that makes no sense to me, how do I, as a reader, proceed? Again, this is nothing mysterious or esoteric. I would return to the text, keep on reading, and seek out more clues. Then I would try out alternative readings of the puzzling passage until I saw how a sensible person could have written it. But then, as Kuhn says, when this passage makes sense, other passages which I thought I had understood before might now change their meaning and create new puzzles. To resolve these new puzzles, I would return to the text and repeat this process.

This reasoning moves in a circle, but the reasoning is *not* circular. Palmer states (1979: 87): 'We understand the meaning of an individual word by seeing it in reference to the whole of the sentence; and reciprocally, the sentence's meaning as a whole is dependent on the meaning of individual words.' This interlocking system, from which meaning emerges, is well known; it is the hermeneutical circle—which I demonstrated above in Fig. 1.1.

Correspondingly, in the situation where I am reading human behaviour —in particular, where I have just observed a person acting in a way that seems silly or irrational—how do I, as an interpretative researcher, proceed? I would return to the text itself—the text of this person's actions, as well as the whole of the organisational setting of which these actions are a part. And I would use the idea of the hermeneutical circle here: I would come to understand any single action by relating it to the whole of the organisational setting; and reciprocally, I would come to understand the whole of the organisational setting by relating it to the individual actions. Just as when I am reading the text of a book, I would continue reading the text of an organisational setting *and* its individual actions until the apparent absurdities dissolve.

There are two more points regarding hermeneutic interpretation that require attention. First, whether the text I am reading is a book or a person's behaviour, I could extend the hermeneutical circle to the social context immediately surrounding the text. For instance, when I am trying to make sense of a biblical passage, I might take advantage of archaeological knowledge about the ancient Middle East. Likewise, when I am trying to understand the behaviour of systems analysts in a corporate headquarters in Boston, I might take advantage of knowledge about the systems profession in the United States. With a larger hermeneutical circle, I would have additional passages on which to draw for clues to make sense of the passages that I find puzzling.

The second point is that, whenever I read, I necessarily approach the words of the text with my own pre-existing 'dictionary' of definitions. Whether I am reading a book or I am reading human behaviour, I necessarily form an understanding with the help of a pre-existing understanding that I carry with me and apply to the text. The 'dictionary' that I bring with me is part of what I am as an instrument of observation.

Summary

Interpretativism, no less than positivism, is itself a socially constructed world, populated with social science researchers whose shared beliefs include the following four concepts. First, the subject matter of interpretative research involves the 'life world', which includes humanly created meanings, whether those that are individually held or those that are shared by groups. This is a subject matter whose study requires procedures that have no counterparts among those of the natural sciences. Second, the researcher himself or herself must inevitably serve as an instrument of observation. Third, interpretation is iterative; in a sense, an interpretation is always 'in process'; the possibility of encountering a 'breakdown' (Agar, 1986) in one's interpretative understanding (i.e. a newly appearing instance of absurd or irrational behaviour, in the light of one's most recently revised interpretation) is always present and is, in fact, to be welcomed as an opportunity for further refining the interpretation. Fourth, the validity or goodness of an interpretation can be assessed. There are numerous ways to do this (cf. Sanday, 1979: 529). With a good interpretation, any apparently absurd or irrational behaviours would no longer appear so. With a good interpretation, new observations would not surprise the observer. With a good interpretation, new observations would not surprise a different observer, to whom the interpretation has been communicated. With a good interpretation, an observer would be able to enter the organisational world of the observed human subjects, whereupon he or she could communicate with them.

How would I respond to a critic who insists that he or she does not understand or agree with my interpretation, and demands conclusive proof? I believe that such a demand would be inappropriate. After all, when I am reading, the burden is on me, the reader, to reach an understanding of the text. Likewise, if a critic is reviewing my interpretation of human or organisational behaviour, the burden is on the critic to reach an understanding of my interpretation (where 'understanding' neither implies nor requires agreement). Because the instrument of observation is the person, the failure of a critic to understand is a fault of the instrument, or the critic himself. For the critic who simply does not understand, the political scientist Charles Taylor offers the following advice (1979: 68): 'Change yourself.' In other words, the instrument of observation itself would require adjustment. Then, if the critic indeed so changed himself, he would become able to appropriate my interpretation (and, in turn, be appropriated by it); this would enable him to identify any inconsistencies and suggest improvements in my interpretation, thereby even transcending it. This scenario applies to interpretative research in general, not just hermeneutics.

What Forms Does 'Researching MIS' Currently Take?

The predominance of the world of positivism among MIS researchers is well known. This predominance received formal documentation by Orlikowski and Baroudi (1991) who noted that 96.8 per cent of all the published MIS articles in their sample were positivist, with the rest being interpretative. Since 1991, there have been signs of increasing acceptance of the world of interpretativism by MIS researchers. The editorial board of *MIS Quarterly*, one of the top MIS research journals, has come to include ample representation from interpretative researchers. The International Conference on Information Systems, the leading annual conference for MIS researchers, routinely includes panels and paper presentations involving interpretative research. A relatively new and highly regarded journal, *Accounting, Management, and Information Technologies*, has the open editorial policy and practice of welcoming interpretative research. Another encouraging sign is that MIS doctoral students are showing and pursuing interests in interpretative research. Still, researching MIS through positivism and interpretativism, while not incorrect, is incomplete.

Positivism's natural science model, which is of course well suited to studying the physical subject matters found in nature, is ill suited to capturing the four dimensions, discussed earlier, of what MIS is. With regard to the first dimension, positivism is well suited to studying information technology itself (as in the academic discipline of computer science), but the rich aspects of *human and organisational instantiations* of information technology have no counterparts in the physical subject matters of the natural sciences and therefore are elusive to positivist study. With regard to the second dimension, positivism posits relationships between factors, but the *emergent* nature of the transformational effects of an information system and its organisational context on each other can make such relationships unforeseeable to a positivist researcher. With regard to the third dimension, information technology's being an *intellectual* technology similarly builds unpredictability into how information technology is instantiated, again impeding a positivist researcher's attempt to foresee, formulate, and empirically test relationships. With regard to the fourth dimension, it is positivism's natural science model itself which insists that scientists not 'contaminate' or 'bias' their subject matter with their presence and their values—an insistence that is difficult, if not impossible, to reconcile with the fact that we MIS researchers have an interest and responsibility to serve our research subjects as our constituents and that we *want* our observations ultimately to make a difference, in good ways, to them, to their information systems, and to their organisations. Positivist research can and does contribute to explanations and diagnoses of existing MIS phenomena, but is an incomplete research approach in itself for addressing fully the four dimensions of MIS.

I have argued (1991*b*) that the practice of interpretative research can be integrated with the practice of positivist research. Clearly, interpretativism can and does help to address the humanity and sociality that infuse the first three dimensions; however, interpretativism would only help to complete an understanding or diagnosis of existing MIS phenomena and, therefore, would still leave us wanting a prescription of what *ought* to be done regarding the people, the information systems, and the organisations we are researching.

In a current research effort, Ojelanki Ngwenyama and I (1996) have examined a research instance of the limitations of positivism and interpretativism. In investigating the richness that occurs in the managerial use of electronic mail, we reviewed the past MIS research on communication richness, which employs both positivist and interpretative perspectives. MIS research that follows positivism's natural science model has, predictably, conceptualized communication as if it were a physical process, where humanly created meanings are treated like a physical substance transported from one person to another through a conduit and where the receiving person is conceptualized as nothing more than a passive receptacle that unquestioningly accepts and comes to hold whatever pours or trickles into it. Interpretative MIS research that examines managerial communication has addressed more adequately the phenomenon of humanly created meanings, explicitly acknowledging the concept of 'mutual understanding' between knowledgeable, intelligent, and acting human beings. Significantly, neither the positivist research nor the interpretative research has ventured into the realm of entertaining value judgements on the validity or rightness of what the observed managers are communicating in the first place. What should they be communicating, how should they be communicating, and what is the role of information technology in both? Both the positivist research and interpretative research stop short of these considerations; they only offer a portrayal at a distance. However, because MIS is a profession and corporate function, because we MIS researchers must treat the people whom we study not only as research subjects but also as our constituents, and because we MIS researchers *want* our observations ultimately to make a difference, in good ways, to our constituents, to their information systems, and to their organisations—MIS research ought to include more than just the worlds of positivism and interpretativism.

What Forms Should 'Researching MIS' Take in the Future?

Certainly, different MIS scholars would offer different answers to the question of what forms 'researching MIS' ought to take in the future. One plausible position is that MIS researchers ought to pursue positivism and interpretativism in the manner of pure or basic research, and that such basic research (similar to basic research in physics, astronomy, biology, chemistry, and other natural sciences) will eventually lead to one or another problem-solving application. The position I take is that MIS researchers ought to pursue another form of research that has not received as much attention as it deserves: critical social theory (CST).

In my research with Ngwenyama (1996), we note that, in Bernstein's review of CST (1976: 179–85), he observes that it was the critical theorist Max Horkheimer who, in the 1930s, coined the term 'critical theory' so as to contrast it to 'traditional theory', which refers not only to positivist research, but even includes interpretative research (such as the phenomenology of Edmund Husserl). Whereas positivist and interpretative researchers see themselves as observers or onlookers whose research is completed when they have achieved a sound explanation or understanding of their subject matter, CST researchers believe differently; they believe that no researchers can simply be onlookers, but that researchers themselves influence, and are influenced by, the social and technological systems they are studying, and that the responsibilities of researchers do not end with the development of sound explanations and understandings, but also extend to the critique of unjust and inequitable conditions in society from which people require emancipation. Excellent reviews of CST already exist both inside and outside the MIS research literature (Alvesson and Willmott, 1992; Held, 1980; Ngwenyama, 1991; Orlikowski and Baroudi, 1991; Tice and Slavens, 1983; White, 1988). However, a difficulty of researching MIS through a CST approach is that it awaits extensive development. Hirschheim and Klein (1994) offer the commentaries that the philosophy of neo-humanism, on which CST is built, 'is strong on utopian vision but short on principles for implementation' (p. 99) and that 'critical social theory does not point to effective ways of handling the darker side of organisational life, which blocks the road to emancipation, in particular the distortions arising from vested interests and power' (p. 100). Hirschheim and Klein can be credited for taking an incremental step towards the needed implementation, thereby establishing a direction in which more such steps need to be taken.

Certainly there are other avenues that researching MIS may also take in the future. Action research (Baskerville, 1995), like CST, is a form of research that deserves more attention than it has received. Another potential avenue whose merits I have argued (1991*a*) is to model MIS research not so much on research in the positivist and interpretative sciences, but on research in the professions, such as architecture.

For a productive future for researching MIS, I believe that the effort of attending to a diversity of research approaches, their limitations, and their potentials is necessary, but insufficient. To conclude this essay, I return to two concepts with which I opened the essay: that our MIS research itself is a social construction and that MIS is distinguished by at least four dimensions.

To highlight the significance of research as being a socially constructed activity, I offer an analogy involving Kling and Scacchi's classic notion of 'the web of computing' (1982) which, in Hirschheim and Klein's recent characterisation, 'reveals that information systems are like social institutions in that they are embedded in a complex web of social norms and practices' (1994: 100). Just as we MIS researchers are familiar with the notion of the web of computing, we may also entertain the notion of *the web of researching*. Our own activities of *researching MIS* involve social institutions (journals, conferences, schools of research thought, funding agencies) and are themselves embedded in a complex web of social norms and practices.

The notion of *the web of researching* presents us with a challenge. What is it about our social institutions in the socially constructed world of MIS research that encourages some forms of research but not others? The mere recognition of a new, needed form of research by one researcher or even a group of researchers would not be enough to launch the new research. In addition, what social and political actions would be needed to intervene in the web of researching so as to secure the new form of research? In what ways do MIS researchers themselves require emancipation? What are some equitable and emancipatory ways in which the activities of researching MIS may continue or should change, and exactly who would, or should, decide what is equitable and emancipatory?

Rich complications in meeting this challenge arise from the fact that our research procedures themselves are a form of technology. Research technology richly complicates researching researchers, just as information technology richly complicates researching MIS. The same four interrelated dimensions that characterise what MIS is, described at the outset of the essay, also characterise what researching is. First, researching MIS does not involve research procedures alone, but also the rich aspects of *human and social instantiations* of research procedures. Second, the *emergent* nature of the transformational effects of our research procedures and our research context on each other can pose difficulties to anticipating, studying, explaining, and understanding our own activities of researching. Third, the fact that research procedures are obviously an *intellectual* technology further builds unpredictability into how we end up instanciating our research procedures. And finally, MIS research itself is a profession or academic function, where we each have an interest and responsibility to serve one another as colleagues and where we *want* our self-reflections on our activities of researching MIS to make a difference, in good ways, to one another, to our research procedures, to our research institutions, and thereby eventually to our constituents—people who use information technology in organisations. As rich as these complications are, we must tackle them. If we do not even attempt to tackle them in researching ourselves, how may we profess to tackle them in researching others?

If we are able to investigate the web of computing among people in organisations, we are no less able to investigate the web of researching amongst ourselves. Both logical consistency and the golden rule require that if we profess the validity of research procedures for explaining, understanding, and prescribing for others, we must also profess the validity of the same procedures for explaining, understanding, and prescribing for ourselves. Ultimately, researching MIS requires researching ourselves.

References

Agar, M. H. (1986), *Speaking of Ethnography* (Beverly Hills, Calif.: Sage).
Alvesson, M., and Willmott, H. (1992), *Critical Management Studies* (London: Sage).
Baskerville, R. (1995), 'Action Research Bibliography' (World Wide Web: http://www.som.binghamton.edu/rbask/actres.htm).
Berger, P. L., and Luckmann, T. (1967), *The Social Construction of Reality: A Treatise in the Sociology of Knowledge* (Garden City, NY: Anchor Books).
Bernstein, R. J. (1976), *The Restructuring of Social and Political Theory* (New York: Harcourt Brace Jovanovich).
—— (1983), *Beyond Objectivism and Relativism: Science, Hermeneutics, and Praxis* (Philadelphia: University of Pennsylvania Press).
Boland, R. J. (1985), 'Phenomenology: A Preferred Approach to Research on Information Systems', in Mumford et al. (1985).
Campbell, D. T., and Stanley, J. C. (1963), *Experimental and Quasi-experimental Designs for Research* (Chicago: Rand McNally).
Cook, T. D., and Campbell, D. T. (1979), *Quasi-experimentation: Design and Analysis Issues for Field Settings* (Chicago: Rand McNally).
Copi, I. (1986 edn.), *Introduction to Logic* (New York: Macmillan).
Curley, K. F., and Pyburn, P. J. (1982), ' "Intellectual" Technologies: The Key to Improving White-Collar Productivity', *Sloan Management Review*, 24: 31–9.
Held, D. (1980), *Introduction to Critical Theory: Horkheimer to Habermas* (Berkeley and Los Angeles: University of California Press).
Hirschheim, R., and Klein, H. K. (1994), 'Realizing Emancipatory Principles in Information Systems Development: The Case for ETHICS', *MIS Quarterly*, 18: 83–109.
Jönsson, Sten (1991), 'Action Research', in Nissen et al. (1991).
Kanter, R. M. (1977), *Men and Women of the Corporation* (New York: Basic Books).
Kling, R., and Scacchi, W. (1982), 'The Web of Computing: Computer Technology as Social Organisation', in Yovits (1982).
Lee, A. S. (1989), 'A Scientific Methodology for MIS Case Studies', *MIS Quarterly*, 13: 33–50.
—— (1991*a*), 'Architecture as a Reference Discipline for MIS', in Nissen et al. (1991).
—— (1991*b*), 'Integrating Positivist and Interpretive Approaches to Organisational Research', *Organisation Science*, 4: 342–65.
—— (1994), 'Electronic Mail as a Medium for Rich Communication: An Empirical Investigation Using Hermeneutic Interpretation', *MIS Quarterly*, 18: 143–57.
Markus, M. L., and Robey, D. (1988), 'Information Technology and Organisational Change: Causal Structure in Theory and Research', *Management Science*, 5: 583–98.
Mumford, E., Hirschheim, R., Fitzgerald, G., and Wood-Harper, A. T. (1985) (eds.), *Research Methods in Information Systems* (New York: North-Holland).
Nagel, E. (1979 edn.), *The Structure of Science* (Indianapolis: Hacket).
Ngwenyama, O. K. (1991), 'The Critical Social Theory Approach to Information Systems: Problems and Challenges', in Nissen et al. (1991).
—— and Lee, A. S. (1996), 'Communication Richness in Electronic Mail: Critical Social Theory and the Contextuality of Meaning', unpub. paper.

Nissen, H.-E., Hirschheim, R., and Klein, H. K. (1991) (eds.), *Information Systems Research: Contemporary Approaches and Emergent Traditions* (New York: Elsevier Science).

Orlikowski, W. J., and Baroudi, J. J. (1991), 'Studying Information Technology in Organisations: Research Approaches and Assumptions', *Information Systems Research*, 2: 1–28.

Palmer, R. E. (1979), *Hermeneutics: Interpretation Theory in Schleiermacher, Dilthey, Heidegger, and Gadamer* (Evanston, Ill.: Northwestern University Press).

Popper, K. (1968 edn.), *The Logic of Scientific Discovery* (New York: Harper Torchbooks).

Rabinow, P., and Sullivan, W. M. (1979) (eds.), *Interpretive Social Science* (Berkeley and Los Angeles: University of California Press).

Sanday, P. R. (1979), 'The Ethnographic Paradigm(s)', *Administrative Science Quarterly*, 24: 527–38.

Schön, D. A. (1983), *The Reflective Practitioner: How Professionals Think in Action* (New York: Basic Books).

Schutz, A. (1973 edn.), *Collected Papers*, ed. with introd. by M. Natanson (The Hague: M. Nijhoff).

Straub, D. (1989), 'Validating Instruments in MIS Research', *MIS Quarterly*, 13: 147–69.

Taylor, C. (1979), 'Interpretation and the Sciences of Man', in Rabinow et al. (1979).

Tice, T. N., and Slavens, T. P. (1983), *Research Guide to Philosophy* (Chicago: American Library Association).

White, S. (1988), *The Recent Work of Jürgen Habermas: Reason, Justice and Modernity* (Cambridge: Cambridge University Press).

Yovits, M. C. (1982), *Advances in Computers*, 21 (New York: Academic Press).

Zmud, R. W. (1995), 'Editor's Comments', *MIS Quarterly*, 19, 1: pp. v–viii.

2

Routinisation, Re-engineering, and Socio-technical Design
Changing Ideas on the Organisation of Work

ENID MUMFORD

Introduction

There is a vast literature around on how to organise the work situation. Companies believe that they must rethink this to survive in a new global market or a much broader international market. This reorganisation is to cut costs, improve efficiency, become more competitive, and increase the share price. Most companies claim to be doing it. The questions that need to be addressed are what kind of reorganisation is taking place today and why, and how does this differ from the kinds of restructuring that have been popular in the past? What influences organisational change in the office and on the shop floor and do particular philosophies, theories, and methods produce better results than others?

Work Study

It must be remembered that the wish to reorganise and restructure work is not new, it has been with us for a very long time. For many years it was called work study and it claimed to cut costs by rationalising the work process so that work was broken down into a large number of small tasks. These were then carried out by unskilled and easily replaceable labour. This worked well for mass production factories although, as the labour force became better educated, there were increasing complaints from both blue- and white-collar workers about the boring and tedious nature of the work they were required to do.

The author would like to thank most sincerely the members of the Socio-technical Round Table who were kind enough to provide comments and ideas on socio-technical design and business process re-engineering. These were: Ross Beattie, Charles E. Berezin, Federico Butera, John Cotter, George Gates, Robert Gilbert, Elaine Granata, Bill Jackson, Christian Schumacher, Jim Taylor, Paul Tolchinsky.

The introduction of technology, particularly computer technology, acted as a catalyst for change although when computers first arrived traditional work study principles were still applied. Many early systems had the computer taking over the more interesting manual activities while the clerk, usually female, was left with the boring and onerous input and output tasks. In recent years increasingly complex and flexible technology has meant that a more highly skilled labour force is required. At the same time there has been a considerable displacement of human labour by new technology.

Over the years far-sighted groups and individuals have recognised that intelligent people become frustrated and unhappy when they are required to work in situations that do not offer any scope for intelligent thought and initiative. A group of this kind emerged in Britain at the end of the Second World War. They were the pioneers of socio-technical design which is an approach that tries to combine the effective use of technology with the effective and humanistic use of people.

Socio-technical Design: How it Began

Eric Trist, one of the founder members of what was to become the Tavistock Institute of Human Relations, became aware of the adverse influence technology could have on people when he was working in the jute industry in Scotland, in the late 1930s. He was a member of a small interdisciplinary team studying unemployment when the spinning section of the jute industry was being rationalised. He found that this change in technology caused unemployment, deskilling, and alienation. Trist realised that the technical and social systems were having a negative effect on each other. This aroused his interest in what was to become his life's work—developing a new approach for the design of work organisation. This was called socio-technical systems design (Trist, 1981).

At the end of the Second World War Trist was joined by a group of his wartime colleagues and together they created the Tavistock Institute of Human Relations in London. The Tavistock, or the Tavvy as it is generally known, was established in 1946. A number of the group had been members of the Tavistock Clinic before the war. During the war they had collaborated on projects such as the setting up of group selection boards for officers and the establishment of resettlement units for repatriated prisoners of war. They came from varied academic backgrounds—one, Harold Bridger, was a mathematician; another, Tommy Wilson, had qualified as a doctor.

The Tavistock Clinic was, and is, a therapeutic establishment, led by psychologists concerned with mental health and individual development. This was the initial focus and orientation of the members of the Tavistock Institute, although they were interested in applying their ideas to workers in industry. The founding group were later joined by people from other disciplines: psychologists, sociologists, and anthropologists. Everyone who joined the Institute in its early days was required to undergo psychoanalysis. The belief was that you could not understand the problems and needs of others unless you thoroughly understood yourself.

Influences on the Tavistock

The early Tavistock Group were greatly influenced by their wartime experiences. Trist had been struck by the efficiency of the German panzer divisions which linked men and machines together for military purposes. Bridger had been assigned to a special unit, under the direction of Wilfred Bion and John Sutherland, that was developing ideas about 'leaderless groups' and applying these to officer selection and training. Bridger was later to apply these same ideas to the hospital treatment of some of the psychological casualties of the war. He introduced self-motivated 'leaderless' groups to the Northfield hospital in which he worked, persuading the patients to take responsibility for organising many of their own activities (Cutcher-Gershenfeld, 1983).

Bion had a particularly strong influence on the ideas of the early Tavvy Group. He was a psychologist of the Melanie Klein School who was associated with the Tavistock Clinic and believed in the power of small group therapy. Bion had two major influences on the work of the Tavistock Institute. He convinced them that their role was to work with small groups in industry, helping group members to become aware of those emotional factors that hindered successful performance of the group's task. The Tavistock workers also used Bion's assumptions as a guide to the nature of the work group. This must be of a size to allow close personal relationships, it must have a capacity for co-operation in achieving its primary task, it must be able to derive satisfaction from the successful accomplishment of this task (Bion, 1961).

The ideas of two other researchers also influenced Tavvy thinking. These were Kurt Lewin in the United States and von Bertalanffy in Europe. Lewin had experimented with democratic, autocratic, and *laissez-faire* groups in the late 1930s. (Lewin, 1935). In 1950, Ludwig von Bertalanffy published a paper in *Science* on 'the theory of open systems in physics and biology'. This drew the attention of the Tavistock Group to systems theory and the notion of open systems (von Bertalanffy, 1950).

Early Projects in Coal Mining

The Tavistock Institute made its first major contribution to socio-technical theory in 1949 when it began a number of field projects in the British coal industry (Trist et al. 1963). Prior to this it had been carrying out action research with small groups in the Glacier Metal Company and this had led to the publication of a book by Elliott Jacques called *The Changing Culture of a Factory* (Jacques, 1951). This described how small group meetings had led to the systematic rethinking and solution of problems and resulted in the setting up of consultative mechanisms at Glacier. But the Glacier project had been directed solely at group relations and social organisation.It did not address the question of technology. The coal mining studies were concerned with organisational arrangements that might increase productivity and technology was clearly an important factor here.

The approach adopted was to consider each production unit as a socio-technical system. The theory underlying this is described in the book *Organisational Choice* (Trist et al. 1963). The Tavistock research team was able to make a number of comparative studies in the north-east coalfield which, together with the rest of the British coal industry, had recently been nationalised. The Durham area offered a wide variety of mining methods, often in the same pit or associated with the same seam of coal, although the degree of mechanisation varied considerably from face to face. The research focused on the quality of work roles, the nature of task groups, the prevailing work culture, the climate of intergroup relations, and the character of the managing system.

The team began to recognise that if the technical system is optimised at the expense of the human system, the results obtained will be suboptimal. The goal must therefore be joint optimisation of the technical and social systems. These ideas were formulated into a set of socio-technical concepts that were written up in a seminal paper called 'Some Social and Psychological Consequences of the Longwall Method of Coal Getting' (Trist and Bamforth, 1951).

Some years after the first coal mine project the National Coal Board approached the Tavistock team and asked for a second study. The Tavistock psychologists decided not to undertake this as it would have meant working for management and they wished 'to maintain an independent role'. The Coal Board then approached a research group at Liverpool University of which the author was a member. We accepted the study which was concerned with industrial relations. The question to be researched was 'why are some pits continually on strike while other pits are relatively strike free?' The attempt to answer this question led to the author spending almost a year underground and obtaining an intimate knowledge of the organisation and hazards of the long wall method of mining in the north-west coalfield. This is her description of how the Tavistock reorganised the work situation in their north-east pits.

Work Reorganisation

The long wall method of mining was based on the assembly line production systems of industry but, unlike industry, it had to be operated in complex and volatile underground environments. These could be subjected to flooding, gas, falls of roof, and other hazards, all of which made the coal extraction task extremely difficult and stressful. Coal mining with the long wall system was now a cyclical process with different activities being carried out by different groups of men on each of three shifts. As a result of these innovations many miners were suffering from stress disorders and a number of articles appeared in the *British Medical Journal* describing these. The Coal Board asked the Tavistock Group if they would try and improve conditions for the miners, although they must do this without removing or changing the new long wall technology.

The result was a new team-based work system in which groups of miners were given responsibility for all the activities, on all shifts, of a section of the coal face. These miners became competent at carrying out a variety of tasks, and they were allowed to organize their own work. Here were early examples of what today are called team-working, multi-skilling, and empowerment. Interestingly the coal mine reorganisation was also an early example of a process approach. The new multi-skilled groups had accepted responsibility for each activity in the extraction cycle from the initial shot firing of the coal and its removal to conveyor belts, through the moving forward of roof supports as the face advanced, to the final packing of the worked face and the management of a controlled fall of roof (Scott et al., 1963).

It is important to recognise that, unlike much of today's reorganisation, the rationale behind the Tavistock approach was not to increase production but to reduce stress and to provide a better work environment for the miners. The fact that production did go up once the new system was introduced was an unexpected benefit and a surprise to the Tavistock Group. From the 1950s on this approach spread rapidly, first to Scandinavia, later to other parts of Europe, the United States, and India. Participating firms in each country accepted the philosophy that it was important to optimise both the use of technology and the use of people. Work was restructured to create motivation, job satisfaction, and good working conditions, as well as increased efficiency.

Other Projects

While the mining studies were underway, Ken Rice, a member of the Tavistock Institute, initiated a similar piece of research in the Indian textile industry. This was carried out in the calico mills at Ahmedabad and began in 1953 (Rice, 1958). Work groups were formed so that interdependent tasks could forge interdependent relationships. Socio-technical design still continues in India and for many years was led by a prestigious Indian behavioural scientist whose name was Nitish De (De, 1984).

By the early 1960s Scandinavia was showing great interest in industrial democracy and Einar Thorsrud was a prime mover in introducing the ideas and action research methods of the Tavistock Group into Norway. Hans Van Beinam in the Netherlands was also active in this field and researchers in different countries were working on similar projects. It was during this period that Eric Trist began to work with the Australian social scientist Fred Emery. The international network that was to spread the Tavistock message into many countries was in the process of formation.

During the 1950s and 1960s work continued on the theoretical aspects of the socio-technical approach with more and more ideas being drawn from systems theory, particularly the notion of open systems that interact with their environment (Herbst, 1961).

The Tavistock research had by now produced (1) the concept of a socio-technical system, (2) a view of the organisation as an open system, (3) the principle of organisational choice—the need to match social and technical systems together in the most appropriate way—(4) a recognition of the importance of autonomous groups, and (5) better understanding of the problems of work alienation (Hill, 1971).

The Norwegian Industrial Democracy Experiment

The next stage of socio-technical development occurred in 1962 with the start of the Norwegian industrial democracy project. During the winter of 1962–3 the Norwegian Institute for Social Research was invited to undertake research on the problems of 'industrial democracy' and they asked the Tavistock Institute to co-operate with them on the project. It now became possible to try out experiments in several industries and to develop methods as well as theory.

Interest in the work spread throughout Europe and also overseas. Swedish and Danish firms introduced their own experiments and there were projects in other parts of Europe, India, and North America. For example, General Motors had quality of work projects, incorporating employee and trade union involvement, as well as job redesign, in 140 of its plants (Cutcher-Gershenfeld, 1983).

In the 1970s and 1980s the ideas of the Tavistock Institute were to be found in the philosophies and legislation of many governments, for example, the German 'humanisation of work' programme and the quality of working life legislation of Norway and Sweden.

Socio-technical Design Today

The socio-technical approach has continued to this day, supported in the UK by the Tavistock Institute and in the USA by a dedicated group of change management consultants called the Socio-technical Round Table. Many large and influential companies have used, and are still using, this approach. Their objective has been to associate improved performance with a high quality of work environment for employees. Unfortunately socio-technical design has never been very good at publicising what it has to offer. If case studies were written up they appeared in learned journals and not in the popular management literature.

Most of the early Tavistock work was concerned with shop-floor systems and there was a question mark over whether the approach was equally applicable to offices. Later research by the author and others showed that this was the case (Pava, 1983). The author's projects all involved the introduction of new technology and were carried out in banks, a manufacturer of aero-engines, chemical plants, and computer manufacturers. She has found that there are few problems in using socio-technical principles for the redesign of technically advanced offices, although there is still a need to learn how to apply the principles to the remote network of employees communicating electronically in the automated office of the future (Mumford and MacDonald, 1989; Mumford, 1995, 1996).

There is now a need for research which will help answer such questions as, 'Can an autonomous group be formed from people who are physically distant from each other, and communicating via terminals?' There is also a need for engineers to design a humanistic technology which makes the machine a servant to man and not a controller of man.

The other challenge for the socio-technical approach is to learn how to apply it at the macro-social level. Can it be applied to the design of large multinational establishments? Can it apply to senior management as well as to lower-level employees?

The values and objectives of the Tavistock and of socio-technical design have always been directed at helping companies to manage change successfully by creating work systems which enable individuals, groups, and organisations to work together productively and harmoniously.

The Rise and Fall of Re-engineering

In the 1980s a new, tightly integrated, form of work organisation called lean manufacturing became common in car plants as a result of Japanese philosophy and influence (Berggren, 1992). This was based on a 'just-in-time' approach in which buffer stocks were removed and suppliers were expected to supply parts 'on demand'. It greatly increased efficiency and the speed of production. In the late 1980s a similar philosophy reappeared on a broader scale under the title of business process re-engineering. It was suggested that this could be applied to the redesign of companies and plants as well as to individual units.

A Boston consulting company recommended it as a means for improving efficiency and profits in companies in a wide variety of businesses and industries (Hammer and Champy, 1993). Its developers, Michael Hammer, James Champy, and Tom Davenport, claimed that it was both new and essential. Firms that did not restructure in drastic and revolutionary ways would soon go out of business in the new global market. The message was restructure or die. This message was driven home by books that were sold in their thousands in most industrialised countries. It is claimed that Hammer and Champy's book, *Re-engineering the Corporation*, sold two million copies.

The re-engineering approach was what industry, particularly American industry, already nervous about the future, had been waiting for. It appeared to offer a means for rapidly increasing profits and reducing costs. For many firms it was not so much the restructuring that was attractive as the opportunity it provided for getting rid of staff. It also enabled management to transfer the blame for staff reductions away from themselves to the new technique. They were able to say, 'business process re-engineering requires that we do this.' As more and more companies adopted the approach and reduced costs by removing staff Hammer, Champy, and Davenport began to realise that their initiative had gone astray. They desperately tried to explain to US newspapers and journals that this was not what they had intended. Their objective had been to improve efficiency through the restructuring of work, not to facilitate the slash and burn removal of large swathes of the US labour force. Unfortunately by now many European firms had also read the books, got the message, and begun the same restructuring and redundancy processes.

Because US industry had misinterpreted the goals of business process re-engineering and focused on short-term financial gains its results were not very positive. A series of large-scale surveys carried out by different consultant groups between 1993 and 1996 charted its progress from initial euphoria, through increasing doubts about its benefits, until, finally, Davenport published an article in a US management journal stating that the approach should now be abandoned (Davenport, 1996). He told the world that it is effectively over. In his view this was not because restructuring did not work but because it had been corrupted into a means for removing staff or *downsizing*. It had paid little or no attention to morale, motivation, or the needs of people. He described it as the last gasp of Taylorism.

In the article he criticised the association of re-engineering with cost reduction through layoffs and described how the re-engineering genie had turned ugly. He maintained it had become:

So ugly that today, to most business people in the United States, re-engineering has become a word that stands for restructuring, layoffs, and too often failed change programmes . . . The rock that re-engineering foundered on is simple: people. Re-engineering treated the people inside companies as if they were just so many bits and bytes, interchangeable parts to be re-engineered.

He concluded:

As is always the case with any fad, there was a kernel of truth to re-engineering. Over time that truth got lost. But that doesn't make it any less true. The most profound lesson of business process re-engineering was never re-engineering, but business processes. Processes are how we work. Any company that ignores its business processes or fails to improve them risks its future. That said, companies can use many different approaches to process improvement without ever embarking on a high risk re-engineering project . . . When the Next Big Thing in management is, try to remember the lessons of re-engineering. Don't drop all your ongoing approaches in favour of the handsome newcomer. (Davenport, 1996)

   Socio-technical design had, of course, also focused on the redesign of work processes, associating this with increased job satisfaction and an improved quality of working life. But US industry had apparently forgotten that this well-tried, humanistic approach was still available.

Why did Business Process Re-engineering not Succeed?

Why have so many firms experienced problems with business process re-engineering? This is an interesting, many-faceted question. We will try to answer it by examining some of the factors that influenced company behaviour.

The tendency to copy others

Richard Dawkins, the geneticist, tells us that in times of uncertainty organisations tend to repeat each other's actions in an attempt to feel secure (Dawkins, 1989). With business process re-engineering companies accepted the global economy scenario and were influenced by the importance attached to cost accounting by major business schools and consultants. They then became victims of their own cost-cutting strategies. Recent research has shown that companies that cut staff to reduce costs have been less successful in increasing profits than companies that took a longer-term view and increased and improved their business activities.

The absence of a theory

The socio-technical approach has always had a number of comprehensive and well-established theories associated with it which are related to the successful management of change. These have been derived from biological open systems, psychoanalysis, psychology, and sociology. The re-engineering pioneers accepted that their approach was, as Davenport said, 'a function more of management rhetoric than of management science'. Because of this absence of theory, little guidance was provided on how to manage a form of change that was claimed to be both essential and revolutionary. This neglect led many companies to believe that re-engineering was easy. You just got on and did it. Re-engineering then had an edge over socio-technical design, which required employee participation and more time for problem analysis. Also, the democratic and participative nature of socio-technical design meant that it was difficult to use if employees were going to be made redundant as part of the change (Mumford and Beekman, 1995).

The lack of management involvement

The reaction of many companies to the daunting re-engineering task was not to try and handle it themselves but to hire consultants. Hammer approved of this approach, arguing that most consultants would have a well-tried methodology for handling change. He saw this as a method for identifying major work activities and related tasks; for analysing time frames and resource requirements for each task; and for deciding key milestones, management reviews, and decision points for each stage of the journey. This sounds rather like traditional work study and contradicted his earlier exhortations to innovate without too much analysis or detailed thought. He now seemed to be writing as an engineer trying to achieve order and certainty in a chaotic world.

The fact that Hammer did not offer any detailed methodology himself left consulting firms with the opportunity for using their old and familiar analytical tools and techniques and calling these re-engineering. This was a great advantage from their point of view as it did not require them to do very much of Hammer's revolutionary rethinking. Old projects could now be called re-engineering and when making a sale they could offer their clients what they called a re-engineering methodology.

Unfortunately, as we have seen, major change proved a much more difficult task than most companies had anticipated and instead of rewards there were often financial losses. One reason for problems was that, with some notable exceptions, many consultants did not have a history of experience in managing major change. They had started as highly respected accounting and auditing consultancies, or they had been experts in information technology and used to introducing new payroll and finance systems. Few had a great deal of experience of advising on organisational change. To make matters more difficult they were all expanding and many of their recruits were young men and women in their first consulting jobs.

The lack of concern for people

A lack of concern for human relations can have a number of psychological effects on those affected by restructuring. There will be little enthusiasm for the proposed change and a considerable anxiety about its consequences. If people are laid off then there is likely to be a general drop in morale. Those that remain may feel guilty that their jobs have been saved while their friends have lost theirs. There will be little enthusiasm to make the new system a success. Good relationships between management and employees that may have taken years to develop can be lost virtually overnight.

If the re-engineering does not result in reduced costs or increased profitability, as the evidence suggests is often the case, then a very serious situation can result. The company will have experienced the high cost of change without financial benefits. At the same time it will have lost the support and confidence of its workforce, and it will have paid a large bill for the expensive consultants it has introduced. Davenport has even suggested that the reason some companies made staff redundant was to pay the enormous bills of the consultants they brought in. The price of revolutionary re-engineering will then have been very high indeed.

What can we Learn from a Comparison of Business Process Re-engineering and Socio-technical Design?

If business process re-engineering is compared with socio-technical design it is clear that the restructuring design principles of both are quite similar but that the two approaches differ greatly in their values and visions. Both are concerned with improving efficiency and favour a process approach, team-working, multi-skilling, and decision-taking by those actually doing the job. With business process re-engineering these structures are to assist the speed-up of the work process and can result in increased stress. In contrast, the socio-technical approach is based on a belief that employees have a right to good working conditions and opportunities for learning and personal development. These will contribute to both high morale and increased efficiency. When work is restructured the employees who will use the new system play a major part in the redesign process. In this way they have ownership of the change and a commitment to it.

Many academics and commentators have described the two approaches but the author decided that it would be useful to ask a group of practising consultants who were familiar with both approaches to compare them. She therefore approached the US Socio-technical Round Table for assistance and asked if members who worked as consultants and were familiar with both socio-technical and business process re-engineering approaches would make some comparisons between the two from their own experiences.

Eleven agreed to do this. All were members of the Round Table but they were not all American. One, Chris Schumacher, was British and managed a consultancy called Work Structuring Ltd. in England. Another, Federico Butera, was Italian and for many years had run a very successful research institute in Milan. The remainder were from different parts of the United States. Some operated on their own, others were associated with small groups of colleagues, one was an internal consultant for a large electronics company. Almost all had acted as socio-technical consultants for a wide variety of industries, health care organisations, and government departments.

Clearly the views of individuals in this group are going to be different and we will concentrate on the majority view together with any interesting and relevant differences of opinion. The first two questions asked the consultants if they were able to apply a socio-technical perspective in most of their work and if the opportunities to do this were increasing or decreasing. The answer to the first question was a unanimous 'yes'. All agreed that they could do this and that they had been doing this for many years. The answer to the second question was a little more cautious and hesitant. Most agreed that opportunities were increasing because good human relations were so important as workplaces became increasingly complex. However, they were not increasing a great deal. One reason for this lack of progress was the growing disaffection of companies with what have been described as the 'slash and burn' exercises of re-engineering and downsizing. Many were now avoiding organisational change. Consultants were often invited in to 'clean up the mess' and many companies had become interested in a slower form of change so that they could build up more understanding and support from their employees. However, the fact that re-engineering had failed to incorporate a concern for people had provided some new opportunities for socio-technical consultants, even though many companies were not aware of the term 'socio-technical' and what it meant.

The consultants were now asked how much contact they had had with business process re-engineering, what form this contact had taken, why it was so popular when it first appeared, and how popular it was today.

All had had some contact although the nature of this contact varied considerably. The internal consultant had had little direct contact as his firm practised a policy of continuous business improvement. Others had found that there was an element of business process re-engineering in many of the projects they were offered. Some had incorporated re-engineering techniques into their socio-technical approach while others had followed on from re-engineering projects with more people-centred and participative approaches. Again several said they had been called in to correct re-engineering disasters.

Reasons given for the early popularity of re-engineering were varied. It was seen as a way of admitting that drastic change was necessary by firms that were not carrying out continuous improvement. It offered managers

Enid Mumford

greater efficiency from a technique not too different from industrial engineering, with which they were familiar. It seemed to promise an easy and logical way to considerably improve organisational performance. It therefore appealed to action-oriented management under pressure for short-term results. It also had appeal because managers did not have to share power with their employees as socio-technical design required. There was also a view that its success was greatly assisted by excellent marketing and by the financial opportunities it offered IT vendors and consultants. Also the ideas of 'starting from a clean slate' and 'radical change' struck a chord with many managers.

Its popularity today was seen as greatly on the wane. One consultant said 'It's dead in the US. It's even difficult to find firms that will admit to having tried it. Many companies have now eliminated their re-engineering departments.' The general view was that re-engineering was getting an increasingly bad press and was on the way out.

The consultants were now asked to provide more detail. Could they describe the kinds of business and organisational problems which it had proved most successful in addressing, and also the most unsuccessful ones? Could it be separated from downsizing, or were downsizing and re-engineering now inextricably linked? Had it displaced socio-technical design or was this due for a rebirth? How could this rebirth best be achieved and what were the advantages and disadvantages of re-engineering when compared with socio-technical design?

One consultant saw it as most successful in simple 'paper flow' types of businesses such as insurance, accounting, and engineering. Another said that in the USA it had been most popular in those industries where rapid technical and/or product change was the norm. Here, the pressure to reduce product development cycle time or rapidly to change product capability made the re-engineering approach very attractive. The general view was that it worked best with relatively simple processes or as part of a larger-scale change programme in which other approaches were used as well. Some of its principles could also assist employees taking part in participative projects which required them to improve their own work processes. Its success or failure was seen as depending more on who was introducing it, and why it was being introduced, than on the method itself.

It was seen as generally unsuccessful when technically or expert driven and with cost control as its primary goals. The cost savings were then short term and the organisational consequences often disastrous. It was also unsuccessful when change management and quality of working life issues were overlooked, when obvious improvements had already been made, and when the deeper underlying problems required more than process streamlining. It was always unsuccessful when it was regarded as 'a quick fix'.

There was general agreement that in the USA business process re-engineering was synonymous with downsizing. This was less the view in

Europe. Professor Butera, the Italian organisational expert, said it did not need to be associated with staff reductions. Cost savings could be achieved without these by shortening work flows and increasing productivity.

There was considerable optimism over the possibility of a rebirth for socio-technical ideas. The internal consultant said that the main hindrance to full-scale acceptance was the desire for quick-fix problem-solving. His view was, 'it's much more fun to jump on the fire truck, speed to the fire and fight it than to plan how best to prevent it from spreading'.

This was the view of a number of the consultants who also stressed the need for organisations to move away from 'short-termism' and concentrate on successful change for efficiency and people. The Italian consultant believed that re-engineering and the socio-technical approach did not need to be in opposition. He said, 'socio-technical design can substantially contribute to re-engineering successes as it provides strong foundations for people and change management issues'.

The general view was that communication and education could assist this rebirth. The positive results of socio-technical design needed to be made known to business leaders. Socio-technical consultancies would benefit from being larger and more influential. And a champion was needed, someone with status such as Michael Hammer or W. Edwards Deming, to make it a household name. There was also a dearth of experienced socio-technical practitioners who could offer firms expert help. Methods also needed to be streamlined and speeded up. Firms would not wait while lengthy group consultations took place about design and implementation.

The consultants were finally asked if they would each provide four important criteria that they believed assisted good organisational design and four contributing to its failure. Here are the success factors.

Factors Contributing to Good Organisational Design

Positive management attitudes

- Senior management practising the values it preaches
- Commitment to change from company leadership
- Support from the top for a democratically run company
- Ensuring the commitment of middle management
- Middle management belief in company democracy

Clear vision and clear goals

- A clear, concise, generally accepted vision of change goals
- Design reflecting the strategic needs of the company
- A time frame that fits with the dynamics of the business
- A focus on the key leverage points that will ensure future business success

A well managed change process

- Analysis and design to be a full-time, internal responsibility
- Constant and continual communication with everyone
- Trust in the socio-technical consultant
- A straightforward change process that involves those who will be affected, including trade unions
- Appropriate rewards for successful change
- Time to complete the change process

A good knowledge of organisational design

- A consensus on the principles of good organisational design
- A set of practical tools to help the company arrive at solutions
- Methodologies for ensuring that the principles of socio-technical design are carried into the future
- Methodologies that are clear and understood by all

Desirable features of the new system

- Organisational systems that reward self-management
- Lower-level employees that favour self-management
- A new work structure that is approved and will endure

Factors Contributing to Unsuccessful Organisational Design
Negative management attitudes

- A lack of commitment or involvement by senior management
- Weak autocratic management
- Insufficient resources being allocated to the project
- Managerial impatience—'I want it tomorrow'
- Treating the design process as something separate from running the business
- A desire for rapid gains in productivity without concern for employee gains
- A change of top management in the middle of a project

A poorly managed change process

- The belief that change is for a particular group—e.g. management or the shop floor
- An absence of appropriate goals
- A lack of trust in the consultant
- Using socio-technical design where it is not appropriate
- Organisational problems
- The project becoming the victim of internal politics
- Different philosophies being used to sabotage a socio-technical approach

Final Comments

Where do we go from here? It is very important for firms to be continually reviewing their working practices and seeing if these can be improved. It is also important for them to have motivated employees who are going to share the company's objectives and interests. It is clear that companies need to think carefully about their existing problems, what they want to achieve in the future, and the best strategies for doing this, given their particular environments, interests, and level of knowledge. A fast just-in-time approach may work well in the mass production car industry, but it may work much less well in white-collar situations where quality and service are more important than speed. A focus on process may improve work integration but it may also produce greater vulnerability and new and difficult problems that are more expensive to solve. There will also be major costs if the new extended and tightly linked system breaks down.

The answer seems to be careful diagnosis, the identification of a number of improvement strategies, and the choice of one or more that fits well with the values and long-term objectives of the company. This then has to be carefully and democratically implemented. Even the most positive change will fail if it is not sensitively introduced with the involvement and assistance of those who will be affected. Radical re-engineering surgery, although attractive to the *macho manager* who wants quick-fix, short-term results, has not turned out to be a viable solution. As we have seen, US firms which have drastically reduced the size of their labour forces have proved to be less financially successful than those in the same industry that did not adopt this approach. When looking for an appropriate change strategy, managers are recommended to try a softer approach such as socio-technical design. This was developed in the UK and it has been successfully used in many parts of the world. It has a humanistic set of values, a sound methodology, and a proven record of success.

References

Berggren, C. (1992), *The Volvo Experience* (London: Macmillan).

Bion, W. R. (1961), *Experiences in Groups and Other Papers* (London: Tavistock Institute).

Cutcher-Gershenfeld, J. (1983), 'QWL: A Historical Perspective', *Work Life Review*, 11: 16–24.

Davenport, T. (1996), 'Why Re-engineering Failed: The Fad that Forgot People', *Fast Company*, Jan.: 70–4.

Dawkins, R. (1989), *The Selfish Gene* (Oxford, Oxford University Press).

De, Nitish (1984), *Alternative Design of Human Organisations* (Beverly Hills, Calif.: Sage).

Hammer, M., and Champy, J. (1993), *Reengineering the Corporation: A Manifesto for Business Revolution* (New York: HarperCollins).

Herbst, P. G. (1961), 'A Theory of Simple Behaviour Systems, 1 and 11', *Human Relations*, 14: 71–94 and 193–240.

Hill, P. (1971), *Towards a New Philosophy of Management* (Aldershot: Gower).

Jacques, E. (1951), *The Changing Culture of a Factory* (London: Tavistock).

Lewin, K. (1935), *Dynamic Theory of Personality* (New York: McGraw Hill).

Mumford, E. (1995), *Effective Systems Design and Requirements Analysis: The ETHICS Method* (London: Macmillan).

—— (1996), *Systems Design: Ethical Tools for Ethical Change* (London: Macmillan).

—— and Beekman, G.-J. (1995), *Tools for Change and Progress: A Socio-technical Approach to Business Process Re-engineering* (Leiden: CSG Publications).

—— and MacDonald, B. (1989), *XSEL's Progress* (Chichester: Wiley).

Pava, C. (1983), *Managing New Office Technology* (New York: Free Press).

Rice, A. K. (1958), *Productivity and Social Organisation: The Ahmedabad Experiment* (London: Tavistock).

Scott, W., Mumford, E., McIvering, I., and Kirkby, J. (1963), *Coal and Conflict* (Liverpool, Liverpool University Press).

Trist, E. (1981), *The Evolution of Socio-technical Systems* (Toronto: Ontario Quality of Working Life Centre).

—— and Bamforth, K. (1951), 'Some Social and Psychological Consequences of the Long Wall Method of Coal Getting', *Human Relations*, 4: 3–38.

—— Higgins, G., Murray, H., and Pollock, A. (1963), *Organisational Choice* (London: Tavistock).

von Bertalanffy, L. (1950), 'The Theory of Open Systems in Physics and Biology', *Science*, 111: 23–9.

3

Systems Thinking

PETER CHECKLAND

Introduction

It may appear obvious to an optimist that 'management information systems' (MIS) are a particular kind of 'system' and that systems theory should be there in the background to underpin the creation of such systems. This chapter cannot but dispel that naïve optimism. There is no simple link between systems theory and work on MIS, no spick-and-span body of ready-made theory which can be used in a straightforward way to help in the design of such systems. But all is not lost. The process of *systems thinking*, that is to say: consciously organised thinking using systems ideas, is very relevant to the problems of work in the MIS field. And some of the problems which have been faced and resolved in the development of systems thinking itself are very relevant to the MIS field, and can usefully illuminate its problems. That is the kind of underpinning which this chapter will seek to provide for the book as a whole. At the start it may be useful to illustrate the kind of difficulties which have to be faced in this task.

In the early 1970s, my group at Lancaster University were invited by a director of what was then the British Aircraft Corporation to take a 'systems engineering' approach to the Anglo-French Concorde project. Our aim was to give advice on how we could improve the management of the project. This was at a time when the two pre-production aircraft, one in Bristol, one in Toulouse, were nearing completion, but had not yet flown. The Concorde project was, at the time, the subject of much public debate in the UK, since it was by then very apparent that it was going to take years longer to develop than originally thought and would cost many millions more than originally estimated. As we started the work, we took it as completely obvious, not to be questioned, that this was clearly an engineering project, one which aimed to create the world's first supersonic passenger aircraft; and it seemed obvious too that this project was 'a system to create a supersonic passenger aircraft according to a defined technical specification, within a certain time, at a certain cost, and under the constraints that it must gain the certificate from the Civil Aviation Authority which will enable the public to fly in it, and that it must not unacceptably damage the environment'. We had the idea that we could model this, and work out from the models the implied information requirements and the necessary management activity. Then we could, in the light of the models, examine the project's real-world information and activity, and make suggestions for improvement.

In the event we were amazed when our models seemed to bear no relation at all to real-world structures and activities and, most importantly, engendered little interest in the engineers and managers working on 'the Concorde project'. Our eventual hard-won learning was that there was in fact no 'project' in the accepted sense of the way the word is used in the management literature. Although the phrase 'the Concorde project' was on everyone's lips, used many times each day, project management was not at all in evidence; that is not how Concorde was created.

Realising our mistake provided valuable learning for us. We were beginning to learn that there are great difficulties in an ill-formed and conceptually confused field like *management* (of which study of 'MIS' is a part) which stem from the fact that there is no language available for serious discussion which is separate from everyday language. Physical chemists know *exactly* what they mean by 'entropy', or 'the Q-branch of an infra-red spectrum'. Would-be scholars in the management field, on the other hand, have no shared precise meaning for many of their relevant concepts, for example 'role', 'norm', 'culture', or 'information system'; all these terms are fuzzy as a result of their unreflective use in everyday chat. Serious work in *management* and in *MIS* needs always to be aware of that.

In the Concorde work our initial mistake was due to the fact that we were thinking that when people used the phrase 'the Concorde project' they were actually referring to something in the British Aircraft Corporation which corresponded to an organised *project* in the full sense of the word. We were in fact thinking like systems engineers; we were too ready to accept the everyday language phrase 'the Concorde project' as indicating that there actually was a project in existence, and that we could model it as *a system* and hence engineer improvements to it.

This is a specific example of the untrustworthiness of casual everyday language in the management field, and an illustration of the problem which bedevils understanding of systems thinking in general. In its purest form, the version of this problem for systems thinking is that the word 'system' is used casually in everyday language, just as 'project' was in the British Aircraft Corporation, simply as a label-word to refer to some complex entity in the real world which contains many parts linked together. We talk casually about 'the legal system', 'the prison system', 'economic systems', 'the education system', 'health care systems'—and many other so-called 'systems' which in real life only occasionally and partially actually meet the requirement of the notion 'system'. For that is what 'system' truly is: the name of an abstract concept, that of a complex whole entity of a particular kind.

Of course there are physical correlates for some 'systems': most noticeably those 'designed physical systems' (bicycles, bridges, tunnels, tramcars) which engineers design and construct. But it would be quite wrong, for example, to link the word 'system' in the phrase 'management information system' exclusively to the hardware components of a computer system. The phrase MIS is extremely ambiguous and problematical; but systems thinking, properly understood, can help to clarify its ambiguities.

In order to try to dispel some of the confusion which results from the casual use of the word 'system' in everyday language, this chapter will examine: the origins of systems thinking; the core ideas behind the concept 'system'; the varieties of systems thinking; and the implications of this for work in MIS. It draws on earlier accounts including Checkland (1981, 1983, 1988, 1996) and Checkland and Haynes (1994). (Checkland, 1996, an encyclopaedia article, includes an annotated bibliography.)

The Origins of Systems Thinking

Systems ideas emerged as a generalisation of ideas about organisms which were developed within biology in the first half of the twentieth century. Where classical physics developed its core conceptualisations in the Newtonian revolution of the seventeenth century (to be modified by Einsteinian physics in the twentieth) and chemistry developed its core concepts ('elements', 'compounds', etc.) in the eighteenth and nineteenth centuries, biology was later in emerging as a science with an accepted conceptual framework. As the new science of biology was developed, its concern with living things led to many controversies over the nature of the living, and hence over the proper concerns of the new discipline. Much debate concerned the issue of *vitalism*: did living things, which to many were, intuitively, clearly 'more than the sum of their parts', possess some mysterious non-material component or directing spirit which characterised the living? (The spirit was even given a name, *entelechy*!) In our century the elucidation of molecular genetic mechanisms based upon DNA replication has finally resolved these debates. But within biology itself there was from the second half of the nineteenth century a strand of holistic thinking within the subject which argued that the degree of *organisation* was the crucial characteristic of living organisms, rather than the presence of some metaphysical directing spirit.

The school of thought associated with these so-called 'organismic biologists', based on such work as Woodger's *Biological Principles* of 1929, focused upon the organism as the unit of analysis in biology, and developed ideas about the processes which characterise metabolism and self-reproduction in organisms. It was one of these organismic biologists, the Austrian Ludwig von Bertalanffy, who founded the systems movement by beginning to argue, in the late 1940s, that these ideas about organisms could be extended to complex wholes of any kind: to 'systems' (von Bertalanffy, 1968; Gray and Rizzo, 1973).

Since it was ideas about physically existing organisms which were generalised as ideas about 'systems' in general, it is perhaps not surprising that most people, taking their cue from everyday language, simply assume unquestioningly that *systems* exist in the world. It is the later history of the systems movement which has painfully established that *system* is, truly, the abstract concept of a whole which may or may not turn out to be useful as a descriptive device for making sense of real-world wholes. Unfortunately, from the very start of the work in the systems movement, Bertalanffy himself used the word promiscuously both as an abstract idea (i.e. epistemologically) and as a label-word (i.e. ontologically). (It may be remarked at this point that this chapter's title is 'Systems Thinking'—i.e. the *process* of thinking using systems ideas—rather than 'System Theory' precisely because the latter title would be taken by many to mean 'the theory *of* systems', taking as given the status of systems as 'things in the world'.)

But in spite of this confusion the concept *system* has been found to be useful as an explanatory device in many subject areas: including for example ecology, engineering, economics, anthropology, sociology, psychology, geography, as well as the natural sciences. In fact systems thinking has emerged as a meta-discipline and as a meta-language which can be used to talk *about* the subject matter of many different fields.

An example of the status of systems thinking as a meta-subject is shown by the emergence of cybernetics, which occurred at about the same time that Bertalanffy was advocating the development of general system(s) theory. The mathematician Norbet Wiener worked on mechanical/electrical computing machines to aim and fire anti-aircraft guns, the work representing an attempt to automate what the hunter after a moving quarry does intuitively. Wiener, with Bigelow, was developing feedback systems in which information about current performance modifies future performance. Excess feedback in such systems leads to oscillatory 'hunting' about the desired performance, which cannot then be tightly controlled. Wiener also worked with a Harvard medical scientist Rosenblueth, who was familiar with the pathological condition 'purpose tremor' in which the patient, in trying to pick up a simple object, overshoots and goes into uncontrollable oscillation. The similarity between the human and electro-mechanical cases suggests that these are two different manifestations of a notional control system which can be described as a general case applicable to many different embodiments. Wiener (1948) launched cybernetics as the general (meta-level) science of 'communication and control in man and machine', though Plato had already made the same point more than 2,000 years earlier in making an analogy between a helmsman steering a ship and a statesman steering the 'ship of state' (Checkland, 1981: 82–6). Nowadays cybernetics is a subset of the broad area covered by systems thinking.

From its emergence in organismic biology, systems thinking has both developed core systems ideas and itself been developed in a number of different ways in different areas. The next two sections summarise these developments.

Core Systems Concepts

In the journal *Philosophy of Science* in 1955 it was announced that 'A Society for the Advancement of General Systems Theory is in the process of organisation'. Behind this initiative were the biologist Bertalanffy, an economist (K. E. Boulding), a physiologist (R. W. Gerard), and a mathematician (A. Rapoport). Their idea was that there could be developed meta-level theory and models 'applicable to more than one of the traditional departments of knowledge'—just as, in the example given above, a single model of a feedback control system might give an account which can describe both the behaviour of electro-mechanical servo-mechanisms made by engineers and the behaviour called 'purpose tremor' in human patients. Surely the engineers and medical scientists would find this both intriguing and useful? The society referred to was the Society for General Systems Research, and it still exists, with a small membership, as the International Society for the Systems Sciences. But its original project, the development of a meta-level systems theory into whose language problems within many disciplines could be translated for solution—leading to an anticipated greater unification of the sciences—cannot be declared a success. The kind of meta-level problem-solving envisaged by the pioneers has not occurred.

Rather, systems ideas have made contributions within many different subject areas. In this the original ideas of the protagonists of general system(s) theory have been vindicated to some extent. There is now a set of systems ideas which find application in many fields.

At the core of systems thinking is a concept which clearly derives very directly from our intuitive or casual knowledge of organisms: the concept of a whole entity which can adapt and survive, within limits, in a changing environment. This notion of 'the adaptive whole' is the central image in systems thinking, and the systems movement can be regarded as the attempt to explore the usefulness of this particular concept in many different fields. In order to understand and use this concept we need a handful of further ideas which, together with the idea of the adaptive whole, constitute the bedrock of systems thinking. (For more detailed discussion see Checkland, 1981: chs. 3 and 4.)

First, for an observer to choose to see some complex entity as a whole, separable from its environment, it must have properties which (for that observer at least) are properties of it as a single entity: so-called *emergent properties*. These are the properties which make the whole entity 'more than the sum of its parts'. This is not a mysterious concept, except to those New Age mystics who are drawn to the systems movement by a yearning for an elusive ill-defined holism. The parts of a bicycle, in a sack, are simply an aggregate. When assembled in the particular structure we call 'a bicycle', that entity has vehicular potential, which is an emergent property of the whole. In the structure of DNA, the laws of physical chemistry allow any sequence of amino-acid residues along the double helix. In order to explain experimental findings we have to invoke the idea that certain sequences constitute a 'code' which, in biological reproduction, results in our having red hair or a large nose. The 'genetic code' is an emergent property of the amino-acid sequences. University degrees are awarded not by departments or courses but by the university as a single entity. The power to confer degrees is an emergent property of the institution as a whole, one which the institution itself invents.

Secondly, wholes having emergent properties may well have smaller wholes with their own emergent properties; for example, it is meaningful to think of a department of a university as having autonomous emergent properties (the resources and authority to put on a particular course, for example). Equally, the larger whole (the university) may be only a part in a yet larger whole (the university sector of higher education) with its own emergent properties . . . and so on. In other words systems thinking includes the idea of *layered structure*.

Thirdly, if our entity is to survive in environments which change, it must have available to it ways of finding out about its environments and ways of responding internally to them; it must have processes of *communication* and *control*, which may be automatic (control of core temperature in our bodies for example) or created by human beings (rules within a university, for example), depending on the kind of entity being considered.

These four ideas: emergent properties, layered structure, processes of communication, and control, are the ideas needed to describe the concept of an adaptive whole. They are the core ideas of systems thinking, and have been used in different ways in many different fields, from engineering to economics, from geography to jurisprudence.

Varieties of Systems Thinking

Three broad areas of work can be defined in which these basic systems ideas have been exploited: the study of the wholes which Nature creates (often called 'natural systems'); the study of wholes designed and made by human beings ('designed systems'); and the study of human affairs, including the subject areas of *management* and, within that, *information systems*.

Biologists and ecologists can make sense of many phenomena which involve natural processes by making systems models of, say, the nitrogen cycle or the processes which go on in river basins or, on a larger scale, in the biosphere of our planet. Here systems models can provide a device for the examination of collectable data, leading to hypothesis testing and predictions of behaviour. Engineers, on the other hand, want to create *designed systems*, systems which will exhibit the emergent properties which their designers seek to achieve. Often these will have carefully designed control systems to maintain stability of performance, just as many *natural systems* will reveal control systems which the processes of evolution have developed; by definition, the complex natural wholes which have evolved and survived are those with good processes of communication and control within the range of variables met within our biosphere.

Not surprisingly these two areas of work, involving natural and designed wholes, are ones in which there is in general good mapping between the systems concepts and the observed real world. Nor surprisingly these are areas in which the everyday use of the word 'system' does not lead to too many intellectual difficulties. It is here possible to forget that systems are always, *fundamentally*, abstract concepts, and to refer to systems as existing in the world. Here there are reasonable grounds for equating an entity in the real world (e.g. 'the natural drainage system of the Rhine Valley') with the systems description of it. It is from that kind of work that the use of *system* as a label-word derives.

But such easy mapping is much more problematical in the third broad area of application, that of human affairs. In the 1960s the main development of systems thinking in this area skirted the problem by focusing on arrangements to meet goals or objectives declared in advance to be desirable. If a carefully defined objective could be taken as given then a system to meet the objective could be *engineered*. This was the approach adopted in most of the post-war developments arising from the success of operational research in the Second World War. Bell Telephones formalised their approach to development of new technology in 'systems engineering' (Hall, 1962); RAND Corporation developed 'systems analysis' (Optner, 1973). As mainframe computers were developed the same thinking was adopted to provide an approach to designing and establishing a computer system. (This was reasonable in the early days when computers were used only to transfer to a machine the transaction processing previously done by clerks; but the thinking behind early computer systems analysis became increasingly inappropriate as the technology developed, as this book illustrates.)

This thinking which characterises the first major use of systems thinking within human affairs is essentially *systematic* in character. All the approaches just referred to consist of examining and selecting one among a number of alternative systems to achieve an objective which is defined as desirable at the start. It is thus limited to the small subset of situations in which objectives are undisputed, so that problems are only 'how to do it?' problems, not problems of 'what to do?'

In the 1970s and 1980s, in trying to use systems thinking in real-world problem situations, it was found that what usually made the situations problematic in the first place was the inability to define objectives precisely, given the changing, multiple, ambiguous, and conflicting alternatives (Checkland, 1981). The problems were at the level of 'what to do?' as well as 'how to do it?' The way out of this dilemma was based on the real-world ubiquity of would-be *purposeful* action in human affairs, and on treating a linked set of activities which constitute a purposeful whole as a new system-type: 'a human activity system'. Ways of building models of such notional systems were developed (Checkland, 1981; Checkland and Scholes, 1990), each model being based on a declared world view—this being necessary because one observer's *terrorism* is another's *freedom fighting*. Such models could then be used as devices to structure questioning of the problem situation (so that they were models 'relevant to' debate, not 'of' anything in the real world). This process became known as 'soft systems methodology' (SSM); it is a learning system, a system of enquiry, one which happens to make use of models of activity systems (but other models could be incorporated).

The difference between this *systemic* thinking and the *systematic* thinking in the methods of systems engineering, RAND, and computer systems analysis is now thought of as marking the difference between the *soft* systems thinking of the 1970s and 1980s and the *hard* systems thinking of the earlier approaches. The key difference between them, little understood as yet in the literature, is that the hard tradition assumes that systems exist in the world and can be engineered to achieve declared objectives. The soft tradition assumes that the world is problematical, always more complex than any of our accounts of it, but that the *process of enquiry* into the world can itself be engineered as a learning system, one in which soft systems thinkers have the option *consciously* to adopt the hard stance if they so wish. It is this shift of systemicity, from assuming systems to exist in the world to assuming that the process of enquiry into the world can be organised as a learning system, which defines the two varieties of systems thinking (Checkland, 1983).

More recently Ulrich (1983), building on the work of Churchman (1971) and on Habermas's theories of the constitution of knowledge (1971), has added an external dimension to consideration of the practical use of systems methodologies: that of the real-world constraints on the situations in which the methodologies are used. He wants the normative assumptions which will underlie any practical social planning to be open to scrutiny by lay persons who will be affected by what planners design. In SSM's language, this work seeks to explore how to make the debate about change as open and unconstrained as possible, so that many voices can contribute. The difficulties here are essentially practical and political, not intrinsically to do with systems thinking. They are, however, pertinent to work on the design and implementation of information systems.

Although the detailed design and installation of such systems will in general require some technical expertise, the crucial nature of information systems—as will be argued in the final section—is that they concern not simply the processing of data but the creation of meaning. That is why it is important to distinguish IS from IT.

Implications of Systems Thinking for Information Systems

It might seem surprising that work on information systems is not in any comprehensive way underpinned by what in the literature is called 'information theory'. This is because that phrase is seriously misleading. Information theory was developed from the work done in the 1920s by communication engineers. They were interested in the conditions for encoding a 'message' into a 'signal', feeding it to a 'transmitter', transmitting it via a 'channel', and decoding it at the 'receiver' end of the chain. Their concerns *as engineers*, in developing what is really signal transmission theory, did not extend to the content of the messages: to them 'I have just changed my socks' was as interesting as 'I have just pressed the nuclear button'. One of the pioneers of the theory, Warren Weaver (in Shannon and Weaver, 1949), described as 'disappointing and bizarre' the fact that the theory 'has nothing to do with meaning'. But 'having meaning' is the usual connotation of the admittedly ambiguous concept: 'information'. Although there is no agreed sharp definition of 'information', there is broad agreement in the literature that 'information' is what you get when human beings attribute meaning to data in a particular context (Holwell, 1989; Aiba, 1993).

Working with this idea, we see that 'information system' is a rich concept indeed, far more substantial than the original phrase 'data processing system', which adequately expressed the nature of computing only in the days of transaction processing. An 'information system', in the full sense, will be a 'meaning attribution system' in which people select certain data and get them processed to make them meaningful in a particular context in order to support people who are engaged in purposeful action.

Since the processing will always be of chosen small subsets of data from the mass which *could* be captured and processed, it is a pity that we do not have a word for those items of data which we focus on, have a concern about, define, and select. Since 'data' comes from the Latin 'dare', to give, the word 'capta' from the Latin 'capere', meaning to take, suggests itself

(Checkland, 1982; Checkland and Holwell, 1995). Thus the core process to which information systems are relevant is that in which initially we select certain items of data out of the mass potentially available. They are selected as being relevant to our concerns (they are our capta), and we arrange to process these chosen items in a way which makes them meaningful in context. This creates 'information', which may itself be incorporated into broader structures of what we may describe as 'knowledge'.

Systems thinking offers an important insight into the role of information systems in this sequence from data to capta to information to knowledge. Information systems are not created for their own sake. They serve or support people engaged in what for them is meaningful action. Now, when one system is thought of as serving another, it is a fundamental principle of systems thinking that in order to think carefully about, and conceptualise the system which provides the support, it is *first* necessary to define carefully the nature of the system served (Checkland, 1981; Winter et al., 1995). This is necessary because how we see the system served will define what counts as *support* to it. The information systems needed to support a manufacturing operation will be very different if it is conceptualised as a system to optimise the use of a production facility rather than as a system to meet a market need; the range of information systems needed to support the operations of a university will depend upon where a particular institution sets the balance between teaching and research. The principle is neither obscure nor particularly subtle; but every reader of this book will have experienced instances in which organisations have purchased computers and/or off-the-shelf systems and only then asked themselves what they are going to use them for. Once that is decided they usually wish they had bought a rather different system. Sometimes major problems of this kind become public knowledge, for example: the failure of the £75m Taurus project of the London Stock Exchange; the abandonment of the London ambulance system after twenty-four hours of chaos; the expenditure of millions of pounds on never-satisfactory systems by Wessex Regional Health Authority; the criticism by the UK Audit Commission of the expenditure of £106m on would-be integrated hospital support systems which yielded identifiable benefits of £3.3m. Such failures emphasise the need for clear basic thinking relevant to the provision of information systems.

The argument here is that systems thinking, especially soft systems thinking, can provide a way of conceptualising the social processes in which, in a particular organisational context, a particular group of people can conceptualise their world and hence the purposeful action they wish to undertake. That provides the basis for ascertaining what informational support is needed by those who undertake that action. Only then does it become appropriate to ask how modern information technology can help to provide that support, and to provide it.

This is to see information systems as systems which attribute meaning to selected data in which someone has an interest (i.e. some capta) by processing it—usually by means of IT—in a way which makes it meaningful to users of the system. This broadly defines the nature of the work which will have to be done to create information systems, but the situation will remain a subtle one, for at least two important reasons. First, the possible definitions of meaningful purposeful activity which IT could support may themselves be defined by IT, in the sense that new technical possibilities may make it possible to contemplate new activities. The relation between the technology and the activity which it supports will remain a symbiotic one. Each can help define the other. Secondly, although any information system will deliver output which is meaningful in the way the *designers* of the system defined, *users* of the system will, as autonomous human beings, still be free to assign their own meanings to it. The output from the organisational information system which consists of collated information about sales of the new product will mean different things to the managing director concerned with the company's share price, the salesmen on the road seeking bonus payments, the production planner working on raw material requirements, and the director whose private agenda is to subvert the whole project. Meaning attribution can never be completely institutionalised, which will continue to make IS a rich and fascinating area of work.

References

Aiba, H. (1993), 'The Conceptualising of "Organisation" and "Information" in IS Work', M.Sc. dissertation, Lancaster University.

Checkland, P. (1981), *Systems Thinking, Systems Practice* (Chichester: Wiley).

—— (1982), 'An Organised Research Programme in Information Systems?', Internal Discussion Paper, 1/82, Department of Systems, Lancaster University.

—— (1983), 'Information Systems and Systems Thinking: Time to Unite?' *International Journal of Information Management*, 8: 239–48.

—— (1988), 'OR and the Systems Movement', *Journal of the Operational Research Society*, 34, 8: 661–75.

—— (1996), 'Systems and Systems Thinking', in M. Warner (ed.), *International Encyclopaedia of Business and Management* (London: International Thomson Business Press).

—— and Haynes, M. (1994), 'Varieties of Systems Thinking: The Case of Soft Systems Methodology', *System Dynamics Review*, 10, 2–3: 189–97.

—— and Holwell, S. (1995), 'Information Systems: What's the Big Idea?', *Systemist*, 17, 1: 7–13.

—— and Scholes, J. (1990), *Soft Systems Methodology in Action* (Chichester: Wiley).

Churchman, C. W. (1971), *The Design of Inquiring Systems* (New York: Basic Books).

Gray, W., and Rizzo, N. D. (1973), *Unity through Diversity: A Festschrift for Ludwig von Bertalanffy* (New York: Gordon & Breach).

56 *Peter Checkland*

Habermas, J. (1971), *Knowledge and Human Interests* (Boston: Beacon Press).
Hall, A. D. (1962), *A Methodology for Systems Engineering* (Princeton: Van Nostrand).
Holwell, S. (1989), 'Planning in Shell: Joint Learning through Action Research', M.Sc. dissertation, Lancaster University.
Optner, S. L. (1973) (ed.), *Systems Analysis* (Harmondsworth: Penguin Books).
Shannon, C. E., and Weaver, W. (1949), *The Mathematical Theory of Communication* (Urbana, Ill.: University of Illinois Press).
Ulrich, W. (1983), *Critical Heuristics of Social Planning* (Bern: Haupt).
von Bertalanffy, L. (1968), *General System Theory* (New York: Braziller).
Wiener, N. (1948), *Cybernetics* (Cambridge, Mass.: MIT Press).
Winter, M., Brown, D. H., and Checkland, P. (1995), 'A Role for Soft Systems Methodology in Information Systems Development', *European Journal of Information Systems*, 4, 3: 130–42.

4

Research on Information Systems Development in Scandinavia
Unity in Plurality

JUHANI IIVARI AND KALLE LYYTINEN

Abstract

Scandinavia has had disproportionate significance in the evolution of information systems (IS) as an academic discipline. One characteristic of the 'Scandinavian' IS development (ISD) approaches is a surprising plurality in theories, research approaches, topics, and outcomes which is unparalleled by any area of similar size and population. This chapter reviews and compares eight ISD approaches, which in one way or another can be regarded as 'Scandinavian' due to their origin, approach, or scope, and summarises their major contributions. It paints a broad historical overview of these approaches, emphasising their evolution, their unity and simultaneous plurality. In distinguishing the approaches we used several criteria including genealogical dependencies, distinctive concepts used to clarify the concepts of IS and ISD, explicit or implicit value orientation, and the focus in ISD in terms of process coverage, stakeholders, type of system. The resulting classification provides a broad map of the intellectual genealogy of the Scandinavian approaches, while emphasising their mutual interaction. We compare these eight approaches with regard to their scope, value orientation, their knowledge interests, support for formal vs. informal co-operation, the role of ISD methods (ISDMs), stakeholder relationships, attention paid to the contexts and process principles. The analysis shows that though there are significant differences between Scandinavian ISD approaches, they also share common features. Generally, the Scandinavian approaches can be characterised as 'grass-roots' approaches when compared with the North American MIS tradition. They emphasise IS evolution, user participation, alternative process models, seek varying theoretical foundations for IS and ISD, and apply dominantly anti-positivistic and action-oriented research approaches.

The authors wish to express their gratitude to Prof. Pentti Kerola and Prof. Pål Sørgaard for the detailed comments on an earlier draft of this paper.

Keywords: research traditions, information systems, information systems development, theoretical foundations, research strategies, design, analysis, user participation, modelling

> I'm against my brother. We are against the world.
>
> (An Arabic proverb)

Introduction

Compared to its population, Scandinavia[1] has had disproportionate significance in the evolution of information systems (IS) as an academic discipline. This is an outcome of several factors. First the homogeneous societies, high living standards, one of the highest educational levels in the world with a full literacy of nearly 100 years, and open societies with an advanced technical infrastructure provide a lucrative environment for computerisation. No wonder then that all Scandinavian countries belong to the top ten list of countries in the spread and intensity of the use of both computing and telecommunication technologies. In the use of Internet and cellular phones they are clearly the leading countries in the world. Therefore there is a social need and also lucrative environment to carry out research in the exploitation of information technology.

Second, Scandinavian countries have relatively similar socio-economic institutions and political traditions, share a sense of solidarity and mutual dependency and support, and have a history of fairly intense and casual co-operation at all levels of societies. This is manifested in such institutions as the Nordic Council. Consequently, there is a long tradition of intense co-operation between researchers and research institutions, and joint (often high-quality) Scandinavian research outlets are more like a rule than an exception.

Third, the Scandinavian IS community has been blessed with several innovative figures which have deeply affected the growth of the community. Among these the impact of a Swedish professor, Börje Langefors, cannot be underestimated. He was influential in the 1960s and 1970s in establishing IS research (ISR) communities through his visionary work on ISD (Langefors, 1966) not only in Sweden, but in nearly all Scandinavian countries. This paved the way for the Scandinavian prominence in European ISR in the 1970s and the early 1980s (especially in the area of systems development, which was then known by the non-English word 'systemeering'). This prominence also affected the fact that Scandinavian researchers and Langefors were key players in founding IFIP TC8 (Technical Committee

---

[1] In this article Scandinavia is interpreted to include Denmark, Finland, Iceland, Norway, and Sweden. Its total population is about 23 million. From the viewpoint of this article, it does not make any great difference whether Greenland as a part of Denmark is included or not, because to our knowledge there is no internationally recognised IS research in Greenland.

of Information Systems). A second major figure is Professor Krister Nygaard, who, after his pioneering work on the Simula language and object-oriented programming (Dahl and Nygaard, 1966), initiated the trade union-oriented approach in Scandinavia (Nygaard and Bergo, 1975), being the dynamic powerhouse of both research orientations in Scandinavia.[2]

Fourth, in the 1970s the Scandinavian political environment, due to the dominance of the social democratic parties and the influence of trade unions, was exceptionally favourable for radical approaches of which the best known is the trade unionist approach. Their value orientations and research paradigms differed radically from the contemporary North American MIS tradition, leading to incommensurability of the research problems and approaches.

Thus the early and innovative start and the socio-political history of the Scandinavian societies combined with a rapid and intense utilisation of computers has formed a fertile environment for the establishment of the 'Scandinavian school'. ISR in Scandinavia is not, however, a monolithic disciplinary regime; rather it forms a village of varying and rich theoretical schools. Accordingly characteristic of the 'Scandinavian' school is its plurality, which may escape the eye of an outsider. The plurality is reflected in theories, research approaches, topics, and outcomes and is not paralleled by areas of similar size and population.

One explanation for this variety is the openness and tolerance of the Scandinavian research community. Representatives of different paradigmatic camps have been able to communicate with each other. Such communications take place through standard academic practices such as reviews, assessments, and joint projects. One important mechanism is an annual meeting called IRIS (Information Systems Research in Scandinavia) which is a yearly window into Scandinavian ISR. It was launched in 1978 mainly as a Finnish event, but soon became truly Scandinavian with an even participation from all Scandinavian countries. Currently it is attended yearly by *c.*100 researchers. The success of IRIS has also led to the establishment of the *Scandinavian Journal of Information Systems* since 1988 (see http://www.cs.auc.dk/~sijs/). The journal publishes original Scandinavian research or research reflecting upon Scandinavian IS research.

Another distinctive feature of the Scandinavian ISR is its strong conceptual and philosophical orientation. Several Scandinavian researchers have sought inspiration from philosophy (e.g. Göranzon, 1978; Langefors,

---

[2] Other prominent figures are: Niels Bjørn-Andersen (Copenhagen Business School) and Bo Hedberg (Stockholm University) who established the socio-technical tradition in Scandinavia, and Pentti Kerola (University of Oulu) and Pertti Järvinen (University of Tampere) who pioneered IS research in Finland. The method developers like Janis Bubenko (Swedish Royal Institute of Technology), Mats Lundeberg (Stockholm School of Economics and Business Administration), and Arne Sølvberg (Norwegian University of Technology and Science) have also played a visible role.

1980; Nissen, 1983; Ivanov, 1984; Lyytinen, 1986; Nurminen, 1988; Ehn, 1988; Dahlbom and Mathiassen, 1993). Even though their philosophical positions have varied, the readiness to consider the fundamentals has formed a strong unifying ethos between Scandinavian researchers, which is clearly visible in the proceedings of the IRIS seminars.

The purpose of this chapter is to review and compare eight ISD approaches that can be regarded as 'Scandinavian', and to summarise their major contributions. The chapter seeks to paint a broad historical overview of these approaches, emphasising their evolution especially from the early stages. It examines their unity and simultaneous plurality and covers research from the early 1960s up to the early 1990s. Though we could have used a formal approach like the content and citation analysis to factor out distinct Scandinavian approaches,[3] we follow here a subjective and biographical approach in organising our discussion. We seek to carve out a personal (but hopefully a scholarly) map of an intellectual community seen from within which is based on our participation in building the community for two decades. Accordingly, the references and literature coverage are not complete but provide pointers to major contributions to readers who want to acquaint themselves with the history of Scandinavian ISR. Therefore, we shall mainly refer to works accessible in English and leave out when possible references to works in Scandinavian native languages (Swedish, Norwegian, Danish, and Finnish).

We warn that the eight approaches covered do not exhaust ISR in Scandinavia. Research on other IS topics is conducted in several Scandinavian universities and research laboratories. This covers topics like management of information technology and strategic uses of information technology, end-user computing, decision support systems, expert systems, and knowledge-based technologies, or economics of information technology. The major reason for exclusion is that these areas do not address ISD or exhibit any 'special' Scandinavian orientation (save maybe the preference for using non-positivist research methods). Technology-oriented research on databases, software tools, and hypermedias is also excluded.

The composition of the chapter is as follows: the second section traces the evolution of ISD approaches in Scandinavia and clusters them into eight approaches. Each approach is discussed in more detail by focusing on its research problems, key concepts, and major contributions. The third section analyses and compares the approaches using some established classification schemes. The goal of the section is to clarify more systematically how the plurality in unity is created. The fourth section concludes the chapter by making some observations about the evolution and discussing the future of ISR in Scandinavia.

---

[3] Proceedings of the IRIS seminars and published work in the *Scandinavian Journal of Information Systems* would provide a fairly representative data set for this.

The Evolution of Scandinavian IS Development Approaches

In view of the variety of Scandinavian ISD approaches, their classification into representative traditions is not necessarily trivial. There are a few earlier reviews, for example Bansler (1989), Bubenko (1992), Bjerknes and Bratteteig (1995), and Nilsson (1995). Bansler (1989) identifies three traditions, systems theoretical, socio-technical, and critical, which he claims differ in their knowledge interest (profit maximisation, job satisfaction, industrial democracy), notion of organisation (cybernetic system, socio-technical system, framework of conflicts), notion of labour force (objects, individual subjects, group subjects), and notion of capital/labour relations (common interest, opposing interest).[4] His analysis can be criticised, however, for being dubious on several points. It is unfairly biased in the case of the systems theoretical tradition (Dahlbom, 1993*b*), gives a false impression of the significance of the socio-technical tradition in Scandinavia, does not do justice to the variety of newer approaches, and is totally confined to 'geographical' Scandinavia, excluding the Finnish influence on Scandinavian ISR.[5] Bubenko's (1992) review is his personal account of major events in the evolution of ISD research, especially information modelling. An interesting review by Bjerknes and Bratteteig (1995) discusses the evolution of Scandinavian research on ISD, but restricts the analysis to Bansler's critical tradition and its affiliates. Nilsson's detailed (1995) review focuses on individual methods, but is restricted solely to Sweden.

Despite the variety of Scandinavian ISD research, it is fairly easy to identify major research schools in ISD—especially when we focus on research that has achieved international recognition. Fig. 4.1 solicits eight such approaches. In distinguishing the approaches we used the following criteria: genealogical dependencies (based on the literature references, publication patterns, and mentoring relationships), distinctive concepts used to clarify the concepts of IS and ISD, explicit or implicit value orientation,

[4] Nurminen (1988) provides quite a similar framework to Bansler (1989). He distinguishes systems theoretical, socio-technical, and humanistic perspectives on ISD. Even though his analysis is not explicitly confined to Scandinavian approaches, it strongly reflects a Scandinavian perspective as echoed by the references used.

[5] 'Scandinavia' as a geographical area comprises Denmark, Iceland, Norway, and Sweden. In these countries people speak Scandinavian languages, which are closely related to each other. Finland is thus not geographically part of Scandinavia and the language spoken in Finland—Finnish—is totally different from 'Skandinaviska', and does not relate to any Indo-European language. Because Finland formed a province of Sweden (and Denmark) for 700 years, the culture and administration in Finland is similar to the rest of the Scandinavia. Furthermore, Swedish is the second official language in Finland, and a significant minority of the Finnish population speaks Swedish. Consequently, all Finnish academics can at least read Swedish fluently. When we add Finland to the Scandinavian countries, it is customary to speak about the Nordic countries. This chapter, accordingly, adheres to the broad socio-political interpretation of Scandinavia which covers all the Nordic countries with the same cultural and political inheritance.

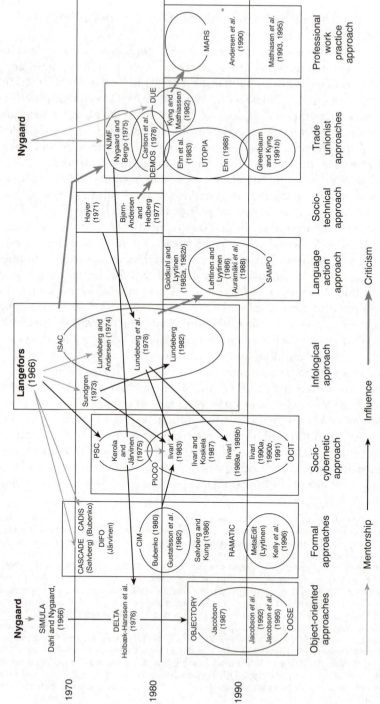

FIG. 4.1. *The genealogy of the Scandinavian approaches*

the focus in ISD (in terms of process coverage, stakeholders, type of system), and the preferred research approach. The resulting classification provides a broad map of the intellectual genealogy of the Scandinavian approaches, while emphasising their mutual interaction. Like all maps it is an abstraction of a diverse, criss-crossing, and idiosyncratic intellectual terrain. We locate the infological tradition in the centre of the map to indicate its role as the root of other approaches. The map also highlights milestones (projects and publications) in the evolution of the eight approaches. They will be described in more detail in the following sections summarising the approaches.

The infological approach

Börje Langefors pioneered the infological approach; 'an engineer from Saab' as Dahlbom (1993*b*) characterises him.[6] Langefors's (1966) monumental work *Theoretical Analysis of Information Systems* records early ideas in the approach, many of which were already outlined in Langefors (1963). It is notable that Langefors developed his ideas independently, being totally unaware of concurrent or earlier works by Young and Kent (1958) and CODASYL (1962). A succinct summary of the infological approach can be found in Langefors (1974) where he summarises the evolution of the approach up to the beginning of the 1970s.

The very idea of the infological approach is to make a distinction between an infological problem of how to define the information to be provided by the *information system* that can satisfy users' information needs, and a datalogical problem of how to design the structure and operations of the *data system* by exploiting information technology (Langefors, 1974). To clarify this difference Langefors proposed a sophisticated vocabulary to develop infology as a distinct area from datalogy (Langefors, 1966, 1977, 1980). Infology in Langefors's sense covers thus the language context and the organisational context in Lyytinen's (1987) taxonomy.[7] Within the language context, the central concepts are: the concept of (irreducible)

---

[6] Dahlbom's (1993*b*) excellent introduction is overtly sympathetic. Even though this may be interpreted as penitence for the 'politically' motivated misinterpretation of Langefors (Bansler, 1989; Nurminen, 1988), it is also a serious attempt to do more justice to Langefors's ideas than has been customary in Scandinavia during the last decade. In addition to Dahlbom (1993*a*), which includes a number of articles by Langefors, the collection of essays (Dahlbom, 1995) in honour of Langefors's 80th birthday is an indication of his rehabilitation in Scandinavia.

[7] The contexts are adopted from Lyytinen (1987) and they encompass different ontological realms for perception and intervention subject to different behaviour and 'laws'. Three contexts are distinguished: organisational context, where organised collections of people/individuals are perceived, language context, where organised collections of symbols and linguistic behaviours are perceived, and technical context, where organised collections of technical artefacts (computers, telecommunication technologies, software) are perceived.

an elementary message, which in its simplest form can be defined as a triple <object, attribute: value, time>, and an elementary concept as a class of elementary messages.[8] The purpose of these was to elaborate a set of concepts that help to solve information system design problems that were seen as distinct from implementation (programming) problems. The idea in developing the infological vocabulary was to free information system design from all aspects of computer technology, and thus to make this problem-solving step more meaningful to users and designers.

Langefors defined IS analysis and design as an analysis and synthesis process in which the designer specifies the information system at the level of elementary concepts, and during the datalogical design synthesises the data system into an efficient technical solution. Consequently, he outlined an approach for information analysis based on precedence and component analysis. During the analysis step one starts from ill-defined information requirements and formalises them using successively precedence analysis and component analysis steps. During precedence analysis one recursively derives the precedent information required to produce the desired information and during the component analysis one decomposes the information sets (non-elementary concepts) into components until elementary messages are reached.

Langefors's interest in information design problems led him (Langefors, 1966) to formulate his famous infological equation $I = i\ (D,\ S,\ t)$. In this equation D denotes the data for a user, S pre-knowledge of the user, t time available to the user for interpreting the data D, I the information conveyed by the data, and i the interpretation process. This equation led him to dig deeper into the problems of knowledge, information, language, and human interpretation. This was later manifested in an attempt to interpret the infological equation as a formulation of the hermeneutic cycle (Langefors, 1980). Within the organisational context, Langefors's ideas were most prominently expressed in his book *System för företagsstyrning* (A System for Steering Companies), dating from 1970. The book outlined a model for cybernetic control of organisations. He pays considerable attention to the definition of goals, starting from the wishes of different interest groups and leading to the uncovering of the ultimate intentions imposed on the organisation. The intentions are further refined to the highest operative goals, which are then further divided into local operative goals. He examines associated decision-making processes and analyses what is required from IS support as a condition for the decision-making. Overall, Langefors's book represents a 'total system approach' in which the IS support is derived from the total control needs of the organisation.

[8] It is beyond the scope of this review to introduce the vocabulary here. One should also observe that there is some confusion between the major proponents of the infological approach (Langefors, Lundeberg, Sundgren) in their use of this vocabulary (see Iivari, 1983, for a synthesis).

Langefors's work has most explicitly been continued by two of his students, Sundgren (1973, 1975) and Lundeberg (Lundeberg and Andersen, 1974; Lundeberg et al., 1978, 1981). At the language level (Lyytinen, 1987), Sundgren (1973) proposed a formalism for conceptual/infological modelling, which was clearly at the forefront of research into conceptual schema formalisms in the mid-1970s (Klimbie and Koffeman, 1974; ANSI/X3/SPARC, 1975). At the same time Lundeberg and his colleagues developed the ISAC method (Lundeberg and Andersen, 1974) which was later extended in two directions: upwards to cover change analysis (which addresses ISD as an organisational change), and downwards to incorporate programme design (see Jackson, 1975) as a method for datalogical design (see Lundeberg et al., 1981). ISAC was one of the first methodologies, based on an integrated set of graphical notations. ISAC was in particular formulated for in-house development for singular applications (or sets of applications) from a greenfield situation.[9] Accordingly, though ISAC formed in many respects an implementation of Langefors's ideas, it did not follow his 'total system approach' (Langefors, 1970a). Accordingly, ISAC derives organisational changes and their IS support using as a starting point problems experienced by the different interest groups.[10] In this respect ISAC's organisational design approach is much closer to the socio-technical school discussed below. Overall, the idea of change analysis was the forerunner of ideas which were heralded by the BPR movement some fifteen years later.

Even though Langefors developed a technique to file and process consolidation using a matrix-based 'systems algebra' (Langefors, 1963; Langefors and Sundgren, 1975), and suggested a theory of imperceivable systems justifying the hierarchical decomposition in information analysis (Langefors, 1966), his major contribution concerns the formulation of the infological problem. This involves three other contributions. First, Langefors and Sundgren's work on the conceptual/infological modelling was pioneering. Secondly, ISAC as the implementer of the Langeforsian programme was the earliest method which organically integrated the idea of ISD with that of organisational development including also modelling of organisational systems and their interactions with the IS. Thirdly, ISAC can be considered the first integrated method that systematically addressed the whole ISD process from an organisational design down to technical design and implementation.[11]

ISAC was 'developed' in several action research projects and it was *de facto* the first method which incorporated an attempt at empirical validation

---

[9] During the 1980s this has been extended to comprise also package-based ISD (Nilsson, 1991).

[10] Lundeberg et al. (1981) refer to Langefors (1970a) in the context of ISAC's goal analysis, but in our view do not follow Langefors's approach.

[11] ISAC largely neglects conceptual modelling of the UoD, however. Later on Lundeberg (1982) incorporated ideas of conceptual analysis by applying Sundgren's earlier work.

(Lundeberg, 1976). It was also successful in the sense that it became relatively widely used in Scandinavia and also in Holland and affected the evolution of 'in-house' methodologies in several countries. Bansler (1989) criticises infology for being Tayloristic and focusing on profit maximisation, adopting a cybernetic view of organisations, reducing human beings to system components, and advocating the notion of a common interest. Even though his criticism is extreme, and misses for example the participatory and work-oriented aspects of ISAC (Dahlbom, 1993*b*), it is obvious that Langefors's (1970*a*) treatment of organisations is predominantly 'rational-structuralistic' (Kling and Scacchi, 1982), resembling the machine metaphor (Morgan, 1986). Yet, the overall attack is too hasty as Langefors on many occasions recognises some 'human relations' issues (Langefors, 1980). In this respect an insider's—Göran Goldkuhl's (1984)—criticism of ISAC is better targeted. Goldkuhl questions the systems theoretic and objectivistic origin of 'infology' for missing the social character of organisations and ISs. In the case of human beings infology does not take into account human agency explicitly in organisational modelling.

Formal approaches

Formal approaches can be regarded as an attempt to develop Langeforsian ideas that relate to the concepts of elementary message, time, and the object system notion and process (precedence) analysis. This has resulted in several rigorous approaches focusing on IS design problems, which lend themselves to formal manipulation, possibly to be carried out by computers. Scandinavian formal approaches to systems design cover two research streams: research on computer aided information systems design (Bubenko et al., 1971) or computer aided systems/software engineering (CASE), and research on conceptual information modelling. The former grew out of attempts to provide tool support for precedence and component analysis, while the latter extended formal analysis of Langeforsian 'object systems'.

Langefors's ideas were influential in establishing in the early 1970s several Scandinavian research projects, which focused on computer aided information systems design. These included projects such as CASCADE (Aanstad et al., 1971), CADIS (Bubenko and Källhammar, 1971), and DIFO (Järvinen, 1971).[12] All these pioneering projects on CASE tools encountered various problems due to poor computing facilities, funding, and the lack of markets and died in the mid-1970s. Not surprisingly, Scandinavians have also been active during the second wave of the CASE tools that started in the late 1980s. This has been prominent especially

---

[12] Langefors has also had considerable influence on the ISDOS project (Teichroew and Sayani, 1971) which can be considered the most ambitious first generation CASE tool.

in the area of flexible CASE tools (Bubenko, 1988; Marttiin et al., 1993) which can support a variety of methods and tailor them to fit a specific ISD situation. This research has even led to commercial products such as RAMATIC (Bergsten et al., 1989), and MetaEdit+ (Kelly et al., 1996). Such metaCASE tools offer the capability to model methods formally using a meta-modelling language. This has opened up novel rigorous means to design (engineer) methods (called computer aided method engineering, CAME) and to analyse them formally (e.g. Rossi and Brinkkemper, 1996).

The second research stream of the Scandinavian formal approaches is tied to the growth of conceptual modelling research in database theory. It combined ideas from systems design, knowledge representation, and databases (Bubenko, 1980). As mentioned above the modelling formalism suggested in Sundgren's dissertation (1973) preceded the conceptual modelling tradition. In Scandinavia, two of Langefors's students, Janis Bubenko and Arne Sølvberg, have been the most visible representatives of this tradition. The community has included also researchers from Finland (e.g. Kangassalo, 1992) and Denmark (e.g. Lindgreen, 1982).[13] The explicit recognition of time in elementary messages explains Bubenko's early focus on the temporal dimension of information modelling (Bubenko, 1977). This led to the development of the conceptual information modelling (CIM) method in which the 'object system' is modelled as a set of events from which all required information can be derived (Bubenko, 1980; Gustafsson et al., 1982).[14] Sølvberg has focused on the integration of behaviour modelling with static structural modelling at the level of conceptual models. Here behaviour modelling is carried out using Petri nets (Kung and Sølvberg, 1986; Sølvberg and Kung, 1986, 1994).

Clearly, the conceptual modelling approaches focus on the language context (Lyytinen, 1987). The behavioural extensions of Sølvberg et al. (Kung and Sølvberg, 1986; Sølvberg and Kung, 1986) include some modelling of activities in the organisational context. This mixing of the language context (the UoD) and the organisational context (host organisation of activities to be supported by the IS) is, however, problematic (Iivari, 1989a), because organisations are regarded as mechanistic entities which comprise events and lawlike relationships between them. Later extensions to object system modelling have extended the models to include also agents (Krogstie, 1995) and goals.

The contributions of the Scandinavian conceptual modelling school have mainly been academic. Suggested extensions to standard modelling

---

[13] The group also organised in the early and mid-1980s several active workshops known as the 'Scandinavian Research Seminar on Information Modelling and Data Base Management' (Kangassalo, 1982 etc.) which were later on extended to a European–Japanese Research Seminar on Information Modelling and Data Base Management (Kangassalo and Jaakkola, 1990 etc.).
[14] Largely based on CIM, Bubenko and Lindencrona (1984) introduce a conceptual modelling language (CMOL), which extends CIM in particular in its graphical notations.

ontologies (like entity, relationship) to address explicitly events, time, or behaviour have not gained wide use in practice. One obvious explanation is that they require rigorous modelling early during the requirements analysis and practitioners are not prepared for this. An indication of the academic significance of the formal ISD approaches in Scandinavia is that Bubenko and Sölvberg initiated in the late 1980s a series of Conferences on Advanced information Systems Engineering (CAiSE) which were at first mainly a Scandinavian event, but soon became the leading annual European conference in the IS design field (Steinholz et al., 1990; Andersen et al., 1991).

The situation with second-wave CASE research is different. Even though the greatest enthusiasm for CASE technology is fading and there is disappointment with the overoptimistic expectations of CASE, it is obvious that ISD without CASE is not a realistic option. In view of the predominance of in-house developed ISDMs (Wynekoop and Rosso, 1993), one can also expect there to be markets for flexible CASE products such as RAMATIC and MetaEdit+ (Kelly et al., 1996). The practical relevance of computer aided method engineering (CAME), reuse of method components, and dynamic configuration of methodologies is still an open question, though Wynekoop and Rosso (1993) report that 89 per cent of respondents suggested that formal ISDMs should be adapted on a project-by-project basis.

The socio-technical approach

Socio-technical design (STD) can be seen as an attempt to extend the Langeforsian ideas into work design. Langefors's original work conceived system design and delivery to include just solving both the infological and the datalogical design problems (Langefors, 1974). Even though Langefors (1977) mentioned users' work processes as a part of the infological problem, and he discussed human motivation in organisational control (Langefors, 1970a), he mostly neglected system impacts on the work environment. But this could be easily added to the Langeforsian programme by incorporating the design of the social system into the IS design space as suggested by the STD approach.

One can identify two inspirations for the development of STD approaches in Scandinavia. These are the Norwegian Industrial Democracy Project in the 1960s (Thorsrud and Emery, 1969) which formed a part of the original Tavistock research programme, and the impact of the ETHICS method for Scandinavian research (Mumford and Ward, 1968; Mumford and Henshall, 1979; Mumford and Weir, 1979). The former did not specifically concern ISD, but was influential during the late 1960s especially in Sweden in attempts to form co-operative industrial relationships. According to Ehn (1988), several STD experiments were initiated in the late 1960s with increased job satisfaction and higher productivity as equally important goals. These experiments encountered, however, severe problems when different interests of management and employees became manifest, which led to the emergence of the more radical trade unionist approach in the early 1970s.

The role of STD in ISD was raised, according to Bansler (1989), by a Norwegian engineer, Rolf Høyer, at the NordData Conference in 1970. Besides Høyer, STD ideas were adopted by such scholars as Bjørn-Andersen in Denmark and Hedbeg in Sweden (e.g. Bjørn-Andersen and Hedbeg, 1977). These researchers had lively connections with Mumford (e.g. Hedberg and Mumford, 1975; Bjørn-Andersen et al., 1979). Their contribution to the theory and practice of STD lies mainly in the empirical validation of STD rather than in developing new methods. The case studies, however (Bjørn-Andersen et al., 1979; Bjørn-Andersen and Eason, 1980; Hedberg, 1980), show that the suggested STD ideals were weakly followed in practice. Characteristically, Mumford (1979) concludes the international study (Bjørn-Andersen et al., 1979) of computer use in banking as follows: 'banks were, at the time of research, very stable organisations with little conflict between management and staff. . . . However, despite their interest in good employee relationships, the banks did not use the opportunity provided by the introduction of a new level of technology to increase the interest and challenge of bank work. Many of the computer systems in the banks studied in this research routinised certain aspects of bank work.' These negative findings are one obvious reason for the emergence of the more militant Scandinavian design approach. Hedberg (1980: 32) observes sharply that 'Socio-technical designs are not enough. Lasting improvements must also involve changing values, rewards, and power structures.' He also contends that 'As long as managerial perspectives dominate problem formulations, design tasks, and reward systems, resulting systems will at best improve organizations from a managerial point of view,' and 'Managerial perspectives must therefore be confronted with worker perspectives, and systems must be designed participatively.' These challenges were tackled at the same time by the trade unionist approach, rather than the STD approach, and Hedberg decided to move from academia to a managerial position in a major Swedish bank.

Even though the golden age of the STD approach was short in Scandinavia, it has influenced generally thinking about ISD in Scandinavia. These influences are visible for instance in the infological tradition (e.g. Lundeberg et al., 1981) and also in some of the formal approaches (Bubenko and Lindencrona, 1984: 298). Also a few individual researchers, such as Kari Thoresen (1994), have continued work in the STD tradition. Most conspiciously, the STD approach has also called for some more or less critical appraisals (Nurminen, 1988) including the trade union approach which will be discussed next.

The trade unionist approach

Even though the proponents of the trade unionist (TU) tradition have used several names to characterise their approach, the label 'trade unionist' emphasises its most distinctive feature. This includes its origin, Scandinavian industrial relations as its institutional background, the role of trade unions as sponsors and partners of its major research projects, and its belief in trade unions as legitimate representatives of resource weak groups.[15] The high level of unionisation among the Scandinavian labour force can largely explain the emergence of the TU approach in Scandinavia. Scandinavian countries have one of the strongest labour federations, and their large social democratic parties have strong links with the national federations and also to national research funding agencies (Ehn and Kyng, 1987). In addition, in contrast e.g. to their UK counterparts Scandinavian trade unions have played often a proactive role in technology and work design agreements, education and health care policies, and so on instead of focusing solely on income distribution problems and conservative employment strategies. Finally, the importance of Professor Kristen Nygaard (e.g. Nygaard and Bergo, 1975) as the intellectual powerhouse for developing trade union-oriented system development methods cannot be too much emphasised (Sandberg, 1979).

Powerful trade unions created a favourable situation for the co-determination arrangements and laws in the mid-1970s which ensured employees and unions the right to participate in the design of and decision-making on computer systems. However, the opportunity to participate posed a considerable challenge to unions for the following reason. They had traditionally dealt on the local level with distribution issues such as pay, working hours, and terms of employment. With the participation rights in ISD, they were confronted with design and manufacturing issues, which are often unstructured, and at the same time technical. Accordingly, there were no formulated union objectives and demands, and the unions' and employees' previous experience was of limited value (Sandberg, 1985). The recognition of this challenge was an important motivation for the formulation of trade union strategies for the development of computer-based systems.

The TU approach can be also regarded as an attempt to seek a radical antithesis to the infological and STD approaches that were viewed as management oriented, because they considered organisations as harmonious assemblages of people and adopted a value-neutral and positivistic world-view. Both of these approaches were regarded as a managerial ploy (Sandberg, 1979), and many researchers in the TU approach assumed a hostile stance towards both infological and STD ideas. They drew on the

---

[15] Sometimes this approach alone has been labelled as the 'Scandinavian approach'.

fact that one presumption of the STD approach is that there is no fundamental conflict between job satisfaction goals and productivity goals
(Mumford, 1983). Bansler (1989) claims that this assumption fails to see
the social origins of the problem: Western capitalism and a fundamental
conflict between the labour and the capital. This led to the 'academic'
confrontation between the STD approach and the emerging TU approach
already in 1974 (Ehn, 1988), an incident which Dahlbom (1993*b*) describes
twenty years later as a crude and unfair attack. In line with this some
Swedish researchers entered the area by starting with severe criticism of
the Langeforsian view of system design and especially its notion of managerial control.[16]

One can identify three generations in the TU approach. The first
covers the first three projects (i.e. NJMF, DEMOS, and DUE),[17] and the
second generation, which its proponents call the 'collective resource
approach', covered initiatives like the UTOPIA project, with the goal
to promote industrial democracy and the quality of work and product.
The generations reflect also a gradual softening of the original, radical
Marxist tones and goals (Nygaard and Bergo, 1975), to more post-modern
attempts to synthesise young Marx, Heidegger, and late Wittgenstein
(Ehn, 1988). A summary of the approach up to the late 1980s can be found
in Ehn and Kyng (1987) and in Ehn (1988). The most recent publications (Bødker et al., 1991; Bødker and Grønbæk, 1991*a*, 1991*b*; Ehn and
Kyng, 1991; Ehn and Sjögren, 1991) describe the third generation, which
emphasises 'co-operative design'. Theoretically it leans more on the
philosophies of Heidegger and Wittgenstein than Marx and deals mostly
with micro-level design issues. Bødker et al. (1991) nevertheless express
their sympathy for users if they are members of 'resource weak groups' (as

---

[16] This was clarified in Ehn's (1973) not well-known but interesting unpublished working
paper titled 'Bidrag till ett kritisk social perspektiv på datorbaserade informationsystem'
which criticised the Langeforsian view of system design for adopting too harmonious and
objectivistic a view of system development. The article draws heavily on Churchman's book
on the *Design of Inquiring Systems* and the idea of dialectic design and inquiry. Marx, who is
only mentioned in Ehn (1973), was much more emphasised in a joint work with Göranzon
(1974) *Perspektiv på systemutvecklingprocessen.* Indicative of 'Scandinavian tolerance' is that this
work was carried out in the same institution where Langefors had a chair!

[17] The most important action research projects were the NJMF project in Norway
(Nygaard and Bergo, 1975), the DEMOS project in Sweden (Carlsson et al., 1978; Ehn and
Sandberg, 1983; Sandberg, 1983), the DUE project in Denmark (Kyng and Mathiassen, 1982),
and the UTOPIA project in Denmark and Sweden (Bødker et al., 1987; Ehn, 1988). Bjerknes
and Bratteteig (1995) interpret also the Florence project as belonging to this same tradition,
even though with less participation orientation. In Finland, two groups can be interpreted
as loose affiliates of the TU approach: a group from the University of Tampere (e.g.
Järvinen, 1987) and a group, the Knowledge and Work project, from the University of Turku
(Eriksson et al., 1988). The group in Tampere took a more radical approach to user participation in the sense that it attempted to develop an application generator (called ABC and Genera)
to support application development without professional programmers (cf. Martin, 1982).
The group in Turku has especially contributed support for informal communication and co-
operation in systems development as will be explained below.

opposed to management or executives), and refer to the TU approach as a means for organising development projects for such resource weak groups (pp. 146–7). In its third generation the TU approach has lost most of its critical edge, and has rather ironically approached its original antithesis, the STD approach, in many respects. Bjerknes and Bratteteig (1995) remark that, despite the intellectual conflict between the STD and the TU approach, it is difficult to see a difference between the two any longer, when in 'co-operative design' the 'design process is viewed as a (rather harmonious) dialogue between a designer and a user about the design of a particular computer application'. The assumption here clearly is that co-operative processes lead to improved work situations and that organisations are willing to introduce the proposed changes (Bjerknes and Bratteteig, 1995).[18]

The 'co-operative design' approach has recently aroused considerable interest (Kuhn and Muller, 1993) in the CSCW community by focusing on technical prerequisites of user participation. To facilitate the engagement of users, it has developed tools and techniques in action research projects to support effective user participation at the level of informal co-operation between users and designers. Clement and Van den Besselaar (1993) report considerable difficulties in sustaining the continued use of the participatory design approaches after the research intervention when the novelty wanes and other work priorities reassert themselves. The attempts to transfer ideas of 'co-operative design' to North America have also aroused considerable debate in Scandinavia (Kraft and Bansler, 1994; Kyng, 1994).

The main contributions of the TU approach comprise its novel value orientation, which challenged the management prerogative to determine the goals of systems development and indicated that ISD can be governed by alternative values.[19] This critical element in the TU approach has, however, been weakening recently. The TU approach also proposed a model for systems development, which suggests employing a union-led 'shadow organisation' in challenging the management-led project organisation and to propose alternative designs (Ehn and Sandberg, 1983). The proponents of the TU approach have also shown that a participatory 'design-by-doing' approach supported by low-technology representations (mock-ups) and co-operative prototyping are feasible ISD in favourable conditions (Ehn, 1988). Such low-level technology representations aim at supporting informal aspects of co-operation between users and designers.[20] In

---

[18] This comes quite close to Mumford's (1983) argument that 'people should be able to influence the design of their own work situations and that if this kind of intervention is encouraged then there are likely to be both job satisfaction and efficiency gains' (p. 1).

[19] On the other hand, from the Scandinavian perspective the TU approach has never looked as radical as seen from outside, from a North American perspective, for example.

[20] To our knowledge, many ideas of supporting the informal aspects of co-operation between users and designers were pioneered by Saaren-Seppälä (1983, 1984, 1988). His 'wall chart technique' was based on interactive creation of wall charts using cardboard stripes,

consequence, the 'collective resource' and 'co-operative design' approaches advocate a tool perspective as a natural ingredient in the model of crafts-manship as an ideal of work.[21] This also fits nicely with the informal co-operative model and the use of technology mock-ups. Originally this was suggested as a new way to understand computer support (Ehn and Kyng, 1987; Ehn, 1988) but, ironically, it grew close to market-driven end user computing. Even though the tool perspective recognises that tools are socially created and used, it can be criticised for imposing a technical view of ISD where computer-based systems are seen solely as technical artefacts. Maybe for this reason the TU approach has never suggested any conceptual means to model and articulate work (in contrast to STD, which it criticises). One reason for this is its romantic craftsmanship model, which claims that professional work is always tacit (Ehn, 1988; Kyng, 1991). A more appropriate title for the TU approach would accordingly be a 'computer artefact oriented design of work', rather than 'work oriented design of computer artefacts'.

The socio-cybernetic approach

The basis idea of Langefors was the distinction between the infological and datalogical problems. Even though he was careful in interpreting these as problem areas rather than sequential phases (Langefors, 1974, 1977), the sequential interpretation was clearly adopted in ISAC which imposes a linear order of five phases for solving these problems.[22] The resultant process model was primitive and confused the WHAT structure and the WHEN structure of the design process (Mathiassen, 1984). This research challenge of formulating a solution to the infological IS design process was taken up by Finnish researchers. This led to innovative amendments to the Langeforsian research programme, which were astonishingly similar to the popular spiral model suggested by Boehm (1988) a decade later.

Kerola and Järvinen introduced their PSC model in the mid-1970s (Kerola, 1975; Kerola and Järvinen, 1975; Kerola, 1980; Kerola and Free-man, 1981).[23] One of its novel contributions was the distinction between

---

photos, etc. The technique, often accompanied by prototyping, is widely used in Finland. The Knowledge and Work project also applied low-technology techniques such as manual simulation (role playing) to support users' learning (Eriksson et al., 1988).

[21] Despite this emphasis, some examples of the nature of the information systems in Kyng (1991) seem difficult to interpret in the tool perspective.

[22] It is interesting to observe that Langefors (1970b) explicitly rejects early spiral models as unrealistic and suggests a more sequential, even though highly iterative, model for the design process.

[23] P stands for pragmatic, S semantic, and C constructive main points of view of systems analysis. These viewpoints were derived mainly from Kerola's and Järvinen's practical experi-ences and from works of prominent system thinkers (e.g. Ackoff and Emery, 1972; Lange, 1965; Mesarovic et al., 1970).

pragmatic and semantic levels, which divided Langefors's infological realm into two 'main viewpoints'. Another was formulating a set of process equations that described the iterative and spiral nature of the design process (Kerola, 1975). This rejected the linear model of ISD and replaced it with a dynamic and hierarchical model. Accordingly, the PSC models suggested that distinct design aspects (or levels of abstraction) such as the infological and the datalogical design aspects can proceed concurrently, that the process is not closed to one process trajectory, and that the process model is recursive in nature.

The ideas of the PSC model were further elaborated by Kerola's students into the PIOCO model (Iivari, 1983; Iivari and Koskela, 1987) and this work continued up to the early 1990s.[24] In most recent publications (Iivari, 1989*a*, 1990*a*, 1990*b*, 1991) the PIOCO model is generalised into an OCIDT model.[25] Compared with the PSC model, the OCIDT model is better aligned with the infological tradition (Sundgren, 1973; Lundeberg et al., 1981), and the formal approaches (especially Bubenko, 1980). Earlier cybernetic views of the original PSC model (Kerola and Järvinen, 1975), and functional organisational models (Iivari and Koskela, 1983) have been replaced here with an interactionist view of organisations emphasising different world-views (inter)subjectivity, and organisational politics (Iivari, 1989*b*).

In the socio-cybernetic (SC) approach underlying the PIOCO and OCIDT models IS design is viewed as human action, which is formalised using the socio-cybernetic theory of acts (Aulin-Ahmavaara, 1977), and information economics (Marschak, 1974). This explains the title 'socio-cybernetic approach' for the process model. In this theory the IS design is viewed as an enquiry process (a set of acts to obtain knowledge about the IS domain) which derives information for decision-makers to decide (another set of decision acts) about the alternatives concerning both the IS product and the ISD process. IS design acts are further conceptualised as either observation/analysis acts or manipulation/refinement acts. The former emphasises the diagnostic aspect of IS design, and the latter the transformation of design artefacts. An IS design process transpires as an execution of sequential and parallel design acts, each act increasing knowledge about the design situation (including the host organisation, user requirements, available technology, and existing IS artefacts) and/or

---

[24] The acronym 'PIOCO' is derived from the three main points of view of systems analysis pragmatic (P), input/output (I/O), and constructive/operative (C/O).

[25] O denotes organisational, CI conceptual/infological, and DT datalogical/technical. Here, the O model for an information system views the system as an integral part of its (re)designed organisational context and defines the application concept of the system, its boundary, and IS services, the C/I model includes a model for the Universe of Discourse (UoD) underlying the system, the specification of the system in terms of information about the UoD processed by the system and the user interface, and D/T model defines the technical solution for the system.

refining the IS artefact. The ISD situation is constantly changing, which calls for in-built flexibility in methods (Iivari, 1989*b*; Avison and Wood-Harper, 1990). Hence, all design acts are subject to uncertainty and risk. Accordingly, there is a need for meta design acts that 'reflect' upon the IS design process in order to plan and select the next design act. This theoretical model (Iivari 1983, 1990*a*) led to several suggestions about IS process models which are surprisingly similar to the risk-driven spiral model of Boehm (1988).[26] There are also differences: the SC approach seeks to balance disciplined model-driven and opportunistic risk-driven process (Iivari, 1990*b*), whilst Boehm (1988) emphasises the latter process.[27]

Retrospectively,[28] the SC approach includes several novel ideas. It extended the Langeforsian design problem covering a two-level abstraction into a three-level abstraction. In particular, it made a clear conceptual distinction between 'the host organisation'—to be supported by an IS—and 'the Universe of Discourse'—to be represented in the IS—which were conceptually bundled together by Langefors in his concept of an 'object system'.[29] The increased number of abstraction levels helped also to draw upon several reference disciplines to analyse the infological design problem and infological equation. These also led to dividing the IS design problem spaces into the organisational, language, and technical contexts of Lyytinen (1986) which has later been used as a basis to develop models of ISR and their interrelations (Hirschheim et al., 1996). The SC approach developed also one of the first meta-models for the IS product (Iivari, 1983). Additionally, the SC meta-model for the ISD can be interpreted as a general reference model, which can be applied to the comparison of ISDMs and approaches (Iivari and Kerola, 1983; Iivari, 1994). Another contribution was the multi-dimensional process model for ISD which integrates decision-making dynamics (O, C/I, and D/T main phases) with a non-linear structure (Kerola and Järvinen, 1975), and learning dynamics with prototyping (Iivari, 1982) and IS evolution (Iivari, 1982). The idea of selecting the next design act and using meta design acts to support this

---

[26] Iivari (1983) used neither the adjective 'spiral' nor a spiral-like graphical representation to describe the process until in Iivari (1990*b*). Interestingly, Kerola and Järvinen (1975) have a graphical model of a converging spiral to describe the ISD process in their PSC model.

[27] Iivari (1983) does not explicitly explain the process in terms of risk but in terms of uncertainty, suggesting that the IS design acts should be in a way complementary existing a priori knowledge. The objective function covering the choice of the next IS design act clearly includes risk as its component.

[28] Retrospectively refers to the fact that the developers of the approach were not necessarily aware of all the innovative implications of the model at the time when it was developed.

[29] This distinction is still exceptional in ISD methods, because the host organisation and the UoD often overlap in business information systems. A similar distinction was adopted by Mathiassen et al. (1993). Their terminology of 'application domain' in the sense of the host organisation and 'problem domain' in the sense of the UoD can be criticised, however, to imply that problems are more closely associated with the UoD than the organisational context of actors and their work where the system is used.

(Iivari, 1983), and the consequent need for reflective design (Iivari, 1983) are still novel. The SC approach includes also a multi-dimensional model of IS quality (Iivari and Koskela, 1979) which recognises the availability of several (incomplete and ambiguous) IS alternatives at each level of abstraction.

The practical use of the SC approach has been modest. One of its weaknesses is its complexity, which results from its generality. The theoretical basis of the model is also eclectic, complex, and loaded with difficult vocabulary, which makes it difficult to understand. It is not complete as an operational method. Especially it lacks detailed procedures for the conceptual/infological design and datalogical/technical design.

The language action approach

The language action (LA[30]) approach in Scandinavia emerged as an evolutionary step from and a radical reinterpretation of the infological tradition. One of its early advocates, Göran Goldkuhl, was also one of the key developers of the ISAC method. In the beginning of the 1980s he distanced himself from ideas in the original Langeforsian theory (Goldkuhl, 1984). This happened at the time when he collaborated with Kalle Lyytinen. Their collaboration led to several articles that established the theoretical basis for the LA approach (Goldkuhl and Lyytinen, 1982*a*, 1982*b*, 1984). Since then the research on the LA approach has taken place primarily in Jyväskylä, Finland (e.g. Lehtinen and Lyytinen, 1986; Auramäki et al., 1988, 1992*a*, 1992*b*) and in Linköping where Goldkuhl moved in the late 1980s. Recently, the approach has been adopted and extended by some researchers that operate within the realm of formal approach (Holm, 1996; Johannesson, 1995; Assenova and Johannesson, 1996). A more detailed and extensive summary of this approach can be found in Hirschheim et al. (1995).[31]

Goldkuhl's and Lyytinen's attempt to reinterpret the Langeforsian programme was radical and in some sense more revolutionary than that advocated by those who followed the TU approach. The main criticism from students of the TU approach was that Langefors adopted too harmonious a view of managerial control, whilst the advocates of the LA view criticised him using ontological and epistemological arguments. They wanted

---

[30] Though this term has now received wide recognition as one valid approach to understanding information system design problems (see e.g. Verharen et al., 1996) it was originally coined by Goldkuhl and Lyytinen (1982*a*).

[31] Besides the LA approach there are a few notable Scandinavian attempts to apply linguistics to IS development. The Florence project included analysis of professional languages of nurses (Kaasboll, 1987). Andersen's book *A Theory of Computer Semiotics* (1990), even though not directly addressing IS development, has connections with user interfaces, work analysis, and systems descriptions which are relevant in IS development. The LA approach based on the speech act theory is, nevertheless, the most explicit attempt.

to reveal several philosophical fallacies underlying the Langeforsian programme (Hirschheim et al., 1995). They concerned: (1) the concept and nature of ISs, (2) the implications of this concept for design strategies, (3) the positivistic concept of elementary message, and (4) the underestimation of the importance of language and intentionality in the use and design of ISs. The LA view attacked the Langeforsian theory using theories of continental and pragmatic philosophy including late Wittgenstein, Schultzian phenomenology, Gadamer's hermeneutics, and Habermas's critical theory. In a way it turned the original programme upside down by changing the concept of an IS from an objective 'thing' into an intersubjective socially constructed institution. Goldkuhl and Lyytinen (1982*a*) formulated this in their slogan: 'Information systems are social systems but only technically implemented.' They changed Langefors's concept of an elementary message which was interpreted originally as a fact (Langefors, 1966) into a notion of an elementary speech act by which users carry out affordances through the IS (Goldkuhl and Lyytinen, 1982*a*). They abandoned the idea of objectivistic 'system modelling' and suggested the idea of system design as a rational reconstruction of implicit (and explicit) rules which make IS communications possible (Goldkuhl and Lyytinen, 1984). The key idea of an IS is its linguistic nature—a system of communication[32]—and the infological design deals primarily with how to understand human communication (Goldkuhl and Lyytinen, 1982*b*).[33] All these developments took place independently of and unaware of the work that was simultaneously carried out by Winograd and Flores (1986).

The LA approach has relied heavily on Austin's and Searle's philosophy of language (Austin, 1962; Searle, 1969, 1979; Searle and Vanderveken, 1985) and to some extent on Apel's (1980) concepts of universal pragmatics, Wittgenstein's (1953) theory of language games, and Habermas's (1971, 1984, 1987) theory of knowledge interests and theory of communicative action. Since the vocabulary of the whole LA approach is complex, our presentation will introduce here the main ideas and concepts of speech act (SA) theory.[34] The SA theory suggests that speech acts form basic

---

[32] Here the impact of one of Langefors's students, Hans-Erik Nissen, cannot be underestimated. To our knowledge he first introduced the idea of understanding computer systems as rendering communication and inferential services in some formal language (Nissen, 1976). This idea was extended in his analysis of the concept of information system represented in Nissen (1980). A similar idea was introduced by Lyytinen in his licentiate thesis in 1981.

[33] An important implication of this result was that the LA approach also gave up the notion of an imperceivable system and replaced it with notions like explicit vs. implicit, vague vs. clear. It argued that the idea of functional decomposition does not work with modelling social systems because rule systems and social institutions can only be understood at the level of actual 'process' thus making functional decomposition useless (Goldkuhl, 1984).

[34] More detailed summaries can be found in Hirschheim et al. (1995) and Lyytinen (1986). IS design issue are outlined in more detail in Lehtinen and Lyytinen (1986), Winograd and Flores (1986), Auramäki et al. (1988), and Dietz and Widdershoven (1991).

units of communication and they always express a human intent, such as making a promise or asserting a claim. To understand the meaning of a speech act the social situation in which it occurs (its context) must be taken into account. It typically consists of the speaker, the hearer, and the time and place of the communication. The context also includes the set of possible worlds covering all features of speakers, hearers, times, and other aspects.

SA theory distinguishes utterance acts, propositional acts, perlocutionary acts, and illocutionary acts as aspects of speech acts: a speech act is performed by uttering an expression, an utterance act (e.g. 'could you please close a door?'). When successful, it will have effects on the hearer, i.e. the speaker performs a perlocutionary act (e.g. the hearer will actually close the door). Performing a speech act also includes a subsidiary act of expressing the propositional content of the speech act, i.e. the propositional act (in our example referring to a particular door, which is currently open). The core aspect of a speech act is its illocutionary act, including its illocutionary force. The illocutionary force is the principal component of a speech act, including among other things the illocutionary point.[35] Searle claims that speech acts can be classified by their illocutionary point into the following five categories: *assertives* telling how the world is or will be (statements of fact or predictions), *commissives* committing the speaker to doing something (e.g. to promise or to agree), *directives* trying to get the hearer to do things (e.g. to order or to request), *declaratives* changing the world by saying so, and *expressives* expressing the speaker's feelings and attitudes. Directives and declaratives can be regrouped into 'imperativa' because they both imply that there is a source of power, which can command that the world needs to be changed to fit the state described in the imperative statement.[36]

In the Langeforsian theory, assertives took a prominent place in that the contents of databases are interpreted as 'statements of fact', i.e. 'elementary messages' (Hirschheim et al., 1995). In distinction to this the LA approach assumes that the task of the IS developer is to recognise all types of speech acts and to use this knowledge in the design of the system.[37] While the direction of fit in the case of assertives is from word-to-world, i.e. to get the word to match the state of affairs in the world, the direction of fit with directives and commissives is world-to-word, i.e. to alter the world to match the word. In the former case predicates such as 'true' and 'false'

---

[35] More exactly, an illocutionary force has seven components. Illocutionary point, mode of achievement, degree of strength, propositional content conditions, preparatory conditions, sincerity conditions, and degree of strength of sincerity conditions.

[36] See Habermas (1971), Dietz and Widdershoven (1991), and Hirschheim et al. (1995) for an alternative classification.

[37] In this sense the LA view takes a broader view on speech acts when compared with Winograd and Flores's work (1986) in that the action diagrams of Winograd and Flores paid attention only to directives and commissives.

characterise how well the matching has taken place while in the latter case adjectives such as 'fulfilled' and 'unfulfilled' can be used to characterise the matching. In the Langeforsian theory elementary messages can be dynamically and functionally related through precedence relationships and these are solely dictated by the data manipulation needs. In LA theory speech acts are seen to form larger wholes, e.g. networks of recurrent conversations (Winograd and Flores, 1986), and these form objects of re-quirements analysis while defining system boundaries (Auramäki et al., 1988). A simple example is the case of a question, which must typically be followed by an answer or a request for clarification, a refusal to answer, or a counter-question. Hence in order to identify the meanings which are exchanged in larger conversations, it is necessary to analyse how sequences of speech acts connect—like the 'moves' in a chess game. Thereby LA suggests recognising speech acts as rule-constituted instances in a larger language game (Goldkuhl and Lyytinen, 1982*a*).

The LA approach consists of a rich set of concepts for the analysis of the original infological problem—seen here as an instance of intricate social communications. In contrast to Langefors, the LA approach takes a different stance on philosophical assumptions, but retains his substance claim that infological (linguistic) design is different from datalogical design. It places high importance on modelling and thereby assumes that some things should be made explicit during the design. One principal strength of the LA approach is its strong theoretical basis. Thereby, in contrast to the original Langeforsian programme, which relied on systems theory in addressing the infological problem, the LA approach has rejected the func-tional system theory and relied on communication theories to develop foundations of IS (see Lyytinen, 1986).[38] The LA approach also illuminates that the received view of regarding information as statements of facts is limited. Compared with the work of Flores and Winograd (Flores and Ludlow, 1980; Winograd and Flores, 1986), this line of work has also been stricter and more formal. At the same time, it has shown the major weak-ness of the LA approach, namely its complexity. It has also been criticised by the proponents of the TU approach (for an extensive discussion see Holm, 1996). Efforts to adopt a simplified version of the SA theory for design have led to several alternative design approaches, which makes the

---

[38] It is interesting to note that the later works of Langefors (1980) extended his theory with some more explicit recognition of the problem of meaning. In these works Langefors tried to analyse his infological equation using Gadamer's hermeneutics. This suggests that he saw the meaning as arising from the process of interpreting the data set that was deliv-ered by the technical system where the context of the user (reader) provided the background for this meaning. In contrast the LA approach 'writes' the meaning into the IS proper by saying that one aspect of the meaning is the rules that impose/constrain behaviours of the speakers/'hearers' of the data in the IS. These rules are always contextualised and therefore all data is contextualised and has meaning in the sense of being outcomes/objects of some social affordances (speech acts).

current status of the LA approach fragmented (cf. Auramäki et al., 1988; Holm, 1996; Verharen et al., 1996). The LA approach has also cross-fertilised other Scandinavian approaches, such as the SC approach (Iivari, 1989*a*) and some formal approaches (Assenova and Johannesson, 1996).

The professional work practice approach

The 'professional work practice' (PWP) approach was developed during the 1980s in Denmark by Mathiassen and his colleagues. They wanted to investigate how systems development was actually carried out (Lanzara and Mathiassen, 1985). They also experimented with different ways of changing work practices (Andersen et al., 1990: p. xii). These action research projects challenged the popular belief that ISDMs and tools would improve the effectiveness of ISD. Hence, they questioned one of Langefors's ideas, that good methods and sound engineering principles —developed through systematic theoretical reflection, analysis, and trials —would solve the IS design problem.

To their surprise PWP developers found that the more experienced the analysts were, the less they followed documented ISDMs. This applied even if the organisation had introduced its own method as its development standard. Methods were at best meant to be recipes for beginners to be tossed aside after a period of apprenticeship. More important for under-standing how systems are actually developed was to analyse work prac-tices of the system professionals. Because of the focus on situated work practices the PWP approach took much influence from the TU approach. This was not coincidence as Mathiassen was closely connected with some researchers in the UTOPIA project (Kyng and Mathiassen, 1982). How-ever, fundamental disagreements about the practicality of the TU approach as a sole basis for professional education prompted Mathiassen to pursue a new strategy. The strength of the PWP approach is its emphasis on the study of professional work practices before attempting to improve them. Its advocates question the value of methods for not paying sufficient attention to what system practitioners actually do and, if they work defi-ciently, taking a realistic look at how this could be changed for the better. In this sense the focus of the PWP approach has been on the relation-ship between methods and practice, which has not been taken up by any other approach in Scandinavia save some action research trials of using methods (Lundeberg, 1976). From this perspective, new methods can be considered but one option for improving the work practices. The empirical base for the PWP approach was derived from investigating con-ditions that determine systems developers' practices. The empirical base of the PWP approach is stronger, however, than its theoretical base, which is weakly documented. In addition to Mathiassen's Ph.D. thesis (1981) the concepts of 'organizational learning' and 'reflective practitioner' (e.g.

Argyris and Schøn, 1978; Schøn, 1983) seem to form the primary source of theoretical inspiration. In addition, though the PWP research seems to have affinity with the grounded theory (Strauss, 1987) there is no awareness of such closeness or reflections on possible methodological problems.

Even though the PWP approach can be seen to challenge the Langeforsian engineering approach with its focus on the situated and reflective designer, it can also be seen to complement it. It has focused on aspects which were largely ignored in the Langeforsian formulation of the design as a *substance* problem; that is, on necessary *engineering practices*: project management and techniques for diagnosing problematic situations (diagnostic, ecological, and virtual maps, Lanzara and Mathiassen, 1985; Andersen et al., 1990), the use of metaphors to discover designs (Madsen, 1989), the use of future workshops to generate visions (Kensing, 1987; Kensing and Madsen, 1991), and the use of diaries to document how decisions were made (cf. Lanzara and Mathiassen, 1985; Jepsen et al., 1989).[39] Accordingly, modelling formalisms, which were the major focus of the infological approach, have largely been neglected in the PWP. In view of its critical attitude towards ISDMs, it is surprising that the main developers of the PWP approach have recently focused on developing object-oriented methods (Mathiassen et al., 1993, 1995). These seem to be only loosely connected—and to some extent contradictory—to the overall strategy of the PWP approach.

The object-oriented approaches

Scandinavia has also been influential in the emergence of object-oriented (OO) approaches. Simula 67 was developed in Norway (Dahl and Nygaard, 1966) and is widely recognised as the major forerunner of OO languages. It was soon followed by object-oriented modelling languages such as Delta in the mid-1970s (Holbæk-Hanssen et al., 1976) and recently by programming environments like Beta (Madsen et al., 1993). To our knowledge Delta was the first attempt to apply OO concepts beyond programming languages. Quite interestingly, Håndlykken and Nygaard (1981) observe the need for improved language support for the ISD as recognised in the NJMF project (Nygaard and Bergo, 1975) as one reason for the development of the Delta language.

Several other OO methods have been developed in Scandinavia such as OCTOBUS (Awad et al., 1996), OOram (Reenskaug et al., 1995), OOSE (Jacobson et al., 1992), object-oriented business process re-engineering (Jacobson et al., 1995), object-oriented analysis and design (Mathiassen et al., 1993, 1995). Among them, Jacobson's books have received most

---

[39] Also here the developers seem not to be aware of the closeness of their ideas to the concept of design rationale and the design of wicked problems.

international recognition. Because his books have a Scandinavian orientation including user orientation and organisational focus, the following is
mainly based on his methods.[40]

The object-oriented software engineering (OOSE) of Jacobson et al.
(1992) is based on two distinctive ideas: the concept of 'use case' and the
division of analysis objects into entity, interface, and control objects in the
spirit of the MVC paradigm of Smalltalk.[41] A 'use case' is a behaviourally
related sequence of transactions performed by an actor in a dialogue with
the system. An actor (a user) can have one or more use cases. OO requirements analysis in OOSE starts with use case modelling. Use cases are
structured into entity objects, interface objects, and control objects. Entity
objects are objects that manage some piece of information, interface
objects encapsulate the functionality to manage a system interface, and
control objects encapsulate the control aspects of one or a few use
cases.

Compared with most methods of OO analysis and design, OOSE is
user oriented. The process starts with use case modelling. Use cases aim
at providing a concrete feel of the functionality inside the system, and
the specific way of using that functionality. The concept of use case has
later been incorporated in several OO methods. OOSE also includes early
attention to user interface (as an integral part of use cases), whereas many
other OO methods neglect it totally or address it quite late (e.g. Coad
and Yourdon, 1991a, 1991b).

The object-oriented business process re-engineering of Jacobson et al.
(1995) applies a conceptual apparatus analogical to OOSE in modelling
organisations. A 'use case' (in a business system) becomes a sequence of
transactions in a business system whose task is to yield a result of measurable value to an individual actor of the business system, 'entity objects' (in
a business system) represent occurrences such as products, deliverables,
documents, and other things that are handled in the business, 'interface
objects' represent a set of operations in the business, each of which
should be performed by one and the same resource who interacts with the
customer, and 'control objects' (in a business system) represent a set of
tasks which should be performed by one resource instance which is not
dealing directly with the customer.

Even though object-oriented business process re-engineering (Jacobson
et al., 1995) forms an interesting attempt to apply OO concepts to organisational modelling, the modelling of organisational phenomena through
use cases, entity objects, interface objects, and control objects seems
mechanistic and ignores many important dimensions of organisational

---

[40] Ironically many of the recent OO developments seem to be totally unaware of their
Scandinavian Langeforsian heritage if one looks at their bibliography etc.
[41] Quite interestingly, the MVC is also of Scandinavian origin (Reenskaug et al., 1995).

behaviour. Finally, although Scandinavia has had an exceptionally strong influence on the evolution of OO approaches, Scandinavians have also contributed significantly to criticisms of object orientation, especially to reading OO analysis as an instance of real-world modelling (Høydalsvik and Sindre, 1993; Opdahl and Sindre, 1994).

Comparison of the Scandinavian Approaches

In this section we analyse differences and commonalities among the eight Scandinavian approaches. We apply Mathiassen's (1981) categories of application area, perspective, and guidelines including techniques, tools, and principles of organisation in comparing the methods. Table 4.1 compares eight Scandinavian approaches with regard to their scope, value orientation, the knowledge interest of the ISD process, support for formal vs. informal co-operation, the role of ISDMs, stakeholder relationships, ISD contexts covered, and principles of the ISD process. Because of the space limitations, we do not report complete quotations, which would justify our classification. Instead, we shall make a few specific comments on issues which beg for explanation.

The scope in Table 4.1 distinguishes whether the approach is—either explicitly or implicitly—*general or specific in terms of the nature or the size of system* to be developed. If the approach does not specify its scope, it is interpreted to be general. As Table 4.1 indicates, all approaches are classified general. To deepen the analysis, we have indicated the major application areas to which the approach can be suitable by applying the classification of systems into transaction processing systems (TPS), office-automation systems (OAS), knowledge work systems (KWS), decision support systems (DSS), management information systems (MIS), and executive support systems (ESS) (Laudon and Laudon, 1994).

The *value orientation* aims at uncovering values underlying the approach. Table 4.1 indicates that most methods emphasise organisational effectiveness, the TU approach being the only exception in its emphasis on the industrial democracy, quality of working life, and quality of work. User-oriented criteria such as job satisfaction (JS) and user information satisfaction (UIS) are also present in the STD approach (JS) and in the SC approach (JS + UIS). The PWP approach expresses increased professionalism as one of its value orientations. The LA approach adopts a broad view of organisational effectiveness, not including only economic outcomes, but also free and open organisational communication and informed choice.

The knowledge interest in Table 4.1 views ISD as an enquiry process in the sense that it must produce valid knowledge. Such validation may be governed by *technical knowledge interest* with the orientation toward the control of the external world, *practical* or *communicative knowledge interest* with

TABLE 4.1. *Comparison of the eight ISD approaches*

Approach	Scope	Value orientation	Knowledge interest of ISD	Aspects supported	Role of methods	Stakeholder relations	ISD contexts covered	Principles of the ISD process
Infological approach	General; in practice mainly TPS and MIS	Organisational effectiveness User-oriented criteria weakly present	Technical (***) Communicative (*+)	Formal (**) Informal (?)	Regulative rules (cookbook)	UP assumed; easily mgmt. and expert led	Organisational (**) Language (**) Technical (**)	Life cycle Blueprint Linear
Formal approaches	General; in practice database-oriented TPS	Organisational effectiveness	Technical (***) Communicative (**)	Formal (***)	Regulative rules	UP assumed; easily expert led	Organisational (*) Language (**+) Technical (***)	Life cycle Blueprint Linear
Socio-technical approach	General; in practice mainly TPS	Organisational effectiveness Job satisfaction	Technical (***) Communicative (*)	Formal (**)	Guidelines	Strong emphasis on UP; easily mgmt. and expert led	Organisational (**) Technical (*)	Life cycle Blueprint Linear
Trade unionist approach	General; in practice tool-oriented small TPS, OAS, or KWS	Quality of working life	Technical (***) Communicative (**) (language game) Emancipatory (*) (critical)	Formal (*) Informal (***)	Reminders	Strong emphasis on UP; ideally co-operative on micro issues	Organisational (*) Technical (*)	Evolution Process mode Non-linear (prototyping)
Socio-cybernetic approach	General; especially TPS, MIS, and DSS	Organisational effectiveness User satisfaction Total efficiency	Technical (***) Communicative (**) Emancipatory (*)	Formal (**) Informal (*)	Guidelines	Steering committee control; easily mgmt. controlled; UP assumed	Organisational (**) Organisational (**) Technical (*)	Evolution Process mode Non-linear (prototyping)
Language approach	General; CSCW-type OAS and KWS	Organisational effectiveness Open communications Informed choice	Technical (**) Communicative (***) Emancipatory (*)	Formal (**) Informal (*)	Guidelines to reconstruct rules	UP a necessity	Organisational (*+) Language (***)	Evolutionary Blueprint Non-linear
Professional work practice approach	General	Organisational effectiveness (productivity); Professionalism in ISD	Technical (***) Communicative (**) (transparency of the process and product)	Formal (*+) Informal (*+)	Guidelines to supplement experience	Possibly a steering committee; UP desired; Professionals essential	Organisational (*) Language (*) Technical (*)	Life cycle Process mode Non-linear (prototyping)
Object-oriented approach	General; in practice mainly TPS	Organisational effectiveness	Technical (***) Communicative (*)	Formal (**+) Informal (*)	Constitutive rules + guidelines	UP assumed; easily expert led	Organisational (*) Language (**) Technical (***)	Evolution/life cycle Process mode Non-linear

* Weakly oriented.
** Moderately oriented.
*** St ... [illegible]

the orientation toward mutual understanding, and *emancipatory knowledge interest* with the orientation toward emancipation from seemingly 'natural' constraints through free and open communication (Habermas, 1971; Lyytinen, 1986). Table 4.1 indicates that all approaches are governed by the technical knowledge interest (to get the desired system technically and organisationally implemented) and thereby they embed the idea of obtaining general and reliable knowledge of 'facts' and 'laws' which can be used to make design acts more efficient. Some of them also adopt a communicative knowledge interest in the sense that ISD interventions should increase mutual understanding about the ISD situation among the stakeholders through engaging in a (multi) dialogue. The emancipatory knowledge interest is rarer. The critical value orientation of the trade unionist approach has an element of the emancipatory knowledge interest, even though it has been weakening. The idea of 'free and informed choice' (Argyris, 1973) as the ideal of the SC approach (e.g. Iivari and Koskela, 1987) has similarity with the free and open communication as a condition for emancipation. The LA approach recognises this idea of emancipation intrinsically by its notion of 'reconstructive' science and the idea of criticising and validating rules embedded in the IS (see Goldkuhl and Lyytinen, 1984; Hirschheim et al., 1995).

The distinction between formal and informal co-operation is adopted from Kraut and Streeter (1995). They mean by 'formal' communication writing (especially using formal or semi-formal notations), structured meetings, and other relatively little interactive and/or impersonal communications, and by 'informal' personal, peer-oriented, and interactive communications. This distinction is used in Table 4.1 to characterise co-operation more generally, including collaboration, co-ordination, and communication. Table 4.1 indicates that almost all the eight approaches have a strong formal orientation, the TU approach being the only exception. Its latest generation in particular has been oriented towards supporting the informal aspects of co-operation. Prototyping as an integral part of the SC approach is also interpreted to support the informal aspects of ISD.

ISDMs may serve a number of functions. They may be intended to serve as ideal models for the ISD process (Parnas and Clements, 1986)—ideals in the sense that they are not be expected to be followed literally—or as heuristics to be followed adaptively. In the former case, one may question to what extent ISDMs form constitutive rules such as rules of games and to what extent they embed regulative rules which only prescribe action without defining it (Searle, 1969). Constitutive rules lead to questioning what are the inherent rules (principles) of an approach the violation of which means that one does not follow the approach. ISDMs may also be interpreted as reminders, 'laundry lists', of the tasks to be performed (Ehn, 1988). They may also be perceived as vehicles of learning (Checkland and

Scholes, 1990) which allow one to make sense of situations and contrast them with one's preconceptions and learn thereby from the experience. As Table 4.1 indicates, most Scandinavian approaches regard methods as guidelines. The cookbook nature of ISAC can be regarded as an example of regulative rules. One could expect every approach to have its core of constitutive rules which define whether one follows the approach or not. These include principles like encapsulation, information hiding, inheritance, polymorphism, communication, and OO approaches (Jacobson et al., 1992). Unfortunately, these regulative rules are not clearly expressed in most approaches, and it is beyond the scope of this chapter to try to nail them down.

All Scandinavian approaches assume some *user participation* but for very different purposes. With the infological, formal, and to some extent the SC approach user participation is seen as a way to ensure the validity of the system specification, and to improve the likelihood of system implementation. With the LA approach the motivation for user participation is ontological and epistemological, and therefore a necessity: IS implements some linguistic rules followed by the user community and therefore to ensure understandable communications through the IS the users must participate in their reconstruction. With the case of the STD and TU approaches the goals of user participation are different: they are to ensure good quality of working life and/or to sustain some power with the workers. In this respect the realities of effective user participation may be different, however. Even though legislation ensures a certain level of user participation in countries like Denmark, Norway, and Sweden, management still has considerable power over decisions, covering also conditions for user participation. The content of user participation can also be different. Most Scandinavian approaches emphasise the significance of using abstractions in user participation. Those abstractions focus on the organisational and language context and help users understand what the system will do and how it will operate in the organisational environment. In contrast, the co-operative generation in the TU approach has focused on micro-level issues in supporting informal user and developer interaction of task-oriented designs.

In the case of ISD contexts Table 4.1 shows, not surprisingly, that the STD approach has paid most attention to the organisational context, the LA approach to the language context, and the formal and the OO approaches are strongest in the technology context.

Table 4.1 identifies three major principles of ISD process: life cycle vs. evolution, blueprint vs. process mode, and linear vs. non-linear process. In general ISD can be conceptualised through metaphors of a (product) life cycle or an evolutionary process similar to that of a species. The life cycle metaphor implies that an IS has relatively well-defined times of birth and death, and during this lifespan the system is developed, used and maintained, and abandoned. The evolution metaphor instead suggests that

ISs are like social institutions, which continuously evolve by just changing their mode of existence and form. Accordingly, the life cycle metaphor emphasises the system's viability and robustness whereas the evolution metaphor underscores its flexibility and change mechanisms. The infological approach like ISAC manifests clearly the life cycle concept. The conceptual information modelling approaches assume the life cycle metaphor because of their idea of an IS as a theory of the application domain. As a theory, one could assume an IS to be relatively permanent. The OO approach illustrates an interesting duality. On the one hand, it emphasises evolution. On the other hand, OO approaches based on conceptual information modelling can be expected to inherit the life cycle view of the conceptual information modelling approaches. Examples of more evolution-oriented approaches are the SC and LA approaches.

The blueprint mode (Faludi, 1973) implies that the ISD process is assumed to proceed according to a well-defined plan or method, possibly supplemented with backtracking, whereas the process mode emphasises that the continuous learning during the development process requires frequent replanning of the development process. Prototyping is a good example of the process mode of planning, even though the process mode does not necessarily require prototyping. The infological approach as manifested in ISAC is a clear example of the blueprint mode, even though ISAC pays considerable attention to learning in more general terms. The LA approach reflects the blueprint mode rather than the process mode, even though the latter is by no means excluded. Otherwise, most of the recent approaches reflect more the process mode, possibly supported by prototypes.

Linear vs. non-linear questions whether the ISD process is assumed to proceed in a linear fashion through analysis/design areas such as requirements analysis, specification, architectural design, detailed design, and implementation or whether they proceed largely concurrently. Again the infological approach as manifested in ISAC is an example of the linear process whereas the SC approach and the PWP approach are most explicitly non-linear. Because prototyping implies a non-linear structure, the TU and OO approaches are also assumed to have a non-linear structure.

Summary and Conclusion

Table 4.2 summarises the Scandinavian approaches indicating their theoretical roots, strengths and weaknesses, and use in practice. It indicates that despite the practical orientation of many Scandinavian approaches, either because of their roots or action research-based development, most of them are mainly academic exercises. Even though not used directly, many approaches have affected the practice indirectly.

TABLE 4.2. *Summary of the Scandinavian approaches*

Approach	Theoretical roots	Strengths and major contributions	Weaknesses	Practical use
The infological approach	Not clearly articulated; eclectic; systems theory	1. The distinction between the infological problem and datalogical problem of ISD 2. The formalism for conceptual/infological formal logic; modelling 3. The ISAC method for information analysis 4. The ISAC method for change analysis	1. Theoretically eclectic and weakly documented 2. Systems theory dominance 3. Structuralist view of organisations 4. Human agency omitted 5. ISAC process oriented (data orientation weakly integrated)	Considerable in the 1980s
The formal approaches	Formal logic, Petri nets, conceptual information modelling formalisms	1. Contributions to the temporal modelling 2. Contributions to the behavioural modelling 3. Innovative ISD methods (e.g. CIM) 4. Pioneering CASE projects 5. Contributions to the metaCASE environments 6. Contributions to the method engineering 7. Formal and quantitative method comparison	1. Mechanistic view of organisations 2. Risk of over-formalisation 3. Conceptual complexity	MetaCASE tools have an increasing usage
The socio-technical approach	The socio-technical design theory	1. Empirical testing of the socio-technical design ideas and ideals in practice	1. Consensus view of organisations	Modest
The trade unionist approach	A synthesis of Marx, Heidegger, and Wittgenstein, which is not fully elaborated	1. The critical value orientation 2. A model of a union-led 'shadow organisation' for ISD 3. The tool perspective of computer artefacts 4. Contributions to the participatory 'design-by-doing' approach supporting informal co-operation in ISD	1. Theoretically eclectic 2. Potential conflict with the critical value orientation and practice 3. Tool orientation 4. Articulation of work omitted	Modest beyond the research projects

Approach	Theoretical background	Strengths	Weaknesses	
The socio-cybernetic approach	Eclectic; systems theory, cybernetics, socio-cybernetic theory of acts, information economics, innovation diffusion theory, theories of organisational decision-making	1. Three levels of abstraction 2. A detailed meta-model for an IS 3. A process model for ISD (the hierarchical spiral model) 4. Quality and choice criteria for an IS 5. A reference model	1. Theoretically eclectic 2. Complexity of the approach 3. Not fully elaborated at the conceptual/infological level and datalogical/technical level 4. Not sufficiently tested in practice 5. No CASE support	Modest
The language action approach	The speech act theory; conversation theory	1. A firm theoretical background 2. Rich understanding of computer-mediated social communication based on the speech act theory 3. Attention to all illocutionary points (assertives, directives, commissives, expressives, and declaratives) 4. SAMPO method	1. Complexity of the approach 2. Not fully elaborated at the organisational level 3. Not sufficiently tested in practice 4. No CASE support	Modest
The professional work practice approach	Not clearly articulated; eclectic; organisational learning; the theory of reflective practitioner, transaction cost economics	1. Empirical understanding of the actual ISD practices 2. Specific techniques such as diagnostic, ecological, and virtual maps, use of metaphors, future workshops 3. Principles of project management	1. Theoretically eclectic and weakly documented 2. Not a complete method	Modest
Object-oriented approach	Not clearly articulated; computer science (programming languages, software engineering, information modelling)	1. The concept of 'use cases' 2. Object categories: entity, interface, and control objects 3. Early attention to user interface 4. An attempt to apply OO concepts to organisational modelling	1. Theoretical background weakly documented 2. Computer science (software engineering) dominance 3. A mechanistic view of organisational work	Considerable interest

The plurality of the Scandinavian approaches portrays on a smaller scale similar trends to those which are visible in the evolution of ISR more broadly. A unique feature is that in many areas Scandinavian approaches have pioneered these trends. In particular, they have paid strong attention to the organisational and human aspects of ISD. Nearly all of them view ISD as an enabler and part of organisational development. In a similar way several Scandinavian approaches have focused on relationships between information technology and work, though their ways of addressing the relationship have varied. The widely known TU approach has adopted an artefact-oriented approach, emphasising the tacit nature of work, whereas especially the SC and the LA approaches have focused on modelling and articulation of work and communications. Typically Scandinavian re-searchers view ISs as inherently social artefacts, which embody multiple social meanings. The socio-technical nature of ISs is widely recognised by nearly all approaches (whether as good or bad). Over the years the inter-pretation of information requirements has also become richer and more nuanced, and faithful to the complexity of ISD. In this regard, the LA approach has been influential in advancing the view of the intersubjective nature of information requirements and questioning their functional 'reading'. The views of ISD process have also evolved towards more varied interpretations, involving IS evolution, a process mode of planning sup-ported by prototypes, and intertwined analysis and design. The role of ISDMs has also changed from regulative rules towards looser guidelines, reminders, and vehicles of learning. Most of the Scandinavian approaches are, however, formal attempts that seek to impose order and discipline on ISD. The latest generation of the TU approach is the clearest exception in this respect.

Generally, the Scandinavian approaches can be characterised as 'grass-roots' approaches when compared with the North American MIS tradition. Partly because of the small size of most Scandinavian organisations, the Scandinavian ISD approaches tend to focus on 'small-scale' development of individual application systems rather than the 'large-scale' development of a total IS. Partly because of the Scandinavian cultural and political environment, they have also paid considerable attention to user participa-tion. Such participation is regulated by legislation in most Scandinavian countries—a fact unheard of in countries like the USA or the rising eco-nomies of the Far East. One explanation for the pressure of higher user participation in Scandinavia is the high level of education among the Scandinavian labour force—workers know, and they know that they know, and therefore they have high demands on their work environments.

Even though there are sharp differences among Scandinavian ISD approaches, they also share common features. The infological tradition pioneered by Langefors led early to attending to organisational, applica-tion, and user issues in ISD. As shown, all other Scandinavian approaches can be construed as varying responses to these infological challenges. At the time of their birth, these responses were mostly viewed as adversary to each other, emphasising conflict, difference, and showing even hostility. Recently, a more 'ecumenical' interpretation has gained acceptance that emphasises the common roots and complementary nature of the approaches. One reason for this is that the political and economic climate of Scandinavia has changed, while sharp ideological and political confrontations have mellowed. This chapter follows this line of reconciliatory interpretation. One aspect in this interpretation is that we have to take into account the notion of *Zeitgeist*, i.e. we have to understand and honour the historical context in which the original ideas were presented. This underlines that research on ISD never occurs in a vacuum. ISDMs tend to be offsprings of their time, reflecting for example dominant research trends and theories of that time. To illustrate our point, it would be quite odd to find an ISDM from the 1960s without any influence from systems theory.

In view of the prevalent Scandinavian political and cultural environment ISR has also led to some paradoxical outcomes. Despite dominant planning-oriented social democratic ideology in Nordic countries, Scandinavian ISD approaches have ironically relied much less on IS planning than corporate America. In contrast, the Scandinavian approaches rely much more on the evolutionary development of individual applications, grassroots initiatives, and *bricolage*. The second paradox is that Scandinavian consensus-oriented corporativism has effectively hindered ISD approaches from emphasising radical organisational changes in the sense of business process re-engineering or redesign. This is almost ironical (though maybe a blessing) when one takes into account how early Scandinavian researchers put IS-induced organisational changes into their research agenda, and how radical were the value orientations the TU approach, in particular, adopted.[42]

The evolution of the Scandinavian school has not halted. Although most of the unique features found in the Scandinavian research have also been taken up elsewhere (as IFIP 8.2 conference proceedings evidence) there is still room for advancing the Scandinavian contribution. At the moment several theoretically inspired approaches have gained a foot in Scandinavia, still are in an embryonic state *qua* ISD approaches. These include approaches based on activity theory (Bødker, 1989; Kuutti, 1991, 1994), critical social theory (Lyytinen, 1992), structuration theory (Karsten, 1996; Käkölä, 1996; Lyytinen and Ngwenyama, 1992, 1996), and actor network theory (Monteiro and Hanseth, 1995). Hopefully, the next ten years will show whether they will evolve to more concrete approaches, possibly with their own Scandinavian flavour.

---

[42] One obvious explanation in this case is that BPR is clearly a management-dominated approach.

References

Aanstad, P., Skylstad, G., and Sølvberg, A. (1971), 'CASCADE: A Computer-Based Documentation System', in Bubenko et al. (1971).

Ackoff, R. L., and Emery, F. E. (1972), *On Purposeful Systems* (Chicago, Aldine-Atherton).

Andersen, N. E., Kensing, F., Lundin, J., Mathiassen, L., Munk-Madsen, A., Rasbech, M., and Sørgaard, P. (1990), *Professional Systems Development: Experience, Ideas and Action* (New York, Prentice Hall) (original in Danish: *Professional systemudvikling: Erfaringer, muligheter og handling*, Copenhagen: Teknisk Forlag A/S, 1986).

Andersen, P. B. (1990), *A Theory of Computer Semiotics: Semiotic Approaches to Construction and Assessment of Computer Systems* (Cambridge: Cambridge University Press).

Andersen, R. J., Bubenko, J. A., Jr., and Sølvberg, A. (1991) (eds.), *Conference on Advanced Information Systems Engineering: CAiSE'91* (Berlin, Springer Verlag).

ANSI/X3/SPARC (1975), 'Interim Report from the Study Group on Data Base Management Systems', *FDT Bulletin of the ACM*, 7, 2.

Apel, K. (1980), *Towards a Transformation of Philosophy* (London, Routledge & Kegan Paul).

Argyris, C. (1973), *Intervention Theory and Method: A Behavioral Science View* (Reading, Mass., Addison-Wesley).

—— and Schøn, D. (1978), *Organisational Learning: A Theory of Action Perspective* (Reading, Mass., Addison-Wesley).

Assenova, P., and Johannesson, P. (1996), 'First Order Action Logic: An Approach for Modelling the Communication Process between Agents', in Verharen et al. (1996).

Aulin-Ahmavaara, A. Y. (1977), 'A General Theory of Acts, with Application to the Distinction between Rational and Irrational "Social Cognition"', *Zeitschrift für allgemeine Wissenschaftstheorie*, 8, 2: 195–220.

Auramäki, E., Hirschheim, R., and Lyytinen, K. (1992*a*), 'Modelling Offices through Discourse Analysis: The SAMPO Approach', *Computer Journal*, 35, 4: 342–52.

—— —— —— (1992*b*), 'Modelling Offices through Discourse Analysis: A Comparison and Evaluation of SAMPO with OSSAD and ICN', *Computer Journal*, 35, 5: 492–500.

—— Lehtinen, E., and Lyytinen, K. (1988), 'A Speech-Act-Based Office Modeling Approach', *ACM Transactions on Office Information Systems*, 6, 2: 126–52.

Austin, J. L. (1962), *How to do Things with Words* (Cambridge, Mass., Harvard University Press).

Avison, D. E., and Wood-Harper, A. T. (1990), *Multiview: An Exploration in Information Systems Development* (Oxford, Blackwell).

Awad, M., Kuusela, J., and Ziegler, J. (1996), *Object-Oriented Technology for Real-Time Systems: A Practical Approach Using OMT and Fusion* (Upper Saddle River, NJ, Prentice-Hall).

Bansler, J. (1989), 'Systems Development Research in Scandinavia: Three Theoretical Schools', *Scandinavian Journal of Information Systems*, 1: 3–20.

Bergsten, P., Bubenko, J., Dahl, R., Gustafsson, M., and Johansson, L.-Å. (1989), 'RAMATIC: A CASE Shell for Implementation of Specific CASE Tools', TEMPORA T6.1, SISU, Stockholm.

Beyer, H., and Holzblatt, K. (1995), 'Apprenticing with the Customer', *Communications of the ACM* (May), 5, 38: 45–52.

Bjerknes, G., and Bratteteig, T. (1995), 'User Participation and Democracy: A Discussion of Scandinavian Research on System Development', *Scandinavian Journal of Information Systems*, 1: 73–98.

Bjørn-Andersen, N., and Eason, K. D. (1980), 'Myths and Realities of Information Systems Contributions to Organisational Rationality', in A. Mowshowitz (ed.), *Human Choice and Computers*, ii (Amsterdam, North-Holland).

—— and Hedberg, B. (1977), 'Designing Information Systems: An Organisational Perspective', *TIMS Studies in the Management Sciences*, 5: 125–42.

—— —— Merceri, D., Mumford, E., and Solé, A. (1979) (eds.), *The Impact of Systems Change in Organisations* (Alphen aan den Rijn, Sijthoff & Noordhoff).

Bødker, S. (1989), 'Through the Interface: A Human Activity Approach to Interface Design', Ph.D. diss., University of Aarhus, Department of Computer Science, DAIMI PB-224, Aarhus.

—— Ehn, P., Kammersgaard, J., Kyng, M., and Sundblad, Y. (1987), 'A Utopian Experience: On Design of Powerful Computer-Based Tools for Skilled Graphic Workers', in G. Bjerknes, P. Ehn, and M. Kyng (eds.), *Computers and Democracy* (Aldershot, Avebury).

—— Greenbaum, J., and Kyng, M. (1991), 'Setting the Stage for Design as Action', in Greenbaum and Kyng (1991*a*).

—— and Grønbæk, K. (1991*a*), 'Design in Action: From Prototyping by Demonstration to Cooperative Prototyping', in Greenbaum and Kyng (1991*a*).

—— —— (1991*b*), 'Cooperative Prototyping Studies: Users and Designers Envision a Dental Case Record System', in J. M. Bowers and S. D. Benford (eds.), *Studies in Computer Supported Cooperative Work* (Amsterdam, Elsevier Science Publishers BV (North-Holland)).

Boehm, B. (1988), 'A Spiral Model of Software Development and Enhancement', *Computer*, May: 611–72.

Booch, G. (1994), *Object-Oriented Analysis and Design with Applications*, 2nd edn. (Redwood City, Calif., Benjamin/Cummings).

Bubenko, J. A., Jr. (1977), 'The Temporal Dimension in Information Modeling', in G. M. Nijssen (ed.), *Architecture and Models in Data Base Management Systems* (Amsterdam, North-Holland).

—— (1980), 'Information Modeling in the Context of System Development', in S. Lavington (ed.), *Information Procession 80* (Amsterdam, North-Holland).

—— (1988), 'Selecting a Strategy for Computer-Aided Software Engineering (CASE)', SYSLAB Report No. 59, SYSLAB, University of Stockholm.

—— (1992), 'On the Evolution of Information Systems Modelling: A Scandinavian Perspective', in K. Lyytinen, and S. Puuronen (eds.), *Computing in the Past, Present and Future* (Jyväskylä, Department of Computer Science and Information Systems, University of Jyväskylä).

—— and Källhammar, O. (1971), 'CADIS: Computer-Aided Design of Information Systems', in Bubenko et al. (1971).

Bubenko, J. A., Jr. Langefors, B., and Sølvberg, A. (1971) (eds.), *Computer-Aided Information Systems Analysis and Design* (Lund, Studentlitteratur).

—— and Lindencrona, E. (1984), *Konceptuell modellering—informationsanalys* (Lund, Studentlitteratur).

Carlsson, J., Ehn, P., Erlander, B., Perby, M.-L., and Sandberg, Å. (1978), 'Planning and Control from the Perspective of Labour: A Short Presentation of the DEMOS Project', *Accounting, Organisations and Society*, 3, 3/4: 249–60.

Checkland, P., and Scholes, J. (1990), *Soft Systems Methodology in Action* (Chichester, John Wiley & Sons).

Churchman, C. W. (1968), *The Systems Approach* (New York, Delacorte).

Clement, A., and Van den Besselaar, P. (1993), 'A Retrospective Look at PD Projects', *Communications of the ACM*, 36, 6: 29–37.

Coad, P., and Yourdon, E. (1991*a*), *Object-Oriented Analysis*, 2nd edn. (Englewood Cliffs, NJ, Yourdon Press).

—— —— (1991*b*), *Object-Oriented Design* (Englewood Cliffs, NJ, Yourdon Press).

CODASYL Development Committee (1962), 'An Information Algebra: Phase I Report', *Communications of the ACM*, 5, 4: 190–204.

Codd, E. F. (1970), 'A Relational Model of Data for Large Shared Data Banks', *Communications of the ACM*, 13, 6: 377–87.

Conklin, J., and Begeman, H. L. (1988), 'gIBIS: A Hypertext Tool for Exploratory Policy Discussion', *ACM Transactions on Office Information Systems*, 6, 4: 303–31.

Dahl, O. J., and Nygaard, K. (1966), 'SIMULA: An Algol-Based Simulation Language', *Communications of the ACM*, 9, 9: 671–8.

Dahlbom, B. (1993*a*) (ed.), *Essays on Infology by Börje Langefors*, Gothenburg Studies in Information Systems (Gothenburg, University of Gothenburg).

—— (1993*b*), 'Introduction: An Engineer from SAAB?', in Dahlbom (1993*a*).

—— (1995) (ed.), *The Infological Equation: Essays in Honor of Börje Langefors*, Gothenburg Studies in Information Systems, Report 6 (Gothenburg: Gothenburg University).

—— and Mathiassen, L. (1993), *Computers in Context: The Philosophy and Practice of Systems Design* (Cambridge, NCC Blackwell).

Davis, G. B. (1974), *Management Information Systems: Conceptual Foundations, Structure and Development* (New York, McGraw-Hill).

Dietz, J. L. G., and Widdershoven, G. A. M. (1991), 'Speech Acts or Communication Action', in L. Bannon, M. Robinson, and K. Schmidt (eds.), *Proceedings of the Second European Conference on Computer-Supported Cooperative Work* (Dordrecht, Kluwer Academic Publishers).

Ehn, P. (1973), 'Bidrag till ett kritisk social perspektiv på datorbaserade informationsystem', University of Stockholm, Department of Information Processing Science, TRITA-IBADB-1023, Stockholm.

—— (1988), 'Work-Oriented Design of Computer Artifacts', Ph.D. diss. Arbetslivscentrum, Stockholm.

—— and Göranzon, B. (1974), *Perspektiv på systemutvecklingprocessen* (Stockholm, Department of Information Processing, University of Stockholm).

—— and Kyng, M. (1987), 'The Collective Resource Approach to Systems Design', in G. Bjerknes, P. Ehn, and M. Kyng (eds.), *Computers and Democracy* (Aldershot, Avebury).

—— —— (1991), 'Cardboard Computers: Mocking-it-up and Hand-on the Future', in Greenbaum and Kyng (1991*a*).

—— —— Sundblad, Y., et al. (1983), 'The Utopia Project', in U. Briefs, C. Ciborra, and L. Schneider (eds.), *Systems Design for, with, and by the Users* (Amsterdam, North-Holland).

—— and Sandberg, A. (1983), 'Local Union Influence on Technology and Work Organisation', in U. Briefs, C. Ciborra, and L. Schneider (eds.), *Systems Design for, with, and by the Users* (Amsterdam, North-Holland).

—— and Sjögren, D. (1991), 'From System Descriptions to Scripts for Action', in Greenbaum and Kyng (1991*a*).

Eriksson, I., Hellman, R., and Nurminen, M. I. (1988), 'A Method for Supporting Users' Comprehensive Learning', *Education and Computing*, 4, 4: 251–64.

Faludi, A. (1973), *Planning Theory* (Oxford, Pergamon Press).

Flores, F., Graves, M., Hartfield, B., and Winograd, T. (1988), 'Computer Systems and the Design of Organisational Interaction', *ACM Transactions on Office Information Systems*, 6, 2: 153–72.

—— and Ludlow, J. J. (1980), 'Doing and Speaking in the Office', in G. Fick and R. H. Sprague, Jr. (eds.), *Decision Support Systems: Issues and Challanges* (Elmsford, NY, Pergamon Press).

Galbraith, J. K. (1967), *The New Industrial State* (Boston, Houghton Mifflin Company).

Goldkuhl, G. (1984), 'ISAC omvärderad', in *Systemutvecling—av Vem, för Vem and Hur?* (Stockholm, Arbetarskyddsfonden).

—— and Lyytinen, K. (1982*a*), 'A Language Action View of Information Systems', in C. Ross, and M. Ginzberg (eds.), *Proceedings of the Third Conference on Information Systems* (Ann Arbor, Mich.).

—— —— (1982*b*), 'Disposition for an Information Analysis Methodology Based on Speech Act Theory', in G. Goldkuhl, and C.-O. Kall (eds.), *Proceedings of the Fifth Scandinavian Research Seminars on Systemeering Models* (Gothenburg, Department of Information Processing, University of Gothenburg).

—— —— (1984), 'Information System Specification as Rule Reconstruction', in T. M. A. Bemelmans (ed.), *Beyond Productivity: Information Systems Development for Organisational Effectiveness* (Amsterdam, North-Holland).

Göranzon, B. (1978) (ed.), *Ideologi och systemutevecking* (Ideology and Systems Development) (Lund, Studentlitteratur).

Greenbaum, J., and Kyng, M. (1991*a*) (eds.), *Design at Work: Cooperative Design of Computer Systems* (Hillsdale, NJ, Lawrence Erlbaum Associates).

—— —— (1991*b*), 'Introduction: Situated Design', in Greenbaum and Kyng (1991*a*).

Gustafsson, M. R., Karlsson, T., and Bubenko, J., Jr. (1982), 'A Declarative Approach to Conceptual Information Modeling', in Olle et al. (1982).

Habermas, J. (1971), *Towards a Rational Society* (London, Heinemann).

—— (1984), *The Theory of Communicative Action*, i: *Reason and the Rationalisation of Society* (Boston, Beacon Press).

—— (1987), *The Theory of Communicative Action*, ii: *The Critique of Functionalist Reason* (Boston, Beacon Press).

Hammer, M., and Champy, J. (1993), *Reengineering the Corporation* (London, Nicholas Brealey Publishing).

Håndlykken, P., and Nygaard, K. (1981), 'The DELTA System Description Language: Motivation, Main Concepts and Experience from Use', in H. Hünke (ed.), *Software Engineering Environments* (Amsterdam, North-Holland).

Hedberg, B. (1980), 'Using Computerized Information Systems to Design Better Organisations and Jobs', in N. Bjørn-Andersen (ed.), *The Human Side of Information Processing* (Amsterdam, North-Holland).

—— and Mumford, E. (1975), 'The Design of Computer Systems: Man's Vision of Man as an Integral Part of the Systems Design Process', in E. Mumford, and H. Sackman (eds.), *Human Choice and Computers* (New York, American Elsevier Publishing Company).

Hirschheim, R., Klein, H. K., and Lyytinen, K. (1995), *Information Systems Development and Data Modeling: Conceptual and Philosophical Foundations* (Cambridge, Cambridge University Press).

—— —— —— (1996), 'Exploring the Intellectual Structures of Information Systems Development: A Social Action Theoretic Analysis', *Accounting, Management and Information Technologies*, 6, 1/2: 1–64.

Holbæk-Hanssen, E., Håndlykken, P., and Nygaard, K. (1976), *System Description and the DELTA Language*, Publication 523 (Oslo, The Norwegian Computing Center).

Holm, P. (1996), 'On the Design and Usage of Information Technology and the Structuring of Communication and Work', Department of Computer and System Sciences, Report 96-009, Ph.D. diss, Stockholm University.

Høydahlsvik, G. M., and Sindre, G. (1993), 'On the Purpose Object-Oriented Analysis', *ACM Sigplan Notices*, 28, 10: 240–55.

Høyer, R. (1971), *Databehandling, organisasjon og bedriftsmiljø* (Oslo, Norsk Produktivitetsinstitut).

Iivari, J. (1982), 'Taxonomy of the Experimental and Evolutionary Approaches to Systemeering', in J. Hawgood (ed.), *Evolutionary Information Systems* (Amsterdam, North-Holland).

—— (1983), 'Contributions to the Theoretical Foundations of Systemeering Research and the PIOCO Model', Ph.D. diss., Acta Universitatis Ouluensis, Series A, No. 150.

—— (1989*a*), 'Levels Abstraction as a Conceptual Framework for an Information System', in E. D. Falkenberg, and P. Lindgreen (eds.), *Information Systems Concepts: An In-Depth Analysis* (Amsterdam, North-Holland).

—— (1989*b*), 'A Methodology for IS Development as Organisational Change: A Pragmatic Contingency Approach', in H. K. Klein, and K. Kumar (eds.), *Systems Development for Human Progress* (Amsterdam, North-Holland).

—— (1990*a*), 'Hierarchical Spiral Model for Information System and Software Development. Part 1: Theoretical Background', *Information and Software Technology*, 32, 6: 386–99.

—— (1990*b*), 'Hierarchical Spiral Model for Information System and Software Development, Part 2: Design Process', *Information and Software Technology*, 32, 7: 450–8.

—— (1991), 'Object-Oriented Design of Information Systems: The Design Process', in F. Van Assche, B. Moulin, and C. Rolland (eds.), *Object Oriented Approach in Information Systems* (Amsterdam, Elsevier Science Publishers BV (North-Holland)).

—— (1994), 'Object-Oriented Information Systems Analysis: A Comparison of Six Object-Oriented Analysis Methods', in A. A. Verrijn-Stuart and T. W. Olle (eds.),

Methods and Associated Tools for the Information Systems Life Cycle, IFIP Transactions A-55 (Amsterdam, North-Holland).

—— and Hirschheim, R. (1996), 'Analyzing Information Systems Development: A Comparison and Analysis of Eight IS Development Approaches', *Information Systems* (in press).

—— and Kerola, P. (1983), 'A Sociocybernetic Framework for the Feature Analysis of Information Systems Design Methodologies', in Olle et al. (1983).

—— and Koskela, E. (1979), 'Choice and Quality Criteria for Data System Selection', in P. A. Samet (ed.), *Proceedings of EuroIFIP 79, European Conference on Applied Information Technology* (Amsterdam, North-Holland).

—— —— (1983), 'HSL: A Host System Language for Pragmatic Specification and Host System Description in Data System Development', in M. I. Nurminen and H. T. Gaupholm (eds.), *Report of the Sixth Scandinavian Research Seminar on Systemeering* (Bergen).

—— —— (1987), 'The PIOCO Model for IS Design', *MIS Quarterly*, 11, 3: 401–19.

Ivanov, K. (1984), 'Systemutveckling och ADB-ämnets utveckling' (Systems Development and the Evolution of the Discipline of Information Systems), in *Systemutveckling: av Vem, för Vem och Hur?* (Stockholm, Arbetarskyddsfonden, K4/84).

Jackson, M. A. (1975), *Principles of Program Design* (London, Academic Press).

Jacobson, I. (1987), 'Object-Oriented Development in an Industrial Environment', *OOPSLA'87 Conference Proceedings* (Orlando, Fla.).

—— Christerson, M., Jonsson, P., and Övergaard, G. (1992), *Object-Oriented Software Engineering: A Use Case Driven Approach* (Wokingham, Addison-Wesley).

—— Ericsson, M., and Jacobson, A. (1995), *The Object Advantage: Business Process Reengineering with Object Technology* (Workingham, Addison-Wesley).

Järvinen, P. (1971), 'DIFO: Design of Information Systems, Especially File Organisation', in Bubenko et al. (1971).

—— (1987), 'On Utilisation of Computers without Computing Experts: The Finnish Metalworkers' Union Case Study', in P. Docherty et al. (eds.), *System Design for Human Development and Productivity: Participation and beyond* (Amsterdam, Elsevier).

Jepsen, L., Mathiassen, L., and Nielsen, P. (1989), 'Back to Thinking Mode: Diaries for the Management of Information Systems Development Projects', *Behaviour and Information Technology*, 8, 3: 207–17.

Johannesson, P. (1995), 'Representation and Communication: A Speech Act Based Approach to Information Systems Design', *Information Systems*, 20, 4: 291–303.

Kaasboll, J. (1987), 'Intentional Development of Professional Language through Computerization', in P. Docherty, K. Fuchs-Kittowski, P. Kolm, and L. Mathiassen (eds.), *System Design for Human Development and Productivity: Participation and beyond* (Amsterdam, North-Holland).

Käkölä, T. (1996), 'Dual Information Systems in Hyperknowledge Organisations', Ph.D. diss., Turku Centre for Computer Science, TUCS Dissertations No. 2, Turku.

Kangassalo, H. (1982) (ed.), *First Scandinavian Research Seminar on Information Modelling and Data Base Management*, Acta Universitatis Tamperensis, Ser. B, Vol. 17, University of Tampere, Tampere.

—— (1992), 'COMIC: A System and Methodology for Conceptual Modelling and Information Construction', *Data and Knowledge Engineering*, 9: 287–319.

Kangassalo, H. and Jaakkola, H. (1990) (eds.), *Advances in Information and Modelling and Knowledge Bases* (Amsterdam, IOS Press).

Karsten, H. (1996), 'Interactions with Collaborative Technology: Lotus Notes in a Network Organisation', Ph.Lic. thesis, University of Jyväskylä, Department of Computer Science and Information Systems, Technical Reports TR-15, Jyväskylä.

Keen, P. G. W., and Scott Morton, M. (1978), *Decision Support Systems: An Organisational Perspective* (Reading, Mass., Addison-Wesley).

Kelly, S., Lyytinen, K., and Rossi, M. (1996), 'MetaEdit: A Fully Configurable Multi-user and Multi-tool CASE and CAME Environment', in P. Constantapoulos, J. Mylopoulos, and V. Vassiliou (eds.), *Advanced Information Systems Engineering* (Berlin, Springer Verlag).

Kensing, F. (1987), 'Generation of Visions in Systems Development', in P. Docherty, K. Fuchs-Kittowski, P. Kolm, and L. Mathiassen (eds.), *Systems Design for Human Development and Productivity: Participation and beyond* (Amsterdam, North-Holland).

—— and Madsen, K. H. (1991), 'Generating Visions: Future Workshops and Metaphorical Design', in Greenbaum and Kyng (1991*a*).

Kerola, P. (1975), 'On Hierarchical Information and Data Systems', in M. Lundeberg, and J. Bubenko, Jr. (eds.), *Systemeering 75* (Lund, Studentlitteratur).

—— (1980), 'In Infological Reserch into the Systemeering Process', in H. C. Lucas, Jr., F. F. Land, T. J. Lincoln, and K. Supper (eds.), *The Information Systems Environment* (Amsterdam, North-Holland).

—— and Freeman, P. (1981), 'A Comparison of Lifecycle Models', *Proceedings of the Fifth International Conference on Software Engineering* (San Diego).

—— and Järvinen, P. (1975), *Systemointi II* (Systemeering II) (Helsinki, Oy Gaudeamus Ab).

Klimbie, J. W., and Koffeman, K. L. (1974) (eds.), *Proceedings of the IFIP Working Conference on Data Base Management* (Amsterdam, North-Holland).

Kling, R., and Scacchi, W. (1982), 'Computing as Social Action: The Social Dynamics of Computer in Complex Organisations', *Advances in Computers*, 29 (New York, Academic Press).

Kraft, P., and Bansler, J. P. (1994), 'The Collective Resource Approach: The Scandinavian Experience', *Scandinavian Journal of Information Systems*, 6, 1: 71–84.

Kraut, R. E., and Streeter, L. A. (1995), 'Coordination in Software Development', *Communications of the ACM*, 38, 3: 69–81.

Krogstie, J. (1995), 'Conceptual Modeling for Computerized Information Systems Support in Organisations', Ph.D. diss., IDT, NTH, Trondheim.

Kuhn, S., and Muller, M. J. (1993), 'Participatory Design', *Communications of the ACM*, 36, 4: 24–8.

Kung, C. H., and Sølvberg, A. (1986), 'Activity Modeling and Behavior Modeling', in T. W. Olle, H. G. Sol, and A. A. Verrijn-Stuart (eds.), *Information Systems Design Methodologies: Improving the Practice* (Amsterdam, Elsevier (North-Holland)).

Kuutti, K. (1991), 'Activity Theory and its Applications in Information Systems Research and Design', in H.-E. Nissen, H. K. Klein, and R. Hirschheim (eds.), *Information Systems Research Arena for the 90's* (Amsterdam, North-Holland).

—— (1994), 'Information Systems, Cooperative Work and Active Subjects: The Activity-Theoretical Perspective', Ph.D. diss., University of Oulu, Department of Information Processing Science, Research Papers, Series A23, Oulu.

Kyng, M. (1991), 'Designing for Cooperation: Co-operating in Design', *Communications of the ACM*, 34, 12: 65–73.
—— (1994), 'Collective Resources Meets Puritanism', *Scandinavian Journal of Information Systems*, 6, 1: 85–96.
—— and Mathiassen, L. (1982), 'Systems Development and Trade Union Activities', in N. Björn-Andersen (ed.), *Information Society, for Richer, for Poorer* (Amsterdam, North-Holland).
Lange, O. (1965), *Wholes and Parts* (Oxford, Pergamon Press).
Langefors, B. (1963), 'Some Approaches to the Theory of Information Systems', *BIT*, 3, 4: 229–54.
—— (1966), *Theoretical Analysis of Information Systems* (Lund, Studentlitteratur).
—— (1970*a*), *System för företagsstyrning* (System for Steering Companies) (Lund, Studentlitteratur).
—— (1970*b*), 'Grunderna för systemanalys', in J. Bubenko, Jr., O. Källhammar, B. Langefors, M. Lundeberg, and A. Sölvberg (eds.), *Systemering 70* (Lund, Studentlitteratur).
—— (1974), 'Information Systems', in *Information Processing 74* (Amsterdam: North-Holland).
—— (1977), 'Information Systems Theory', *Information Systems*, 2: 207–19.
—— (1980), 'Infological Models and Information User Views', *Information Systems*, 5: 17–32.
—— and Sundgren, B. (1975), *Information Systems Architecture* (New York, Petrocelli/Charter).
Lanzara, G. F., and Mathiassen, L. (1985), 'Mapping Situations within a System Development Project', *Information and Management*, 8: 3–20.
Laudon, K. C., and Laudon, J. P. (1994), *Management Information Systems: Organisation and Technology* (New York, Macmillan).
Lehtinen, E., and Lyytinen, K. (1986), 'Action Based Model of Information Systems', *Information Systems*, 11, 3.
Lindgreen, P. (1982), 'The Information Graph', in Kangassalo (1982).
Lundeberg, M. (1976), 'Some Propositions Concerning Analysis and Design of Information Systems', Ph.D. diss., Department of Information Processing Science, TRITA-IBDB-4080, Royal Institute of Technology and the University of Stockholm, Stockholm.
—— (1982), 'The ISAC Approach to Specification of Information Systems and its Application to the Organisation of an IFIP Working Conference', in Olle et al. (1982).
—— and Andersen, E. S. (1974), *Systemering, Information analys* (Lund, Studentlitteratur).
—— Goldkuhl, G., and Nilsson, A. (1978), *Systemering* (Lund, Studentlitteratur).
—— —— —— (1981), *Information Systems Development: A Systematic Approach* (Englewood Cliffs, NJ, Prentice-Hall).
Lyytinen, K. (1981), 'Language Oriented Development of Information Systems: Methodological and Theoretical Foundations', Department of Computer Science, University of Jyväskylä, unpublished licentiate thesis, Jyväskylä.
—— (1986), 'Information Systems Development as Social Action: Framework and Critical Implications', Ph.D. diss., Jyväskylä Studies in Computer Science, Economics and Statistics, University of Jyväskylä, Jyväskylä.

Lyytinen, K. (1987), 'A Taxonomic Perspective of Information Systems Development: Theoretical Constructs and Recommendations', in R. Boland and R. Hirschheim (eds.), *Critical Issues in Information Systems Research* (Chichester, John Wiley & Sons).

—— (1992), 'Information Systems and Critical Theory', in M. Alvesson, and H. Willmott (eds.), *Critical Management Studies* (London, Sage).

—— and Ngwenyama, O. (1992), 'What Does Computer Support for Cooperative Work Mean? A Structurational Analysis of Computer Supported Cooperative Work', *Accounting, Management and Information Technologies*, 2, 1: 19–37.

—— —— (1996), 'Groupware Environments as Action Constitutive Resources: A Social Action Framework for Analyzing Groupware Technologies', *CSCW Journal*, forthcoming.

Madsen, K. H. (1989), 'Breakthrough through Breakdown: Metaphors and Structured Domains', in H. K. Klien, and K. Kumar (1989) (eds.), *Systems Development for Human Progress* (Amsterdam, North-Holland).

Madsen, O. L., Møller-Pedersen, B., and Nygraad, K. (1993), *Object-Oriented Programming in the BETA Programming Language* (Workingham, Addison-Wesley).

Marschak, J. (1974), *Economic Information, Decision and Prediction: Selected Essays*, Vol. ii (Dordrecht, Kluwer).

Martin, J. (1982), *Application Development without Programmers* (Englewood Cliffs, NJ, Prentice-Hall).

Marttiin, P., Rossi, M., Tahvanainen, V.-P., and Lyytinen, K. (1993), 'A Comparative Review of CASE Shells: A Preliminary Framework and Research Outcomes', *Information and Management*, 25, 2: 11–31.

Mathiassen, L. (1981), 'Systems Development and Systems Development Method', Ph.D. diss., DAIMI PB-136, Department of Computer Science, Aarhus University.

—— (1984), 'Summary of the Working Group "Systems Development and Prototyping"', in R. Budde, K. M. Kuhlenkamp, L. Mathiassen, and H. Züllighoven (eds.), *Approaches to Prototyping* (Berlin, Springer Verlag).

—— Munk-Madsen, A., Nielsen, P. A., and Stage, J. (1993), *Objektorienteret analyse* (Aalborg, Forlaget Marko).

—— —— —— —— (1995), *Objektorienteret design* (Aalborg, Forlaget Marko).

Mesarovic, M. D., Macko, D., and Takahara, Y. (1970), *Theory of Hierarchical, Multilevel, Systems* (New York, Academic Press).

Monarchi, D. E., and Puhr, G. (1992), 'A Research Typology for Object-Oriented Analysis and Design', *Communications of the ACM*, 35, 9: 35–47.

Monteiro, E., and Hanseth, O. (1995), 'Social Shaping of Information Infrastructure: On Being Specific about the Technology', in W. Orlikowski, G. Walsham, M. Jones, and J. DeGross (eds.), *Information Technology and Changes in Organisational Work* (London: Chapman & Hall).

Morgan, G. (1986), *Images of Organisations* (Beverly Hills, Calif., Sage Publications).

Mumford, E. (1979), 'Conclusions', in Bjørn-Andersen et al. (1979).

—— (1983), *Designing Human Systems for New Technology: The ETHICS Method* (Manchester, Manchester Business School).

—— and Beekman, G. J. (1994), *Tools for Change and Progress: A Socio-technical Approach to Business Process Re-engineering* (Leiden, CSG Publications).

—— and Henshall, D. (1979), *A Participative Approach to Computer Deisgn* (London, Associated Business Press).

—— and Ward, T. B. (1968), *Computers: Planning for People* (London, Batsford).

—— and Weir, M. (1979), *Computer Systems in Work Design: The ETHICS Method* (London, Associated Business Press).

Nilsson, A. G. (1991), 'Anskaffning av standardsystem för att utveckla verksamheter, Utveekling och prövning av SIV-metoden', Ph.D. diss., Stockholm Handelshögskolan, Stockholm.

—— (1995), 'Evolution of Methodolgies for Information Systems Work: A Historical Perspective', in Dahlbom (1995).

Nissen, H.-E. (1976), 'On Interpreting Services Rendered by Specific Computer Applications', unpublished Ph.D. diss., University of Stockholm, Department of Information Processing Science, Stockholm.

—— (1980), 'Towards a Multisubject Groups Conception of Information Systems', in K. Lyytinen and E. Peltola (eds.), *Report of the Third Scandinavian Research Seminar on Systemeering Models* (Jyväskylä, University of Jyväskylä, Department of Computer Science).

—— (1983), 'Subject Matter Separability in Information Systems Design Methods', in Olle et al. (1983).

Nurminen, M. I. (1986), *Kolme näkökulmaa tietotekniikkaan* (Three Perspectives to Information Systems) (Juva, WSOY).

—— (1988), *People or Computers: Three Ways of Looking at Information Systems* (Lund, Studentlitteratur/Chartwell-Bratt) (original in Finnish: *Kolme näkökulmaa tietotekniikkaan*, Juva, WOSY).

Nygaard, K., and Bergo, O. T. (1975), 'The Trade Unions: New Users of Research', *Personnel Review*, 4, 2: 5–10.

Olle, T. W., Hagelstein, J., MacDonald, I., Rolland, C., Sol, H., Assche, J., and Verrijn-Stuart, A. (1988), *Information System Methodologies: A Framework for Understanding* (Reading, Mass., Addison-Wesley).

—— Sol, H. G., and Tully, C. J. (1983) (eds.), *Information Systems Design Methodologies: A Feature Analysis* (Amsterdam, North-Holland).

—— —— and Verrijn-Stuart, A. A. (1982) (eds.), *Information Systems Design Methodologies: A Comparative Review* (Amsterdam, North-Holland).

Opdahl, A. L., and Sindre, G. (1994), 'A Taxonomy for Real-World Modelling Concepts', *Information Systems*, 19, 3: 229–41.

Parnas, D. L., and Clements, P. C. (1986), 'A Rational Design Process: How and Why to Fake it', *IEEE Transactions on Software Engineering*, SE-12, 2: 251–66.

Reenskaug, T., Wold, P., and Lehne, O. A. (1995), *Working with Objects: The OOram Software Engineering Method* (Greenwich, Cann., Manning Publications).

Rittel, H. W. J. (1972), 'On the Planning Crisis: Systems Analysis of the First and Second Generations', *Bedriftsekonomen*, 8: 390–6.

Rossi, M., and Brinkkemper, S. (1996), 'Complexity Metrics for Systems Development Methods and Techniques', *Information Systems*, 21, 2: 209–27.

Saaren-Seppälä, K. (1983), *Seinätaulutekniikka: Systeeemin suunnittelun opas* (Wall Chart Technique: A Guide to Systems Design), Tietojenkäsittelyliiton julkaisu 68 (Helsinki, Titetojenkäsittelyliitto).

—— (1984), Oral presentation in the 'Confrontation Session: The Needs of the Software Industry: Problems, Needs and Products' in the Seventh Scandinavian Research Seminar on Systemeering in Helsinki, 28 Aug.

—— (1988), *Wall Chart Technique: The Use of Wall Charts for Effective Planning* (Helsinki, Kari Saaren-Seppälä Ky).

Sandberg, A. (1979) (ed.), *Computers Dividing Man and Work* (Stockholm, Arbetslivscentrum).

—— (1983), 'Trade Union-Oriented Research for Democratization of Planning in Work Life: Problems and Potentials', *Journal of Occupational Behavior*, 4, 1: 59–71.

—— (1985), 'Socio-technical Design, Trade Union Strategies and Action Research', in E. Mumford, R. A. Hirschheim, G. Fitzgerald, and A. T. Wood-Harper (eds.), *Research Methods in Information Systems* (Amsterdam, North-Holland).

Schøn, D. (1983), *The Reflective Practitioner: How Professionals Think in Action* (London, Temple Smith).

Searle, J. R. (1969), *Speech Acts: An Essay in the Philosophy of Language* (Cambridge, Cambridge University Press).

—— (1979), *Expression and Meaning: Studies in the Theory of Speech Acts* (Cambridge Cambridge, University Press).

—— and Vanderveken, D. (1985), *Foundations of Illocutionary Logic* (Cambridge, Cambridge University Press).

Sølvberg, A., and Kung, C. H. (1986), 'On Structural and Behavioral Modelling of Reality', in T. B. Steel and R. Meersman (eds.), *Database Semantics (Ds-1)* (Amsterdam, North-Holland).

—— —— (1994), *Information System Engineering* (Reading, Mass., Addison-Wesley).

Stamper, R. (1987), 'Semantics', in R. Boland, and R. Hirschheim (eds.), *Critical Issues in Information Systems Research* (Chichester, John Wiley & Sons).

Steinholz, B., Sölvberg, A., and Bergman, L. (1990) (eds.), *Proceedings Second Nordic Conference on Advanced Information Systems Engineering: CAiSE'90* (Berlin, Springer Verlag).

Strauss, A. (1987), *Qualitative Analysis for Social Scientists* (Cambridge, Cambridge University Press).

—— (1988), 'The Articulation of Project Work: An Organisational Process', *Sociological Quarterly*, 29, 2: 16–178.

Sundgren, B. (1973), 'An Infological Approach to Data Bases', Ph.D. diss., Skriftserie utgiven an statistiska centralbyrån, No. 7, Statistiska Centralbyrån, Stockholm.

—— (1975), *Theory of Data Bases* (New York, Petrocelli/Charter).

Teichroew, D., and Sayani, H. (1971), 'Automation of System Building', *Datamation*, Aug.: 25–30.

Thoresen, K. (1994), 'Socio-technics Revisited', NR notat IFIP/08/94, Norwegian Computer Center, Oslo.

Thorsrud, E., and Emery, F. (1969), *Mot en ny bedriftsorganisasjon: eksperimenter i industrielt demokrati* (Oslo, Tanum).

Verharen, E., Rijst, N., and Dietz, J. (1996) (eds.), *The Language Action Perspective* (Berlin, Springer Verlag).

Winograd, T., and Flores, F. (1986), *Understanding Computers and Cognition: A New Foundation for Design* (Norwood, NJ, Ablex).

Wittgenstein, L. (1953), *Philosophical Investigations* (Oxford, Basil Blackwell).

Wynekoop, J. L., and Rosso, N. (1993), 'Systems Development Methodologies: Unanswered Questions and the Research–Practice Gap', in J. I. DeGross, R. Bostrom, and D. Robey (eds.), *Proceedings of the Fourteenth International Conference on Information Systems* (Orlando, Fla.).

Young, J. W., and Kent, H. (1958), 'Abstract Formulation of Data Processing Problems', *Journal of Industrial Engineering*, Nov.–Dec.: 471–9.

5

Structuration Theory

MATTHEW JONES

Introduction

Structuration theory emerged as a significant development in European sociology in the late 1970s. Urry (1982) traced its origins to Berger and Luckman's (1967) concept of the mutual constitution of society and individuals, and identified several different strands of structurational analysis including the work of Bourdieu (1977), Bhaskar (1979), and Giddens. In the IS context, however, it is only Giddens that has received any significant attention and his work will therefore be the primary focus of this chapter.

It should be emphasised at the outset that structuration is a general theory of social organisation rather than a theory specific to IS. Moreover, as will be discussed later, Giddens has never directly discussed IS issues in his writings. To the extent, however, that IS are seen as social systems, existing in social and organisational contexts that influence their development and use, and are also implicated in sustaining and changing these contexts, then structuration offers potentially significant insights on IS phenomena as this chapter will seek to illustrate.

This view would seem to be borne out by the evidence that, despite only having been introduced in the IS field just over a decade ago, structurational analyses have gained an increasing popularity, to the extent that many organisational IS researchers would now probably claim an awareness of Giddens's writings. Whether, however, this awareness amounts to an appreciation of the subtle implications of structuration is less clear. Certainly some of the purported offshoots from Giddens's work adopt perspectives that are significantly at odds with the ideas he has presented. The purpose of this chapter will therefore be to describe Giddens's structuration theory and some of the key issues related to it, to review some of the ways in which it has been used in the IS field and in the management field more generally, and to consider an agenda for structurationally informed IS research.

Given the increasing volume of IS research citing Giddens, much of it quite recent, the discussion in this chapter will not attempt a comprehensive review. Although several on-line searches were conducted for articles referring to Giddens's work, the number that these turned up was fairly limited and did not include a number of contributions quite widely cited in the IS literature. The aim has therefore been to identify the main issues that structuration raises for IS research in the hope that if particular articles are missing from the following discussion it may nevertheless address topics that would permit an evaluation of their contribution to the field.

Structuration Theory

A brief sketch of Giddens's theory

Structuration theory is set out by Giddens in three main works, *New Rules of Sociological Method* (Giddens, 1976, second edition 1993), *Central Problems in Social Theory* (Giddens, 1979), and *The Constitution of Society* (Giddens, 1984), and is also discussed in *A Contemporary Critique of Historical Materialism* (Giddens, 1981, second edition 1994). It may be seen as an attempt to resolve a fundamental division within the social sciences between those who consider social phenomena as products of the action of human 'agents' in the light of their subjective interpretation of the world, and others who see them as caused by the influence of *objective*, exogenous social structures. Giddens attempts to 'square this circle' by proposing that structure and agency be viewed, not as independent and conflicting elements, but as a mutually interacting duality. Thus social structure is seen as being drawn on by human agents in their actions, while the actions of humans in social contexts serve to produce, and reproduce, the social structure. Structure is thus not simply a straitjacket, but is also a resource to be deployed by humans in their actions: it is enabling as well as disabling.

More specifically, Giddens identifies three dimensions of structure, drawing from earlier work of Durkheim, Marx, and Weber, which he describes as signification, domination, and legitimation. These are seen as interacting through *modalities* of, respectively, interpretative schemes, resources, and norms, with human action of communication, power, and sanctions as shown in Fig. 5.1. The separation of these dimensions is simply for analytical convenience, since they are, in practice, intimately interlinked. For example the operation of norms depends upon power relationships for its effectiveness and is deployed through symbolic and linguistic devices.

An everyday example may help to illustrate these concepts, albeit at the cost of presenting structuration in a rather more mechanistic way than might be desirable. Thus, when buying an item at a shop we draw on structures of signification which tell us that items have prices and that we may expect these to be displayed on or near them and that the pieces of paper or metal (money) in our pockets are valid forms of exchange for these items. Our interpretative schemes allow us to translate the symbols on the price tag into an idea of how much money we will need to buy them. Similarly we draw on structures of domination that indicate that money gives you the right to acquire the item and expect the shopkeeper to hand over the item in exchange for the money. There are also structures of legitimation which define the appropriate norms of exchange in the particular cultural context—in Britain we usually do not haggle over the price and would expect to receive sanctions if we tried to take the item without paying. In acting in the established way we reinforce these existing structures. For example, in proffering the appropriate amount of money for the items we reproduce the structure of signification, in receiving the item in exchange for the money the structure of domination is reproduced, in paying the ticket price for the goods we reinforce the structure of legitimation. In each instance, however, there is the possibility (since we are active agents) that we may fail to reproduce the structure. We could argue with the shop-keeper over the meaning of the symbols on the price tag, arm-wrestle with him or her to decide the right to acquire the item, or take the item without paying. If enough people behaved in that way then one might expect the existing structures to change.

Giddens emphasises that social structures do not exist independent of human action, nor are they material entities. He describes them as 'traces in the mind' and argues that they exist only through the action of humans. This leads to a view of human beings as being in a constant state of reflexive monitoring of their situation and to the omnipresent potential for change. That we may not be aware of this monitoring or of the continuous opportunities for change is ascribed by Giddens to the existence of two types of consciousness: practical and discursive. The former relates to our ability to act in a knowledgeable way and the latter to our incomplete explanations for those actions. We therefore, Giddens argues, know more than we can say. In addition, humans cannot determine exactly the way in which structure is produced and reproduced. Giddens therefore draws attention to the unacknowledged conditions and unintended consequences of intentional action. For example, the reproduction of the legitimation of certain forms of metal and paper as valid currency in our shop example may promote the production of counterfeit money to 'cash in' on this a cceptance. The reproduction of lawful behaviour therefore helps to promote illegal behaviour as an unintended consequence.

Key issues in structuration theory

From the above brief outline of Giddens's ideas a number of key issues may be identified that give structuration its distinctive character. Given the scale of the project it claims to address, nothing less than 'an attempt to transcend, without discarding altogether, three prominent traditions of thought in social theory and philosophy' (Giddens, 1994: 26) and the reconstruction of 'some of the basic premises of social analysis' (Giddens, 1991*b*: 205), it is not surprising that these have also been the focus for, sometimes severe, criticism. An examination of the 'controversy' (Clark et al., 1990) around these issues, to which in a number of cases Giddens himself has sought to respond, may help to clarify the underlying assumptions of structuration theory and serve as a basis for assessing the way in which it has been used in organisational and IS research and its future potential.[1]

It should also quickly become apparent that the topics discussed below share many common points, and that the analytical convenience of chopping up structuration theory in this way is at the expense of some potential distortion of its essential message. This is a problem that Giddens himself faces in a number of aspects of his description of the theory and may help to account for the situation that some of those drawing on his work have interpreted it in ways that appear to contradict some of his central arguments. This is not to suggest that the current chapter offers a definitive reading, indeed one of the problems for anyone wishing to get to grips with structuration theory is that Giddens's productivity (at least twenty books in the past twenty-five years) has provided plenty of opportunity for subtle restatement of the main tenets of his position. Combined with his adoption of a deliberately idiosyncratic definition of certain key terms and a fluency of expression that can sometimes seem to cover up for a lack of precision in the statement of his own position on particular issues, a concise exposition, even in Giddens's own words, is not easily arrived at. This has not escaped the notice of his critics, for example Bernstein (1989: 27) describes him as 'foxlike' and notes his tendency, in the face of difficult problems, to 'introduce a plethora of distinctions and schemas' which, while illuminating, often fail to be sufficiently specific about the criteria of their applicability. For this reason, the current chapter will make perhaps more than usual use of quotations, both from Giddens and those who have drawn on his work, to enable readers to reach their own conclusions, although of course this cannot be an adequate substitute for a detailed consultation of the original sources.

The character of structuration theory

In Giddens's own view, the origins of structuration theory represented a reaction to the perceived deficiencies of the two major prevailing schools of sociological thought. On the one hand there was 'naturalistic' sociology

---

[1] It should be emphasised that space limitations of a chapter of this sort mean that the ensuing discussion can only touch on some of the central debates around structuration theory rather than provide a systematic critical appraisal of the theory as a whole. There is however already a large literature on Giddens's work including at least five books (Bryant and Jary, 1991; Clark et al., 1990; Cohen, 1989; Craib, 1992; Held and Thompson, 1989). Interested readers are therefore encouraged to consult these sources for a fuller discussion of the topics raised and, more importantly, to read Giddens's own writings to assess the validity of the analyses they present.

(a term Giddens prefers to the 'more diffuse and ambiguous label *positivism*', 1993: 1), in particular functionalism (especially as developed by Parsons), but also structuralism and post-structuralism. These approaches, particularly functionalism, he argues, are 'strong on structure, but weak on action' (1993: 4), underplaying the importance of human agency, and imputing purposes, reasons, and needs to society rather than to individuals. On the other hand, Giddens is also critical of interpretative sociology, such as Schutz's phenomenology, Garfinkel's ethnomethodology, and post-Wittgensteinian language philosophy, which, he argues, are 'strong on action, but weak on structure' (1993: 4), having little to say on issues of 'constraint, power and large-scale social organisation' (ibid.). Structuration is thus seen as a means of breaking out of this unsatisfactory dualism of action and structure and also that between individual and society.

Not surprisingly Giddens's rejection of both naturalistic and interpretative sociology and his claim to provide a means of transcending their differences has provoked considerable criticism from adherents of both schools and accusations of syncretism (accepting incompatible positions) and wilful eclecticism. Certainly the wide range of sources on which he has drawn in developing the theory (often, it must be said, providing in the process a most concise and telling précis of others' work), his multiple elaborations of the central concepts, and the idiosyncratic terminology already alluded to, mean that it is often difficult to pin down the character of structuration theory. This has led, for example, to it being identified both as post-modern (Macintosh and Scapens, 1990) and as insufficiently pluralistic (Craib, 1992) and irredeemably modernist (Wilson, 1995). This issue cannot be resolved here, but the more general point that structuration was set up in opposition to both functionalist/determinist and interpretative/voluntarist models of social action is an important one that should not be lost in efforts to slot it into a particular theoretical pigeonhole.

The other significant feature of structuration concerns methodology where, as Bryant and Jary (1991) note, Giddens adopts a post-empiricist and anti-positivist stance. This denies the existence of universal laws of human activity and emphasises the centrality of the interpretative endeavour, describing social science as 'irretrievably hermeneutic' (1993: 13). Giddens (1991*b*: 219), however, does not reject the potential contribution of 'technically-sophisticated, hard-edged' research. Indeed in (1984: p. xxx) he specifically states that 'I do not try to wield a methodological scalpel . . . there is [nothing] in the logic or the substance of structuration theory which would somehow prohibit the use of some specific research technique, such as survey methods, questionnaires or whatever'. Rather, he argues that 'the intellectual claims of sociology do not rest distinctively upon [hard-edged research]. All social research in my view, no matter how mathematical or quantitative, presumes ethnography' (Giddens, 1991*b*: 219).

The duality of structure and its status

For Giddens the duality of structure refers to the 'essential recursiveness of social life, as constituted in social practices: structure is both medium and outcome of the reproduction of practices' (1979: 69). His emphasis is therefore on structuration as an ongoing process rather than structure as a static property of social systems. In order to drive this home Giddens adopts quite specific and non-standard meanings for certain key terms (1979: 66):

STRUCTURE	Rules and resources, organised as properties of systems. Structure only exists as 'structural properties'
SYSTEM	Reproduced relations between actors or collectivities, organised as regular social practices
STRUCTURATION	Conditions governing the continuity or transformation of structures, and therefore the reproduction of systems

The particular meaning of rules in this context is also the subject of extended discussion (1984: 17–23) in which Giddens distinguishes between the 'rules of social life [which are] techniques or generalisable procedures applied in the enactment/reproduction of social practices' and 'formulated rules', such as those of a game or a bureaucracy, which are 'codified interpretations of rules rather than rules as such' (1984: 21). As an illustration of the type of rules he is referring to Giddens cites the mathematical formula $a_n = n^2 + n - 1$. As he stresses, this does not mean that 'social life can be reduced to a set of mathematical principles' (1984: 20), but that the formula provides a rule for how to carry on in any given situation (n) and that an individual may be able to state the formula without understanding its meaning or observe a sequence of numbers that obey it without being able to describe the principle involved. Two types of resources are also distinguished: allocative, which involve 'transformative capacity generating command over objects, goods or material phenomena', and authoritative, which involve 'transformative capacity generating commands over persons or actors' (1984: 33).

Although at first sight this might seem to provide some clarification, Thompson (1989) is typical of a number of critics in arguing that it 'generates more confusion than it dispels and . . . tends to obscure some important issues', drawing attention to ambiguities of the term 'rule' and Giddens's concern with a general notion of structure at the expense of specific features of social structure. Giddens (1989) does not accept these criticisms, however, arguing that they reflect a misunderstanding of his usage and that structuration is capable of explaining both individual and institutional features of social life. Again, this is not the place to adjudicate on this question, but it draws attention to the need to get inside Giddens's terminology and to understand his concepts in his own terms.

One particular implication of Giddens's conceptualisation of structure relevant to IS research is that it is 'a "virtual order" of transformative relations . . . that exists, as time-space presence, only in its instantiations in [reproduced social] practices and as memory traces orienting the conduct of knowledgeable human agents' (1984: 17). This is true, Giddens argues, even in the case of the apparently material allocative resources (such as land) which 'might seem to have a "real existence" ' but which 'become resources only when incorporated within processes of structuration' (1984: 33). This has led Giddens to be identified as an idealist, although New (1994) argues that his view that structure is causally generative implies that it is real and that structuration is therefore able to transcend the objective/subjective divide. While Layder (1987) argues that Giddens's complete rejection of any objectivist element in his ontological position is both unnecessary and theoretically problematic, what remains true is that, as Giddens himself presents it, the rules and resources constituting structure exist only in the agents' heads. To talk of structure being inscribed or embedded in artefacts is therefore inconsistent with Giddens's views, as it fixes one half of the duality in which action and structure are seen to be inseparably linked.

Practical and discursive knowledge and unintended consequences

Giddens views human agents as essentially knowledgeable about their actions. He argues that this may include 'unconscious sources of cognition' (1979: 5) as well as those at level of practical consciousness embodied in what actors know 'about how to "go on" in the multiplicity of contexts of social life' (1983) and at the discursive level, at which they are able to provide explanations for them (1984: 7). They are thus seen to be continuously engaged in reflexive monitoring of conduct, rather than as the 'cultural' or 'structural dopes . . . of stunning mediocrity' (1979: 52) suggested by traditional views of structure as constraint on action. This has important implications for the understanding of social action, as we have seen, as 'every member of society must know . . . a great deal about the workings of that society by virtue of his or her participation in it' (1979: 250). Giddens uses the term 'discursive penetration' to describe this awareness of social actors of their engagement in social reproduction and production. This leads, he argues, to a 'double hermeneutic' whereby the concepts that sociological observers describe are already constituted as meaningful by social actors and can themselves become elements of the actors' understanding of their own condition.

This knowledgeability of social actors might seem to suggest that they are always in control of action. Giddens avoids this however by emphasising the unacknowledged conditions and unintended consequences of action. Thus 'the production or constitution of society is a skilled accomplishment of its members, but one that does not take place under conditions that are either wholly intended or wholly comprehended by them' (1993: 108). This of course is a reformulation, as Giddens acknowledges, of Marx's famous dictum that men (*sic*) make history, but not in the circumstances of their own choosing. This has a further implication, however, that universal laws in the social sciences are 'markedly implausible' (1984: 345) if not impossible. Social generalisations can therefore, at best, only be 'historical', i.e. temporally and spatially circumscribed.

Agency and constraint

Structuration theory has been the subject of significant criticism by a number of authors who contend that, unacknowledged conditions and unanticipated consequences notwithstanding, it assumes an inappropriately voluntaristic view of human agency (e.g. Bhaskar, 1979). This comes from Giddens's contention that structure is not simply constraining, but is also enabling, and that, except in situations where they have been drugged and manhandled by others, human agents always 'have the possibility of doing otherwise' (Giddens, 1989: 258). Thus 'the seed of change is there in every act which contributes towards the reproduction of any "ordered" form of social life' (1993: 108). This is linked to a relational model of power based on a dialectic of control whereby the operation of power relationships relies upon the compliance of subordinates.

His critics, however, suggest that it does not make sense to argue that structural constraint simply places 'limits upon the feasible range of options open to an actor in a given circumstance' (Giddens, 1984: 177). Individuals, such as a landless peasant at the start of the capitalist era, they argue, had effectively only one feasible option if they wished to survive, to sell their labour-power. Archer (1990) therefore proposes a morphogenetic approach in which constraint and action operate sequentially, while Layder (1985: 146) argues for a notion of structural power which is 'not simply a negotiable outcome of routine and concrete interactions and relationships' in the specific context. Barbalet (1987), in particular, criticises Giddens's assumption that material existents (which, as we shall see, are a potentially significant issue in relation to a structurational theory of information systems) cannot be social structural resources in power relations. Similarly Storper (1985) argues that 'the *durée* of the material, although not imposing absolute constraints on system change, does mean that at any moment not everything is possible'.

Giddens, however, does not accept these views, suggesting that the alternative to his conception is a form of determinism. All sanctions, he argues, no matter how oppressive and comprehensive, even the threat of death, carry no weight without the acquiescence of those threatened with them, in this case the individual's wish not to die (1984: 175). In insisting on power as being instantiated in action rather than a type of act or a resource to be drawn on, he therefore provides a distinctive approach to a central issue in organisational analysis.

Time, routines, and time-space distantiation

Time, for Giddens, is one of the central, but frequently neglected, topics of social science and each of his major writings gives considerable attention to it. In particular, he identifies (1994: 28) three intersecting planes of temporality involved in every moment of structuration—*durée* (the temporality of daily experience), Heidegerrian *dasein* (the temporality of the life cycle, being-unto-death), and Braudel's *longue durée* (the temporality of institutions). In this way, he argues, structuration ties together the individual and institutional levels of social practice and points to the recursive nature of social life.

The idea of structure being continuously produced and reproduced through action also leads to another significant aspect of structuration, that of routinisation. Giddens argues that routine is 'integral to the continuity of the personality of the agent . . . and to the institutions of society' (1984: 60). In particular, individuals acquire ontological security through their engagement in predictable routines and encounters. Because these encounters are also constitutive of social institutions they enable the continuity of social life, the classic sociological 'problem of order'.

Giddens permits a distinction between two levels of integration, or regularised relations of relative autonomy and dependence, in respect to social practices. The first is defined as 'social integration' and refers to 'systemness', in terms of the definition given above, at the level of face-to-face interaction, while the second, 'system integration', refers to systemness on the level of relations between social systems or collectivities (1979: 76). What this highlights, apart from the differentiation of micro and macro spheres of sociological analysis, is the significance of space and presence in social relations. This forms an important strand of Giddens's later analysis of modernity (see below), drawing on the work of time-geographers. From an IS standpoint this is particularly significant in view of the role of IT in the changing temporal and spatial character of modern organisations.

The critics of Giddens's treatment of agency, however, question the view that social order is produced and reproduced entirely through individual action. Focusing on the dependency of social structure on agency, some, such as Harré (1983), suggest that in well-ordered institutions, such as monasteries, social rules may dominate social reproduction and that individual structurational agency is thus insignificant or even absent. Others argue that all aspects of structure may not be equally amenable to agency, suggesting that there may be a 'differentiated (and thus limited) topography for the exercise of agency rather than an endlessly recursive plain' (Storper, 1985: 419), or that some structural constraints may be 'relatively independent' (Layder, 1987). Although, as has been noted, Giddens would reject such views, these criticisms draw attention once again to the distinctive character of structuration and the need for structurational analyses of IS to be sensitive to its particular perspective.

The role of theory and its relationship to empirical research

The final aspect of structuration to be considered will be its relevance to empirical research, where some critics, such as Gregson (1989) have suggested that it operates at too high a level of generality to provide guidance in specific empirical settings. Giddens, himself, also shows a certain ambivalence about the appropriate use of his ideas. Thus, on the one hand: in (1984: 281–4) he provides a ten-point summary of the key features of structuration (see Table 5.1) that, he argues, suggest 'guidelines for the overall orientation of social research'; in Giddens (1989: 300) he describes four features of a 'structurationist programme of research'; in Giddens (1991*b*: 311) he simplifies the ten principles of (1984) to just three (contextual sensitivity, the complexity of human intentionality, and the subtlety of social constraint) and (p. 313) mentions four aspects of structuration 'most generally relevant to social research' (reproduction of practices, dialectic of control, discursive penetration and the double hermeneutic); and in Giddens (1983; 1984: ch. 6; and 1991: 213–18) he discusses various attempts by researchers to use structuration in empirical research projects.

At the same time he frequently states that structuration is not intended as a concrete research programme (Giddens, 1983: 77; 1992: 310) and that his principles 'are essentially procedural and do not supply concepts useful for the actual prosecution of research' (Giddens, 1990*b*: 311). He is also critical of those who 'have attempted to import structuration theory *in toto* into their given area of study', preferring those 'in which concepts, either from the logical framework of structuration theory, or other aspects of my writings, are used in a sparing and critical fashion' (Giddens, 1991*b*: 213). Another favoured description of the role of structuration in empirical research is the use of principles derived from it as 'sensitising devices' or to 'provide an explication of the logic of research into human social activities and cultural products' (Giddens, 1991*b*: 213).

Craib (1992: 108) suggests that this is because the focus of structuration is primarily ontological: 'it tells us what sort of things are out there in the world, not what is happening to or between them; it does not give us anything to test or to find out', or, as Archer puts it, structuration is 'fundamentally non-propositional'. This is effectively acknowledged by Giddens (1989: 295) in his distinction between theory, as a generic category, and *theories*, or explanatory generalisation. Structuration, he argues, is clearly

TABLE 5.1. *Aspects of structuration theory that impinge most generally upon problems of empirical research in the social sciences*

1 All human beings are knowledgeable agents
2 The knowledgeability of human agents is always bounded on the one hand by the unconscious and on the other by the unacknowledged conditions/unanticipated consequences of action
3 The study of day-to-day life is integral to the analysis of the reproduction of institutionalised practices
4 Routine, psychologically linked to the minimising of unconscious sources of anxiety, is the predominant form of day-to-day social activity
5 The study of context, or of the contextualisation of interaction, is inherent in the investigation of social reproduction
6 Social identities, and the position–practice relations associated with them, are 'markers' in the virtual time-space of structure
7 No unitary meaning can be given to 'constraint' in social analysis
8 Among the properties of social systems, structural properties are particularly important, since they specify overall types of society
9 The study of power cannot be regarded as a second-order consideration in the social sciences
10 There is no mechanism of social organisation or social reproduction identified by social analysts which lay actors cannot also get to know about and actively incorporate into what they do

Source: Giddens (1984: 281–4).

of the first type. A number of authors have therefore suggested that structuration is best considered as a meta-theory, a way of thinking about the world rather than as an empirically testable explanation of social behaviour, indeed Weaver and Gioia (1994) propose it as *the* integrating meta-theory for organisational studies (although this is contested by DeCock and Rickards, 1995).

Other, related writings of Giddens

The breadth of application of structuration theory means that it has implications across the entire range of social phenomena and Giddens has not neglected to develop a substantive sociology consistent with his structurational principles addressing issues from the condition of traditional and modern societies to the micro-politics of gender relations. While these topics might seem to have little to do with IS, or even organisational research, and indeed Whittington (1992) observes that Giddens's writings on these topics have received almost no attention in the management literature, a number of aspects of this research may be argued to deserve serious consideration in the IS field. In particular attention will be paid to two works, *The Consequences of Modernity* (Giddens, 1990*a*) and *Modernity and Self Identity* (Giddens, 1991*a*).

In (1990*a*) Giddens suggests that the current era is one of radicalised, reflexive, or 'high' modernity (rather than some form of post-modernity) which acquires its dynamism through the separation of time and space, the development of disembedding mechanisms involving symbolic tokens and 'expert systems' (not, it is important to note, in the IS sense), and the reflexive appropriation of knowledge, filtered by differential power, the role of values, the impact of unintended consequences, and the circulating of social knowledge in the double hermeneutic. Each of these concepts will now briefly be discussed.

Time and space have already been identified in the context of routinisation as significant features of structuration. Giddens's argument is that time has become separated from space, for example whereas in pre-modern societies time might have been measured by the movement of the sun relative to the features of a specific locale, or even by a public clock, in modern society time throughout the world follows a common, abstract, and standardised order. Space is also dislocated from place as the common physical environment of interaction in pre-modern societies, gives way to interactions between individuals widely separated from any situation of face-to-face interaction, whether communicating over a telephone or corresponding with a pen-pal or customer in another country. In this, IT, not least the Internet, may be seen to have a potentially significant role.

The concept of disembedding refers to the 'lifting out' of social relations from specific contexts and their 'restructuring across indefinite spans of time-space' (1990*a*: 21) and is viewed, with reflexivity, as a major source of the globalising character of modernity. Disembedding is seen as being achieved by two forms of 'abstract systems': symbolic tokens, pre-eminently money, and 'expert systems', here seen as 'systems of technical accomplishment or professional expertise' (1990*a*: 27) such as those involved in designing and building a car or software programme or in medical diagnosis. Individuals, who cannot hope to acquire all the necessary technical expertise to understand how these 'expert systems' work, nevertheless have to trust in their enduring and generalised efficacy. Thus, even if Giddens adopts a non-standard definition of the term 'expert system', IS are likely to be implicated in many disembedding mechanisms.

The reflexive appropriation of knowledge describes the way in which knowledge about social practices comes to be drawn upon in their reproduction. For example, concepts of the information society such as information poverty or the virtual organisation help us to make sense of and talk about the way that society is perceived to be changing. This knowledge is not uniformly appropriated however and certain groups may be better placed to draw on it in the pursuit of sectional interests. Moreover this appropriation does not necessarily have a fixed relationship to changes in values. As a result of unintended consequences reflexivity does not necessarily lead to more effective social action and this is further complicated by way in which social knowledge re-enters and transforms its own subject.

These ideas are taken forward in Giddens (1991*a*), predominantly at the level of the individual. Here the focus is on how modernity contributes to a reflexivity of the self which Giddens links with existential anxiety and the problematisation of identity. Electronic media are seen as an insepar-able component of modernity, contributing to a 'collage effect', whereby news about the world becomes a patchwork of unconnected events not linked to any particular sense of place, and to the increasing intrusion of distant events into everyday life. They are also identified as contributing to the plurality of lifestyle choices that individuals face.

This brief outline of some of the main features of these two works obvi-ously involves an extreme simplification of Giddens's argument. They may serve, however, as pointers to issues deserving of further attention. Before discussing what this might mean, attention will first be turned to a review of some of the research in the management and IS fields that has sought to draw on structuration, particularly in the context of empirical research.

Structuration in the Management Literature

Organisation studies

Ranson et al. (1980) is widely cited as one of the first attempts to utilise structuration in the management literature. Their discussion of organisa-tional structure cites Bourdieu and Giddens and emphasises the continual production and reproduction of structure through the action of organ-isational members. They also suggest, however, that structures 'embody and become constitutive of . . . provinces of meaning' which are mediated by contingent size, technology, and environment and that 'the influence of structural constraints upon organisational structuring can be quite inde-pendent of an individual's perception of them' (p. 11). These points were picked up by Willmott (1981) who argued that Ranson et al. had applied Giddens inconsistently based on an inappropriate, functionalist model of organisation.

Another widely cited early study is Manning (1982). While not expli-citly referencing Giddens, it referred to 'structuration of environments' arguing that organisations 'prefigure, organise and then enact the social environment in which they operate'. Riley (1983) also employed structura-tion in an analysis of organisational culture. Her focus was on 'organisa-tional symbols and language that embody political intentions or display the trappings of political power' (p. 418) and involved interviews in two subsidiaries of a large organisation, which were identified as engaged in respectively routinised, and non-routinised, tasks. Issues of power are taken up in another significant stream of structurational analysis by Knights,

Willmott, and others (e.g. Knights and Willmott, 1985; Willmott, 1987; and Knights and Willmott, 1989). A particular focus of this work has been on the relationship between power and identity, seeking to extend Giddens's dialectic of control to consider how individuals' pursuit of self through social identity may contribute to the reproduction of conditions of subordination.

One of the earliest case studies of structuration in a management context was a paper by Smith (1983) discussing the pure-bred beef business in Canada. While Giddens (1983) describes the paper as 'interesting and ingenious' he is also critical of its attempt to 'insert structuration [so] directly into a research context'. As Craib (1992: 107) observes, this may be because Smith's paper is 'largely a translation of empirical data, much of it derived from participant observation, into the categories of structuration theory, with one or two of Smith's own categories where the data does not fit so easily'.

As Whittington (1992) shows, interest in structuration in the management literature grew considerably during the 1980s, with forty-seven citations in *Administrative Science Quarterly, Organisation Studies,* and *Journal of Management Studies* alone. There was also an extensive secondary literature based on Ranson et al. (1980), more than half of which did not cite Giddens himself. Whittington identified Pettigrew (1985) and Willmott (for example, 1987) as particularly influential interpreters of Giddens, but also comments that the particular use of structuration adopted by Ranson et al. was 'characteristic of later attempts'. Despite this level of interest, however, knowledge of structuration appears to be quite localised within particular subareas of the organisational literature and its diffusion a relatively slow process. Thus Sarason (1995) in the 'best paper' issue of the *Academy of Management Journal* was engaged in an exposition of the basic principles of structuration to illustrate their relevance to organisational transformation and strategic management.

Finally, one other significant interpreter of Giddens in the organisational literature should be mentioned, namely Karl Weick (for example, 1993). Rather than 'apply' structuration, however, he has drawn on Giddens as part of his own distinctive organisational theorising. Moreover, as Garnsey (1993) argues, Weick's work, and in particular his concept of enactment (Weick, 1979), may be seen as a parallel development to Giddens's on structuration, describing both as examples of 'constitutive process' theories. In Garnsey and Kelly (1995) a framework is proposed for combining these approaches with ideas from systems thinking to produce a simpler conceptualisation that, it is argued, is more easily able to address the dynamics of social and organisational change.

Accounting

A subject area of management research that has taken considerable interest in structuration has been the behavioural accounting literature.

Roberts and Scapens (1985) used the duality of structure to propose a re-orientation of accounting research, distinguishing between the abstract, potential 'accounting system' and the systems-in-use that they termed 'systems of accountability'. While the former had been the traditional focus of accounting research, they argued, the latter needed to be studied to understand accounting practices in their context of use.

Taking up from Roberts and Scapens (1985), Macintosh and Scapens (1990) sought to use structuration to analyse a longitudinal case study of accounting practice, showing how management accounting systems: 'are the interpretive schemes which management use to interpret past results, take actions and make plans'; 'communicate a set of values and ideals about what is approved and what is disapproved'; and 'are a facility that management at all levels can used to co-ordinate and control participants'. In a careful reworking of the data from the original source of Macintosh and Scapens's analysis, however, Boland (1993) argued that this was a misinterpretation of Giddens's ideas which ignored the agency of individual managers and the way in which they created meaning for themselves from the accounting reports. Although Scapens and Macintosh (1996) responded by suggesting that Boland's critique did not acknowledge the social and institutional dimensions of the interpretative act, Boland (1996) in turn emphasised that Scapens and Macintosh's analysis assumed the existence of shared meanings, the rejection of which, he argues, is a central element of structuration.

Structuration and IS

Giddens himself has written very little that could be seen as directly discussing IS, indeed he would readily admit to being largely ignorant of how IT is specifically implicated in organisational and social change, although well aware of the potential social significance of IT-based systems in a general sense. In Giddens (1984) there is reference to the role of IT in time-space distantiation, and he suggests that email and video may substitute to some extent for face-to-face interaction in achieving social integration. This can be justified in terms of his attitude toward empirical research and the primarily ontological orientation of structuration as a whole. For those seeking to 'apply' structuration theory in IS research, Giddens's reservations notwithstanding, however, this means that they are very much 'on their own'. No advice is available beyond the generalised oracular pronouncements discussed above. Moreover, there is a particular problem for structurational IS research which may be argued not to exist for organisational research, that is the material character of technology. This is not to say that technology should be understood simply as material artefacts, but that all computer-based IS have some component that has a physical existence, even if the IS itself is much more than that.

Structuration, however, is a theory of the social which has little to say about the material. Thus Giddens argues that 'some forms of allocative resources (such as raw materials, land etc) might seem to have a "real existence" in a way that structural properties as a whole do not. In the sense of having time-space "presence" in a certain way this is obviously the case. But their "materiality" does not affect the fact that such phenomena become resources, in the manner in which I apply the term here, only when incorporated within processes of structuration. The transformational character of resources is logically equivalent to, as well as inherently bound up with the instantiation of, that of codes and normative sanctions' (1984: 33). Material properties are also considered through Giddens's adoption of the time-geography concepts of coupling and capability constraints. These, however, relate primarily to the corporeality of the human body and the physical features of locales of human interaction which limits the potential for spatial and temporal co-presence. Although, following Hirschheim (1985) it may be argued that 'IS are social systems that rely increasingly on computer-based IT for their operation', there still remains a stubbornly material aspect of technology which sits uneasily with Giddens's insistence on structure being 'traces in the mind' instantiated only through action.

An outline of structurational research in the IS field

Many IS researchers have made reference to structuration in their work. As was explained above, however, rather than attempt to provide a comprehensive survey of all such studies a relatively few articles will be selected to identify some of the main contributors and to illustrate some of the different ways in which the theory has been used in the IS field.

Although not explicitly identified as an IS article, the paper by Barley (1986) is generally recognised as among the first to address IT, in this case computed tomography scanners, from a structurational perspective. As its title indicates, Barley's paper saw the introduction of CT scanners into the radiology departments of two hospitals as an 'occasion for structuring', describing how the same equipment led to quite different social organisation in the two nominally similar environments. It also adopted the (curiously functionalist) concept of scripts from Schank (e.g. Schank 1990) to 'parse structuring's ceaseless flow into temporal phases' and concluded that structuration theory was a form of 'soft determinism'. This study was extended by Barley (1990) to examine how roles and social networks mediate technology's 'structural effects', arguing that 'technically-driven social change is likely to be rooted in a technology's material constraints', but that these must be transformed into social forces if technology is to have a significant effect on social organisation.

One of the most prolific and acute writers using structuration in the IS field has been Orlikowski. In a series of significant articles she has not

TABLE 5.2. *Framework for investigating the interaction of human actors and social structure during information system development*

Realm of social structure	Systems developers are informed by systems development methodologies and knowledge about their organisation to build information systems	System developers work within the constraints of time, budget, hardware, software, and authority to build information systems	System developers draw on the values and conventions of their organisation, occupation, and training to build information systems
Modalities	*Interpretative schemes*	*Resources*	*Norms*
Realm of human action	System developers create meaning by programming assumptions and knowledge into the information systems	System developers build information systems through the organisational power or capabilities they wield in their organisational roles	System developers create sanctions by designing and programming legitimate options and conventions into the information systems

Source: Orlikowski and Robey (1991).

only 'applied' structuration theory in a number of different contexts, but has also sought to employ structurational insights to the development a new model of the relationship between technology and organisation. This model will be considered in more detail in the next section, but for the moment attention will be focused on her other contributions.

Orlikowski and Robey (1991) presents an outline of Giddens's ideas, largely in the context of a contrast between 'subjective and objective' treatment of IT in the IS and computer science literature. Discussing the treatment of technology in Barley (1986) it is argued that CT scanners are not typical of IT in general in that users have little control over their form and functioning, whereas users of other IT 'often continually shape and reshape applications, so that technology ceases to be a fixed, tangible constraint'. This is used to introduce the structurational model elaborated in Orlikowski (1992) and then to develop frameworks for investigating the interaction of human actors and social structure during information systems development and use as shown in Tables 5.2 and 5.3. This framework was taken up by Jones and Nandhakumar (1993) in the analysis of a case study of executive information systems development.

Orlikowski's empirical research has included studies of CASE tools in a consultancy (Orlikowski, 1991), electronic mail and conferencing technology in a Japanese R&D project group (Orlikowski et al., 1995), and Lotus Notes in two consultancies (Orlikowski, 1995). She has also applied

TABLE 5.3. *Framework for investigating the interaction of human actors and social structure during information system use*

Realm of social structure	Using information systems, users draw on embedded knowledge, assumptions, and rules and through such use reaffirm the organisation's structure of signification	Using information systems, users work within the rules and capabilities built into them and through use reaffirm the organisation's structure of domination	Using information systems, users work within the authorised options, values, and sanctions built into them and through such use sustain the organisation's structure of legitimation
Modalities	*Interpretative Schemes*	*Resources*	*Norms*
Realm of human action	Users appropriate the rules, knowledge, and assumptions embedded in information systems to perform tasks, or they may modify patterns of use to create new structures of meaning that potentially alter institutionalised practices	Users appropriate the rules and capabilities embedded within information systems to achieve authorised outcomes, or they may modify patterns of use to create new structures of domination that potentially alter institutionalised practices	Users appropriate the legitimate conventions of use within information systems to execute sanctioned action, or they may modify patterns of use to create new structures of legitimation that potentially alter institutionalised practices

Source: Orlikowski and Robey (1991).

structuration in the analysis of genres in organisational communication (Yates and Orlikowski, 1992), noting how electronic mail carries over some of the conventions of paper-based memos. This work has employed structuration to varying degrees, sometimes as an explicit framework and in others as a source of useful concepts. A number of the papers also employ a sequential model of the structuring process (Barley, 1986) in which particular episodes are identified in the flow of events.

Another significant contribution to the use of structuration theory in IS research has come from Walsham. His work has included a review of the application of structuration in IS research (Walsham and Han, 1991), analyses of case studies in a variety of domains drawing on structurational concepts (Walsham, 1993; Walsham and Han, 1993), and the use of structuration as a sensitising device in studies employing other analytical approaches (Barrett and Walsham, 1995; Walsham and Sahay, 1996).

Walsham and Han (1991) provides a useful overview of early work on structuration in the IS field with thoughtful commentaries on Barley (1986) and Orlikowski (1992) and discussion of the ways in which structurational concepts may be used in IS research. Some of these ideas are developed in Walsham (1993) which locates structuration within a synthesised analytical framework for the interpretative study of IS and organisational change. This is used to analyse the context/process linkage in a number of empirical case studies, of IS strategy, design, and policy development.

Even from these few writers, it is clear that there are several different modes of use of structuration in the IS literature. These may be classified into four main types. The most ambitious use of structuration has been the attempts to reconstruct the theory to accommodate technology. The most notable of these, adaptive structuration theory (DeSanctis and Poole, 1994) and the structurational model of technology (Orlikowski, 1992), are discussed in the next section. Less ambitious, but similarly comprehensive in their approach to structuration, have been some of the attempts to 'apply' the theory to the analysis of IS cases. Karsten (1995*b*) provides a good example of this type in systematically employing the elements of structuration to a case study of Notes implementation in three organisations. Jones and Nandhakumar (1993) perform a similar analysis, based on Orlikowski and Robey (1991), but seek to take it rather further by using the experience to reflect back on the strengths and limitations of the framework and structuration more generally in empirical research.

The third type of structurationally informed IS research uses it as a meta-theory. There appear to be two main connotations to this concept. The first, given in Walsham and Han (1991), is as a perspective 'within which to locate, interpret and illuminate other approaches', which is illustrated by an analysis of Kling's web models (Kling, 1987) in structurational terms. A more extended example of this approach may be found in the analysis of CSCW by Lyytinen and Ngwenyama (1992) or in the 'culture, control and competition' framework for the study of IT in organisations of Coombs et al. (1992), based on the analysis of power and subjectivity of Knights and Willmott (1985). In Barrett and Walsham's (1995) analysis of innovation in the Jamaican insurance industry, however, structuration's use as a meta-theory is described as means of 'focusing research attention on actions, mental models and processes of reproduction and change', while in Walsham and Sahay's (1996) study of GIS in India it is described as a 'general approach to what one is looking for whilst planning, conducting and analysing fieldwork [which] induces the researcher to constantly look at actions, perceptions and slow-to-change structure, and to try to trace the links between these over time'.

The latter usage of structuration as a meta-theory may be quite close to the last category of structurationally informed IS research which is where particular concepts from Giddens's writings are adopted. Walsham and Han (1991) illustrate this with respect to a number of concepts such as practical and discursive consciousness, routinisation, and unanticipated consequences. Similarly Karsten (1995*a*) lists a number of 'key ideas and concepts of structuration theory' to be applied in the analysis of a specific case. While this 'pick and mix' approach to theory can, in the right hands, lead to insightful analysis which remains true to Giddens's principles (i.e. retains the meta-theoretical assumptions of structuration whether explicated or not), in other situations it can lead to the appropriation of concepts into frameworks which may contradict many of structuration's key tenets, or which juxtapose them with incompatible concepts from other writers. Contractor & Eisenberg (1990) provide an example of this, and by no means a particularly bad one, in which Giddens's duality of structure is paired with an approach based on Archer's morphogenetic principles in the analysis of computer-mediated communication. Unfortunately, as Archer and Giddens have both forcefully argued in Clark et al. (1990), their positions are fundamentally different; structure cannot be both a duality and a dualism, and the combination of the two approaches therefore betrays a lack of appreciation of the underlying positions.

Finally, a possible indication of structuration's maturity as a concept in the IS field may be seen in the emergence of attempts to link it with newer theories, at least in IS terms, particularly actor-network theory (Callon, 1986; Latour, 1987) or to criticise it in comparison with these theories. Two papers employing both structuration and actor-networks are Lea et al. (1995) and Walsham and Sahay (1996). The former, an analysis of the development of a computer-mediated communication system in a professional services organisation, is critical of the tendency of some structurationally informed analyses to view technology as a 'black box', and to treat the distinction between content and context of IS use as unproblematic. Walsham and Sahay (1996) make a clearer distinction between structuration, which they employed as a meta-theory, and actor-network theory which they employed as a 'more detailed methodological and analytical device', incorporating not just 'an emphasis on stakeholder groups, on context and process and their linkage, and on the view of technology as socially-constructed', but also novel concepts such as non-human actors incorporated into actor-networks and the processes of translation and enrolment.

Lack of specificity about technology is also the focus of Monteiro and Hanseth's (1995) critique of structurational research in the IS field. Orlikowski (1991) is cited as typical in describing the focus of her study simply as 'a CASE tool', despite the fact that there may be a wide variety of such tools. They argue that actor-network theory, with its explicit commitment to the equal treatment of technological and human actors is therefore more promising as a means of understanding how specific elements and functions of an IS relate to organisational issues. Monteiro and Hanseth concede, however, that this may not be an inherent weakness of structuration and that it may provide a more appropriate analysis of institutional influences than actor-network theory.

Extensions of Structuration as applied to IS

Two approaches within the IS literature have sought to recast structuration so as to make it more suitable to IS research. These will now be considered in more detail.

Adaptive structuration theory (AST)

AST was developed by DeSanctis and Poole (DeSanctis and Poole, 1994; Poole and DeSanctis, 1990) as a way of considering the mutual influence of technology and social processes. In DeSanctis and Poole (1994: 125) they identify a number of propositions of AST; these include that: 'social structures serve as templates for planning and accomplishing tasks'; 'designers incorporate some of these structures into the technology' with the result that the structures may be reproduced or modified, 'thus creating new structures within the technology'. In a similar way to Orlikowski (1992) they also argue that advanced IT have 'greater potential than traditional business computer systems to influence social aspects of work'.

AST suggests that 'the social structures provided by an advanced information technology can be described in two ways: structural features of the technology and the spirit of this feature set' (DeSanctis and Poole, 1994: 126). Examples of structural features for a group decision support system are identified as voting algorithms and anonymous recording of ideas. These are said to bring meaning and control (Giddens's signification and domination) to group interaction. A particular advanced information technology can therefore be 'described and studied in terms of specific structural features' (ibid.). Poole and DeSanctis's concept of spirit, which they derive from the dictionary definition of the term, is described as the general intent with regard to values and goals underlying a given set of structural features' and is said to equate to Giddens's legitimation dimension of structuration. This 'property of a technology as it is presented to users' can be identified, it is argued, by 'reading' the philosophy of the technology based on an analysis of: '(a) the design metaphor underlying the system; (b) the features it incorporates and how they are named and presented; (c) the nature of the user interface; (d) training materials and on-line guidance materials; and (e) other training or help provided with the system.'

Because IT is only one source of structure for groups, Poole and DeSanctis (1994) argue, it is therefore necessary to consider other sources of structure such as work tasks and the organisational environment in analysing the use of a particular technology. Another important concept in AST is that of 'appropriations'. These are described as the 'immediate visible actions that evidence deeper structuration processes' (DeSanctis and Poole, 1994: 128) and are seen as equivalent to Giddens's modalities of structuration (Poole and DeSanctis, 1990). Groups, it is explained, may choose to appropriate structural features through a variety of 'appropriation moves', for example by directly using technology structures, or making judgements about them; they may appropriate technology 'faithfully' or 'unfaithfully'; they may appropriate the features for 'different instrumental uses or purposes'; and display a variety of 'attitudes' as structures are appropriated such as 'comfort', 'respect', and 'challenge'.

Through the use of AST, it is suggested, it will be possible to develop propositions of the form: '*Given* advanced information technology and other sources of social structure n_1 to n_k *and* ideal appropriation processes, *and* decision processes that fit the task at hand, *then* desired outcomes of advanced information technology will result' (DeSanctis and Poole, 1994: 131—emphasis in original). If group interaction processes are inconsistent with technology's structural potential, however, then the outcomes will be less predictable and generally less favourable. This is said to illustrate the 'dialectic of control between the group and the technology'. DeSanctis and Poole (1994) suggest that AST is therefore able to overcome the limitations of previous structurational approaches which, they argue, gave only weak consideration to IT, were exclusively focused at the institutional level, and relied on purely interpretative methods. As an illustration of its potential, AST has now formed the basis of a research programme by Bostrom and a variety of co-authors Gopal et al. (1992), Miranda and Bostrom (1993), Nagasundram and Bostrom (1994), in which it is used as a framework for experimental studies to test a causal model of group support system use.

In terms of the description of structuration given in this chapter, it should be clear that AST bears very little resemblance to Giddens's ideas. Although a number of terms are borrowed from Giddens and comments are made about the ongoing production and reproduction of structure, AST's view of 'structure within technology', its identification of other independent 'sources of structure', and its concept of a dialectic of control between 'the group and the technology' are all directly contrary to Giddens's principles. That these ideas are then elaborated through underspecified concepts, such as 'spirit' and 'appropriation', for which no substantive theoretical justification is offered, to produce a contingency-type model of technology 'impacts' of a type which Giddens has specifically criticised, may make sense in terms of the 'limitations' of structuration as DeSanctis and Poole (1994) identify them, but is almost completely incompatible with the central tenets of structuration theory itself. Telling evidence of the depth of AST's misreading of structuration is provided by its use as a framework for the positivist experimental studies of GDSS.

Orlikowski's duality of technology

Orlikowski's model of the duality of technology is developed most fully in Orlikowski (1992). Starting with a critique of prior conceptualisations of technology, in particular the hardware and social technology views on the scope of technology, and the 'technological imperative', 'strategic choice', and 'technology as a trigger of structural change' (Barley, 1986) models of the role of technology in organisations, it is argued that structuration can provide a new conceptualisation on which to base future research.

Orlikowski defines technology (p. 403) as 'material artefacts (various configurations of hardware and software)', but also claims that this does not imply an 'exclusive focus on technology as a physical object'. Rather, it is argued, the 'analytic decoupling of artefacts from human action allows ... material artefacts [to be conceptualised] as the outcome of co-ordinated human action and hence inherently social'. This leads to the first premiss of the structurational model of technology that 'technology is created and changed by human action, yet it is also used by humans to accomplish some action'. This is termed the 'duality of technology'. Technology is thus seen as 'interpretatively flexible', although it is argued that this is often neglected in the traditional IS literature, which treats technology largely as a 'black box'. In part, this is seen as being due to the 'time-space discontinuity' of design and use of IS which 'typically' occurs in different organisations (those of the vendor and customer). It is also stated, however, that 'interpretive flexibility is not infinite', being constrained by the material characteristics of the technology and the institutional contexts of its design and use, and the power, knowledge, and interests of the relevant actors. Thus 'initial designers of a technology have tended to align with managerial objectives ... with the result that many technologies reinforce the institutional status quo, emphasizing standardisation, control and efficiency' (p. 409).

Orlikowski's model (Fig. 5.1) depicts the relationships between institutional properties, human agents, and technology. Thus technology is identified as the 'product of human action' (arrow *a*), coming into existence and being sustained through human action, and being constituted through use. Only through the appropriation of technology by humans, therefore, does it exert influence. Technology, however, is also 'the medium of human action' (arrow *b*). It conditions, rather than determines, the performance of social practices, both constraining and enabling them. The influence of institutional properties on human agents (arrow *c*) is a more conventional component of structuration, although Orlikowski also slants this towards technology in emphasising how the form and function of a specific technology will 'bear the imprint' of the social and historical conditions under which it is built and used. The last relationship, of technology on institutional contexts (arrow *d*), reflects the influence of technology in reinforcing or transforming the institutional properties of organisations. For example

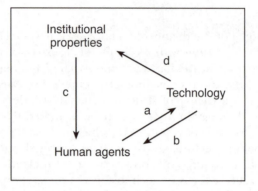

F IG . 5.1. *The structurational model of technology*
Source: Orlikowski (1992).

it is argued that 'when users conform to the technology's embedded rules
and resources they unwittingly sustain the institutional structures in which
the technology is deployed'. It is also emphasised, however, that the different relationships may vary in their relative strength over time and may
be in contradiction with one another, thus precluding determinism and
creating points of tension and instability that may give rise to change and
transformation.

The model is applied to an analysis of the case study of the introduction of CASE tools in the Beta software consultancy (Orlikowski, 1991).
In this, reference is made to knowledge and norms of interaction being
'embedded in' the tools, and the way in which this 'directs the manner in
which problems are interpreted and work is conducted' (p. 417), and to
the reinforcement of 'Beta's shared reality, assumptions and values' (p. 418).
In the discussion it is also suggested that time may reduce interpretative
flexibility as the interpretation and use of technologies becomes habitu-
alised, and it is proposed that further research might be directed toward
analysing how 'different organisational forms may engender certain kinds
of technologies, and how these technologies in turn may reinforce or transform the structural configurations' (p. 423).

Compared to AST, it should be evident that Orlikowski's model is
much closer to the spirit of structuration theory as Giddens has described
it, and there are many instances in her description of structuration and
the structurational model of technology that illustrate Orlikowski's subtle
appreciation of nuances of Giddens's work. As described in Orlikowski
(1992), however, there are a number of aspects of the model of technology that fit uneasily with some of the essential principles of structuration.
Thus, although she proposes that her model avoids seeing technology in
exclusively material terms and emphasises its social construction, the definition of technology as material artefact confuses the ontological status

of Fig. 5.1. From Giddens's standpoint institutional properties are 'traces in the mind' which are inseparable from the human agency with which they are mutually constituted, and material phenomena are resources only when drawn upon in processes of structuration. Technology as both material entity and existing outside the duality of structure and agency is therefore anomalous in this context.

The material character of technology also creates difficulties for the concept of interpretative flexibility. For example some material properties of information technology such as power supplies, screen resolution, processing speed may be only indirectly interpretatively flexible. From a structurational standpoint this is not a problem, as it could be envisaged that a human actor might believe that the computer was working when there was no power supply, see detail not represented by the screen resolution, or consider the system to be working faster than it actually was. So long as these structures are 'virtual', in the mind of the agent, and instantiated in their actions then the material properties are not significant. If it is argued, however, as Orlikowski does, that technology is distinctively material then it does not fit in this schema. This is the problem of dealing with material artefacts in a theory of the social raised in the introduction to this section. Since Giddens himself provides no indication of how this might be resolved it is no particular criticism of Orlikowski that she has not come up with the answer, but it weakens the structurational model at the outset.

Further problems arise with the concepts of knowledge, norms and rules, and resources 'embedded' in technologies, since, from a structurational perspective, these only exist in the instance of action by knowledgeable agents. To suggest that structure may be somehow fixed into the technology is to separate it from agency and hence to turn Giddens's carefully constructed duality back into a dualism. It might also suggest that this structure fixed in the technology could be transplanted with predictable effects into another context, for example that Beta's structures of domination, legitimation, and signification could be coded into the CASE tools such that their use in other organisations would reproduce the structures in some way independently of the agency of their social actors. If CASE tools are used in similar ways in different organisations, then from a structurational perspective, this is not because of structures embedded in the technology, but because actors in the different organisations draw on broader social structures (of capitalism, of employee relationships in the software industry).

A similar separation of agency and structure is also evident in the model's rather sequential view of the relationship between structure and action, and to some extent in the case description, despite the discussion of the simultaneous and potentially contradictory interaction between the different relationships of technology and structure. More generally, although it could be argued that the emphasis on technology in the model is a necessary simplification, particularly as represented in Fig. 5.1, it gives an undue prominence to technology, making it the dominant element in terms of interaction, with three relationships, and the only one with a reciprocal relationship. In structurational terms, however, technology is a minor aspect of social practice, if indeed it is considered at all. Moreover, bearing in mind the way in which structuration has been misunderstood in other contexts, such a representation risks further misinterpretation.

An Agenda for IS Structuration Research

A number of conclusions about the future agenda for structurational research in the IS field may be drawn from this brief review. The first is that the case for the relevance of structuration, whether as a source of concepts or as a meta-theory, has been well and eloquently made. There are already a number of examples of IS papers that make effective use of ideas from structuration and this particular wheel does not need to be reinvented. This is not to say that all future IS researchers will avoid the misinterpretations that have been made in the past (although one would hope that the sort of careful analysis of the writings of Giddens and his critics that this chapter has sought to illustrate might reduce their recurrence), but that we have good evidence that the perspective that structuration offers is a fruitful one for the analysis of IS and this does not need to be 'proved' again.

While this may be true at a general level, it is also evident that the specific attempts to adapt structuration to incorporate the material aspects of IS have encountered a number of serious problems which remain as yet unresolved. While, as Joerges (1988) points out, there are similar deficiencies in the treatment of technology in many other forms of social theory, in the current context they may be seen to cast doubt on the suitability of structuration in the study of specific instances of IS development and use. This need not be the case, however, if we see these 'difficulties' as opportunities to reassess our understanding of the character of IS. Thus, while the virtual character of structure in Giddens's theory may be incompatible with its being embedded in technology, this may be more of a problem with our conceptualisation of IS than with structuration itself. Barley's (1986) concept of 'occasions for structuring', while problematic in its episodic rather than continuous treatment of the process of structuration, may suggest a way forward. Similarly the recent attention of Orlikowski (1995) to 'technologies in use' may point to a way of conceiving IS that fits with the notion of material allocative resources being structurational *resources* only when drawn upon in the production or reproduction of structure.

This provides a much more idealist ontology than many IS researchers would probably be happy with, but is a necessary implication of Giddens's position on the irretrievably hermeneutic character of social science. Alternatively, if we accept the arguments of writers such as Storper (1985) and Layder (1987) that structuration need not be incompatible with a realist ontology, then a more conventionally acceptable resolution may be possible. The development of such a position would seem a valuable contribution to IS research.

Another, possibly complementary, approach would be to develop ideas arising from Giddens's attempts to draw on time-geography, where he acknowledges the influence of the corporeality of the human body and the physical characteristics of the contexts of interaction. As IS play an increasing role in social interactions in future, these ideas would seem to require modification to address the ways in which the different affordances of the information space may affect the binding of time and physical space in social systems. For example, how do computer-mediated interactions fit into, or alter, the processes of social production and reproduction within organisations? Ideas from other theories with a more explicit concern with technology may also be used to suggest how structuration might better address IS. Actor-network theory, for example, is currently attracting considerable attention and is producing some interesting analyses (Monteiro and Hanseth, 1995). This is not to suggest that these have all the answers or that they may be seamlessly synthesised with structuration to yield a complete theory, but that they may facilitate reflection upon the unresolved issues in structuration's treatment of technology.

A further implication of structuration is that IS research needs to be not only, as Monteiro and Hanseth (1995) suggest, more specific about the technology (and actor-network theory is not necessarily the only way to do this), but also more specific about use. Given that structuration takes place in every instant of action, each of which is a potential moment of transformation, then we need to look at use in much more detail. This is difficult when considering IS at the organisational level, where tracking the minutiae of every interaction risks overwhelming the broader picture (and in practical terms would require a density of description that would probably be unpublishable in most normal fora), but does suggest that such micro-studies could enrich our appreciation of the processes of structuration around IS. Following Boland (1993, 1996), this may also help to direct the attention of IS researchers to the agency of individual actors and to avoid inappropriate reification of social structures. This is not to contradict the earlier conclusion that we do not need more demonstrations of the applicability of structuration, but to suggest that structuration theory highlights a generally neglected aspect IS research that might also contribute to a better understanding of its insights.

At the same time, however, structuration also points to the insepar-
able linkage of micro-level, individual action and institutional processes;
again a frequently neglected aspect of IS research. If structuration encourages IS researchers to pay greater attention to the way in which the design
and use of IS is not just influenced by, but also helps to the stabilise and
transform, broader social structures, then this would seem a positive development. For example, as Jones (1994) discusses, the actions of individuals
involved in the formation and implementation of an IS strategy in a District Health Authority could be seen as contributing to significant changes
in the UK National Health Service associated with the introduction of the
'internal market' and also to the growth of a discourse of managerialism
in the UK and, in principle, internationally.

Structuration theory in itself provides a framework for addressing such
issues, but Giddens's development of the concept of 'radicalised modernity' in CM and MSI offers an interpretation of social developments in
which IS are strongly implicated that would seem to provide a rich vein
of potential research. Given Giddens's own recognition of his lack of expertise on such issues, this might even be an area in which IS researchers
could make a significant contribution to theoretical development. Indeed,
one particular aspect of structuration that Giddens has repeatedly stressed
as central to his concerns, and in which IS play an increasingly important
role, is issues of time-space distantiation. For example the use of IS to support the globalisation of organisations, especially those such as professional
service organisations for whom their product is the intangible expertise of
their members, provides what would appear to be a particularly fruitful site
for the exploration of these issues. This might also enable IS researchers
to take the lead in responding to Whittington's (1992) implicit criticism
of the selective way in which Giddens's work has been used in the management field.

Despite Giddens's own reservations about particular 'applications' of
his work, therefore, it would seem that there is still a place for structurationally informed, empirical IS research. It is essential, however, that such
research should seek to engage fully with the richness and complexity of
Giddens's ideas and not to treat them as a grab bag of assorted concepts
to be used wherever they appear to provide a suitable catchphrase. As this
chapter has sought to suggest, this sort of engagement is unlikely to be
possible without close reading of Giddens's own works and those of his
interpreters and critics. Indeed it could be argued more generally that attention to the primary literature is essential in any area where IS researchers
are seeking to draw on theoretical concepts from reference disciplines.

For structurational research this also means that IS researchers need to
take seriously its philosophical basis, recognising the distinctive ontological
and epistemological stance Giddens adopts. In Markus and Robey's (1988)
terms, structuration implies an 'emergent' perspective; indeed Barley

(1986), despite his references to 'soft determinism', is cited as an example of this position. It is also a 'process' theory and addresses multiple levels of analysis. Attempts to use structuration with methods that ignore the 'irretrievably hermeneutic' character of social science, with causal models, or with a focus solely on a single level of analysis (particularly where individual agency is excluded), are therefore at odds with central principles of the theory.

Looking positively, if not prescriptively, the way forward would seem to be suggested by Giddens's approval of 'sparing and critical' use of the logical framework of structuration. This is not to propose that all such IS research should explicitly adopt structurational concepts, but that it should be informed by Giddens's more general theoretical position. In view of the way in which his ideas have been misinterpreted it would unfortunately seem necessary to supplement this by stating that such use needs to reflect the spirit as well as the logic of Giddens's theory. IS researchers could also gain from attention to his guidelines for empirical research, either in the elaborated ten-point form in or the three principles of attention to: contextual sensitivity; the complexity of human intentionality; and the subtlety of social constraint. Indeed, whatever the particular merits or deficiencies of structuration, these would seem sensible recommendations for any piece of IS research.

References

Archer, M. (1990), 'Human Agency and Social Structure: A Critique of Giddens', in Clark et al. (1990).

Barbalet, J. M. (1987), 'Power, Structural Resources and Agency', *Current Perspectives in Social Theory*, 8: 1–24.

Barley, S. R. (1986), 'Technology as an Occasion for Structuring: Evidence from Observation of CT Scanners and the Social Order of Radiology Departments', *Administrative Science Quarterly*, 31: 78–108.

—— (1990), 'The Alignment of Technology and Structure through Roles and Networks', *Administrative Science Quarterly*, 35: 61–103.

Barrett, M., and Walsham, G. (1995), 'Managing IT for Business Innovation: Issues of Culture, Learning and Leadership in a Jamaican Insurance Company', *Journal of Global Information Management*, 3, 3: 25–33.

Berger, P. L., and Luckmann, T. (1967), *The Social Construction of Reality: A Treatise in the Sociology of Knowledge* (Harmondsworth: Penguin).

Bernstein, R. J. (1989), 'Social Theory as Critique', in Held and Thompson (1989).

Bhaskar, R. (1979), *The Possibility of Naturalism* (Brighton: Harvester).

Boland, R. J. (1993), 'Accounting and the Interpretive Act', *Accounting, Organisations and Society*, 18, 2/3: 125–46.

—— (1996), 'Why Shared Meanings have no Place in Structuration Theory: A Reply to Scapens and Macintosh', *Accounting, Organisations and Society*, 21, 7/8: 691–7.

Bourdieu, P. (1977), *Outline of a Theory of Practice* (Cambridge: Cambridge University Press).

Bryant, C. G. A., and Jary, D. (1991), 'Introduction: Coming to Terms with Anthony Giddens', in Bryant and Jary (1991*b*).

Callon, M. (1986), 'Some Elements of the Sociology of Translation: Domestication of the Scallops and the Fishermen of St Brieuc Bay', in J. Law (ed.), *Power, Action and Belief: A New Sociology of Knowledge?* (London: Routledge).

Clark, J., Modgil, C., and Modgil, J. (1990), *Anthony Giddens: Consensus and Controversy* (Brighton: Falmer Press).

Cohen, I. (1989), *Structuration Theory: Anthony Giddens and the Constitution of Social Life* (Basingstoke: Macmillan).

Contractor, N. S., and Eisenberg, E. M. (1990), 'Communication Networks and New Media in Organisations', in J. Fulk, and C. Steinfeld (eds.) *Organisations and Communication Technology* (Beverly Hills, Calif.: Sage).

Coombs, R., Knights, D., and Willmott, H. (1992), 'Culture, Control and Competition: Towards a Conceptual Framework for the Study of Information Technology in Organisations', *Organisation Studies*, 13, 1: 51–72.

Craib, I. (1992), *Anthony Giddens* (London: Routledge).

DeCock, C., and Rickards, T. (1995), 'Of Giddens, Paradigms and Philosophical Garb', *Organisation Studies*, 16, 4: 699–704.

DeSanctis, G., and Poole, M. S. (1994), 'Capturing the Complexity in Advanced Technology Using Adaptive Structuration Theory', *Organisation Science*, 5, 2: 121–47.

Garnsey, E. W. (1993), 'Exploring a Critical Systems Perspective', *Innovation on Social Sciences Research*, 6, 2: 229–56.

—— and Kelly, S. B. (1995), 'Structuration and Enacted Social Systems', in K. Ellis, A. Gregory, B. R. Mears-Young, and G. Ragsdell (eds.), *Critical Issues in Systems Theory and Practice* (New York: Plenum).

Giddens, A. (1979), *Central Problems in Social Theory* (Basingstoke: Macmillan).

—— (1983), 'Comments on the Theory of Structuration', *Journal for the Theory of Social Behaviour*, 13: 75–80.

—— (1984), *The Constitution of Society* (Cambridge: Polity).

—— (1989), 'A Reply to my Critics', in Held and Thompson (1989).

—— (1990*a*), *The Consequences of Modernity* (Cambridge: Polity).

—— (1990*b*), 'Structuration Theory and Sociological Analysis', in Clark et al. (1990).

—— (1991*a*), *Modernity and Self-Identity* (Cambridge: Polity).

—— (1991*b*), 'Structuration Theory: Past, Present and Future', in Bryant and Jary (1991*b*).

—— (1993), *New Rules of Sociological Method* (Cambridge: Polity (1st edn. 1976)).

—— (1994), *A Contemporary Critique of Historical Materialism* (Basingstoke: Macmillan (1st edn. 1981)).

Gopal, A., Bostrom, R. P., and Chin, W. W. (1992), 'Applying Adaptive Structuration Theory to Investigate the Process of Group Support Systems Use', *Journal of Management Information Systems*, 9, 3: 45–69.

Gregson, N. (1989), 'On the Ir(relevance) of Structuration Theory to Empirical Research', in Held and Thompson (1989).

Harré, R. (1983), 'Commentary from an Ethogenic Standpoint', *Journal for the Theory of Social Behaviour*, 13: 69–73.

Held, D., and Thompson, J. B. (1989) (eds.), *Social Theory of Modern Societies: Anthony Giddens and his Critics* (Cambridge: Cambridge University Press).

Hirschheim, R. (1985), *Office Automation: A Social and Organisational Perspective* (Chichester: John Wiley).

Joerges, B. (1988), 'Technology in Everyday Life: Conceptual Queries', *Journal for the Theory of Social Behaviour*, 18, 2: 219–37.

Jones, M. R. (1994), 'Learning the Language of the Market: Information Systems Strategy Formation in a UK District Health Authority', *Accounting Management and Information Technology*, 4, 3: 119–47.

—— and Nandhakumar, J. (1993), 'Structured Development? A Structurational Analysis of the Development of an Executive Information System', in D. Avison, J. E. Kendall, and J. I. DeGross (eds.), *Human, Organisational and Social Dimensions of Information Systems Development* (Amsterdam: North-Holland).

Karsten, H. (1995a), 'Converging Paths to Notes: In Search of Computer-Based Information Systems in a Networked Company', *Information Technology and People*, 8, 1: 7–34.

—— (1995b), 'It's like Everyone Working around the Same Desk': Organisational Readings of Notes', *Scandinavian Journal of Information Systems*, 7, 1: 3–32.

Kling, R. (1987), 'Defining the Boundaries of Computing cross Complex Organisations', in R. J. Boland, and R. Hirschheim (eds.), *Critical Issues in Information Systems Research* (Chichester: John Wiley).

Knights, D., and Willmott, H. (1985), 'Power and Identity in Theory and Practice', *Sociological Review*, 33, 1: 22–46.

—— —— (1989), 'Power and Subjectivity at Work: From Degradation to Subjugation in Social Relations', *Sociology*, 23, 4: 535–58.

Latour, B. (1987), *Science in Action: How to Follow Scientists and Engineers through Society* (Milton Keynes: Open University Press).

Layder, D. (1985), 'Power, Structure and Agency', *Journal for the Theory of Social Behaviour*, 15: 131–49.

—— (1987), 'Key Issues in Structuration Theory: Some Critical Remarks', *Current Perspectives in Social Theory*, 8: 25–46.

Lea, M., O'Shea, T., and Fung, P. (1995), 'Constructing the Networked Organisation: Content and Context in the Development of Electronic Communication', Organisation Science, 6, 4: 462–78.

Lyytinen, K. J., and Ngwenyama, O. K. (1992), 'What Does Computer Support for Co-operative Work Mean? A Structurational Analysis of Computer Supported Co-operative Work', *Accounting, Management and Information Technology*, 2, 1: 19–37.

Macintosh, N. W., and Scapens, R. W. (1990), 'Structuration Theory in Management Accounting', *Accounting Organisations and Society*, 15, 5: 455–77.

Manning, P. (1982), 'Organisational Work: Structuration of Environments', *British Journal of Sociology*, 33, 1: 118–34.

Markus, M. L., and Robey, D. (1988), 'Information Technology and Organisational Change: Causal Structure in Theory and Research', *Management Science*, 34, 5: 583–98.

Miranda, S. M., and Bostrom, R. P. (1993), 'The Impact of Group Support Systems on Group Conflict and Conflict Management', *Journal of Management Information Systems*, 10, 3: 63–95.

Monteiro, E., and Hanseth, O. (1995), 'Social Shaping of Information Infrastruc-
ture: On Being Specific about the Technology', in W. J. Orlikowski, G. Walsham,
M. R. Jones, and J. I. DeGross (eds.), *Information Technology and Changes in
Organisational Work* (London: Chapman & Hall).
Nagasundram, M., and Bostrom, R. P. (1994), 'The Structuring of Creative Pro-
cesses Using GSS: A Framework for Research', *Journal of Management Information
Systems*, 11, 3: 87–114.
New, C. (1994), 'Structure Agency and Social Transformation', *Journal for the
Theory of Social Behaviour*, 24, 3: 197–205.
Orlikowski, W. J. (1991), 'Integrated Information Environment in Matrix of
Control: The Contradictory Implications of Information Technology', *Account-
ing, Management and Information Technology*, 1, 1: 9–42.
—— (1992), 'The Duality of Technology: Rethinking the Concept of Technology
in Organisations', *Organisation Science*, 3, 3: 398–427.
—— (1995), *Action and Artifact: The Structuring of Technologies-in-Use* (Cambridge,
Mass.: Sloan School of Management, Massachusetts Institute of Technology).
—— and Robey, D. (1991), 'Information Technology and the Structuring of
Organisations', *Information Systems Research*, 2, 2: 143–69.
—— Yates, J., Okamura, K., and Fujimoto, M. (1995), 'Shaping Electronic Commun-
ication: The Metastructuring of Technology in the Context of Use', *Organisation
Science*, 6, 4: 423–44.
Pettigrew, A. (1985), *The Awakening Giant: Continuity and Change in ICI* (Oxford:
Blackwell).
Poole, M. S., and DeSanctis, G. (1990), 'Understanding the Use of Group
Decision Support Systems: The Theory of Adaptive Structuration', in J. Fulk, and
C. Steinfeld (eds.), *Organisations and Communication Technology* (Beverly Hills,
Calif.: Sage).
Ranson, S., Hinings, B., and Greenwood, R. (1980), 'The Structuring of Organisa-
tional Structures', *Administrative Science Quarterly*, 25: 1–17.
Riley, P. (1983), 'A Structurationist Account of Political Culture', *Administrative Science
Quarterly*, 28: 414–37.
Roberts, J., and Scapens, R. (1985), 'Accounting Systems and Systems of Account-
ability: Understanding Accounting Practices in their Organisational Contexts',
Accounting, Organisations and Society, 10, 4: 443–56.
Sarason, Y. (1995), 'A Model of Organisational Transformation: The Incorpora-
tion of Organisational Identity into a Structuration Framework', *Academy of
Management Journal*, Best Papers Proceedings 1995: 47–51.
Scapens, R. W., and Macintosh, N. B. (1996), 'Structure and Agency in Manage-
ment Accounting Research: A Response to Boland's Interpretive act', *Accounting,
Organisations and Society*, 21, 7/8: 675–90.
Schank, R. C. (1990), *Tell Me a Story: A New Look at Real and Artificial Memory* (New
York: Charles Scribner).
Smith, C. W. (1983), 'A Case Study of Structuration: The Pure-Bred Beef Business',
Journal for the Theory of Social Behaviour, 13: 3–18.
Storper, M. (1985), 'The Spatial and Temporal Constitution of Social Action: A
Critical Reading of Giddens', *Environment and Planning D: Society and Space*, 3:
407–24.

Thompson, J. B. (1989), 'The Theory of Structuration', in Held and Thompson (1989).

Urry, J. (1982), 'Duality of Structure: Some Critical Issues', *Theory, Culture and Society*, 1, 2: 100–6.

Walsham, G. (1993), *Interpreting Information Systems* (Chichester: John Wiley).

—— and Han, C.-K. (1991), 'Structuration Theory and Information Systems Research', *Journal of Applied Systems Analysis*, 17: 77–85.

—— (1993), 'Information Systems Strategy Formation and Implementation: The Case of a Central Government Agency', *Accounting, Management and Information Technology*, 3, 3: 191–209.

—— and Sahay, S. (1996), *GIS for District-Level Administration in India: Problems and Opportunities*, Management School Working Paper SM 02/96 (Lancaster: University of Lancaster).

Weaver, G. R., and Gioia, D. A. (1994), 'Paradigms Lost: Incommensurability vs Structurationist Inquiry', *Organisation Studies*, 15, 4: 565–90.

Weick, K. E. (1979), *The Social Psychology of Organizing*, 2nd edn. (Reading, Mass.: Addison-Wesley).

—— (1993), 'The Collapse of Sense-Making in Organisations: The Mann Gulch Disaster', *Administrative Science Quarterly*, 38: 628–52.

Whittington, R. (1992), 'Putting Giddens into Action: Social Systems and Managerial Agency', *Journal of Management Studies*, 29, 6: 693–712.

Willmott, H. (1981), 'The Structuring of Organisational Structure: A Note', *Administrative Science Quarterly*, 26: 470–4.

—— (1987), 'Studying Managerial Work: A Critique and a Proposal', *Journal of Management Studies*, 24, 3: 249–70.

Wilson, D. (1995), 'Excavating the Dialectic of Blindness and Insight: Anthony Giddens' Structuration Theory', *Political Geography*, 14, 3: 309–18.

Yates, J., and Orlikowski, W. J. (1992), 'Genres of Organisational Communication: A Structurational Approach to Studying Communication and Media', *Academy of Management Review*, 17, 2: 299–326.

6

A Theory of Information Systems Based on Improvisation

CLAUDIO U. CIBORRA

Discovery, that is a mix of instinct and method!
(E. Husserl)

The man of affairs, despite his constant use of the words 'logical', 'sound reasoning', 'reasonable', etc., in his rationalizations, even more distrusts the formal reasoning processes for the fields in which he works. This distrust . . . is well founded.

(C. Barnard)

Life is what happens to you while you're making other plans.
(From a sign on a refrigerator door)

Introduction

Improvisation is situated performance where thinking and action occur simultaneously and on the spur of the moment. It is purposeful human behaviour which seems to be ruled at the same time by chance, intuition, competence, and outright design. In improvising features of a situation are 'suddenly' (from the Latin 'improviso') framed and combined by the actor, so that they become resources at hand for intervention. 'During' the suddenness the contours of the problematic situation, the problem-solving strategy, and the deployment of resources for implementation precipitate into a burst of action. Improvisation is intentional but looks extemporaneous ('ex tempore'—outside the flow of time) and 'without known causes or relationships' (Webster, 1973).

In a previous paper the author has put forward the idea that so-called strategic applications of information technology (IT) are largely the outcome of tinkering and *bricolage* during systems development and use (Ciborra, 1994). As a consequence, the design of strategic information systems ought to be based on the systematic appreciation and nurturing of emerging practices of improvised, serendipitous development and use of computer-based information systems (IS). Furthermore, *planning* for strategic IT applications would entail the solicitous management of those learning processes which turn emerging, idiosyncratic applications into strategic resources and core competencies of the organisation (Andreu and Ciborra, 1995). In this chapter, improvisation is seen as playing a much broader and foundational role for business and IT. It challenges the received theories of information systems, and provides an opportunity to reflect in a new light upon key IS concepts, such as the structure of individual and organisational decision-making; the nature of business processes in markets and hierarchies; the data vs. information distinction; and last but not least, the scope for new generations of technology to support or enable business processes of an improvised nature.

The focus of this chapter is smart or competent improvisation, which contributes to individual and organisational effectiveness. That is, it is not just acting extemporaneously for the sake of acting. Nor is it the novice's improvised performance, i.e. an action with no effective link with the demands of the situation. On the other hand, the expert's smart improvisation might appear to have no links with the task environment, but, after the fact, it turns out to be highly competent behaviour. How to align IT to smart improvisation is at the heart of the discussion.

To be sure, (smart) improvisation is an intriguing process as far as IT is concerned. For one thing, it shows contradictory features. In a *slow motion*, after the fact analysis, one could trace in its dynamics the ingredients germane to rational decision-making: goal definition, information-gathering, planning, choice, and so on. Still, whether there are physical symbols in the improviser's brain representing the situation and the plans for action (Newell and Simon, 1972; Vera and Simon, 1993) seems to be a minor issue, since it would be very hard to access those which may be determinant when the action is suddenly performed. Improvisation is simultaneously rational and unpredictable; planned but emergent; purposeful but opaque; effective but irreflexive; discernible after the fact, but spontaneous in its manifestation. These characteristics make improvisation a difficult target for systems modelling and support, so difficult, that one could question the very fact that IT applications have anything to do with improvisation. More in general, is improvisation just a marginal phenomenon in economic organisations, a side-effect of dysfunctional routines or an outcome of artistic performance, or is it frequent and important enough to demand a special effort in developing appropriate IS?

This chapter argues for the latter scenario, invoking a different awareness of what is routinised and what is spontaneous in an organisation (Schön, 1983; Suchman, 1987). In doing so it celebrates the role played by human experience in creating and using information and systems. Its contents unfold as follows. First, the importance of improvisation in organisations is spelled out for those situations where routines do not work, i.e. in emergencies. Next, the everyday life in economic institutions such as markets and bureaucracies is revisited in order to show how improvisation is there both ubiquitous and economically relevant. Then, the *structure* of improvisation is explored and contrasted with rational, planning-driven decision-making: on the one hand, improvisation does contain elements of planning and design, oriented to the future; on the other, what may look like planned, structured decision-making appears to be intrinsically improvised, since it is grounded on an opaque stock of past experience.

A small Copernican revolution is suggested: competent actions which seem improvised are in reality deeply rooted, while structured decisions based on abstract representations and models appear to be improvised, i.e. lacking any relationship to context. The next two sections deal with design issues. The first criticizes current systems design principles, moulded by the idea of planned decision-making, and shows how they lead to the automation of incompetent behaviour. The next section is constructive, for it identifies new design strategies and systems to support and enable improvisation. In such an emerging field conclusions are bound to be temporary.

Improvisation in Economic Institutions

In music, improvisation is defined as extemporising, or creating all or part of a composition at the moment of performance. To improvise effectively the musician ought to know the conventions and the rules of a given musical style, since they provide a sort of library of musical resources that can be recombined to generate new instances of the score. The resulting, reinvented music has at the same time a sense of unity and coherence, while allowing room for spontaneous activity (*Encarta*, 1994; Sudnow, 1978). A parallel between musical practice and rational, albeit limitedly so, management may indeed seem improvised (though not new, see Weick, 1993*a*, and his analysis of the Amsterdam Symphony Orchestra). On closer inspection, however, if one considers the art and science of organising, rather than organisation (Weick, 1979), the analogy is much more grounded. Namely, we can truly appreciate the importance of improvisation, if we look at organisations less as a stable outcome of a hierarchical, functional decomposition of tasks, and more as an ongoing process of design and sense-making. Consider, in order, organisational settings with an increasing degree of stability: emergencies, markets, and hierarchies.

Improvisation in emergencies

Improvisation is a key success factor which can hold together a faltering organisation in extreme situations. An original study of the aftermath of an earthquake in the south of Italy provides a telling case of how improvisation, rather than planned organisation, led to the establishment of an effective network of local recovery initiatives (Lanzara, 1983). It all started when an ordinary citizen opened a makeshift coffee bar (actually a bench) on the main square of an isolated village in ruins. The coffee bar proved to be a primary support for the survivors and an important co-ordination point for the first, local rescue operations, before the army and the government forces were able to reach the disaster area. While the official recovery organisation came late and proceeded slowly, if not clumsily, the improvised coffee bar functioned as a knowledge brokerage house, allowing the quick allocation of resources available locally to those who needed them most. It effectively decreased the transaction costs of co-ordination and provided an essential organisational continuity to the community.

In his ground-breaking reconstruction and interpretation of the Mann Gulch forest fire accident, where almost all of the members of a consummate fire-fighting team died, Weick (1993*b*) concludes that improvisation and *bricolage* were an effective, albeit partial antidote to panic and ensuing collapse of the team organisation. The survivors were able to devise and try out ad hoc tactics to escape the fire. For example, tactics included the paradoxical recombination of resources left at hand. The captain deliberately provoked a fire in the bushes ahead of him and the rest of the team, and threw himself into it, in order to stop at least locally the larger fire front by destroying its very fuel sources. Those who thought he was a lunatic and did not follow him died a few minutes after as isolated (disorganized) individuals. Weick further suggests that various forms of improvisation helped the few survivors to keep their minds busy on a specific project and preserved their identity as team members taking different functional roles in the implementation of that project. Improvisation was especially effective in countering the true source of organisational failure: panic, a paralysis of sense-making which leads to the collapse of the team.

Improvisation, however, is not just an individual or collective antidote to panic and disruption in emergency situations. If this were the case, its role would be confined to the design of ad hoc organisations in emergencies or disasters. We submit, instead, that improvisation is a part of everyday economic behaviour. It is the very stuff market choices and hierarchical routines are made from.

Improvisation on markets

Hayek (1945) is possibly unsurpassed in portraying the functioning of the market institution, or price system. For Hayek, the market is essentially a discovery process, where new opportunities and innovations are relentlessly found out, and the news of such findings is transmitted instantaneously through the price system. On markets, change dictates improvisation. Namely, decision-making on markets is, like any relevant economic process, linked to change (Knight, 1964): 'So long as things continue as before, there arise no new problems requiring a decision, no need to form a new plan . . . The economic problem of society is ultimately one of rapid adaptation to change' (Hayek, 1945).

In market behaviour one can find the key components of improvisation: immediacy; situatedness; idiosyncrasy; local knowledge; access to and deployment of resources at hand. Take for example *situatedness*: adaptation occurs through decisions based on knowledge of the particular circumstances of time and place. And relevant knowledge is ultimately in the hands of those actors 'who are familiar with such circumstances, who know directly of the relevant changes and the resources immediately available to them' (Hayek, 1945). No such knowledge of the here and now can be efficiently communicated to a central board, which, after integrating it, issues its orders. The highly situated and fragmentary nature of knowledge which lies at the heart of improvised decision-making on markets defies the efficacy of economic calculus based on 'data'. 'Data' is never actually 'given' to a single mind. Knowledge concerning the circumstances in which economic action is performed cannot obtain in an integrated form, 'but solely as dispersed bits of incomplete and frequently contradictory knowledge which all the separate individuals possess' (Hayek, 1945).

Improvisation in work organisations

At first glance, it is hard to imagine a role for improvisation in hierarchies. We exit the world of adjustment to change and relentless exploration of new opportunities (the market), and we enter the world of exploitation of the already known and carefully planned, the world of hierarchical routines (March, 1991). That is, thanks to the division of labour and specialization, work routines are generated to freeze both explicit and tacit knowledge necessary to make decisions and carrying out activities (Nelson and Winter, 1982). Organisational structures are there to influence, possibly in the smallest detail, decision-making at all levels of the hierarchy, through sophisticated mechanisms of communication and authority (March and Simon, 1958). This picture of organisational decision-making which seems to rule out improvisation derives from a particular approach to the analysis and design of organisations, the information-processing perspective (Galbraith, 1977).

The adoption of other perspectives (e.g. the one which looks at organisations as interpretative systems (see Daft and Weick, 1984), coupled with a closer observation of the organizing processes which take place daily in any work organisation, would delineate a quite different picture, where routines are virtual and improvisation is for real.

Consider, for example, the empirical studies on the role of 'practical thinking' in the execution of mundane, highly routinized tasks in dairies

(Scribner, 1984); supermarkets (Lave, 1988); offices (Wynn, 1979); and in the use of new technologies (Suchman, 1987) and when repairing them (Orr, 1990). These studies indicate that 'contrary to much conventional wisdom, people continually learn and improvise while working' (Brown and Duguid, 1991). Improvisation in organisations is systematic, not haphazard. People plan to improvise, by *playing by ear*, or by *taking things as they come*. Competent members respond to unforeseen contingencies 'by making it up as they go along' (Rosaldo, 1985).

In her studies of work routines in a modern milk-processing plant, Scribner (1984) finds that in a variety of jobs, ranging from the manual assembly of products, to accounting, picking delivery tickets, and taking inventory, intricate forms of improvisation are successfully performed to meet production goals. In most instances, even preset problems are subjectively reformulated on the basis of experience or hunch. Actual problem definition is made to fit 'good solutions', where good solutions are what circumstances have to offer. For example, product assemblers may convert a loading problem, formally expressed in an addition of units to be sent out to the loading dock, into a subtraction problem: how many units should be subtracted from available cases in order to reach the desired amount of units. Or, inventory people are able to manipulate in a sophisticated way the physical areas where cases are piled up in order to translate a counting problem in inventory-taking into a multiplication of physical space problem. Here, improvisation is systematic in the sense that formal accounting procedures are bypassed, and new calculus procedures are set in place by a quick registering of the situation, according to a principle of *least mental effort* and maximum exploitation of the affordances provided by the physical layout.

A second empirical feature of improvisation is the flexibility in which the same problem is solved 'now one way, now another, each way finely fitted to the occasion' (Scribner, 1984). Such flexibility comes in handy, since improvisation is deployed to fill the unavoidable gaps between standard operating procedures and events as they occur in the flow of daily work (Wynn, 1979; Suchman, 1983; Zimmerman, 1973). During improvisation an intense commerce takes place between what are analytically known as body, mind, and (task) environment. Specifically, what is reputed to lie outside the body or the mind (functions, activities, artefacts) gets internalized; and what is reputed to belong to mind or body is externalized in the surrounding environment (the group, the artefacts, the layout). Thus, the good jazz improviser has the music in his or her fingers (Sudnow, 1978); while the dairy men use the layout as an external memory. Or, secretaries learning how to use a new copying machine do not follow written instructions, but as a group construct methods to overcome many situations the instructions fail to anticipate (Suchman, 1987). Also, Orr (1990) and Lave and Wenger (1991) point out that improvisation, understood as a process of making sense of incoming working events and developing ad hoc solutions, takes place within *communities of practice*, and consists of *non-canonical* routines deployed to circumvent the inadequacies of formal ones. Local, specialized language of work groups, often unintelligible to outsiders, is an important sign of the deeply social nature of improvised work. Such an idiosyncratic language, which consists of jargon, slang, and war stories developed and used *in situ*, appears as an external medium to support the development of ad hoc, novel ways of formulating problems and finding out solutions. It allows members immediately to access relevant knowledge of local circumstances, close to the events to be faced, rather than relying on the *distant* and abstract representation of events one finds in the organisation manuals. The ecological nature of improvisation results from the intricate commerce between problem formulation and implementation, and the environment (situation) where it takes place. For example, tools and artefacts which populate the task environment, such as workstations, pencils, desks, are always annotated, if not 're-invented' (De Certeau, 1984), with personalized adaptations, such as 'hacks', 'macros', and a plethora of 'add-ons'. The annotations indicate the richness of the 'inventive calibration, calculation and workarounds' (Brown and Duguid, 1991).

More subtly, Scribner (1984) suggests that practical thinking and improvisation take place through sophisticated processes by which the task environment and its affordances (people, artefacts, information) (Gibson, 1977; Norman, 1988) are internalized into problem setting and solving, to the point that even written, formal instructions are interpreted by experienced workers, not as the (pre-planned) way to solve a problem or execute an action, but as an 'input to an, as yet, unspecified problem' to be addressed (Gerson and Star 1986). Here, we come full circle in our study of improvisation in economic institutions. Seen as a last resort in emergencies, improvisation seems to represent the essence of competent behaviour in a highly decentralized (authority-free) institution such as the market. But also the image of work in highly routinized, hierarchical settings, as conveyed by the ethnographic studies reported above, shows that the daily work life is punctuated by myriads of instances of improvisation.

In all the contexts examined a reason why improvisation tends to appear without known causes or relationships lies in the intense, but disconcerting, trade between internal and external cognitive and behavioural functions. The expected boundaries, drawn from the prevailing organisational, technological, and cultural representations, between mind, body, and environment are criss-crossed. Functions get recombined in a way that does not square with customary images of a permanent and univocal assignment of functions to the mind, the body, and the environment during both problem setting and solving (Zuboff, 1988). In this perspective, improvisation is not just a fluctuation in regular organisational routines, but is a practice which contains a different vision of work in organisations. Such practice and vision challenge the prevailing, objectivist paradigm which governs organisation and IS design (Husserl, 1970; Daft and Weick, 1984).

Improvisation, Planning, and Experience

Before tackling the issue of what kind of information processing is needed for improvisation, we pursue further our line of argument by submitting that improvisation has not only a paramount importance *per se*, but also permeates structured decision-making: this would explain the ubiquitous role of improvisation found even in hierarchical organisations.

Contrast two different worlds: the one of improvisation and the one of planned decision-making and action (Winograd and Flores, 1986; Vera and Simon, 1993; Agre, 1993; Clancey, 1995). Limitedly rational decision-making is about the choice of an appropriate means–ends chain to achieve a given goal. Though based on value premises of a different sort (Weber, 1964; Simon, 1976), the study of rational decisions focuses on selection criteria, planning and choice processes, control, and ensuing adjustments. As a conscious, future-oriented activity, decision-making seems to be improvisational only in those circumstances where planning is impossible: that is, contingencies of high uncertainty and unpredictability (the realm of non-programmable decisions (Simon, 1965).

According to Weber and Simon rational decision-making and action can be analysed objectively, as the planned selection and deployment of means to achieve a goal, without further enquiring into their consistency and unity. On the other hand, the phenomenological study of the internal time-consciousness of the decision-maker, due to Bergson (1927), Husserl (1962), and Schutz (1967), indicates that choice processes are intrinsically subjective and transient (in Hayek's words: 'linked to the here and now'). For Weber and Simon the meaning of the decision can be traced in the objective circumstances, in the value premises and preferences of the actor, in the act of selecting alternatives, and so on.

Phenomenologists advise us differently: any choice process is constituted from preceding projects of acts, and derives its unity (sense) from the range and scope of such projects. But, these are highly dependent upon the here and now of their formulation and evocation, so that the meaning of an action is merely relative to the particular moment in time, and the recollections the actor is able to perform in those particular circumstances (Schutz, 1967). In other words, the meaning of an action depends upon the intensity and direction of a (retrospective) beam of light (attention) thrown back to illuminate past experience. The *positioning* of the light beam itself is continuously shifting, making an action highly subjective (i.e. tied to the subject at a given moment of time), and ephemeral (i.e. tied to shifting local circumstances).

One may recall, further, our initial definition of improvisation as purposeful behaviour, which contains elements of planning and design, even if on the fly, or the examples of practical thinking which show cognitive and behavioural variety, flexibility but also calculus. How can the orientation to the future, which seems to characterize both improvisation and planned decisions, be reconciled with a view where subjective, highly circumstantial interpretation of the past gives the ultimate meaning to action?

According to Schutz (1967), every action is indeed carried out according to a project, which contains a vision of the act as if already accomplished in the future. The unity of the action (its meaning) is constituted by the image of that project: the actor-in-action is led by the vision of the accomplished project. The meaning embedded in such a project and its constituent elements (plans, goals, means, etc.), represent what Schutz calls the *in-order-to* motives of action. It is precisely these motives which are the special object of the analysis and design of rational decision-making processes, in the fields of IS, AI, DSS, and MIS (Simon, 1976). However, the in-order-to component is just the tip of the decision-making 'iceberg' (Garfinkel, 1974). Below, there are the actor's past experiences—selectively evoked according to the existential circumstances valid at the moment of making the decision. Such a deeper and wide-ranging bundle of motives is called the *because-of* component of the action. It is the latter bundle which conveys the ultimate meaning and motivational thrust to the devising and performance of the action. The *in-order-to* project deals with the actor's explicit and conscious meaning in solving a problematic situation, while the *because-of* motives can explain the reasons why and how a situation has been perceived as problematic in the first place.

The asymmetry between the orientation of attention to the past and to the future, intrinsic to any decision or action, has important implications for the study of improvisation. The because-of motives are tacit and lie in the background of the explicit project at hand. They fall outside the glance of rational, awake attention during the action. They could be inferred by an outsider, or made explicit by the actor, but only as a result of a reflection after the fact.

We can now try to explain why ordinary decisions on markets and in hierarchies are de facto improvised, no matter the extent to which rules and norms guide and constrain behaviour. For sure, the plans, the *means–ends* chain are there and they are relevant, but they are just the tip of the iceberg. Even more relevant is the drifting mass at the bottom, which provides the raw materials, the leftovers out of which plans are put together, particular problem definitions are selected, and the *means–ends* chains are assembled. The improvised component, *caché* even in structured decision-making, comes from the highly circumstantial fashion in which the bottom of the iceberg is brought to bear in the situation at hand, the ensuing formulation of the problem and construction of a solution.

The bottom is there, but we are not aware of its selective influences on our plans and projects at the moment of action. Hence, even a carefully planned and explicit decision is extemporaneous and pasted up, since it may be based on motives which are opaque and remote. Note, furthermore, that the very act of interpretation of the because-of motives may well be *improvised*, for it is in itself an act based on yet different bundles of because-of and in-order-to motives, some of which fall outside the awake attention of the actor while he or she is doing the planning. That is, the beam of light that can be thrown on the meanings of a (past) decision is also highly situated, and constantly shifting. The same action performed in the past may reveal new meanings depending upon the circumstances in which the actor or the observer reconsiders it.

Exit now the life world of people condemned to improvise, i.e. to act semi-blindly by trying to steer the iceberg of experience to match circumstances, and enter the clean, rational world as envisioned by the business and IT models in good currency. Structured analysis and design methodologies assume that plans and decisions can be analysed and executed objectively, and deny the intrinsic improvised nature of decision-making and action (Garfinkel, 1974). In doing so, such methodologies create artificial worlds (e.g. the 'enterprise models') made of deceivingly univocal and objective *entities, data, processes*, and *activities*. That improvisation be ruled out from such an artificial world is only an illusion. Decision-makers who perform actions taking this world for real are bound to meet surprises, and possibly be puzzled by the impredictabilities generated by the gaps between artificial routines, programmes, and structures and the practicalities of their use in the flow of daily activities. In fact, the surprises are so common, that it is a sign of competent organisational behaviour not to panic when gaps and surprises occur, and acknowledge that manuals, automated procedures, and instructions should not be followed blindly, but regarded as an input, not always reliable, to get the job done (Zimmerman, 1973; Suchman, 1987).

To conclude, we submit that there is much more intuition, instinct, and background experience even in carefully planned actions than meets the eye when analysing rational decision-making. The deep nature of decision-making appears to be one of improvisation. Routines and programmable decisions, and the institutions which host them, appear to be more 'on the edge' (Unger, 1987) than is admitted by mainstream management and IS literature. Ironically, we can submit that improvisation is far from being the Cinderella of organized work; indeed, it is *routines, plans, and business processes* that are *fantasized*, second-order constructs belonging to a virtual world of organisations. A virtual world with limited and indirect impact onto the flow of micro improvised actions which punctuate the here and now of human life in organisations (Gerson and Star, 1986). In other words, we envision a small Copernican revolution.

What appeared at the beginning as an extemporaneous process, improvisation, without known causes and relationships, appears to be grounded in deep-seated human experience, while what is usually presented by mainstream management and systems models as structured, planned, and well thought out looks makeshift, artificial, and de-rooted. Indeed, the only chance for such models to have an impact on the actual workflow is to be constantly *worked at* by competent members, who by *fiddling around* and *bricolage* fill the frequent gaps between the artificial models and the unfolding circumstances of work.

A Critique of Present-Day Automation

We have mentioned above that most systems (and software) design approaches not only ignore the ubiquitous role of improvisation in human affairs, but also, whenever they spot it, they aim at cleansing it through structured procedures and formalization of information. This practice of designing and building systems leads to two paradoxes, which capture in a nutshell the reasons why many systems fail when they are put in use. The two paradoxes consist in:

- the automation of incompetent behaviour, and
- the backlash of experience.

What is competent behaviour on markets, in hierarchies, or in teams? In our perspective, it is a sustained ability to develop and implement a project of action most suited to a (changing) situation, to the here and now of the work flow, to the ongoing co-operation with other team members, or to the unpredictable unfolding of market transactions. A competent agent is able to deploy knowledge of local circumstances, set feasible goals, come up with a plan, and choose a satisficing alternative. Thus, competent behaviour includes:

- effective registering of the situation;
- peripheral attention to local subtleties and nuances;
- development of an ad hoc plan (or on-line modification of an already existing plan);
- implementation that fully exploits local affordances ('let the world help you');
- flexibility in generating and switching between alternative courses of action, if required by the changing situation.

Incompetent behaviour, on the other hand, may lead to technically sound plans and their orderly implementation, but the outcome of such efforts does not square with the circumstances at hand. Hence, the inadequacy, inefficiency, and general clumsiness of incompetent actions (Dreyfus and Dreyfus, 1986).

Recall now the distinction between the in-order-to and the because-of motives. What appears to the agent, or to the external observer, as competent behaviour is a set of actions carried out in relation to one or more *in-order-to* projects. Such projects convey to the agent before and during the action a meaning about what is going on. Actually, incompetent behaviour is also guided by *in-order-to* projects, the difference being that they do not seem to match the requirements of the problem at hand. The projects tell very little, at the moment of action, about the internal process which led to the particular way of setting the problem or the selection of those resources which have become the means–ends components of the project itself. On the other hand, it is the because-of motives (the bottom of the iceberg) which underlie the perception and framing of the situation as problematic, direct attention to specific subsets of past experience, set the horizon and scope for the intervention, evoke a limited number of ways of formulating the problem, and so on.

What distinguishes competent from incompetent behaviour is the tacit component (Polany, 1962), the one *below the line*, as well as the type of project explicitly formulated. Competent behaviour is situated, i.e. it achieves a good matching (alignment) between the because-of motives and the registering of circumstances. Improving the competence level means learning how to flexibly select relevant because-of motives, and align them with the characteristics of the situation, so that the direction and thrust of the action is accompanied by an effective retrieval of relevant experience, a good framing of the problem, the development of a sound plan, and a sensible implementation, in a way that avails itself of the resources at hand, here and now. The introduction of computer-based information systems, instead, is oriented by structured design methodologies towards the formalisation and the automation of the 'tip of the iceberg', i.e. the in-order-to component of decision-making. What is missing is an effective link between the planned, automated decision process and all those tacit aspects, such as the because-of motives, or past experience, which give *life* and deep meaning to the development and implementation of a decision. This is why automated procedures tend so often to be under-utilised, for they do not match changing circumstances; badly mimic the know-how of even a novice; feel unnatural and clumsy; seem to lack meaning and be out of context; are full of loopholes which have to be filled by (improvised) human intervention; in one word, they seem to internalise all the main features of incompetent behaviour.

To introduce the second paradox, recall the textbook distinction between data and information. Data is just signs over a physical support, while information is data endowed with meaning. According to the conventional wisdom information needed for better decision-making can be obtained by improving the quality/quantity of data, since (it is implicitly assumed that) the decision-maker will be capable of providing enough meaning to transform the incoming data into new and relevant information. Realities of use suggest that this picture is an idealised one: what happens frequently is that more data leads to information overflow, and incompetent use/production of information, so that, paradoxically, one is better off relying on less, highly localised information. That is, since the competence available is limited, if compared to the actual complexity of the task at hand, data gets associated with wrong or lacking meanings, and information thus generated leads to errors in decision-making (Heiner, 1983).

Interestingly, the way computer specialists try to fix the problem is very often worse than the initial situation. To avoid the faulty associations of meanings to data, they narrow down the margins for interpretation. For example, company-wide data dictionaries and enterprise models are created to decrease ambiguity in definitions and interpretations of data performed by the users. The result is that very little data, and few events or situations, appear to have meaning. On the one hand, variety and speed in the change of business circumstances lead to an increasing number of exceptions to the existing definitions; on the other, agents are incompetent in dealing with such exceptions, since these occur outside the narrow repertoire of events/situations/actions endowed with meaning by their past experience. In the artificial, closed world defined by the data dictionary and enterprise models, any event which falls outside the precoded meaning is difficult to interpret and handle. In such a world, incompetent behaviour is bound to occur more, not less, frequently.

The phenomenological study of decision-making would show instead that behind meaning lies experience, and the span of attention towards past experience (Schutz, 1967). Thus, behind the notion of information there is nothing else but experience and attention. The past lurks in the back of even the latest information we can get on line. By restricting the meaning which can be attributed to data as it emerges in situations, one reduces the sources of past experience which can be tapped to come up with an interpretation, i.e. one multiplies the chances of generating poor or wrong information. Moreover, opportunities for learning and effective knowledge transfer are also restricted, thus endangering competent behaviour in the future. In sum, by wiping out the roots of ad hoc interpretation, and improvised, situated action, the backlash of experience condemns decision-makers to the incompetent use of the surplus of data made available by the new, powerful systems.

Implications for Design

The canonical design of organisations and information systems delivers systems which may undermine the goal for which they were designed in the first place: to enable users to process information (experience) relevant for economic action. What many current systems do, irrespective of their degree of sophistication, is to process data with little or no meaning; restrict access to experience and hamper its growth; impose meanings that do not match changing circumstances; dilute the chances for data to be converted into useful information; automate incompetent behaviour.

Our analysis so far, however, contains a few hints to explore new criteria and goals for the design of more effective information systems in economic institutions. Our discussion at this stage need not be purely conceptual or visionary. Indeed, if one looks carefully at the variety of IT applications being developed and in use in a few R&D labs, one can find many already functioning systems able to support decision-making and action, conceived as improvised processes. The theme of improvisation can help establish a common framework among what at present may seem scattered experiments or peculiar applications. Our review will be neither exhaustive nor totally consistent, since we cannot do justice here to the diversity of technological solutions, or to the complex and varied design rationales.

Just a few criteria will guide our navigation in such a dispersed and emerging archipelago of applications. First, the concept of improvisation and its different facets, rather than the sheer technical characteristics, will guide our review. Second, we will limit ourselves to consider a few avant-garde applications, disregarding that even legacy systems are used in some instances to support/enable improvised decision-making. That is, we consider systems for which their design rationale includes a vision of decision-making as an intrinsically improvised process. Third, we will stay away from two domains which deserve a special study: Internet and AI. The former can be regarded as the most powerful example of global, distributed application, born out of 'instinct and method', which supports a myriad of forms of improvisation. It is up to the ethnographers who study how the Internet is used in action, or the hackers themselves, to report about the multiple practices which mushroom around the largest distributed information system on Earth, and tell us the thousand stories of improvisation over the net. AI constitutes a complex domain of sophisticated applications, some of which seem to run, at least in their design rationale, against improvisation (the rule-based systems), while others aim at capturing aspects of situated, spontaneous decision-making (Gasser, 1991). The debate between the two camps is far from being exhausted (see for example the special issue of *Cognitive Science*, 1993). Here too we leave it to the AI community to position their systems and emerging designs in respect to the notion of improvisation. Having delimited the boundaries of our review, let us examine the new applications and systems according to the key dimensions of improvisation which have emerged from our analysis.

Situatedness: systems for the here and now. These systems, such as the various devices included in the 'ubiquitous computing' research program at Xerox PARC (Weiser, 1991); the electronic badge of Olivetti; the 'Forget-me-not' application developed at Europarc (Newman et al., 1991), aim at capturing electronically, for future use (unspecified at the moment of collection, Robinson, 1993), location and time of events in the life of a person, a document, an artefact (e.g. a picture), a conversation. They register 'the Now' and make it accessible for later use, in general as a 'time and place' labelling of more complex events (an action, a decision, the writing of a document). These systems help to index events for fast retrieval: they fix the *durée* (Bergson, 1927) of documents, decisions, and conversations, so that they can be directly accessed when one needs to have a better grasp of the because-of motives which lie behind these documents, decisions, or actions. Also, such systems augment the scope and range of peripheral awareness (Lave, 1988; Brown and Duguid, 1991; Goodwin and Goodwin, 1993).

Resources for improvisation: systems to access and retrieve experience. Lévi-Strauss (1966) suggests that 'exhaustive observation and systematic cataloguing of relations and connections are necessary for successful *bricolage*' (see also Weick, 1993a). Such systems, which go under the label of corporate memory (Stein and Zwass, 1995), allow the actor to index, store, and retrieve in a variety of ways (e.g. full text retrieval) distributed (over networks) fragments of past experience (again, documents, email messages, images, conversations). Programs like WAIS (Press, 1992) enable a flexible and focused search of information, thus enlarging and strengthening attention that underlies improvisation. Data warehouses (Cronk, 1993) can also be harnessed for similar purposes, although their link with legacy systems may reduce the chances for truly improvised access and use. In other words, systems which in one way or another assume that data has a fixed meaning, or should be used according to a limited (pre-planned). set of criteria, are not well suited for improvisation, a process whereby the meaning of data, or any other resource for that matter, depends heavily upon the conditions of use (Weick, 1993*a*).

Communication and shared context: systems which constitute a shared context for interpretation. Improvisation in organisations is based on acts of interpretation supported by a shared context (Daft and Weick, 1984). Context is created through sharing views, opinions, stories (Orr, 1990) between members. Improvisation reflects a changing set of competencies and resources, which are recombined in continuously novel fashions. Availability of such competencies and resources needs to be communicated and exchanged on a permanent basis. Groupware systems, conceived as 'common artefacts' (Robinson, 1993), enable (highly dispersed) individuals to establish or reinforce shared meanings, seen as organisational resources for individual or group improvisation. Groupware can be looked at not only as a co-ordination tool (Malone and Crowston, 1994), but also as a means for collective memory and consensual validation of experience (Ciborra, 1993). Groupware applications can become a collective repository, where members can access vast collections of because-of motives on a shared basis.

Reflection and learning: systems which can support reflection-in-action (Argyris and Schön, 1978) and learning for smart improvisation. These systems, like the Answer Garden (Ackerman and Malone, 1990), gIBIS (Conklin and Begeman, 1988), or Grapevine, keep track of *ex post* reconstructions, by an observer or the actor, of the rationale of performed actions or any organisational move (Pentland, 1992). They establish precedents endowed with interpretation. They constitute another form of memory which can be looked up and deployed at the moment of new deliberations and actions. These systems allow users to build maps of situations and convey, in a somewhat stylized form, compact interpretations which can be utilized to share the meaning of past experience, and as platforms for simulating future events. More in general, simulation software can be utilized to accumulate substitute *past experience*, that is to enlarge the pool of because-of motives which can be tapped for new projects of action. Finally, systems, still to be designed, could act as dynamic mirrors of ongoing experience, help users to be better aware of the context and situations in which they are immersed at the moment of action (Ciborra and Lanzara, 1994), and enable them to engage in activities that transcend such contexts (double-loop learning).

The systems mentioned so far seem to support and enable the trade of functions between mind, body, and task environment which emerged at the outset of our study of improvisation. They support mainly the externalization of functions from the mind (memory) and the body (movement in space and time) into electronic artefacts. Note that such systems can represent forms of indirect control (Perrow, 1986) on improvisation, precisely by their influence on the premises of decision-making, on the 'formative context' (Unger, 1987) out of which improvisation emerges. Finally, consider how the design of these systems is regulated by criteria that go beyond the issues of efficiency. The *answers* one can get from these systems are open and point to a multiplicity of meanings. They do not convey a single meaning, nor do they comply with a single efficiency criterion. Rather, they deliver a variety of possible meanings and criteria out of which, in the here and now of the action, one can select an ad hoc criterion best suited for the circumstances. Efficiency criteria become part of the interpretative bundle that is associated with the circumstances. Such flexibility makes these systems preserve adaptability and openness (Hewitt, 1991).

Conclusion

The challenge which improvisation sets for our conceptions of decision-making, information, and systems consists in abandoning the neat but artificial world of models, structures, and univocal meanings and entering the world of the ordinary, of sense-making and experience in the every-day life of organisations. The increasing complexity and rate of change of circumstances put strain on and limit planning and structure in decision-making. Correspondingly, we have pointed to a family of system solutions which does not consist of *more sophisticated techniques* or *more structured systems*, rather of systems and applications that focus on a ubiquitous practice in mundane situations: improvisation. Such a practice plays an import-ant role in complex economic institutions. Instead of trying to eradicate it through automation, we should more modestly appreciate its flexibility and effectiveness, and thus try to support/enable it, albeit indirectly. By trusting the role of improvisation, our chances to make sense of complex situations increase and we are in closer touch with human experience when developing and using systems. If we want to improve the effectiveness of IT in organisations, and society at large, due consideration for the role played by improvisation in human affairs advises us to stay more attached to those everyday micro-practices and means developed by mankind over the centuries to survive. Indeed, behind competent improvisation one can find work practices or operational logics that go as far back as the age-old ruses of fishes and insects, of fishermen and sailors (De Ceretau, 1984). Information systems to support improvisation should not just provide functionalities which allow users to interact with systems in a more intuit-ive way (Winograd, 1995), rather they should be designed to enable *tout court* the free exercise of intuition and ingenuity in daily affairs.

References

Ackerman, M. S., and Malone, T. W. (1990), Answer Garden: A Tool for Growing Organisational Memory', in *Proceedings of ACM Conference on Office Information Systems, Cambridge, MA, April.*

Agre, P. E. (1993), 'The Symbolic Worldview: Reply to Vera and Simon', *Cognitive Science,* 17: 61–9.

Andreu, R., and Ciborra, C. U. (1995), 'Core Capabilities and Information Tech-nology: An Organisational Learning Approach, *EFMD Review,* 1: 37–43.

Argyris, C., and Schön, D. A. (1978), *Organisational Learning: A Theory of Action Perspective* (Reading, Mass.: Addison-Wesley).

Barnard, C. (1938), *The Functions of the Executive* (Cambridge, Mass.: Harvard Univer-sity Press).

Bergson, H. (1927), *Essai sur les données immédiates de la conscience* (Paris: Presses Universitaires de France).

Brown, J. S., and Duguid, P. (1991), 'Organisational Learning and Communities of Practice', *Organisation Science*, 2, 1: 40–57.

Ciborra, C. U. (1993), *Teams, Markets and Systems* (Cambridge: Cambridge University Press).

—— (1994), 'From Thinking to Tinkering: The Grassroots of Strategic Information Systems', in C. U. Ciborra and T. Jelassi, *Strategic Information Systems: A European Perspective* (London: Wiley).

—— and Lanzara, G. F. (1994), 'Formative Contexts and Information Systems: Understanding the Dynamics of Innovation in Organisations, *Accounting, Management and Information Systems*, Dec., 2, 4: 61–86.

Clancey, W. J. (1995), *Situated Cognition: On Human Knowledge and Computer Representations* (Cambridge: Cambridge University Press).

Conklin J. E., and Begeman, M. L. (1988), 'gIBIS: A Hypertext Tool for Exploratory Policy Discussion', *Proceedings of CSCW 88, Portland, OR, September*.

Cronk, R. D. (1993), 'Unlocking Data's Content', *Byte*, Sept.: 111–20.

De Certeau, M. (1984), *The Practice of Everyday Life* (Berkeley and Los Angeles: University of California Press).

Daft, R. L., and Weick, K. E. (1984), 'Toward a Model of Organisations as Interpretation Systems, *Academy of Management Review*, 9, 2: 284–95.

Deryfus, H. L., and Dreyfus, S. E. (1985), *Mind over Machine* (New York: Macmillan).

Encarta Encyclopedia (1994), Microsoft.

Galbraith, J. (1977), *Organisation Design* (Reading, Mass.: Addison-Wesley).

Garfinkel, H. (1974), 'The Rational Properties of Scientific and Common-Sense Activities', in A. Giddens (ed.), *Positivism and Sociology* (London: Heinemann).

Gasser, L. (1991), 'Social Conceptions of Knowledge and Action: DAI Foundations and Open Systems Semantics', *Artificial Intelligence*, 47: 107–38.

Gerson, E. M., and Star, S. L. (1986), 'Analyzing Due Process in the Workplace', *ACM Transactions on Office Information Systems*, 4, 3: 257–70.

Gibson, J. J. (1977), 'The Theory of Affordances', in R. E. Shaw and J. Bransford (eds.), *Perceiving, Acting, and Knowing* (Hillsdale, NJ: Erlbaum).

Goodwin, C., and Goodwin, M. (1993), 'Formulating Planes: Seeing as Situated Activity', in Y. Engestrom and D. Middleton (eds.), *Communication and Cognition at Work* (New York: Cambridge University Press).

Hayek, F. (1945), 'The Use of Knowledge in Society', *American Economic Review*, 35: 519–30.

Heiner, R. (1983), 'The Origin of Predictable Behavior', *American Economic Review*, Sept., 73, 4: 560–95.

Hewitt, C. E. (1991), 'Open Information Systems Semantics for Distributed Artificial Intelligence', *Artificial Intelligence*, 79–106.

Huber, G. P. (1990), 'A Theory of the Effects of Advanced Information Technology on Organisation Design, Intelligence and Decision Making', *Academy of Management Review*, 15: 47–71.

Husserl, E. (1962), *Ideas* (New York: Collier Books).

—— (1970), *The Crisis of European Sciences and Transcendental Phenomenology* (Evanston, Ill.: Northwestern University Press).

Knight, F. H. (1964), *Risk, Uncertainty, and Profit* (New York: A. M. Kelley).

Lanzara, G. F. (1983), 'Ephemeral Organisations in Extreme Environments: Emergence, Strategy, Extinction', *Journal of Management Studies*, 20: 71–95.

Lave, J. (1988), *Cognition in Practice* (New York: Cambridge University Press).

—— and Wenger, E. (1991), *Situated Learning: Legitimate Peripheral Participation* (Cambridge: Cambridge University Press).

Lévi-Strauss, C. (1966), *The Savage Mind* (Chicago: Chicago University Press).

March, J. G. (1991), 'Exploration and Exploitation in Organisational Learning', *Organisation Science*, 2, 1, Feb.: 71–87.

—— and Simon, H. A. (1958), *Organisations* (New York: Wiley).

Nelson, R. R., and Winter, S. G. (1982), *An Evolutionary Theory of Economic Change* (Cambridge, Mass.: Harvard University Press).

Newell, A., and Simon, H. A.(1972), *Human Problem Solving* (Englewood Cliffs, NJ: Prentice Hall).

Newman,W. M., Eldridge, M., and Lamming, M. G. (1991), 'Pepys: Generating autobiographies by automatic tracking', *Proceedings E-CSCW 91* (Amsterdam, Kluwer).

Nonaka, I. (1994), 'A Dynamic Theory of Organisational Knowledge Creation', *Organisation Science*, 5, 1: 14–37.

Norman, D. (1988), *The Psychology of Everyday Things* (New York: Basic).

Orr, J. (1990), 'Sharing Knowledge, Celebrating Identity: War Stories and Community Memory in Service Culture', in D. S. Middleton and D. Edwards (eds.), *Collective Remembering: Memory in Society* (London: Sage).

Pentland, B. T. (1992), 'Organizing Moves in Software Support Hot Lines', *Administrative Science Quarterly*, 37: 527–48.

Perrow, C. (1986), *Complex Organisations: A Critical Essay*, 3rd edn. (New York: Random House).

Polany, M. (1962), *Personal Knowledge* (London, Routledge).

Press, L. (1992), 'Personal Computing: Collective Dynabase', *Communications of the ACM*, June: 26–32.

Robinson, M. (1993), 'Design for Unanticipated Use . . .', in G. De Michelis et al. (eds.), *Proceedings of the Third European Conference on CSCW* (Dordrecht: Kluwer).

Rosaldo, R. (1985) 'While Making Other Plans', *Southern California Law Review*, 58, 19: 19–28.

Schön, D. A. (1983), *The Reflective Practitioner* (New York: Basic Books).

Schutz, A. (1967), *The Phenomenology of the Social World* (Evanston, Ill.: Northwestern University Press).

Scribner, S. (1984), 'Studying Working Intelligence', in B. Rogoff and J. Lave (eds.), *Everyday Cognition* (Cambridge, Mass.: Harvard University Press).

Simon, H. A. (1965), *The Shape of Automation* (New York: Harper & Row).

—— (1976), *Administrative Behavior*, 3rd edn. (New York: Free Press).

Stein, E. W., and Zwass, V. (1995), 'Actualizing Organisational Memory with Information Systems', *Information Systems Research*, 6, 1.

Suchman, L. A. (1983), 'Office Procedures as Practical Action: Models of Work and System Design', *ACM Transactions on Office Information Systems*, 1, 4: 320–28.

—— (1987), *Plans and Situated Actions: The Problem of Human–Machine Communication* (New York: Cambridge University Press).

Sudnow, D. (1978), *Ways of the Hand: The Organisation of Improvised Conduct* (London: Routledge & Kegan Paul).

Unger, R. M. (1987), *False Necessity* (Cambridge: Cambridge University Press).

Vera, A. H., and Simon, H. A. (1993), 'Situated Action: A Symbolic Interpretation', *Cognitive Science*, 17: 7–48.

Weber, M. (1964), *The Theory of Social and Economic Organisation* (New York: Free Press).

Webster (1973), *Collegiate Dictionary* (Springfield, Mass.: Merriam Co.).

Weick, K. E. (1979), *The Social Psychology of Organizing*, 2nd edn. (Reading, Mass.: Addison-Wesley).

—— (1985), 'Cosmos vs. Chaos: Sense and Nonsense in Electronic Contexts', *Organisational Dynamics*, Autumn: 51–64.

—— (1993*a*), 'Organisation Redesign as Improvisation', in G. P. Huber and W. H. Glick (eds.), *Organisational Change and Redesign* (New York: Oxford University Press).

—— (1993*b*), 'The Collapse of Sense-making in Organisations: The Mann Gulch Disaster', *Administrative Science Quarterly*, 38, 4: 628–52.

Weiser, M. (1991), 'The Computer for the 21st Century', *Scientific American*, 265: 94–105.

Winograd, T. (1995), 'From Programming Environments to Environments for Design', *Communications of the ACM* 38, 6: 65–74.

—— and Flores, F. (1986), *Understanding Computers and Cognition* (Norwood, NJ: Ablex).

Wynn, E. S. (1979), 'Office Conversation as an Information Medium', Ph.D. thesis, Berkeley, University of California.

Zimmerman, D. (1973), 'The Practicalities of Rule Use', in G. Salaman and K. Thompson (eds.), *People and Organisations* (London: Longman).

Zuboff, S. (1988), *In the Age of the Smart Machine* (New York: Basic Books).

PART II

Information Systems, Strategic Management, and Performance Evaluation

Introduction

In this section, we consider four contributions which broadly cover one of the above two themes of strategic management and performance evaluation in the context of information systems. Within management research, the subject of corporate strategy has been of immense interest to researchers within the IS field. This is also true when we look at the rich contributions from finance and accounting which consider the behavioural aspects of accounting and information systems and performance measurement and evaluation. In fact, some of the more interesting and critical research over the last decade which is relevant to IS has originated from the finance and accounting discipline compared with less critical contributions from the strategy field, many of which are derivative from the earlier work of Michael Porter.

Key debates within the strategy area have focused upon the relationship between competitive advantage and IT, and in some ways, an unholy alliance has developed between these terms.[1] The origins of the link between strategy and technology may be traced back to the popular paper by Kantrow in *Harvard Business Review* in 1980, on 'The Strategy–Technology Connection'.[2] More recently, writers have considered the issue of strategic alignment and IT,[3] arguing that, since technology is no longer just a traditional back office support function, and is now an integral part of an organisation's activities, it should be included in the overall corporate strategy.

Our first chapter by Michael Earl considers 'Strategy-Making in the Information Age'. Here, he argues that society is transforming from an industrial economy towards an information economy. This is marked by the emergence of major new technological and informational changes such as the Internet, electronic commerce, voice and data networks. He claims that it is now 'just about possible to claim that every business is an information business'. *Infopreneurs* is a term used to describe those who

---

[1] W. Currie (1995), *Management Strategy for IT* (London: Pitman).

[2] A. M. Kantrow (1980), 'The Strategy–Technology Connection', *Harvard Business Review*, 58, 4, July–Aug.: 1–21.

[3] J. C. Henderson, and N. Venkatraman (1994), 'Strategic Alignment: A Model for Organizational Transformation via Information Technology', in T. J. Allen and M. Scott-Morton (eds.), *IT and the Corporation of the 1990s* (Oxford: Oxford University Press).

exploit the information and information service sectors for profit-making in this new age.

In her chapter provocatively entitled 'Thinking the Unthinkable: What Happens if the IS Field as we Know it Goes away?', Lynne Markus discusses the strategic position of the subject within the academic IS (AIS) field. To reiterate the issues posed in the preface to this volume, the state of IS in some academic institutions worldwide is rather parlous. Views vary as to whether IS is a discipline in its own right or merely an adjunct to mainstream management or computing. What is evident is a lack of consensus about the role of IS within the academic community. She calls for an expanded research agenda for IS which encapsulates both the behavioural and technical issues within the AIS community.

Our third chapter is in the realm of performance evaluation of IS and looks at three major empirical research projects undertaken by Barbara Farbey, Frank Land, and David Targett over the last decade. They suggest that although financial investment in IS/IT in the UK is considerable, the *productivity paradox* demonstrates that greater productivity and shareholder value is not necessarily positively correlated with higher investment. The authors cover a comprehensive range of literature on IS evaluation and explore the reasons why few organisations conduct ongoing rigorous evaluation of their IS/IT resource.

In the final chapter in this section, Dick Boland focuses attention on the construction and use of accounting representations (income statements, balance sheets, funds flow statements, budgets, and cost statements) as a distinctive body of research for which the IS field has few offerings. He traces the use of accounting practices used for management control of organisations back to the thirteenth century in English manor farms. The factory cost accounting and budgeting analysis used in industrial firms several centuries later were similar to those used today. He demonstrates the distinctive features of management accounting and information systems research respectively and argues that the 'craft of representation is an integral part of accounting practice'.

The chapters presented in Part II are diverse in topic and scope, yet offer a rich analysis of issues relating to the strategic management and performance evaluation of IS. What emerges strongly from these discussions is that both IS as a discipline within business and management, and IS as an organisational and management tool, are continually being evaluated, often using measures and techniques which are no longer applicable or relevant. Whilst our contributors are unable to offer definitive answers to many pertinent questions, the various discussions offer a detailed analysis of past, present, and possible future developments. Such discussions are therefore relevant in Part III where we explore the development and implementation of change programmes.

7

Strategy-Making in the Information Age

MICHAEL J. EARL

The Information Age

Most scholars might agree that we are by now well on our way through the transition from an industrial economy to an information economy. The convergence of computing, telecommunications, and software is not only enabling new forms of competition and organisation to evolve, but the digital convergence of various states of information—data, text, voice, graphics, audio, and video—is also spawning new business opportunities and new ways of communicating. Only the most reclusive Luddite could argue that business and economic activity today is untouched by information technology.

Indeed, it is just about possible (at least in a reorienting volume like this) to claim that every business is an information business. Managers always spent much of their time on information processing, broadly defined, according to Mintzberg (1973) and Stewart (1982) and now often do so mediated by technology in the form of executive information systems, groupware, video-conferencing, and the like. Organisations have been seen in the past as forms of information processing (Galbraith, 1973) and now have gathered technocratic descriptors like 'networked', 'knowledge based', and 'virtual' as telecommunications in particular have been deployed to co-ordinate remote workers or share information across enterprises. Business processes increasingly are information-systems dependent and are being 're-engineered' (Davenport and Short, 1990; Hammer, 1990), partly by asking, what can IT allow us to do which was not possible before in terms of time compression, co-ordination, integration, automation, and communication? And at least in my institution would-be entrepreneurs are turning to the information and information service sectors as their potential arenas for profit-making. This new breed might be called 'infopreneurs' (Earl, 1996).

Every Business is an Information Business

There is, however, another more telling trend. Industrial sectors also are converging. We see telecommunications companies, entertainment

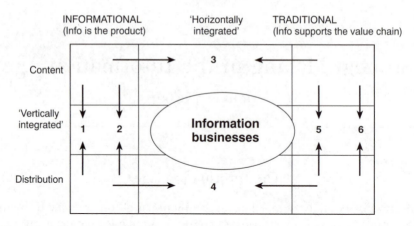

F I G. 7.1 *Information business convergence*

companies, and software companies merging or creating alliances to form the 'infotainment' sector as the information superhighway begins to take shape. Indeed we now talk about 'Silicon Alley' as well as 'Silicon Valley'. Perhaps these always were information businesses, but the classification looks more robust now. In the same way, publishing houses or advertising companies link up with database providers and electronic distribution channels as both the content and context of the media change. More surprisingly, perhaps, pharmaceutical companies buy prescription processing companies and health care management organisations for their information potential in diagnostic work, drug discovery, and treatment. And retailers, transportation companies, and oil companies fight for, or collaborate in, customer and market share to gain consumer information. The list goes on.

Fig. 7.1 attempts to show that in businesses we historically would have classified as traditional or informational, various forms of horizontal and vertical integration are occurring, explained by an information thread. To keep the matrix clean, I only suggest a few examples. However, these and many other companies are recognising that they are information businesses.

Viacom's acquisition of Blockbuster (1) is a channel acquiring content. Disney's acquisition of the ABC (2) is the reverse. Horizontally we can see Microsoft's agreements with Dreamworks (3) and NBC (4) as a business comprising both content and channel acquiring respectively content and distribution from the informational side. On the traditional side, vertical integration is evidenced by Smith Kline Beecham's acquisition of Diversified Prescriptions Management (5) for prescription patterns and practice information. On the customer card alliance front, Sainsbury's (a retailer) deal with British Airways (6) potentially opens up the information pool to both parties.

While this might be a useful description of events in the corporate world, it has deeper implications at the level of the firm. Put simply, it suggests that firms need to have an information business mindset in their strategy-making. This in practice raises at least three issues for business strategy-making:

1. Information technology developments, threats, and opportunities have to be included in strategy formation.
2. The value creation potential of information has to be included in strategy formation.
3. The future has to be brought back into strategy-making in order to analyse, anticipate, and prepare for the information age.

Information Business Strategy

It is not the first time that a claim has been made that IT considerations should be included in strategy-making. Kantrow argued this in a rather crusading abstract way in 1980 and it was implied by the early 1980s articles on IT and competitive advantage (McFarlan, 1981; Porter and Millar, 1985). There is modest attention to technology in the mainstream business strategy literature (McGee and Thomas, 1989) and in the MIS or information management field, the last fifteen years or so have seen considerable interest in strategy, particularly information systems strategy formulation. This is not surprising. The IT function has to grapple with far from trivial problems in constructing information systems strategic plans. Unavailability or poor clarity of business plans and strategies, low awareness of IT capabilities, rapid business and environmental change, weak managerial involvement, and a plethora of implementation problems are among the problems identified by McFarlan (1981), A. L. Lederer and V. Sethi (1988), Galliers (1991), Earl (1993)—and others.

Most of this research and the on the ground efforts of practitioners can be seen (Fig. 7.2) as concern with the 'alignment problem'. The business question being pursued is what information systems and IT investments are required to support the business strategy. (The strategic alignment model of Henderson and Venkatraman (1989) took a somewhat broader and more conceptual view than this.) Probably over 90 per cent of organisational activity in IT strategy-making has focused on this question.

A second, complementary question which seems to receive only occasional or sometimes accidental attention is 'the opportunity problem'. This is concerned with what opportunities for doing business differently are presented by IT. The 'IT for competitive advantage' articles referred to earlier highlighted the question and some writers offered techniques of opportunity search (Wiseman, 1988; Ives and Learmonth, 1984). Others,

Michael J. Earl

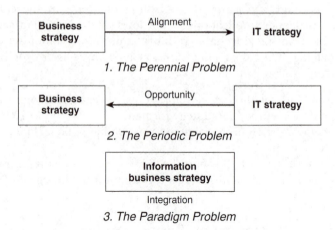

1. *The Perennial Problem*

2. *The Periodic Problem*

3. *The Paradigm Problem*

FIG. 7.2. *The evolution of IT strategy-making*

based on field research, adopted a more processual perspective (Runge, 1985; Lockett 1996; Ives and Vitale, 1996) often drawing on, or parallel-ing studies on, innovation. Perhaps some of the business re-engineering literature has contributed to this domain; for example Hammer and Champy (1993) talk of the need for 'inductive thinking' or the ability first to recognise a powerful solution and then to seek the problems it [an IT application] might solve.

The third perspective in Fig. 7.2 argues differently. If every business is an information business, perhaps it is unhelpful to think of a business strat-egy *and* an IT strategy. Perhaps they should be one: an integrated informa-tion business strategy.[1] Here business strategy becomes a statement of intent about the future, much as advanced by Hamel and Prahalad (1994) and Hamel (1996). More than this, however, the business threats and oppor-tunities posed by IT and information resources more widely are addressed and worked out in the strategy-making process. So the future becomes an explicit vision of the information age.

The remainder of this article addresses this third perspective, more particularly how to craft an information business strategy. In the spirit of Fig. 7.1, it assumes all businesses—informational or traditional (a dichot-omy which now should seem historical and somewhat false)—should have one. The ideas are drawn from an ongoing investigation into how firms formulate IT-based business strategies. The research is not complete, but the ideas here have been prompted by the actions, experiments, and

[1] As an aside, in my 1993 work on IS strategic planning, the seemingly most successful companies—those that adopted the "organisational approach"—often had either just a busi-ness strategy with IT references in it or no formal business or IT strategy at all, but a theme which captured how the company was trying to win.

experiences of corporations in the UK and USA. Why I suggest in Fig. 7.2 that information business strategy-making is a paradigm problem is left to the conclusion.

Crafting Information Futures

I am about to offer a high-level methodology. This may seem odd for one who has previously stressed the importance of process in strategic information systems planning and where in the organisational approach (1993) which I advocated method was not overly important. My purpose here however is to bring together a number of steps which I have seen practised by the companies I have studied and which seem to be helpful. No one company has followed this methodology or procedure or adopted all of the steps; it is an amalgam of ideas—except that perhaps one or two firms followed it intuitively or implicitly.

I am about to be bold—even outrageous! (If one cannot do so in a 'new directions' volume like this, when can one?) The methodology to be advanced is a six-step procedure with a convenient acronym: AVENIR. Coincidentally (I can see the sceptics, cynics, and iconoclasts reaching for their swords), French speakers will recognise that this translates into 'future'. However, I have been impressed by those companies who have analysed future trends, painted a plausible future for themselves, taken steps towards building that future—and recognised that the future is also uncertain. To those like me who originally were taught that business strategy-making is about the future, it is a welcome turn of the cycle after the competitive immediacy of Porter-like (1980) product-market analysis, the general management grand theories of resource-building (Wernerfelt, 1984), and the bureaucratic models of strategic planning (Ansoff, 1987; Vancil and Lorange, 1977).

The first step of AVENIR (Fig. 7.3) is *Analysis,* unsurprising and in some ways comprising an even older acronym or model. There are three possible components. To begin, it can be helpful to identify and codify agreed business trends—about markets, products, competitors, regulation, and the like—not only to link any future picture with today and the past, but also to convey almost always a sense of change, for few firms are enjoying static environments. The obvious aim is, however, to identify and agree any substantial force for change which is likely to continue for some years and/or become more significant. The equally important reason is because few executives have faith in the analysis of, or plans for, the future which are not grounded in the present.

The second component of analysis is identifying and agreeing mega trends—to borrow Naisbitt's (1990) term—into the future. This, of course, impels the firm to identify its strategic horizon. I have come across a range

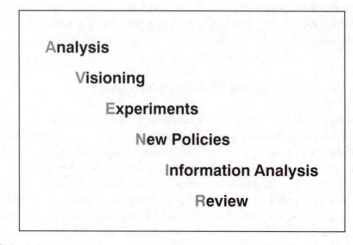

Analysis

Visioning

Experiments

New Policies

Information Analysis

Review

FIG. 7.3. *Information business strategy-making*

of time frames in my investigations: the furthest out is twenty-five years and the shortest is five years. It is here where the old acronym applies: PEST. In other words, we seek mega trends in the political, economic, social, and technological environments. By technological we mean not just IT; for pharmaceutical companies it clearly includes biotechnology; for many manufacturing companies, material sciences.

The third component is information technology forecasting. For information business strategy-making this is a *sine qua non*. The aim is to identify both breakthrough technologies and killer applications. The longer the time frame under analysis, there is a frustrating paradox. Some technological possibilities will have become commonplace, some will have been rejected or overtaken, and some will not have been identified at all. The early history of IT forecasting was not promising; pundits tended to get both the directions and the timing wrong. In the nearer time horizons, however, some sensible practices are possible. A recent pilot survey of UK firms (Earl, 1996) found that primary 'research and development' outperformed secondary or vicarious learning. For example study tours of labs and state of the art adopters, technology development projects with vendors, and technology pilots were rated more effective than scanning literature, attending exhibitions and conferences, and volunteering Beta-test sites. Furthermore since a breakthrough technology or killer application is somewhat firm or industry specific, managements may have to see a new or emerging technology, try it, and learn about it for themselves.

The output of the analysis phase is an agreed set of trends which together could either (*a*) threaten the future of the business or (*b*) provide an avenue to explore for creating new value in the future or competing differently. What is striking about analyses which appear to have helped firms paint a future to invest in is that they are combinatorial; there is something about the future political, economic, or social domain which when combined with a technology trend suggests an information future that must be addressed. An example is a pharmaceutical company's identification of various forms of tele-medicine offering ways of mitigating the effects of, or bypassing, increasing regulatory constraints and also reaching an ageing population.

Who does the analysis? Staff planners can do much of the initial trend analysis and also codify the eventual outputs. However senior general and line executives must debate and agree the trends and significant combinations in order to add relevance and achieve buy-in. If primary IT forecasting is done, it is paramount that business executives take part; again to bring relevance but also to prompt learning and cultivate enthusiasm.

The principal purpose of analysis is to inform and influence the second, substantially creative step of AVENIR, namely, *Visioning*. Here some companies seem to construct powerful scenarios of the future. These are not alternative pictures or scenarios drawn up by staff planners to inform the routine business planning process, as practised by Shell in the past (Wack, 1985). They are discrete, clear, believable statements of the business to be in, or more often how business will be done, in the future. They will be pursued and invested in; thus they are not options or alternatives but descriptive statements of intent. Importantly, they will not have been possible without exploiting information and technology. For the pharmaceutical company mentioned above, a scenario could be the provision of remote or home-based surgeries. For an apparel manufacturer it could be interactive customer-driven design of bespoke outerwear.

Visioning, or scenario imagining, then, is usually led by analysis. Next, the scope of scenarios has to be agreed: for example are we tackling products and services or market and customer reach or business scope or distribution and selling? And what is the time frame? Scoping is necessary to help participants focus on manageable domains. Participants will be general and line executives, perhaps with planners, definitely with IT executives, and possibly aided by outside catalysts and gurus. However, it seems important not to crowd out inspirations, wild ideas, pet projects, and borrowed visions at this stage. But it is useful to test them against the outcomes of the earlier analysis stage.

A potentially valuable scenario seems to paint a picture in words. It becomes more plausible when it is examined for what it says about the positioning of the firm, the capabilities needed, possible partnerships required, and next steps that can be taken. Incidentally, threatening scenarios can be as informative as positive ones. Schoemaker (1995) has some valuable advice on the properties of good scenarios or visions including that they are seen to 'ring true' by the firm's executives and that they will endure for some time.

Those companies that then translate scenarios or visions into action, rather than file them away as planning documents, commonly *Experiment*. In other words, the next step of AVENIR is to build stepping stones towards the future. A stepping stone is an experiment which takes the scenario forward but does not 'bet the farm'. It tests an idea, starts to build a capability, or tries an intermediate learning approach. A firm can go forwards, sideways, or backwards from the stepping stone, rather like crossing a turbulent river. Rarely are the first steps to implement the vision or scenario the end-game; they are moves towards an end which is not perfectly envisioned or known. Stepping stones comprise not only technology developments, but experiments in products, markets, channels, and organisation.

Commonly, these experiments require alliances, joint ventures, or acquisitions to assemble infrastructure, capture information content, build electronic distribution channels, develop information age skills, or make market entries to be able to achieve the scenario. So stepping stones may not be small; it is only when they become classified as 'mega-deals' that shareholders worry.

Simpler experiments include ventures on the Internet which may create revenue, but more likely yield learning for doing business on future embodiments of the information superhighway. And some of the firms I have studied have invested in alternative or complementary channels and infrastructures in order to understand the characteristics of those which are likely to be adopted or survive and to take stakes should ownership or participation opportunities become limited.

More obvious experiments are proactive development of new technologies with vendors and laboratories. Examples I have recorded include a bank working on new encryption techniques, a brewer developing gaming machines, and an airline developing new in-flight shopping technology.

Not all experiments are technical. Paul Allen, co-founder of Microsoft, has set up Interval Research at Palo Alto where multidisciplinary teams act out life on superhighways in order to discover possible future product and service needs. Team members include software developers, electrical engineers, VR designers, and videographers together with anthropologists, musicians, artists, writers, and actors. Clearly this is also one way of scenario-building. On a more modest scale, we see companies building their own experimental IT workshops, cybercafés, and exploration spaces.

An accompanying step often is the formulation of *New Policies*. Crafting strategies for the information age frequently involves a change in corporate mindset, together with agreement on the need to build new capabilities. Four policy areas have been addressed by the companies under study. One is a new frame of reference on information, usually recognising the value of information. For example an advertising agency revisited its practice in releasing copy; old advertisements could be a source of revenue in new channels. A bank debated how much it could afford in data storage to preserve possible experience content in the mass of transactions accumulated each day. An insurance company redefined agreements with allies and intermediaries to include two-way information-sharing.

A second policy area is technology. Here we can be reassessing postures on risk and coverage of emerging technologies. Firms who are building information futures often find that they have to break policy rules of the past; in a few technologies, they have to be 'leading edge'. Others find that redefining themselves as information businesses means building new capabilities in technologies they previously thought they would buy and learn later on when they were mature.

Related to this challenge is the third key policy change: acquisition and development of human resources. An advertising company seeks new hybrids of creative/multi-media professionals. A pharmaceutical company is considering hybrids combining IT and biotechnology. And we can foresee some creative companies being bought by more technocratic companies for their artistic talent.

Because these policy steps tend to be radical and also because some of the experimental actions mentioned above are a departure from 'business as usual', some corporations have set up new divisions, business units, or lines of business through which to build their new futures. This is the fourth new policy area: new organisation. It is not yet clear that this is essential for success, but if creating the future is about rule-breaking, rather than rule-making or rule-taking, to use Hamel's (1996) distinction, then creating a new ventures division may be an appropriate way to encourage and not impede risk-taking, entrepreneurship, and radical policy-making.

Another analytical step in the AVENIR model employed by some companies is *Information Analysis*. This is the search for value-generation opportunities in information content or information processing. To use the language of Rayport and Sviokla (1995), this activity assumes not that information systems are required just to support the functioning of the value chain, but that information flows in the value chain can be a source of value too. Rayport and Sviokla talk of virtual value chains and information value chains. The latter recognise five possible steps in the way information can generate value:

- gather;
- organise;
- select;
- synthesise;
- distribute;

Fig. 7.4 shows how one pharmaceutical company employed information analysis in decomposing critical stages of the traditional value chain into three, not five, information activities: acquisition (which is meant to raise awareness not just of information which can be captured, but that which

Michael J. Earl

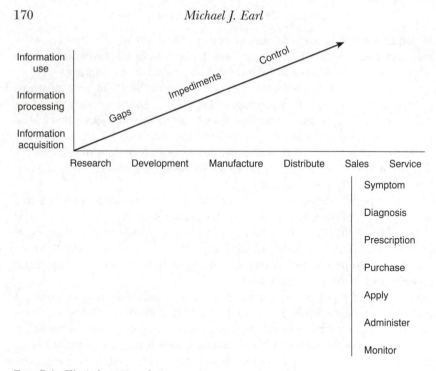

FIG. 7.4. *The information chain*

should not be lost); processing (which could include the above steps of organizing, selecting, synthesising, and distributing); and use (which covers correct use but also potential value-adding or creating use). I label these *Information chains.*

The important point is that without explicit attention to value creation by information resources, futures only of a technologically enabled kind may be envisioned. If information is the thread which provides the synergy between the alliances and mergers described in the information business matrix of Fig. 7.1, then such information analysis is one way of analysing threats and opportunities. Indeed since this is an 'ideas paper', let us also coin the term *Information Threads* as the basis of diversification and acquisition in the information age and a source of synergy across the corporation.

If this is so, then information chain analysis also must look at extended value chains (value system according to Porter, 1980, and business network according to Short and Venkatraman, 1992), which incorporate actual and potential customers, suppliers, rivals, and allies. We then see why airlines do deals with retailers, banks, and hoteliers, why pharmaceutical companies buy medical equipment and service companies, and why sports coverage agencies do deals with news corporations and on-line service companies.

Finally, future trend analysis is uncertain; visions and scenarios are partly imagination; experiments fail, new policies hit buffers, and information is full of surprises and so all strategies for the future must be *Reviewed*. There are at least two review questions. The first is to review the economic case for, and benefits of, the future which is being built or developed. In all strategic investments, two characteristics are common. Management often 'moves the goalposts'; the initial rationale or aim is forgotten and harsher management criteria are introduced. This can never be stopped altogether; after all *ex ante* justification cases are often emotional and *ex post* ones are liable to be so too. However, the role of sponsors and champions is critical in maintaining strategic investments. We have documented one major information futures venture by a financial institution which was aborted by the main board. The director who had been the sponsor apparently never passed on the decision to the venture team who carried on their experiment regardless. Today the experiment is a new line of business for that institution and its partners. An alternative, more rational tactic is to try and continue the experiment on a smaller scale.

A learning review is the other necessity. Whatever the economic outcome, there are likely to be lessons to share, including learning on consumer behaviour, technology adoption, information quality, regulating context, and internal skills. Indeed since most early investments for the future are experiments or stepping stones, we expect to step backwards or sideways sometimes—but we also were planning to learn. Clearly, the review process is as much the responsibility of general management as of the line executives and specialists involved.

Beyond AVENIR

AVENIR is a convenient acronym to organise five steps identified in some businesses who have set out to be prepared for and prosper in the information age. It is unlikely to be complete and it will not cover all successful case histories. At this stage it is a deposit of ideas suggested and prompted by fairly unstructured investigation of both 'informational' and 'traditional' businesses as well as analysis of related literature. There is a research agenda prompted by this work.

The very obvious questions include (1) deeper understanding of the process of crafting futures, especially where information and technology are involved; (2) development and assessment of techniques used in this process; and (3) guidance on roles and skills required. This may be a research domain where strategic management and information management academics can collaborate.[2]

---

[2] As a member of a strategy group myself, I expect some robust reactions to this chapter—well beyond the draft stage.

For practice, there are at least implications. Whether business strategy or IT strategy has been the concern hitherto, there could be merit in pursuing formulation of an information business strategy as conceived here. This again could require collaboration, this time between CIOs and IT executives on the one hand and strategic planners and general managers on the other. Indeed in a show of hands at a recent CIO conference in the USA, I found about 30 per cent of CIOs were being invited into business strategy-making for the first time. Third, AVENIR provides a framework for those companies taking up the challenge of information business strategy-making.

In Fig. 7.2, I suggested that this challenge represented a paradigm problem. I conclude this chapter with seven observations from my own research in, and work with, companies on the nature of the paradigm shift required in strategic management. Information business strategy is typified by the following:

- It confronts the FUTURE . . . which executives find uncomfortable.
- It centres on INFORMATION . . . which is a neglected, complex resource.
- It requires some TECHNOLOGY-LED thinking . . . which worries the risk-averse.
- It benefits from BOLD ACTIONS . . . which can go wrong.
- It needs creativity and IMAGINATION . . . which is not the planning tradition.
- It should involve the IT FUNCTION . . . which is not normal.
- It is based on FAITH in the information age . . . which has been asked for before.

A few companies have 'bitten these bullets' and are seeing returns. More are recognising that time is running out. There could hardly be a more exciting agenda for executives—or for strategy and information management researchers.

References

Ansoff, H. (1987), *The Concept of Corporate Strategy* (Homewood, Ill.: Irwin).

Davenport, T. H., and Short, J. E. (1990), 'The New Industrial Engineering: Information Technology and Business Process Redesign', *Sloan Management Review*, 31, 4: 11–21.

Earl, M. J. (1993), 'Experiences in Strategic Information Systems Planning', *MIS Quarterly*, 17, 1: 1–24.

—— (1996), *The Practices of Large Corporations in Understanding New Technologies: A Pilot Survey*, CRIM Working Paper 96/5 (London: Centre for Research in Information Management, London Business School).

Galbraith, J. (1973), *Designing Complex Organisations* (Reading, Mass.: Addison-Wesley).

Galliers, R. D. (1991), 'Strategic Information Systems Planning: Myths, Reality and Guidelines for Successful Implementation', *European Journal of Information Systems*, 1, 1: 55–64.

Hamel, G. (1996), 'Strategy as Revolution', *Harvard Business Review*, 74, 4, July–Aug.: 69–71.

—— and Prahalad, C. K. (1994), 'Competing for the Future', *Harvard Business Review*, 72, 4, July–Aug.: 122–8.

Hammer, M. (1990), 'Reengineering Work: Don't Automate, Obliterate', *Harvard Business Review*, July–Aug.: 68, 4: 104–12.

—— and Champy, J. (1993), *Reengineering the Corporation: A Manifesto for Business Revolution* (New York: Harper Press).

Henderson, J. C., and Venkatraman, N. (1989), *Strategic Alignment: A Framework for Strategic Information Technology Management*, CISR Working Paper No. 190 (Cambridge, Mass.: Centre for Information Systems Research, Massachusetts Institute of Technology).

Ives, B., and Learmonth, G. P. (1984), 'The Information System as a Competitive Weapon', *Communications of the ACM* 27, 12, Dec.: 1193–1201.

—— and Vitale, M. (1996), 'Strategic Information Systems: Some Organisational Design Considerations', in M. J. Earl (ed.), *Information Management: The Organisational Dimension* (Oxford: Oxford University Press).

Kantrow, A. M. (1980), 'The Strategy–Technology Connection', *Harvard Business Review*, July–Aug.: 1–21.

Lederer, A. L., and Sethi, V. (1988), 'The Implementation of Strategic Information Systems Planning Methodologies', *MIS Quarterly*, 12, 3 (Sept.): 444–61.

Lockett, M. (1996), 'Innovating with Information Technology', in M. J. Earl (ed.), *Information Management: The Organisational Dimension* (Oxford: Oxford University Press).

McFarlan, F. W. (1981), 'Problems in Planning the Information System', *Harvard Business Review*, Sept.–Oct.: 142–50.

McGee, J., and Thomas, H. (1989), 'Technology and Strategic Management: A Research Review', in M. J. Earl (ed.), *Information Management: The Strategic Dimension* (Oxford: Clarendon Press).

Mintzberg, H. (1973), *The Nature of Managerial Work* (New York: Harper & Row).

Naisbitt, J. (1990), *Megatrends* (London: Sidgwick & Jackson).

Porter, M. E. (1980), *Competitive Strategy* (New York: Free Press).

—— and Millar, M. E. (1985), 'How Information Gives you Competitive Advantage', *Harvard Business Review*, July–Aug.: 149–60.

Rayport, J. F., and Sviokla, J. J. (1995), 'Exploiting the Virtual Value Chain', *Harvard Business Review*, 73, 6, Nov.–Dec.: 75–85.

Runge, D. A. (1985), 'Using Telecommunications for Competitive Advantage', unpublished doctoral dissertation, University of Oxford.

Schoemaker, P. J. H. (1995), 'Scenario Planning: A Tool for Strategic Thinking', *Sloan Management Review*, Winter: 25–40.

Short, J. E., and Venkatraman, N. (1992), 'Beyond Business Process Redesign: Redefining Baxter's Network', *Sloan Management Review*, Fall, 34, 1: 7–21.

Stewart, R. (1982), *Choices for the Manager: A Guide to Managerial Work and Behaviour* (New York: McGraw Hill).

Vancil, R. F., and Lorange, P. (1977), *Strategic Planning Systems* (Englewood Cliffs, NJ: Prentice Hall).

Wack, P. (1985), 'Scenarios: Uncharted Waters Ahead', *Harvard Business Review*, Sept.–Oct.: 72–89.

Wernerfelt, B. (1984), 'The Resource Based View of the Firm', *Strategic Management Journal*, 5, 2: 171–80.

Wiseman, C. (1988), *Strategic Information Systems* (Homewood, Ill.: Irwin).

8

Thinking the Unthinkable
What Happens if the IS Field as we Know it Goes Away?

M. LYNNE MARKUS

Introduction

One of the central questions asked in this volume is the extent to which the academic IS field (AIS)[1] is at a crossroads. One sign points toward a solid identity for AIS as a unified 'discipline' within business schools. Another indicates lost identity, with AIS incorporated into other fields such as organisational behaviour or marketing. Many IS academics share the editors' concerns, pointing to such evidence as denials of tenure to some well-respected AIS researchers, introductory AIS courses dropped from some MBA programme cores, and even closure of some visible AIS programmes. Do these events simply represent normal 'churn' in the academic industry? Or do they portend the end of our intellectual community?

IS academics have a natural tendency to frame these questions in terms of disciplinary 'turf'. We bemoan the fact that intellectual communities like organisational behaviour, operations management, and marketing are 'discovering' information technology (IT) as an important topic for *their* teaching and research. Whether their interests lie in IT impacts, software engineering, or electronic commerce, we see them as laying claim to research domains that we think of as ours. We deplore their ignorance of our contributions, and bridle when they question the value of AIS. As the newest business school discipline, we believe AIS to be vulnerable in faculty hiring and promotion decisions and curriculum debates.

I wish to thank those people who contributed to my thinking about the issues in this chapter, especially: Steve Alter, Cynthia Beath, Bob Benjamin, Mary Culnan, Jonathan Grudin, Burt Swanson, Mark Silver, Bob Zmud, and my colleagues at the Claremont Graduate School Programs in Information Science.

[1] The field is known by a variety of names, including management information systems, information systems, and, increasingly, information technology. In this chapter, I will use the term AIS to refer to the academic field so that it is clearly differentiated from the subject of study and from the functional unit in computer-using organisations.

Regardless of the validity of these views, we cannot escape the fact that developments in IT itself are raising serious questions about the future of our field. As computers increasingly become embedded in every aspect of personal and organisational life, it is less and less possible to distinguish between computing and 'everything else'. Looking even twenty years out, it is hard to imagine any branch of knowledge that is not in some way transformed by IT, whether as a learning/research tool, a tool of professional practice, or an object of study. Given the ubiquity of computing, why does the world need a field that specializes in IT, independent of, or abstracted from, particular substantive applications? In a world of inevitable resource constraints, why should business school deans and heads *not* try to achieve excellence in IT without the expense of an AIS unit by hiring IT-knowledgeable non-IS faculty?

In my view, the AIS field must squarely confront the increasingly common argument that IT does not need 'disciplined' attention (that is, attention by members of an AIS discipline), because IT is ubiquitous. If we do not have an effective response to this argument, we will miss opportunities to influence colleagues and events. The nature of our response is important, too. Appeals to logic[2] are attractive. But, to economically minded deans and heads, market-based responses may be more compelling. Ideally, our response would show that disciplined attention to AIS is good for the business of business schools by attracting funds.

In the long run, the fortunes of professional[3] academic disciplines like finance, marketing, and AIS vary with their access to, and control over, key resources. In many schools, a large portion of funding varies directly with the number of students (via tuition revenues or government allocations). Alumni contributions are another important source of funds. With the decline of federal government research support (in the USA at least), private funding sources are growing in importance. Since organisations that employ a field's students are among the most likely funders of its research, we can view students as *the* critical resource for the future of the AIS field. Therefore, the question 'will the AIS field go away?' can be rephrased as 'will there be any AIS students in the future, who will they be, and what will they need in the way of AIS education and research?'

In this chapter, I explore these questions by examining historical AIS assumptions about our customers and their intellectual needs and by identifying some likely future trends that conflict with our past assumptions. I argue that recent technical, economic, and institutional trends are pressuring our field to change. If we change with the trends, the future of our field as a field looks considerably more certain than if we do not.

---

[2] Money and people are also ubiquitous organisational resources; yet the need to focus on *them* independent of specific uses is well understood. Why should IT be different?'

[3] As distinguished from the liberal arts or sciences.

The Early Roots of AIS

The field of AIS originated as a functional academic speciality paralleling the growth of information systems (IS) units in business organisations. In the USA, most academics who identify themselves with AIS (or related names such as management information systems, information systems, or information technology) are located in business schools.[4] In continental Europe, AIS academics are more commonly located in computer science departments (which in the USA are often located in schools of engineering).

Business uses of computers date from the mid-1950s. At that time, organisations that saw business potential in computers had no choice but to write their own programs. There was no 'packaged' software for sale, and there were few trained programmers. Naturally, there was much trial and error in early system-building. Nevertheless, there were many rewards for the organisations that succeeded in developing workable software. Most early 'electronic data processing' (EDP) systems automated clerical record-keeping about business transactions—primarily accounting and sales records—where the potential for cost savings was great. Business interest in EDP grew rapidly.

In universities, professors with backgrounds in accounting, engineering, and the emerging field of computer science began teaching and researching the principles of effective software development. Among the primary areas of interest were the information systems life cycle, systems analysis and design, programming, and project management.

This activity was promptly challenged by colleagues in other business school disciplines. Why, they wondered, was system-building and programming not being taught with other design and development specialities —in computer science departments or schools of engineering? AIS specialists took great pains to differentiate themselves from computer scientists, who, for their part, also wanted to differentiate themselves from the former group. Between the two groups, it is clearly understood that computer science is more technical, 'theoretical' (in the sense of the theory of computation), and abstract than AIS. AIS is more applied, more managerial than technical in focus, and more attuned to the needs of computer-using businesses. However, this distinction is difficult to draw, since IS academics share many common interests with computer scientists, including software engineering methods and metrics, requirements analysis and interface development, and even organisational informatics (a hybrid of computer science and sociology). As a result, the distinction between AIS and computer science remains fuzzy to most non-IS academics colleagues in business schools and completely incomprehensible by academics outside business schools other than computer scientists.

---

[4] Some are located in library/information science programmes.

Eventually, business interest in computers expanded beyond clerical cost reduction to the use of data for managerial decision-making. Transaction-processing systems generated volumes of data about business operations and resource use. Secondary analyses of this data produced numerous suggestions for organisational improvements. Database management systems and techniques were created to facilitate data access and retrieval. New analysis and reporting techniques were pioneered.

This new and potentially more important use of computing merited a grander name. 'EDP' gave way to 'management information systems' (MIS), a title designed to merit a legitimate place on the MBA curriculum. Teaching and research began to focus on the information requirements of individual managers, reporting formats, data-modelling and analysis techniques, the principles of 'decision support', decision-making effectiveness, and related areas. When failures remained high despite improved system-building practices, interest in 'implementation' and user involvement in software development grew (Friedman, 1989).

Since then, many additional business uses for computing, known as 'applications', have been developed and named, including expert systems, executive information systems, and personal productivity and group support tools. As applications grew in type, number, size, and age, organisations began to experience problems maintaining them and managing the growing numbers and types of IS personnel. The corporate manager of IS was promoted to chief information officer (CIO) and headed up a unit that dwarfed other staff functions like accounting and human resources.

Corresponding to these changes, AIS teaching and research began to tackle the *impacts* of information systems on individuals, groups, and organisations. As a result, the *management of information systems* (MOIS) emerged as a distinct speciality concerned with the structure of the IS function, the policies needed to guide its operation, and IS personnel management.

Several basic assumptions and beliefs that continue to characterise the AIS field today can be identified in its early history. These core elements may provide a springboard for change or may inhibit adaptation to changing conditions. Thus, to confront effectively the various challenges facing the field, it is important to identify core assumptions, values, and beliefs of the field's members. Important among the basic cultural values of the AIS field are implicit notions about the 'customer' and the 'core mission' of AIS teaching, research, and practice.

The customer: user organisations

In general, AIS texts and publications implicitly assume that the key customers of the field are organisations that use computers. (We might call these customers 'user organisations' to distinguish them from organisations whose primary orientation is the production of computing products and services for consumption by other organisations.) The important members of user organisations are individual users and IS specialists. Especially important among individual users are managers who use computer-generated analyses and reports to make business decisions. IS specialists include system analysts, programmers, computer operators, IS managers, and CIOs.

One important consequence of this core element of our field is that there has been relatively little focus on IT producer organisations. Until the recent trend toward IT outsourcing, there has been almost no research on computing products or services vendors. Strikingly absent are studies of the structure of the computer world and the influences of vendors on computer-using organisations.

A second consequence is that the unit(s) of analysis in the AIS field (organisations or individuals/groups embedded in organisations) set(s) it apart from other similar fields. The AIS perspective differs quite a bit, for example, from human–computer interaction (HCI, a hybrid of computer science and cognitive psychology) and from library/information science (LIS), both of which focus primarily on individuals independent of organisational context. (However, organisational informatics is similar to AIS in its focus on organisations.) On the other hand, the focus on work groups is arguably not as strong in the AIS field as it is in HCI. In addition, until quite recently the focus of the AIS field has been on organisations' *internal* operations and data. Increasingly important to organisations are external data sources and electronic links to suppliers, customers, and end consumers. This suggests a growing need for an *inter*-organisational, as well as an *intra*-organisational, focus in the field of AIS.

The mission: in-house development of numeric applications

Leaders in the AIS field often describe its mission as 'to develop useful computing applications (software) efficiently and effectively'. And, indeed, roughly half of AIS research in the field can be categorized as 'software engineering' (Morrison and George, 1995).

Less often, but with increasing frequency, the core mission of the field is phrased in terms of 'management' rather than 'development'. However, there is considerable dissensus about what is to be managed and by whom. This alternative core mission is variously described as 'the management of *information systems*' (or of 'the IS function'), as 'the management of *information*', or as 'the management of information *technology*' (or of 'the IT function'). Since the terms information systems, information, and information technology have quite different connotations (and since the technology itself differs from the organisational units that provide or manage it), the essence of this mission remains ill defined. A further complication concerns who is assumed to do the managing. Historically, IS managers or executives have been viewed as the primary managers *of* information systems, information, or technology. Increasingly, however, IS/I/IT management is conceptualized as a role of general managers in partnership with internal IS specialists and external vendors. Even when it is not viewed as the core mission of the AIS field, IS/I/IT management is generally regarded an important advanced subject in the AIS curriculum, with its own texts and research agenda.

The ambiguity surrounding the AIS core mission exhibits a tension in the field between more technically oriented colleagues who focus on the 'production' of in-house IT services and more managerially or behaviourally oriented colleagues who focus on IT 'consumption' (or 'use'). The former tend to accuse the latter of being 'too soft', the latter to accuse the former of being 'too technical'. These accusations create considerable intramural tensions in hiring and curriculum decisions. Because the *more* technically oriented colleagues must continue to differentiate themselves from the really *technical* computer scientists, they are outraged at being called 'too technical' and deny it vehemently. Nevertheless, the curriculum remains 'too technical' in the perceptions of behavioural IS academics, most non-IS business school academics, and many bewildered MBA students. Ironically, it is entirely 'too soft' for MBA students with strong technical backgrounds or an interest in enterpreneurial high-tech firms.

A second implication relates to the field's heavy emphasis on the computational end of the IT spectrum. Since AIS began, the technology of numeric data-oriented computing has begun converging with telephony, document- and image-oriented computing, and video. Nevertheless, academic AIS has continued to emphasise numeric, data-oriented computing. AIS treatments of 'telecommunications' usually ignore telephony, voice-response systems, and video. Much of the research on telephony and video-conferencing has been done in the communications fields. Similarly, much of the document-oriented IT research has been done in LIS. Finally, although research on group support systems is an important subfield within AIS, the majority of groupware research has been done in HCI.

Summary

The academic AIS field originated in the needs of large business organisations to develop computer software. As the technical capabilities of computers grew, the business uses of computing expanded, and the number and types of in-house IS specialists devoted to developing, operating, and maintaining computing services increased. For several decades, the teaching and research of IS academics generally paralleled these developments in the in-house IS departments of large user organisations. The next section will outline some of the recent developments, technical, economic, and institutional, that are straining the core elements of the AIS field.

What Has Changed?

Since the establishment of the AIS field, a bewildering variety of changes have occurred in the technology of organisational computing. The field has striven to incorporate these changes into its basic paradigm. However, outside the academic field, alternative perspectives on the changes have emerged. These perspectives clearly highlight the nature of pressures for change in AIS teaching and research. What follows is a brief sketch of IT change since about 1980 from the AIS point of view, contrasted with two alternative perspectives.

The canonical AIS view

IS academics note that the rapidly decreasing size and price of mini-computers and personal computers greatly expanded the economic uses of computers and the number of computer users. This enabled office automation, personal productivity software, and end-user computing to emerge as important application areas. What were originally standalone personal computers began to be linked in local area networks and connected by gateways to wide-area networks (WANS). Organisations interfaced their in-house transaction-processing systems and databases to those of their organisational customers and suppliers. These *strategic information systems* became sources of competitive advantage, and the IS function finally earned its place in the corporate boardroom. Even traditional product-oriented businesses discovered the value of their information resources; information became increasingly seen as a *product* that could be sold or leveraged in commercial transactions.

Simultaneously, electronic communication systems, group support systems, and groupware came into vogue as organisational management tools. The cost advantages of computer hardware *downsizing* coupled with developments in telecommunications and software development led many organisations to pursue applications designed for *client-server* rather than traditional mainframe architectures. Recently, business organisations have discovered the Internet, and *electronic commerce* was born. Today, organisations are developing *intranets* for internal use and Internet interfaces for use by consumers.

This AIS view of recent developments promises a bright future for in-house IS specialists. Because organisations are ever expanding their needs for computer-based applications, they will continue to need IS specialists who can identify organisational requirements for applications and data, design and build custom applications, or specify, select, install, and customize generic packages, operate computers and networks, and support and train users. On the academic side, existing teaching and research on software engineering and management of IS/I/IT forms a strong base from which to expand into new offerings for future in-house IS specialists as well as for general managers.

The world according to Microfirm

A very different view of the same fundamental IT trends can be seen in the writings and presentations of human–computer interaction (HCI) specialists. According to members of this field, many of whom work in computer product and service firms, the course of computing history changed fundamentally with the advent of *interactive systems*. AIS specialists also speak of interactive systems, contrasting them with the 'batch processing' of transactions. But HCI specialists use the term to refer to the characteristics of the interface between computers and users rather than to the nature of within-computer processing *per se*. Thus, while AIS specialists would describe as interactive most modern mainframe-based systems, HCI specialists would not. To the latter, interactive systems differ from traditional in-house information systems in several important ways.

The most obvious hallmark of interactive systems is their *graphical user interface*. But more importantly, they are generally developed by software product development firms (like Lotus and Microsoft) or by the software product development groups of hardware manufacturers (such as Apple or Sun), rather than by IS specialists employed by user organisations. In most cases, in-house IS specialists do no development, modification, customisation, or maintenance of interactive systems, although in-house IS specialists may select and purchase them and provide installation, training, and support services.

Many of the important new classes of information technology applications are interactive systems. Examples include groupware (such as Lotus Notes), interactive information retrieval systems (such as Web browsers), and multi-media systems (such as computer-aided design, CAD, and desktop video-conferencing). Interactive systems have been responsible for the migration of computing from the back offices of large corporations onto desktops everywhere, including the home. In addition, most of what might be called *embedded* systems[5] (Strassmann, 1995) are interactive systems. As a rule, embedded systems are much more likely than traditional IS applications to be acquired and actively managed by line business leaders than by central IS staffs.

Because interactive systems are developed as products for sale to consumers or buyers in other organisations, the process by which they are designed and developed differs substantially from the AIS system devel-

---

[5] Systems that are integrated into the core operations of a business, such as CAD in an engineering firm or Loutus Notes in a consulting firm.

opment life cycle (Grudin, 1991). 'Requirements' may be determined by marketing specialists assessing competitive products, rather than by interviewing users. Developers (in contrast to marketing specialists) are much less likely to have access to users than is usually the case with in-house IS development (Poltrock and Grudin, 1994). Detailed descriptions of the software development practices of product development firms (Cusumano and Selby, 1995) show few similarities to the traditional in-house IS development approach. When users are studied by members of product development firms, anthropological observational methods are preferred to the survey-based interview methods favoured in AIS.

As they look toward the future, proponents of interactive systems see a world in which packages—developed and provided by specialized IT industry firms—will completely replace traditional in-house custom IS development. As interactive systems improve, they will increasingly become *environments* (an amalgam of infrastructure, applications, and networking), which users can (without the intervention of IS professionals) effortlessly tailor to their own unique needs. Within these environments, users will increasingly make use of *content* provided by third party data or information vendors rather than (or in addition to) data collected and maintained by in-house IS groups.

These trends will apply, it is claimed, as much to large organisations with heavy transaction-processing needs as they do today to small companies and to organisations such as professional services firms that need document- and communication-oriented, rather than data-oriented, systems. The new management theories of *worker empowerment* and *networked* or *virtual* organisations are decentralising decision-making enabled by flatter hierarchies. Consequently, what AIS calls management or executive information systems are collapsing into embedded systems and groupware environments. Further, with the advent of worldwide high-bandwidth *network computing*, organisational members will be able to download *applets* on demand from vendors, eliminating the onerous tasks of software installation, version control, and network management that plague in-house IS specialists today.

In short, according to this alternative view, the same technology trends that portend a rosy future for in-house IS specialists when viewed through the lenses of AIS signal the eventual demise of the in-house IS function when understood in light of interactive systems and network computing.

Outsiders' onlook: OutSultants Inc.

Developments among the larger user organisations in recent years provide yet another take on the traditional AIS domain. Much has changed since the first flush of excitement over CIOs and strategic information systems. For years, many large user organisations maintained sizeable IS units with strong central control over critical operational and management information systems. As long as the economy was strong and confidence in information technology remained high, these companies generally shied away from software packages for their enterprise-wide transaction-processing and MIS needs. Their business practices were unique, and they were reluctant to change them to conform to packages. Since making major modifications to packages is expensive and risky, building custom software remained the preferred option, despite the growing number of software product options in the market place.

But hard times and the *productivity paradox* changed large user organisations' traditional approach to IS management. When academic research began to challenge the business value of IT investments, businesses acted on pent-up frustrations with long system development lead-times, restrictive controls, and the arrogant behaviour of in-house systems experts. They quickly cut costs and took back control of a major chunk of the business overhead budget.

One result has been widespread *decentralisation* of the information systems function. Throughout the history of organisational computing, there have been periodic swings in IT governance fashions. A broad-based shift toward decentralization began when companies expanded their purchases of departmental minicomputers and PCs. It accelerated during the productivity paradox years, as line managers struggled to take back control over the resources of money, people, and technology that enabled them to make a profit (or prevented them from doing so). In many large user organisations today, business units rather than IS units now have broad authority over IT applications and processing. Because business unit heads generally have shorter time frames and tighter budgets than corporate executives, they often prefer *outsourcing* and *packages* to in-house operations and development. Some companies have turned over all their IT processing equipment and personnel to large IT vendors. Total outsourcing generates cash that can be used to turn around financially troubled operations or invested to upgrade IT systems and services. It improves cost management by converting fixed costs to variable costs. It also assuages a sore spot in companies with non-responsive or ineffective IS departments.

With dollars and people moving from corporate IS units to business units (and even further out to IT industry firms), central IS units (not just hardware) have been *downsized*. Corporate IS groups that once hired hundreds of people are today mere shadows of their former selves—sometimes only five or six people. Often they focus on corporate purchasing agreements and enterprise standards for an IT *architecture* that ensures adequate connectivity among business units. Usually, central IS units retain operational responsibility for what has come to be called the *IT infrastructure* (corporate telecommunications networks, data centres, and central applications development/operations) only in firms with integrated business operations (e.g. airlines, banks).

Other organisations faced up to economic woes by re-engineering their business processes. This activity often highlighted the dependence of business performance on seriously inadequate *legacy* mainframe systems. Organisations began to realize that delays in improving their systems would decrease or eliminate the financial benefits of *process re-engineering*. In this environment, packaged software looked much more appealing than it had just a few years earlier. Packages might still not fit every nuance of the business, but business practices were bound to change anyway, and speed is the critical factor in business success. More and more companies decided to select the best fitting package and use it without modification, changing business practices as needed to make this strategy work.

Developments in the large-system software package market place made this strategy even more attractive. In recent years, a number of integrated application suites, also known as *enterprise packages*, based on the client-server architecture, have appeared on the market (e.g. SAP and Peoplesoft). These products simultaneously support multiple application areas, such as order entry, inventory, invoicing, payables, payroll, and general ledger. Adopting organisations can avoid the time and cost involved in tailoring custom interfaces among separately developed systems, and they can gain improvements in secondary data analysis and reporting. Many integrated packages also facilitate multi-country operations by providing several language versions and automated currency conversions. Although installing an integrated system is a much bigger job than implementing a single application package, many organisations are delighted at the prospect of lightening their legacy systems' maintenance burden by eliminating some of it and transferring much of the rest to the package vendor. Some companies anticipate sizeable reductions in their in-house IS staffs once hundreds of interfaced legacy applications are replaced by an integrated package and a handful of custom systems.

The benefits of integrated packages come at a price. The packages are very complex, containing hundreds or thousands of tables of parameters to be set during installation. Vendors run training schools for the technical personnel of their clients. But it is difficult for any individual to develop expertise in all of a major package's application areas. So, user organisations often augment in-house technical personnel with external consultants and contractors. But even when the technical work is outsourced, the process of installing an integrated package usually requires considerable involvement of the user company's non-technical personnel.

The popularity of enterprise software packages has been a bonanza for *professional services firms* as well as for package vendors. For years, the so-called *system integrators* (firms such as Andersen Consulting and Ernst & Young) did a brisk business in custom software development as well as general technology consulting services. Today, installing integrated enterprise software packages comprises roughly 50 per cent of their billings. Clients like the comfort of working with consultants who have already experienced successful installations in other companies. To enhance their expertise, system integrators specialize in a small number of enterprise packages. The vendors, in turn, refer their customers to integrators that specialize in their products.

Many user organisations hail enterprise software packages as the 'end of legacy systems'. While they may get rid of their old mainframes and the COBOL programming language, the new systems still need to be 'maintained' and eventually become legacy systems themselves. But from the perspective of user organisations, much of the maintenance burden can be shifted out of house to vendors, whose periodic *releases* fix bugs, add features, and allow for upgrades to more powerful computing equipment. After the initial software setup, most of the effort of data maintenance is borne by process workers rather than IT staff.

These developments portend an acceleration, rather than a halt or reversal, of the shift in the locus of application development and maintenance from user organisations to IT industry firms. One major reason involves electronic commerce among organisations and between organisations and consumers. For years now, many large user organisations have pursued the advantages of computer-based links to their customers and suppliers. But, despite the promised benefits, the diffusion of *electronic data interchange* (EDI) among businesses has considerably lagged expectations, largely due to the need to build expensive custom software interfaces with each business partner (in a process called *system integration*). A few firms are experimenting with *electronic commerce* to extend their reach to consumers in their homes. But just as electronic commerce depends on bandwidth, security, and payment schemes, interenterprise computing also needs infrastructure and standards.

EDI and electronic commerce could get a major boost from the evolution of *interenterprise packages*. Such packages would reduce the hassles of interfirm interface development—again, at a price. If many organisations today engage system integrators to help them with enterprise system installation, they are even more likely to do so in a future of interenterprise software. The typical organisation is unlikely to trust even preferred business partners with the details of its core business systems, since that would render it vulnerable to abuse. And, since the business partners are likely to feel exactly the same way, a trusted or bonded third party *system integrator* is the obvious choice. Industry associations and consortia of user organisations may join professional services firms in supplying such services, but the overall trend would be an accelerated migration of technical IS specialists out of user organisations into IT specialist firms.

Again, this view of recent IT developments suggests a very different future from the canonical AIS view.

Summary

The next decade will see the information processing workloads migrate from internal services to marketplace offerings. . . . [A]bout half the current information technology employees will leave their jobs and seek careers and jobs as contractors, consultants, and part-time specialists. . . .

Currently, organisations primarily depend on themselves to satisfy most of their computing needs. They buy their own equipment, select the operating systems, purchase the software, write the applications, and manage the telecommunications links. I do not believe even very large organisations will sustain the required expertise to do all these tasks very well, and certainly not at competitive costs. The future belongs to [external] specialists who market and deliver network services in every way the customer needs them. (Strassmann, 1995: 469–71)

The AIS field emerged in an era when user organisations developed custom, numerically-oriented transaction and management information systems. Since then, the software products and services segment of the computer world has grown and matured into a powerful alternative to in-house IS departments (the historic customers of AIS teaching and research). Two very different lines of development can be identified, one involving interactive environments and multi-media content, the other involving enterprise software vendors, third party consultants and integrators, and external processing and support services companies (outsourcers). Both alternatives enable reductions in in-house IS personnel, offset by increases in external providers. The future of organisational computing will probably involve some combination of smaller in-house staffs and greater use of both alternatives.

Overall, the growth of both the software and the professional services markets seems likely to have major effects on computer-using firms. First, consumers, small organisations, and knowledge-intensive firms are likely to become much heavier users of computing than they were in the past. At the same time, they are unlikely to rely heavily on specialized in-house IS technical expertise and support services. Second, an increasing number of large user organisations will find it possible and advantageous to forgo in-house processing, data management, and custom application development. As a result, the human resource requirements of both user organisations and IT products and services firms may change considerably. These effects, in turn, have major implications for AIS teaching and research, addressed in the next section.

Implications

According to Peter Drucker, any enterprise needs to answer two key sets of strategic questions, one dealing with customers, the second with mission: Who are our customers, and what do they consider value? What is our mission with respect to customers' needs, and what core competencies do we have and need to fulfil this mission? As discussed above, the answers to these questions were relatively clear in the early days of the AIS field. The customer was the computer-using organisation, its in-house IS unit, and its general managers, and these customers' needs centred on the development of custom application software. The field's mission was to facilitate software development, and its core competencies were the life cycle, the applications portfolio, and the management of IS/I/IT.

Today and into the future, the needs of user organisations in terms of the size, tasks, and skill requirements of their in-house IS units appear to be changing. Package purchase and outsourcing are reducing the number of IS specialists employed in-house, and changing what they do. Small organisations are often able to dispense entirely with in-house IS specialists, with vendors taking charge of computing *environments* (consisting of hardware, networking, and an integrated applications suite) while process workers take responsibility for managing internal and accessing external *content*. Larger organisations are differentiating new or specialized *applications* (managed by business unit managers and their IT/IS suppliers) from *infrastructure* (platforms, telecommunications, standards, corporate data, and corporate systems such as email, groupware, data access and analysis software, and enterprise systems). Systems integration, training, and support work is displacing new software development by in-house IS specialists, and the re-engineering or replacement of legacy systems is reducing their system maintenance work. General managers and process workers are becoming more aware of users and purchasers of external IT products and services. However, they may not require skill in the traditional processes of IS application development and the management of in-house IS specialists.

Who is our customer?

All in all, the needs of user organisations, the traditional customer of the AIS field, are changing so significantly that they may no longer be met adequately by the field's existing intellectual capital in application development and in-house MOIS. New research and teaching programmes are required to address the emerging IT knowledge and skill needs of user organisations in such areas as vendor selection and management and information product development. Conversely, customer groups that the AIS field has *not* traditionally served are growing in size and importance, both in sheer economic terms and relative to the needs of user organisations. Among the most important of these potential new AIS customer groups are:

- software product development firms (e.g. makers of PC tools, group-ware, and enterprise software),
- third party developers, integrators, and product consultants (firms that specialise in the customisation of the products of a particular development firm, e.g. Lotus Notes or SAP's enterprise software),
- general IT consultants (those who employ the methods of IT planning, re-engineering, etc.),
- facilities managers and help services (outsourcers who run data centres and support services on contract for user organisations),
- third party data or content suppliers (e.g. stock quotation and news services), and
- telecommunications service providers.[6]

These IT products and services firms represent potentially important new customers for IT educational and research programmes. Already, for example, firms like Andersen Consulting are said to be hiring large numbers of undergraduate IS majors and MBA students with IS concentrations. However, it will be no simple matter to serve any or all of these customer groups with the existing intellectual capital and core competencies of the AIS field. Software product development firms are a case in point. While the IT specialists in these firms may use the newer development languages and object-oriented paradigm taught in many AIS departments, they often use development *strategies* that differ radically from the traditional AIS life cycle (cf. Grudin, 1991; Cusumano and Selby, 1995).[7] 'Information product' firms (third party data and content providers) also appear to require very different development approaches (Meyer and Zack, 1996). System integrators, likewise, do not follow the traditional AIS development life cycle.

Even the outsourcing vendors who take over the operations and support of a user organisation's computing facilities may require different skills from those that have traditionally been taught to in-house IT service providers. Recently, I had an opportunity to participate in a management development seminar for a major outsourcing vendor. When I asked about the goals for the programme, my contact showed me a diagram with two adjacent triangles. The first triangle was labelled something like 'What the XYZ account executive needs to do to provide value to our clients.' It strongly resembled the Gorry and Scott Morton framework that was used for many years to explain the different kinds of IS applications. At the bottom level, the XYZ account team was expected to perform traditional IS work efficiently and effectively; at the top level, the outsourced IS

---

[6] Some large organisations like IBM, EDS, Andersen Consulting, and AT&T may operate in multiple segments.
[7] Grudin points out that the traditional AIS life cycle pre-dates interactive systems and is not suited to their particular development challenges.

function had to demonstrate the ability to understand the strategic needs of the client and to deliver business value.

But the second triangle was different. It showed what the outsourced IS function had to do, operationally and strategically, to deliver business value *to XYZ*, for example, make a profit and sell new business. One of my students at the Claremont Graduate School described rather graphically the change of mind needed when an in-house IS specialist goes to work for an outsourcing firm. Mark was formerly employed by an aerospace company, but became an employee of XYZ Corp. when his company outsourced IS. At first, he felt shocked and betrayed by the change, which left him working at the very same desk but changed all his other conditions of employment, including employee benefits. A few weeks later, he was feeling much better about the change. But he said that some of his 'clients' (his former colleagues at the aerospace company) were having more difficulty making the adjustment than he was: 'They don't seem to understand that I work for XYZ now.'

Mark's mindset changed along with his incentives. His incentives changed because his employer changed, and his new employer had a different value equation from his old employer. Now doing IS work for external clients instead of for his employer, Mark needs different business, political, and technical skills from those he did before. This is an area which the AIS field today does not know much about. Not all of these needs will be met by traditional AIS teaching and research programmes that assume IS work is performed in-house. New courses and research are needed if AIS is to make a demonstrable contribution to firms like XYZ and the students they will employ.

In short, recent developments in information technology and the computer world are confronting the AIS field with a critical strategic choice: whether to stay with the field's historical customer group—IS specialists and general managers in user organisations—or to shift to one or more new customer groups of IT producers. Each choice has pros and cons. As a business school case study might ask: Given this situation, what should the AIS field do?

Pursue new customers?   The choice to pursue new customers may enable substantial growth in the markets for AIS graduates and research. But developing this market will require forging new relationships and accumulating new intellectual capital. It is conceivable, for example, that a curriculum appropriate for system integrators would differ considerably from one appropriate for content and applications product developers, and that both would differ substantially from a curriculum for general managers or in-house IS specialists. Developing a new market may also result in increased competition from other academic fields and schools that already target these customers successfully. (For instance, computer science currently supplies students and research to software product development firms, and LIS and communication programmes supply third party information product vendors.) In addition, this strategy may create risks in academic resource politics. The interests of IT producer firms are not completely aligned with those of the general managers of user organisations. How well could a single academic field balance the needs of two such different customer groups? Supporting IT producers at the expense of user organisations might undermine the legitimacy of IS academics with business school colleagues in other disciplines who are more aligned with the general management perspective.[8]

Remain with existing customers? The choice to remain with our historic customer group preserves a comfortable relationship that was nurtured over years. However, we can expect the general management audience to become increasingly impatient with an AIS curriculum rooted in the era of mainframes. User organisations will probably hire fewer IS specialists over time, with predictably negative impacts on AIS enrolments and funding. Furthermore, the remaining IS specialists employed by user organisations are likely to require rather different skills from those they do today.

Today, the majority of the IS specialists in traditional user organisations perform technical tasks such as operations, designing software, coding, and capacity planning. A minority perform work that involves much greater interaction with people, such as requirements analysis, user help, consulting, and vendor management. In general, one would expect user organisations to be much more likely to outsource tasks involving predominantly technical skills than those involving predominantly people skills, for several reasons. First, technical specialists are more likely to prefer the career development opportunities available in vendor organisations to those in user organisations, so user organisations may encounter difficulty attracting and retaining the needed technical specialists. Second, IS people work is more likely than IS technical work to require organisation-specific knowledge that cannot be obtained from vendors or that should not be shared with them. Further, in-house IS specialists with strong people skills can easily be redeployed in other managerial or professional jobs. These factors suggest that the in-house IS specialists of the future may require a much less technical skill set and a much stronger grounding in interpersonal aspects of IS work than either today's in-house IS specialists or tomorrow's entry-level IT vendor personnel.

If this analysis is correct, user organisations may become increasingly reluctant to hire IS personnel trained in traditional AIS programmes. Their options would be to retrain existing employees in the necessary

---

[8] It is perhaps to avoid the politics of business schools that some AIS academics are being attracted to new schools that collocate specialists from computer science, LIS, and AIS.

information technologies and methodologies (perhaps by contracting with commercial educational providers) or to hire seasoned IT vendor personnel who have left the technical ranks.[9] Thus, a strategic choice for the AIS field to continue to serve its current customer group would require a significant reinvestment in the curriculum and the research required to support it. Among the areas where new curriculum development is most required to support user organisations are the following:

• *Change agentry, political skills, 'soft skills', user training, implementation, project management, and experimental approaches:*

    As noted above, the outsourcing of IS technical work does not reduce the required involvement of non-IS specialist personnel and managers. Facilitating this involvement often requires considerable interpersonal and political skill. While much knowledge about change management exists outside the AIS field (cf. Benjamin and Levinson, 1993), considerable effort is required to adapt this knowledge to the IS context (cf. Markus and Benjamin, 1996). For instance, while Buchanan and Boddy (1992; Boddy and Buchanan, 1992) have developed materials that cover the interpersonal and political aspects of general 'project management', strong AIS education requires similar materials that are specialised to *IT projects*. Further, effective in-house IS specialists also need *non-project* change management skills. From the perspective of user organisations, time is *the* critical variable in business success. User organisations often cannot wait for lengthy 'IT projects' to begin achieving results. Thus, IS specialists will need to acquire the skills associated with disciplined experimentation, sometimes called 'organisational prototyping' by re-engineering specialists (cf. Markus, 1994; Schaffer and Thompson, 1992). These skills help organisations obtain maximum benefits from existing information technologies instead of, or while waiting for, new ones.

• *Feasibility analysis, requirements analysis, and technical change design:*

    The re-engineering tradition suggests that business processes cannot be successfully redesigned unless other aspects of the organisation, such as jobs and reward systems, are also changed to support them. That this is also true of ordinary information systems has long been known, as demonstrated by socio-technical systems IS methodologies (cf. Mumford and Weir, 1979; Checkland, 1981). Nevertheless, the relevant concepts and techniques have generally not yet made their way into mainstream IS education and practice in the USA (cf. Markus and Keil, 1994). There is much more emphasis in most AIS texts on data flow analysis than on organisational analysis.

---

[9] For example, managers in system integration firms who do not 'make partner'.

Increasingly, user organisations are recognising that IS specialists need to work more closely with human resource management practitioners and quality specialists when planning organisational change. Several high-technology companies have organisationally collocated these different functional groups. The AIS field could make a major contribution to user organisations by developing and evaluating holistic organisational redesign methodologies.

One particular area in which considerable fragmentation exists is requirements analysis. In the USA, AIS emphasizes individual interview techniques, while group techniques are increasingly preferred in practice. In Scandinavia, 'participatory design' approaches prescribe a much more active role for users. The HCI community advocates ethnographic approaches. The AIS field could make a major contribution by pursuing the rapprochement and integration of these diverse traditions.

- *Vendor management:*

The growth of outsourcing has begun stimulating AIS research on contracting and vendor management. The AIS curriculum has been slower to change. The topic is usually considered as part of the IS specialists' software 'make or buy' decision or as a chapter in the 'management *of* IS', rather than as an overall philosophy of user organisations as 'intelligent consumers' of IT products and services. Much can be gained by examining the literature on technology and innovation management for insights that can be tested for their fit to the situation involving information, rather than manufacturing, technology.

Summary

There is no right or wrong answer to the question: 'Who is our customer?' The answer is a strategic *choice*. However, the success of a choice will depend in large part on how the enterprise attempts to serve the customer(s) it chooses. The preceding analysis suggests that the AIS field could fumble the future in several ways. First, it could attempt to pursue new customer groups, such as system integrators and outsourcers, with traditional curricula and research. For reasons articulated above, the traditional intellectual capital of AIS does not closely fit the needs of the new customer groups. Second, it could attempt to continue serving its traditional customer—the user organisation—with existing curricula and research. Because of the shift of application development work from user organisations to IT industry firms, the needs of user organisations are no longer met by historic AIS intellectual capital. Third, it could attempt to be all things to all customers without thinking through the similarities and differences in needs between user organisations and vendors. The attempt to do so might lead to loss of focus, infighting among different factions in the field, and negative external perceptions of the field's mission and quality.

On the other hand, many benefits could accrue to the field from a clear consensus about the field's preferred customer group(s) and a careful articulation of the customers' emerging needs (with special emphasis on the common and unique dimensions of need). As in IS planning, the benefits of the *process* could far outweigh the specific analytic results of such a customer segmentation analysis. The effort could generate new excitement and commitment among the field's members which could translate into improved teaching and research outcomes and enhanced credibility among customers and other stakeholders. The major risks of customer identification and choice are the risks that come from not doing it.

What is our Mission?

The second key strategic question concerns the mission of the enterprise with respect to the customers and their needs. As discussed above, the mission of the AIS field has historically been 'to deliver usable systems on time on budget'. Recent developments in technology, in user organisations, and in the IT industry cast doubt on the long-term viability of this mission for AIS. In one sense, from the perspective of user organisations, this historical goal has been achieved (or shortly will be), if more through the efforts of software product development organisations than those of in-house IS specialists. (From the perspective of user organisations, the easiest way to avoid software development budget and schedule overruns is to purchase a package and install it without modifications.) Like the March of Dimes after the discovery of a cure for polio, AIS needs a new mission—ideally, one that is not likely to go away any time soon. We need the AIS equivalent of the March of Dimes' change in mission from 'eliminating polio' to 'eliminating birth defects'.

Within the AIS field today, it is possible to discern at least two possible candidate new missions for the field. These alternatives can be understood as movements *in opposite directions* away from our historical mission. Consider the process by which an investment in IT adds business value to computer-using organisations; this process has several prerequisites (Soh and Markus, 1995). Closest to the 'value end' of the process is favourable market response. (For example, in a consumer products firm, if consumers do not buy the firm's products, it does not matter whether or not the firm's IT enabled faster product development cycle time, better product design, or lower cost. The firm still goes out of business.) Further away, but still close to the value end, is appropriate and effective use of an IT application. (To continue the example, if people in the firm did not use the IT that was installed to reduce cycle time, cycle time would not be reduced.)

Further away yet is an IT application that is capable of achieving value, if used. (In the example, this might be a groupware application designed to link product designers and manufacturing engineers.) Further away still is the IT infrastructure to support the application. (Running the groupware application requires PCs, servers, networks, etc.). One candidate new mission for AIS moves closer to the value end by focusing on activities that ensure that IS/IT are *used* effectively. The other moves away from the value end by focusing on the *infrastructure* that applications run on.

'Organisational improvement' as a mission for AIS?

The historic mission of AIS—to develop *usable* applications within certain constraints—is somewhat distant from business value, because unless the application is actually *used*, the application produces no benefits (Markus and Keil, 1994). Clearly, a large part of good application *development* involves attempts to ensure use. However, much of what is involved in ensuring use has been historically defined as outside the IS development mission (Markus and Keil, 1994; Markus and Benjamin, 1996), such as deciding the business objectives for the software and ensuring that process workers are using it effectively. Thus, one alternative new mission for IS involves moving away from application development closer to the business value end of IT investment payoff process. This might be called an 'organisational improvement mission' of AIS. It would tap into the sizeable body of behavioural AIS research devoted to explaining and predicting systems use. Adopting the organisational improvement mission for AIS would shift technical and development activities into the background and would shift into the foreground behavioural (people-oriented) activities such as: user training, consulting, change agentry, holistic business process design (designing the entire business system, not just the information system), etc.

'IT infrastructure' as a mission for AIS?

In the opposite direction along the IT value process from the historical AIS mission is a potential new mission for AIS around IT infrastructure. Today, as a result of IS decentralization, package purchase, and outsourcing, many CIOs are redefining their roles as 'chief *technology* officers' rather than as 'chief *information* officers'. Their duties, which focus on designing the framework for shared corporate IT services (and sometimes also providing the services), exclude developing applications that are unique to individual business units. In the AIS field, a burgeoning area of research involves defining the IT infrastructure and identifying what is involved in its effective design and management (cf. Weill, 1993).

A new 'IT infrastructure mission' for AIS has the advantage that it parallels observable developments in user organisations. But it has the disadvantage, as Peter Keen (1991) warns us, that 'infrastructure is *all cost*'. By contrast, he claims, all the business value in the IT investment is in the *application* of IT.[10] This does not, of course, mean that IT infrastructure is unimportant. Indeed, a robust infrastructure is an essential precondition for achieving sustained business value from IT applications. However, focusing on the cost end of the value process rather than on the value end entails sizeable political risks both for CIOs and for the AIS community. A well-known business methodology called activity value analysis (among other names) seeks to improve organisational performance by eliminating or outsourcing low-value activities and increasing the attention that organisational employees devote to high-value activities. Line managers are conditioned to 'value' high-value activities and the people who perform them. Conversely, they tend to disregard low-value activities and the people whose work is seen as remote from the business value-producing core. Thus, a new mission for AIS that moves away from IT applications toward IT infrastructure could be perceived both by line managers and by academic colleagues in other disciplines as a retreat from value (or, conversely, an advance into marginalism). Reduced credibility is an obvious risk of adopting the IT infrastructure as the new mission of the AIS field.

By contrast, adopting organisational performance improvement as the new mission for AIS avoids this particular disadvantage, but it does have others. For one thing, this mission is likely to be opposed by more technically oriented IS teachers and researchers, exacerbating existing tensions in the field. Second, this redefined mission is likely to be contested by other management disciplines, especially by organisation behaviour and development specialists, but also by strategy and policy specialists, technology and operations management specialists, and managerial accountants. Third, and perhaps most important in light of the earlier discussion of customers, organisational performance improvement as a new mission for AIS may be inappropriate for some customers that the AIS field may choose to serve. It is certainly appropriate for user organisations and some IT industry consultants. However, it is not a good fit for other IT industry firms, such as facilities managers or software product development firms (The same is also true of the IT infrastructure mission for AIS: it works for user organisations and for some technology firms and services vendors, but not for general IT consultants and many external applications and content developers.)

Toward a more integrative new mission for AIS

The two candidate missions for the field discussed above—organisational improvement versus IT infrastructure—both suffer from several drawbacks.

[10] I would revise Keen's statement to say that the business value of IT comes from favourable market response to the impacts that result from the effective use of a well-designed application.

First, each fails to cover some potential customer group that AIS field members may choose to serve. Second, each creates conflicts of interest between the technical and managerial/social/behavioural sides of the AIS field. Third, each focuses explicitly on the intra-organisational level of analysis, thereby obscuring issues at the levels of consumers and households, inter-organisational networks, industries, or nations. Is there another potential new mission that might overcome these disadvantages?

I believe that a preferable new mission for AIS would focus on *the electronic integration of socio-economic activity.* 'Socio-economic activity' covers the behaviour of households, organisations, industries, and nations, and it includes education and leisure as well as work and commerce. 'Electronic' refers to the role of IT in integration and in socio-economic activity. This role is manifold. Some ITs are the means of integrating socio-economic activity (e.g. EDI and email); yet most ITs must themselves be integrated, in at least two senses: technically (e.g. an operating system with hardware, network software, and applications software) and socio-economically (e.g. home banking into a consumer's financial routines, into a bank's business processes, into the activities of numerous third parties from retail establishments to financial clearing houses and telecommunications process, and into the relationships among all these parties). Further, IT is both produced and consumed, and therefore it needs to be assessed as both the input and the output of various production functions. As a result of the manifold role played by IT in both integration and socio-economic activity, this new mission 'works' both for user organisations and for many other different potential customers of the AIS field. In addition, the new mission 'integrates' the activities and interests (both intellectual and political) of different factions within the AIS community today.

I would like to emphasise that to adopt 'integration' as the mission for AIS is a bigger job than simply renaming what we are doing now. To discharge this mission seriously would require us to rethink some of our core concepts and competencies. For example, our field today is highly skilled in understanding how a single application can integrate across different 'users' in the same business process. It is less well skilled in the equally important area of helping single users integrate effectively across the different applications and technologies they use in related or unrelated business process.

Consider this illustration. For years now, I have been assigning student teams course projects to analyse a business process and the information technologies that support it. This type of analysis usually reveals major gaps and duplications in the business process, fumbled handoffs between organisation units adjacent in the business process flow, and the lack of technological integration among various transaction-processing systems and databases supporting the process. In short, this type of analysis, which is an institutionalised part of AIS teaching as well as the subject of much AIS research, is a useful business tool.

Recently, I experimented with a different student assignment. I asked teams to select one major job type or organisational unit and to consider all the different business processes and information technologies used by the person or group. This analysis produced, from my perspective, some startlingly different kinds of results from my usual assignment. The reports revealed the large numbers of different IT devices and systems used (many of which were not 'supported' by the in-house IS function), the difficulties or 'seams' that users often encountered when transitioning from one business process or technology to another, and the resulting inefficiency or ineffectiveness in organisational performance. A similar analysis could be done to identify the problems users experience in co-ordinating with different suppliers of IT products and services. The usefulness of these analyses suggests that the AIS field and our customers could benefit from the intellectual renewal that follows from embracing—not just mouthing—the new mission of integration.

IT integration teaching and research encompasses the following areas, among others:

- *Technical integration issues:*

  What roles do different technologies, features, packages, standards, etc. play in promoting or inhibiting *interoperability* at different levels of analysis? How effective are they? What strategies can organisations and other entities use to reduce the risks of inappropriate IT selection? How must old applications change to exploit the full potential of multi-media convergence? What improvements in business value can be traced to multi-media integration? What are best practices in product development, when the product involves software or information content? How does or should the product development process differ from that for developing enterprise systems? What are the different skill requirements for product developers versus enterprise package developers versus in-house IS specialists?

- *Socio-technical integration issues:*

  What technical features promote or inhibit the ability of users, work groups, organisations, and alliances to assimilate new ITs? How can user organisations anticipate the impacts (social, financial, etc.) of adopting integrated packages with different 'best practice' business processes embedded in them? What policies and practices foster the effective integration of IT into the workplace? What related changes in support arrangements, job design, incentives, spatial arrangements, etc., must be made to obtain full value from IT investments? How can potential negative effects of IT on worklife be avoided or reduced? What are the relative merits and problems of 'project-oriented approaches' versus 'experimental' approaches to IT introduction?

- *IT governance and policy integration issues:*

  From the perspective of users, user organisations, and inter-organisational alliances, IT is often viewed as a public good. As a result, change agents often have difficulty in selling IT or funding it adequately and in ensuring appropriate levels and types of use. What economic and social arrangements (e.g. chargebacks, pricing, contracts, structures, standards) promote or inhibit payoffs from IT public goods? What security and reliability issues are most critical to the long-term success of user organisations? How do current governance arrangements in large organisations change as myriad applications collapse into a small number of integrated packages? What does this mean for the size, structure, and locus of IS support services? How much of what we know about IT management in very large business organisations applies to very small organisations and to not-for-profit organisations?

- *Managerial integration issues:*

  What are the risks and best practices in introducing enterprise software and IT-based products and services? What are the payoffs? How can the risks and opportunities best be assessed and managed? What are the differences, if any, in IT-based product/service development/acquisition and enterprise software acquisition/installation? What are the most effective ways to select and work with IT vendors and/or business partners on IT projects? Under what circumstances should organisations pursue custom development today, and how can they manage the considerable risks it entails?

- *Vendor integration issues:*

  IT vendors have contradictory interests in electronic integration. On the one hand, integration can expand the market for their products and services. On the other hand, integration can reduce their ability to capture benefits from their investments in product development. What strategies do vendors use (including everything from pricing and standards to interfirm alliances) to promote or inhibit integration, and why? How should user organisations cope (proactively or reactively) with these strategies? How is the IT world changing shape as a result of alliances among vendors and service providers, and what are the implications for user organisations? What distinguishes the ITs (or vendors) that become dominant in the market place from those that become marginal or fail?

- *Socio-economic integration issues:*

  IT enables substantial increases in the speed of economic processes. How strong is this effect in various sectors of the economy, and what are the social effects? Which industry 'middlemen' prosper, which are eliminated, and why? How does consumer and household behaviour change as a result of an increasingly electronic economy? Can we develop early warning systems for potentially irreversible negative social effects? How can we intervene effectively at the industry or societal levels of analysis? What types of public policy changes are needed and effective?

What's in a name?

As far as the name of our field is concerned, a focus on 'integration' might provide a way around the discomfort created by current terminological fashions. The term MIS (management information systems) become prominent, even predominant, for AIS in the 1970s. But in the 1980s, many academics came to prefer the label IS (information systems), possibly because the technology was now for everyone, not just managers, possibly because the same acronym was widely used in industry to refer to departments that supply information services. In the 1990s, most IS specialists have come to prefer the term IT (information technology) for their departments as well as for the technology, possibly because systems (applications) are moving out of their sphere of influence, possibly because of the growing importance of information technologies that do not require user organisations to perform procedural programming (e.g. cellular telephones, personal digital assistants, the World Wide Web).

At the present time, the AIS field has not caught up with industry terminology, and both IS and IT are used widely and interchangeably. This indiscriminate usage blurs the important distinctions between them. (Not all information technologies are information systems, although all ITs have both production and use systems. Conversely, not all information systems are electronically-mediated.) Further, it intensifies confusion over what the field is all about. As an example of this confusion, I mention three recent personal experiences in which the name we give our field was an issue.

My first title for this chapter referred to the 'MIS field' to mirror the volume editors' usage. When I shared an earlier version, two colleagues at different institutions urgently pleaded '*Please* don't call it MIS. Our field is so much more than just *management* information technology.'

Last year, at a SIM (Society for Information Management) International board meeting (I am current serving as Vice-President of Academic Community Affairs), I heard a CIO angrily protest against a new SIM mission statement that featured 'information management'. He insisted on having 'technology' in the mission statement, since 'after all, *technology* is why we're all here'.

Somewhat later, my colleague Peter Drucker remarked to me that 'The problem with your field, is that you haven't figured out that it's about *information,* not about technology.' This is a statement with which some other IS academics will agree (Tom Davenport among them). Yet, I personally remain uncomfortable with substituting 'information management' for 'information systems and/or technology', since the term 'information' does not to me adequately connote 'communication' (which is important and different enough from information to warrant separate mention), and since there are undeniable technical issues that affect, for example, the quality of business information.

My own personal contribution to the terminological turmoil is 'Integration Teknowledgy', where 'integration' is shorthand for 'electronic integration of socio-economic activity' and 'teknowledgy' is my term for 'knowledge and skill in the area of electronic content, information, communication, technologies, and systems'. And, whenever you use the acronym term 'IT' to refer to our field, I will know exactly what you mean.

Concluding Thoughts

In this chapter, I have argued that the AIS community must directly confront arguments that there is no need for an IT discipline because the technology is ubiquitous and embedded in other areas of knowledge, and that we should view this argument, not simply as an issue of disciplinary *turf,* but rather as a manifestation of major technological, social, and institutional changes that challenge our historic definitions of customer and core mission. I have argued that whether we choose to support our historic customer—the organisation that uses IT—or whether we choose to pursue growing new customer segments in the IT industry—e.g. outsourcers, integrators, consultants, vendors—we must rethink our mission and update our intellectual capital. In addition, I have examined the obvious alternatives to our historic mission of systems development and/or management of IS—organisational improvement and IT infrastructure—and have found them both limited. On the other hand, I argued that a focus *on electronic integration of socio-economic activity* would unite the technical and behavioural segments of our field, would work for current and potential customer groups, and would work for both existing and emerging technologies for the foreseeable future. Taken seriously, this new mission for AIS would do far more than just suggest a new name for our field. It would suggest new lines of curriculum development and an expanded research agenda for both the technical and the behaviour subgroups in the AIS community.

I would be remiss to close this chapter without at least mentioning two important uncertainties that might affect the ability of the AIS field to set its own course for the future. One involves the nature of competition among business schools, the second involves the structure of business knowledge.

Information technology offers the potential for educational institutions to extend their offerings to students at a distance, and some schools are already doing so. The possibility exists for this use of IT to combine with demographic, social, and economic trends leading to aggressive competition, mergers, or alliances among schools, shakeouts, etc. A likely response to increased competition is differentiation among educational institutions by customer, mission, or both. Recent changes in AACSB guidelines would in fact support schools in presenting the same subject matter to students in very different ways depending on institutional mission. Institutional differentiation could, in turn, promote fragmentation within academic disciplines, particularly those like ours with pre-existing tensions and subgroups.

Recent years have seen a broad rebalancing of business focus from functionally oriented (e.g. sales and marketing) toward process oriented (e.g. order fulfilment, new product development) management. Business schools, by and large, remain functionally organised, as does the production of academic business knowledge. However, a number of business schools are introducing cross-functional courses into their curricula; some are virtually dismantling the functional structure of management education by means of redesigned courses and team teaching. It remains to be seen how widespread and lasting these innovations will be and how great, if any, will be their effect on the academic business disciplines and their research programmes. Nevertheless, almost any such effect would be in the direction of dissolving boundaries among existing disciplines and promoting new hybrid specialities.

Both increasing differentiation of business school missions and increasing cross-functionality in academic management knowledge production would tend to intensify identity conflict within the AIS field, perhaps to the point of crisis. The best insurance against such conflict in the future is to address the identity issue in the present. Let's not worry about whether the AIS field will go away. Let's *make* the AIS field of the past go away, so that we can create the IT field of the future!

References

Benjamin, Robert I., and Levinson, Eliot (1993), 'A Framework for Managing IT-Enabled Change', *Sloan Management Review*, Summer: 23–33.

Boddy, David, and Buchanan, David (1992), *Take the Lead: Interpersonal Skills for Project Managers* (New York: Prentice Hall).

Buchanan, David, and Boddy, David (1992), *The Expertise of the Change Agent: Public Performance and Backstage Activity* (New York: Prentice Hall).

Checkland, Peter (1981), *Systems Thinking, Systems Practice* (Chichester: John Wiley & Sons).

Cusumano, Michael A., and Selby, Richard W. (1995), *Microsoft Secrets: How the World's Most Powerful Software Company Creates Technology, Shapes Markets, and Manages People* (New York: Free Press).

Friedman, A. L. (1989), *Computer Systems Development: History, Organisation and Implementation* (Chichester: John Wiley & Sons).

Grudin, Jonathan (1991), 'Interactive Systems: Bridging the Gaps between Developers and User', *IEEE Computer*, 24, 4, Apr.: 59–69.

Keen, Peter G. W. (1991), *Shaping the Future: Business Design through Information Technology* (Boston: Harvard Business School Press).

Markus, M. Lynne (1994), 'Do-It-Yourself Reengineering', *Drucker Magazine*, Spring: 13–16.

—— and Benjamin, Robert I. (1996), 'Change Agentry: The Next IS Frontier', *Management Information Systems Quarterly*, Dec.

—— and Keil, Mark (1994), 'If We Build It They Will Come: Designing Information Systems that Users Want to Use', *Sloan Management Review*, Summer: 11–25.

Meyer, Marc H., and Zack, Michael H. (1996), 'The Design and Development of Information Products', *Sloan Management Review*, 37, 3, Spring: 43–59.

Morrison, Joline, and George, Joey F. (1995), 'Exploring the Software Engineering Component in MIS Research', *Communications of the ACM* 38, 7, July: 80–91.

Mumford, Enid, and Weir, Mary (1979), *Computer Systems in Work Design: The ETHICS Method* (New York: John Wiley & Sons).

Poltrock, S. E., and Grudin, J. (1994), 'Organisational Obstacles to Interface Design and Development: Two Participant Observer Studies', *ACM Transactions on Computer–Human Interaction*, 1, 1: 52–80.

Schaffer, Robert H., and Thompson, Harvey A. (1992), 'Successful Change Programs Begin with Results', *Harvard Business Review*, Jan.–Feb.: 80–9.

Soh, Christina, and Markus, M. Lynne (1995), 'How IT Creates Business Value: A Process Theory Synthesis', *Proceedings of the Sixteenth International Conference on Information Systems* (Amsterdam): 29–41.

Strassmann, Paul A. (1995), *The Politics of Information Management: Policy Guidelines* (New Caanan, Conn.: Information Economics Press).

Weill, Peter (1993), 'The Role and Value of Information Technology Infrastructure: Some Empirical Observations', in Rajiv D. Banker, Robert J. Kauffman, and Mo Adam Mahmood (eds.), *Perspectives on the Strategic and Economic Value of Information Technology Investment* (Middletown, Pa.: Idea Group Publishing).

9

IS Evaluation
A Process for Bringing Together Benefits, Costs, and Risks

BARBARA FARBEY, FRANK LAND, AND DAVID TARGETT

Introduction

Investment in information technology (IT) and associated information systems (IS) in the UK is substantial. Fifty-eight of the top 150 companies spend more than 2 per cent of turnover on IT and 96 more than 1 per cent (Spikes Cavell, 1996). In 1995/6 central government spending in the UK was of the order of £2.31bn (Taylor, 1996). Statistics from other countries reveal massive IT expenditure throughout the industrialised world. At the same time IT spending is under pressure from the perception of a 'productivity paradox'. At firm, industry, and economy level the relationship between IT spending and return in the form of greater productivity and shareholder value is seriously questioned (for example, Loveman, 1994). However, these findings are much debated (for example, Brynjolfsson, 1993) and a number of reasons why purely statistical findings could be misleading have been suggested, one of which is that inadequate evaluation practices have resulted in poor selection and management of projects.

At the level of the IT practitioner there has been relentless pressure on IT departments and businesses generally to cut costs and account for money spent, yet few organisations appear to be satisfied with their evaluation procedures. Very few evaluate IT investment consistently, either within IT or as between IT and other investments. The 'value for money' question has been a major concern for a number of years (Price Waterhouse, 1990–5).

These debates and concerns have been reflected in increased activity in researching IT evaluation in recent years. In this chapter we review this research and go on to make theoretical and practical proposals which stem from the literature and from three major research projects carried

Some of this work was supported by the ESRC research grant R000 23 3758. The authors are most grateful for this support.

out by the authors in the years 1989–96. The first section describes the role of evaluation and its relationship to other matters of concern such as benefits and risks. The second reviews the current state of the art as reflected by the literature. We then describe briefly our three projects. The core of the chapter is in the next four sections which discuss four major themes that have emerged from our research, which employs an interpretativist approach, and the literature. The themes are the variety of evaluation methods available, how to select the best method to use in a given situation, the impact of evaluation on the IT decision-making process, and the increasingly important factor of project dynamics. The penultimate section offers some recommendations for best practice before we conclude by speculating on the future.

Defining the Role of Evaluation

Evaluation is often spoken of as if it were a once-for-all episode happening close to the commencement of a project with the principal intention of comparing measurable benefits and costs in order to decide whether the project should go ahead. However, in both theory and practice the concept is much broader.

Definition

The first broadening is in terms of the meaning of evaluation. The origin of the word 'evaluation' is that of 'drawing the worth out'. This expression carries two important implications. The first is that the *worth* being drawn out is not just, as is sometimes assumed, the positive quantitative benefits. The 'worth' could include negative and qualitative factors. It might be helpful to think of evaluation in terms of Fig. 9.1.

Hard benefits are the quantifiable positive outcomes, typically cash savings from staff reduction. 'Hard Costs' are the measurable costs of the system's hardware. However, this cell is not as clear-cut as it may appear. It should also include many measurable but overlooked costs such as training, restructuring, and the acquisition of employees, often with new skills. *Soft benefits* refers to items such as job enrichment but it also includes some elements which are the whole rationale of a strategic IS—competitive advantage, improved customer service, and so on.

Risks is the most complex cell. Risk includes all the things that can go wrong, not just the measurable finances that could turn sour. This cell incorporates resistance to changing work practices, changing market situations, changing strategy and so on. It also incorporates uncertainty. This might simply mean uncertainty over the level of costs and benefits streams, or their time horizon. Or it might mean uncertainty over the causal factors

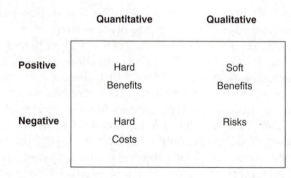

Fig. 9.1. *Broad evaluation*

which link the project with its impacts, for example whether the managers of the branches of a retail chain will make profitable use of the management information the new system makes available to them. See Farbey et al. (1993) for a detailed categorisation of benefits and costs.

The second implication of 'drawing the worth out' is that the *worth* has to be sought. The full range of costs and benefits will almost certainly not be obvious and it may require considerable effort to discover what they are. Research (Farbey et al., 1993) has shown that many projects bring unanticipated benefits but also that anticipated benefits may not be realised. Likewise there are unexpected costs and many projects go over budget. So, the task of evaluation is as much to do with discovering what the costs and benefits are as putting numerical values to them.

Evaluation dynamics

The second broadening is in terms of the dynamics of evaluation. An organisation may want to evaluate a project at any of several stages in its development and implementation. The main stages are when:

1. The decision to outsource the IT function is taken. The outsourcing of IT-related parts of the core business is now so prevalent and its impact on investments and projects so great that this stage must be seen as a pre-strategy stage of evaluation.
2. Strategy is being developed. An IT strategy should be being developed alongside the business strategy and the role of IT will have to be assessed in general terms before either strategy can be finalised.
3. A specific project has been defined. This may be an application or a decision to install IT infrastructure. At this stage the project has usually to be cost justified in the context of other capital investments.
4. The project is in the developmental stage. Checks must be made to ensure that internal and external changes have not affected the feasibility of the project.

5. The project has reached the point of 'sign off'. Responsibility is being transferred from the IT department to the user department. The users have to sign that the system does what is required.
6. The project has just been implemented. The system is checked to ensure that it is working as planned and is beginning to deliver the anticipated benefits.
7. The project has been in operation for some time. Evaluation at this stage monitors the project's impact, compares actual costs and benefits with planned costs and benefits, identifies unexpected benefits and costs, and records lessons for the future.
8. The project is nearing the end of its life and the feasibility of replacement options is being investigated.

Kumar (1990) has suggested that organisations are not clear about the different purposes of evaluation and may confuse these stages. In particular what is seen as an evaluation by an IT manager, and even by senior general management, may not be so. It may merely be the 'sign off' or closure of the project. In different organisations there may well be other stages and substages when evaluation is carried out. It may even be better to view evaluation as a continual process.

Our working definition of evaluation for the rest of the chapter is therefore as follows. It is a process, which takes place at different points in time or continuously, for searching for and making explicit, quantitatively or qualitatively, all the impacts of an IT project (or group of projects, i.e., a programme, or the overall application of IS, i.e. a strategy).

State of the Art: A Literature Review

The outline of a contemporary approach to IT evaluation began to emerge in the 1980s. A spate of journal papers and books in the late 1980s and early 1990s complemented earlier writing, picking up older, unsolved problems and proposing new perspectives and new solutions. The earlier writing included for example Emery (1976) and Land (1976). In the UK the theme of evaluation was taken up in the late 1980s by among others Earl (1989), Hochstrasser (1990), Silk (1990), Symons (1990), Symons and Walsham (1991), Farbey et al. (1993), Walsham (1993*b*), Ward (1990), and Willcocks (1992). There was similar interest elsewhere (for example Bjorn-Andersen and Davis, 1988; Remenyi et al., 1991; and Weill, 1992). In particular the newer writing addressed the question of the so-called strategic information systems (SIS) which were perceived as different in kind from the older 'transaction' systems and thus requiring new methods of evaluation (Earl, 1989).

There were a great number of methods on offer. These ranged from the IT specific, for example return-on-management (Strassmann, 1985), to the general, for example, return-on-investment (ROI) (Brealey and Myers, 1991). They included methods relying on quantitative assessment of costs, benefits, and risks such as information economics (Parker et al., 1988). There were also 'softer' methods, for example multi-criteria, multi-objective methods (Chandler, 1982) as well as those based on modelling and experiment, for example systems dynamics models (Wolstenholme et al., 1993).

Nonetheless research showed that in practice little attention was paid to formal evaluation of IT investment. Instead many substantial investments were defended as 'acts of faith' or 'got to do' or simply 'strategic'. Where formal evaluation did take place it tended to be a version of ROI or other finance-based technique, undertaken very early in the project life cycle or at the point where the system was handed on from the developers to the users (Willcocks, 1992; Kumar, 1990). Post-implementation audit was rare. Appraisal and evaluation[1] were viewed negatively as hoops which had to be jumped, an organisational imposition which took up valuable working time. They were not perceived as positive activities leading to better decisions, tighter control, happy users, and greater benefits.

In fact neither practice nor theory saw much of a role for mechanical cost–benefit calculation albeit for different reasons. Academic writing highlighted specific concerns (Galliers, 1995; Symons, 1990; Ward, 1990; Willcocks, 1992; among others):

- the treatment of costs, risks, and benefits was unsatisfactory;
- the difficulty of dealing with intangible benefits was leading to neglect of important aspects of the investments;
- conversely the emphasis on tangible costs, benefits, and risks was leading to the bending of rules;
- there had been a failure to create a strategic climate in which IT could be related to the strategic direction of the organisation;
- the focus of evaluation was too narrow, concentrating on the system in itself, rather than the intervention as a whole of which the (new) system was just a part;
- evaluation methods were aimed in the main at project level. Other levels were important too, for example the IT portfolio.

Academic prescriptions followed the diagnosis, calling for:

- a more accurate view of the strategic value of systems: Earl (1989);
- a broad view of what was to be evaluated, including portfolio evaluation: Ward (1990);

---

[1] Following the convention in public sector practice, we will use the terms 'appraisal' to refer to evaluation activity which takes place before system implementation, i.e. *ex ante*, and 'evaluation' for activity after implementation, i.e. *ex post*. Where the distinction is not required we use 'evaluation' as the generic term.

- a more holistic approach: Galliers (1995), Wolstenholme et al. (1993);
- recognition of the role of evaluation in organisational learning: Symons (1990);
- greater appreciation of the wider purposes served by evaluation, including its political and persuasive effects: Farbey et al. (1993);
- more attention to accounting systems in theory and practice: Willcocks (1992);
- further exploration of softer methods for determining costs, benefits and risks: Symons and Walsham (1991), Walsham (1993*a*), Keen (1995), among others;
- greater emphasis on post-implementation audits: Farbey et al. (1993).

Taken together these prescriptions represented if not exactly a new consensus, then at least a fresh approach: broader, more insistent on the social nature of evaluation, and perhaps as a consequence less mechanistic, more situated and contingent than before.

Three Projects

Our own research is based on three major projects carried out over the years 1989–96.

Project One: 1989–1991

Our research investigated sixteen IT projects all of which had just been implemented or were about to be implemented. The main focus of the research was to study how the projects had been evaluated. The systems concerned were management related and in the area of office automation. Broadly, eleven of the sixteen were specific applications, three were providing infrastructure, and two were senior management support systems. The projects were located in a wide range of private and public sector organisations.

Evidence about each of these systems, from the original conception through to the latest position, was collected from relevant documentation and from interviews with the people involved in the development and running of the systems. In particular the research sought to interview the 'champions', the people who had a major influence in getting the project accepted.

As far as evaluation was concerned *ad hoc procedures* were used in the majority of systems investigated. Even when a formal prescribed method was used it was frequently customised to suit the exigencies of a particular situation. The ad hoc methods used in the cases studied can be classified under the following headings.

1. *Top-Down Strategic*: senior management believes IT is fundamental to the success.
2. *Top-Down by Dictat*: corporate headquarters make rules on what divisions can do.
3. *Incremental Change*: next step is determined by technological change or obsolescence.
4. *Competitive Imperative*: the organisation must use IT to survive.

For a full description of the overall findings of the research, see Farbey et al. (1993).

Project Two:[2] 1993–1996

Besides the general concerns about evaluation, specific concerns arose from Project One.

• Project One investigated projects that had gone ahead, relying on recollection. It would be valuable to carry out longitudinal research, investigating projects as they happened and including those which were not completed according to plan.
• For the same reason Project One had little sense of project dynamics. We now wished to research how project decision-making processes evolved.
• A method for matching project to evaluation method was developed empirically in Project One. It worked effectively but we wished to develop a theoretical basis.

These concerns led to the formation of Project Two. The methodological approach was to develop an in-depth, interpretative study, following the progress of planned investments over a sustained period. Case studies were the primary research instrument, based on action research, collaborative enquiry, interviews, documentation, and literature. We followed twelve main projects in nine organisations. The projects ranged across the systems life cycle from strategy formation through development and implementation to benefits management, maintenance, and decommissioning. Each represented a significant capital investment.

To collect data we attended company meetings, wrote reports, participated in workshops, maintained telephone contact, and conducted interviews. The interviewees were key personnel including project sponsors, project managers, senior IS managers, and users. Some of the data was provided by our collaborators directly, in the spirit of collaborative enquiry. A systematic framework was employed to keep the accounts coherent both within and between cases. In addition the research team kept a series of

[2] This project was supported by the ESRC research grant R000 23 3758. The authors are most grateful for this support.

informal research notes to record ideas and comments which might otherwise have been lost in the long time scale of action research.

The results of this project have not been published at the time of writing. However, a number of the findings are reported as part of the 'four themes' described later in the chapter.

Project Three: 1995/6

The third project stemmed from interest in the early results of the second. Our remit was to investigate the appraisal and evaluation of IT investments and projects in the public sector and consider the extent to which benefits had been achieved from them. We were then to recommend improvements to the appraisal and evaluation processes.

Based on the remit, it was decided to carry out research into six IT projects in six different public sector organisations. In choosing the cases we were looking for significant projects, that is projects which by virtue of the size of the investment, newness, or widespread application would be likely to yield insights of interest beyond the six cases studied. All six were either fully implemented or close to implementation. They covered a range from clear success to probable failure. In each case we were looking at appraisal and evaluation but it was not possible to do this in isolation from the whole process by which these systems are developed, managed, and implemented: appraisal and evaluation were threads running through that process with substantial influence at all parts of it. For each project we studied relevant documents and interviewed key members of staff, including both providers and users of the systems as well as senior managers as appropriate.

The findings from this research include practical suggestions for improving the evaluation process. They form a significant part of the 'best practice' recommendations reported later in the chapter.

Four Themes

Theme 1: the variety of evaluation methods available

Our research has shown that not many organisations rely only on formal techniques to appraise IT investments; those that do usually restrict calculations to return-on-investment methods. However, a range of evaluation methods for IT investments is available. The following is a brief list.

- return-on-investment (ROI);
- cost–benefit analysis;
- multi-objective, multi-criteria decision-making (MOMC);
- boundary values;
- return-on-management;

- value analysis;
- business process enhancement;
- information economics;
- experimental methods:
    - prototyping;
    - simulation;
    - gameplaying;
- methods from non-business areas:
    - critical appraisal
    - adversarial debate
    - connoisseurial judgement.

Each method has its own distinctive characteristics which dictate the situations in which it can be used. There is no one method which is universally applicable but they have all been developed to enable organisations to cope with common evaluation problems. For example, MOMC can help with the problem of determining what the benefits of a project are and can also help to reduce resistance to changed working practices.

Theme 2: matching technique with project

The characteristics of an information system which affect evaluation. Evaluations are needed at different stages in the development of an information system, and for different purposes. These factors, purpose and timing, are two of the many influences on the way an evaluation is carried out. The range of factors is wide because every IT project, and its organisational context, has characteristics which influence the choice of a suitable evaluation technique. At the same time every evaluation technique has characteristics which point to the set of circumstances in which it could be applied. A first step in deciding how to evaluate is therefore to understand more about these factors. Our empirical findings suggest that the factors affecting the evaluation of an IT project can be classified into five main groups.

1. The role of evaluation. The role of an evaluation is defined by the time (stage of the project) and level (seniority) at which it is carried out.

2. The decision environment. The environment in which a decision has to be made may be more or less constrained. IT decisions do not occur in a vacuum, and the choice of a method of justification must, at the very least, match the culture of the organisation and the prior history of implementing information systems.

3. The system underlying the IT investment. The system can be summarised as two variables. The first is the nature of the system: whether it is a specific application or provides an infrastructure. The second is the relation of the system to the business: whether the system is in a supporting role or core.

4. The organisation making the investment. The competitive position of the organisation may also effect evaluation. One factor is the industry situation: whether it is stable or turbulent. A second is the leadership role of the organisation: whether it aims to pioneer or to follow.

5. Cause and effect relationships. The degree to which it is possible to predict the impact of the new system is an important factor in determining how to do an evaluation (Kydd, 1989). The impact of the new system may be direct (immediate staff reductions) or indirect ('better' information which will depend on the skill of a manager to use it). The degree of uncertainty is equally important. The impact of a system may be clear (the number of staff saved can be calculated precisely) or it may be uncertain (the reduction in stock-outs at a supermarket is not so easy to calculate). These factors are described in detail in Farbey et al. (1997).

From a knowledge of evaluation techniques and from the characteristics of a particular system, it should be possible, in theory at least, to match an IT investment with a suitable method of evaluating it but the process would be both lengthy and imprecise. The purpose in the next section is to find a *systematic* means of performing the matching process.

A *matching process*

In our earlier research (Farbey et al., 1992) we developed, empirically, a process for matching a system with an evaluation technique. The process has three stages:

1. Represent the circumstances of the project as crosses on a series of 2 × 2 matrices.
2. Locate each evaluation technique at some point on another 2 × 2 matrix.
3. Overlay the matrices to match project with technique.

The location of the crosses, whether clustered or dispersed, is used to suggest the range of techniques that might be applied. In some cases all crosses may fall within the same quadrant giving a strong indication of exactly which techniques might be suitable. In other cases the crosses might be spread around indicating that the choice is not clear-cut and that several techniques could be used.

In subsequent research we validated the matching process and developed a theoretical basis for it (Farbey et al., 1997). As described above, the matrices describing project characteristics were derived empirically, abstracting from interviews and the literature. The evaluation methods were assigned to cells according to their dominant features following our definitions of the two axes as: 'well-defined' vs. 'fuzzy' evaluation constraints and 'conservative' vs. 'radical' role of IT.

The method has proved to be effective for the projects we were studying and also for other researchers working independently. However, there is a theoretical platform which explains why the method works. The classification, which is due to Hellstern (1986), comes from the 'evaluation research' body of work. It is also available in the IS literature in an article by Earl and Hopwood (1987) where it is discussed in terms of strategic decision-making. Taking all three classifications together, it becomes clear that they are essentially the same. In particular, the logic which underpins the Hellstern categorisation and the language which he uses provide a rationale for our empirically discovered method.

Hellstern is writing about the problems of evaluating programmes in the context of public policy. The sorts of programme with which he is concerned are major governmental programmes, such as Head Start in the USA. They are social interventions and he writes that,

'technical' program evaluations . . . may prove to be successful for well defined problems with clear goals and clear causal relations . . . most problems . . . are ill-structured . . . with substantive problems varying from actor to actor and over time; they are dynamic. Such problems are not mechanical and cannot be separated from the context.

This adds a new dimension to the argument which we have been making. We have argued for consideration of different methods principally on the grounds that a variety of methods was necessary to match the variety of situations encountered in evaluating IT. Following Hellstern, it is possible to argue for variety on the grounds not only that the problems are often ill structured, as is suggested in some of our descriptions of situations, but also that the lack of structure itself has two bases: lack of structure with respect to objectives and lack of structure with respect to knowledge of cause and effect.

Expanding the argument: if information systems are complex and pervasive socio-technical systems whose life extends over several months or even years then investment in IS can be understood as a programme of social action, based on a complex technology and taking place over a substantial period in time. Such investments are in many ways like the programmes of social action which are the subject of evaluation research. In particular they generally present problems to the evaluator which are poorly structured. The lack of structure has two bases: lack of clear objectives and a lack of knowledge as to the potential impact of the systems and hence a lack of knowledge as to cause and effect.

Looking at the axes of our matrices, it can be seen in most cases that the distinction being made follows this same split. The vertical axes (constraints on evaluation) of the individual matrices represent situations where the objectives are not clear, whether the objectives of the system or the objectives of the evaluation. The horizontal axes reflect uncertainty about cause and effect. By definition, conservative action is action undertaken in known circumstances; radical action is not.

Looking next at the matrix of methods against which the descriptions are to be matched, and using Hellstern's description of the contexts, we now assert that the critical features of each method are those which determine:

1. how far they contribute to, or are based upon, a knowledge of cause and effect;
2. how far they assume, or contribute to the formation of, clear and agreed objectives.

Theme 3: evaluation as part of decision-making

One of the major objectives of Project Two was to investigate the IT decision-making processes of which evaluation forms a part. Decision-making in general tends to be complex and confusing, and early research concentrated on conceptual simplifications which attempted to make some sense of it. For example, Simon (1955) developed 'bounded rationality' and Lindblom (1959) saw decision-making as incremental, 'muddling through'. In the 1980s researchers tried to improve our understanding by categorising different types of decision process. For example, Hickson et al. (1989) identified three types of process: sporadic, fluid, and constricted.

More recently research has moved in the opposite direction, attempting to expose the full intricacy of decision-making. Langley et al. (1995) proposed a model of decision-making which tried to capture the complexity and included a range of interacting factors which could affect the process. Our research, which is based on interpretativism and grounded theory, has led us in this same direction. In the spirit of this approach a number of complex issues have emerged from our work. The findings have not yet been fully analysed or published but some of the issues are presented here in descriptive mode.

Formal evaluation methods The case research in Project Two showed that formal appraisal and evaluation procedures have become more common. All except one of the investments observed were formally appraised. The exception was a case in which disaster recovery procedures were under consideration and an unexpected drop in the cost of providing security rendered evaluation unnecessary.

The formal evaluation was, however, not always decisive in determining the initiation or continuation of a project. Other factors, political or strategic, entered into the decision. The basic scheme was a return-on-investment calculation supplemented by a statement of the expected contribution to strategic aims. The most sophisticated appraisal procedures were found in the financial sector.

Organisations used evaluation procedures that were not always part of the formal evaluation or recognised for what they were. Examples of such techniques were the procedures used by a manufacturing organisation which set up a 'panel of experts' to deal with the technical and financial evaluation of six product offerings and a financial services organisation which carried out a requirement by requirement analysis, with some RAD, which amounted to a form of value analysis.

Adversarial methods were implicit in many organisations. In one organisation a 'project board' had a role as arbitrator of disputes which could not be settled at a lower level. The resolution of these disputes remained adversarial, with each side putting its case for the board to decide. If a decision could not be reached, it was likely that more senior people would be drawn in, thus keeping the process adversarial.

Evaluation, i.e. *post hoc* evaluation, was not well done although many organisations paid lip service to the concept. The most advanced procedures were in the public sector where they are often mandatory, although even here the implementation of post-project reviews was fraught with practical difficulties. On the other hand one health authority developed and implemented a well-thought-out benefits management project.

Criteria   The research took place against the backdrop of a distinctive economic climate. The need to remain competitive by cutting costs was seen to be paramount and the way to cut costs was by cutting staff. But towards the end of the research there were some signs that the cost-cutting approach was changing and with it the criteria for formal evaluation. In the later interviews additional factors such as control and customer value were part of the discussion. Some organisations were thinking in terms of strategic benefits. For example, one organisation was looking at projects which added value and/or enhanced control; another had a system for project selection and prioritisation which allowed the portfolio to track the current strategic thrust; another used criteria for acceptance which were adapted as time went by to reflect new strategic thinking.

Ideas of business process re-engineering were common currency and although few of the cases were implementing BPR, most were apologetic or regretful that they had not done so. Also BPR, and the values it implies, are now regularly challenged in the literature and one would expect this to filter through quite quickly to organisations like the ones in Project Two (Grint et al., 1996).

Actors   With prolonged observation it became apparent that there were three principal groups of actors within the project situation: the sponsors, the users, and the systems people. This is in contrast, partly, with the more commonly implied view in IS writing of two groups: users and systems people (developers).

The significance of the difference is most easily explained using game theory (for example Friedman, 1991). Game theory suggests that three-person games are fundamentally different from two-person games. More-over, most noticeably in one organisation where we were able to observe more than one case, these were repeated games, again fundamentally different from two-person, single-shot games. As it happened in this organisation the actors in each game (project) overlapped, so that what we were witnessing was a series of similar games, with shifting particip-ants, interests, and coalitions. At times it felt as though one were part of a 'segmented' society (Gellner, 1991) in which small groups would be in opposition to one another in some contexts, say the project context, but would band together to fight a larger battle beyond it. At others it felt more Hobbesian 'each against all'.

An important side-effect was that many project participants were not aware of, or were unable to fathom, the larger picture. Metaphorically they were like Rosencrantz and Guildenstern in Tom Stoppard's play of the same name (and, as in the play, some projects ended up dead). Moreover, in both Projects Two and Three we found instances of two people stand-ing in two different hierarchical relationships to each other. In Project Two, despite an initial goodwill and considerable intelligence on both sides, the position became unsustainable. One was caught in a political pincer movement and withdrew. Internal competition and internal mar-ket organisation reinforced these internal tensions and multiple games.

In other words, relationships between stakeholders in a project were not necessarily confined to that project but extended beyond it. These relationships were 'multi-stranded' (Gellner, 1991). The project was one meeting ground among others, so that for example, if there were pre-existing tensions between IS and the business, or between two user depart-ments, they would carry through into the project. The project became a continuation of the war by other means.

The roles played by each group, users, sponsors, and developers, varied. 'Users' came in different flavours. The 'user' on a project board was most likely to be a representative of the sponsoring department or a manager with experience of the area affected by the new system but no longer active within it, rather than a hands-on user. This could create problems if the user representatives were out of touch with current practice, or 'went native' (Farbey et al., 1995).

The role of the business sponsor was critical. A powerful sponsor could act either to rescue a project or to sink it. An investment in one organ-isation lost momentum when it lost senior management support. In another two investments were finally lost because they could not attract the financial support of a senior business sponsor.

Two further sets of actors were unexpectedly prominent: 'suppliers', i.e. hardware vendors and software contractors or outsourcers, worked very closely indeed with some of the organisations studied. Hardware suppliers were part of and influential on at least one project board where outside analysts would work shoulder to shoulder with in-house analysts. 'Consultants' were also very influential. They were for example responsible for setting ball-park targets, which in-house actors would then try to match.

The levels at which decisions are made   Many evaluation methods focus on single projects. However in theory as well as practice evaluation is conducted at many levels. Writers within IT who address questions at levels other than the individual project include Barua and Kriebel (1995, single business units), Dos Santos et al. (1993, market value), CCTA (1992, portfolio analysis), Monk (1993, infrastructure), Parker et al. (1988, information economics and linkage), Rivard and Kaiser (1989, value analysis), Ward (1990, portfolio), Weill (1992, firm performance). Many of these problems are addressed outside of the 'traditional' IT investment evaluation literature. According to Galliers (1995), 'the concept of considering investments of a synergistic nature as a "bundle" rather than as individual, isolated investments within a bundle, is gaining considerable ground in accounting circles'.

There may also be analogies to be drawn with other disciplines. For example, when considering portfolios with limited resources, ecological ideas of competition, survival, and balance may be appropriate (Bateson, 1987).

The research showed that in practice evaluation was required at the levels of:

- subproject;
- project;
- programme;
- portfolio;
- IS strategy;
- corporate;
- industry;
- IT department.

The purposes of evaluation   Appraisal and evaluation are not simply undertaken for the purposes of deciding whether or not to initiate or continue a project. As well as feedback studies organisations may undertake feedforward and predictive studies. Examples provided by our studies included a *feedback* study assessing the performance of an existing system as well as a *feed-forward* study assessing what could usefully be brought to bear on a proposed new system from existing system components: hardware, software, training, and experience (Canavet, 1995—a doctoral thesis linked to our research).

Evaluation may be summative, emphasising performance and attainment of objectives, or formative, that is, designed to illuminate and learn. Methods like ROI are essentially summative, their purpose is accounting and control. Formative evaluation is a common notion within the discipline of 'evaluation'. It has recently gained ground in IS writing, for example Kaplan (1995) and Keen (1995). Formative evaluation was often asked for in meetings and interviews by senior managers. However in the constricted climate of recession which affected most of the organisations, this was not usually taken up.

Theme 4: project dynamics

One of the most rewarding findings of Project Two, which went beyond the original objectives, was the increased awareness of the vulnerability of projects, the volatility of their value, and the ability to differentiate some of the causes. Projects were vulnerable to cancellation at any stage.

At the initial (feasibility) stages they had to compete with other projects for resources, both money and skills, in a situation where there were ever-tighter controls on projects accepted for development. Only two of the projects accepted for development reached the implementation phase. One project fell when the organisational procedure it was supposed to support was scrapped at very short notice. A second could not proceed because the people concerned were not able to agree the numbers which were to go into the business case. A third could not continue following a review of business cases. The project was part of a series of interrelated projects, all of which were reviewed and each of which had to show that there was either a sound business case, or a business sponsor who was prepared to take it on. The project concerned did not meet either criterion. One project stalled when the systems supplier collapsed. Another was held up (although not for long) when management decided to change supplier. The value of projects could change dramatically. The value of one system dropped very suddenly when the market which it was intended to support collapsed. Parts of the system were implemented, but the project had an operational rather than a strategic focus and finished up as a feeder system in a larger scheme. Its value in the end came from the learning experience it provided in developing systems and handling suppliers.

Investments took time to customise and deliver. Meanwhile value seeped away. For example, one project was intended to replace an existing, but outdated, purchasing system. Delays to this project meant that savings from the new system were delayed too. In another organisation a system required major customisation effort at each local site, again delaying implementation.

Interest and attention from senior management fluctuated. For example in one organisation it was hardly surprising that senior management became preoccupied elsewhere when the organisation was subject to a hostile takeover bid. In another the organisation itself was split in two parts and again senior management attention was 'otherwise engaged'. Interest in evaluation itself and evaluation activity fluctuates across the life cycle (Savolainen, 1995).

Some Best Practice Recommendations

In Project Three a major feature of our remit was to recommend improvements to the appraisal and evaluation processes. Our recommendations were based on the literature and all three of our research projects. Some of the main recommendations, which fell into four categories, are summarised here. The full recommendations are described in a restricted report (Farbey et al., 1996).

1. Factors which are known but not applied in practice

A number of the projects we investigated were to some extent failures. Often and surprisingly, the primary causes of failure stemmed from factors and errors which are well known and often feature in development methodologies. In practice they are sometimes ignored with disastrous results. Here is a list of the main ones.

- Project boards could learn from analogous projects but we came across virtually no attempts to do this.
- Business cases should include all benefits, tangible and intangible, certain and uncertain, so that the benefits can be managed and therefore realised. But benefits are frequently omitted because they are difficult to handle or politically embarrassing or hinder the approval procedures.
- We found few formal processes for realising benefits.
- For a major strategic project, affecting the core of the business, evaluation needs to be a more or less continual process.
- Costing estimates should include the full cost of ownership not just the hardware.
- Supply risk should be calculated and minimised, perhaps via a reliability panel; a number of projects got into serious difficulties because of supplier inadequacy or failure.
- Organisations should respond to known risks. For example, one organisation identified a series of risks in a new strategic plan but went ahead with it without making appropriate adjustments or developing contingency plans. It was as if noting the risks was sufficient.

2. *Additions/amendments to existing methodologies*

Failure and difficulty also arose from factors which could easily be corrected by minor amendments to development methodologies.

- Workshops for the project board and other important stakeholders at the outset of a project could help to promote consistency; different groups of actors can hold remarkably contrasting perspectives on a project—and often no one is aware of these differences.
- Potential benefits should be updated and pursued throughout the project's life cycle; this relates to the need for a continuing evaluation process.
- Project boards were usually surprised by the major problems that arose; a formal and explicit constraints analysis at the project outset would ameliorate the situation.
- A range of evaluation methods and techniques should be considered.
- *Post hoc* project evaluations were often based solely on the objectives set out in the original project brief; for major systems the business and its strategy has nearly always moved on by the end of the project. It was sometimes the case that a project was branded a failure (when evaluated against the original objectives) whereas if it had been evaluated against the changed current situation it would probably have been deemed a success.

3. *Shifts in principles or mindsets*

Other recommendations are more fundamental and required significant shifts in current thinking about projects by practitioners.

- Strategic thinking, i.e. considering all the business aspects of the project not just the IT, needs to be present from the outset and maintained throughout projects. Senior management's delegation of a project to less senior members of staff on a project board often means the original strategic thinking, and the ability to maintain it, is lost.
- Project boards which are often located centrally within an organisation usually perceive projects differently from the ultimate users who may well be on the periphery, i.e. in branches or local offices. The dissonance between the two groups can be the root of failure; a cultural analysis of organisations/offices in which the system is to be implemented would be helpful.
- Local offices should be classified in selecting trial sites and preparing for implementation.
- Projects are usually seen as 'fixed' from the moment the go-ahead is given, and therefore the task is to implement the specification on time and within cost; but major projects exist in a fluid environment and

methodologies would better focus on strategy and benefits, rather than requirements and costs.

4. New techniques and tools

These recommendations imply that two major new techniques are required by organisations developing major information systems:

- a process for carrying out a cultural analysis of target organisations and groups;
- a process for managing and realising benefits.

Conclusions

The evaluation of IS investments is better done than formerly but is not yet a tame problem. A 'tame' problem is 'one which can be specified in a form agreed by any relevant parties, ahead of the analysis, and which does not change during the analysis'. A 'wicked' problem, by contrast, is 'ill-defined' (H. W. I. Rittel and M. M. Webber, as quoted in Rosenhead, 1989). The evaluation of IS is a little 'tamer' than it was only a few years ago. The technology itself is more familiar, as are its uses and applications. Continuing recession, strenuous competition, and pressure on costs have forced management to take a grip on IT budgets and to compare them with other areas of corporate expenditure. The mystique which protected some budgets is no longer credible. Evaluation is demanded and done.

However, the continuing sources of wickedness need to be taken into account.

Change. There is substantial and significant change within projects throughout the life cycle. Regarding the project as an intervention in an organisational context there are two types of change to be taken into account. The first is the 'natural' change that one would expect from a complex, creative activity, the kind that would be dealt with in routine if occasionally acrimonious meetings and 'requests for change'. It is the *nature of the intervention* which changes. The second, which has shown up very clearly in this research, is *contextual* change: to markets, strategy, structure, and policy. Towards the end of the research there were signs of an even broader change to the dominant philosophy itself. Since value derives from the 'intervention-in-its-context', tameness in one part of the problem does not imply the tameness in the other. Most of the projects were wicked on both dimensions.

Multiple stakeholders. The research, particularly in Project Two, showed that there are many relevant stakeholders in a major project and this leads of itself to complexity. The research also showed that the stakeholders often stand in multiple relationships with each other (multi-strandedness). The choices they make may be influenced not only by the project in hand but by all the other connections. When there are many relevant stakeholders the decision that is being made is a social choice as opposed to an individual choice (Elster and Hylland, 1989). Social choice needs to be structured, as do the criteria for supporting choice, and a mechanism for making the choice must be developed

Multifactorial problems. Tracing cause and effect relationships is extremely difficult, if not impossible. The introduction of a new system is always accompanied by other changes, for example: new work practices in business process re-engineering, new marketing initiatives, new business relationships using EDI. Such changes interact with those implemented in the new systems and with each other. Singling out one factor, the new system, for evaluation is at best conditional and at worst counter-productive as managers attempt to control the part instead of managing the whole.

Programmes. Projects may have intricate links with other projects in a major programme. The value to the organisation is ultimately the value of the whole, but this may be too complex to comprehend. There is a danger of suboptimisation.

This chapter has concentrated almost exclusively on findings which relate to evaluation. However, evaluation is simply one of many inter-related management activities and there are equally many findings and recommendations which relate to general management. It is anticipated that these will form a 'second front' for future work. Three broad management issues stand out as relating to the progress of a project and determining the climate for evaluation. (1) *Proactive management,* especially to gain commitment, is crucial to the advancement of projects at every stage. (2) IS departments find it very difficult to appreciate the urgency and pace required by general management in the 1990s. Nor do they always appreciate the need to 'market' the system constantly. The assumption that once a project had been accepted that is the end of the matter is false. Projects must be continuously fought for and related to present and future management concerns. (3) It is at least possible that emotion plays a greater part in decision-making than has been recognized in IS writing. In many organisations we studied, the behaviour at project boards was overtly political. People were there to represent their own patch and, where necessary, formed alliances and coalitions. However, the emotional overtones of some of the discussions were also evident. People were afraid of losing their jobs, or that someone close to them would lose theirs. Project board chairs often played on an emotional palette, not a political one, to gain commitment. Fear, embarrassment, pride were the levers, not power, or not only power. Our work has revealed several issues for further research. They can be grouped into three broad categories.

1. Evaluation

Allocation of costs. Companies find themselves in a considerable dilemma when attempting to justify common infrastructure. This is dealt with either by taking a 'strategic' decision, i.e. not justifying it, or by allocating all the cost to the first or very early projects which use it. This distorts the value of individual projects. Cost allocation is a particular problem for inter-dependent projects.

Portfolio construction. Although there are examples of sound common sense in accepting or rejecting projects within a programme or portfolio there is very little theoretical work that bears on the problem. Some clues are available from accounting theory. A different line of attack would be to regard the portfolio as an ecology in which different projects stand as different life forms competing for resources. This would change the perspective from the parts to the whole (Bateson, 1987).

Neutrality. Evaluation is not a neutral tool. The methods used profoundly affect the outcome and which projects are accepted. The criteria for investment, even when they have the appearance of objectivity, as does the hurdle rate, are socially determined (Miller, 1994). Both methods and criteria affect the power structures and reflect them. The use of whole life costing for example, changed the numbers sufficiently to cause great anxiety among those whose projects were affected.

Influence. Culture, strategy, and organisation structure are determinants of meaning and value within an organisation. Evaluation is an activity addressing the value of an investment in terms which are meaningful in the organisation. At the same time, the process of articulating values for an evaluation exercise is a formative activity, affecting among other things the terms of discourse and hence the concept of value.

2. Management

Project guidelines for managing large-scale, interdependent projects. These projects present a series of management problems. Should they be managed top-down or bottom up? What control and decision structures should be in place? How should the overall programme be split up? How should the rewards and financing of these subprojects be organised so that the whole is not jeopardised by suboptimal behaviour in the parts?

Stakeholders. The identification and role of a wide range of stakeholders were issues in nearly all the projects yet little in-depth work has been done in this area.

3. Processes

Appraisal and evaluation occur across the life cycle. There may be a way to design either individual ongoing evaluations or a series of evaluations in different periods, taking into account principles of factorial design.

New techniques such as case-based reasoning (Allen, 1994) and genetic programming (Levy, 1992) could be considered in the context of evaluation. CBR is rather like boundary values in that it looks to external experience. It provides far more detailed comparisons than does boundary values, leads to exploration and learning, and could be used to surface assumptions and gain agreement. Genetic programming uses evolution to optimize complex functions and in so doing provides a window for the workings of evolution, i.e. for greater understanding of how projects work (evolve).

Problem-structuring methods could form a useful front-end to evaluation procedures (Rosenhead, 1989). These are methods which structure decisions and problems rather than attempting to solve them. They include for example, cognitive mapping (C. Eden) and soft systems methodology (P. B. Checkland), as well as decision conferencing (L. Phillips), analytic hierarchy process (T. Saaty), and systems dynamics modelling (J. Morecroft) (all are referenced in Rosenhead, 1989). Their function would be to clarify goals and constraints, possibly in tandem with, say, MOMC methods.

References

Allen, B. P. (1994), 'Case Based Reasoning: Business Applications', *Communications of the ACM* 37, 3: 40–2.

Barua, A., Kriebel, C. H., and Mukhopadhyay, T. (1995), 'Information Technologies and Business Value: An Analytic and Empirical Investigation', *Information Systems Research*, 6, 1: 3–23.

Bateson, G. (1987), *Steps to an Ecology of Mind: Collected Essays in Anthropology, Psychiatry, Evolution and Epistemology* (Northvale, NJ: Jason Aaronson Inc.).

Bjorn-Andersen, N., and Davis, G. (1988), *IS Assessment: Issues and Challenges* (Amsterdam: North-Holland).

Brealey, R. A., and Myers, S. C. (1991), *Principles of Corporate Finance*, 4th edn.: international (New York: McGraw-Hill Inc.).

Brynjolffson, E. (1993), 'The Productivity Paradox of Information Technology', *Communications of the ACM*, 56, 12: 67–77.

Canavet, S. (1995), 'The Role of Information Systems Evaluation across an Extended System Lifecycle', unpublished Ph.D. thesis, University of London.

CCTA (1992), *Prioritisation: A Brief Guide*, ISD Planning Subject Guides (London).

Chandler, J. S. (1982), 'A Multiple Criteria Approach for Evaluating IS', *MIS Quarterly*, 6, 1: 61–74.

Dos Santos, B., Peffers, K., and Mauer, D. C. (1993), 'The Impact of Information Technology Investment Announcements on the Market Value of the Firm', *Information Systems Research*, 4, 1: 1–23.

Earl, M. (1989), *Management Strategies for Information Technology* (New York: Prentice Hall).

226   *Barbara Farbey, Frank Land, David Targett*

Earl, M., and Hopwood, A. (1987), 'From Management Information to Information Management', in E. K. Somogyi and R. D. Galliers (eds.), *Towards Strategic Information Systems*, vol. i, Strategic Information Systems Management series (Tunbridge Wells: Abacus Press).

Elster, J., and Hylland, A. (1989), *Foundations of Social Choice Theory* (Cambridge: Cambridge University Press).

Emery, J. C. (1976) (ed.), *We Can Implement Cost Effective Systems Now* (Princeton: EDUCOM).

Farbey, B., Land, F. F., and Targett, D. (1992), 'Evaluating Investments in IT', *Journal of Information Technology*, 7: 109–22.

—— —— —— (1993), '*How to Assess your IT Investment: A Study of Methods and Practice* (Oxford: Butterworth Heinemann).

—— —— —— (1995), 'A Taxonomy of Information Systems Applications: The Benefits' Evaluation Ladder', *European Journal of Information Systems*, 4: 41–50.

—— —— —— (1996), *Report to HM Treasury* (Bath: School of Management, University of Bath) (confidential).

—— —— —— (1997), 'Evaluating IT Investments', in L. Willcocks (ed.), *Evaluating IT Investments* (London: Chapman & Hall).

Friedman, J. W. (1991), *Game Theory with Applications to Economics*, 2nd edn. (Oxford: Oxford University Press).

Galliers, R. (1995), 'Rethinking IT Evaluation in the Context of Business Systems Strategy', in B. Farbey, F. F. Land, and D. Targett (eds.), *Hard Money—Soft Outcomes* (Henley-on-Thames: Alfred Waller in association with UNICOM).

Gellner E. (1991), *Plough, Sword and Book: The Structure of Human History* (London: Paladin Grafton Books).

Grint, K., Case, P., and Willcocks, L. (1996), 'Business Process Reengineering Reappraised: The Politics and Technology of Forgetting', in W. J. Orlikowski, G. Walsham, M. R. Jones, and J. I. DeGross (eds.), *Information Technology and Changes in Organisational Work* (London: Chapman & Hall).

Hellstern, G-M. (1986), 'Assessing Evaluation Research', in F. X. Kaufmann, G. Majone, and V. Ostrom (eds.), *Guidance, Control and Evaluation in the Public Sector* (Berlin: de Gruyter).

Hickson, D., Butler, R., Cray, D., Mallory, G., and Wilson, D. (1989), 'Decision and Organisation Processes of Strategic Decision-Making and their Exploration', *Public Administration*, 67, 4: 373–90.

Hochstrasser, B. (1990), 'Evaluating IT Investments: Matching Techniques to Project', *Journal of Information Technology*, 5, 4: 215–21.

Kaplan, B. (1995), 'Information Technology and Three Studies of Clinical Work', *ACM SIGBIO Newsletter*, 15, 2: 2–5.

Keen, J. (1995), 'The Evaluation of Leading Edge Technologies', in B. Farbey, F. F. Land, and D. Targett (eds.), *Hard Money—Soft Outcomes* (Henley-on-Thames: Alfred Waller in association with UNICOM).

Kumar, K. (1990), 'Post-implementation Evaluation of Computer Based IS: Current Practice', *Communications of the ACM*, 33, 2: 203–12.

Kydd, C. T. (1989), 'Understanding the Information Content in MIS Management Tools', *MIS Quarterly*, 13, 3: 277–90.

Land, F. (1976), 'Evaluation of Systems Goals in Determining a Decision Strategy for Computer-Based Information Systems', *Computer Journal*, 19, 4: 290–4.

Langley, A., Mintzberg, H., Pitcher, P., Posada, E., and Saintmacary, J. (1995), 'Opening up Decision-Making: The View from the Black Stool', *Organisation Science*, 6, 3: 260–79.

Levy, S. (1992), *Artificial Life: The Quest for a New Creation* (London: Penguin Books).

Lindblom, C. E. (1959), 'The Science of "Muddling Through"', *Public Administration Review*, 19: 79–88.

Loveman, G. (1994), 'An Assessment of the Productivity Impact of Information Technologies', in T. J. Allen and M. S. Scott Morton (eds.), *Information Technology and the Corporation of the 1990s* (Oxford: Oxford University Press).

Miller, P. (1994), 'Accounting as Social and Institutional Practice: An Introduction', in A. G. Hopwood and P. Miller (eds.), *Accounting as Social and Institutional Practice* (Cambridge: Cambridge University Press).

Monk, P. (1993), 'The Economic Significance of Infrastructure Systems', *Journal of Information Technology*, 8: 14–21.

Parker, M. M., Benson, E. W., and Trainor, H. E. (1988), *Information Economics: Linking Business Performance to Information Technology* (Englewood Cliffs, NJ: Prentice Hall).

Price Waterhouse (annual), *Information Technology Review*, Price Waterhouse.

Remenyi, D. S. J., Money, A., and Twite, A. (1991), *A Guide to Measuring and Managing IT Benefits* (Oxford: NCC, Blackwell).

Rivard, E., and Kaiser, K. (1989), 'The Benefits of Quality I/S', *Datamation*, Jan.: 53–8.

Rosenhead, J. (1989), 'Introduction', in J. Rosenhead (ed.), *Rational Analysis for a Problematic World: Problem Structuring Methods for Complexity, Uncertainty and Conflict* (Chichester: John Wiley & Sons).

Savolainen, V. (1995), 'Analysis of the Dynamic Nature of Information Systems Performance Evaluation', in B. Farbey and V. Serafeimides (eds.), *Proceedings of the Information Systems Evaluation Workshop, European Conference on Information Systems, Athens, Greece*.

Silk, D. J. (1990), 'Managing IS Benefits for the 1990's', *Journal of Information Technology*, 5, 4: 185–93.

Simon, H. (1955), 'A Behavioural Model of Rational Choice', *Quarterly Journal of Economics*, Feb.: 99–118.

Spikes Cavell (1996), *Corporate IT Strategy* (Newbury: VNU Business Publications).

Strassmann, P. (1985), *Information Payoff: The Transformation of Work in the Electronic Age* (New York: Free Press).

Symons, V. (1990), 'Evaluation of Information Systems: IS Development in the Processing Company', *Journal of Information Technology*, 5: 194–204.

—— and Walsham, G. (1991), 'The Evaluation of Information Systems: A Critique', in R. Veryard (ed.), *The Economics of IS* (Oxford: Butterworth Heinemann).

Taylor, P. (1996), 'Squeeze on the Big Spenders', *Financial Times*, 4 Sept. 1996.

Walsham, G. (1993a), 'Interpretive Case Studies in IS Research: Nature and Method', *European Journal of Information Systems*, 4: 74–81.

—— (1993b), *Interpreting Information Systems in Organisations* (Chichester: John Wiley & Sons).

Ward, J. (1990), 'A Portfolio Approach to Evaluating Information Systems Investments and Setting Priorities', *Journal of Information Technology*, 5, 4: 222–31.

Weill, P. (1992), 'The Relationship between Investment in IT and Firm Performance: A Study of the Valve-Manufacturing Sector', *Information Systems Research*,
3, 4: 307–33.

Willcocks, L. (1992), 'Evaluating Information Technology Investment: Research
Findings and Re-appraisal', *Journal of Information Systems*, 2, 4: 243–68.

Wolstenholme, E. F., Henderson, S., and Gavine, A. (1993), *The Evaluation of Management Information Systems: A Dynamic and Holistic Approach* (Chichester: John Wiley
and Sons).

10

Accounting as a Representational Craft
Lessons for Research on Information Systems

RICHARD J. BOLAND, JR.

Introduction

In order to deal with the broad topic of how the traditions of research in accounting can provide lessons for our approach to thinking about research in information systems, I have found it necessary to narrow the scope of this study considerably. I will focus on financial and managerial accounting, and will not be touching on other topics of accounting research, such as taxation or auditing. I have also chosen to avoid accounting research based on agency theory, behavioural decision-making, capital markets, and so-called positive theory. This narrowing still leaves a large domain, and as an organising theme for considering that body of research I will focus on the construction and use of accounting representations such as income statements, balance sheets, funds flow statements, budgets, and cost statements. I take these representations to be a distinctive feature of accounting for which the information systems field has no counterpart.

Information systems are designed to create reports, report-generating systems, decision systems, work flow systems, group systems, and enquiry systems of all sorts, but none of those systems is associated with well-defined representations such as those that have been developed in the practice of accounting. Accountants have extensive experience in developing accounting statements which constitutes a representational craft. In the information systems field, we have a craft for developing information systems (Hirschheim et al., 1996), but not one for developing representations.

The categories, classifications, measurements, codings, and summarizing techniques employed by a particular information system are a function of its design, and the direction of research in information systems is towards making the possibilities for creating representations as open ended and flexible as possible. Accounting representations, in contrast, are relatively well defined and stable. Techniques of financial accounting, for instance, have evolved over many centuries (Littleton, 1933; Mattessich, 1987) being first documented over 500 years ago in Luca Pacioli's 1494 treatise *Summa de arithmetica, geometria, proportioni: et proportionalita*.

Accounting practices have been integrated with the process of govern-ance since ancient Mesopotamia (Mattessich, 1987), and have been relied upon for managerial control of organisations since at least the thirteenth-century English manor farm (Oschinsky, 1971). Factory cost accounting and budgeting analysis essentially similar to those of today have been in use by industrial firms since the mid-nineteenth century (Johnson, 1972; Chandler, 1977; Kaplan, 1984). The accounting curriculum in American universities has taught the making of these representations throughout the twentieth century, and before that apprentice programmes had been training young accountants in the proper construction of accounting rep-resentations for several centuries (Previts and Marino, 1979).

I will explore some of the features of accounting research which derive from its established craft of making representations and will contrast them with our tradition of research in the information systems field. This contrast makes possible an understanding of ways in which information systems research follows a different strategy in its relation to the firm and to management from that of accounting. I conclude by suggesting how developing a concern with representations can strengthen research in information systems.

How a Concern with 'Getting it Right' Leads to a Unique Reflexivity in Accounting Research

Accounting representations have a formal logic that restricts the forms they may take (Nehmer, 1988). The basic rules of construction and interrela-tionships of double entry bookkeeping, the balance sheet, and the income statement provide a limited set of forms and methods for producing ac-counting representations of a firm (Littleton, 1933; Mattessich, 1957). Within these rather well-defined constraints for creating a representation of the financial status of a firm, accountants have a long tradition of trying to 'get it right' with those representations (Young, 1995*b*). To 'get it right' means to make a representation that is a truthful depiction of a firm's financial results and position. This search for a truthful depiction leads to a continuing concern with fairness, relevance, and accuracy of the rep-resentations themselves. The profession of accountancy solidified itself as an institution in financial markets during the 1930s when key practitioners claimed in testimony on the Securities Exchange Act to have general principles for constructing and evaluating 'right' representations of a firm using the restricted, formal language of accounting. Accountancy's claims to possess general principles for 'getting it right' with financial represen-tations were unfounded at the time, and remain so today (Boland, 1982).

Professional claims to expertise have, not surprisingly, become an object of accounting research in their own right, as have the peculiar problems posed by the limitations of the formal language of accounting. Regardless of the false claims that justified an expertise in making such representations, the profession has endured and flourished. Claims of expertise aside, accountants as a profession have established their representations of the financial condition of a firm as an institutionalised practice.

The unique strategies of accounting research associated with a concern for the established representations of accounting will be surveyed under two broad headings: research on accounting representations as part of organisational control systems and research on accounting representations as interventions in social and economic processes. Because of the well-developed and relatively stable character of accounting representations, each of these topics includes historical research on the development of accounting representations as well as cross-cultural research on differing practices with them.

The stability of accounting as a representational practice over the last few centuries has provided a unique opportunity for accountants as a community of practice (Lave and Wenger, 1991) to elaborate and refine their income statement, balance sheet, and managerial accounting statements. These representational forms involve practices of categorisation, measurement, and logics of assemblage that have been subject to careful examination and critique during this period of relative stability. This has been a process of perspective-making (Boland and Tenkasi, 1995) that has resulted in a strong, community-wide knowledge of what accounting representations are, what their limitations are, and how they should be employed in different circumstances. Representational forms such as the income statement and balance sheet are applied uniformly to a wide variety of organisational types, but managerial accounting representations for responsibility reporting, flexible budgeting, or investment centre reporting are closely associated with specific organisational structures and practices.

It is in part because of the extensive analysis and experimentation with these few representational forms that we see accounting researchers displaying a higher degree of reflexivity about their practice than we do in the information systems arena. By this I mean reflexivity on the limitations of any particular representational form, reflexivity on the history of those representational forms, and reflexivity on the way those representational forms affect and are affected by organisations and social systems. These heightened forms of reflexivity enable accountants to approach their research with a more strategic orientation than we tend to see in information systems. They enable an approach to research that puts the process of making and using representations into a larger, richer, more elaborate set of contexts than that available to researchers in the information systems area.

The relatively fixed representational forms of accountancy are a self-imposed constraint on their practice, and are undoubtedly a limitation

232 *Richard J. Boland, Jr.*

to their ability to represent different aspects of socio-economic systems. Accountants have attempted to broaden their representations into areas such as the environment or society at large, with proposals for new forms of accounting, including non-financial statements, to represent these non-traditional domains. New areas such as environmental accounting and social system accounting have been under discussion for decades, but have not been well received and are not generally accepted as part of accounting practice.

I argue, though, that it is just because accountancy has worked under rather strict limitations of its representational forms that it has been able to make more fundamental and important enquiries into the strategic analysis of representational practice that both accounting and information systems share as a professional concern. Working on problems of representation within the limits of a well-specified formal language such as the language financial and managerial accounting provides (Mattessich, 1957; Carlson and Lamb, 1981; Nehmer, 1988; Bailey et al., 1992) means that accountants will 'bump up against' the limits of representations in a way that information systems practice does not. Accountants have come to recognize that representations of the firm and its activities have an arbitrariness associated with them that cannot be ignored or overcome.

In the financial accounting domain, for instance, accountants' long history of attempting to produce income statements and balance sheets that were 'right' has led to an awareness that they cannot portray both the process of change over time (as in an income statement) and the conditions at a point in time (as in a balance sheet) using a consistent vocabulary and set of rules. If, for instance, they use current market values to represent assets and liabilities on a balance sheet in a more 'accurate' way, they will distort the representation of costs in the income statement. They also recognize that representation necessarily requires allocations of costs and revenues among categories, and that such allocations are incorrigible. Transfer pricing mechanisms for allocating revenues and expenses among divisions in a multi-divisional company produce representations that are inherently flawed and unable to meet the multiple demands that managers place upon them (Tricker and Boland, 1982). Allocations across time, such as the assignment of depreciation expense to calendar periods, or allocations across space, such as the assignment of production costs to products, have an unavoidable arbitrariness to them (Thomas, 1969; 1997).

Supplying the 'Right' Accounting Representation versus Providing Desired Information

This awareness of the limits of representation that accountants have developed is important in shaping their strategic sense of what accounting is and how it should be researched in a way that has not happened in the information systems field. Information systems practice, in part because it has not confronted the limits of representation, takes as its mission the satisfaction of 'user needs' (Boland, 1979). The emphasis is on methods of identifying what information the intended user of a system desires or should have, without particular concern that a representation might not be able meaningfully and coherently to satisfy them. This lack of reflexivity on the limits of representational practice places information systems practitioners in a different strategic relation with their clients from that of accountants, and in a different strategic relation to their status as professionals. Accountants, when confronted with challenges to their representations, tend to stand in place and confront them, whereas information systems researchers either ignore them or place their hopes on the development of new technologies to solve their representational problems.

Representations that have a relatively stable history of presence in organisations are able to serve as potent boundary objects which provide a focus of conversation within and between managers and others (Star, 1989). Accounting representations of a firm's specific circumstances are such a boundary object. They have an identifiable and stable shape, vocabulary, and logic of use which readers can use as a focal point for engaging in critical dialogue. They are open to endless, irresolvable debates, which stimulates the analysis of assumptions and meanings, or at least the raw material for such analysis. When confronted with the limits of their representations, accountants stand before them and work on improving them. They move towards 'getting it right', through slow and continuous adjustments which include:

- innovations of form (categories, classifications, genre),
- innovations in precision (measures, data management, speed), and
- innovations in analysis (logics, criteria, values).

Even seemingly large steps like activity-based costing (Cooper and Kaplan, 1988; Kaplan, 1992*b*) are really quite modest as far as a transformation of practice is concerned. By standing still when faced with a problem of representation, accountants remain within their traditions of representation and work to refine their established forms and methods of analysis. This is the locus and driver of their heightened reflexivity on practice compared to information systems practitioners or academics.

Information systems researchers in contrast do not have specific representations to refine with innovations in form or analysis. Instead, they work on innovations in precision and on innovations in the methods of system design and development including requirements analysis, system-building, and project management (Hirschheim et al., 1996). The difficulties they encounter with representations are difficulties in the construction of representations in general, and can be side-stepped by invoking the future power of computers. In a manner of speaking, when faced with a problem of representation, they 'flee forward' into their hopes for a future technology.[1] They can look forward to a new processor, a new storage and retrieval system, or a new development methodology to solve their problem with representations in general. The accountant, grappling with the limits of a specific representation, reflects upon and innovates with the representational forms themselves.

With a specific and relatively stable set of representations, accountants have been able to institutionalize as a profession, with claims to an expertise in the construction, validation, and reading of their representational forms. This enables accounting researchers to display a reflexivity on their representations and on the professional status of accounting practice that is not available to information systems researchers. That is, accounting researchers ask if their representations are true, appropriate, and fair. They ask how the representations came to be the way they are. They also ask if a representation can be an intervention into the culture and process of an organisation. They ask if accountants' claims to expertise are valid, and what the limits of that expertise might be. The information system researcher, in contrast, deals with representation in general and tries to improve information systems by listening to the customer and satisfying needs. The accounting researcher is concerned about needs, too, but that concern is subservient to the accountants' determination to get the representations right, and to the research questions that follow from a realisation that no representation can make such a strong claim to truthfulness.

The accountant is thus in a supply-driven information economy, believing that the right accounting representations will satisfy needs. Creating refinements in accounting representations so that they are relevant and meaningful is the market imperative for the accounting information economy. The information systems researcher, in contrast, is in a demand-driven information economy, believing the customer is always right when it comes to a demand for information. Providing a flexible response to customers' requests and facilities to search the way they want for information to satisfy needs are the market imperatives for the information systems information economy.

Research on Accounting Representations as Control Systems

Accounting has been associated with the process of organisation control since the earliest prehistory of storage records on clay tablets in Assyria and Babylon (Chiera, 1938; Mattessich, 1987). From its role in monitoring

---

[1] The image of 'fleeing forward' into the hopes for an improved, future technology was brought to my attention by Ulrike Schultze and comes from the German expression 'Flucht nach vorne'.

medieval English manor farms (Oschinsky, 1971), through to the modern factory's integrated costing systems (Anthony, 1965), there has been a close historical association between accounting representations and organisation control systems. The structure of a firm's accounting function has long been understood as critical to the successful control of a firm's operations. Within the hierarchy of the firm, the accountant was seen as torn between the dual roles of making representations within guidelines set by top management and of interpreting those representations to inform the action of local management (Simon et al., 1954). The organisational structure of accounting services enabled and constrained the ability of accountants to perform these dual competing roles.

The use of accounting representations by managers was in turn seen as enabling and constraining their interpretation of events as well as their motivation to act (Hopwood, 1974; Watson and Baumler, 1975; Otley and Berry, 1980). I argue that it is in large part due to the stability and well-formed quality of accounting representations that this kind of research on organisational and behavioural dimensions is made possible. These representations provide a public and visible object around which questions of organisation structure, enabled and constrained behaviours, and social consequences can be addressed.

The relatively stable set of management accounting representations has allowed accounting researchers to theorize the form and function of representations in the organisation from a wide variety of perspectives, including organisation theory (Cooper et al., 1981; Covaleski and Dirsmith, 1983; Macintosh, 1981; Spicer and Ballew, 1983; Fisher, 1994), social theory (Collins, 1982), corporate strategy (Simons, 1987; Miller and O'Leary, 1994) and manufacturing strategy (Miller and O'Leary, 1994; Abernethy and Lillis, 1995). More recently, the role of multiple representations and multiple logics in organisational control systems has been highlighted (Munro, 1993; McSweeney, 1995).

The stability and visibility of accounting representations in an organisation, and the accounting profession's refined sense of expertise in their construction and deployment, has also led to a reflexive critique of the profession and a questioning of their claims to such an expertise (Burchell et al., 1980; Hoskin and Macve, 1986; Cooper and Hopper, 1987; Dillard and Burris, 1993). This reflexive look at the profession and its practices includes an examination of the social and organisational context in which accounting representations are crafted (Hopwood, 1983, 1987) and ethnographic studies of accountants and managers practising their crafts (Tomkins and Groves, 1983; Preston, 1986).

As part of the critical analysis of accounting and its claims to expertise in crafting representations, the role of institutional forces in creating and sustaining accounting practice is raised (Meyer, 1986; Richardson, 1988). These analyses challenge the official history of the profession (Hunt and

Hogler, 1993) and the taken for granted understanding of its practices and their foundations (Power, 1992; Humphrey, 1994; Chua, 1995). The integrity of their profession and its operations in the political process of standard setting and enforcement are also brought under critique (Young, 1995a, 1996; Bealing et al., 1996).

The relatively stable set of accounting representations also allows for a concern with the history of those representations—how did they come to be in their current form? Histories that trace sequences of events in the development of the profession and its representations as a progressive evolution have a long tradition in accounting research (Littleton, 1933; Staubus, 1987; Wardell and Weisenfeld, 1991; Edwards, 1992; Bhimani, 1993; Bryer, 1993). The involvement of accounting representations in shaping and being shaped by significant historical periods such as Stalinism (Bailey, 1990) or South African Apartheid (Arnold and Hammond, 1994) are also evident. Unique adaptations of accounting representations to non-traditional settings such as religious communes (Flesher and Flesher, 1979) and utopian movements (Sotto, 1982) have also been studied. This kind of historical research on the development of representational forms and their role in a broad array of social and economic practices has no counterpart in the information systems field. We do see histories of information technologies and their genres of use in organisations (Yates, 1993; Beniger, 1986), but these have been from historians and other scholars outside the information systems field.

Research on Accounting Representations as Social Interventions

The long period of time during which accountants have crafted their set of relatively stable representations has allowed them to become sensitive to the ways that such representations shape and are shaped by social and economic practices (Scott, 1933; Hopwood, 1983, 1994; Boland and O'Leary, 1991). Accounting representations, in part because of the claims to expertise that lie behind their construction, were taken to be generalizable across wide domains of human activity (Birnberg and Gandhi, 1976). Yet, the problem of meaning and equivocality in even the most well-formed accounting representations was also recognized (Boland, 1979; Colville 1981; Boland and Pondy, 1983). The power of accounting representations to carry logics and values, enabling authority to act at a distance, is well recognised in accounting research (Hoskin and Macve, 1986; Robson, 1992, 1994). The power of accounting representation to transform practices and logics operates on work groups in the kindergarten (Jönsson, 1992) as well as on the factory floor (Jönsson and Grönlund, 1988). But it is recognized that accounting representations are not a monolithic power. They have multiple forms and can present an ecology of views with which actors frame and reframe organisational issues (Dermer, 1990).

Careful orchestration of political rhetoric and calculative practices with accounting representations can shape social transformation as in the Progressive Movement in America (Covaleski and Dirsmith, 1995). It can also transform the nature of work and the identity of the worker on the factory floor (Miller and O'Leary, 1987, 1994). Accounting research is increasingly concerned with uncovering the active role of accounting representations in governance. This movement is especially evident in the work of Miller and O'Leary (1987, 1994) who have inspired others to track the way calculative practices shift over time, bringing multiple expertise and the many practical details of governing in the economic and political spheres into tenuous alignments. Young's (1995*b*) study of the shifting uses of accounting representations in the savings and loan crisis is a good example of this type of research.

This tradition of research in accounting also explores the way that the construction and use of representations includes the shaping of cognitions, beliefs, and behaviours in a community practice (Czarniawska-Joerges, 1992). Accounting representations are an intervention in the life of an organisation and its members. Accounting representations as interventions are inextricably intertwined with a wide range of cultural and social practices that are increasingly becoming objects of research in their own right (Hopwood, 1994).

The interrelations are complex, multiple, and dynamic, calling for careful study of their development over time. Hoskin and Macve (1986, 1988) demonstrate how this complex development is part of a larger societal process of knowledge/power relations through which the very idea of managerialism is produced. Miller and Napier (1993), following a similar line of argument, show how our technologies of calculation are discursive in nature and do not flow from a point of origin, but emerge from the contingent conjunction of disparate practices and ideals. Bhimani (1994) explores how such interdependencies include the way that changes in concepts of human subjectivity and human sensitivity to economic motivations interact with changes in the logic and structure of organisation control systems. Colignon and Covaleski (1988) trace one such interaction, showing the way that an organisational crisis can trigger a process of change, with an unfolding set of adjustments between managerial practice and accounting representations. Pinch et al. (1989) dramatize the unfolding, reflexive quality of an intervention with accounting representations in a public health care setting.

Boland and Pondy (1983) also contrast how different management groups engage with accounting representations as they confront a revenue crisis in their organisations. In that study, Boland and Pondy highlight the way that accounting representations are experienced by the actors as inadequate for the complex political and moral choices that are being enacted. In a highly automated factory setting, Jönsson and Grönlund (1988) trace the way several sets of operators of integrated brake drum production lines take quite different paths in alternately changing their work practices and their locally recorded accounting representations. In an office setting, Den Hertog and Wielinga (1992) follow different ways that engineers reshape their practices with the introduction of initially similar accounting control systems.

Accounting representations as interventions are inevitably located in points of tension between the local and the global, the task and the strategy. Jönsson (1982) traces these tensions of organisational hierarchy and the role of trust in working with budgets in that near universal context. Interventions with accounting representations are dramatically evident in health care, where incorporating the logic of business and its associated accounting representations promises to remake and control the delivery of medical services. Bloomfield et al. (1992) and Preston et al. (1992) report on an extended study of the deployment of accounting as an organisational and political intervention in the British National Health Service, tracing the changes in health care administration and in the role of accounting representations.

A key element in the tension between the local and the global as reflected in accounting representations is the way that such representations shape the experience of time. Frederick Taylor's use of time studies in the construction of cost accounting systems (Chen and Pan, 1980) and Loft's depiction of time in the accounting for labour (1991) show the intimate relation between the construction of accounting representations and the construction of organisational experience. Ezzamel and Robson (1995) provide a compelling analysis of how accounting can structure the experience of time in organisations so as to affect its power and politics. Kavanagh and Araujo (1995) take this argument further with an insightful case study of how a manufacturing control system reshapes the possibilities for experiencing time and employing logics by both workers and managers.

Implications for Research on Information Systems

In this chapter I have contended that research in accounting, especially research in managerial accounting, has several distinctive features from research in information systems, and that these distinctive features derive from the craft of representation that is an integral part of accounting practice. The craft of representation opens unique questions and approaches in accounting research which are not evident in information systems research. Accounting representations, whether they be a balance sheet for an entire organisation or a management accounting report for a division or work unit, are constructed within the relatively stable forms and methods of accounting representational practice. A responsibility accounting statement, for instance, is constructed with a very specific notion of the structure of managerial authority that is in place in the organisation. Similarly, a transfer pricing mechanism is constructed to compensate for and work with other managerial practices and reward systems to maintain organisational control. There is no comparable set of logics guiding the design of reports or structuring of queries in a management information system. Whereas accounting is concerned with specific types of representations and the ways to 'get them right', information systems is concerned with representation in general. Information systems professionals are concerned with constructing representations, but they tend to be one-off, ad hoc responses to requests of the managers or staff being served by a system. As a result, the information systems area has a well-established concern with the process of developing systems, but little evidence of reflecting upon the various kinds of representations our systems are employed to create.

Only if we are concerned with the qualities and characteristics of specific types of representations are we in a position to ask questions such as 'how does this representation affect the control process in this organisation?', or 'how does this representation constitute an intervention into the socio-political process of this organisation?' Unless we have specific representational forms to observe in action, to redesign over time, and to argue about their underlying logics, we do not have a place to stand and reflect upon our practice of representation. When faced with a problem, we find ourselves instead 'fleeing forward' in hopes that a new round of technology advances in processors, storage, transmission, or display devices will eliminate the difficulty.

There are some rudimentary representational forms in the information systems field that we might use as boundary objects for taking a stand and reflecting upon our representational practice. The idea of 'critical success factors' has been discussed for a considerable time, with no evidence that it has been used by researchers to construct representations and reflect upon their logics, vocabularies, and consequences in practice. Similarly, the 'balanced scorecard' is being promoted as a new representational form for guiding managerial dialogue on organisational control (Kaplan, 1992*a*, 1993) but it has not become an object of information system research. The possibility of constructing representational forms with these two rudimentary ideas is only put forward as one alternative. It is not so important which representations we begin to explore. What is important is that we do begin exploring some representations in ways that parallel the research strategies in accounting. Standing before representations and reflecting upon the way their vocabularies and logics participate in the construction of organisational practices is the important point. Fleeing forward into technology will not get us nearly as far in our research as standing still in that way.

References

Abernethy, M. A., and Lillis, A. M. (1995), 'The Impact of Manufacturing Flexibility on Management Control System Design', *Accounting, Organisations, and Society*: 241–58.

Anthony, R. N. (1965), *Planning and Control Systems: Framework for Analysis* (Boston: GSBA Harvard University).

Arnold, P., and Hammond, T. (1994), 'The Role of Accounting in Ideological Conflict: Lessons from the South African Divestment Movement', *Accounting, Organisations, and Society*: 111–26.

Bailey, A. D., Jr., Han, K. S., Stansifer, R. D., and Whinston, A. B. (1992), 'A Formal Algorithmic Model Compatible with the Conceptual Modeling of Accounting Information Systems', *Accounting, Management and Information Technologies*: 57–76.

Bailey, D. (1990), 'Accounting in the Shadow of Stalinism', *Accounting, Organisations, and Society*: 513–25.

Bealing, W. E., Dirsmith, M. W., and Fogarty, T. (1996), 'Early Regulatory Actions by the SEC: An Institutional Theory Perspective on the Dramaturgy of Political Exchanges', *Accounting, Organisations, and Society*: 317–38.

Beniger, J. R. (1986), *The Control Revolution: Technological and Economic Origins of the Information Society* (Cambridge, Mass.: Harvard University Press).

Bhimani, A. (1993), 'Indeterminacy and the Specificity of Accounting Change: Renault 1898–1938', *Accounting, Organisations, and Society*: 1–39.

—— (1994), 'Accounting and the Emergence of "Economic Man"', *Accounting, Organisations, and Society*: 637–74.

Birnberg, J. G., and Gandhi, N. M. (1976), 'Toward Defining the Accountant's Role in the Evaluation of Social Programs', *Accounting, Organisations, and Society*: 5–10.

Bloomfield, B. P., Coombs, R., Cooper, D. J., and Rea, D. (1992), 'Machines and Manœuvres: Responsibility Accounting and the Construction of Hospital Information Systems', *Accounting, Management and Information Technologies*: 197–219.

Boland, R. J., Jr. (1979), 'Control, Causality and Information System Requirements', *Accounting, Organisations, and Society*: 259–72.

—— (1982), 'Myth and Technology in the American Accounting Profession', *Journal of Management Studies*: 109–27.

—— and O'Leary, T. (1991), 'Technologies of Inscribing and Organising: Emerging Research Agendas', *Accounting, Management and Information Technologies*: 1–7.

—— and Pondy, L. R. (1983), 'Accounting in Organisations: A Union of Natural and Rational Perspectives', *Accounting, Organisations, and Society*: 223–34.

—— and Tenkasi, R. V. (1995), 'Perspective Making and Perspective Taking in Communities of Knowing', *Organisation Science*: 350–72.

Bryer, R. A. (1993), 'Double-Entry Bookkeeping and the Birth of Capitalism: Accounting for the Commercial Revolution in Medieval Northern Italy', *Critical Perspectives on Accounting*: 113–40.

Burchell, S., Club, C., and Hopwood, A. G. (1980), 'The Roles of Accounting in Organisations and Society', *Accounting, Organisation, and Society*: 5–28.

Carlson, M. L., and Lamb, J. W. (1981), 'Constructing a Theory of Accounting: An Axiomatic Approach', *Accounting Review*: 554–73.

Chandler, A. D. (1977), The Visible Hand: The Managerial Revolution in American Business (Cambridge, Mass.: Harvard University Press).

Chen, R. S., and Pan, S. (1980), 'Frederick W. Taylor and the Evolution of Standard Overhead Costing', Working Paper 42 (n.p.: Academy of Accounting Historians).

Chiera, E. (1938), *They Wrote on Clay* (Chicago: University of Chicago Press).

Chua, W. F. (1995), 'Experts, Networks and Inscriptions in the Fabrication of Accounting Images: A Story of the Representation of Three Public Hospitals', *Accounting, Organisations, and Society*: 111–45.

Colignon, R., and Covaleski, M. (1988), 'An Examination of Managerial Accounting Practices as a Process Adjustment', *Accounting, Organisations, and Society*: 559–79.

Collins, F. (1982), 'Managerial Accounting Systems and Organisational Control: A Role Perspective', *Accounting, Organisations, and Society*: 107–22.

Colville, I. (1981), 'Reconstructing Behavioral Accounting', *Accounting, Organisations, and Society*: 119–32.

Cooper, D. J., Hayes, D., and Wolf, F. (1981), 'Accounting in Organized Anarchies: Understanding and Designing Accounting Systems in Ambiguous Situations', *Accounting, Organisations, and Society*: 175–91.

—— and Hopper, T. M. (1987), 'Critical Studies in Accounting', *Accounting, Organisations, and Society*: 407–14.

Cooper, R., and Kaplan, R. S. (1988), 'Measure Costs Right: Make the Right Decisions', *Harvard Business Review*: 96–103.

Covaleski, M. A., and Dirsmith, M. W. (1983), 'Budgeting as a Means for Control and Loose Coupling', *Accounting, Organisations, and Society*: 323–40.

—— —— (1995), 'The Preservation and Use of Public Resources: Transforming the Immoral into the Merely Factual', *Accounting, Organisations, and Society*: 147–73.

Czarniawska-Joerges, B. (1992), 'Budgets as Texts: On Collective Writing in the Public Sector', *Accounting, Management and Information Technologies*: 221–39.

Den Hertog, F., and Wielinga, C. (1992), 'Control Systems in Dissonance: The Computer as an Inkblot', *Accounting, Organisations, and Society*: 103–27.

Dermer, J. (1990), 'The Strategic Agenda: Accounting for Issues and Support', *Accounting, Organisations, and Society*: 67–76.

Dillard, J. F., and Burris, B. H. (1993), 'Technocracy and Management Control Systems', *Accounting, Management and Information Technologies*: 151–71.

Edwards, J. R. (1992), 'Companies, Corporations and Accounting Change, 1835–1933: A Comparative Study', *Accounting and Business Research*: 59–73.

Ezzamel, M., and Robson, K. (1995), 'Accounting in Time: Organisational Time-Reckoning and Accounting Practice', *Critical Perspectives on Accounting*: 149–70.

Fisher, Joseph (1994), 'Technological Interdependence, Labor Production Functions and Control Systems', *Accounting, Organisations and Society*: 493–505.

Flesher, T. K., and Flesher, D. L. (1979), 'Managerial Accounting in an Early 19th Century German-American Religious Commune', *Accounting, Organisations, and Society*: 297–304.

Graves, O. F., Flesher, D. L., and Jordan, R. E. (1996), 'Pictures and the Bottom Line: The Television Epistemology of U.S. Annual Reports', *Accounting, Organisations, and Society*: 57–88.

Hirschheim, R., Klein, H. K., and Lyytinen, K. (1996), 'Exploring the Intellectual Structures of Information Systems Development: A Social Action Theoretic Perspective', *Accounting, Management and Information Technologies*: 1–64.

Hopwood, A. G. (1974), *Accounting and Human Behaviour* (Englewood Cliffs, NJ: Prentice Hall).

—— (1983), 'On Trying to Study Accounting in the Context in which it Operates', *Accounting, Organisations, and Society*: 287–305.

—— (1987), 'The Archeology of Accounting Systems', *Accounting, Organisations, and Society*: 207–34.

—— (1994), 'Accounting and Everyday Life', *Accounting, Organisations, and Society*: 299–301.

Hoskin, K. W., and Maceve, R. H. (1986), 'Accounting and the Examination: A Geneology of Disciplinary Power', *Accounting, Organisations, and Society*: 105–36.

—— —— (1988), 'The Genesis of Accountability: The West Point Connections', *Accounting, Organisations, and Society*: 37–74.

Humphrey, C. (1994), 'Reflecting on Attempts to Develop a Financial Management Information System for the Probation Service in England and Wales: Some Observations on the Relationship between the Claims of Accounting and its Practice', *Accounting, Organisations, and Society*: 147–78.

Hunt, H. G. III, and Hogler, R. L. (1993), 'An Institutional Analysis of Accounting Growth and Regulation in the United States', *Accounting, Organisations, and Society*: 341–60.

Johnson, H. T. (1972), 'Early Cost Accounting for Internal Management Control: Lyman Mills in the 1850's', *Business History Review*: 466–74.

Johnson, S. (1982), 'Budgetary Behavior in Local Government: A Case Study over 3 Years', *Accounting, Organisations, and Society*: 287–304.

Jönsson, S. (1992), 'Accounting for Improvement: Action Research on Local Management Support', *Accounting, Management and Information Technologies*: 99–115.

—— and Grönlund, A. (1988), 'Life with a Sub-contractor: New Technology and Management Accounting', *Accounting, Organisations, and Society*: 513–32.

Kaplan, R. S. (1984), 'The Evolution of Management Accounting', *Accounting Review*: 390–418.

—— (1992*a*), 'Putting the Balanced Scorecard to Work', *Harvard Business Review*: 134–47.

—— (1992*b*), 'In Defense of Activity Based Costing', *Harvard Business Review*: 58–63.

—— (1993), 'The Balanced Scorecard: Measures that Drive Performance', *Harvard Business Review*: 71–8.

Kavanagh, D., and Araujo, L. (1995), 'Chronigami: Folding and Unfolding Time', *Accounting, Management and Information Technologies*: 103–21.

Lave, J., and Wenger, E. (1991), *Situated Learning: Legitimate Peripheral Participation* (Cambridge: Cambridge University Press).

Littleton, A. C. (1933), *Accounting Evolution to 1900* (New York: Russell & Russell).

Loft, A. (1991), 'Accounting in Time', Working Paper (Copenhagen Business School).

Macintosh, N. B. (1981), 'A Contextual Model of Information Systems', *Accounting, Organisations, and Society*: 39–52.

McSweeney, L. B. (1995), 'Accounting in Organisational Action: A Subsuming Explanation or Situated Explanations', *Accounting, Management and Information Technologies*: 245–82.

—— 'The Unbearable Ambiguity of Accounting', *Accounting, Organizations and Society*, 22, 7: 691–712.

Mattessich, R. (1957), 'Towards a General and Axiomatic Foundation of Accounting: With an Introduction to the Matrix Formulation of Accounting Systems', *Accounting Research*: 328–55.

—— (1987), 'Prehistoric Accounting and the Problem of Representation: On Ancient Archeological Evidence of the Middle East from 8000 BC to 3000 BC', *Accounting Historians Journal*: 71–91.

Meyer, J. W. (1986), 'Social Environments and Organisational Accounting', *Accounting, Organisations, and Society*: 345–56.

Miller, P., and Napier, C. (1993), 'Genealogies of Calculation', *Accounting, Organisations, and Society*: 631–47.

—— and O'Leary, T. (1987), 'Accounting and the Construction of the Governable Person', *Accounting, Organisations, and Society*: 235–66.

—— —— (1994), 'Accounting, "Economic Citizenship" and the Spatial Reordering of Manufacture', *Accounting, Organisations, and Society*: 15–44.

Munro, R. (1993), 'Just When you Thought it Safe to Enter the Water: Accountability, Language Games and Multiple Control Technologies', *Accounting, Management and Information Technologies*: 249–71.

Nehmer, R. (1988), 'Accounting Information Systems as Algebras and First Order Axiomatic Models', unpublished Ph.D. dissertation, University of Illinois at Urbana-Champaign.

Oschinsky, D. (1971), *Walter of Henley and Other Treatises on Estate Management and Accounting* (Oxford: Clarendon Press).

Otley, D. T., and Berry, A. J. (1980), 'Control, Organisation and Accounting', *Accounting, Organisations, and Society*: 231–44.

Pinch, T. M., Mulkay, M., and Ashmore, M. (1989), 'Clinical Budgeting: Experimentation in the Social Sciences: Drama in Five Acts', *Accounting, Organisations, and Society*: 271–301.

Power, M. K. (1992), 'From Common Sense to Expertise: Reflections on the Prehistory of Audit Sampling', *Accounting, Organisations, and Society*: 37–62.

Preston, A. (1986), 'Interactions and Arrangements in the Process of Informing', *Accounting, Organisations, and Society*: 521–40.

—— (1991), 'The "Problem" in and of Management Information Systems', *Accounting, Management and Information Technologies*: 43–69.

—— Cooper, D. J., and Coombs, R. W. (1992), 'Fabricating Budgets: A Study of the Production of Management Budgeting in the National Health Service', *Accounting, Organisations, and Society*: 561–93.

Previts, G. J., and Marino, B. D. (1979), *A History of Accounting in America: An Historical Interpretation of the Cultural Significance of Accounts* (New York: John Wiley & Sons).

Richardson, A. J. (1988), 'Accounting Knowledge and Professional Privilege', *Accounting, Organisations, and Society*: 381–96.

Robson, K. (1992), 'Accounting Numbers as "Inscription": Action at a Distance and the Development of Accounting', *Accounting, Organisations, and Society*: 685–708.

244 Richard J. Boland, Jr.

Robson, K. (1994), 'Inflation Accounting and Action at a Distance: The Sandilands Episode', *Accounting, Organisations, and Society*: 45–82.

Scott, D. R. (1933), *The Cultural Significance of Accounts* (Lawrence, Kan.: Scholars Book Club; reprint 1976).

Simon, H. A., Kozmetsky, G., Guetzkow, H., and Tyndall, G. (1954), *Centralization and Decentralization in the Controllers Department* (New York: Controllership Foundation).

Simons, R. (1987), 'Accounting Control Systems and Business Strategy: An Empirical Analysis', *Accounting, Organisations, and Society*: 357–74.

Sotto, R. (1982), 'Scientific Utopia and Accounting', *Accounting, Organisations, and Society*: 57–71.

Spicer, B. H., and Ballew, V. (1983), 'Management Accounting Systems and the Economics of Internal Organisation', *Accounting, Organisations, and Society*: 73–96.

Star, S. L. (1989), 'The Structure of Ill-Structured Solutions: Boundary Objects and Heterogeneous Distributed Problem Solving', in M. Huhns and L. Gasser (eds.), *Readings in Distributed Artificial Intelligence*, vol. ii (Menlo Park, Calif.: Morgan Kaufmann).

Staubus, G. J. (1987), 'The Dark Ages of Cost Accounting: The Role of Miscues in the Literature', *Accounting Historians Journal*: 1–18.

Thomas, A. L. (1969), *The Allocation Problem in Financial Accounting Theory*, Studies in Accounting Research no. 3 (Sarasota, Fla.: American Accounting Association).

Tomkins, C., and Groves, R. (1983), 'The Everyday Accountant and Researching his Reality', *Accounting, Organisations, and Society*: 361–74.

Tricker, R. I., and Boland, R. J., Jr. (1982), *Management Information and Control Systems* (Chichester: John Wiley & Sons).

Wardell, M., and Weisenfeld, L. W. (1991), 'Management Accounting and the Workplace in the United States and Great Britain', *Accounting, Organisations, and Society*: 655–70.

Watson, D. J., and Baumler, J. V. (1975), 'Transfer Pricing: A Behavioral Context', *Accounting Review*: 466–74.

Yates, J. (1993), *Control through Communication: The Rise of System in American Management* (Baltimore: Johns Hopkins University Press).

Young, J. J. (1995a), 'Defending an Accounting Jurisdiction: The Case of Cash Flows', *Critical Perspectives on Accounting*: 173–200.

—— (1995b), 'Getting the Accounting "Right": Accounting and the Savings and Loan Crisis', *Accounting, Organisations, and Society*: 55–80.

—— (1996), 'Institutional Thinking: The Case of Financial Instruments', *Accounting, Organisations, and Society*: 487–512.

PART III

Developing and Implementing Change Programmes

Introduction

The theme of developing and implementing change programmes is one which is central to business and management education internationally. From a computer science perspective, a variety of methodologies and approaches have emerged for information systems development. Within business and management more generally, the focus has been largely on developing project management methods and approaches to integrate both the technical and managerial aspects. Whilst some criticise the concept of formal project or systems methodologies and techniques, others claim they are useful, not least because of the history of computer project disasters. Yet managing change, both technically and politically, is fraught with difficulty and not conducive to a purely recipe-driven approach. Methodologies, procedures, tools, and techniques frequently show their limitations when put into practice. Indeed, the relationship between developing and implementing change programmes is one which continues to receive much attention within business and management research. Beer et al. claim that,

In a four year study of organisational change at six large corporations, we found that . . . the greatest obstacle to revitalisation is the idea that it comes about through company-wide change programs, particularly when a corporate staff group such as human resources sponsors them. We call this 'the fallacy of programmatic change'. Just as important, formal organisation structure and systems cannot lead a corporate renewal process.[1]

In Part III we present five chapters on developing and implementing change programmes in the context of IS. The first chapter by David Avison and Guy Fitzgerald on 'IS Development' is divided into four sections. First they trace IS Development from the early 1970s when no formal methodology was adopted. Second, they examine what they describe as 'the motivation to develop a formal approach to system development', commonly known as the 'system development life cycle'. Third, they reacquaint us with the 'waterfall model' which consists of phases, procedures, rules, techniques, and documentation. In tracking the development

---

[1] M. Beer, R. A. Eisenstat, and B. Spector (1990), 'Why Change Programs Don't Produce Change', *Harvard Business Review*. 159.

of methodologies, the authors analyse their strengths and weaknesses in what is termed the 'methodology period'. They demonstrate that no single approach is without its problems. Finally, they examine the role of methodologies in the 'post-methodology era' and the backlash against their use. CASE tools, incremental development, external development, and contingency approaches bring the chapter to a close.

Our second chapter in this section considers the important subject of IS failures. In recent years, there have been a spate of high-profile IS failures, most notably in the UK, the Taurus fiasco,[2] and the London Ambulance Service and Wessex Regional Health Authority computer failures. In his comprehensive chapter on IS failures, Chris Sauer examines the theoretical and empirical literature on this subject. He asserts that risk control, risk containment, and incrementalism are different ways of approaching IS development and implementation with differing levels of risks and benefits. Yet none gives IS professionals a deeper understanding of the reasons for failure or, more importantly, how to avoid failure.

The following three chapters are concerned with implementing change programmes in a variety of organisational settings. Frank Land argues that we can learn a great deal about developing and implementing information systems by analysing historical processes and practices. He illustrates this by examining the British food and manufacturing catering company J. Lyons. The chapter demonstrates how J. Lyons and Co. grew from a specialist caterer serving a niche market to a major food manufacturer and caterer. Part of this change involved the growth and diffusion of information systems within the company and the associated structural changes to the hierarchy and business processes and units.

Mary Lacity and Rudy Hirschheim offer a comprehensive discussion of IS outsourcing. They contrast the benefits and pitfalls of outsourcing and insourcing options based upon their extensive case study research into the subject. Six key findings are presented which compare the initial expectations of the client with the outcome of the outsourcing decision. Here we can often discern a wide gap between expectations and reality, frequently with disappointing results. The authors further analyse their research findings with other contributions on IS outsourcing.

The final chapter is offered by Bob Galliers and Jacky Swan. It considers the subject of business process re-engineering from a trans-disciplinary perspective. Utilising material from the organisational literature on technology diffusion and innovation in combination with the IS literature on implementation and, to a degree, failure, they provide a critical review of BPR and propose how the subject of IT and organisational change might

---

[2] W. Currie (1994), 'The Strategic Management of a Large Scale IT Project in the Financial Services Sector', *New Technology, Work and Employment*, 9, 1: 19–30. See also W. Currie (1997), 'Computerising the Stock Exchange: A Comparison of Two Information Systems', *New Technology, Work and Employment*, 12, 2: 75–90.

be approached—as against the more superficial bedmate of BPR, to be found in much of the popular literature on the topic.

Part III attempts to link development and implementation to illustrate the processual and problematic nature of change programmes within organisations. Clearly, initatives such as outsourcing and BPR become increasingly complex when we track their conceptual development to the implementation stage. As the chapters on these subjects illuminate, the problems associated with outsourcing and BPR increase over time. This is also the case with other large-scale management change programmes in the form of IS projects. In Part IV, we continue to explore the consequences of developing and implementing change programmes by considering organisational and managerial issues.

11

Information Systems Development

DAVID E. AVISON AND GUY FITZGERALD

Introduction

In this chapter we examine information systems development. We discuss information systems development in the period from the early 1970s when there was no formal methodology to develop information systems. We look at the motivation to develop a formal approach to system development, known as the system development life cycle, which is described below. This 'waterfall model' consists of phases, procedures, rules, techniques, documentation, and so on. This particular approach had a number of weaknesses and these were addressed in the many approaches and methodologies that were specified and practised in the 1980s. We call this the 'methodology period' because in some ways it represents their heyday. They were adopted to attain a better end product, that is the information system itself, through a better development process and a standardised process. These methodologies of the time varied in philosophy, general approach, and in many other ways. But it seems that no approach was considered ideal. Finally, the chapter discusses criticisms and disillusionment with methodologies. In this 'post-methodology era', which we are presently undergoing, there has been a backlash against methodologies. The use of CASE tools, incremental development, external development, and contingency approaches are all described in the final part of the chapter.

The Pre-methodology Era

Early computer applications—say, until the early 1970s—were developed and implemented without an explicit or formalised information systems development methodology. In these early days, the emphasis of computer applications development was on programming and the solution of various technical issues. Most of the problems were perceived to be in the technical arena particularly those resulting from the rather limited hardware of the time. Thus the emphasis was on technical skills with the two major skills required being that of the computer programmer, to ascertain requirements and write, test, and implement the programs, and the computer operator, to run them on the computer once implemented.

We have termed this the 'pre-methodology era' but others have used different terms. Friedman (1989), for example, has called this the 'hardware era', an era in which hardware and capacity constraints dominated systems development. The key issue of systems development was certainly to get the program working given the hardware limitations, particularly memory, which led to a prime emphasis on program efficiency.

This emphasis meant that the requirements of the users and of the organisation were somewhat neglected. This was originally not such a great problem as the systems were usually relatively straightforward, with requirements well defined. Applications were typically limited functional copies of existing manual systems. But as the complexity of the systems being developed increased, it became more of a problem. The developers were technically trained but rarely fully understood the business or the organisational context in which the systems were being implemented, and they were typically not very good at communicating with non-technical people. The needs of the users were rarely well established with the consequence that the system designs were often inappropriate to the real requirements of the application and the business.

This does not mean that effective systems were not developed at this time; indeed, given the constraints, there are some excellent examples (see, for example, Caminer et al. 1996). However, the dominant approach, or 'methodology', of development was rule of thumb and experience based, conducted by technically focused people. This often led to poor control and management of projects. For example, estimating the date on which the system would be operational was difficult, and applications were frequently behind schedule. Programmers were usually overworked, and spent a very large proportion of their time correcting and enhancing the applications that were operational. Emphasis had to be placed on maintaining operational systems to get them working properly and to evolve them into systems that would meet the needs of users and the business. This left relatively little time and resources to devote to the development of new systems. Perhaps as much as 70–80 per cent of time was spent on maintaining operational systems rather than developing new ones.

However, despite these problems the demand for computer-based business systems was steadily increasing and management were demanding more appropriate systems for their expensive outlay. This led to a number of changes. First, there was a growing appreciation that the part of the development of the system that concerned analysis and design required a different person with different skills from that of the programmer. This led to the systems analyst as the person (or persons) with the key role in systems development. Second, there was a growing appreciation of the desirability for a more disciplined approach to the development of information systems to overcome the problems of systems being delivered late and over budget. Thus the first information systems development methodologies were established.

The Early Methodology Era

The early methodology era is characterised by an approach to building computer-based applications that focused on the identification of phases and stages that it was thought would help control and enable the better management of systems development and bring some much needed discipline. This approach has come to be known as the systems development life cycle (SDLC) or, more commonly in the USA, the 'waterfall model'. It should be stated that at the time the term methodology was not used to describe the SDLC, although in fact that is what it was. Maddison et al. (1983) define a methodology as 'a recommended collection of philosophies, phases, procedures, rules, techniques, tools, documentation, management, and training for developers of information systems' and the SDLC meets the requirements of this definition.

The life cycle approach had its origins in systems theory, operations management, and operational research and was a generalised approach to problem-solving. It was widely applied to systems development with the move away from programming as the primary emphasis of applications development. It consisted of a sequential set of phases or steps, each of which contained a series of defined tasks, often requiring different skills and/or people involved. It also embodied the notion that one phase had to be completed before the next one began (which is said to be the reason for the term waterfall). Each phase had a set of defined outputs that had to be produced before the phase could be deemed complete. This helped it to be used as a mechanism for project control. In systems development it also became associated with a set of techniques, such as flowcharting, that were applied in particular phases.

There are a large number of variations on the SDLC theme. For example, Daniels and Yeates (1971) define the phases as those of feasibility study, systems investigation, analysis, design, and implementation, followed by review and maintenance. This National Computing Centre (NCC) methodology was widely used in the 1970s and early 1980s in the UK. The feasibility study attempts to assess the costs and benefits of alternative proposals enabling management to make informed choices. From the potential solutions, one is chosen. Included in the study are human and organisational costs and benefits as well as economic and technical ones. The systems investigation stage takes a detailed look at the functional requirements of the application, any constraints imposed, exceptional conditions, and so on, using techniques such as observation, interviewing, questionnaires, and searching through records and documentation. Armed with the facts about the application area, the systems analyst proceeds to the systems analysis phase, and analyses the present system by asking such questions as:

- Why do the problems exist?
- Why were certain methods of work adopted?
- Are there alternative methods?
- What are the likely growth rates of data?

Through consideration of such factors, the analyst moves on to designing the new system. The design documentation set will contain details of:

- input data and how the data is to be captured (entered in the system);
- outputs of the system (sometimes referred to as the deliverables);
- processes, many carried out by computer programs, involved in converting the inputs to the outputs;
- structure of the computer and manual files which might be referenced in the system;
- security and back-up provisions to be made;
- systems testing and implementation plans.

Implementation of the design will include program-writing, purchasing new hardware, training users, writing user and operations documentation, and cutover to the new system. A major aspect of this phase is that of quality control. The manual procedures, along with the hardware and software, need to be tested to the satisfaction of users as well as analysts. The users need to be 'comfortable' with the new methods. Once the application system is operational, there are bound to be some changes necessary due to corrections or changes in the organisation itself. These changes are made in the review and maintenance phase.

The SDLC had a number of features to commend it. It has been well tried and tested. The use of documentation standards helps to ensure that proposals are complete and that they are communicated to users and computing staff. The approach also ensures that users are trained to use the system. There are controls and these, along with the division of the project into phases of manageable tasks with deliverables, help to avoid missed cutover dates and disappointments with regard to what is output. Unexpectedly high costs and lower benefits are also less likely. It enables a well-formed and standard training scheme to be given to analysts, thus ensuring continuity of standards and systems.

However, there are serious limitations to the approach, as well as limitations in the way it is used. Some potential traps have been identified as follows (Avison and Fitzgerald, 1995):

- failure to meet the needs of management (due to the concentration on single applications, particularly at the operational level of the organisation);
- unambitious systems design (due to the emphasis on the existing system as a basis for the new computer system);
- instability (due to the modelling of processes which are unstable because businesses and their environments change frequently);
- inflexibility (due to the output-driven orientation of the design processes which makes changes in design costly);
- user dissatisfaction (due to problems with the computer-oriented documentation and the inability for users to 'see' the system before it is operational);
- problems with documentation (due to its computer rather than user orientation and the fact that it is rarely kept up to date);
- application backlog (due to the maintenance workload as attempts are made to change the system in order to reflect user needs).

The Methodology Era

As a response to one or more of the above limitations or criticisms of the SDLC, a number of different approaches to systems development began to emerge and what we term 'the methodology era' began. In this era the term methodology was probably used for the first time to describe instances of these different approaches. It has been estimated that there are over 1,000 'brand name' methodologies worldwide (Jayaratna, 1994). Although we are rather sceptical of such a high figure, there is no doubt that methodologies proliferated during this period. Many of these were essentially similar, and were differentiated only for marketing purposes. Nevertheless, a variety of methodologies began to emerge.

We have said that the term methodology emerged during this period and it has been widely used ever since, but there is little agreement as to what the term means other than at a very general level. This loose use of the term does not of course mean that there are no definitions, simply that there are no universally agreed definitions. At the general level, it is regarded as a recommended series of steps and procedures to be followed in the course of developing an information system.

Above, we gave Maddison's (1983) definition of a methodology. In our view, the notion of a 'philosophy' should be singled out for special attention as in practice it is often ignored, particularly by methodology vendors. The philosophy relates to the underlying theories and assumptions that the authors of the methodology believe in, which have shaped the definition of the methodology. This identifies those usually unwritten aspects and beliefs that make a methodology an effective approach to the development of information systems (at least in the eyes of their authors). These may lead to the particular emphasis of the approach. This emphasis may lie in the documentation or human, data, or process aspects and so on.

Utilising this interpretation of the term 'information systems methodology' makes it very much more than just a series of techniques and tools. This extended view of a methodology implies that a methodology needs to be closely and carefully described in order for it to be usable. This fits in with the commercial situation, where a methodology is usually a product which is 'packaged' and might include:

- manuals;
- education and training;
- consultancy support;
- CASE tools;
- pro forma documents;
- model-building templates, and so on.

Some (for example, Flynn, 1992) have argued that the term methodology is not apt in the context of systems development and that the term 'method' is perfectly adequate to cover everything that we mean by a methodology. Indeed Flynn states that 'the term methodology was popular for a time in the 1980s', implying that it is no longer much used. This is contrary to our experience, although it is true that the term method is also used. For us, this seems to substitute one ill-defined word for another. We believe that the term methodology has certain characteristics that are not implied by method, for example the inclusion of 'philosophy'. Methodology is thus a wider concept than method.

Checkland (1981) has distinguished between the two terms, arguing that a methodology 'is a set of principles of method, which in any particular situation has to be reduced to a method uniquely suited to that particular situation'. Later, Checkland (1985) argues that information systems development must be seen as a form of enquiry in the context of the general model of organised enquiry, which consists of three components: an intellectual framework, a methodology, and an application area.

The first element is the intellectual framework, which consists of the ideas that we use to make sense of the world. This is described as the philosophy that guides and constrains the enquiry. It consists of ontological assumptions, that is beliefs about the fundamental nature of the physical and social world and the way it operates, and epistemological assumptions, that is the theory of the method, or grounds of knowledge. It also consists of ethical values, which should be articulated, that may serve to guide or constrain the enquiry. The second element is the methodology. This is the operationalisation of the intellectual framework of ideas into a set of prescriptions or guidelines for investigation that require, or recognise as valid, particular methods and techniques. The third element is the application area, that is, some part of the real world that is deemed to be problematical and worthy of investigation.

This is a useful framework for discussions of research and enquiry, but the question is: 'how well does it relate to the world of information systems development methodologies?' Working backwards, it would seem that the application area is that of information systems development in general. The methodology element is equivalent to the collection of phases, procedures, rules, methods, and techniques that are usually considered to be a methodology in the information systems world. The intellectual framework is the element that is usually missing from commercial methodologies, or rather it is not missing, for it exists, but is not explicitly articulated. In our definition, much of this intellectual framework element is included in what we term the underlying philosophy, which we include in the definition of methodology itself. Checkland has it as a separate element, and it encompasses somewhat wider notions about the underpinnings of knowledge and beliefs.

Methodologies came from two sources: practice and theory. Methodologies in the first category often evolved from use and experience in organisations, many of them consultancy companies. Approaches were often based on one technique or on a series of closely related techniques, such as entity modelling or data flow diagramming (but usually not both). This technique was the foundation of the approach and it was then developed into a commercial methodology product. Slowly methodology authors began to formalise their approaches by expanding them to include prescriptions and phases or stages and these informal and somewhat ad hoc procedures or 'cook-books' evolved into methodologies. Methodologies in the second category were typically based on some theoretical concept and developed in universities or research institutions. These were usually not developed into commercial products, but written up in books and journals. Nevertheless the concepts and ideas were sometimes highly influential.

During the methodology era most organisations concerned with systems development adopted a methodology. It may not have been a commercial methodology purchased from a vendor. Often it was an in-house set of methodology standards that were adopted. Nevertheless organisations went through the process of selecting a methodology for systems development. Their rationales for adopting a methodology varied between organisations and individuals, but we identify three main categories of rationale: a better end product, a better development process, and a standardised process.

A better end product

People wanted a methodology to improve the end product of the development process, that is, they wanted better information systems. This should not be confused with the quality of the development process. It is difficult to assess the quality of information systems produced as a result of using a particular methodology. We cannot know that the use of the methodology produced the particular results. The same results might have occurred if the system had been developed using another methodology or without using a methodology at all. In systems development we do not have the luxury of developing a control with which we can compare results. However, the choice of methodology is crucial to the achievement of a better end product, and one that fits with the organisation's perception of 'the best way' of developing information systems would be the best choice. Clearly, the philosophy underpinning the methodology would be an important factor in understanding this. However, many organisations did not choose their methodology in this way. It appears that they often thought they were all the same and their selection appears to have frequently been based on criteria such as 'how comprehensive is it?' or 'which has the best CASE software?' rather than 'which best fits our system of beliefs about the key factors that are needed to develop the information systems?'

A better development process

Under this heading came the benefits that accrue from tightly controlling the development process and identifying the outputs (or deliverables) at each stage. This resulted in improved management and project control. It was usually argued that productivity was enhanced, that is, either systems were built faster, given specific resources, or they used fewer resources to achieve the same results. It was sometimes also argued that the use of a methodology reduced the level of skills required of the analysts, which improved the development process by reducing its cost.

Some methodologies sought to accredit their quality, and thus hopefully increase marketability, by adopting the quality standards that had proved popular in manufacturing and industrial processes, for example, BS5750/ISO9001. These standards have been designed to ensure the quality of processes rather than the end product and this sometimes led to emphasis on conformance to the standard, irrespective of whether it helped the quality of the system. Another problem, according to Avison et al. (1994), is that the traditional manufacturing process is quite different from the process of developing software products. The software product is a 'one-off' rather than a mass replication of a design.

A standardised process

The needs associated with this category related to the benefits of having a common approach throughout an organisation. This meant that more integrated systems could result, that staff could easily change from project to project without retraining being necessary, and that a base of common experience and knowledge could be achieved. In short, it was thought that all the normal benefits of standardisation, including the specific benefit of easier maintenance of systems, could be achieved by adopting a standardised methodology across an organisation.

All the reasons contained in the above categories were specified, in some form or other, by the authors or vendors of methodologies as being benefits of adopting their particular methodologies. In contrast, a survey of benefits that purchasers looked for in a methodology showed that the most important factors for them were (Gray, 1985):

1. improved systems specifications;
2. easier maintenance and enhancement.

Some of the new methodologies were actually very similar to the earlier SDLC (indeed this was not so surprising as they often evolved from the SDLC), but others were quite radically different. Avison and Fitzgerald (1995) have classified the various methodologies that emerged in this period into a number of broad themes as follows:

- structured;
- data;
- strategic;
- participative;
- prototyping;
- object-oriented;
- tools;
- systems.

One of the most important developments of this era was the structured methodology which some say has been the most widely used of the methodologies in practice (Yourdon, 1989). Structured methodologies are broadly based on the principle of functional decomposition, that is, the breaking down of a complex problem into more manageable units in a disciplined way. This is particularly true of the top-down concept of identifying the broad elements or big picture first, and getting the overall structure right, and subsequently adding more and more layers of detail.

The development of structured methodologies stemmed from the benefits that had been achieved in the programming arena by the application of structured design methods. Information-hiding, coupling and cohesion, and the use of structure charts had helped bring discipline to the previous 'spaghetti code'. Similar structured concepts were applied to analysis, leading to the adoption of the data flow diagram (DFD), probably the most important of the structured analysis techniques. This enabled the top-down analysis and representation of complex processes.

The separation of the analysis of the logical system from the physical implementation was also an important element of structured analysis. This separation allowed a concentration on the principles of *what* the system should do rather than *how* it might be achieved in the context of a specific implementation. It also enabled changes to be more easily accommodated. Other techniques, such as structured English, decision trees, decision tables, functional hierarchy diagrams, and data structure diagrams, and tools, such as the data dictionary or systems repository, were also introduced. Most of the documentation of the structured systems approach was graphical. This was easier to follow than traditional text or technically oriented representations, and is said to have helped understanding and communication between analysts and users.

Although the approach was quite revolutionary at the time it was not really an alternative to the SDLC as the phases were much the same. Rather it enhanced the SDLC by adding a number of specific techniques and concepts based upon the principles of structure. The only major area of change to the SDLC was the separation of the single design phase into two (logical design and physical design). The approach adopted by Yourdon (1989) is typical of the structured systems approach and follows the earlier works of DeMarco (1979) and Gane and Sarson (1979). The structured approaches are primarily concerned with the analysis of processes, with data being identified as a by-product of those processes.

The data-oriented approaches are somewhat different but have also been highly influential in systems development. Whereas structured analysis and design emphasises processes, data analysis concentrates on understanding and grouping common data, and identifying the relationships between these groupings. The philosophy is that data is the most important element in the development of the system. Getting the 'master' data right is seen as the key to the development of successful systems because it is the most stable of the elements involved, more stable than inputs, outputs, or processes. When an application changes, the data structures and the data already collected are still likely to be relevant to the new or revised system and therefore need not be changed or collected and validated again. Data analysis involves the collection, validation, and classification of the entities, attributes, and relationships that exist in the area being investigated, the construction of the entity model being the key activity. Information engineering (Martin, 1989), for example, has the data approach at its heart.

Strategic approaches stress the pre-planning involved in developing information systems and the need for an overall information systems strategy that supports and enables the objectives of the business or organisation to be met. This involves top management in the analysis of the objectives of their organisation. Planning approaches address the criticism of the SDLC, that it treats information systems development in a piecemeal fashion, focusing on a single project at a time, and not taking an integrated or strategic approach. IBM's business systems planning (IBM, 1975) is an early example of a more strategic approach and more recent examples are found in Bullen and Rockart (1986), Earl (1989), and Lederer and Mendelow (1989). Business process re-engineering (BPR) (Davenport and Short, 1990; Hammer and Champy, 1993) is also a development approach that adopts a focus on strategy.

In participative approaches, the role of all users is stressed, and the role of the technologist may be subsumed by other stakeholders of the information system. If the users are involved in the analysis, design, and implementation of information systems relevant to their own work, particularly if this takes the form of genuine decision-making (as against lip-service consultation at the other extreme), these users are likely to give the new information system their full commitment when it is implemented, and thereby increase the likelihood of its success. ETHICS (Mumford, 1995) stresses the participative nature of information systems development, following the socio-technical movement, and embodies a sustainable ethical position. Related approaches, where systems are developed which permit emancipation through rational discourse, are typified by the UTOPIA project (Bodker et al., 1987).

A prototype is an approximation of a type that exhibits the essential features of the final version of that type. By implementing a prototype first, the analyst can show the users inputs, intermediary stages, and outputs from the system. These are not diagrammatic approximations, which tend to be looked at as abstract things, or technically oriented documentation, which may not be understood by the user, but the actual representation of the system on the screen with the relevant outputs. Data dictionaries, fourth generation systems, CASE tools, and workbenches of various kinds can all enable prototyping. These have become more and more powerful over the last few years. Rapid application development (Martin, 1991) is an example of a prototyping approach.

A methodology which incorporates formal methods uses mathematical precision and notation in the specification and design of an information system. Some systems requirements can be expressed mathematically rather than through the use of natural language and this can be translated into computer language. This version of the specification can be tested for correctness. Software engineering approaches, which we have included in the structured school, aim at producing quality software incorporating the rigour of formal methods.

Object-oriented information systems development has become the latest 'silver bullet' (Booch, 1991; Coad and Yourdon, 1991). Yourdon's (1994) exposition argues that the approach is more natural than data- or process-based alternatives. The basic concepts of the object-oriented approach, of objects and attributes, wholes and parts, and classes and parts, are basic and simple to understand and the approach unifies the information systems development process.

Tools include project management software, data dictionary software, systems repositories, drawing tools, and computer-assisted software (or systems) engineering (CASE) tools. The incorporation of these developments addresses some of the criticisms discussed above. The data-modelling techniques suggest that the waterfall models now are more balanced between process and data. The documentation has improved, thanks to the use of drawing and CASE tools, and it is more likely to be kept up to date for the same reason. Further, CASE tools can be used to develop prototypes which enable users to assess the proposed information system in a far more tangible way and can speed up delivery of the operational system.

General systems theory attempts to understand the nature of systems which are large and complex. Organisations are open systems, and the relationship between the organisation and its environment are important. Systems approaches attempt to capture this 'holistic' view, following Aristotle's dictum that 'the whole is greater than the sum of the parts'. By simplifying a complex situation, we may be reductionist, and thereby distort our understanding of the overall system. The best-known approach in the information systems arena to address this issue is Checkland's soft systems methodology (SSM), found in Checkland (1981) and Checkland and Scholes (1990), although perhaps the account of most relevance to information systems is found in Wilson (1990).

As has been mentioned, each of the above themes (and the methodologies embodying those themes) addresses one or more of the perceived weaknesses of the SDLC. As the methodology era progressed, a number of further developments can be perceived. One development concerned the expansion of the scope of methodologies to fill various gaps. As a result of their historical development, which had typically involved a concentration on a single development technique (or a small set of them), many methodologies did not address anything like the whole of the systems development process. Sometimes whole development phases might be missing. For example, methodologies might concentrate on analysis and design to the exclusion of implementation. Some did not address the early stages of the process, such as systems justification. Few ensured that any system developed successfully fitted in with the overall business strategy. Even if the methodologies did not have complete gaps, they often had areas that were treated much less thoroughly than others. So as the methodology era progressed most methodology vendors expanded the scope of their methodologies to ensure they covered all the necessary stages required to develop and implement information systems.

Another development was the coming together, or blending, of a number of themes within one methodology. For example, a methodology based on entity-modelling techniques might have been very powerful for data analysis and database design, but not so comprehensive when it came to specifying functions and designing applications, and might not provide any support for dialogue design. This was not just an expansion of scope as described above, but more a blending of previously separate philosophies in one methodology. Such blended approaches include Merise (Quang and Chartier-Kastler, 1991) and SSADM (Eva, 1994).

We characterise the above as the methodology era because of the apparent proliferation of methodologies and approaches to systems development. The practical world was full of vendors pushing their particular methodologies and the academic world full of papers advocating and comparing methodologies (see for example Olle et al., 1982, 1983, 1986, 1988). However, it is probable that even at the peak of the methodology era and at the time of most 'hype' concerning methodologies, many organisations were still not using a specific commercial methodology for developing their information systems. The relatively few empirical studies that have been undertaken to ascertain the adoption of methodologies often tend to indicate that the use of methodologies is by no means universal (for example, Palvia and Nosek, 1993; Fitzgerald, 1996) and that methodology use is less widespread than vendors would have us believe. Vendors suggest that any company which has expressed interest in their methodology, or has bought an evaluation version, is a 'user'. Wasserman et al. (1983) produced a survey of 24 methodologies and found that nearly half had been used on 10 or fewer projects. A survey by Informatics of about 70 users (cited in Eurogroup, 1990) found that 19 used SSADM, 12 Jackson Systems Development, 9 Information Engineering, and 8 Yourdon Systems Method, with 11 using in-house methods. This coincides with a number of other surveys that suggest that SSADM is the most frequently used methodology in the UK, with over 250 organisations represented in the SSADM User Group. In France, surveys cited in Eurogroup (1990) suggest that Merise is used in developments in between 20 and 61 per cent of cases. In Europe as a whole 55 per cent of organisations are using brand-name methodologies.

Those organisations not using a brand-name methodology appear to be either still using the traditional SDLC, or using their own in-house variations or approaches developed to suit themselves based on their own experience and development environment. Of course many of these variations may be closely based upon one or more commercial methodology.

The Post-methodology Era

The era that we term post-methodology is relatively recent, indeed we may only just be entering this period. It is characterised by a serious reappraisal of the concepts and practicalities of the methodologies of the methodology era. As a result some organisations have turned to yet different methodologies and approaches, some have abandoned their use of traditional methodologies completely, whilst others have adopted a more contingent approach.

Criticisms of methodologies

In the same way that the SDLC was criticised, many of the methodologies that replaced it are themselves being criticised and are recognised as having their own limitations. For example, some of the methodology themes identified above have been the subject of criticism as follows:

- The structured approach in breaking down a system into manageable units offers a simplistic view of a complex system and fails to identify fully the importance of the links between systems.
- Data analysis may not solve underlying problems that the organisation might have. Indeed it may have captured the existing problems into the data model, and made them even more difficult to solve in the future.
- Participation leads to inefficient systems designed by those who are good managers, clerks, or salespeople, but poor, and unwilling, systems analysts. Further, it is demotivating to people trained and experienced as 'true' systems analysts.
- Systems theory represents an idealistic academics' position and is not relevant to the practitioner.
- Prototyping is only concerned with the user interface and does not address the fundamental problems of systems analysis, it simply makes poor systems palatable to users.

Backlash against methodologies

Methodologies were often seen as a panacea to the problems of traditional development approaches, and were often chosen and adopted for the wrong reasons. Some organisations simply wanted a standardised approach or a better project control mechanism, others a better way of involving users, still others wanted to inject some rigour or discipline into the process. For many of these organisations, the adoption of a methodology has not always worked or been the success its advocates expected. Indeed, it was very unlikely that methodologies would ever achieve the more overblown claims made by some vendors and consultants. Some organisations have found their chosen methodology not to be successful or appropriate for them and have adopted a different one. For some this second option has been more useful, but others have found the new one not to be successful either. This has led some people to reject methodologies in general.

Indeed we have previously described this as a backlash against formalised information systems development methodologies (Avison and Fitzgerald, 1995).

This does not mean that methodologies have not been successful for some. It means that they have not solved all the problems that they were supposed to. Many organisations are using methodologies effectively and successfully and conclude that, although not perfect, they are an improvement on what they were doing previously, and that they could not handle their current systems development load without them.

However, many have rejected all methodologies listing a number of criticisms, for example:

Productivity. They fail to deliver the suggested productivity benefits. It is said that they do not reduce the time taken to develop a project. Instead, their use may increase systems development lead-times usually because the methodology specifies many more activities and tasks that have to be undertaken. Methodologies may specify the construction of many more diagrams and models, and in general the production of considerably more documentation at all stages. Much of this may be felt by users to be unnecessary. As well as being slow, they are resource intensive, in terms of the number of people required, from both the development and user side, and from the point of view of the costs of adopting the methodology (for example, purchase costs, training, CASE tools, organisation costs, and so on).

Complexity. Methodologies have been criticised for being over complex. They are designed to be applied to the largest and most comprehensive development project and therefore specify in great detail every possible task that might conceivably be thought to be relevant, all of which is expected to be undertaken for every development project irrespective of its specific characteristics.

'Gilding the lily'. Methodologies develop any requirements to the ultimate degree, often over and above what is legitimately required. Every requirement is treated as being of equal weight and importance, which results in relatively unimportant aspects being developed to the same degree as those that are essential. It is also said that they encourage the creation of 'wish lists' by users.

Skills. Methodologies require significant skills. These skills are often difficult for methodology users and end users to learn and acquire. It is sometimes also argued that the use of the methodology does not improve system development skills or organisational learning.

Tools. Some argue that the tools that the methodology advocates are difficult to use and do not generate enough benefits. They increase the focus on the production of documentation rather than leading to better analysis and design.

Not contingent. The methodology is not contingent upon the type of project or its size, nor upon the environment and organisational context. Therefore the standard becomes the application of the whole methodology, irrespective of its relevance.

One-dimensional approach. The methodology usually adopts only one approach to the development of projects and whilst this may be a strength, it does not always address the underlying issues or problems. In some applications, systems development might require a more political or organisational dimension.

Inflexible. The methodology might be inflexible and does not allow changes to requirements during development. This is problematic as requirements, particularly business requirements, frequently change during a long development process.

Invalid assumptions. Most methodologies make a number of simplifying yet invalid assumptions, such as a stable external and competitive environment. For example, many methodologies that address the alignment of business and information systems strategy assume the existence of a coherent and well-documented business strategy as a starting point for the methodology. This does not always exist in practice.

Goal displacement. It has been claimed that the existence of a methodology standard in an organisation might lead to its unthinking implementation and to a focus on following the procedures of the methodology to the exclusion of the real needs of the project being developed. In other words, the methodology obscures the important issues. De Grace and Stahl (1993) have termed this 'goal displacement' and talk about the severe problem of 'slavish adherence to the methodology'. Wastell (1996) talks about the 'fetish of technique' which inhibits creative thinking. He takes this further and suggests that the application of a methodology in this way is the functioning of methodology as a social defence which he describes 'as a highly sophisticated social device for containing the acute and potentially overwhelming pressures of systems development'. He is suggesting that systems development is such a difficult and stressful process that developers often take refuge in the intense application of the methodology in all its detail as a way of dealing with these difficulties. Developers can be seen to be working hard and diligently, but this is in reality goal displacement activity because they are avoiding the real problems of effectively developing the required system.

Difficulties in adopting a methodology. Some organisations have found it hard to adopt methodologies in practice. They have found resistance from developers who are experienced and familiar with more informal approaches to systems development and see the introduction of a methodology as restricting their freedom and creativity and perceive it as a slight on their skills. In other cases it has been the users that have objected to a methodology, because it did not embody the way they wished to work and included techniques for specifying requirements with which they were not familiar and which they did not see a good reason to adopt.

No improvements. Finally, and perhaps the acid test, is the conclusion that methodology use has not resulted in better systems. This is obviously difficult to prove, but nevertheless the perception of some is that 'we have tried it and it didn't help and may have actively hindered'.

Strictly speaking not all these criticisms are levelled against methodologies in general, some are more specific criticisms of a particular methodology. In making such criticisms a distinction should really be made between the poor application and use of a methodology and an inadequate methodology itself. Unfortunately, such distinctions are rarely made and, fairly or unfairly, they tend to be used to condemn methodologies as a whole.

One reaction of organisations that are critical of methodologies has been to reject the use of a methodology altogether. Others suggest that it is not the use of a methodology that is the problem, it is simply the inadequacy of current methodologies. What is needed, they argue, is better methodologies. Some see information systems development as essentially a technological process and believe that the increased use of CASE tools will overcome the problems currently being experienced. Another reaction is for methodology authors to use developments elsewhere as a prescription to refine, improve, and develop existing methodologies, in particular to make them increasingly comprehensive. Some organisations, however, are looking for more flexibility, and have adopted a contingency-based framework. Another flexible approach is that provided by incremental development (or RAD). Alternatively some organisations are rejecting the notion of developing systems internally and turning to the market and having their systems developed externally, either partially or completely through the use of application packages and outsourcing. We now look at some of these alternatives in more detail.

Development with tools

The approach of some people and organisations to the continuing problems of systems development is to pin their faith on the evolution of tools increasingly to automate the development process. CASE is the term used to describe software support tools that help in the applications software and information systems development process as a whole. We use CASE as a generic term applying to systems development in general (computer-aided *systems* engineering) rather than the more narrow (computer-aided *software* engineering). CASE tools help to cope with complexity, improve project control, enhance quality, enforce standards, and automate consistency checking. In addition, more advanced tools incorporate the automatic production of complete application systems by the generation of code, including embedded calls to a standard database. They can also produce screen definitions, graphical user interfaces, database definitions, referential integrity triggers to control database deletions, and transaction control programs. The code generated is based on the logic specified in the various diagrams and models formed in the earlier stages of development. Developers are able to test and modify the program without tampering with the source code. The traditional form of maintenance is made obsolete, because any changes required are not made by directly reworking the code in response to errors and changing requirements, but by going right back to the analysis and design stages and amending the original diagrams and specifications and regenerating the code automatically. This helps eliminate the frequently encountered problem of introducing new errors as a result of correcting existing ones. The productivity gains of such CASE tools is potentially large, indeed it is argued to 'revolutionise' systems development. However, the benefits have not yet been clearly seen or demonstrated in practice. The generated code is often inefficient and requires change and tuning, which can reduce the benefits significantly. Further, the learning period for CASE tools is long. Both developers and users need time to learn, assimilate, and become effective with the tools. In terms of productivity, it has been suggested that the learning curve (productivity benefits plotted against time) may actually dip below that of non-CASE tools, in the early stages. The length of this early stage, before improved performance is achieved, has been estimated to be between six months and two years. Clearly CASE is not an instant panacea but some organisations are prepared for the kind of long-term investment that is required.

In addition to the potential benefits of code generation, many advocates who see CASE tools as the way forward for systems development also point to other benefits. For example, further productivity benefits can be achieved by the reuse of existing development objects. The information captured by a CASE tool over a number of projects may eventually provide a repository of models or objects of various kinds that can be used again. These may include analysis and design models of all types and libraries of common code that can be utilised in future developments. Depending on circumstances, these models may be used in their entirety or are amended according to the requirement of the new project. This can save a significant amount of development effort and also help achieve consistency between applications, as the standards in the original models will be incorporated into the new developments.

A further potential benefit is in the re-engineering (or reverse engineering) of existing systems. The problem in many organisations is not so much that of developing new systems, but the maintenance and enhancement of their old, legacy systems, some of which are based on 1960s designs, third generation languages, and dated file and access methods. The normal use of CASE tools provides support for 'forward development', that is, the top-down, linear approach to the development of new systems, but CASE tools can support reverse engineering as well, providing the ability to capture the primary elements from current systems, such as their process logic and the data they use, including entities, attributes, names, locations, sources, edit criteria, relationships, etc. From this captured information, the tool can help to clean up the data definitions, produce entity models, restructure the process logic and build process hierarchies, and construct the repository for the old system. The CASE tool can then be used in the normal forward development mode to produce new systems. The degree of automation of the reverse engineering process varies, and currently there still needs to be a high degree of manual intervention at most stages. Nevertheless, it is argued that CASE tools can be very helpful in this context.

CASE tools are continually changing and meta-CASE tools are not fixed in their functionality but have the ability to be changed according to the needs of the developers and the development environment. Meta modelling is the specification of the data stored, represented, and manipulated in the repository, and the process to specify the content and functionality of that repository. The tool itself has facilities that can be used to define the way in which it will function.

This enables Excelerator, for example, to be specified differently for each user or group of users or for each project or organisation. Currently there are limits to the degree of customisation that can be achieved, but in the future it may be possible to develop the meta modelling characteristics and power to the extent that developers will be able to specify a 'tool' to reflect their own preferences and, in effect, their particular tool-set for their own development approach. This flexibility will enable a more contingent approach to the use of CASE tools, that is, to customise the tool according to the characteristics and environment of the project being developed. It may also enable an improved ability to learn what works well in an organisation and what does not, by experimenting with different approaches and configurations of the tools. It may mean that developers do not have to adhere to one particular methodology, but may be able to mix and match elements from a variety of approaches and be able to specify how these should work.

The integration of CASE tools with expert systems concepts, known as intelligent CASE, is likely to continue. Some tools already have knowledge bases in their repositories that contain the rules of the methodology and use expert system techniques to perform a number of checks, to identify standards violations, to analyse the impact of changes, and to transform from analysis models to design specifications. The potential is perhaps even greater than this. One possibility is for the expertise of systems development to be incorporated. It may be possible to capture and use it to provide knowledgeable assistance to developers when building systems. This already happens to some extent, but may well be enhanced with interactive dialogue sessions between the developer and the tool. For example, the expert system element of the tool might ask whether the developer has realised that some critical design decisions hinge on the specification of a particular relationship between two entities, and the expert system might suggest that the developer check with the users that this is actually what was required. This type of expertise might be described as a kind of sensitivity analysis that the expert system can apply.

Obviously the range of expert support that the tool might be able to apply is dependent on the knowledge concerning information systems development that can be elicited from experts, and up to now there has been little agreement amongst experts. However, in future, an expert system CASE tool itself may be able to capture some of this knowledge on the basis of experience of a number of projects in an organisation. Indeed, knowledge might be able to be captured from a number of organisations using the same tool.

In a similar way, knowledge concerning a particular application and a particular organisation might also be able to be captured and utilised by an expert system. For example, the tool might 'know' from past projects the characteristics of a particular department and be able to identify that some analysis information is already available in the system or that something in this system conflicts with information previously specified in an earlier project and therefore should be carefully rechecked.

A further development of CASE might be in the area of enhanced support for interpersonal communication and co-ordination amongst the various groups involved in information systems development. In other contexts there have been some advances in these human interaction support capabilities, for example, in group decision support systems (GDSS) and computer-supported co-operative work (CSCW). These developments could be integrated with CASE in the future. Facilities like electronic mail, video-conferencing, meeting support, and the co-ordination and communication between developers of documents (and other objects such as graphs and spreadsheets) are certainly relevant to CASE tools. Additionally, it can support the co-ordination of remote groups working in different locations, even in different countries. One organisation is attempting to utilise the world's different time zones to speed up the development of a project by having two groups of developers in different zones. After a day's work when the first group goes home the work is taken up by a new team of developers in a different time zone of the world. This obviously requires not only a great deal of work group co-ordination but also a shared repository of some kind.

Incremental development

Another alternative approach being adopted is incremental or evolutionary development. This has the characteristic of building upon, and enhancing, the previous versions of systems rather than developing a whole new system each time. It has evolved as a way of overcoming specific problems. First, it aims to reduce the length of time that it takes to develop a system and second, it addresses the problem of changing requirements during the process of development.

Incremental development has also been termed RAD (rapid application development) or 'timebox' development (Martin, 1991). The system to be developed is divided up into a number of components that can be developed separately. The most important requirements and those with the largest potential benefit are developed first. Some argue that no single component should take more than 90 days to develop (others suggest 180 days). Whatever length of timebox is chosen, the point is that it is relatively quick.

The idea of this approach is to compartmentalise the development and deliver early and often (hence the term timeboxing). This provides the business and users with a quick, but, it is hoped, useful part of the system in a refreshingly short time scale. The system at this stage is probably quite limited in relation to the total requirements, but at least something has been delivered. This is radically different from the conventional delivery mode of most methodologies which is a long development period of typically two to three years followed by the implementation of the complete system. The benefits of incremental development are that users trade off unnecessary (or at least initially unnecessary) requirements and wish lists (that is, features that it would be 'nice to have' in an ideal world) for speed of development. This also has the benefit that if requirements change over time, the total system has not been completed and the next timebox can accommodate the changes that become necessary as requirements change and evolve. It also has the advantage that the users become experienced with using and working with the system and learn what they really require from the early features that have been implemented.

Fig. 11.1 illustrates three chunks, or timeboxes, of development and although the overall time to achieve the full implementation could be argued to be the same as with conventional development, the likelihood is that the system actually developed at the end of the three timeboxes will be radically different from that developed at the end of one large chunk as a result of the learning process and changes made to each specification at each stage.

Obviously such an approach requires a radically different development culture from that required for formalised methodologies. The focus is on speed of delivery, the identification of the absolutely essential requirements,

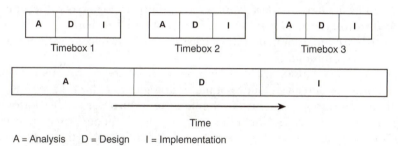

Time

A = Analysis   D = Design   I = Implementation

F IG. 11.1. *Comparison of evolutionary/timebox development and traditional development*

implementation as a learning vehicle, and the expectation that the requirements will change in the next timebox. Clearly such radical changes are unlikely to be achieved using conventional techniques.

External development

Some organisations are attempting to satisfy their systems' needs by buying application packages. The purchase of packages has been commonplace for some time, but the post-methodology era is characterised by some organisations deciding not to embark on any more in-house system development activities and to buy in all their requirements in the form of packages or 'turn-key' systems. This is regarded by many as a quicker and cost-effective way of implementing systems for organisations that have fairly standard requirements. Only applications that are strategic or for which a suitable package is not available would be considered for development in-house.

The package market is becoming increasingly sophisticated, and more and more packages which are highly tailorable are becoming available. Integrated packages which address a wide range of standard business functions, purchasable in modular form, such as SAP, have emerged in the last few years and have become particularly popular with large corporations. These packages are tailorable to the needs of individual companies. This is achieved by setting a large number of parameters usually stored in tables. Such package modification and integration with the business and existing systems is a non-trivial task and may be undertaken in-house or by external consultants. The development focus for such organisations shifts from the selection of the best development approach or methodology to the process that ensures that the best package is chosen. The key for these organisations is ensuring that the correct trade-off is made between a standard package, which might mean changing some elements of the way the business currently operates, and a package that can be modified to reflect the way they wish to operate. Although packages save the cost and time of developing systems in-house from scratch, there are dangers of becoming locked in to a particular supplier and of not being in control of the features that are incorporated in the package, especially to cope with new and emerging requirements.

For other organisations, the continuing problems of systems development, and the perceived failure of methodologies to deliver, have resulted in them outsourcing systems development to a third party. The outsourcing of elements of IT, including systems development, to a specialist vendor, such as EDS or CSC, is now widespread both in the public and private sectors. Outsourcing is different from buying in packages or solutions, because the management and responsibility for the development of appropriate systems are given to the vendor (Willcocks and Fitzgerald, 1993). The client organisation is no longer so concerned with how a system is developed, that is, what development approach or methodology is used, but is concerned with the end results and the effectiveness of the system that is delivered. The outsourcing vendors are usually large companies with wide ranges of skills and experience in systems development. Whether economies of scale operate in systems development is questionable, but the vendor companies argue that they can often provide a quicker and cheaper service. Some argue that it is better for the client organisation, because it pays only for what is delivered, and that the payment of real money (often coming directly from the business users) serves to 'focus the mind' and results in more accurate and realistic specifications. The client company has to develop skills in selecting the correct vendor, specifying requirements in detail, and writing and negotiating contracts.

Contingency

Most methodologies are designed for situations which follow a stated or unstated 'ideal type'. The methodology provides a step-by-step prescription for addressing this ideal type. However, some argue that situations are all different and there is no such thing as an 'ideal type' in reality. Such thinking suggests a contingency approach to information systems development (as against a prescriptive methodology), where a framework is presented but tools and techniques are expected to be used or not (or used and adapted), depending on the situation.

Situations might differ depending on, for example, the type of project and its objectives, the organisation and its environment, the users and their skills, the developers, and so on. The type of project might differ in its purpose, complexity, structuredness, degree of importance, the projected life of the project, and its potential impact. The organisation might be large or small, mature or immature in its use of IT, its experience of systems development, and so on. Different environments might exhibit different rates of change, the number of users affected by the system, their skills, and those of the analysts. All these characteristics are likely to affect the choice of development approach that is required.

An extreme example of different situations requiring different approaches are software for a 'fly by wire' aircraft and a sales information system to support management decision-making. One is safety critical; the other might be business critical. Most managers would not like the 'fly by wire' system of the aircraft that they fly to the sales conference developed in the same way as their sales system. One requires fast response, absolute adherence to the specification, and a degree of cross-checking and zero failure that can only be achieved by a very rigid and engineering approach to development. The other requires flexibility and changeability to respond to the diverse requirements of a marketing team which perhaps can only be achieved by an evolutionary prototyping approach to development.

Contingency can take a number of forms. It might be that an organisation chooses a particular methodology depending on the contingent factors and has systems developers available to use the most appropriate methodology for each particular application (Davis, 1982). Euromethod (Jenkins, 1994) is a framework enabling the use of European approaches (SSADM, Merise, and five others) as appropriate to the application. Another form of contingency is to have a contingent methodology or framework which allows for different approaches depending on situations. It might be that some phases could be omitted, or carried out in a different sequence, or in parts that are developed further and in more detail than defined by the methodology. Similarly, particular techniques and tools may be used differently or not used at all in some circumstances. In this form of contingency the methodology should help in identifying the situations and conditions which would prompt different actions. Multiview (Avison and Wood-Harper, 1990) is an example of a contingency methodology and Avison and Taylor (1997) suggest different situations for different approaches.

There are, however, potential problems with the contingent approach. First, some of the benefits of standardisation might be lost. Second, there is a wide range of different skills that are required to handle many approaches. Third, the selection of approach requires experience and skills to make the best judgements. Finally, it has been suggested that certain combinations of approaches are untenable because each has different philosophies that are contradictory.

Yet another alternative is the growing treatment of information systems development as a social and political process. The traditional methodologies of the methodology era are often criticised for being over-technical and ignoring the importance and influence of social and political factors. Some organisations are attempting to address this more directly in systems development. Multiview, for example, now includes a more direct recognition of information systems development as a social process with three aspects. These are the role of the systems analyst and the paradigm of assumptions constructed in practice; the political nature of the change process; and the way that methodologies are interpreted. These aspects are described in Wood-Harper and Avison (1990).

The theory about the role of the systems analyst and the paradigm of assumptions constructed in practice (Burrell and Morgan, 1979) can perhaps be explained best by giving examples of systems analysts in different situations. Four different stereotypical views of the systems analyst may be given as functionalist, interpretative, objective, and subjective. The last three, to a greater or lesser degree, suggest that information systems development is more of a social than a technical process. Roles, ideals, and metaphors for each might be as follows (Avison and Wood-Harper, 1990):

- *In the functionalist perspective*, the information system consists of interactions which function independently of outside manipulation. The analyst assumes that the situation can be readily understood, indeed there is an assumption of rational behaviour by the actors which makes understanding easier. The systems are well controlled, can be well understood, and can be formally defined. The systems analyst might be seen as technical expert, the ideals are objectivity, rigour, and formality. A metaphor of the analyst might be a medical doctor. This is very much a technical and process view and one where information systems development is seen as a technical rather than as a social process.
- *In the interpretative perspective*, it is assumed that the analyst is subjective and interprets the problem situation. The analyst hopes to understand the intentions of the actors in the situation. Participation and involvement will be the best way to obtain detailed information about the problem situation, and later to be able to predict and control it. The systems analyst might be seen as facilitator, the ideal might emphasise the importance of meaning, and a metaphor of the analyst might be a liberal teacher.
- *In the radical structuralist view*, the situation will appear to have a formal existence but require radical change due to, for example, contradictory and conflicting elements. The systems analyst is assumed to be an agent for change and social progress, emancipating people from their socio-economic structures. The systems analyst might be seen as an agent for social progress, the ideals lean towards change of the socio-economic class structures. A metaphor of the analyst here might be a warrior.
- *In the radical humanist view*, the situation is seen as external and complex. There is an emphasis on participation to enable a rapport

between the actors and this leads to emancipation at all levels, including the socio-economic and psychological. The systems analyst might be seen as change analyst, the ideals lean towards change of the socio-economic structures and psychological barriers. A metaphor of the analyst might be an emancipator.

Kling and Scacchi (1982) identified four perspectives within which problem-solvers may view the content of the problem situation in which information technology is embedded. The importance of these perspectives for the information systems definition concerns the fact that different strategies should be adopted dependent on the perspective embraced. The first is the formal rational perspective, which emphasises the formal organisational structure and procedures. With this perspective, we see the extreme of reductionist thought. Again, this is a traditional technical perspective. The second perspective, the structural perspective, includes considerations of the situation's formal subunits and recognises that communication must occur between them. The third perspective is the interactionist viewpoint which recognises that the pieces of the information resource are neither independent nor formally defined. The social groups of interest cross intra-organisational and inter-organisational boundaries and are possibly in a constant state of flux. The process of change is founded on negotiation. The fourth perspective, organisational politics, assumes that interactions in the organisation are based on the political machinations and resulting manifestations of power. As development progresses through the four perspectives, less emphasis is placed on the technical and structural and more emphasis on the social and potentially emancipatory. It has to be said that these concepts have not influenced the practising world of systems development much as yet, but the ideas are well founded and reflect a move away from the typical approach of the methodology era.

We have described above some alternative approaches that organisations are taking as a result of what we have termed the backlash against the traditional methodologies of the methodology era. However, they are not all alternatives to methodologies; some are new or putative methodologies. Others are complements to conventional methodologies, or simply shifts from developing in-house purchasing to packages or outsourcing. They are not necessarily mutually exclusive: some can be used together, providing a greater variety of approaches in a more contingent manner.

The post-methodology era is thus not about the abandonment of methodologies altogether. We identify the continuing refinement and improvement of existing commercial information systems methodologies, in terms of the products and techniques, and particularly in the use of CASE tools. We expect the tools to support more and more phases of methodologies including improvements in code generation systems.

This does not mean that programming and programmers will become obsolete, but that they are likely to be of declining importance in the development of standard information systems. The advent of object-oriented systems development is likely to have an important effect on current commercial methodologies. The market push is certainly in this direction, and we expect to see a number of methods, particularly those that currently separate the analysis of data and process in a rigid fashion, evolve with the incorporation of object-oriented concepts.

Thus the post-methodology era is characterised by a large number of different types of methodologies and we do not expect to see the development of one 'common' methodology. Rather we believe that systems development will become more contingent, and there will continue to exist different methodologies and approaches for different situations and purposes. For example, one approach is unlikely to be suitable, for example, for the development of management information systems, safety critical systems, business critical systems, expert systems, and so on. Further, with the backlash against methodologies, it is clear that some people are looking to move away from the constraints of traditional bureaucratic methodologies and are seeking new and alternative directions. One direction is the growth of packages, and we expect to see the development of methods that support the selection of packages and the tailoring and integration of these.

In conclusion, we expect that standard methodologies will decline in importance in the development of information systems within organisations, with the post-methodology era providing a greater focus on contingent and alternative approaches. However, predicting the future is always problematical and has a habit of making fools of those who attempt it!

References

Avison, D. E., and Fitzgerald, G. (1995), *Information Systems Development: Methodologies, Techniques and Tools*, 2nd edn. (Maidenhead: McGraw-Hill).

—— Shah, H. U., and Wilson, D. N. (1994), 'Software Quality Standards in Practice: The Limitations of Using ISO-9001 to Support Software Development', *Software Quality Journal*, 3: 105–11.

—— and Taylor, V. (1997), 'Information Systems Development Methodologies: A Classification According to Problem Situation', *Journal of Information Technology*, 15, 1: 73–81.

—— and Wood-Harper, A. T. (1990), *Multiview: An Exploration in Information Systems Development* (Maidenhead: McGraw-Hill).

—— —— Vidgen, R., and Wood, R. (1998), *Multiview: A Further Exploration in Information Systems Development* (Maidenhead: McGraw-Hill).

Bodker, S., Ehn, P., Kammersgaard, J., Kyng, M., and Sundblad, Y. (1987), 'A UTOPIAN Experience: on Design of Powerful Computer-Based Tools for

Skilled Graphic Workers', in G. Bjerknes, P. Ehn, and M. Kyng. (eds.), *Computers and Democracy: A Scandinavian Challenge* (Aldershot: Avebury).

Booch, G. (1991), *Object Oriented Design with Applications* (Redwood City, Calif.: Benjamin/Cummings).

Bullen, C. V., and Rockart, J. F. (1984), *A Primer on Critical Success Factors*, CISR Working Paper 69 (Boston: Sloan Management School, MIT).

Burrell, G., and Morgan, G. (1979), *Sociological Paradigms and Organisational Analysis* (London: Heinemann).

Caminer, D., Aris, J., Hermon, P., and Land, F. (1996), *User-Driven Innovation* (Maidenhead: McGraw-Hill).

Checkland, P. B. (1981), *Systems Thinking, Systems Practice* (Chichester: Wiley).

—— (1985), 'From Optimising to Learning: A Development of Systems Thinking for the 1990s', *Journal of the Operations Research Society*, 36, 9.

—— and Scholes, J. (1990), *Soft Systems Methodology in Action* (Chichester: Wiley).

Coad, P., and Yourdon, E. (1991), *Object Oriented Analysis*, 2nd edn. (Englewood Cliffs, NJ: Prentice Hall).

Daniels, A., and Yeates, D. A. (1971), *Basic Training in Systems Analysis*, 2nd edn. (London: Pitman).

Davenport, T. H., and Short, J. E. (1990), 'The New Industrial Engineering: Information Technology and Business Process Redesign', *Sloan Management Review*, 31, 4: 11–21.

Davis, G. B. (1982), 'Strategies for Information Requirements Determination', *IBM Systems Journal*, 21, 2.

De Grace, P., and Stahl, L. (1993), *The Olduvai Imperative: CASE and the State of Software Engineering Practice* (Englewood Cliffs, NJ: Prentice Hall).

DeMarco, T. (1979), *Structured Analysis and System Specification* (Englewood Cliffs, NJ: Prentice Hall).

Earl, M. J. (1989), *Management Strategies for Information Technology* (Englewood Cliffs, NJ: Prentice Hall).

Eurogroup (1990), 'Euromethod Project, Phase 2, Deliverable 1', *State of the Art Report*, 2 (n.p.: Eurogroup).

Eva, M. (1994), *SSADM Version 4: A User's Guide*, 2nd edn. (Maidenhead: McGraw-Hill).

Fitzgerald, B. (1996), 'An Investigation of the Use of Systems Development Methodologies in Practice', in J. Coelho et al. (eds.), *Proceedings of the Fourth European Conference on Information Systems, Lisbon*.

Flynn, D. J. (1992), *Information Systems Requirements: Determination and Analysis* (Maidenhead: McGraw-Hill).

Friedman, A. (1989), *Computer Systems Development: History, Organisation and Implementation* (Chichester: Wiley & Sons).

Gane, C. P., and Sarson, T. (1979), *Structured Systems Analysis: Tools and Techniques* (Englewood Cliffs, NJ: Prentice Hall).

Gray, E. M. (1985), 'An Empirical Study of the Evaluation of Some Information Systems Development Methods', *Proceedings of Conference of the Information Systems Association, Sunningdale Park, Reading*.

Hammer, M., and Champy, J. (1993), *Reengineering the Corporation: A Manifesto for Business Revolution* (New York: Harper Business).

IBM (1975), 'Business Systems Planning', in J. D. Couger, M. A. Colter, and R. W. Knapp (1982), *Advanced Systems Development/Feasibility Techniques* (New York: Wiley).

Jayaratna, N. (1994), *Understanding and Evaluating Methodologies, NIMSAD: A Systemic Framework* (Maidenhead: McGraw-Hill).

Jenkins, T. (1994), 'Report Back on the DMSG Sponsored UK Euromethod Forum '94', *Data Management Bulletin*, Summer Issue, 11, 3.

Kling, R. K., and Scacchi, W. (1982), 'The Web of Computing: Computing Technology as Social Organization', *Advances in Computers*, 21.

Lederer, A. L., and Mendlelow, A. L. (1989), 'Information Systems Planning: Incentives for Effective Action', *Data Base*, Fall.

Maddison, R. N. (1983) (ed.), *Information System Methodologies*, (Chichester: Wiley Heyden).

Martin, J. (1989), *Information Engineering* (Englewood Cliffs, NJ: Prentice Hall).

Martin, J. (1991), *Rapid Application Development* (Englewood Cliffs, NJ: Prentice Hall).

Mumford, E. (1995), *Effective Systems Design and Requirements Analysis: The ETHICS Method* (Basingstoke: Macmillan).

Olle, T. W., Sol, H. G., and Tully, C. J. (1983), *Information Systems Design Methodologies: A Feature Analysis* (Amsterdam: North-Holland).

―― ―― and Verrijn-Stuart, A. A. (1982), *Information Systems Design Methodologies: A Comparative Review* (Amsterdam: North-Holland).

―― ―― ―― (1986) (eds.), *Information Systems Design Methodologies: Improving the Practice* (Amsterdam: North-Holland).

―― Verrijn-Stuart, A. A., and Bhabuta, L. (1988) (eds.), *Computerized Assistance during the Information Systems Life Cycle* (Amsterdam: North-Holland).

Palvia, P., and Nosek, J. (1993), 'A Field Examination of System Life Cycle Techniques and Methodologies', *Information and Management*, 25: 73–84.

Quang, P. T., and Chartier-Kastler, C. (1991), *Merise in Practice*, trans. D. E. and M. A. Avison (from the French *Merise appliquée*, Paris: Eyrolles, 1989) (Basingstoke: Macmillan).

Wasserman, A. I., Freeman, P., and Porchella, M. (1983), 'Characteristics of Software Development Methodologies', in Olle et al. (1983).

Wastell, D. (1996), 'The Fetish of Technique: Methodology as a Social Defence', *Information Systems Journal*, 6, 1: 25–40.

Willcocks, L., and Fitzgerald, G. (1993), 'Market as Opportunity? CASE Studies in Outsourcing Information Technology and Services', *Journal of Strategic Information Systems*, 2, 3.

Wilson, B. (1990), *Systems: Concepts, Methodologies and Applications*, 2nd edn. (Chichester: Wiley).

Wood-Harper, A. T., and Avison, D. E. (1992), 'Reflections from the Experience of Using Multiview: Through the Lens of Soft Systems Methodology', *Systemist*, 14, 3.

Yourdon, E. (1989), *Modern Structured Analysis* (Englewood Cliffs, NJ: Prentice Hall).

―― (1994), *Object-Oriented Systems Design: An Integrated Approach* (Englewood Cliffs, NJ: Prentice Hall).

Yourdon Inc. (1993), *Yourdon Systems Method: Model-Driven Systems Development* (Englewood Cliffs, NJ: Yourdon Press).

12

Deciding the Future for IS Failures
Not the Choice You Might Think

CHRIS SAUER

Introduction

> If I define a successful system as one that is developed *on time and within budget*; is *reliable* (bug-free and available when needed), and *maintainable* (easy and inexpensive to modify); *meets its goals and specified requirements*; and *satisfies the users*, how many of you would say that your organisation builds successful systems? I've asked this question of hundreds of people at all levels of data processing, and the overwhelming response is one of silence.
>
> (Robert Block, 1983)

Block's experience still has a sad ring of familarity. In the pioneering years of the field, information systems (IS) were subject to high failure rates. Today, the situation is little better. Throughout the current decade major failures have been publicised in a variety of countries demonstrating that failure remains a problem worldwide. This is not a situation we have willingly chosen. Substantial efforts have been made to understand failure and avoid it but without apparent success. The question now is whether we can learn to be more successful in the future. Experience does not encourage optimism. However, there are changes unfolding in practice and research which could result in significantly reduced failure rates. The first is a shift in practice toward risk containment, a relatively new approach which promises to reduce the high incidence and cost of failure. The second is the growing research interest in IS failures.

This chapter places IS failures research in its historical context to help us see what has and has not been achieved in the past, what is happening today, and where current trends are taking us. The main purpose is to demonstrate that we face a choice between reducing risk through containing it and accepting high risk but trying to control it. The dilemma is this —in an ideal world there would be no IS failures, but a world in which there are no IS failures will not necessarily be ideal. A world in which risk containment is the dominant approach to IS will be one in which ambition for the business value of IS applications is diminished. So, for as long as there remains a real prospect of bringing risk under control without sacrificing ambition there is reason not to pursue a reduced rate of failure in the short term. The choice that faces us is not just about the acceptability of IS failures, it is a choice with profound implications for the future business importance of IS. For this reason, what we should do is not as obvious as it might appear at first. This chapter helps managers, practitioners, and researchers to make a more informed decision by setting out the nature and parameters of the choice. In particular it outlines what needs to be done if failures research is to bring risk under control and hence make available the full business potential of IS before risk containment circumscribes that potential.

The chapter starts by describing the continuing importance of IS failure, and explaining why such a major problem has been tolerated for so long. This helps to explain the risk control approach that has dominated IS professionals' attempts to solve the problem. This approach is described and its limitations are spelled out to show why so little has been learnt from IS failures in the past. The chapter then describes how practice is changing by moving toward risk containment. Changes in research trends are also described. The choice that faces managers, practitioners, and researchers is set out and the implications of the possible alternatives drawn. We conclude by offering suggestions about how IS failures research should proceed if it is to make progress on risk control in the window of opportunity available to it.

The Problem of Failure

IS failures have been and continue to be a serious problem for practitioners and researchers. While there have been periods in the last thirty years when failure has been less in the industry eye, there is no reason to think that it has been less serious at any time. Table 12.1 provides indicative survey findings from a range of computer-based technologies. In the late 1960s and 1970s, no informed industry commentator would have denied that failures were a critical issue. The term 'software crisis' was common currency (Friedman, 1989). Mowshowitz (1976) estimated that 40 per cent of all projects were failures. Subsequent data have not contradicted him. By the 1980s, though, IS failure was less discussed. At the time, it was not clear whether this was because IS professionals were bringing the problem under control. Table 12.1 suggests retrospectively that this was not the case.

The ubiquity and magnitude of the problem of IS failure have become more openly apparent in the 1990s. No countries are immune. Recent high-profile examples in the USA include the Denver International Airport

TABLE 12.1. *Summary of survey results indicating levels of failure for a range of computer-based information systems*

Source	Findings
Lehman (1979)	57-project survey—46% overdue (mean delay 7 months), 59% over budget
Comptroller-General (1979)	9-project survey—$3.2m never delivered, $2m delivered but never used, $1.3m abandoned or reworked, $0.2m used after change, $0.1m used as delivered
Gladden (1982)	Survey—75% of systems development not completed or not used
Bikson and Gutek (1984) (cited in Long, 1989)	2000-company survey—40% of office systems failed to achieve intended results
New and Myers (1986) (cited in Zammuto and O'Connor, 1992)	239-company survey—poor or negative returns on investment for CAD and CAM (46% of companies), FMS (67%), robotics (76%)
Ettlie (1986) (cited in Majchrzak, 1991)	55-manager, 41-company survey—50% of CAM systems fail
Works (1987) (cited in Majchrzak, 1991)	75% of production and inventory control systems fail
Lyytinen (1988)	34-systems analyst survey—70% find between 20% and 50% of projects fail
Ewusi-Mensah and Przasnyski (1994)	82-respondent survey—22% had abandoned more than 5 systems development projects in the last 5 years, 69% had abandoned at least one
Phan et al. (1995)	143-project survey—25% do not meet requirements
Johnson (1995)	365-company survey—31% projects cancelled before completion, 53% overrun overrun costs and budget and have impaired functionality; only 12% of 3,682 current projects on time and on budget

baggage-handling system (Gibbs, 1994; Montealegre et al., 1996*a*, 1996*b*) and American Airlines' CONFIRM (Oz, 1994). In France, difficulties with the SNCF's SOCRATE reservation system have been in the headlines (Eglizeau et al., 1996; Mitev, 1996). The UK has been beset with equally newsworthy failures including the London Ambulance Service's (LAS) command and control system (Beynon-Davies, 1995; Wastell and Newman, 1996), the London Stock Exchange's Taurus project (Drummond, 1996), and the Wessex Health Authority's IS project (Kirby-Green, 1993). In Australia, Westpac Bank's CS90 failure has achieved industry folklore status (Plunkett, 1991) while in New Zealand, the Education Department's failure was front-page news (Myers, 1994). The really bad news is that this list is far from exhaustive.

There are many facets to IS failure including undelivered functionality (Comptroller-General, 1979; Phan et al., 1995), schedule overruns (Lehman, 1979; van Genuchten, 1991), resistance (Hirschheim and Newman, 1988), and costs. Costs include risk to human life and health (e.g. LAS) although actual loss of life is relatively rare (Mackenzie, 1994). A more common cost is the wasted investment. Unofficial estimates of the London Stock Exchange's abandoned Taurus project put the total cost as high as £400 million (Kane and Whitebloom, 1993). Delay with the Denver International Airport's system reportedly cost more than $US1 million per day (Gibbs, 1994). The abandonment of a relatively unambitious project such as the California vehicle registration and driver licensing system still cost $50 million (Johnson, 1995; Keil, 1995a). The costs of IS project failures can be competitively important too. The chief executive of an Australian company whose systems integration projects are worth tens of millions of dollars sees budget and schedule overruns as a major competitive issue for him and his competitors. The macroeconomic costs are startling. Johnson (1995) estimated that abandoned projects alone would cost the USA $81 billion in 1995, equivalent to 1 per cent of GDP. The full cost of all types of failure is substantially more.

IS failure clearly continues to trouble the industry. The magnitude of the problem is evident. Its relevance to all companies using IT is high. American Airlines' experience with CONFIRM should be a salutary lesson. If the company that achieved so much with its developments of the SABRE reservation system can suffer a massive failure, anybody can. We might therefore have expected IS failure to be top of the agenda for both practice and research, instead of which it has been tolerated almost as a necessary evil.

More than the Price of Progress

The problem of failure has not prevented the IS field from advancing on many fronts. The dynamics of practice have maintained such momentum that failure has come to be tolerated as an undesirable fact of life—the price of progress.

Information systems practice over the last thirty years has been influenced by two related dynamics—the *dynamic of capability* and the *dynamic of opportunity*. The dynamic of capability can be characterised in terms of the development of a robust technological core for IS. This has seen practitioners' attention move initially from hardware issues, which until the diffusion of integrated circuitry were the critical component of any IS, to software development through the period of the 'software crisis', and on into the late 1970s and early 1980s when attention turned to the individual's IS use in terms of decision support and expert systems, and human computer interaction (Friedman, 1989). Since then, with the development of technologies such as client-server, attention has turned to the organisation. And, arguably, with electronic data interchange (EDI) and other boundary-spanning technologies, it has now moved even further to inter-organisational relationships. At each stage in this historical development the core of what has been considered robust has been expanded.

As the dynamic of capability has unfolded, by defining what is viewed as robust, it has also defined what is leading edge. This is where new work has been directed, and this is where success has been hardest won and failure most likely. Thus, for example, before GUIs became standard, attempts to build them or some alternative friendly interface required developers to innovate at the leading edge. There was less knowledge of what was needed and few robust tools to help. Consequently, a new interface was a risky undertaking. Not only were the developers attempting to deliver something new for their organisation, they were at the same time pushing at the frontier of technological capability. As Petroski (1992) has argued in respect to construction engineering, it is as engineers seek to expand the limits of what is known and technologically robust that failures occur. The rapid development of the capabilities of IS has therefore ensured a steady flow of failures.

Practice has also been influenced by the dynamic of opportunity. Perceptions of the opportunities presented by IS have developed over time from automating to informating to transforming (Zuboff, 1988). Just as the dynamic of capability has pushed technological ambition further and further, so too the dynamic of opportunity has pushed organisational ambition further and further. This has continually extended the degree of organisational change demanded into territory not well understood with consequential risk of failure. The more extreme versions of business process re-engineering (BPR) are the current representatives of this extended ambition. Not only is it therefore not surprising that BPR should have experienced high failure rates (Davenport, 1993; Davenport and Stoddard, 1994; Hammer and Champy, 1993), in an intriguing reversal its proponents have advertised its propensity to failure as if to say if failure is so high the opportunity must be unparalleled.

The dynamic of opportunity is a dynamic of *IS* practice. Despite its name, it should not be thought of as exclusively reflecting *business* demand. Rather, it reflects the technology-driven marketing efforts of IS. BPR exemplifies the point. It is a product of information technology-based consulting rather than of business-initiated demand.

The dynamic of capability and the dynamic of opportunity have formed complementary constituents of the way in which practice has developed historically and continues to develop today. The development of new capabilities has stimulated the recognition of opportunities which have further stimulated the development of capabilities and so on. The rapid momentum generated for progress has fixed IS professionals' eyes on the prizes of the future and away from the casualties of the past.

The dynamics of practice have been underpinned by certain assumptions about the value and the application of IS. Value has been defined by dazzling opportunity or potential so that little trouble has been taken to identify what is realisable. Once an organisational opportunity has been recognised, this has typically been regarded as sufficient justification for pursuing it. Thus, opportunities might be passed up for lack of resources but not because of doubts about whether the opportunity can be successfully grasped. In order to sustain such beliefs consistently it has been necessary to make assumptions about the application of IS, through both the systems development process and the implementation of packages. Application has been viewed as a technical process which can be managed by rational principles of engineering (Hirschheim et al., 1995). The strong engineering culture of much of the IS profession has ensured that such assumptions are easily, indeed unconsciously, adopted.

These assumptions about the value and application of IS have resulted in practice adopting a *risk control* orientation. This implies that whatever risk there might be in the deployment of IS can be fully controlled through appropriate engineering management such that employment of the right engineering practices will guarantee that there is (1) a successful systems outcome, and (2) no relevant risk in terms of achievement of business value. In its most extreme form, the implication of the risk control approach is that any opportunity can be pursued because any possible risk can be brought under control. This risk control orientation is manifested in the popular decision-making practice of relying solely on cost–benefit evaluations rather than subjecting them to a probabilistic risk analysis.

The persistence of risk control in practice has been sustained by the IS industry's unflagging optimism—while there may have been failures in the past, they will be controlled in the future. This optimism has been possible because like a suitably programmed poker machine, or one-armed bandit, practice has delivered just enough success to encourage companies to continue to believe in the promise of risk control. The dynamic of opportunity has sustained that optimism particularly through the 1980s with the promise of strategic information systems (SIS). Moreover, because failure has been sufficiently widespread that if one company in an industry has sustained IS losses, there has been a good chance that its competitors will have done so too, there has been less incentive for business and practice to challenge the risk control orientation.

The fly in the ointment is that failures have not been confined to leading edge applications or even inflated organisational ambitions. The risk control orientation has not tamed the supposedly robust core. Unadventurous personnel and payroll systems still fail readily (Auditor-General, 1991;

Myers, 1994); mature though more complex applications such as MRP likewise (Ciborra and Schneider, 1992; Works, 1987). For a long time the combination of momentum and optimism have been sufficient to generate business tolerance of IS failures, but business managers have begun to waken to the fact that the IS profession has not yet brought risk under control and that they are paying more than the price of progress.

The Failure of Risk Control

While IS failure may have been accepted, it has not been accepted passively. Practitioners and researchers have worked hard to achieve advances in risk control, that is to reduce substantially the probability of failure associated with achieving a given level of ambition in respect of IS functionality and performance. Whatever these efforts may have achieved, they do not appear to have made a substantive, general advance in risk control as far as the incidence of failures is concerned. It is arguable that there have been advances but they have been offset by the new opportunities for failure created by the dynamic of capabilities. Unfortunately, there have been no rigorous studies to shed light on the question of whether risk control has made real advances. If there are individual organisations and researchers who have discovered how to control risk to a significant degree, the IS community is not abuzz with the news. All too often today's failure analyses point to the same old familiar suspects that shouldered the blame for earlier failures—inadequate top management support, insufficient user involvement, poor project management, and so on. However, both practice and research are changing. If we are to understand these changes and if we are to assess the prospects for making progress with risk control in the future, it is necessary to understand the approaches that have been taken in the past, the types of study that have been conducted, and the reasons we have learnt so little from them.

Approaches to learning from failure

For the purposes of trying to understand why we have not yet learnt how to control risk, we need to know what the analyses of practitioners have been as well as those of researchers. Practice has usually studied failures informally so that individual practitioners have been expected to learn from experience. Managers have rarely sought to achieve formal organisational learning—post-mortem analyses are the exception rather than the rule and where they occur, their outcomes are usually restricted to the particular organisational context (Abdel-Hamid and Madnick, 1990; Boddie, 1987). There are no studies to show that organisations that do review their failures are less prone to subsequent failure. Institutional reviewers such as government audit offices commonly complain that the recommendations of their earlier reviews have not been acted on (GAO, 1983).

The other route through which it has been expected that the lessons of experience would be made available is through their distillation and codification into methodologies and statements of good practice. Neither the evidence of adoption (Beck and Perkins, 1983) nor the project performance achieved suggest that whatever lessons have been thus distilled have significantly helped control risk.

Although practitioner analyses are typically part of the industry's folklore rather than having been explicitly recorded, researchers have asked practitioners about the causes of failures, so their analyses are embedded in our existing research knowledge (Keider, 1984; Ewusi-Mensah and Przasnyski, 1994). We can therefore treat research findings as capturing the bulk of the IS profession's knowledge of IS failures. More advanced knowledge that may be embedded in the competencies of individual organisations has to be ignored because, not being codified, it is not currently generalisable.

Research studies of IS failure

IS failure and IS success have never been sufficiently separable for failures research to be conducted entirely independently of the broader programme of IS implementation research. Nevertheless, enough work has been directed toward understanding failure for us to be able to focus on failures research, drawing on broader implementation research where appropriate.

IS failure is not a well defined concept. It is an evaluation that can be applied to a system or project in respect of the expectations of one or many stakeholders (Lyytinen and Hirschheim, 1987). Consequently, IS failure covers a variety of familiar experiences and outcomes. Lyytinen and Hirschheim have identified three different failure concepts commonly used in research studies. Correspondence failure refers to failure of IS to meet the specified objectives such as staff savings, improved efficiency of resource allocation, greater productivity, and the like. Process failure refers to outcomes of the systems development process such as project abandonment, schedule overruns, and budget blowouts. Interaction failure refers to failure to use an IS. Implementation studies are broader than IS failure studies because they include attention to success and system adoption which may not always be explained by the same reasons and causes as failure and rejection.

Failures research has been strongly influenced by the changing dynamics of practice and by the assumptions of practice. It has changed

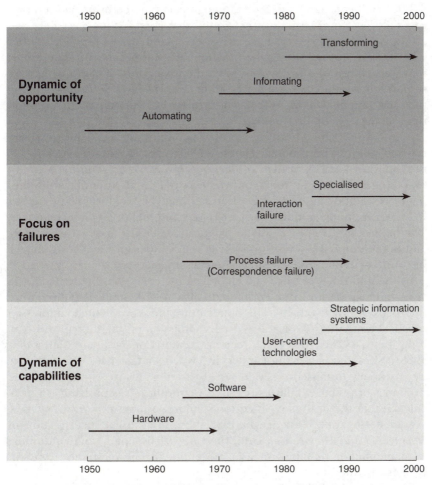

FIG. 12.1. *The changing focus of failure studies against the changing dynamics of practice*

with the times, but like practice it has often moved on leaving unfinished business behind. Tracing its development against the unfolding dynamics of practice permits us to see what phenomena have been studied and when, and how satisfactory closure has not been achieved. As the dynamics of capabilities and opportunities have developed, so the focus of failure research has turned to each new frontier between the robust core of technology and its context where new types of failure were occurring. Fig. 12.1 provides a schematic depiction of the changing focus of failure studies in relation to the dynamics of practice.

IS failure studies originated at the end of the 1960s at the same time as the software crisis was recognised and after the worst sources of hardware failure had been stabilised. Software engineers focused principally on process failures. IS professionals recognised that correspondence failure was also a problem. However, they perceived it as a *systems* problem. Either systems were not delivering the functionality that had been requested or they were, but it was turning out to be the wrong functionality. Thus, correspondence failure was conceived to be a problem of process—building the right system. The focus for analysis and prescription was therefore on the systems development process.

In the late 1970s, the dynamic of capabilities advanced into its user-centred phase. The problem of resistance began to surface regularly, so the focus for analysis turned to users because however good the software development process, if users, for whatever reason, did not like an IS they might resist and cause an interaction failure. The technical response was to focus on understanding user psychology and building better interfaces. The behavioural response was to try to understand the structure of user and organisational interests and power, and to design for that or engage in counter-counter-implementation tactics (Keen, 1981).

By the mid-1980s practice had embraced the competitive potential for IS (Ives and Learmonth, 1984; Porter and Millar, 1985). Strategic IS (SIS) were the focus of much activity. The opportunity they represented suppressed practical awareness of, or at least open admission of, the difficulty of realising them. As they took many years to create (Copeland and McKenney, 1988), SIS failures were not much in evidence. The risks of SIS failure were scarcely discussed or evaluated. Following this development in the dynamics of practice, failures research went quiet. It is probably no coincidence that the journal devoted to IS failure, *Systems, Objectives, Solutions*, ceased its separate existence in 1983, becoming just a small section of *Information and Management*. Until the early 1990s, apart from continuing implementation research on user adoption, IS failure studies were virtually suspended.

This account of the development of IS failure studies shows that the field has historically understood failure in terms closely associated with its technical capabilities. It has never taken the opportunity or trouble to understand failure in terms of the organisation's business and the way it organises and manages. Failures research has not been able to throw off the shackles that have confined practice to its organisational role as a functional specialism rather than an integral part of core business. It has left unchallenged the conception of IS which is widely held in practice that IS should be able to deliver black box systems which other parts of the organisation are then responsible for making work for the business. It has twice missed opportunities to pursue this line of enquiry, first when correspondence failure was interpreted as a problem of technical process, and second in not taking up the challenge of SIS in the 1980s.

If we look at what IS failures research has found, we discover that the dominant stream of work has been devoted to discovering factors associated with failure. An alternative stream of research, starting more recently, has explored the processes by which IS have failed. The study of IS failures, whether alone or in combination with IS success, has been predicated on the assumption that if we can detect what causes failure, we can thereby discover the sources of risk and by eliminating those causes control risk.

The earliest studies of IS failures looked for simple causes. They were inclined to focus on the shortcomings of individuals, 'incompetents' Dearden (1972) called them, such as systems professionals (Ackoff, 1967) and the chief IS executive (Morgan and Soden, 1973). Colton (1972) found that most of the difficulties being encountered in his study of police departments were social and behavioural rather than technical. Lucas (1975) in his review of findings to that date confirmed the generality of Colton's conclusion. By 1985 the social and behavioural basis of IS failure was a firmly fixed research result (Boland and Hirschheim, 1985). The bulk of the research undertaken has therefore addressed the issue of which social and behavioural factors are associated with IS failure. The factors that have been consistently identified are now familiar to most in the field. They include lack of top management support, lack of value in the system, inadequate resources, and non-involvement of users. Appendix 12.1 provides a representative list of factor classes, factors, and the studies that have identified them. It bears witness to the complexity that factor studies have uncovered.

The factors discovered in these studies have typically been treated as causes of IS failure. In some cases, this is because the research design involved asking respondents about what they perceived to be the causes of failure (Keider, 1984; Ewusi-Mensah and Przasnyski, 1991, 1994). The pursuit of risk control has led researchers to make recommendations for practice based on their results. Those recommendations have been based on the engineering assumptions implicit in practice, namely that the causes discovered are straightforwardly related to failure in such a way that IS development and implementation can be easily brought under control. In the most extreme instances, prescription has involved researchers advising practitioners to avoid doing those things practitioners have told researchers cause failure! As Appendix 12.1 shows, factors are usually described with limited specificity. Some of the prescriptions based on them have spawned mini-industries of researchers developing methods, methodologies, and good practices through which the specifics of, for example, user requirements elicitation are fully and correctly specified.

Research into failure factors has been pursued for over twenty years. Some researchers have moved beyond the identification of factors to developing more general implementation frameworks (Schultz and Slevin, 1975; Kwon and Zmud, 1987; Swanson, 1988; Davis, 1989; Cooper and Zmud, 1990). Attempts at completeness are necessarily very complex—Lucas et al.'s (1990) framework includes twenty-seven variables and thirty-four relationships. Such frameworks need to be tested not only because they posit relationships among factors, but also because the validity of the original factor studies has not been adequately demonstrated. For example, notwithstanding an almost universal belief in the importance of user involvement in IS development, Ives and Olson (1984) found that the evidence from research studies did not justify the conclusion drawn. However, testing of the frameworks has not generated any fully validated models (Lucas et al., 1990; Brancheau and Wetherbe, 1990). This lack of convincing validation, the dearth of new insights from factor research, and the continuing evidence of failures in practice strongly suggest that the factor-based approach to failures research has not been successful.

Alternative approaches began to emerge in the early 1980s when interaction failure first surfaced on the main failure studies agenda. Resistance studies have gradually increased our awareness of the extent of the phenomenon to include rejection because of task inadequacy (Miller, 1983), shop-floor politics (Wilkinson, 1983), executive resistance (Argyris, 1971), IS professionals' resistance (Rudelius et al., 1982), governmental politics (Dutton, 1981), and organisational culture (Sloane, 1991). Hirschheim and Newman (1988) conclude that resistance defies simple explanation. With studies of resistance has come appreciation of the need to explain aspects of IS failure in terms of the processes of organisational politics (Markus, 1981, 1983; Markus and Pfeffer, 1983). Research into resistance has thus highlighted the value of process analysis distinct from the traditional factor approach.

Process research has not been restricted either to interaction failure or to political theory. Analytical frameworks and approaches for understanding process have been developed to different degrees of detail and with different emphases including the interactionist perspective (Markus, 1984), the interpretativist perspective (Walsham, 1993; Myers, 1994; Myers and Young, 1995), and the exchange/dependence perspective (Sauer, 1993a). Some studies have attempted partial tests of these frameworks (Beynon-Davies, 1995; Myers and Young, 1995). None has been widely accepted or convincingly rejected. None has received extensive, rigorous validation. While, individually, they give rise to interesting analyses, they have not resulted in any breakthroughs in risk control.

Factor research has generated a number of very similar results, but has not satisfactorily isolated causes in a way that allows them to be eliminated in practice. Process research has probed closer to causes but has been more fragmented, not resulting in consensus, and consequently has also not made an impression on actual failure rates.

Why have we learnt so little from IS failure studies?

IS failure studies have not been more useful because of limitations in both factor and process research. Factor studies have encapsulated a research strategy which has proved too simple for the complexity of the phenomenon. Consequently, its prescriptions have not proved effective. By contrast, process research is more appropriate to the complexity, but has typically been more individualistic, has developed little by way of cumulative knowledge, and has not generated simple prescriptions. Neither approach has fully broken out of the narrow conception of IS that has kept researchers from conducting their analyses in terms of *business* factors and processes. Both approaches have been handicapped by the limited interest shown in their research findings by practitioners, and by theoretical and practical difficulties in undertaking failures research.

The factor-based research strategy has many attractive features which explain its adoption. It elicits key dimensions of failure situations across a range of organisational settings. It is straightforwardly replicated and validated. It is easy to develop prescriptions from it. The engineering assumptions underlying practice have encouraged the belief that failure would be susceptible to a simple factor research strategy. This would identify factors as failure causes; prescription would recommend their avoidance and permit the design of engineering practices which would eliminate failures.

There are two possible reasons why the factor research strategy has not brought risk under control. One is that it has not identified the true causes of failure. So many studies have focused on the same widely cited failure factors without asking whether the continuing problems in industry suggest that these factors are not true causes. Perhaps the familiar old failure factors are merely symptoms, and attacking the symptoms does not cure the underlying disease. The second possible reason is that the factors *are* causes but they are not readily avoidable. Kling (1987) has pointed out the difficulties of identifying appropriate, controllable causes in the complex social webs in which IS are set. It is quite possible therefore that deeper organisational conditions prevent the causal factors identified from being changed unless the organisational conditions themselves are changed. An example of this kind of analysis is that of Arnold (1982) who analyses the failure of the UK Prestel system in terms of apparently obvious errors but shows that they were strongly influenced by deeper and more powerful industry conditions that constrained management choice. Researchers in the factor tradition have been reluctant to explore such possibilities thereby limiting the further development of their research.

Whether or not factor studies have found the true causes of IS failures, the prescriptions based on them have suffered from practical shortcomings. The visible effect is that organisations continue to do the things identified as factors associated with or causing failure. There are several reasons for this. The first is that the majority of prescriptions are insufficiently specific. For example, collecting user requirements has long been prescribed; virtually every project can claim to respect this prescription *to some extent* but there are no adequate guidelines about what is a sufficient extent. Only *post hoc*, that is post-implementation when it is too late to do anything differently, is their adequacy confirmed, and this by the very result, success or failure, that the prescription is designed to influence.

The second reason is that other conditions do sometimes determine whether prescriptions can be followed. For example, clear objectives are often prescribed, but lack of structural alignment can prevent business and the IS function reaching agreement. If IS is centralised but much business decision-making is decentralised, there is a structural barrier to the agreement of clear objectives.

Thirdly, some prescriptions are not easily acted upon. For example, the importance of gaining top management support is continually asserted by practitioners and researchers alike, but it is difficult advice on which to act because there are no foolproof ways of detecting the absence of top management support when a project has been approved, and even if there were, there is little advice about how an IS professional might influence top management to make its support available.

Fourthly, like physicians of old leeching their patients, our cures can contribute to the disease. For example, although methodologies are promoted as securing the discipline of good practices, they come at a cost which is not always acceptable. The profusion of detail in a methodology like SSADM and the time it takes to develop a system can be counterproductive (Baskerville et al., 1992; Dhillo and Hackney, 1996). Another dysfunctional cure is the unqualified prescription for top management commitment which in cases of escalation simply makes matters worse (Keil, 1995*b*; Newman and Sabherwal, 1996). The strategy of identifying factors and then prescribing their elimination is too simplistic.

Process research has been stimulated by the need to enquire more incisively into the causes of failure. The potential of process research is that by analysing more information and by examining relationships over time it is possible to identify phenomena inaccessible to cross-sectional eyes. Process studies are able to trace causal linkages better than factor studies and are better equipped to provide explanations of complex social and organisational interactions (Markus and Robey, 1988). The drawbacks of the process-oriented approach have been that the frameworks and analyses have been complex, their theoretical foundations diverse, and they have not been the focus of accumulated research efforts comparable to those lavished on the factor stream. Their practical value derives less from specific findings and more from internalising a framework usually incorporating a new way of thinking. For obvious reasons this has limited appeal to practitioners who have gained little value from process research so far.

Both factor and process studies have been constrained by their choice for the scope of their studies. By focusing most strongly on the behaviour of the IS project organisation and the end users, researchers have often not attended to the wider context. In consequence they have not only forgone the possibility of identifying deeper causes, they have also been seduced into assuming that the factors and causes they have identified are behaviours that are within the autonomous power of IS professionals and users to change.

The difficulty of making IS failure research useful has been compounded by the special problems of researching IS failure. These consist of theoretical difficulties associated with the nature of the phenomena of failure and practical problems. There are three difficulties. The first is that while practitioners and many researchers talk about failure as if it were a single phenomenon, it is in fact a diverse set of phenomena. The emergence of new kinds of failure over time such as BPR and outsourcing failures further complicates matters (Clemons et al., 1995; Earl, 1996).

Second, the complexity associated with the combination of technical, human, and organisational characteristics of IS makes theorising very difficult. Third, studies of failures in other fields have provided no ready made answers. To the extent that other technologies share the distinctive characteristics of IS their fields of study are equally lacking in powerful explanatory theory. Complex and tightly coupled technologies are precisely the systems whose behaviour we cannot predict and even struggle to explain *ex post* (Perrow, 1984).

As well as there being problems associated with theorising about IS failure, there are practical research problems too. Most obviously organisations do not like to air dirty linen (Dutton et al., 1995). DeMarco and Lister (1987) talk of a conspiracy of silence. Organisations suppress publicity and tell their staff not to discuss failures (Maiden, 1996). They may decline to return survey forms and refuse permission for study. As a result, obtaining data about failures can be difficult. Once access has been gained to study a failure, organisational subjects are often keen to rationalise their own part. It is to be expected therefore that the data they provide is selective. Publication too may be problematic if an organisation or individuals are identified and they object to what has been written. The possibility of litigation is a real threat (Dutton, 1993). Prudent lawyers will advise that however defensible the research, the costs and difficulties of defending a lawsuit make it worth avoiding even if this is to the detriment of the research. For these reasons IS failures have often not been studied and where they have, the research has been partial.

In summary, we have not learnt more from IS failures because our approaches have been limited in their assumptions and their scope, because they have suffered from limited applicability, and are subject to both theoretical and practical difficulties. What is not clear is whether we ever will learn substantially more from IS failures.

Changing Practice

Business dissatisfaction with the inability of IS professionals to bring risk under control has been growing over the last decade (Strassmann, 1985). Business managers are taking an increased interest and active part in the management of IS with a view to avoiding many of the problems they have experienced in the past. This has resulted in practice starting to change its emphasis from risk control. The systems development paradigm has begun to shift from in-house development to the increasing use of standard commercial packages and the outsourcing of development work. Both of these reflect a new approach to IS management which reduces the downside of high-risk systems projects for the organisation. The essence of the new approach is that it favours *risk containment*. Risk containment is based on a recognition that risk control is not and may not ever be available. Rather than strive for the impossible, business managers are increasingly directing their IS departments toward practices which buy off risk to the organisation in one way or another.

Adoption of packages reduces the risk associated with systems development by minimising the technical activity required. The trend is to try to change the organisation to fit the package. Any risk is limited to whatever organisational change is required. The organisation thus contains risk at the expense of accepting an IS which is equally available to its competitors and hence offers no sustainable advantage.

Outsourcing, by contrast, does not offer the organisation a system with guaranteed functionality but rather relocates the development risk to the outsourcing vendor. Contractual arrangements can ensure that if the desired functionality is not supplied, the costs are not incurred by the purchaser. Again, the risks of organisational change associated with implementing the system remain.

The current situation is that as a result of increased business interest in IT investments the optimism that has favoured risk control for the last twenty years is no longer dominant. The shift from engineering to business dominance is a shift in the *balance* of what is important in the dynamics of practice, not a total shift. The dynamic of capabilities is still active, promoting enthusiasm for inter-organisational systems and the Internet as the newest frontier. Risk containment is not as yet the dominant systems development strategy in the industry and there are still forces tending to promote risk control. Any number of outcomes may reverse the trend including advances in risk control and difficulties making risk containment work.

The Current State of Failures Research

We are currently seeing a resurgence of interest in IS failure studies among academics. More researchers are explicitly addressing failures. More studies are being published—the 1996 European Conference on Information Systems included four papers on recent European IS failures. A new journal, *Failure and Lessons Learned in Information Technology Management*, is about to be launched.

In the past, research had a single failure concept (Lyytinen and Hirschheim, 1987) and treated it as a single phenomenon common to all failure contexts. This more holistic approach has not borne fruit, so the new strategy is to specialise in the hope of smaller but more useful results. Risk will not be brought under control through a single large breakthrough on this approach but in smaller piecemeal advances.

Research is focusing on different types of failure phenomena, different types of system, different sectors, and popular IS-enabled organisational change initiatives. The single most studied phenomenon is IS adoption and implementation. Two other phenomena currently being actively researched are project and system abandonment (Ewusi-Mensah and Przasnyski, 1991, 1994, 1995; Sauer, 1993*a*, 1993*b*; Martin and Chan, 1996; Johnson, 1995) and escalation of commitment to failing projects (Drummond, 1996; Keil, 1995*b*; Keil et al., 1995; Newman and Sabherwal, 1996). Studies of the failure of different types of system include group systems (Grudin, 1989), manufacturing systems (Kling, 1987; Kling and Iacono, 1984; Webster and Williams, 1993; Ciborra and Schneider, 1992), and safety critical systems (Mackenzie, 1994; Rochlin, 1991; Beynon-Davies, 1995; Wastell and Newman, 1996). Studies of sector-specific failures include the health industry (Palley, 1991; Dhillon and Hackney, 1996; Southon et al., forthcoming; Yetton et al., 1994*b*) and public service failures (Margetts, 1991; Margetts and Willcocks, 1993; Sauer, 1993*a*; Korac-Boisvert and Kouzmin, 1995). In addition, some recent studies are beginning to focus on the failures of popular IS-enabled approaches to organisational and change management including BPR failures (Clemons et al., 1995) and strategic alignment (Sauer and Burn, 1997).

The other development in failures research has been the exploration of different theories and frameworks. This tactic is currently being tried with interpretativism (Walsham, 1993), critical theory (Myers, 1994; Myers and Young, 1995), and actor-network theory (McMaster and Vidgen, 1995; Vidgen and McMaster, 1995). For the most part, recent developments reflect researchers' continuing preoccupation with and commitment to risk control although research on adoption and use is also pertinent to risk containment. The new work constitutes a bet that specialisation or new frameworks can succeed where past ones have not.

Some researchers have followed the change in practice and are studying risk containment strategies. There is increasing attention given to risk in the literature (Willcocks and Griffiths, 1994; McGaughey et al., 1994; Yetton et al., 1995) where risk is understood as a prudent, probabilistic focus on systems outcomes rather than being a mere euphemism for failure. Other researchers are studying specific risk containment strategies. Sometimes they are finding them to be unsuccessful as with cases of outsourcing (Lacity and Hirschheim, 1993; Earl, 1996).

Thus, rather than unify work on IS failure, recent research has developed the scope and complexity of the phenomenon. It remains an open question whether in the fullness of time common elements might emerge which would warrant a partial reunification of the disparate types of failure.

Deciding the Future of IS Failures

The argument of this chapter has been that in the past organisations have been prepared to pay the cost of high risk of failure in return for developing and implementing individualistic systems which latterly have been recognised to have the potential to be a competitive advantage. IS professionals have believed that it would be possible to control the risk so that the full potential of IS could be gained without failure. There is no evidence that this has been achieved. In consequence, organisations have started to take a risk containment approach which reduces the risk of failure. This means that, surprising as it may seem, we are currently in the position of being able partially to *decide* the future of IS failures. The reason there is a decision to be made is that there are alternatives and risk containment, despite promising lower failure rates, has its own costs.

There are three main options for businesses: risk containment, risk control, and compromise. The first is risk containment. There are strong reasons for expecting this to be successful in the long run. Packaged software is likely to enjoy a lower probability of failure because systems development is not an issue. Packages are also increasingly maturing into products which can be used effectively without tailoring throughout an industry. Therefore, all that needs to be managed is the organisational change to fit the organisation to the package. This is made easier because the application's characteristics are relatively certain and attention and focus will not be distracted from organisational change toward systems development as has often been the case before. Also, because other companies have the same package, skilled and experienced staff can be found.

The other risk containment strategy, outsourcing, relocates risk to the vendor. Much of the hype associated with outsourcing suggests that outsourcing vendors will incur less risk because they will be better developers than in-house IS groups. This may prove to be the case, but if it does, it will be because they have made advances in risk control which are not available to the outsourcing company. A more likely reason is that to the extent that they act as an insurance for their clients, vendors' business survival will require them to minimise risk. Thus, they will promote packages, and they will discourage their clients from pursuing ambitious developments.

As risk containment matures as a strategy, it is to be expected that it will reduce the incidence of IS failures. In the meantime, there will be failures as organisations learn to manage the new approach. Some risk will remain. Both package solutions and outsourcing require organisational change to be managed and many organisational change programmes fail (Kotter, 1995). Packages require competence in selection and acquisition while outsourcing requires contract management skills. In the absence of either of these, failure will continue to be a risk. In the longer term, this is likely to be a lesser risk for the organisation than it would encounter through current risk control strategies.

The advantages of risk containment are that it reduces risk and is easier to manage. The disadvantage is that it will lead to more uniform, less ambitious systems and hence to less competition on IS. If it becomes the dominant approach, it will seriously downgrade the business status of IS.

The second option is to continue to pursue risk control. This holds the promise of delivering competitive systems not easily imitated by competitors. It would be folly to expect a complete turnaround in the short term with risk suddenly becoming completely manageable. In the longer term, there can be no certainty. It is possible that the problem will continue to be intractable with the consequence of continuing high failure rates. However, conditions are better than ever before for this strategy to begin to pay off because business managers are now paying attention to IS. In the past, however much research may have implicated management and organisation in IS failures, it has not made a difference because only IS practitioners have heard. The call for top management support is futile if addressed to IS personnel but may be highly efficacious if heard by top management. Likewise, the identification of organisational structural sources of failure changes nothing unless it is heard by managers with the authority and power to change structures. Organisational conditions previously deemed uncontrollable by IS professionals become manageable with the involvement of business managers.

The third alternative is a compromise. Some are trying this in the form of selective outsourcing (Lacity et al., 1996). However, the organisational competencies required to design and deliver systems are different from those needed to manage contracts. Consequently it is likely to be a difficult compromise to manage. A more promising approach is *incrementalism*. This involves partitioning IS projects into smaller units which incur less risk than large projects. A new IS is only designed when the last one is complete and forms a stable base for its successors. Its advantage over risk containment is that it retains the potential for the organisation to achieve distinctive, competitive systems (Yetton et al., 1994*a*). The costs are that there remains a development risk and a possibility that the resulting systems will not achieve the desired competitive ends. It also requires IS professionals to accept suboptimality because the clean, elegant, and efficient designs are too large to fit into the scale of a single incremental step. Its advantage over risk control is that it incurs lower development risk but the cost is the uncertainty of the resulting system's competitive value.

Business managers will make their choices among the various options. There will be far less system development activity, and much of that is likely to be the incremental development of existing packages. If businesses choose risk control, then correspondence and process failures will also continue to require resolution. In the short to medium term researchers will also need to give attention to outsourcing failures to help resolve them. If businesses opt for incrementalism then correspondence failures should decline because of the less ambitious nature of systems development. Process failures will be restricted in that problems of scale and extended time frames should not occur. On all three alternatives, interaction failure will continue to be an issue.

The Future of Failures Research

Whatever decisions companies make over the coming years there will continue to be risks of failure to a greater or lesser extent. Although the dynamics of practice cannot sustain business commitment to ineffective risk control strategies forever, there is currently a window of opportunity in which to develop a practically useful understanding of IS failure. Despite the trend toward risk containment, business still has a strong belief in the potential of IS. While that commitment is there, IS professionals have an opportunity to refashion our understanding of failure in a way which both involves and makes sense to business. The resurgence of researcher interest in failure is a promising sign that some will grasp the current opportunity.

The crucial advance that needs to be made in overcoming the difficulties of past work is to abandon the engineering assumptions about IS. IS are an organisational technology. Managers do not manage by devising exhaustive algorithms of their subordinates' tasks. We should not expect to find a theory which will specify all the conditions that would allow us to eliminate failure. In particular, we would do well to abandon our commitment to 'best practices'. Most IS projects are conducted under difficult conditions such as resource constraints, limited skill sets, changing market conditions, organisational turnover, and so on. What we need to discover is minimum practices. What is the least we can get away with without failing?

For failures research to take advantage of the window of opportunity, it will need to address itself more directly to the interests and conceptual frameworks of senior business managers. In this respect frameworks such as MIT'90s (Scott Morton, 1991) are useful because their major constituents are concepts with which managers are familiar and which represent elements of organisations which they typically manage. What IS failures researchers need to do is to conceptualise IS development and implementation in these terms and to explain failures accordingly. This should include the *dynamics* of IT-based organisational change. It might integrate earlier findings about IS failures, perhaps by reconceptualising them in the context of the more business-oriented framework. For example, the norms of IS project organisation are typically seen as defining the right way to manage an IS project. However, reconceptualised as structures and processes for management control, they may be seen as inconsistent with the business structures and processes which define the organisation's culture. Inadequate IS project management may then be understood not as a problem for the CIO to rectify by selection and training of project managers but as an organisational problem whose remedy is in the hands of senior managers.

Research progress in failure studies will be assisted by taking a more innovative approach to the investigation of causes. We can approach this in several ways. First, we can exploit known valuable research approaches such as making detailed comparisons between success and failure (Robey and Zeller, 1978; Markus, 1981; Buechi, 1982; Wastell and Newman, 1996). This tactic helps us concentrate on essential differences without being distracted by preconceived notions of good and bad practice.

Second, we can explore approaches which come at the data from a new direction. One opportunity here is to seek 'deviant' approaches to success (Yetton, 1997). The strong attachment of many researchers to normative models makes it difficult to view failures other than through normative lenses. One way of rectifying this research astigmatism is to seek examples of success which have bucked the norms.

Scott Sagan suggests studying near misses (Dutton et al., 1995). In the context of safety critical systems these may be straightforwardly recognised. In the case of commercial/administrative systems it is more difficult to identify a system which nearly failed since it may look just like a success. Nevertheless, signs of near misses can be found, for example, in counterfactual statements from project participants such as, 'if X had been in charge then, he'd have cancelled the project'. The value of examining near misses is that they can help identify critical factors. They also help to identify the buffers and slack which may prevent failure.

A related suggestion is for us to study project turnarounds (e.g. Jelassi et al., 1994). Like near misses it offers an opportunity to study the elements of failure and success in the same context. It has the particular benefit of covering the identification of danger signals, and the dynamics of change and recovery. Its relevance for practitioners is high.

To be successful, research will need to overcome the barriers that have prevented progress in the past. The problem of prescription will have to be solved. Rejection of the engineering assumptions will help this. If prescriptions take on the character of heuristics rather than algorithms, and managers understand them as requiring the same common-sense application as any other managerial advice, then some progress will have been made.

Many of the difficulties of failures research will remain. The complexity of the technology and its social setting have not been simplified. We shall not suddenly find business welcoming the failures researcher as a long-lost friend. The data will still be partial. For these reasons, the research community needs to make the most it can of its research data. Sharing data and exposing it to review by colleagues with different perspectives may lead to researchers collecting data that can be used in multiple ways and may also lead to some fruitful, and sometimes unlikely, collaborations.

Correspondence, process, and interaction failures are all susceptible to a more business-oriented research strategy. Thus even if the move to risk containment becomes an avalanche and correspondence and process failures decline in importance, the same principles should guide research.

Conclusion

Risk control, risk containment, and incrementalism are different ways of approaching IS development and implementation with differing levels of risks and benefits. None of them gives IS professionals better understanding of how to avoid failures. That can only come through developments in knowledge. In the absence of such knowledge business continues to have to choose. The opportunity lies with risk control. The prospects for making progress are better than ever. But, we may not succeed. If business prefers risk containment, then the IS field will change considerably. Fewer staff will be needed. The skills base will alter as implementation and organisational change become the critical activities. The organisational status and position of IS will be reduced. For IS professionals, no further incentive is surely needed for grappling with the problem of IS failure.

References

Abdel-Hamid, T. K., and Madnick, S. E. (1990), 'The Elusive Silver Lining: How we Fail to Learn from Software Development Failures', *Sloan Management Review*, 39, Fall.

Ackoff, R. L. (1976), 'Management Misinformation Systems', *Management Science*, 14, 4, Dec.

Argyris, C. (1971), 'Management Information Systems: The Challenge to Rationality and Emotionality', *Management Science*, 17, 6, Feb.: B-275–92.

Arnold, E. (1982), 'Information Technology in the Home: The Failure of Prestel', *Systems, Objectives, Solutions*, 2: 219–28.

Auditor-General (1991), *Audit Report No 24 1990–1991: Department of Veterans' Affairs—Transport Services—Personnel and Pay Administration System* (Canberra: Australian Government Publishing Service).

Baskerville, R., Travis, J., and Truex, D. (1992), 'Systems without Method: The Impact of New Technologies on Information Systems Development Projects, in K. E. Kendall, K. Lyytinen, and J. I. DeGross (eds.), *The Impact of Computer Supported Technologies on Information Systems Development* (Amsterdam: North-Holland).

Beck, L. L., and Perkins, T. E. (1983), 'A Survey of Software Engineering Practice: Tools, Methods, and Results', *IEEE Transactions on Software Engineering*, SE-9, 5, Sept.: 541–61.

Beynon-Davies, P. (1995), 'Information Systems "Failure": The Case of the London Ambulance Service's Computer Aided Despatch System', *European Journal of Information Systems*, 4: 171–84.

Bignell, V., and Fortune, J. (1984), *Understanding Systems Failures* (Manchester: Manchester University Press).

Bikson, T. K., and Gutek, B. (1984), *Implementation of Office Automation* (Santa Monica, Calif.: Rand Corporation).

Block, R. (1983), *The Politics of Projects* (New York: Yourdon Press).

Boddie, J. (1987), 'The Project Postmortem', *Computerworld*, 7 Dec.: 77–82.

Boland, R., and Hirschheim, R. A. (1985), Series foreword in Hirschheim (1985).

—— (1987), *Critical Issues in Information Systems Research* (Chichester: Wiley).

Brancheau, J. C., and Wetherbe, J. C. (1990), 'The Adoption of Spreadsheet Software: Testing Innovation Diffusion Theory in the Context of End-User Computing', *Information Systems Research*, 1: 115–43.

Buechi, H. (1982), 'Success and Failure in edp Project Development: Two Examples', *Systems, Objectives, Solutions*, 2: 39–47.

Ciborra, C. U. (1991), 'From Thinking to Tinkering: The Grassroots of Strategic Information Systems', *Proceedings of the Twelfth International Conference on Information Systems, New York, 16–18 Dec.*

—— and Schneider, L. S. (1992), 'Transforming the Routines and Contexts of Management, Work and Technology', in P. Adler (ed.), *Technology and the Future of Work* (New York: Oxford University Press).

Clemons, E. K., Thatcher, M. E., and Row, M. (1995), 'Identifying Sources of Reengineering Failures: A Study of the Behavioral Factors Contributing to Reengineering Risks', *Journal of Management Information Systems*, 12, 2, Feb.: 9–36. [1]

Coelho, J. D., Jelassi, T., König, W., Krcmar, H., O'Callaghan, R., and Sääksjärvi, M. (1996) (eds.), *Proceedings of the 4th European Conference on Information Systems, Lisbon, Portugal, July 2–4.*

Colton, K. W. (1972), 'Computers and Police: Patterns of Success and Failure', *Sloan Management Review*, Winter: 75–98. [2]

Comptroller-General (1979), 'Report to Congress', FGMSD-80–4.

Cooper, R. B., and Zmud, R. W. (1990), 'Information Technology Implementation Research: A Technological Diffusion Approach', *Management Science*, 36: 123–39.

Copeland, D. G., and McKenney, J. L. (1988), 'Airline Reservation Systems: Lessons from History', *MIS Quarterly*, 12, 3, Sept.: 353–70.

Davenport, T. H. (1993), *Process Innovation: Reengineering Work through Information Technology* (Boston: Harvard Business School Press).

—— and Stoddard, D. B. (1994), 'Reengineering: Business Change of Mythic Proportions?', *MIS Quarterly*, June: 121–7.

Davis, F. D. (1989), 'Perceived Usefulness, Perceived Ease of Use, and User Acceptance of Information Technology', *MIS Quarterly*: 319–40.

Dearden, J. (1972), 'MIS is a Mirage', *Harvard Business Review*, Jan.–Feb.: 90–9.

DeLone, W. H., and McLean, E. R. (1992), 'Information Systems Success: The Quest for the Dependent Variable', *Information Systems Research*, 3: 60–95.

DeMarco, T., and Lister, T. (1987), *Peopleware* (New York: Dorset House).

Dhillon, G., and Hackney, R. (1996), 'Developing Integrated Solutions in the Health Care Environment: A Case Study', paper presented at ECIS 96, 4th European Conference on IS, Lisbon, 2–4 July, vol. ii. [3]

Drummond, H. (1996), *Escalation in Decision Making: The Tragedy of Taurus* (Oxford: Oxford University Press).

Dutton, W. H. (1981), 'The Rejection of an Innovation: The Political Environment of a Computer-Based Model', *Systems, Objectives, Solutions*, 1, 4: 179–201.

—— (1993), private communication to the author, 4 May.

—— MacKenzie, D., Shapiro, S., and Peltu, M. (1995), 'Computer Power and Human Limits: Learning from IT and Telecommunications Disasters', PICT policy research paper 33 (Uxbridge: Brunel University).

Eardley, A. (1995), book review of *Why Information Systems Fail: A Case Study Approach*, *Journal of Strategic Information Systems*, 4, 4: 383–5.

Earl, M. J. (1996), 'The Risks of Outsourcing IT', *Sloan Management Review*, Spring: 13–25.

Eglizeau, C., Frey, O., and Newman, M. (1996), 'Socrate: An implementation débacle', in Coelho et al. (1996). [4]

Ein-Dor, P., and Segev, E. (1981), *A Paradigm for Management Information Systems* (New York: Praeger). [5]

Ettlie, J. (1986), 'Implementing Manufacturing Technologies: Lessons from Experience', in D. D. Davis (ed.), *Managing Technological Innovation: Organisational Strategies for Implementing Advanced Manufacturing Technologies* (San Francisco: Jossey-Bass).

Ewusi-Mensah, K., and Przasnyski, Z. H. (1991), 'On Information Systems Project Abandonment: An Exploratory Study of Organisational Practices', *MIS Quarterly*, Mar.: 67–86.

—— (1994), 'Factors Contributing to the Abandonment of Information Systems Development Projects', *Journal of Information Technology*, 9, 3: 185–201.

—— (1995), 'Learning from Abandoned Information System Development Projects', *Journal of Information Technology*, 10: 3–14. [6]

Fitzgerald, G., and Willcocks, L. (1994), *Information Technology Outsourcing Practice: A UK Survey* (London: Business Intelligence Ltd).

Friedman, A. L. (with Cornford, D. S.) (1989), *Computer Systems Development: History, Organisation and Implementation* (Chichester: John Wiley).

Fuerst, W. L., and Cheny, P. H. (1982), 'Factors Affecting the Perceived Utilization of Computer-Based Decision Support Systems in the Oil Industry', *Decision Sciences*, 13: 554–69. **[7]**

GAO (1983), 'Social Security Needs to Better Plan, Develop, and Implement its Major adp Systems Redesign Projects—Part 1' (US General Accounting Service), reprinted in *Systems, Objectives, Solutions*, 3: 105–23.

Gibbs, W. (1994), 'Software's Chronic Crisis', *Scientific American*, 271, 3, Sept.: 72–81.

Ginzberg, M. J. (1981), 'Early Diagnosis of MIS Implementation Failure: Promising Results and Unanswered Questions', *Management Science*, 27, 4, Apr.: 459–78. **[8]**

Gladden, G. R. (1982), 'Stop the Life-Cycle, I Want to Get off', *Software Engineering Notes*, 7, 2: 35–9.

Gosden, J. A. (1979), 'Some Cautions in Large-Scale System Design and Implementation', *Information and Management*, 2: 7–13. **[9]**

Grudin, J. (1989), 'Why Groupware Applications Fail: Problems in Design and Evaluation', *Office: Technology and People*, 4, 3: 245–64. **[10]**

Guimares, T., Igbaria, M., and Lu, M. (1992), 'The Determinants of DSS Success: An Integrated Model', *Decision Sciences*, 23: 409–30. **[11]**

Hammer, M., and Champy, J. (1993), *Reengineering the Corporation: A Manifesto for Business Revolution* (New York: HarperCollins).

Herzlinger, R. (1977), 'Why Data Systems in Non-profit Organisations Fail', *Harvard Business Review*, Jan.–Feb.: 81–6. **[12]**

Hirschheim, R. A. (1985), *Office Automation: A Social and Organisational Perspective* (Chichester: John Wiley). **[13]**

—— Klein, H. K., and Lyytinen, K. (1995), *Information Systems Development and Data Modeling: Conceptual and Philosophical Foundations* (Cambridge: Cambridge University Press).

—— and Newman, M. (1988), 'Information Systems and User Resistance: Theory and Practice', *Computer Journal*, 31, 5: 398–408. **[14]**

Howard, G. S., and Mendelow, A. L. (1991), 'Discretionary Use of Computers: An Empirically Derived Explanatory Model', *Decision Sciences*, 22: 241–65. **[15]**

Ives, B., and Learmonth, G. P. (1984), 'The Information System as a Competitive Weapon', *Communications of the ACM*, 27, 12, Dec.: 1193–201.

—— and Olson, M. H. (1984), 'User Involvement and MIS Success: A Review of Research', *Management Science*, 30, 5, May: 586–603.

Jelassi, T., Dutta, S., and Valentine, N. (1994), 'BP Chemicals' Commercial System: IT Risk and Project Management', in C. Ciborra and T. Jelassi (eds.), *Strategic Information Systems: A European Perspective* (Chichester: Wiley).

Johnson, J. (1995), 'Chaos: The Dollar Drain of IT Project Failures', *Application Development Trends*, Jan.: 41–7. **[16]**

Kane, F., and Whitebloom, S. (1993), 'Stock Exchange Boss Resigns over Computer Fiasco', *Guardian Weekly*, 21 Mar.: 4.

Keen, P. G. W. (1981), 'Information Systems and Organisational Change', *Communications of the ACM*, 24, 1: 24–33.

—— and Scott Morton, M. S. (1978), *Decision Support Systems: An Organisational Perspective* (Reading Mass.: Addison-Wesley). **[17]**

Keider, S. (1984), 'Why Systems Development Projects Fail', *Journal of Information Systems Management*, 1, 3: 33–8. **[18]**

Keil, M. (1995*a*), 'Identifying and Preventing Runaway Systems Projects', *American Programmer*, 8, 3, Mar.: 16–22.

—— (1995*b*), 'Pulling the Plug: Software Project Management and the Problem of Escalation', *MIS Quarterly*, 19, 4, Dec.: 420–47.

—— Mixon, R., Saarinen, T., and Tuunainen, V. (1995), 'Understanding Runaway Information Technology Projects: Results from an International Research Program Based on Escalation Theory', *Journal of Management Information Systems*, 11, 3, Winter: 65–85.

Kirby-Green, F. (producer) (1993), 'Wessex Man', *Panorama* (London: BBC News and Current Affairs, 12 July).

Kling, R. (1987), 'Defining the Boundaries of Computing across Complex Organisations', in Boland and Hirschheim (1987).

—— and Iacono, S. (1984), 'The Control of Information Systems Developments after Implementation', *Communications of the ACM*, 27, 12, Dec.: 1218–26.

Korac-Boisvert, N., and Kouzmin, A. (1995), 'Transcending Soft-Core IT Disasters in Public Sector Organisations', *Information Infrastructure and Policy*, 4: 131–61.

Kotter, J. P. (1995), 'Leading Change: Why Transformation Efforts Fail', *Harvard Business Review*, Mar.–Apr.: 59–67.

Kumar, K., and Welke, R. J. (1984), 'Implementation Failure and Systems Developer Values: Assumptions, Truisms, and Empirical Evidence', in L. Maggi, J. L. King, and K. L. Kraemer (eds.), *Proceedings of the 5th International Conference on Information Systems, Tucson, Arizona.* [19]

Kwon, T. H., and Zmud, R. W. (1987), 'Unifying the Fragmented Models of Information Systems Implementation', in Boland and Hirschheim (1987).

Lacity, M., and Hirschheim, M. (1993), *Information Systems Outsourcing: Myths, Metaphors and Realities* (Chichester: Wiley).

—— Willcocks, L. P., and Feeny, D. F. (1996), 'The Value of Selective IT Sourcing', *Sloan Management Review*, Spring: 13–25.

Lehman, J. H. (1979), 'How Software Projects are Really Managed', *Datamation*, Jan.: 119–29. [20]

Long, R. J. (1989), 'Human Issues in New Office Technology', in T. Forester (ed.), *Computers in the Human Context: Information Technology, Productivity and People* (Oxford: Basil Blackwell).

Lucas, H. C., Jr. (1975), *Why Information Systems Fail* (New York: Columbia University Press). [21]

—— (1976), *The Implementation of Computer-Based Models* (New York: National Association of Accountants). [22]

—— Ginzberg, M. J., and Schultz, R. L. (1990), *Information Systems Implementation: Testing a Structural Model* (Norwood, NJ: Ablex Publishing Corp).

Lyytinen, K. (1988), 'Expectation Failure Concept and Systems Analysts' View of Information Systems Failures: Results of an Exploratory Study', *Information and Management*, 14, 1: 45–56. [23]

—— and Hirschheim, R. (1987), 'Information Systems Failures: A Survey and Classification of the Empirical Literature', *Oxford Surveys in Information Technology*, 4: 257–309.

McCosh, A. M. (1984), 'Factors Common to the Successful Implementation of Twelve Decision Support Systems and How they Differ from Three Failures', *Systems, Objectives, Solutions*, 4: 17–28. [24]

McGaughey, R. E., Jr., Snyder, C. A., and Carr, H. H. (1994), 'Implementing Information Technology for Competitive Advantage: Risk Management Issues', *Information and Management*, 26: 273–80.

Mackenzie, D. (1994), 'Computer Related Accidental Death: An Empirical Exploration', *Science and Public Policy*, 21: 233–48.

McMaster, T., and Vidgen, R. (1995), 'Implementation Planning for Information Systems: Promoting the Transition with a Communications Strategy', in K. Kautz, J. Pries-Heje, T. Larsen, and P. Sørgaard (eds.), *Conference Notebook for First IFIP 8.6 Working Conference on Diffusion and Adoption of Information Technology* (Oslo: Norwegian Computing Center).

Maiden, M. (1996), 'Revealed: How CBA Fell into the Techno-trap', *Sydney Morning Herald*, 3 May: 21 and 24.

Majchrzak, A. (1991), 'Management of Technological and Organisational Change', in G. Salvendy, *Handbook of Industrial Engineering*, 2nd edn. (New York: John Wiley & Sons).

Margetts, H. (1991), 'The Computerization of Social Security: The Way Forward or a Step Backwards?', *Public Administration*, 69, 3, Autumn: 325–43.

—— and Willcocks, L. (1993), 'Information Technology in Public Sectors: Disaster Faster?', *Public Money and Management*, 13, 2, Apr.–June: 49–56.

Markus, M. L. (1981), 'Implementation Politics: Top Management Support and User Involvement', *Systems, Objectives, Solutions*, 1: 203–15.

—— (1983), 'Power, Politics and MIS Implementation', *Communications of the ACM*, 26, 6, June: 430–44.

—— (1984), *Systems in Organisations: Bugs and Features* (Marshfield, Mass.: Pitman).

—— and Pfeffer, J. (1983), 'Power and the Design and Implementation of Accounting and Control Systems', *Accounting, Organisations and Society*, 8, 2/3: 205–18.

—— and Robey, D. (1988), 'Information Technology and Organisational Change: Causal Structure in Theory and Research', *Management Science*, 34, 5, May: 583–98.

Martin, A., and Chan, M. (1996), 'Information Systems Project Redefinition in New Zealand: Will we ever Learn?', *Australian Computer Journal*, 28, 1, Feb.: 27–40.

Mata, F. J., Fuerst, W. L., and Barney, J. B. (1995), 'Information Technology and Competitive Advantage: A Resource-Based Analysis', *MIS Quarterly*, 19, 4, Dec.: 487–505.

Meredith, J. (1988), 'Project Monitoring for Early Termination', *Project Management Journal*, 19, 5: 31–8.

Miller, C. L. (1983), 'How to Successfully Resist a Computer System and Avoid its Benefits: A Victory for the Bureaucracy?', *Systems, Objectives, Solutions*, 3: 3–12.

Mitev, N. (1996), 'Social, Organisational and Political Aspects of Information Systems Failures: The Computerised Reservation System at French Railways', paper presented at 4th European Conference on 15, Lisbon, 2–4 July, ii. 1213–22.

Montealegre, R., Knoop, C. I., and Applegate, L. M. (1996*a*), *BAE Automated Systems (A): Denver International Airport Baggage-Handling System*, Harvard Business School Case Study N9-396–311, 12 Apr. (Boston: Harvard Business School).

—— —— Nelson, J., and Applegate, L. M. (1996*b*), *BAE Automated Systems (B): Implementing the Denver International Airport Baggage-Handling System*, Harvard Business School Case Study N9-396–312, 26 Apr. (Boston: Harvard Business School).

Morgan, H. L., and Soden, J. V. (1973), 'Understanding MIS Failures', *Data Base*, 5, Winter. **[25]**

Mowshowitz, A. (1976), *The Conquest of Will: Information Processing in Human Affairs* (Reading, Mass.: Addison-Wesley).

Myers, M. D. (1994), 'A Disaster for Everyone to See: An Interpretive Analysis of a Failed IS Project', *Accounting, Management and Information Technologies*, 4, 4: 185–201.

—— and Young, L. W. (1995), 'The Implementation of an Information System in Mental Health: An Ethnographic Study', *Proceedings of the 6th Australasian Conference on Information Systems, Perth, September.*

New, C. C., and Myers, A. (1986), *Managing Manufacturing Operations in the UK, 1975–1985* (Cranfield: British Institute of Management).

Newman, M., and Sabherwal, R. (1996), 'Determinants of Commitment to Information Systems: A Longitudinal Investigation', *MIS Quarterly*, 20, 1, Mar.: 23–54.

Oz, E. (1994), 'When Professional Standards are Lax: The CONFIRM Failure and its Lessons', *Communications of the ACM*, 37, 10: 29–36.

Palley, M. A. (1991), 'Hospital Information Systems and the DRG Reimbursement: The Adaptation of Large Transactions Processing Systems to Radical Rule Changes', *Information and Management*, 20: 227–34.

Perrow, C. (1984), *Normal Accidents: Living with High Risk Technologies* (New York: Basic Books).

Petroski, H. (1992), *To Engineer is Human: The Role of Failure in Successful Design* (New York: Vintage Books, Random House).

Phan, D. D., Vogel, D. R., and Nunamker, J. F., Jr. (1995), 'Empirical Studies in Software Development Projects: Field Survey and OS/400 Study', *Information and Management*, 28: 271–80.

Pinto, J. K., and Slevin, D. P. (1987), 'Critical Factors in Successful Project Implementation', *IEEE Transactions on Engineering Management*, 34, 1, Feb.: 22–7. **[26]**

Plunkett, S. (1991), 'Westpac Abandons High-Tech Hopes', *Business Review Weekly*, 8 Nov.: 26–7.

Porter, M., and Millar, V. E. (1985), 'How Information Gives you Competitive Advantage', *Harvard Business Review*, 63, 4: 149–60.

Ramiller, N. C. (1994), 'Perceived Compatibility of Information Technology Innovations among Secondary Adopters: Towards a Reassessment', *Journal of Engineering Technology and Management*, 11: 1–23. **[27]**

Robey, D., and Zeller, R. (1978), 'Factors Affecting the Success and Failure of an Information System for Product Quality', *Interfaces*, 8, 2: 70–5. **[28]**

Rochlin, G. I. (1991), 'Iran Air Flight 655 and the USS Vincennes: Complex, Large-Scale Military Systems and the Failure of Control', in T. R. La Porte (ed.), *Social Responses to Large Technical Systems* (Amsterdam: Kluwer Academic Publishing).

Rudelius, W., Dickson, G. W., and Hartley, S. W. (1982), 'The Little Model that Couldn't: How a Decision Support System for Retail Buyers Found Limbo', *Systems, Objectives, Solutions*, 2: 115–24.

Sambamurthy, V., and Zmud, R. W. (1997), 'At the Heart of Success: Organisational Management Competencies', in C. Sauer, P. Yetton, and Associates, *Steps to the Future: Fresh Thinking in Management of IT Based Organisational Transformation* (San Francisco: Jossey-Bass).

Sauer, C. (1993*a*), *Why Information Systems Fail: A Case Study Approach* (Henley-on-Thames: Alfred Waller).

—— (1993*b*), 'Partial Abandonment as a Strategy for Avoiding Failure', in D. E. Avison, J. deGross, and J. Kendall (eds.), *Information Systems Development: Human, Social and Organisational Aspects* (Amsterdam: North-Holland).

—— and Burn, J. (1997), 'The Pathology of Alignment', in C. Sauer, P. Yetton, and Associates *Steps to the Future: Fresh Thinking in Management of IT Based Organisational Transformation* (San Francisco: Jossey-Bass).

Schultz, R. C., and Slevin, D. P. (1975) (eds.), *Implementing Operations Research/ Management Science* (New York: American Elsevier).

Scott Morton, M. (1991) (ed.), *The Corporation of the 1990s: Information Technology and Organisational Transformation* (Oxford: Oxford University Press).

Seddon, P. B., and Kiew, M. Y. (1994), 'A Partial Test and Development of DeLone and McLean's Model of IS Success', *Proceedings of the Fifteenth International Conference on Information Systems, Vancouver, BC, December.*

Sloane, S. B. (1991), 'The Use of Artificial Intelligence by the United States Navy: Case Study of a Failure', *AI Magazine*, Spring: 80–92.

Southon, G., Sauer, C., and Dampney, C. N. D. (forthcoming), 'Anatomy of a Failed Project', *Journal of the American Informatics Association.*

Strassmann, P. A. (1985), *Information Payoff: The Transformation of Work in the Electronic Age* (New York: Free Press).

Swanson, E. B. (1974), 'Management Information Systems: Appreciation and Involvement', *Management Science*, 21, 2: 178–88. **[29]**

—— (1988), *Information System Implementation: Bridging the Gap between Design and Utilization* (Homewood, Ill.: Irwin).

van Genuchten, M. (1991), 'Why is Software Late? An Empirical Study of Reasons for Delay in Software Development', *IEEE Transactions on Software Engineering*, 17, 6, June: 582–90.

Vidgen, R., and McMaster, T. (1995), 'Black Boxes, Non-human Stakeholders and the Translation of IT through Mediation', in W. J. Orlikowski, G. Walsham, M. R. Jones, and J. I. DeGross (eds.), *Information Technology and Changes in Organisational Work* (London: Chapman & Hall).

Walsham, G. (1993), *Interpreting Information Systems in Organisations* (Chichester: John Wiley).

Wastell, D., and Newman, M. (1996), 'Information Systems Development in the Ambulance Service: A Tale of Two Cities', in Coelho et al. (1996). **[30]**

Webster, J., and Williams, R. (1993), 'The Success and Failure of Computer-Aided Production Management: The Implications for Corporate and Public Policy', Research Report No. 2 (Edinburgh: PICT Research Centre for Social Sciences, University of Edinburgh).

Wilkinson, B. (1983), *The Shopfloor Politics of New Technology* (London: Heinemann).

Willcocks, L., and Griffiths, C. (1994), 'Management and Risk Issues in Large-Scale IT Projects: A Comparative Analysis', Oxford Institute of Information Management Research and Discussion Paper (RDP94/7) (Oxford: Templeton College).

Works, M. (1987), 'Cost Justification and New Technology: Addressing Management's No! to the Funding of CIM', in L. Bertain and L. Hales (eds.), *A Program Guide for CIM Implementation*, 2nd edn. (n. p.: SME).

Yetton, P. W. (1997), 'False Prophecies, Successful Practice and Future Directions in IT Management', in C. Sauer, P. W. Yetton, and Associates, *Steps to the Future: Fresh Thinking in Management of IT Based Organisational Transformation* (San Francisco: Jossey-Bass).

—— Craig, J. F., and Johnston, K. (1995), 'Fit, Simplicity and Risk: Multiple Paths to Strategic IT Change', *Proceedings of the Sixteenth International Conference on Information Systems, Amsterdam, Netherlands, Dec. 10–13*.

—— Johnston, K. D., and Craig, J. F. (1994a), 'Computer-Aided Architects: A Case Study of Strategic Change and IT', *Sloan Management Review*, 35, 4, Summer: 57–67.

—— Southon, G., and Craig, J. (1994b), 'The Impact of Strategic Conflict on the Management of Information Technology in a Hospital', Working Paper 94–003 (Kensington: Australian Graduate School of Management, University of NSW).

Zammuto, R. F., and O'Connor, E. J. (1992), 'Gaining Advanced Manufacturing Technologies' Benefits: The Role of Organisation Design and Culture', *Academy of Management Review*, 17, 4: 701–28.

Zells, L. (1994), 'Litigated Disaster: The Anatomy of a Major Product Failure', *Application Development Trends*, Nov.: 43–8. [31]

Zuboff, S. (1988), *In the Age of the Smart Machine: The Future of Work and Power* (New York: Basic Books).

Appendix 12.1. Common factor classes, factors, and their sources

Factor Class	Factors	Sources[a]
User involvement	User involvement	2, 6, 8, 14, 16, 22, 28, 29, 30
	User consultation/communication	18, 26
	User acceptance	6
	Early user commitment	17
	Conscious user involvement	17
Management commitment	Management support	2, 6, 11, 14, 15, 16, 17, 28
	Management style	22, 30
	Management decisions	5
	Management understanding	4, 10, 12, 24
Value basis	User has felt need	14, 17
	Who benefits	10
	Relevance of output	7
	Output accuracy	7
Mutual understanding	User–developer understanding	5, 6, 8, 25
	Technical and economic orientation of designers	13, 14, 19
	Designer self-image	23
	Designer lack of understanding of human aspects	19

	Lack of understanding of business needs	1, 3
	Conservatism	14
Design quality	Technical quality	6, 14, 21, 30
	Technical characteristics	22, 25
	Complexity	23
	Interface	2
	Task compatibility	15
Performance level	System performance	25
	Project performance	6, 25
Project management	Project objectives	9, 26
	Priorities	2, 25
	Lack of plan	18, 26
	Poor estimates	18, 20
	Unclear scope	18, 31
	Evaluation difficulties	10
	Scale	9
Resource adequacy	Time	30
	Funds	6
	Control over resources	20, 31
	HR quality, selection, training	2, 6, 7, 14, 15, 18, 26, 30
Situational stability	Complex, informal user organisation	28
	Industrial relations problems	30
	Change in requirements	20
	Loss of critical personnel	5, 6
Management processes	Funding processes	12
	Control processes	5
Implementation process	Implementation process	8, 23
	Poor change management	1, 31
	User requirements not known	9, 16
	Specifications not complete	9
Individual differences	Personal factors	22
	Cognitive style	14

[a] Numbers given under 'Sources' refer to bold numbers in square brackets following entries in References.

13

A Historical Analysis of Implementing IS at J. Lyons

FRANK LAND

Introduction

Now is a good time to bring together management information systems (MIS) experts to publish their thoughts on the development of the subject. It is exactly fifty years since two senior executives were sent to the USA by the British food manufacturing and catering company J. Lyons to study what advances in office facilities and office methods had taken place during and since the Second World War (Hendry, 1986; Bird, 1994; Caminer et al., 1996; Land, 1997). In May 1947 the two executives, T. R. Thompson and Oliver Standingford, visited Professor Goldstine at Princeton University and were introduced to the latest news on the development of electronic computers.

Thompson and Standingford immediately recognised that computers could be the solution to the problems of business data processing faced by the growing Lyons company. In a remarkable report they outlined their vision of what computers for business use should look like, and how they might be applied to help solve business problems. Their report went on to recommend that J. Lyons should either acquire a computer from a supplier, or, as few companies were interested in building a computer to the Lyons specification, that the company should fund a university to help develop a computer for the use of Lyons. A quotation taken from their report gives an indication of the importance they attached to their recommendation.

We believe that we have been able to get a glimpse of a development which will in a few years time, have a profound effect on the way in which clerical work (at least) is performed. Here, for the first time, there is a possibility of a machine which will be able to cope, at almost incredible speed, with any variation of clerical procedures, provided the conditions which govern the variations are predetermined. What effect such machines could have on the semi-repetitive work of the office needs only the slightest effort of imagination. The possible savings from such a machine should, be at least £50,000 a year. The capital cost would be of the order of £100,000. We feel, therefore, that the Company might well wish to take a lead in the development of the machine and indeed that, unless organisations such as ours, the potential users, are prepared to do so, the time at which they become commercially available will be unnecessarily postponed for many years.

A further quotation from the report reads:

Our first concern is, of course, the advantage which Lyons may gain from the commercial development of electronic machines, but there is a wider aspect which cannot be overlooked. This machine may well be a prime factor in relieving the present economic distress of the country. In this respect we cannot help but feel that Lyons occupies a key position; no-one else here, as far as we can learn, has realised the far-reaching possibilities of electronic machines.

We assume that Lyons will want to take full advantage of these machines for their own offices. It is possible for us to play a passive role by merely keeping in touch with developments, and in due course buying machines as they become available, probably from American sources. But such a role would not enable us to have any influence on the kind of machine built, and without commercial influence they may be built in a form more suited to handling mathematical and census calculations owing to the influence of the large governmental concerns.

Finally they laid out five possible strategies for the Lyons board to consider to enable the company to apply computer technology. These include the suggestion that Lyons should support the efforts of Hartree and Wilkes at Cambridge University with a financial grant and at the same time to provide them with 'clerical procedures' to use in programming experiments. An alternative strategy suggests that: 'We could build a machine in our own workshops drawing on information and advice from Harvard University.' The Lyons board accepted the recommendation and in November 1947 agreed to provide financial aid, plus the services of a young Lyons electrical engineer, to Cambridge University to complete the EDSAC.

Conventional models of the history of MIS suggest that applications progressed from early attempts to automate defined business processes, without making noteworthy changes to the business itself, to the increasing complexity of applications involving integration of processes and functions, and leading to the transformation of the business itself (Nolan, 1983; Venkatraman, 1991; Galliers and Sutherland, 1991). Early applications, in these models, provided the required payback, principally, by reducing the costs of the processes automated by the use of information technology. Later the business case for the deployment of the technology was based on adding value or gaining advantage over competitors (Porter, 1985).

In this chapter we argue that it is a mistake to date the development of information systems (MIS) from the first use of computers in data processing and that, as at present, events unfold in diverse and often unexpected ways. Hence, whilst the models fit reality for some organisations—perhaps even the majority—the behaviour and developments of other organisations do not fit the models at all. There are valuable lessons to be learned today if we do not disregard earlier experiences because they are perceived to conform to an earlier phase of some theoretic model of the development of the history of MIS. Perhaps we have to reinvent the history of MIS before we can reinvent MIS itself! This chapter uses the case of J. Lyons as an illustration of pioneering applications of information technology which are of interest as history, but also provide useful lessons for the future.[1]

MIS before Computers

J. Lyons and Co., founded in the nineteenth century (1887), had by the 1920s grown from a specialist caterer serving a niche market to a major food manufacturer and caterer. Senior management—primarily members of the founding families, the Salmons and Glucksteins, plus a few trusted senior employees such as George Booth, the company secretary—recognised that progress could only be maintained if the company selected people of high academic standing to join the company. In 1923 they hired John Simmons direct from Cambridge University where he had been a wrangler with a first class honours degree in mathematics to join them as a management trainee and statistician. A few years later they again recruited a Cambridge University wrangler, T. R. Thompson. In an interview with Chris Evans at the Science Museum about 1970, Simmons explained, 'In fact I was engaged to try to build up a system of information for the management of the company which would be superior, more sensible, than just depending upon the profit and loss account and such like. . . . in this respect the company was already ahead.' (Simmons, 1980).

Simmons rose rapidly in the management hierarchy and was responsible for introducing a number of far-reaching changes in practice and organisation designed to cope with the growth of the business and to achieve the control necessary for the maintenance of profits. Simmons ensured that the company kept up a continuous striving for improving practice, and in doing this introduced many innovations, in particular, to the management support services which enabled management to keep their business under constant cost-effective review.

In the early 1930s Simmons set up an office, the Systems Research Office (SRO), whose function was to review existing systems, trawl the world for better ways of supporting management activities, and invent, test, and implement improvements. The SRO working with line managers produced a stream of business process innovations from the time of its establishment. Examples include the notion that each sales representative, having a customer group of many small retailers, would not only be responsible for

[1] The author worked with LEO between the years 1952 and 1967, so that much of the material is based on personal recollections.

selling to his customer group, but be totally responsible for the accounting, credit, and payment functions conventionally carried out at arm's length by a separate accounting office. The introduction of 'traveller covered credit' was a radical business process innovation which increased efficiency and the effectiveness of the representative.

Whilst Lyons were one of the leaders in applying systems ideas to the improvement of business practice, they were in no sense alone. The Ford Motor Company had pioneered the notions of scientific management to transform the work practices of manufacturing industry. People like Simmons and his colleagues in Lyons were similarly attempting to transform the way information was processed and used in their business with the aim of making the business more responsive and more effective. By the 1930s the ideas and innovations stemming from Simmons were widely disseminated via the Institute of Administrative Management in which he played a leading role.

Before the Second World War the Systems Research Office had begun investigating ways of coping with the mass of transaction data by some kind of mechanisation or automation for many years. They had already investigated the possibility of devising a document reader for transaction data prior to the Second World War. They had researched the possible application of unit record systems based on punched cards, but rejected these as too localised, too constraining, and too costly. Lyons had only one punched card installation and that had a very limited application. Instead they had installed alternative types of office mechanisation based on accounting machines and calculators. For Lyons and many other companies adopting similar ideas, MIS was a matter of common practice a decade before the arrival of the electronic computer. Nevertheless the company was not satisfied and sought continuously for ways to improve its business processes. It was this search for improvements which led the company to send Simmons's senior colleagues in the administration to visit the USA in 1947.

The Impact of Electronic Computers on MIS[2]

Between 1947, when the Lyons board made its offer to help finance the development of EDSAC at Cambridge University, and 1951 Lyons had assembled a team of engineers, programmers, and systems analysts and designed a business version of the EDSAC computer which they named LEO.

[2] Much of the material of this section is derived from talks given by John Aris (Aris, 1996) and Frank Land (Land, 1996) during a seminar at the Science Museum on 18 May 1995 and subsequently printed as an edited version in the Summer 1996 issue of *Resurrection*, the journal of the Computer Conservation Society.

On Thursday, 29 November 1951 LEO ran the first regular business application. The job carried out was concerned with the valuation of the variety of bread, cakes, and pies produced in the several bakeries and the assembly and dispatch to the company's retail and wholesale channels and to the many catering establishments. This, the first job, was intended to demonstrate that it was possible to use an electronic computer on a regular basis to carry out an important task for the business and at the same time to reduce the cost of carrying out that task.

Interestingly there was very little resistance within Lyons to the possibility of using computers to carry out jobs previously undertaken by an army of white-collar labour. Management ensured that all employees were given information about the introduction of LEO, and this was reinforced with demonstrations of the computer system. Lyons had acquired a reputation for their innovations in business methods, and the new computer was simply one of many developments.

Between 1952 and 1956 a stream of new applications were planned and implemented. Looking back at these applications for first LEO I and then the faster, larger LEO II, the characteristic which strikes one most forcefully is the very high level of ambition. Each application involved what in current terminology might be described as business process re-engineering (BPR), but without the implicit brutality of the methods espoused by some of its advocates (Hammer, 1990; Davenport, 1993). This chapter focuses on three early applications to illustrate that designers and users alike aimed at more than the automation of transaction processes.

Case I: the teashop ordering job

The first, and perhaps most radical, was the tea shop ordering job. Analysis carried out by the Lyons Systems Research Office, once the strategic decision to re-engineer the teashop ordering process had been taken, had shown that teashop manageresses tended to order to a pattern dictated by season and by day of the week. By and large, today's order was similar to the order placed on the same day the previous week. As the seasons changed adjustments were made to the daily order. From this analysis stemmed the notion of the standard order. This idea led in turn to the idea of triggering new action by the principle of exception. The concept of exception reporting had been used many times before, but not as part of the way the system carried out operational tasks. The daily teashop order to the central kitchens comprised the standard menu plus or minus exceptions requested by each teashop.

Within this framework, the shop manageress had total freedom to order what she wanted to, although as with all systems running on the LEO there was always a possibility of an override, because of later information (for example, a weather forecast suggesting a fall in temperature, triggering a reduction in ice cream sales), or because management wanted to do something special (for example, attempting to boost the sales of mince pies by a special offer in the post-Christmas period).

The second major novelty introduced by the system was the notification of the order data in as close to real time as it was possible to get economically with the technology then available. Each teashop was telephoned at a specified time of the day, when the teashop manageress would read out the variations from the standard order to an order-taker equipped with a card punch. Once the variations from the standard order for all teashops (nearly 200 at the peak) had been punched, they were entered into the computer for processing.

Not all the teashops had telephones: with those that did not, someone had to go to a public telephone booth at the specified time, and hope that there was nobody else in the way, and wait for the telephone call. Amazingly, the system worked! The system had to convert orders received in the afternoon into schedules for overnight production and assembly, ready for dispatch to the teashops before the morning breakfast rush.

Another innovation was the way the various components of the system were integrated. The SRO investigated the whole process from order-taking to delivery of the goods from various sources. The process involved the teashops and their management, the separate manufacturing departments, kitchens, bakeries, ice cream, purchasing and warehousing dealing with bought-out items, the assembly and dispatch departments, and the administration and accounts departments. Each of these had their own management and often a culture built up over many years of working together.

The basic data—standard menus, teashop changes, and management interventions—was used to do calculations for the manufacturing and purchasing divisions. At the same time the computer produced assembly lists in the correct order for loading the Lyons transport fleet which called on the teashops at least once, and for the busiest twice, a day. Packing material and pallets were also called up via the computer system.

All items were costed at 'realisation' (selling price) and at standard cost in order to compute gross margins for each teashop and for each line of sale. A full reconciliation was produced to demonstrate for example that the values credited to a manufacturing division, say the kitchens, exactly matched the charges from the division to the teashops.

The system was designed to produce a wide range of management statistics intended to provide local and senior management with information relating to each teashop's performance. However, the teashop management had been selected and trained to be good at man-management, but were, with some exceptions, not skilled at business management. As a result some carefully thought-out management outputs had far less impact on the business than had been anticipated. It is interesting to note that the designers followed what they took to be best business practice without examining carefully whether their model of best practice actually fitted in with the culture and practice of the users.

For many years, the teashop job ran along the same lines as it was initially conceived. However, the market for the teashop style of catering gradually fell away. Perhaps a middle management selected for skills in business management might have changed the nature of the teashops in line with contemporary needs, and permitted them a niche in the market place. But a management style suitable for an earlier period was no longer relevant in the 1960s.

Case II: reserve stores allocation

The reserve stores job arose directly out of the problems created for a food-manufacturing company of food rationing and a general shortage of some materials. When the application was planned in the early 1950s food rationing was still in force. Lyons had to use a range of alternative or substitute materials, for example, sweetened fat as a substitute for sugar. The purchasing department had to obtain materials when it could. Just-in-time (JIT) was not an option. Materials were held in often remote reserve stores and drawn upon by the manufacturing units (the bakeries, kitchens, confectionery, and ice cream plants) on the basis of scheduled production. Some materials might be stored in a number of reserve store warehouses.

The problem was to provide the production units with the best available raw material to meet production and quality needs, and, at the same time, schedule the deliveries of the same material to different production units in such a way that existing transport facilities were used as efficiently as possible.

The requirements of the application were ambitious. The production scheduling was itself complex, and short-term variations were inevitable. The designers recognised that a simple automation of existing procedures would not solve the problems. The system had to compute the best way to allocate stock from the reserve stores on the basis of the production schedules, but permit management intervention and overrides to cope with sudden variations in both production needs and availability of supplies.

The reserve store job was killed when rationing stopped and the reserve stores and substitute materials where no longer needed. The application had lost its *raison d'être*. From a systems point of view it was well conceived, but from a business point of view it had ceased to add value.

Case III: the tea-blending job

The third application was concerned with Lyons' extensive tea-blending and -packing business. Like all LEO jobs it was rooted in office procedures which served the needs of the business. Lyons, under the tutelage of Simmons, did everything it could to avoid the heavy overheads of a swollen bureaucracy and to prevent the accumulation of paper. The tea-blending job was an early example of a decision support system (DSS), though that name had not yet been invented. The application was designed to give management control over tea-blending in two respects: the quality of the particular blend and the cost. The job had to reconcile the cost of the very wide range of teas purchased at the Mincing Lane auctions or acquired on long-term contract from India, Ceylon, and the Rhodesias (as they then were) with the needs of the tea blenders who had to achieve a standard quality (taste, colour, and fragrance) of products sold in the shops. In designing the application a bond had to be forged between the highly skilled and elite tea blenders, the tea buyers, the administrative management, and the systems analysts.

Each chest of tea had its own individuality with respect to the characteristics it added to the blend. Hence LEO had to be able to maintain the identity of the chest throughout its life. As part of the job the movements of tea to and from warehouses and the company's tea factories had to be planned and accounted for. The system was able to provide senior management with rapid information about the stocks that had been wanted —information that had never been available before. Given the very restricted facilities in modern terms of the LEO computer, the systems analysts had to find the most ingenious methods to maximise what could be got out of the data once it had been entered into the computer system. In he phrase of John Aris, one of the LEO analysts, the 'data had to be made to sweat'. Once again this was a very ambitious job, especially as it had to be carried out on a daily basis. In practice the job was run on a succession of LEO and later IBM machines for about thirty years.

The LEO Approach: The First Ten Years

Visitors to the group of people responsible for the design and execution of the early LEO applications noted the prevalent spirit of enthusiasm and excitement. Each day involved the discovery of new ways of doing things. In the excitement of finding a better way of doing something, or overcoming a problem which had seemed insurmountable, meal times and breaks were always full of discussions about the latest problem identified and overcome.

There was no reference manual or established methodology on how to analyse an application domain and there were no training courses in systems analysis available. Hence the system of learning resembled the notions of apprenticeship—a novice working closely with a more experienced mentor. The Systems Research Office, established in the 1930s, had developed some effective working practices and these provided the ground rules for the analysis.

The main precepts of these practices derived from a long history of innovative thinking, many of which had been developed by John Simmons. Some of the more important aspects of the practices developed in the Systems Research Office are discussed below.

First, there was a need for close interworking between users and the analysts. Simmons had wisely said that there should be a symbiotic relationship involving a process of mutual learning. Second, the recognition that valuable ideas can come from anywhere, including the peer group, played an important role in developing successful systems. This is where the lunchtime discussions were so enormously helpful. Third, any proposed changes would need to add value or reduce costs in some identifiable form. Each potential application had to pass the test of where and how it would be useful to the organisation. Fourth, risk was consciously minimized, very often by designing and carrying out experiments designed to verify the feasibility of some new approach.

Today the approach used by the Lyons team would be called prototyping, but it had its roots in the approach to radical change implemented decades earlier. An example was the introduction of document-reading, which was to play an important part in many Lyons applications. Lyons had developed a mark-reading document reader capable of inputting data from marked documents directly (or off-line) into the computer. One of the first applications for which the reader was designed was to read order data taken by salesmen on their regular visits to some thousands of small retailers. The salesman had to make a mark on the pre-printed order form to indicate the product line and quantity ordered, instead of writing in the actual quantity required. Each row on the form indicated a different product and each column a different quantity. The problem was to design the form so that the salesman found it acceptable to use, and at the same time the order form was reliable under a variety of conditions. Variables which could affect reliable performance included paper quality, paper colour, type of printing (for example, fonts), row and column spacing, number of relevant columns—the maximum was 16—the type of mark to be made, and the marking agent. A series of laboratory experiments was designed, followed by a series of field tests, before a design was selected which achieved the hoped-for outcomes.

Another important practice was keeping records of what was taking place. The management was absolutely insistent that records were kept documenting all decisions, and how these were arrived at, as well as flow charts, store layouts, etc. It was expected that applications should be understood at two levels, at the level of first principles—understanding the logic of the processes undertaken—and at the level of actual practice. It was always possible to pretend that the slate could be wiped clean—obliterate, in terms of Hammer's rhetoric (Hammer, 1990)—in order to achieve a set of business outcomes. But the experience of the Systems Research Office over many years showed that it was often the detail of actual operation which had to be understood. In the real world all sorts of things happen which are not accounted for by first principles.

Management stressed the importance of providing reconciliations based on standard accounting practice and auditing practice, even if the application had no specific accounting function. All jobs had to be capable of showing visibly that the operations had been correctly carried out and all elements in the job balanced together. Quite recently, in 1993, a very large multinational company had to abandon a major MIS system, costing many millions of pounds, because it provided no reconciliation of income and expenditure flows between different business units of the company. They could not make those things balance. This could not have happened with the kind of thinking and discipline adopted by the Lyons team.

A stream of applications covering a wide range of business and technical processes were implemented in the ten years following the first application. Some were abandoned because the business process they had supported had changed beyond all recognition. Most were modified in line with business changes or to take advantage of improvements in the technology. In addition to preparing applications for the Lyons operation work was carried out for numerous other companies on a contract basis, some of whom would later acquire their own LEO computers. Many of these service jobs were themselves pioneering in the sense that they were the first examples of carrying out that kind of work on a computer.

As experience was gained more details of good practice became part of the stock-in-trade of the LEO systems analyst and designer. Trainee analysts were taught to recognise:

(*a*) What could be squeezed out of the underlying transaction data which would add value to the business. Hence most applications developed for Lyons had elements of what today would be called transaction processing, management information systems, decision support systems, and even executive support systems.

(*b*) Which attributes of a system were likely to be permanent and which were more likely to change through time. The latter were dealt with by designing special systems change data forms rather than by implementing expensive and error-generating program changes. Of course, the analyst would sometimes miss elements of a system which later changed; nevertheless most applications had an extended life time because of the flexibility built into the design.

(*c*) The importance of building restart procedures into any computer-based system. The relative lack of reliability of the earliest machines made the possibility of restarts essential if work was to be completed in a regular routine. As a result LEO achieved a very high reliability rating in terms of delivered outputs despite working with equipment with a fault rate that would not be tolerated today.

(*d*) The importance of providing back-up facilities to protect the user against unforeseen accidents or catastrophic failures. Equally important was the recognition that it was essential to keep back-up facilities up-to-date and to test them under realistic simulated failure conditions.

In most systems a relatively small number of all possible types of transaction account for a significant proportion of the total data flow in terms of traffic and value. The so called Pareto principle suggests that often 20 per cent of possible transaction types account for 80 per cent of the total traffic. A well-known design principle states that it is possible to save very substantial design and implementation costs by focusing the design of the computer system on the most active 20 per cent of transaction types. However, the designer has to balance the reduction in design and implementation costs against the increased costs of operating the system, stemming from the need to synchronise and co-ordinate the automated and non-automated elements of the system. In practice coping with the costs of synchronisation and co-ordination and correcting the consequential errors can wipe out the expected benefits of the application.

It is interesting to note that as early as 1958, one of the first issues of the *Computer Journal* was devoted to the problem of the failure of computer-based information systems. David Caminer, who had been manager of the Systems Research Office, and became the Systems and Programming Manager for LEO, argued in the *Computer Journal* that one reason for failure was that applications did not attempt to deal comprehensively with a business process (Caminer, 1958).

The LEO approach began to be incorporated into training courses for systems analysts. Rapid expansion meant it was no longer possible to assign a trainee to a mentor on a one-to-one basis. Thus the apprenticeship system was gradually replaced by formal training. Training courses are fine but the loss of the apprenticeship system made it more difficult for the new generation to get the kind of understanding taken for granted by the pioneers of the early years.

One problem with the LEO culture was the constant danger of 'analyst arrogance'—the conviction that the LEO people and only the LEO people had the key to the Holy Grail of successful computer application development. Elsewhere attempts to use computers for business processes seemed to the LEO people to be simplistic and often landed the sponsors in a mess. Few organisations seemed to be developing the standards and quality control methods deemed necessary in the LEO environment.

In the 1950s when Lyons worked with service customers or potential clients for LEO computers, the initiative regarding the design of applications often lay with the LEO systems people. Gradually the initiative shifted to the client—partly as the result of the growing confidence of clients, but more importantly because the competitive basis for the marketing of computers had changed. Clients prepared a specification and evaluated competing bids against that specification. It was no good LEO telling the client that the specification was flawed—other suppliers were prepared to bid for the contract and gained the major share of the rapidly growing market. And so gradually over the 1960s, the way things had to be done altered, and in particular instead of LEO people regarding their role primarily as that of systems analysis, they had to change to accept the more conventional role of computer salesman.

In the end the qualities which had led to the innovations of the 1950s and the successful birth of business computing were insufficient to maintain LEO as a viable international computer supplier. The story ended effectively in 1967 when the last LEO computer was delivered to a London municipal borough.

Discussion and Analysis

To many observers the notion of a catering company in England, shortly after the Second World War, pioneering successfully what is now called the information revolution, by not only recognising the potential role of electronic computers for business data processing, but actually designing and building such a machine, seems unlikely and incredible. Indeed, the American edition of the book *User-Driven Innovation: The World's First Business Computer* (Caminer et al., 1996) is to be called *The Incredible Story of LEO the World's First Business Computer.*

Yet, looking at J. Lyons and Co. in the period after the Second World War, their recognition of computers as a way ahead, and the decision to build their own, should not have been regarded as surprising. There are a number of features in the way the company had developed and was organised in the immediate post-war period (1945–55) that provide the basis for the pioneering move into business computing. In summary these are:

The nature of the business

The business was characterised by the very large range of food products and food-providing services. This was supported by a range of company-owned and -managed services. The company sold its products direct to the retail trade or through its catering outlets direct to the public. This resulted in a mass of transactions with relatively low average values.

Competitiveness depended on keen pricing of its products. Thus the company was constantly fighting to contain or reduce its transaction costs. Hence its constant search for improving its business processes in all aspects of the business—manufacture, distribution, supply, and, most relevant to the decision to experiment with electronic computers, the support services provided by the office. The latter were responsible for the standard processes associated with bookkeeping and accounts, payment of suppliers, charging customers, and paying the staff, but also with the management support activities of providing management information. Already by the middle 1930s the company had established a systems research office to put the search for improved methods onto a more formal footing.

Personnel and leadership

Senior management recognised that to sustain the growth and competitiveness of the company it had to have top-class management. Lyons was one of the earliest companies to establish a management trainee scheme and many of the people later involved with the LEO enterprise first joined Lyons as management trainees. These included Oliver Standingford, who, together with T. R. Thompson, visited the USA in 1947, and whose joint report alerted the company to the possibility of electronic computers. David Caminer, probably the world's first programming manager, joined Lyons as a management trainee in 1936, became head of the Systems Research Office, and joined the LEO team as one of its first members.

The recruitment of people with top-class academic qualifications, such as Simmons and Thompson, and permitting these to take leadership roles in the management of the company, ensured that the company was never short of ideas on how to improve itself. This was reflected in the esteem in which the company was held in the first half of the twentieth century. Their leading role in developing 'systems' was widely acknowledged beyond the boundaries of their industry sector. It is in keeping with this tradition that Thompson and Standingford could claim in their report that it was almost a duty for Lyons to get directly involved in the design of a computer for business applications to solve the critical problems of the nation (see quotation from the report above).

Self-sufficiency

The economist Oliver Williamson (Williamson, 1975, 1986) suggests that firms have two types of strategies for coping with transaction costs. The first which he call 'hierarchies' involves vertical integration. The firm attempts to minimise transaction costs and retain control by becoming as self-sufficient as possible. The second strategy which he calls 'markets' involves going to the market (or 'outsourcing' in today's parlance) for all but the core activities of the business. Costs are minimised by using the mechanisms of the market place, and control is retained through contractual arrangements with suppliers.

Lyons, in general, preferred the first strategy because they had the confidence and experience to believe they could provide the relevant goods or services more effectively than any contractor. Of course, some goods and services had to be subcontracted or purchased when investigations showed that appropriate suppliers were available. But even then, Lyons, like Marks and Spencer plc, set up an organisation which set standards and ensured that suppliers themselves were efficient and always sought improvements. Thus it did not take Lyons long to realise that outside suppliers capable of meeting the requirements as seen by Simmons and Thompson simply did not exist in the late 1940s. They had the confidence based on previous experience, including the very recent experiences of the war, that they were capable of effectively organising businesses remote from their core food business.

Conclusion

John Aris (Aris, 1996) analyses the differences and similarities between the issues and concerns of the LEO analysts and designers and those prevalent today. He sets out the design principles on which the LEO systems analysts based their approach as follows:

Systems design principles
- design radically;
- check everything;
- document design is crucial;
- specifications must be detailed, agreed, and frozen;
- computers are expensive, programmers are cheap;
- configure cautiously.

And we might add:

- The devil is in the detail.

The first three elements can be traced back to the experience and influence of the Systems Research Office. Value could only be added if the analysis was thorough and of sufficient depth to suggest significant changes. But nothing could be taken at face value. It had to be checked and double checked and if necessary experiments set up to test the validity of assertions and the feasibility of designs. Document design was the equivalent of today's ergonomic concerns and crucial to the usability and hence robustness of the object system.

The last four elements came directly from the experience of the first applications. The LEO team quickly learned the importance of clarity and, for the time being, finality in the specification. Combined with the management insistence on documentation the group built up its own very thorough specification standards. The ratio of human resource costs against computer costs has been shifting year by year with the relative cost of information technology falling at an exponential rate. The importance of configuring conservatively is perhaps obvious for an organisation like Lyons configuring for its own use. It is less obvious for a vendor engaged in a competitive bidding battle with a rival, and knowing that the under-configured buyer will in the end buy more equipment to make up the deficit. In the later market conflicts with rivals, the LEO analysts, basing their strategy on what was appropriate for the parent company, lost out to more hard-nosed rivals. In pre-computer systems the designers could often leave the detail to later—human activity systems relying on human operators have an inherent flexibility, which permits late adjustments to the system to be made. The nature of preparing tasks for a computer by programming makes it essential that all the details are properly specified and understood long before the final implementation can take place. This was particularly true in the days before operating systems and high-level languages made programming somewhat more straightforward.

Today there are a range of issues which the LEO pioneers would have found surprising. One of these is the notion of business sponsorship. In Lyons it could be taken for granted that each application had the backing of senior management. Today, despite the continuous increase in spending on information technology, and the deep penetration of IT into business processes, sponsorship is much harder to achieve. There have been too many partial successes and too many failures. For the same reason the emphasis on justification has increased with ritual cost–benefit evaluations. The easy options have all been taken—those which provide obvious benefits in the form of manpower savings.

Modern technology provides far more options than were available to the LEO people. But the majority of these would have been absorbed and utilised without going against basic principles. However, there is one development which seems to run counter to the whole LEO approach. It stems from something very obvious which would not have caused much concern —the notion of the application package. It is perhaps surprising that the LEO team never developed the concept of a generalised application package. What would have caused consternation is the current trend towards adopting the SAP solution. The notion that the organisation is built around the package and not the other way round would have been regarded as putting the cart before the horse.

It is clear that some of the features of the LEO approach are still as valuable today as they were decades ago and today's systems analysts would do well to study the LEO approach. It is equally true that the LEO pioneers would have improved their performance with the use of some of the methods and tools available to the analyst and designer today.

References

Aris, J. B. B. (1996), 'Systems Design—Now and Then', *Resurrection*, Summer.

Bird, P. J. (1994), *LEO: The First Business Computer* (Workingham: Hasler Publishing).

Caminer, D. T. (1958), '. . . And How to Avoid Them', *Computer Journal*, 1, 1.

—— Aris, J. B. B., Hermon, P. M. R., and Land, F. F. (1996), *User-Driven Innovation: The World's First Business Computer* (Maidenhead: McGraw-Hill).

Davenport, T. (1993), *Process Innovation: Reengineering Work through Information Technology* (Cambridge, Mass.: Harvard Business School Press).

Galliers, R. D., and Sutherland, A. R. (1991), 'Information Systems Management and Strategy Formulation: The "Stages of Growth" Model Revisited', *Journal of Information Systems*, 1, 2: 89–114.

Hammer, M. (1990), 'Reengineering Work: Don't Automate, Obliterate', *Harvard Business Review*, July–Aug., 68, 4: 104–12.

Hendry, J. (1986), 'The Teashop Computer Manufacturer: J. Lyons', *Business History*.

Land, F. F. (1996), 'Systems Analysis for Business Applications', *Resurrection*, Summer.

—— (1997), 'Information Technology Implementation: The Case of the World's First Business Computer', in *Proceedings of IFIP W.G. 8.6 Conference: On the Diffusion, Transfer and Implementation of Information Technology, Kendal, July 1997.*

Nolan, R. L. (1983), 'Managing the Computer Resource: A Stage Hypothesis', *Communications of the ACM*, 16, 7, July.

Porter, M. L. (1985), *Competitive Advantage: Creating and Sustaining Superior Performance* (New York: Free Press).

Simmons, J. R. M. (1962), *LEO and the Managers* (London: Macdonald).

—— (1980), interview between J. R. M. Simmons, director and chief comptroller of J. Lyons & Co., and the Science Museum (London, c.1970s. Copyright © 1980 The Trustees of the Science Museum, London).

Venkatraman, N. (1991), 'IT-Induced Reconfiguration', in M. Scott Morton (ed.), *The Corporation in the 1990s: Information Technology and Organisational Transformation* (Oxford: Oxford University Press).

Williamson, O. E. (1975), *Markets and Hierarchies: Analysis and Antitrust Implications* (New York: Free Press).

—— (1986), *Economic Organisation* (Brighton: Wheatsheaf Books).

14

Information Technology Outsourcing
What Problems are we Trying to Solve?

MARY C. LACITY AND RUDY HIRSCHHEIM

Introduction

When Eastman Kodak announced that it was outsourcing its information systems (IS) function in 1989 to IBM, DEC, and Businessland (now Entex Information Services) it created quite a stir in the IS industry. Never before had such a well-known organisation, where IS was considered to be a strategic asset, turned it over to third party providers. Since then both large and small companies have found it acceptable, indeed fashionable, to transfer their IS assets, leases, and staff to outsourcing vendors.

Although companies outsource IS for many reasons, industry watchers generally attribute the growth of the IS outsourcing market as a consequence of a shift in business strategy. Many companies have recently abandoned their diversification strategies (once pursued to mediate risk) to focus on core competencies. Senior executives have come to believe that the most important sustainable competitive advantage is strategic focus by concentrating on what an organisation does better than anyone else while outsourcing the rest.

As a result of the this focus strategy, IS came under scrutiny: is IS a competitive weapon or merely a utility? In many companies, senior executives perceive that IS failed to deliver the competitive advantage promised in the 1980s. Subsequently, senior executives frequently view the entire IS function as a non-core activity, and believe that IS vendors possess economies of scale and technical expertise to provide IS services more efficiently than internal IS departments. Consequently, many senior executives view IS as an overhead; an essential cost but one to be minimized.

Attributing the growth and acceptance of outsourcing to a re-focus to core competencies provides only a superficial understanding of sourcing decisions. Our research suggests a much more complex interaction among stakeholders drives sourcing decisions and their ultimate outcomes. Senior executives often make decisions based on false assumptions about the nature and contribution of IS, fuelled by the legitimacy offered by the *sound* core-competency rationale. Consequently, we have some major concerns about the long-term viability of these deals. We are not alone.

Some prominent IS professionals have cautioned against the wholesale transferral of the management and control of a *strategic asset* such as IS. Harbingers of disaster include articles titled 'Outsourcing: The Scam May Be on You' (Gantz, 1994); 'Outsourcing: A Game for Losers' (Strassmann, 1995), and 'Selling One's BirthRight' (Dorn, 1989). In a number of cases, these concerns proved valid, with outsourcing *partnerships* experiencing grave problems. A few companies have paid out significant sums of money to extricate themselves from outsourcing contracts and then rebuilt their internal IS capability (Lacity and Hirschheim, 1993a). On the other hand, some IS managers who have refused to deal with outsourcing vendors or ignored them have either been fired or had their jobs marginalised when their IS shops have failed to demonstrate value for money. So clearly outsourcing must be taken seriously.

What appears to be happening is that an important change is taking place in the sourcing of IS activity. The high-profile outsourcing events alluded to above have tended to obscure the real issues:

- How do we determine the current and potential contribution of the IS portfolio?
- How do we source the IS portfolio to minimise costs and maximise service to deliver real value?

These issues require an appreciation and understanding for the complexity of such decisions in terms of stakeholder perceptions and agendas for IS, assessment of market vs. in-house IS capabilities, and contract management (in the case of outsourcing) to ensure that value is delivered.

In this chapter, we offer significant insights into the complex issues surrounding sourcing decisions, particularly the pre-decision context of sourcing evaluations. Before making sound sourcing decisions, there are many problems to diagnose and understand properly, such as conflicting stakeholder perceptions of IS, the popular press's influence on these perceptions, the organisational issues which continue to mask IS's contribution. We believe that until these circumstances are understood, sourcing decisions will be made based on false assumptions and practitioners will continue to address symptoms rather than problems.

The insights we share are founded from our in-depth study of twenty-one organisations, which included both outsourcing and insourcing decisions. Based on interviews with multiple stakeholders within organisations, we discovered many underlying problems which affect the expectations, processes, and ultimate outcomes associated with IS sourcing. This rich research base, which includes both sourcing successes and failures, provides an opportunity for other academics and practitioners to learn from participants' experiences with various sourcing decisions.

Outsourcing and Insourcing Options

The terms *outsourcing* and *insourcing* do not capture the complexity of sourcing options available on the market place. There are several taxonomies of sourcing decisions that have been adopted. Our research distinguishes among three:

> *Total Outsourcing: the decision to transfer IS assets, leases, staff, and management responsibility for delivery of IS services from an internal IS function to a single third party vendor which represents more than 80 per cent of the IS budget.*
>
> *Total Insourcing: the decision to retain the management and provision of more than 80 per cent of the IS budget internally after evaluating the IS services market.[1]*
>
> *Selective Sourcing: the decision to source selected IS functions from external provider(s) while still providing between 20 per cent and 80 per cent of the IS budget internally. This strategy may include single or multiple vendors.*

The use of percentages of IS budget as differentiating total from selective decisions is consistent with the studies done by Willcocks and Fitzgerald (1994) which show that selective sourcing usually takes up between 25 per cent and 40 per cent of the formal IS budget. Other authors have further categorised the variety of outsourcing options. Millar (1994) defines four basic types of outsourcing arrangements:

General outsourcing encompasses three alternatives:

  (a) *selective outsourcing* where one particular area of IS activity is chosen to be turned over to a third party, such as data centre operations;
  (b) *value-added outsourcing* where an area of IS activity is turned over to a third party who is thought to be able to provide a level of support or service which adds value to the activity that could not be cost-effectively provided by the internal IS group;
  (c) *co-operative outsourcing* where some targeted IS activities are jointly performed by a third party provider and the internal IS department.

Transitional outsourcing involves the migration from one technological platform to another. Such transitional outsourcing has three phases: (a) management of the legacy systems; (b) transition to the new technology/system; and (c) stabilisation and management of the new platform.

---

[1] Included in our definition of insourcing is the buying-in of vendor resources to meet a temporary resource need, such as the need for programmers in the latter stages of a new development project or the use of management consultants to facilitate a strategic planning process. In these cases, the customer retains responsibility for the delivery of IT services—vendor resources are brought in to supplement internally—managed teams.

Any one or all of these three phases could be turned over to a third party provider. The Sun Microsystems deal with CSC to handle the maintenance of Sun's legacy systems for a three-year period is a good example of such transitional outsourcing (*I/S Analyzer*, 1993).

Business process outsourcing is a relatively new outsourcing arrangement. It refers to an outsourcing relationship where a third party provider is responsible for performing an entire business function for the client organisation. According to Millar (1994), a number of industries are considering business processing outsourcing; in particular, government, financial services (banks and insurance companies), health care, transportation, and logistics. Targeted services include hotlines, help desks, call centres, claims management, and document processing.

Business benefit contracting is also a relatively recent phenomenon. It refers to a 'contractual agreement that defines the vendor's contribution to the client in terms of specific benefits to the business and defines the payment the customer will make based upon the vendor's ability to deliver those benefits. The goal is to match actual costs with actual benefits and to share the risks.' Given the risks associated with traditional outsourcing, there is considerable interest in this form of outsourcing. Millar notes, however, that while business benefit contracting is frequently used in the marketing of outsourcing services by third party providers, it typically is not actually adopted because of the difficulty associated with measuring benefits. Benchmarking in this area is particularly problematic. Because vendor revenue and margin potential are directly tied to the benchmarks, it is not surprising that getting agreement by both parties on the benchmarks proves especially thorny.

Research Methodology

To investigate the consequences of outsourcing and insourcing, we studied the sourcing decisions of twenty-one organisations from 1990 to 1994, including total outsourcing, total insourcing, and selective sourcing decisions. We conducted in-depth interviews with multiple stakeholders including senior executives, IS managers, and vendors. We saw a range of outcomes, including total disasters as well as substantial successes in terms of cost savings achieved, up to 54 per cent in one case we studied.

Table 14.1 describes the twenty-one organisations in terms of industry type, size in terms of annual revenue, IS budget, and data centre MIPS, sourcing decisions scope, decision sponsor, evaluation process, and in instances of outsourcing, contract length, and type.

The twenty-one organisations represent a wide variety of industries, including aerospace, banking, chemical, metals, mining, petroleum refining, and transportation. We studied some very large companies with annual

TABLE 14.1. *Case study profiles*

Firm	Industry	Annual revenue ($m.)[a]	Annual IS budget ($m.)[b]	Sourcing decision(s)[c]	Year of decision	IT headcount	Data centre MIPS	Formal RFP?	No. of bids	Contract length	Expected cost savings	Cost savings achieved?	Decision sponsor
1	Chemicals	5,000	17	Insourcing	1991	60	28	Yes	3	n/a	No cost savings estimated	No cost savings achieved	IS manager and senior manager
2	Diversified services	3,000	30	(a) Insourcing (b) Selective sourcing	(a) 1991 (b) 1992	184	<150	(a) n/a (b) Yes	(a) n/a (b) 2	(a) n/a (b) 5 years	(a) No cost savings estimated (b) 20%	(a) No cost savings achieved (b) Too early	(a) IS manager (b) Senior manager
3	Petroleum refining	35,000	240	Insourcing	1988	1,800	>300	n/a	1 informal	n/a	No cost savings estimated	No cost savings achieved	Senior manager
4[a]	Petroleum refining	10,000	32	Insourcing	1991	134	200	Yes	2 plus internal	5 years	43%	Yes, achieved within 5 years	Senior manager
5	Petroleum refining	3,000	6	Insourcing	1990	25	17	Yes	2	Open time limit	0%, remain as is	Yes, costs remained the same	IS manager
6	Commercial bank	6,000	25	Outsourcing	1990	160	180	No	1	10 years	15–18%	Yes, as of 1994	Senior manager
7	Diversified services	6,000	100	(a) Insourcing (b) Outsourcing	(a) 1988 (b) 1988	530	135	(a) No (b) No	(a) 0 (b) 1	(a) n/a (b) 10 years	(a) 0% (b) 20%	(a) None (b) No, customer threatened to sue vendor	(a) IS manager (b) Senior manager
8	Petroleum refining	400	4	Selective—data centre	1991	40	<150	Yes	2	5 years	16%	Unable to determine	IS manager
9	Metals	2,000	20	Outsourcing	1990	40	20	Yes	2	10 years	16%	Unable to determine	IS manager
10	Transportation	6,000	300	Outsourcing	1991	2,000	880	No	1	10 years	20%	Unable to determine	Senior manager
11	Mining	500	7	Outsourcing	1991	45	150	No	1	10 years	Savings anticipated but not quantified	Some savings achieved	Senior manager

No.	Industry			Decision	Year						Outcome	Decision-maker
12	Chemicals	700	4	(a) Outsourcing (b) Insourcing—return in-house	(a) 1984 (b) 1988	40	<150	(a) No (b) No	(a) 1 (b) 0	(a) 7 years (b) Indefinitely	(a) and (b) Savings anticipated but not quantified	(a) No, contract terminated early due to costs (b) Yes	(a) Senior manager (b) IS manager
13	Rubber and plastics	6,000	240	(a) Outsourcing (b) Insourcing—return in-house	(a) 1987 (b) 1991	1,000	>150	(a) No (b) n/a	(a) 1 (b) n/a	(a) 7 years (b) n/a	(a) and (b) Savings anticipated but not quantified	(a) No, IS costs rose to 4% of sales; contract terminated early (b) Yes	(a) Senior manager (b) IS manager
14	Aerospace	16,000	300	Outsourcing	1993	1,450	>300	Yes	1	10 years	No savings estimated	Unable to determine	Senior manager
15	Apparel manufacturer and retailer	2,000	27	Insourcing	1988	125	56	No	1 informal	n/a	54%	Yes, achieved within 4 years	IS manager
16	Public university	250	7	Insourcing	1992	110	106	No	1 + internal	n/a	20%	Yes, achieved within 1 year	IS manager
17	Food manufacturer	7,000	18	Insourcing	1988	80	180	No	1 + internal	n/a	45%	Yes, achieved within 3 years	Senior manager
19	Telecommunications	500	7	Insourcing	1991	39	32	Yes	2 + internal	5 years	46%	Yes, achieved within 2 years	Senior manager
20	Energy			Insourcing	1989			Yes	3	5 years	25%	Yes, achieved within 2 years	Senior manager
21	Retail			Insourcing	1993			No	n/a	n/a	Not specified	Too early	Senior manager

[a] Dollar figures are rounded to protect company identity; banks show deposits; university shows annual budget.

[b] IS budget, headcount, and MIPS were gathered only for the organisation conducting the sourcing evaluation. The organisation either equates to the entire company or an SBU within the company.

[c] Some companies made multiple sourcing decisions.

TABLE 14.2. *Job positions of participants*

Participants' job positions	Number of participants
Senior manager (CFO, controller, treasurer)	7
CIO or equivalent title	16
IS staff member involved in evaluation	29
Vendor account manager	4
Consultant	5
TOTAL	61

revenues exceeding $300 billion, IS headcounts of 2,000, and annual IS budgets of $300 million. We also studied some very small organisations, with revenues under $400 million, IS headcounts under 40 people, and IS budgets of $7 million. Decision sponsors included senior-level executives such as CEOs and CFOs, as well as decisions made by IS managers and their staff. Evaluation processes varied, with some companies making hasty decisions based on informal data gathering, with others rigorously bench-marking, creating RFPs, and evaluating both internal and external bids. Finally, in the instances of outsourcing, some participants signed relational contracts while others signed very detailed ones. While such diversity may result in every situation being unique, strong patterns across the cases were evident. These patterns provide the foundation of the lessons learned.

In total, we interviewed sixty-one people (see Table 14.2), including senior managers, IS managers, IS staff, and vendor account managers. The senior managers held titles of CFO, controller, VP of planning, and treas-urer. IS managers held titles of CIO, VP of IS, director of IS. Information systems staff people we interviewed were usually responsible for gathering the technical and financial details for the request for proposals. In some cases, these participants were placed in awkward positions. They assisted the outsourcing effort even though it would eliminate their jobs. Four out-sourcing vendors were interviewed. After these initial interviews, it was realised that the vendors were reticent to talk about their outsourcing experi-ences because they felt the interviews breached their supplier–client con-fidentiality agreements. They advised us to direct all questions to the client. Two consultants, both experts in outsourcing contracts, were interviewed. Rather than let their clients sign the vendor contracts, these consultants insisted that a custom contract be designed that included service-level measures and penalties for non-performance. Interestingly enough, the companies that used a consultant considered the investment worthwhile.

The most important characteristic of the group interviewed in the out-sourcing research is that all participants were privy to the details of the outsourcing decisions in their respective companies. Whether they initiated outsourcing, compiled information, analysed bids, participants had strong opinions about the decisions their companies made about outsourcing. The disparity of views expressed by different stakeholders provided a rich picture of these outsourcing decisions.

The duration of the interviews, on average, was one and a half hours. Although some interviews were shorter or longer, all interviews followed the same protocol which proceeded from a very unstructured to a very structured format. During the unstructured portion, participants were merely asked to tell their insourcing or outsourcing story. This allowed the participant free rein to convey his or her interpretation of events. After they completed their stories, participants were asked semi-structured questions designed to solicit information on specific insourcing/outsourcing issues that may have been absent from their previous recollections. In addition, all participants were assured of anonymity.

Where possible, an organisation's insourcing or outsourcing story was cross-checked by interviewing several individuals at each organisation and against collected documents. In cases where there were differences in opinion between participants at the same organisation, follow-up telephone calls were conducted with participants to clarify their positions. In many instances, interesting differences of opinion persisted. These differences provided us with new insight into how individuals variously perceived their organisation's insourcing/outsourcing evaluation. It provided a richer interpretation than might have otherwise been possible.

All interviews were tape-recorded, transcribed into a 637 single-spaced document. In addition to the interviews, the following supporting documentation was gathered: outsourcing request for proposals, internal bids, external bids, bid evaluation criteria, annual reports, and organisation charts. From this data, individual cases were written, then analysed to uncover patterns across the cases. In the following sections, we present the findings and lessons learned from these organisations. We first address the pre-decision context we witnessed across organisations. This context includes perceptions about the contribution of IS for various stakeholders, the role of the trade press in formulating outsourcing expectations, and the actual reasons why participants investigated outsourcing in our case companies.

Findings

The first three findings address the pre-decision expectations and motivations for evaluating sourcing alternatives as well as perceptions of the value (or lack of value) of IS. The first finding demonstrates the varying expectations for IS performance prior to the sourcing evaluations. The conflict among stakeholders caused a general perception that IS cost too much and added too little value. The second finding describes how this internal perception, combined with the promises of outsourcing popularised in the trade literature, caused many senior executives to view outsourcing as the answer to the perceived problems with IS. The third finding details actual expectations participants articulated for evaluating outsourcing.

Finding 1: conflicting stakeholder expectations place IS managers in the precarious position of providing a Rolls Royce service at a Chevrolet price

We discovered that many companies investigated outsourcing as a consequence of IS managers' failure to demonstrate the value of IS to various stakeholders within the organisation. Many different stakeholders (senior managers, business unit managers, IS managers, IS staff, and end users) possessed different preferences, expectations, perceptions, and agendas for IS. Although IS practitioners and academics have argued for strategic alignment of IS and business strategy, we found that participating organisations failed to achieve such alignment. Instead, different stakeholders wanted different things. Consequently, IS was often set up to fail in the participating companies.

Based on our case studies, we have characterised the following stakeholder expectations and agendas for IS:

- In general, senior management perceived the entire IS function as a utility, and therefore set the IS agenda to be cost minimisation.
- In general, business units and end users perceived that IS critically contributed to business operations, and therefore set the IS agenda to be service excellence.
- In general, IS managers were frustrated because senior managers and users set conflicting agendas for IS, expecting IS managers to deliver a Rolls Royce service at a Chevrolet price.

This conflict is depicted in Fig. 14.1. It captures the different stakeholders' perceptions and expectations of IS as they related to IS costs and service levels. In general, costs are directly proportional to service levels, i.e. the better the service, the higher the costs. This relationship was evident in virtually all IS activities we studied. Consider, for example, software costs. Users' demands for service excellence required that packaged software be customized to their idiosyncratic needs, a practice that drove up IS development and maintenance costs. When IS managers tried to contain costs by implementing packaged software 'as is', users complained their needs were not being met. An example of the cost/service trade-off in the area of hardware was response time. Users demanded service excellence, defined by them as sub-second response time all the time. This increased hardware costs because IS managers purchased excess capacity or other devices to deliver service excellence.

Another surprising example of the cost/service trade-off was data centres. Senior management in all of our cases perceived data centre operations

	MINIMAL COST	PREMIUM COST
PREMIUM SERVICE	**Superstar** Senior management's and users' *expectations* of IS	**Differentiator** Realm of possible IS performance
MINIMAL SERVICE	**Commodity/ low cost producer** Realm of possible IS performance	**Black hole** Senior management's and users' *perceptions* of IS

FIG. 14.1. *IS cost/service trade-off*

to be a utility that should be cost minimised. On the other hand, business managers and end users perceived that their data centres provided critical support and wanted a differentiated service. Unlike senior managers, business unit managers and users asserted that data centres are hardly homogeneous. Different companies used different hardware configurations, operating software, software utilities, facilities for cooling/lighting/fire prevention, levels of software automation, and disaster recovery strategies. All of these contributed to service levels in terms of response time, availability, and, in particular, support. Users wanted their own dedicated support staff who understand what systems they run at what times with what particular problems.

Because of the direct relationship between service and costs, IS can be realistically expected to perform in one of two boxes: IS can provide a premium service for a premium cost *or* IS can provide a minimal service for a minimal price. If organisations perceive that a given IS function is a critical contributor, then IS can be expected to perform in the *Differentiator* quadrant. As a differentiator, IS can provide customised IS products and services to meet idiosyncratic business needs. If organisations perceive that a given IS function is merely a utility, IS can be expected to perform in the *Commodity* or *Low Cost Producer* quadrant. As a commodity, IS can be expected to deliver a standard service at a minimal cost. Unfortunately, the failure to align senior management's priorities for IS with user's priorities created precarious expectation of IS operating in the *Superstar* quadrant; a goal few IS departments can realistically achieve. IS managers attempted to respond to conflicting goals by compromising on both cost and service. The result: neither stakeholder group was satisfied and began to perceive that IS performed in the *Black Hole* quadrant. The black hole analogy seems particularly appropriate as management simply perceived IS as a bottomless cost pit in many of the participating companies.

As a consequence of the differing views of the nature of data centre operations, stakeholders expected IS to perform in the *Superstar* quadrant.

IS managers attempted to meet these inconsistent expectations by giving senior managers *some* cost savings and providing users *some* level of service. Such compromise strategies backfired. Inevitably, IS managers were unable to meet the conflicting expectations of providing a superior, differentiated service at a minimal cost. Consequently, IS was perceived by three stake-holders, senior management, business unit managers, and end users, as operating *Black Holes.*

Senior managers eventually doubted that IS managers would meet their cost reduction mandates and decided that outsourcing was the solution. The outsourcing threat served to align all stakeholders to their cost min-imisation agenda. By creating this shared agenda, some IS managers were able to compete with vendor bids by proposing to replicate their cost reduc-tion tactics. Business unit managers and users realised that either their familiar IS managers or external vendors would implement cost reduction tactics. Many elected to support IS managers with their new insourcing bids that contained cost-reduction schemes users had previously resisted. For companies that chose insourcing, firms moved to the *Commodity* quadrant, providing a minimal acceptable service level for a reduced cost.

The IS cost/service trade-off is something of a double-edged sword. While companies desperately attempted to reduce IS costs, most IS executives preferred to believe that customer service is crucial. In spirit (if not necessarily in deeds) IS attempted to highlight the criticality of customer support. The recent emergence of the function relationship management within IS is a case in point. This function ostensibly creates an account manager role between IS and its business unit customers, and clearly demonstrates that customer service is valued. However, customer service does suffer if cost considerations become the guiding light. This is clearly documented in the cases. For example, FIRM17 increased response time, reduced its software portfolio, eliminated testing (which could lead to errors in installation); yet senior management applauded this reduced service be-cause IS costs are 40 per cent lower. The people who made the decisions (senior management) were different from the recipients of the service (the users). The same was true for FIRM18. They now provide a 'Chevrolet' instead of a 'Rolls Royce' level of service. The IS manager's job is to run the legacy systems into the ground. These insourced centres basically run like outsourcers, trying to meet some minimum service level while reducing costs as much as possible.

One might argue that too often IS provides a 'Rolls Royce' service when a 'Chevy' will do. Of course this notion of service is highly perceptual. What to one is a 'Rolls Royce', is but a 'Chevy' to another. Furthermore, there is the issue of whether a Rolls Royce is justified in the first place. If the firm differentiates itself on the basis of service then such a high class of service, i.e. Rolls Royce, adds value. Taking the analogy further, a Chevy might be fine until the first time one gets into an accident. Then suddenly the Rolls Royce appears no longer a luxury, but a necessity. As usual, such decisions involve trade-offs. Reduced service (Chevy) may be acceptable in the short run but what about the long run? Is a firm potentially mortgaging away its future for short-run savings now? Such questions may not have simple answers but organisations must consider the long-run implications of their actions. It is indeed worrying if long-term gains are sacrificed for short-term cost savings.

Finding 2: the published literature portrays an overly optimistic view of IS outsourcing

The previous finding characterised the pre-decision context we witnessed in participating organisations. Senior managers perceived that IS cost too much and despaired that IS managers would ever reduce costs on their own. They began to perceive that outsourcing was the answer to their problems. Senior executives were bombarded with messages in the trade press and by *wooing* vendors that IS is a utility that is best managed by outside experts. But the overall finding from scrutinising the published literature is that these sources often portrayed an overly optimistic view of outsourcing, promising an IS utopia with costs reductions up to 50 per cent, significant service-level improvements, access to new technologies, and low levels of capital investment. Furthermore, vendors would run IS, allowing senior managers to focus on their core competencies.

Three reasons can be identified to explain the optimism. First, reports are made during the honeymoon period when clients first sign an outsourcing contract. At this point, the client and vendor possess high outsourcing expectations (cf. Hamilton, 1989; Kass, 1990; Gillin, 1990; Radding, 1990; Anthes, 1991; Rochester and Douglas, 1990). Second, the literature only reports projected savings instead of actual savings. American Standard, for example, expects their data centre operations and network costs to be reduced by 40 per cent through outsourcing (Rochester and Douglas, 1990). Southeast Corporation expects a 20 per cent savings in IS costs over the ten-year life of their outsourcing contract (Kass, 1990). Hibernia National Bank projects savings of between $25 million and $100 million over their ten-year outsourcing deal (Kass, 1990). Therefore, the preponderance of literature that suggests that outsourcing can save 20 to 50 per cent on IS costs is largely based on expectations. But have these expectations been met? Third, public reports under-represent outsourcing failures because few companies wish to advertise a mistake. Therefore, the literature misrepresents the spectrum of outsourcing experiences by focusing on the success stories.

The enthusiasm for IS outsourcing in the trade press is not unique—any new management trend promises to be the panacea to organisational problems. Through radical change, be it business process re-engineering, total quality management, virtual corporations, etc, practitioners are offered yet another utopia. Such positive press tempts many senior executives to jump on the latest bandwagon (DiMaggio and Powell, 1983), but subsequent research shows that many organisations fail to improve radically. For example, in a recent study of 100 companies seeking radical transformation through BPR, TQM, 'right-sizing', and restructuring, Kotter (1995) found that only a few achieved a radical transformation, a few were 'utter disasters', and most achieved incremental improvements. We found the same with total outsourcing. Initially viewed as a route to radical change, most found that total outsourcing is not a substitute for IS management.

Finding 3: organisational members initiated outsourcing evaluations for a variety reasons

An analysis of participants' motives to investigate outsourcing can only be appreciated by understanding the pre-decision context discussed so far. Conflicting stakeholder perceptions created unrealistic agendas for IS performance, resulting in disappointment with IS. To participating senior managers, and even some high-level IS managers, the increasing popularity of outsourcing seemed a viable alternative. Their expectations, fuelled by the trade press, were very high. They expected a number of financial, business, and technical benefits. To some IS managers, however, outsourcing was perceived as a threat, and they displayed political behaviours during the evaluation process. Below, we discuss the participants' reported expectations for initiating outsourcing evaluations, which we classified into four broad categories:

1. *financial*—cut costs (FIRMs 4, 6, 7, 9, 10, 11, 15, 16, 17, and 19), improve cost controls (FIRMs 6, 16), and restructure the IS budget (FIRMs 3, 10, 14);
2. *business*—return to core competencies (FIRMs 14, 19), facilitate mergers and acquisitions (FIRM9), provide IS for start-up companies (FIRMs 1, 12), and devolve organisational and management structures (FIRMs 18, 19, 20);
3. *technical*—improve technical services (FIRMs 9, 13), gain access to new technical talent (FIRMs 9, 11, 13), provide access to new technologies (FIRMs 9, 13), and focus the internal IS staff on core technical activities (FIRMs 14, 18, 20);
4. *political*—react to the efficiency imperative (FIRMs 1, 2, 4, 5, 6, 11, 12, 13), acquire or justify additional resources (FIRMs 1, 3, 5, 7, 9, 11, 13), react to the positive outsourcing media reports (FIRMs 1, 2, 4, 6, 8, 11), reduce uncertainty (FIRMs 8, 9), eliminate a burdensome function (FIRMs 1, 4, 11), and enhance personal credibility (FIRMs 3, 5, 8).

Financial Reasons

Many participants in our research, especially senior managers, cited financial reasons for outsourcing. In particular, participants viewed outsourcing as a way to cut costs, improve cost control, and restructure the IS budget.

Reduce costs

Many participants expected that outsourcing would save them money. They perceived that vendors enjoy economies of scale that enable then to provide IS services at a lower cost than internal IS departments. In particular, participants believed that a vendor's unit costs are less expensive due to mass production efficiencies and labour specialization.

Improve cost control

Another financial rationale for outsourcing described by participants was gaining control over IS costs. As any IS manager will attest, IS costs are directly related to IS user demands. In most organisations, however, IS costs are controlled through general allocation systems which motivate users to demand and consume resources excessively. General allocation systems are analogous to splitting a restaurant tab—each dinner companion is motivated to order an expensive dinner because the cost will be shared by the other parties. Participants saw outsourcing as a way to control costs because vendors implement cost controls that more directly tie usage to costs. In addition, users no longer call their favourite analysts to request frivolous changes, but instead must submit requests through a formal cost control process. This results in the curtailing of excessive user demands and thus reduces overall IS costs.

Restructure IS budgets

Some participants stated that the reason for initiating outsourcing was for restructuring their IS budgets from cumbersome capital budgets to more flexible operating budgets. Through outsourcing, organisations could more efficiently purchase IS resources as needed rather than invest in capital. For example, rather than retain a $15 million mainframe on the books, participants could sell the asset to the vendor and merely buy the number of MIPs they need each year from the vendor. The sale of the asset also generates cash up front, which increases the participants' cash flow. In addition, some vendors will purchase stock and postpone the bulk of IS payments to the latter part of the contract, making the overall net present value extremely attractive to participants. In return for these financial incentives, vendors require long-term contracts, typically ten years in duration.

Business Reasons

A number of participants expressed three business rationales for out-sourcing: return to core competencies, facilitate mergers and acquisitions, and start up new companies.

Return to core competencies

During the 1990s, many large companies abandoned their diversification strategies—once pursued to mediate risk—to focus on core competencies and outsourcing the rest. As a result of this core competencies focus, IS came under scrutiny: is IS a competitive weapon or merely a utility? Even within companies, perceptions over IS's contribution to core activities varied. In general, senior executives tended to view the entire IS function as a non-core activity whereas IS managers and some business unit managers contended that certain IS activities are core to the business.

Facilitate mergers and acquisitions

Because the participants were from large companies, as indicated by their presence in *Fortune* 500 list, many of the companies pursue a growth strategy through mergers and acquisitions. Mergers and acquisitions create many IS nightmares for IS managers because they are required to absorb acquired companies into existing systems. Participants expected outsourcing to solve the technical incompatibilities, absorb the excess IS assets, such as additional data centres, and absorb the additional IS employees generated by mergers and acquisitions.

Provide IS for start-up companies

Some participants explained that they outsourced IS when the company was first incorporated. At the time, participants expected that outsourcing was a quicker and cheaper way to provide IS services. As start-up companies, participants simply could not afford the capital investment required to erect internal IS departments.

Devolution of organisational and management structures

Participants from a number of organisations initiated outsourcing evaluations in response to devolution of organisational and management structures occurring in a wider business context. Often termed *downsizing*, participants intended to use outsourcing as a means to reduce headcount and thus the costs associated with salaries, pensions, and benefits.

Technical Reasons

Technical issues associated with why participants considered outsourcing involve the technical difficulties associated with providing effective IS; more specifically, the desire to either improve technical services, gain access to technical talent not currently available in the organisation, and/or provide access to new technologies.

Improve technical service

Some participants were dissatisfied with the technical services provided by their in-house IS departments. In particular, the IS departments delivered systems late and over budget and did not respond in a timely manner to user requests. Participants viewed outsourcing as a way to improve technical service, reasoning that outsourcing vendors possess a technical expertise lacking in internal IS departments.

Access to technical talent

Some participants thought outsourcing would provide access to technical talent. Many participants found it difficult to find and/or retain staff with the state-of-the-art technical skills. Vendors are felt to have core competencies in technology skills which allow them to bring these skills to the organisation through outsourcing. Numerous companies consider outsourcing partly for the access to greater IS expertise it would bring.

Access to new technologies

Some participants felt outsourcing would provide a conduit to new, emerging technologies. They viewed outsourcing as a way to hedge bets on emerging technologies, providing them access to the products of the vendors' large research and development departments. Participants were particularly interested in client/server technology, expert systems, new development methodologies, and CASE tools.

Focus the internal IS staff on core technical activities

Participants from a number of companies initiated outsourcing evaluations to focus the internal IS staff on *core* technical activities, such as the development of new applications, while outsourcing *non-core* technical activities, such as the support of legacy systems.

Political Reasons

Political reasons for why participants considered outsourcing revolved around the desire to deal more effectively with the subjective nature of assessing the value of IS. In short, the political dimension of outsourcing involves the behaviour of the various parties associated with the outsourcing decision-making process. In contrast to the rational description of outsourcing evaluation surrounding the above-mentioned financial, business, and technical reasons, the political perspective interprets the behaviour of the organisational actors in a subjective light, seeing outsourcing as one piece of a large puzzle involving the shaping of senior management's perception about IS. Political rationale for why organisations consider outsourcing includes: proving efficiency (as a reaction to the efficiency imperative), justifying new resources, reacting to the positive media reports, reducing uncertainty, eliminating a troublesome function, and breaking the so-called 'glass ceiling' (i.e. enhancing credibility).

Reaction to the efficiency imperative

A commonly cited reason for initiating outsourcing evaluations by participants was the reaction to the efficiency imperative. Because twelve of the fourteen companies are accounted for as an overhead function, senior managers tended to evaluate the function solely on cost efficiency (Quinn et al., 1990). Because no concrete measures of *actual* efficiency exist, senior managers formulated only a *perception* of efficiency. When senior managers perceived that IS was inefficient, they initiated outsourcing evaluations to improve efficiency. In a similar vein, IS managers themselves initiated outsourcing evaluations. This way, IS managers *proved* that the IS department was already efficient or was making strides to become efficient.

The need to acquire new resources

Participants initiated outsourcing decisions to acquire new resources, such as machine upgrades, additional personnel, or cash. IS managers were well aware that their requests for capital funds would be met with questions such as, 'isn't it cheaper to outsource this?' Outsourcing evaluations helped participants acquire resources by showing that outsourcers could not provide the additional resources at a lower cost. The participants adopting this strategy were usually granted the resource.

Reaction to the bandwagon

Another reason identified was the reaction to the proverbial bandwagon. Favourable outsourcing reports triggered participants to initiate outsourcing for two reasons. First, participants, especially senior managers, wanted to duplicate the success stories they read in the literature. Because these senior managers didn't truly value the IS function anyway, they hoped to at least reduce costs to the levels their competitors allegedly achieved through outsourcing. Second, participants, particularly IS managers, feared that the favourable reports would seduce their managers into outsourcing. By taking the initiative, participants used outsourcing evaluations to temper the many exaggerated claims made in public information sources.

Reduce uncertainty

Participants initiated outsourcing evaluations to respond to their desire to reduce uncertainty. Because IS demand is erratic, IS managers have difficulty planning for IS services. Rather than react to demand fluctuations, IS managers outsourced. By including a clause that varies fees with volumes, IS managers effectively dispensed with the risks associated with uncertainty.

Eliminate a troublesome function

Another political reason identified was the desire of participants to eliminate a troublesome function. Since senior executives do not fully value IS, IS administrators receive few accolades for managing the function. When the function runs smoothly, senior executives do not notice. When the function experiences problems, senior management screams. Participants in the research felt, quite frankly, who needs the aggravation? Since no one cares about the function, why not outsource it and let the vendor worry about it?

Enhance credibility

The final reason identified by the participants was the use of outsourcing evaluations to enhance personal or departmental credibility. Since senior managers do not fully value the services of the IS department, they may not value the contribution of the people who run the function. Studies have repeatedly shown that IS personnel rarely break into the upper echelons of management. Several participants initiated outsourcing decisions to enhance their credibility. By showing that they are willing to outsource their kingdom for the good of the company, they prove to management that they are corporate players.

Finding 4: successful sourcing evaluations compared vendor bids against a newly submitted internal bid, not against current IS performance

Because beliefs about the outsourcing were so positive, many participants failed to perform a thorough evaluation. Some CEOs (i.e. FIRM2, FIRM9, FIRM12) engaged in long-term outsourcing contracts without thoroughly understanding how vendors proposed to reduce costs. Other participants actually created requests-for-proposals, but only compared vendor bids with current IS costs (i.e. FIRM3, FIRM8, FIRM11). But lower external bids were often based on efficient managerial practices that could have been replicated by internal IS departments if they were empowered to act. By far the most rigorous evaluations we studied carefully assessed current IS costs and service levels, prepared requests-for-proposals, and invited both internal and external bids (i.e. FIRM4, FIRM16, FIRM17). Below we discuss the rational and political reasons why this process was the most likely route to a successful outcome.

Many senior managers assume that outsourcing vendors submit lower bids because they are inherently more efficient due to economies of scale. The theory of economies of scale states that large-sized companies achieve lower average costs than small-sized companies due to mass production and labour specialisation efficiencies. In the outsourcing arena, however, the applicability of the economies of scale model may be questioned. In an analysis of sixty-one sourcing decisions, Lacity and Willcocks (1996) found that size of IS operations in terms of MIPS, IT headcount, and IT budget did not differentiate successful from unsuccessful decisions. Managerial practices were the major contributor to efficiency in IT—not economies of scale.

Thus, when vendors submit bids that indicate savings, companies must question how the vendor proposes to reduce costs, and not just attribute savings to economies of scale. In many cases, vendor bids were based on efficient managerial practices such as standardisation, consolidation, centralisation, and tighter controls—practices that internal IS managers may be able to replicate if empowered to do so. Many senior executives argued against inviting an internal bid because they believed that if internal IS managers were capable of change, they would have done so already. In the past, however, the lack of IS power combined with conflicting stakeholder pressures often prohibited IS managers from implementing change.

Implementing cost savings measures requires IS to adopt policies which may not be readily agreed to by the business units in the organisation. Internal politics often drives what can and cannot be implemented. For example, in a number of cases, there was a recognition that consolidating data centres would yield cost savings; however, corporate politics precluded it from happening. Each business unit felt that 'their' data centre provided special services which could not be provided from a single, consolidated centre. Their data centres understood the idiosyncrasies of their particular business requirements, were responsive to their needs, and were, fundamentally, more controllable by the business units. They owed their allegiance to the business units they supported rather than to the corporation as a whole. Hence the business units vehemently resisted any form of consolidation. In such an environment, it was often impossible for IS to push through consolidation; the business units had too much power. Only when senior management empowered the IS department did IS actually have the authority, i.e. the political muscle, to implement consolidation.

There are other examples in our case studies where IS knew of ways to reduce costs but simply could not convince the business units to agree to implement them. For example, the implementing of a full-cost chargeback scheme is one of the best mechanisms for getting the user departments to recognise the true costs of providing various services to them. Many organisations have chargeback schemes, but they are simply allocation schemes agreed to by some IS steering committee to apportion costs. And the way these costs are apportioned is often very unfair. Unfortunately, it is not an easy task to change the allocation scheme. Business units tended to resist because they felt that, with full-cost chargeback, they would be charged for services that previously were absorbed by someone else (often another department or the corporation as a whole). IS costs rise because the business units can demand whatever they want knowing (or even not knowing) that the costs will be shared with others. Of course one can just imagine how such a scenario might play out. Business unit A requests a particular expensive type of service (e.g. reports produced in colour), so business unit B, not wanting to be outdone, requests something equally exotic (e.g. multimedia interface to some corporate database). One can imagine how this might escalate. The implementation of a true chargeback scheme would stop such potentially frivolous requests as the user department requesting such services would have to pay the full amount of IS providing that service. But implementing such a chargeback scheme is problematic, and will only be possible if senior management empowers and supports IS to do so. To put it differently, IS needs a 'big stick' to hammer resistance with in order to implement cost saving policies. This big stick can only come from senior management.

In all instances that we studied when internal IS managers were allowed to compete with external vendor bids, they won the bid and implemented the savings. One could conceive of an outcome when an external bid would beat an internal bid, but such an occurrence would be based on a vendor's capabilities that simply could not be replicated in-house. Below we discuss the IS cost drivers, which can be used to answer the question, 'where can vendors provide capability more efficiently than we can?'

Finding 5: internal IS departments actually possess superior cost advantages for some IS cost drivers

Another major benefit of allowing internal IS managers to compete is that it often surfaced the real IS cost drivers. Rather than merely accepting platitudes such as, 'the vendor can do it cheaper because that is their core competency,' these practitioners analysed the relative advantage of in-house

TABLE 14.3. *IS cost drivers*

Sources of IS costs	Internal IS Departments	Outsourcing vendors
Data centre operating costs	Comparable to a vendor for 150–200 MIP range	Comparable to large IS departments. Inherent advantage over small IS departments
Hardware purchase costs	Large companies: volume discounts comparable to a vendor	Volume discounts comparable to large IS departments. Inherent advantage over small companies
Software licensing costs	Comparable due to group licences	Comparable
Cost of business expertise	Inherent advantage	
Cost of technical expertise		Inherent advantage
Cost to shareholders (the need to generate a profit)	Inherent advantage	
R&D costs		Inherent advantage
Marketing costs	Inherent advantage	
Opportunity costs		Inherent advantage
Transaction costs	Inherent advantage	

versus market capabilities. By decomposing the cost drivers of information technology, practitioners can better evaluate the relative advantages of insourcing and outsourcing. Although such an analysis will have unique outcomes depending on the individual firm, we identified some general lessons across the cases (see Table 14.3). Based on our research, the major cost drivers are data centre operating costs, hardware purchasing costs, software licensing costs, labour costs to acquire both business and technical expertise, shareholder costs (the need to generate a profit), research and development costs, marketing costs, opportunity costs, and transaction costs. This analysis also sheds insights into the previous finding on economies of scale. In the context of IS, economies of scale may be achieved at a size which creates a level playing field between vendors and IS departments for some IS cost drivers. As is discussed below, internal IS departments may find they actually possess an inherent advantage on some of these cost drivers.

Data centre operating costs

In the area of data processing, economies of scale are achieved in the 150 to 200 MIP range, which is approximately equivalent to the size of a large mainframe. Thus, most large companies have the critical mass required to achieve economies of scale. In cases where companies operate multiple smaller data centres, economies of scale could be achieved through data centre consolidation. Indeed, many outsourcing vendors generate bids for large companies based on the premiss that they will consolidate the data centres once the contract is signed. From our cases, internal IS departments can accomplish consolidation through insourcing. Given the internal IS departments' inherent cost advantage for other cost drivers, insourcing is more cost efficient than outsourcing to achieve data centre economies of scale.

We also note that smaller companies can achieve similar average costs to a vendor even though they operate data centres below the 150–200 MIP range. As documented in Lacity and Hirschheim (1993*a*), small companies are often willing to lag one or two generations behind, allowing them to capitalize on the large savings of the used computer market. Theoretically, vendors could also duplicate these savings, but vendors sensibly position themselves as technology leaders rather than laggards.

Hardware purchase costs

The theory of economies of scale suggests that lower average production costs are partly achieved through volume discounts. Suppliers are willing to offer large customers volume discounts to secure the business. In the area of IS, most hardware suppliers do indeed offer significant discounts off published price lists to their larger clients. Thus, large companies typically purchase heavy iron for approximately the same costs as outsourcing vendors. For example, one consultant claims that mainframes that retail for $15 million may be sold to large companies such as Exxon or EDS for as little as $11 million. Thus, large internal IS departments and outsourcing vendors possess comparable economies of scale for hardware purchases.

Smaller companies may indeed be at a disadvantage. FIRM19, for example, diligently tried to negotiate lower costs with their hardware suppliers. Due to their size, however, the suppliers were unwilling to offer the same volume discounts enjoyed by their larger customers. Thus, outsourcing vendors possess an inherent cost advantage for hardware purchases over smaller IS departments.

Software licensing costs

As discussed in Lacity and Hirschheim (1993*b*), at one time vendors possessed an inherent cost advantage over internal IS departments because of site licences. With site licences, outsourcing vendors spread licensing fees over multiple customers, yielding lower average software costs than internal IS departments. As a backlash to lost revenues due to outsourcing, software houses have restructured their licensing practices. Instead of offering site licences, software houses now offer group licences in which the customer is charged based on the size of machine. Thus, internal IS departments typically possess a comparable cost advantage to vendors for software licences.

Cost of business expertise

The cost of acquiring business expertise is a major cost driver, particularly in the areas of applications development and support. The critical skill required to deliver these functions is understanding how business requirements can be met through available technology. Most internal IS departments possess superior knowledge of their users' business requirements. As company employees, internal IS managers and systems analysts understand the idiosyncratic business requirements required to deliver a cost-effective service. For example, every company possesses significant quirks even in their allegedly *commodity* type applications such as payroll, inventory control, purchasing, order processing, etc. As any business person will attest, it is the exceptions that potentially cripple an application. Internal IS staff have acquired significant understanding of these quirks and thus have an inherent advantage over vendors.

Technical expertise costs

The cost of acquiring technical expertise is also a major IS cost driver, particularly in the area of emerging technologies. The vendors are primarily the creators of new technologies, such as LANs, expert systems, and neural networks, and therefore possess an inherent cost advantage over internal IS departments. We do not, however, suggest that all new technologies should be outsourced; rather, it is the combination of applying business requirements to emerging technologies that yields value to the firm. Technology in and of itself is of no value; it is merely a general purpose vehicle.

In cases where companies wish to develop applications involving new technologies, companies can access vendor expertise while still maintaining control over applications development. For example, rather than outsource the entire development of an application using a new technology to an outsourcing vendor, companies can maintain managerial control, use the internal IS staff to determine business requirements, and merely hire vendor resources to learn about the new technology. In this scenario, companies can exploit the inherent efficiencies of both internal IS departments and vendors.

Shareholder costs

Shareholders purchase company stock in return for sharing in company profits. In the area of IS, outsourcing vendors must generate a profit for their shareholders whereas internal IS departments merely need to re-cover costs. Some participants claimed that this cost driver alone provides internal IS departments with a significant cost advantage. As is evident from this analysis, a vendor cannot undercut internal IS departments on most cost drivers. When participants were asked how vendors can operate without such an advantage, participants responded that vendors often underbid contracts in hopes of selling more lucrative excess services and products to their customers.

Research and development costs

IS research and development costs are incurred to fuel the development of new technologies. Few internal IS departments have the critical mass to justify large expenditures in research and development. Rather, vendors possess an inherent advantage because they can recover R&D costs by sell-ing the new technology to many customers. Also included in R&D costs are the costs of environmental scanning and retraining staff. Here too, a vendor possesses an inherent cost advantage. An outsourcing vendor can recover the costs of environmental scanning by selling selected tech-nologies to multiple customers. In addition, an outsourcing vendor can efficiently train their staff, which may include as many as 50,000 people. Internal IS departments simply cannot reach the critical mass required to achieve economies of scale in these areas.

Marketing costs

Marketing costs are incurred to attract IS customers. For internal IS departments, marketing costs are minimized because they have to a large extent a captive audience. Outsourcing vendors, however, incur con-siderable costs to attract customers and submit bids. Thus, internal IS departments possess an inherent advantage over vendors in the area of marketing.

Opportunity costs

Opportunity costs are an important cost driver, but often ignored because they are not captured in accounting calculations. When management choose to focus resources in one area, they lose the opportunity of apply-ing those resources elsewhere. In the area of IS, some senior managers consider opportunity costs in their sourcing decisions. Willcocks and Fitzgerald (1994) describe several companies that decided to outsource their legacy systems so that the internal IS department could focus on the development of more strategic applications. Even though these legacy systems could have been efficiently run and maintained in-house, the opportunity cost of not developing strategic applications was significantly high to warrant outsourcing.

Transaction costs

Transaction costs may be the single most important cost driver. Transaction costs are the management costs associated with co-ordinating, monitoring, and controlling the delivery of products or services. Transaction costs explain why many companies produce goods and services internally rather than acquire them on the market. Internal organisations minimise transaction costs because they presumably administer an efficient system of rewards and punishments that discourage employee opportunism (Williamson 1975, 1979, 1991). When goods or services are acquired through a vendor, the transaction costs increase because the vendor may behave opportunistically by being untrustworthy, dishonest, or purporting unfair representations. Thus, companies incur transaction costs to negotiate sound contracts, monitor vendor performance, solve vendor disputes, etc. Transaction cost economists also suggest that transaction costs increase when only a small number of suppliers exist in the market. With few competitors, a vendor may take advantage of their captive customer. Thus in general, economists argue that internal companies possess an inherent transaction cost advantage over external vendors.

In the area of IS, the transaction costs associated with outsourcing can be considerable. Companies accrue significant management costs creating requests for proposals, soliciting vendor bids, analysing vendor bids, negotiating contracts (which may take six months), monitoring vendor performance, paying bills, and solving disputes. With large companies, outsourcing increases transaction costs due to the few number of vendors large enough to provide their IS services. Typically, only one or two vendors responded to bids solicited by the *Fortune* 500 firms we studied. Some participants feared that if they outsourced, they would have no other sourcing alternatives in the short run if their vendors did not perform. Thus, internal IS departments possess a significant transaction cost advantage over vendors.

From this analysis, it becomes apparent that vendors only possess an inherent cost advantage for IS functions whose cost drivers are dominated by new technologies, R&D costs, and opportunity costs. Conversely, large internal IS departments possess equivalent or superior economies of scale to vendors for several major cost drivers: data centre costs, hardware purchasing costs, software licensing costs, business expertise costs, marketing costs, and shareholder costs. When considering sourcing alternatives that are primarily driven by these cost drivers, managers should consider whether insourcing is the most efficient sourcing strategy.

The limitation of the analysis of the theoretical economies of scale is that it ignores the political aspects of organisational life. Just because an internal IS department can theoretically achieve efficiency does not mean that the political environment is receptive to changes required to achieve efficiency. Political obstacles must be overcome to empower the internal IS department to implement cost reduction tactics.

The last finding discusses the last phase of decision process. Companies that decided to outsource followed one of two general contracting strategies: strategic partnerships and detailed contracts. Despite the popularity of the former in the trade press, the latter was much more successful.

Finding 6: when companies decided to outsource, detailed contracts were more likely to be successful than relational contracts

When some companies decide that outsourcing is the preferred mechanism for achieving IS objectives, they often like to view their vendors as partners. A Kodak manager told an audience of practitioners: 'We think of our strategic alliances as "partnerships" because of their cooperative and long term qualities' (Hovey, 1991). Kodak sealed their partnerships with IBM, DEC, and Businessland with little more than a gentleman's agreement. While such arrangements might work in the Kodak case, we feel the general assumption that the outsourcing vendor is a partner is dangerously flawed. Vendors are not partners unless profit motives are shared (see Willcocks 1994, 1995 for a thorough discussion of the limitations of the strategic partnership model in IT outsourcing). In the companies we studied, a dollar out of the client's wallet was a dollar in the vendor's wallet; thus they were not true partners, there was no shared profit motive. An outsourcing contract is the only way to ensure an equitable balance of power. Service-level measures, arrangements for growth, penalties for non-performance, and other contract provisions must be stipulated prior to outsourcing commencement.

Lacity and Willcocks (1996) describe the limitations of strategic partners as follows:

In our research base, we found that weaker companies who view their IT outsourcing suppliers as 'strategic partners' signed relational contracts which strongly favored the vendor. The customer, relying on the trust and spirit of a partnership to ensure success, failed to recognize they have little leverage in the partnership once they signed the contract. These relational contracts provided minimal obligations for vendor performance, specified no shared risks or rewards, gave the vendor power of sole supplier, and provided no means to translate the promised 'added-value' into a reality.

Consider the example of FIRM12. Senior executives signed a seven-year, total outsourcing deal using a relational contract. They selected a particular vendor partly because vendor representatives promised access to industry-specific systems used by other chemicals customers. Because vendor representatives presented themselves as *partners*, senior executives from the chemicals company neglected contract negotiations and hastily signed an incomplete contract. The first month into the contract, the vendor's excess charges for items missing in the contract exceeded the fixed monthly price. As time went on, promises of access to additional software vaporized, and instead the chemical company paid the vendor to build new systems. When these systems were late and over-priced, users purchased cheaper PC-based solutions, funded through discretionary money. Rather than continue the *partnership* with the outsourcing vendor, senior executives terminated the contract, purchased hardware and software, and hired a new IS staff of forty people.

The outsourcing vendor provides the level of IS services specified in the contract using the technological platform it deems appropriate. In such an environment, vendors typically run mainframes and mainframe software applications *into the ground* as they are sunk costs. Unless specifically spelled out in the contract, the flexibility of moving to new computing platforms is lost. Or if not lost, the vendor is likely to be the sole benefactor of any cost advantage of moving to new, more cost-effective technology. More worrying, however, is that outsourcing could constrain how an organisation reacts or adapts to a changing business environment. Without the flexibility of having an internal IS capability, it might prove difficult (and/or expensive) to have the vendor provide a changed set of IS services.

We do not mean to imply that vendors are sneaky. Again, an understanding of the failure of strategic partnerships requires an appreciation for varying stakeholder expectations. Customers often expected vendors' fixed fees to include access to new technologies, new talent, new software, etc. But these services are outside the scope of the vendor's bid, and represent a significant cost to the vendor to introduce them. In the case of FIRM12, the vendor's promise for new software was, from their perspective, a verification that they have the expertise to deliver such systems if the customer wants them. But was it realistic to expect that the vendor should pay for new technology and new software from their profit share?

Outsourcing expectations are best met when those expectations are well defined in a detailed contract. Customers who understand the underlying costs and service levels and articulate these requirements with concrete measures in detailed contracts were most satisfied. The relational model was used when customers could not articulate their requirements. But this is analogous to going to a car mechanic and saying, 'I trust your judgement, do whatever you think needs to be done as long as it only costs me $X.' How do customers outsource IS activities that they do not understand or cannot predict very well? Not with a relational contract.

Lacity, Willcocks, and Feeny (1996) argue that IS activities which are characterised by a high degree of uncertainty require a *buy-in* contracting strategy. With a buy-in strategy, companies buy in vendor resources to supplement in-house abilities, but manage the activity internally. This strategy was most successful for the development of technically immature activities. In these cases, companies wished to access vendor expertise but could not negotiate a detailed contract because they did not understand requirements, nor could they afford to miss a learning opportunity. An example of this buy-in strategy is the development of a first client/server system. Companies they studied (a food manufacturer, an insurance company, and a high-tech manufacturer) lacked the technical skills to develop the client/server systems, but felt that their own business expertise was required for the applications, which included manufacturing scheduling, customer order processing, and claims processing. Outside experts were hired on an hourly basis to participate on the project team. After the systems were completed, the knowledge had been transferred and these companies opted to support the systems internally.

Lessons Learned

There are many lessons for practitioners in the previously discussed findings, including the need to align stakeholder perceptions, understand the cost and contribution of IS before making sourcing decisions, overcoming internal obstacles to change, etc. In addition, two other lessons are noteworthy.

The metaphor that IS is merely a commodity/utility is misguided

It is possible to find in the published literature numerous examples of practitioner statements that compare the entire IS department to electricity, cafeterias, fruit stands, and laundry services. For example, Henry Pfendt of Kodak claims that outsourcing comes down to one question: 'Do you want to manage commodities?' (Kass and Caldwell, 1990: 14). Similarly, Elliot McNeil of Southlands claims that IS is largely a utility; rather than pay for the entire plant, why not just pay for wattage used? 'It's like the electricity company; you use less, you pay less' (Ambrosio, 1991). Ward states: 'Like shoppers at a fruit stand, companies are picking an apple here or an orange there until they have selected a menu of outsourcing services' (1991: 40). Gardner writes: 'Outsourcing takes over all information systems functions, much the way an outside company would manage food service or laundry' (1991: 35). These metaphors are based on the assumption that IS services are homogeneous—one unit of IS service is equal to any other.

The problem with this metaphor is it ignores the idiosyncratic nature of an organisation's information needs. A true commodity is defined as a product or service that is so standardized that the buyer and seller need not engage in special contracts. Indeed, they may not even need to *meet*.

True commodities in IS include buying off-the-shelf software (we do not need to meet Bill Gates to buy Microsoft Office), personal computers, some printers, etc. But few significant IS activities are true commodities. Close communication between the organisation and IS usually must occur to relay requirements accurately. As utility users, we do not have to call the power company to communicate our complicated changing business needs. We simply use more of the power when and as needed. As IS users, however, we do. So how is an IS department like electricity?

Selective sourcing which treats IS as a portfolio is the key to right-sourcing

Taken as a whole, the previous lessons point to the conclusion that selective sourcing is the key to right-sourcing (Feeny et al., 1993; Lacity et al., 1996). Total outsourcing proved a poor sourcing strategy because the entire IS function cannot be treated as one homogeneous utility. By outsourcing the entire IS function, senior executives realised that they lost control of core IS activities, such as strategic planning, scanning the environment for new technologies applicable to business needs, development of business-specific applications, and support of critical systems. Consequently, companies engaged in total outsourcing experienced significant difficulties a few years into the contract. After the initial honeymoon period, companies complained of a loss of alignment between IS strategy and business strategy, failed promises to access new technologies, and contractual costs which were significantly greater than current market prices. Although total outsourcing 'war stories' (which are by no means atypical) rightfully discourage total outsourcing, they do not suggest that total insourcing is necessarily the answer. By ignoring the external services market altogether, senior executives had unwittingly created an environment of complacency and erected political barriers for continuous improvement.

With the failures of treating IS as a either a utility to be totally outsourced or a differentiator to be totally insourced, a more selective sourcing strategy appears warranted. Such a strategy treats IS as a portfolio of activities. While some well-defined, isolated, and mature IS activities can be safely handed to a vendor, other IS activities require senior management's attention, protection, and nurturing to ensure current and future business success. Consider the case of Sun Microsystems. They signed a three-year, $27 million deal with CSC to handle all of Sun's mainframe operations while the in-house IS staff rewrites its mainframe-based manufacturing and financial applications to run on a client/server platform (*I/S Analyzer*, 1993). Sun's use of selective sourcing is suggestive of how this can be an effective sourcing strategy. But while selective sourcing offers much promise, the greater choice of options increases the complexity of the sourcing decision.

The Future of IS Sourcing

Issues associated with new technologies and the management of such have a habit of maturing very rapidly. Outsourcing is no exception. Since we concluded our research studies of outsourcing and insourcing—the results of which were reported above—a number of changes have begun to emerge. Subsequent research will be needed to assess the viability of these new trends.

Change in focus

Although companies outsource for a variety of reasons, the view that the primary reason is cost savings appears to be falling out of favour. More and more companies appear to be entering into outsourcing 'deals' not so much to reduce costs but for the sake of management focus (Halvey, 1994). In other words, they outsource certain parts of IS in order to free up management and IS personnel to work on specific value-added functions; turning their attention to those areas where the internal skill sets add strategic value to the organisation.

The growth in alliances/partnerships

In the early days of outsourcing, deals were often struck on the basis of *partnerships*. As our outsourcing research showed, however, this concept was fallacious. Outsourcing vendors were not partners because, ultimately, these arrangements were simply transactions: the vendor provided a set of services for which it received compensation from the client. Sometimes the deals sounded like a form of *alliance* because the vendor provided up-front cash (either through low-interest loans or stock purchases) to sweeten the deal. This gave the appearance of an alliance because the vendor was acting on the client's behalf. The truth was that these financial sweeteners were simply that: inducements to sign long-term outsourcing deals where the vendor would ultimately get back its investment during the life of the contract. Recently however, alliances are being entered into by the vendor and client which seem much more like *real* alliances. New entities are being formed which offer synergistic skills aimed at specific markets. Such a targeted focus offers the possibility of real gain which was lacking in previous alliance or partnership deals.

Equity holding deals

Concomitant with the growth in alliances and partnerships has been the emergence of a number of large equity-holding deals. These include:

vendors taking some stake in outsourcing client; clients taking some stake in the outsourcing vendor; and, as noted above, both parties taking stake in the formation of a new entity. Swiss Bank, for example, signed a twenty-five-year outsourcing deal with Perot Systems worth $6.25 billion. In so doing, they also took a 24.9 per cent equity holding in Perot Systems. Perot, in turn, took a 40 per cent stake in the Swiss Bank-initiated venture Systor AG. In Australia, Lend Lease outsourced all its information systems to ISSC but took a 35 per cent holding in ISSC Australia. Similarly, Telstra (Australia's telecommunications company) is negotiating to outsource its IS to ISSC which in turn would outsource its network operations and management to Telestra. Additionally, Telstra would take a 26 per cent stake in ISSC. In Canada, Bell Canada and IBM Canada are reportedly negotiating a similar kind of deal. Rumours of analogous deals in the USA and around the globe abound. Of course the real question is: will such equity-holding and alliance deals prove successful? And while it is too early to pass judgement on such arrangements, the trend is very clear. Future research will need to be done to see if the new wave of outsourcing arrangements and deals offers value to both the vendor and client which was not present in earlier outsourcing deals.

Conclusion

The interest in IS sourcing is growing and changing. The increasing numbers of vendors and services available in the market place provide more opportunities, but also complicate the decision-making, contracting, and management issues. As the market evolves and long-term contracts mature, our learning about IS sourcing and the implications for sound practices will also evolve. There are many opportunities for further research in the area. However, our research found that practitioners must first address some very significant challenges before even considering market offerings. These challenges include:

1. aligning stakeholder expectations for the IS portfolio;
2. understanding the current and future business contribution of the IS portfolio;
3. properly assessing the underlying cost drivers for the IS portfolio.

On point 1, we have merely diagnosed the problem but have concerns over the adopted *solution*. In our case studies, alignment was achieved, but always to the cost minimisation agenda. This inhibits the potential of IS to contribute significantly to competitive advantage.

On point 2, we diagnosed that IS was not perceived as contributing much, but we believe this is because IS's contribution is masked. In our cases, IS was accounted for as an overhead which highlighted only costs, not value. We talked to IS managers who noted that the user departments receive the credit for the benefits of technology, while IS gets blamed for the costs. For example, a silicon manufacturer implemented a worldwide client/server system that reduced order-processing from three weeks to four hours. The credit for the system went to the business unit, while IS was credited only with the costs of the system. Several factors that seem correlated with demonstrated value are the IS accounting structure, reporting level of the IS manager, use of IS to support corporate strategies, top management support, and some measures (however pitiful) of effectiveness (particularly evaluations coming from benchmarking against other companies) (Applegate and Elam, 1992; Feeny et al., 1992; Jarvenpaa and Ives, 1991). The identification of these factors, however, provides few insights into *how* IS managers can politically and economically enact these policies. The problem is essentially one of the chicken and the egg: does demonstrated value come before or after top management support?

We have perhaps shed the most light on point 3. Customers must question how vendors propose to deliver a given IS activity at their bid price. The best way is through an analysis of cost drivers. What cost advantages does a vendor have that cannot be replicated in-house? We strongly believe that practitioners can only outsource, i.e. turn over the management and delivery to a vendor, when they understand exactly what they want and can articulate those expectations in a detailed contract. For IS activities characterised by a high degree of certainty, vendor expertise can be brought in to transfer knowledge. Or perhaps the new forms of alliances, ones with contractually shared risks and rewards, will prove effective.

References

Ambrosio, J. (1991), 'Outsourcing at Southland: Best of Times, Worst of Times', *Computerworld*, 25, 12 (25 Mar.): 61.

Anthes, G. (1990), 'HUD Set to Outsource IS', *Computerworld*, 24, 49 (3 Dec.): 1, 119.

—— (1991), 'Perot Wins 10-Year Outsourcing Deal', *Computerworld*, 25, 14 (8 Apr.): 96.

Applegate, L., and Elam, J. (1992), 'New Information Systems Leaders: A Changing Role in a Changing World', *MIS Quarterly*, 16, 4 (Dec.): 469–90.

—— and Montealegre, R. (1991), 'Eastman Kodak Organisation: Managing Information Systems through Strategic Alliances', Harvard Business School Case 9-192-030, Boston.

Brown, B., and Eckerson, W. (1990), 'Kodak Turns Nets over to IBM and DEC; Farming out Net Operations Can Trigger Staffing Issues', *Network World*, 7, 3 (15 Jan.): 1, 4, 61, 63.

Caldwell, B. (1994), 'Special Counsel: Outsourcing Lawyers can Help Corporate Clients Avoid Nasty Pitfalls when Signing Billion-Dollar Deals', *InformationWeek*, 499 (31 Oct.).

—— (1995), 'Outsourcing Megadeals: More than 60 Huge Contracts Signed since 1989 Prove they Work', *Information Week*, 552 (6 Nov.).

Clark, T., Zmud, R., and McCray, G. (1995), 'The Outsourcing of Information Services: Transforming the Nature of Business in the Information Industry', *Journal of Information Technology*, 10, 4: 221–37.

DiMaggio, P., and Powell, W. (1983), 'The Iron Cage Revisited: Institutional Isomorphism and Collective Rationality in Organisational Fields', *American Sociological Review*, 48: 147–60.

Dorn, P. (1989), 'Selling One's Birth Right', *Information Week*, 241 (16 Oct.): 52.

Feeny, D., Edwards, B., and Simpson, K. (1992), 'Understanding the CEO/CIO Relationship', *MIS Quarterly*, 16, 4 (Dec.): 435–48.

—— Willcocks, L., Rands, T., and Fitzgerald, G. (1993), 'Strategies for IT Management: When Outsourcing Equals Rightsourcing', in S. Rock (ed.), *Director's Guide to Outsourcing IT* (London, Institute of Directors, IBM).

Gantz, J. (1994), 'Outsourcing: The Scam May Be on You', *Computerworld*, 28, 16 (18 Apr.): 41.

Gardner, E. (1991), 'Going on-line with Outsiders', *Modern Healthcare*, 15 July: 35–47.

Gillin, P. (1990), 'EDS Rides Outsourcing to Riches', *Computerworld*, 24, 42 (15 Oct.): 113–17.

Halvey, J. (1994), 'No Longer a Last Resort: Companies Used to Consider Outsourcing Only When they were in Financial Straits. But no more', *Information Week*, 486 (1 Aug.).

Hamilton, R. (1989), 'Kendall Outsources IS Chief', *Computerworld*, 23, 46 (13 Nov.): 1, 4.

Hammersmith, A. (1989), 'Slaying the IS Dragon with Outsourcery', *Computerworld*, 23, 38 (18 Sept.): 89–93.

Henderson, J. (1990), 'Plugging into Strategic Partnerships: The Critical IS Connection', *Sloan Management Review*, Spring: 7–18.

Hovey, V. (1991), Presentation to the University of Houston's Information Systems Research Center, 22 Jan. 1991.

Huber, R. (1993), 'How Continental Bank Outsourced its Crown Jewels', *Harvard Business Review*, 71, 1 (Jan.–Feb.): 121–9.

I/S Analyzer (1993), 'New Wrinkles in Outsourcing', 31, 9 (New York): 1–8.

Jarvenpaa, S., and Ives, B. (1991), 'Executive Involvement and Participation in the Management of Information Technology', *MIS Quarterly*, 15, 2: 205–27.

Kanter, R. (1994), 'Collaborative Advantage: The Art of Alliances', *Harvard Business Review*, July–Aug.: 96–108.

Kass, E. (1990), 'EDS Shifts to the Fast Lane', *Information Week*, 268 (30 Apr.): 30–4.

—— and Caldwell (1990), 'Outsource Ins and Outs', *Information Week*, 260 (5 Mar.): 14.

Kelleher, J. (1990), 'The Dollars and Sense of Outsourcing: Sometimes a Great Notion', *Computerworld*, 24, 2 (8 Jan.): 76–7.

Kotter, J. (1995), 'Why Transformation Efforts Fail', *Harvard Business Review*, Mar.–Apr.: 59–67.

Krass, P. (1990), 'The Dollars and Sense of Outsourcing', *Information Week*, 259 (26 Feb.): 26–31.

Lacity, M., and Hirschheim, R. (1993*a*), 'The Information Systems Outsourcing Bandwagon: Look Before You Leap', *Sloan Management Review*, 35, 1 (Fall): 72–86.

—— —— (1993*b*), *Information Systems Outsourcing: Myths, Metaphors and Realities* (Chichester, Wiley).

—— and Willcocks, L. (1996), 'An Empirical Investigation of Information Systems Outsourcing: Findings from Experience', Oxford University working paper.

—— —— and Feeny, D. (1995), 'Information Technology Outsourcing: Maximizing Flexibility and Control', *Harvard Business Review* (May–June): 84–93.

—— —— —— (1996), 'The Value of Selective IT Sourcing', *Sloan Management Review*, 37, 3 (Spring): 13–25.

Loh, L., and Venkatraman, N. (1992*a*), 'Determinants of Information Technology Outsourcing: A Cross Sectional Analysis', *Journal of Management Information Systems*, 9, 1: 7–24.

—— —— (1992*b*), 'Stock Market Reaction to IT Outsourcing: An Event Study', Sloan School of Management, Massachusetts Institute of Technology, Working Paper.

—— —— (1992*c*), 'Diffusion of Information Technology Outsourcing: Influence Sources and the Kodak Effect', *Information Systems Research*: 334–58.

McFarlan, F. W., and Nolan, R. (1995), 'How to Manage an IT Outsourcing Alliance', *Sloan Management Review*, 36, 2 (Winter): 9–23.

Millar, V. (1994), 'Outsourcing Trends', paper presented at the Outsourcing, Co-sourcing and Insourcing Conference, University of California, Berkeley, 4 Nov.

Morse, P. (1990), 'Big Business in Outsourcing', *Computer Data*, 15, 1 (Jan.): 23.

O'Leary, M. (1990), 'The Mainframe Doesn't Work Here Anymore', *CIO* 6, 6 (June): 27–35.

Oltman, J. (1990), '21st Century Outsourcing', *Computerworld*, 24, 16 (16 Apr.): 77–9.

Palvia, P. (1995), 'A Dialectic View of Information Systems Outsourcing: Pros and Cons', *Information and Management*, 29: 265–75.

Peak, D. (1994), 'The Risks and Effects of IS Outsourcing on the Information Systems Function and the Firm', Ph.D. thesis, University of North Texas, Denton.

Pfeffer, J. (1981), *Power in Organisations* (Marshfield, Mass., Pitman Publishing).

—— (1992), *Managing with Power* (Boston, Harvard Business School Press).

Quinn, J., Doorley, T., and Paquette, P. (1990), 'Technology in Services: Rethinking Strategic Focus', *Sloan Management Review*, 31, 2 (Winter): 79–87.

Radding, A. (1990), 'The Ride is no Bargain if you can't Steer', *Computerworld*, 24, 2 (8 Jan.): 67, 70–2.

Rochester, J., and Douglas, D. (1990) (eds.), 'Taking an Objective Look at Outsourcing', *I/S Analyzer*, 28, 8 (Sept.): 1–16.

Strassman, P. (1995), *The Politics of Information Management* (New Canaan, Conn.: Information Economics Press).

Ward, B. (1991), Hiring Out: Outsourcing is the New Buzzword in the Management of Information Systems', *Sky Magazine*, 20, 8 (Aug.): 37–45.

Willcocks, L. (1994), 'Collaborating to Compete: Towards Strategic Partnerships in IT Outsourcing', Oxford Institute of Information Management working paper series, RDP94/11.

—— (1995), 'A Source of Collaboration', *Best Practice*, Mar.: 31–7.

Willcocks, L., and Fitzgerald, G. (1994), *A Business Guide to Outsourcing Information Technology* (London, Business Intelligence).

Williamson, O. (1975), *Markets and Hierarchies: Analysis and Antitrust Implications. A Study in the Economics of Internal Organisation* (New York: The Free Press).

—— (1979), 'Transaction Cost Economics: The Governance of Contractual Relations', *Journal of Law and Economics*, 22, 2 (Oct.) 233–61.

—— (1991), 'Strategizing, Economizing, and Economic Organisation', *Strategic Management Journal*, 12 (Winter): 75–94.

—— (1994), 'Efficiency, Power, Authority, and Economic Organisation', paper presented at 'The Conference of Transaction Cost Economics and beyond', Erasmus University, Rotterdam, June.

—— and Ouchi, W. (1981), 'Markets and Hierarchies: Origins, Implications, Perspectives', in A. Van de Ven and W. Joyce (eds.), *Perspectives in Organisational Design and Behavior* (Chichester, John Wiley & Sons).

15

Information Systems and Strategic Change
A Critical Review of Business Process Re-engineering

BOB GALLIERS AND JACKY SWAN

To every complex question there is a simple answer—and it's always wrong.

(H. L. Mencken, quoted in Sauer, 1993: 315)

Introduction

BPR (Davenport and Short, 1990; Hammer, 1990) has become big business. The market for BPR services is estimated to be $51bn in 1995 (Davenport, 1996). Senior executives indicate that BPR is one of the most vital issues they face in the late 1990s (Galliers et al., 1994; Brancheau et al., 1996; Watson et al., 1997), and interest is still keen. This is despite the failures arising from its narrow, IT focus (Watts, 1993); despite the criticisms (Mumford, 1994, 1996; Land, 1996); and despite the warnings from one of its founders that the original concept was flawed (Davenport, 1996).

This chapter focuses on BPR because it is but one example of the various fads that have been taken on board with apparent alacrity by the IS community over recent years. We might have focused on IS outsourcing (Lacity and Hirschheim, 1993), on IS for competitive advantage (e.g. Ives and Learmonth, 1984; McFarlan, 1984; Porter and Millar, 1984), on the chief information officer (Synott, 1987) or hybrid manager (Earl and Skyrme, 1992) concepts, or, going further back in time, on decision support systems (DSS) (Keen and Scott Morton, 1978) or database as a means of delivering executive information (Martin, 1982). Each has enjoyed a period of considerable interest, and each has often been heralded as *the* answer to the gaining of strategic advantage from information technology (IT). We might expect to see, and already are seeing in fact, similar attention lavished on electronic data interchange (EDI) and, more recently, on the Internet and the World Wide Web—on electronic commerce—as we approach the millennium (Holland et al., 1992, 1994; Mukhopadhyay et al., 1995).

Clearly, in a field like IS, there are bound to be rapid changes in the way we view IT's role and the manner in which we approach the management of IS—and the IS topic itself for that matter. IS is a young discipline; developments in IT are occurring at an incredible speed. In this sense, fads might be expected to come with the territory. What is worrying, though, is the IS community's apparent predisposition to accept new ideas as *the* solution, no matter how untested or poorly architected they might be. Certainly, there appears to be a tendency to accept many new ideas without due consideration and evaluation. What is more, there appears to be a propensity in IS to dismiss as outmoded or irrelevant what we might already know about an issue, often learnt at some considerable cost, in both human and financial terms, simply because it is seen as being passé. Thus, in IS there has been a tendency to reject ideas that may be demonstrably technically efficient and to accept more readily new, untested and possibly inefficient ideas (Abrahamson, 1991).

The paradox is that in seeking to be modern, innovative, and forward thinking, there is a danger that IS is brought into disrepute and is seen as being unable to deliver promised solutions, because key lessons have not been retained and applied (Galliers, 1992). As we shall see as the chapter unfolds, BPR is a case in point. The idea here is not to dismiss BPR out of hand, but to show that the lessons drawn from relevant literatures can be helpful in avoiding the problems that have already been encountered in implementing organisational change and in developing more robust models of the change process. This chapter seeks to draw from research in the fields of information systems (IS) implementation and failure and organisational innovation to construct a critique of business process re-engineering (BPR). This is done in order to understand and illustrate the role for information systems in strategic change.

The chapter is structured as follows. We start with a brief introduction to BPR, identifying its key characteristics and objectives, as well as the major arguments that have been raised—both pro and con. This is followed by a review of the key lessons that can be drawn from the organisational literature on innovation and innovation diffusion, and from the IS implementation literature with reference to the IS failures literature (see also Chapter 12). As a result of these reviews, we identify a number of convergent issues from these literatures and relate these back to BPR. The final section attempts to identify the key lessons that emerge—for BPR, IS implementation, and technological and organisational innovation. We conclude by drawing broader implications from our analysis for the role of IS in strategic change.

The Focus on BPR

Business process re-engineering (BPR) has been hailed as the latest break-through in programmed organisational change and change management. Aimed at radical, rather than incremental improvement, BPR uses IT and tools such as TQM and JIT to enable the analysis, redesign, and improvement of operational effectiveness along the entire supply chain with particular emphasis on customer satisfaction, competitive advantage, and cost reduction (Hammer, 1990; Hammer and Champy, 1993). In its various guises, BPR essentially represents a planned, rational, and phased approach to the management of organisational change encompassing, for example: *discovery*—where the organisation is audited, key processes identified, and potential and scope for re-engineering is planned; *redesign*—where the core processes to be changed are examined in more detail and change management goals, issues, and potential problems are identified; and *realisation*—where the change programme is implemented and communicated and the organisation is transformed from top to bottom in line with identified improvement goals. Thus BPR has synergies with TQM and other planned change approaches except that BPR is purported to be a more radical and holistic solution requiring current organisational structures and practices to be dismantled and rebuilt into a process-oriented business.

Despite the failures alluded to above, claims of BPR successes abound and BPR has been widely disseminated and credited across academic and business communities alike.[1] However, opinions about both the newness and success of BPR appear to be extremely polarised. The opposing pole sees BPR as the latest in a long line of management fads. At best BPR is seen as little different, in terms of its underlying principles and methodologies, from other long-established and well-researched and recognised approaches to organisational redesign. Mumford (1994: 316), for example, argues that BPR is similar in terms of procedures to socio-technical redesign: 'Today BPR is being hailed as an entirely new approach to efficiency improvement. However, it is difficult to see how it differs from socio-technical design.' Similarly Passmore (1994) suggests that BPR incorporates many of the essential ingredients of socio-technical approaches including attention to the horizontal integration of technical processes and the emphasis on multifunctional and empowered work teams. At worst BPR has been deemed to be potentially disruptive or even doomed to failure. Mumford (1994), for example, suggests that BPR is impoverished relative to socio-technical design both because it has a weaker theoretical and methodological foundation, and because it de-emphasises the value of the social system in favour of the technical system and competitive advantage.

---

[1] See, for example, *Knowledge and Process Management: The Journal of Corporate Transformation*, incorporating *Business Change and Re-engineering*, vols. 1–4 (1994–7), published by Wiley.

Egan (1995) takes a stronger standpoint arguing, from the broader perspective of strategic management, that BPR offers nothing new, nothing tangible, nothing strategic, and nothing demonstrable in terms of sustainable advantage. 'Organisations are far more likely to "muddle through", to adapt incrementally rather than "reinvent" themselves' (1995: 111).

Despite these criticisms, one of the major successes of BPR has been its rapid and widespread diffusion among communities of industrialists and academics both within and across nations. The disillusionment felt by some advocates of socio-technical systems approaches in terms of the apparent lack of enthusiasm for these approaches by management (Passmore, 1994) has yet to be felt by proponents of BPR. Perhaps ultimately BPR will be deemed yet another management fad or new fashion (Jackson, 1995). However, even if this is the case, management fads and fashions are also worthy of investigation and conceptualisation. Fads and fashions do not necessarily harm organisations but may offer advantages as powerful symbols for efficiency and legitimacy (Abrahamson, 1991). For example, companies that claim to be 're-engineering' can potentially gain an image of innovativeness that may help them to attract customers (Nystrom and Starbuck, 1981). Even if fads or fashions are technically inefficient, they may still act as mechanisms for change and organisational action by allowing companies to label, attend to, interpret, and make sense of complex and uncertain problems and from this process appropriate solutions could be iterated. 'Fads and fashions may constitute vital processes that animate random variations from which increasingly efficient innovations can evolve' (Abrahamson, 1991: 609; see also Anderson and Tushman, 1991).

The purpose of this chapter, then, is not to repeat or to resolve ongoing debates about the relative competitive advantages and/or novelty of BPR approaches. These debates are covered very well elsewhere (see, for example, Sauer, Yetton, and Associates, 1997), nor will we focus on the tools, techniques, and methodologies of BPR (Kettinger et al., 1997). Rather, the aim is to offer new insights into BPR by drawing upon a range of theoretical perspectives encompassed by the literatures on organisational and technological innovation and on IS implementation and failure, in particular focusing on issues relevant to adoptions and implementation of BPR. These literatures are characteristically highly fragmented and individual phenomena tend to be understood from particular narrow theoretical perspectives. While Rogers (1992) warns of the problems of granularity in using different literatures interchangeably, thinking about a single 'innovation'—in this case, BPR—from a range of rather different theoretical perspectives widens the scope of enquiry and pools the lessons derived from research that spans disciplines and methodologies. This may help to extend the depth and breadth of understanding of the adoption, implementation, and likely outcomes of the innovation process with BPR as the focus.

IS Implementation . . . and IS Failure: Organisational Innovation and IS Implementation Perspectives

In this section an attempt is made to bring together the various strands of research from the organisational innovation and the IS implementation and failures literatures. As argued above, these literatures tend to be highly fragmented,[2] although notable exceptions include Kwon and Zmud (1987) and Swanson (1994). An attempt is made here to synthesise the issues raised in the literatures with a view to highlighting the implications for BPR and IS and strategic change.

Organisational innovation

The study of organisational innovation has attracted a wide following from researchers across a range of disciplinary perspectives. However, despite the abundance of research on innovation, there have been few consistent findings regarding the causes, consequences, or management of the innovation process: 'the results of innovation research have been inconclusive, inconsistent, and characterised by low levels of explanation' (Wolfe, 1994). Wolfe and others argue that this apparent lack of consistency in the organisational innovation literature is due in large part to the complex, contextually embedded nature of the innovation process. Because of this complexity researchers tend to focus on different aspects of the innovation process (e.g. diffusion, design, adoption, implementation) and use different methodologies. This body of research tackles different types of innovation process, at different points in time, and across a range of organisations in different industries at different stages of their development and is therefore highly unlikely to produce consistent findings. Thus reviewers argue that 'there can be no one theory of innovation, as the more we learn the more we realise that the "whole" remains beyond our grasp' (1994: 406). However, all is not lost because particular theoretical perspectives may offer useful insights into particular aspects of the innovation process. The development and use of BPR, as with other types

---

[2] An example of this fragmentation is Wolfe (1994). While providing a comprehensive treatment of the innovation literature, Wolfe fails to cite *any* of the IS implementation literature, let alone that which explicitly attempts to unify the two literatures (e.g. Kwon and Zmud, 1987).

of innovation, has entailed a time-phased and iterative process in which the concepts and languages have been generated, communicated, adopted, and implemented by firms across a range of industries. Different theoretical perspectives may help in the analysis and understanding of particular points in this process.

Recent reviews identify discernible streams in the literature on organisational innovation (Wolfe, 1994; Slappendel, 1996). For example, Wolfe (1994) identifies three streams of research as: *diffusion of innovation; organisational innovativeness*; and *process theory research.* The first, innovation diffusion, focuses on understanding the communication, spread, and adoption of new ideas through social communities. Diffusion research therefore offers potentially useful insights into the reasons surrounding the widespread uptake of new ideas such as BPR by communities of firms. However, it remains largely silent on the implementation of such ideas at firm level and concurrent problems surrounding implementation.

Organisational innovativeness research focuses on understanding the factors or variables that make some organisations more likely to develop innovations than others. These studies identify factors, both at the level of the organisation (e.g. firm size, firm strategy) and the individual (e.g. personality characteristics; cognitive styles), that predict the development and implementation of innovation in firms (e.g. as measured by dependent variables such as rates of adoption of new technologies or R&D expenditure). These perspectives offer useful insights into the complex array of micro- and macro-level variables that potentially influence innovation. However such approaches fail fully to address the complex interactions between individual and organisational variables and the ways in which processes of innovation are socially shaped and constructed (Slappendel, 1996). Process theory research seeks to fill these gaps by analysing and understanding the processes (cognitive, social, and political) through which new ideas are developed, designed, and implemented within firms (Wolfe, 1994; Slappendel, 1996). These streams are neither tightly bounded nor mutually exclusive. Some studies of innovation, for example Rogers's (1962, 1987) work on innovation diffusion (see below), have properties that fall across streams. However, distinguishing different streams of research offers a useful structure for an analysis of particular innovation processes such as BPR.

IS implementation

Similarly, while it may be argued that there is no general agreement in the IS literature regarding a comprehensive framework for IS implementation (Myers, 1994), there is a long tradition of research in this area which is relevant to a consideration of IS/IT and strategic change. An early work in the IS development literature which focuses particular attention on the significance of implementation issues in the successful take-up of IS was written by Hank Lucas (Lucas, 1981)[3] and this has had considerable influence on both the IS implementation and IS failures fields (cf. Sauer, 1993). Its emphasis on the organisational as opposed to technical issues in IS implementation, while apparently fairly obvious in the latter half of the 1990s, was, with hindsight, a landmark feature of work published in the early 1980s—a feature which did not receive immediate or universal recognition by the IS community at the time.

Myers (1994), after Lucas (1981), identifies two dominant themes in IS implementation research, namely what he calls *factor research* and *process research*. The former is normally an investigation into those factors that lead to successful innovation (however interpreted), while the latter argues that it is the process of innovation itself, of which implementation is a crucial part, that really matters. These themes parallel, respectively, the organisational innovativeness and process theory research streams identified in the organisational innovation literature. This suggests some convergence across disparate academic disciplines on what are identified as central issues in innovation.

Kwon and Zmud (1987) echo Myers's argument but, in addition, identify three additional streams: *mutual understanding* research which focuses on designer–user interaction (cf. Churchman and Schainblatt, 1965; Boland, 1978; Ginzberg, 1981; Ives and Olson, 1984); the *political stream* that looks into the different motives of multiple stakeholders in implementing IS (cf. Kramer, 1981; Markus, 1983); and a *prescriptive stream* that includes generic risk factors requiring to be taken into account in implementation projects (cf. Alter and Ginzberg, 1978; Keen, 1981; McFarlan, 1981). These similarly address processes of implementation as well as factors that influence these processes, with the level of analysis being the firm. What is particularly helpful about Kwon and Zmud's (1987) work in the context of this chapter, however, is the use they make of both the IS implementation and innovation literatures. It is for this reason that we make reference to their analysis in the sections that follow.

Research on IS implementation and organisational innovation appears then to converge at least to some extent. That is they both identify three broad areas for analysis of innovation: diffusion research, factor research, and process research. What follows is an attempt to draw from these three areas of analysis a more critical understanding of BPR, synthesising lessons learned from both IS implementation and organisational innovation literatures.

---

[3] Following earlier work on information systems failures (Lucas, 1975).

IS Adoption: Diffusion Perspectives and BPR

Diffusion research has been aimed at developing a better understanding of the dissemination of new ideas through communities of potential adopters who may then make the decision to adopt the idea. Sociological and organisational perspectives on diffusion have been dominated by the work of Everett Rogers who developed a supply-focused framework premissed on assumptions about best practice (e.g. Rogers, 1962, 1983). The focus of diffusion perspectives is on developing models that will enable central supply agencies to promote more rapid diffusion of best practice innovations to communities of potential adopters. Innovation tends to be defined as a new form of 'best practice' with fixed parameters that, if adopted, will improve the efficiency or effectiveness of any organisation. Thus innovation is treated as a fixed entity or 'thing' to be diffused (i.e. a noun) rather than as a process (i.e. a verb). Since there is a (single) definable best practice, success is measured by the rate at which potential users adopt a particular innovation.

Diffusion research has contributed to understanding about factors that predict the rate of adoption of innovation over time and space. Central factors concerned with the rate and extent of adoption have been highlighted as (i) characteristics of the innovation, such as its complexity, relative advantage, trialability, compatibility (Rogers, 1983); (ii) characteristics of potential adopters so that those who are likely to be early adopters can be targeted in the initial diffusion process by central supply agencies, and (iii) social networks that enable the ideas to be communicated within and across communities of organisations (Wolfe, 1994). An important point here then is that it is crucial to understand the attributes of the new idea in order to understand its diffusion and development across organisations (Wolfe, 1994). This concurs with research on technological and organisational innovation which identifies attributes such as radical versus incremental; altering versus entrenching (Clark and Staunton, 1989); informating versus automating (Zuboff, 1988); and technical versus administrative (Damanpour, 1987) as important mediators of the innovation process.

Using these types of categorisations, BPR is perhaps best categorised as a complex, possibly advantageous, certainly incompatible, not easily observable or trialable, altering innovation involving major or radical technical and administrative change. Given that BPR has many of the characteristics that might be expected to retard its diffusion, however, how can the apparently rapid diffusion of BPR among communities of firms and academics alike be explained? Why are firms persuaded to adopt BPR when it appears to be inherently problematic? Part of the explanation lies in the fact that these are perceived characteristics and are therefore shaped by cognitive, social, and political processes. BPR, like many other technical and administrative technologies, is best represented as a complex, multifaceted bundle of ideas which can be embedded in a variety of ways including technical artefacts; organisational routines; languages; symbols (the three-letter acronym is probably a powerful symbol); equipment; decision-making structures, and so forth (Clark and Staunton, 1989). The attributes of technologies such as BPR are able to be unpacked and selectively communicated by those who have a vested interest in promoting their adoption. For example, research investigating suppliers of complex computeraided production management systems (CAPM; such as manufacturing resources planning—MRP2) found that IS suppliers presented highly simplified and codified visions of such systems, emphasising technical advantages and artefacts and downplaying the degree of organisational change that was often needed to implement such systems (Clark and Staunton, 1989). This served the suppliers' interests in selling the systems, that is in adoption rather than in implementation. Users, seduced by the idea of a technical fix, often adopted these technologies with very little real understanding about their complexity, with a resultant high level of failure (Swan and Clark, 1992; Wilson et al., 1994).

The diffusion literature has been criticised for its emphasis on adoption and its assumptions about best practice (Clark, 1987). As the many failures of BPR attest, innovation clearly does not stop at adoption. The literature is littered with cases in which organisations have adopted new ideas or technologies and have failed to implement them. Therefore the focus on adoption, whilst appropriate for a model aimed at informing technology suppliers, is at best misplaced or at worst downright dangerous as far as the adopters of innovation (i.e. the users) are concerned. The assumption that there is a single technically efficient best practice is rarely the case. In many cases of innovation, users are faced with a bewildering array of choices about the design and implementation of technologies and approach these choices with selective information about the attributes of particular technologies. Again, this can be seen clearly in research on CAPM. Users needed to be able to appropriate new technologies—that is they needed to unpack and reconfigure technologies alongside existing organisational and technical systems in order to develop firm-specific solutions (Newell et al., 1993). Supplier-focused models are problematic from the perspective of users. This is because suppliers are mainly interested in adoption whereas users are mainly interested in implementation and appropriation of new ideas. It is in suppliers' interests to disseminate notions of 'best' practice (therefore you must adopt it to survive), whereas it is in users' interests to design and customise new ideas so that they work within their own organisation.

The different political interests of stakeholders in the diffusion process which tend to be neglected in diffusion research are recognised by more recent perspectives on the diffusion of fads and fashions (Abrahamson, 1991, 1996). This recognises that new ideas, such as BPR, generate important market opportunities for a range of suppliers. For example, BPR may be favourably promoted by IT vendors because they emphasise the notion of IT-led change, by management consultants because they emphasise the notion of facilitating the change process, and by academics in IS/IT fields because IS is central to the study of and critique of BPR. The notion of a definable best practice that organisations must adopt to remain competitive is seen clearly in the heavily prescriptive language of many of the original proponents of BPR. '*Don't* automate, obliterate' was the message (Hammer, 1990). 'Existing approaches to meeting customer needs are so functionally based that incremental change will *never* yield the requisite interdependence' (Davenport, 1993: 4). Using IT for competitive advantage was pronounced as *the* best route towards achieving competitive advantage: 'IT for process innovation is a virtual *necessity*' (1993: 5). Whilst acknowledging potential pains involved in its implementation, BPR has nonetheless been hailed as *the* hottest trend in management. Done well re-engineering delivers extraordinary gains in speed, productivity, and profitability. BPR claims, however, to be more than just another fashionable idea. As Grey (1994) notes in a critique of BPR, 'it also aspires, according to its classic exegesis, to be a revolutionary creed' and 'like most creeds, BPR is proselytising: it "must be done"' (Grey, 1994: 1). The main thrust from the supply side (including consultants, IT suppliers, and some academics), then, has been on getting organisations to buy into the revolutionary vision and to recognise the strategic opportunities created by BPR. The result of this revolutionary fervour is a strong focus on adoption and a relative neglect of issues surrounding the implementation of BPR or its appropriateness in particular contexts (Galliers, 1995).

The diffusion literature has made a crucial contribution in emphasising the importance of social networks within and across organisations that enable new ideas to be communicated. Rogers's (1983) work focuses mostly on the communication network that is formed between central supply agencies and the population of potential adopters. Other research has highlighted the importance of a wide variety of other types of interorganisational network in the diffusion process (e.g. Alter and Hage, 1993; Robertson et al., 1996). For example, Robertson et al. found that information about CAPM was shaped by the social network created by a professional association. Practitioners in manufacturing industry frequently used information gained through their involvement in professional associations to help them to understand and design CAPM solutions. Further, information gained in this way was perceived by practitioners as more complete and less partial than that gleaned directly from IT suppliers. In other words, the information diffused through professional associations was credited with higher status in terms of quality and reliability relative to other sources of information (see also Swan et al., 1996). However, it was also notable in this case that the information disseminated through the formal communication channels of the professional association (e.g. its conferences and journals) was heavily shaped by an active minority of IT suppliers and consultants who penetrated such networks and who wrote or presented much of the formal material. Thus the professional association network reinforced supply-led notions of best practice.

Professional groups are likely to diffuse innovations that increase the power or status of their members (Drazin, 1990). For example, Newell et al. (1993) found that, in the UK in the late 1980s, the major production control association was heavily involved in disseminating information about MRP2 systems, which relied centrally on production management expertise, as the best practice technology for logistics. During the same period, the main purchasing association prioritised just-in-time approaches for managing logistics, which relied on purchasing expertise. BPR is an approach which explicitly sets out to destroy traditional boundaries between functional groupings and therefore threatens knowledge domains which are protected by professional specialists within these groupings. The professional group most likely to gain from BPR is that formed by IS professionals, given BPR's advocacy of IT as the main enabler of change. Therefore it is not surprising that IS professionals have been key agencies in the diffusion of BPR.

The diffusion literature usefully highlights the importance of both strong and weak ties for diffusion of new ideas (Granovetter, 1973; Rogers, 1983). Strong ties are close associations among firms, for example, contractual links between a firm and its customers or suppliers or between a firm and an IT supplier. These will promote rapid diffusion of ideas among organisations within a particular community. An illustration is the strong ties among UK firms in the banking sector being a possible explanation why BPR has been so widely diffused in this sector (Grey, 1994). Whilst strong ties may promote rapid diffusion, they may also constrain the *invention* of new ideas because organisations in the same community tend to encounter the same kinds of ideas. On a related point, Di Maggio and Powell (1990) suggest that, when many strong ties exist among organisations in a particular field, processes of 'isomorphism' can lead organisations to become more similar to one another. For example, an organisation may adopt ideas that are accepted as norms of best practice in order to gain legitimacy in their particular field, regardless of whether or not they are the most appropriate ideas for that organisation. In this way technically inefficient ideas (fads or fashions) can be diffused (Abrahamson, 1991). Given that innovation is typically highly dependent on context, it is very unlikely that BPR could be efficient in all circumstances (and there is a growing literature that is questioning BPR as the panacea, as we have already pointed out). Despite this, firms might still adopt BPR in sectors where it is seen as an established best practice, especially where IT suppliers are active in promoting this.

Weak ties link individuals from organisations across different sectors or communities that would not normally make contact during their day-to-day business. These can be equally important in the diffusion process because, through weak ties, organisations can encounter ideas that are outside established modes of operating. For example, educational programmes and research allow weak ties to develop among academics and industrial practitioners; professional associations allow weak ties to develop among members who attend meetings and conferences (Robertson et al., 1996). Communications technologies such as electronic mail and the Internet could also play an important role in encouraging weak ties across a wide variety of individuals and organisations. IS professionals have been central agencies in the diffusion of BPR and are also likely (though not necessarily) to be active users of communications technologies. Through electronic mail, for example, there is an abundance of information about conferences and meetings at which BPR is a central theme. Therefore it is not surprising that information about BPR has spread so rapidly. In explaining the rapid diffusion of BPR, then, it is important to recognise the influence of a wide variety of networks of both strong and weak ties including networks formed by academics, technology suppliers and consultants, and IS professionals.

Diffusion perspectives offer an explanation of why it is that new ideas such as BPR can diffuse widely despite their efficiency being questionable. A problem with diffusion perspectives is that they tend to assume a broadcaster–receiver perspective on the communication of ideas where ideas are created centrally and broadcast to an audience of potential users. This under-emphasises the active role that users can play in constructing and reconstructing ideas encountered through diffusion networks. For example, Robertson et al. (1996) found that innovation was more successful where users actively and selectively unpacked and redesigned the prescriptive IT solutions marketed by suppliers. The diffusion literature, with its emphasis on the adoption of portable best practice technologies with fixed parameters, also under-emphasises problems users face in implementing solutions that solve their particular problems. In contrast, factor and process research on innovation takes more account of the importance of the organisational context surrounding the design and implementation of new technologies.

IS Implementation: Factor and Process Research

As indicated previously, we shall in this section attempt to synthesise something of the information systems implementation and organisational innovation literatures under the two headings proposed by Myers (1994) and Wolfe (1994), namely factor research and process research. In addition, mention will be made of the information systems failures literature (e.g. Lucas, 1975; Sauer, 1993; Poulymenakou and Holmes, 1996).

Factor research

Numerous attempts have been made to identify factors that predict greater or lesser success with IS implementation and with organisational change more broadly. These cover both micro individual level factors and more macro organisational and environmental factors (Slappendel, 1996). Kwon and Zmud draw from the IS implementation and diffusion of technological innovation literatures the following components as key to the implementation process: adoption behaviours; structural arrangements; technological issues; task-related factors; and environmental factors. *Adoption behaviours* such as receptivity to change are highly correlated to individual level factors such as job tenure (institutional legitimacy), educational background, and organisational role: the more gregarious and less parochial the stakeholders in the change process, the more they are open to external influences, outside contacts, and networking (Becker, 1970; Rogers and Shoemaker, 1971; Robertson et al., 1996), and the greater the likelihood of successful implementation. As regards organisational *structural arrangements*, both formal and informal structures have been found to influence the implementation of IS (Tichy, 1981). Kwon and Zmud (1987: 235), citing Steers (1977), summarise the research undertaken by organisational theorists in this area as identifying 'specialization (complexity and functional specialization), centralisation (concentration of decision making), and formalization (functional differentiation) as key factors for successful organisational change'. In terms of *technological issues*, Tornatzky and Klein (1982) identify an innovation's compatability to an adopting organisation, and the degree to which an innovation is seen to provide relative benefits, as positive influences on the adoption and implementation process. Conversely complexity and the degree of difficulty users experience in understanding and using an innovation have a negative impact (Kwon and Zmud, 1987). *Task-related factors*, such as uncertainty (March and Simon, 1958; Tushman and Nadler, 1978; Van de Ven and Ferry, 1980), can have both positive and negative effects on implementation. Uncertainty can motivate information search (Blandin and Brown, 1977; Culnan, 1983) for example, but may also be seen as a constraint to implementation (Thompson, 1967). As regards *environmental factors*, while 'studies of [their] influence on innovation processes are relatively rare ... assertions regarding [their] influence frequently appear' (Kwon and Zmud, 1987: 239). While the environment may be viewed as a source of information, another view is that it is a stock of resources (Aldrich, 1979; Scott, 1981).

Thus, we appear to have a considerable amount of research to draw upon when identifying implications regarding the process of strategic change involving IT. Despite this there are only a small set of factors that have been identified as having any consistent bearing on IS implementation 'success' or 'failure' and these are defined only in very broad terms (Wolfe, 1994). For example, 'critical success factors' or CSFs (Rockart, 1979) include: the need for a top management champion for the implementation effort; a relevant, good-quality design for the IS which is to be implemented; appropriate designer–user interaction during the IS implementation; and motivated, capable users (Kwon and Zmud, 1987).

Thus the simplistic prescriptive view of 'identifying what has to be done, then doing it' associated with the more crass writings on BPR (cf. the earlier quote from Hammer and Champy, 1993) is clearly inadequate. Issues associated with, *inter alia*, individual motivations and perceptions, organisational structures and group dynamics, the innovation's 'fit' (cf. Ein-Dor and Segev, 1981) with the organisation, and boundary spanning behaviours and opportunities—i.e. surrounding the more dynamic *process* of implementation—are all key. These conclusions parallel those arising from some of the, albeit sparse, literature on IS failures. For example, Oz (1992) in reviewing four typical forms of IS failure—namely: correspondence failure (objectives not having been met); process failure (such as cost and time overruns); interaction failure (between users and IS professionals), and expectation failure (cf. Lyytinen and Hirschheim, 1987)—concludes that successful implementations depend on:

- securing organisational and stakeholder commitment;
- involving prospective system users;
- ensuring managerial decision-making consensus; and
- outlining a realistic implementation timetable.

To this, Baker (1995) would add reinforcement mechanisms arising from periodic post-implementation reviews. Implementation is considered to be a crucial, transitional stage between IS development and operation: 'Implementation can be distinctly traumatic, for it is the time when flaws will make themselves felt and when operational user resistance may become apparent' (Sauer, 1993: 69). The tone of this sentence is enlightening. It is often the case that the IS literature will talk of 'user resistance' to the introduction of a new IT-based system. An underlying message has often been that the introduction of the new IS is perceived to be 'a good thing', and that resistance is irrational or unwarranted. This assumption is questioned in the *mutual understanding* research on the topic, in which the exchange and interpretation of information between designer and user is highlighted. Ives and Olson (1984) cite the desirability of designer–user interaction and the cognitive functioning of these two stakeholder groups as being the two most significant CSFs in this stream of research on the topic (Kwon and Zmud, 1987). A lighthearted article by Oliver and Langford (1984) highlights six common myths or (self-fulfilling) prophecies held about users by IS developers. The six 'myth-takes' are:

1. Users don't know what they want.
2. Users keep changing their minds.
3. Users want everything yesterday.
4. Users react emotionally and illogically.
5. Users are stupid.
6. Users resist change.

These may be seen as the negative platitudes associated with the topic of user resistance. Just as these are overly simplistic and potentially misleading, if taken at face value, so are the positive platitudes highlighted by Hirschheim and Newman (1988), such as 'build a prototype', 'involve users', enlist a sponsor', or 'create user-friendly interfaces' that are so common in the IS literature. As Hirschheim and Newman (1988: 406) point out: 'resistance is a complex phenomenon which defies simple explanation and analysis . . . only those development strategies which view such change in terms of social and political processes are likely to prove satisfactory.'

Clearly then—at the risk of being *prescriptive*—IS innovation/implementation may be eased when different perspectives are taken into account, and an IS solution to organisational problems is not assumed. Indeed, the argument is extended by those who focus on *political* dimensions, with the realisation that "Many motives can induce individuals to promote, engage in, or resist IS implementation efforts [with] many seemingly irrational or inconsistent implementation behaviours and outcomes [being] understood when all of the consequences of IS implementations on all stakeholders are considered" (Kwon and Zmud, 1987: 230).

Another aspect of the IS literature on implementation relates to the identification of the risks associated with IS innovations (Rainer et al., 1991; Tate, 1988; McGaughey et al., 1994).[4] For example, McGaughey et al. argue that significant risks may arise from external sources and, as a result of the implementation process, an appropriate implementation strategy depends on nature of that risk 'and other situational variables that influence the organisation's range of choices' (1994: 273). They identify four components of risk, namely threats, resources, modifying factors (that influence the probability of any threat), and consequences, and advocate the use of four primary methods of handling these aspects of risk. These are: *reduction* (i.e. taking action to eliminate or reduce the severity of a risk); *protection* (i.e. using physical means to achieve the same result as reduction);

---

[4] For a treatment of the subject of reducing risks in BPR, see Galliers (1997).

transfer (i.e. making arrangements for some other party to carry all or part of the risk), and *financing* (i.e. providing for the risk in the operating budget, e.g. via insurance). In doing so they point out that a distinction should be made between historical and new risks.

This analysis has clear implications for BPR, which has a tendency towards a single, profit-maximisation, objective (Galliers, 1997), and is often described in such terms as 're-engineering determines first *what* a company must do, then *how* to do it' (Hammer and Champy, 1993: 33). Implementation in BPR is thus relegated to little more than a set of simple steps and procedures (Craig and Yetton, 1997: 191). Different (dissident?) perspectives are not allowed. In Davenport's (1996) own words, it has become 'the fad that forgot people'. Thus, if we are to draw but one, single message from this analysis it is that the very *process* of implementation should be considered key, and it is to this aspect of the IS implementation literature that we shall now turn.

Process research

Innovation can be defined as 'the development and implementation of new ideas by people who over time engage in transactions with others within institutional context' (Van de Ven, 1986: 591). Defined in this way, innovation is seen not as an entity or thing to be implemented but as a context-specific process of invention, diffusion, adoption, and implementation. As long as the idea is seen as new by the people concerned (i.e. invented elsewhere) then the process can be defined as innovation (Zaltman et al., 1973). In the past, process theory research has been dominated by stage models, for example, with invention followed by diffusion followed by adoption, implementation, and usage (e.g. Rogers, 1983).[5] Such stage-model thinking fits comfortably with linear, rational assumptions about cause and effect sequences. Research on innovation, predicated on stage-model assumptions, has therefore tended to focus on particular aspects of the innovation process discretely. Diffusion research, for example, has focused more on diffusion and adoption of new ideas, and less on the process of implementation within organisations. In contrast, process research studies have looked more thoroughly at the processes involved in implementation of new ideas, and at factors that influence successful outcomes, and less so at their generation and diffusion (Wolfe, 1994).

More recently, stage models have been criticised as being inadequate explanations of all bar the most simple innovation processes (e.g. Clark and Staunton, 1989). Although stages have been demonstrated, the extent to which these occur in a predictable sequence is questionable (Wolfe,

---

[5] cf. Kwon and Zmud's (1987: 233) six-phase model: initiation; adoption; adaptation; acceptance; use; and incorporation.

1994). Clear stages appear to be confined to particular situations in which identifiable organisational populations are able to borrow ideas with easily definable parameters from external supply agencies (Ettlie, 1980). Researchers in the field of IS management will see strong parallels with the early 'stages of growth' models developed by Nolan (Gibson and Nolan, 1974; Nolan, 1979) and subsequent criticisms of a similar nature to those raised by Clark and Staunton (1989) and Wolfe (1994), for example, by King and Kraemer (1984) and Benbasat et al. (1984).

Refinements to the 'stages' concept have attempted to deal with criticisms with some degree of success (e.g. Galliers and Sutherland, 1991). However, in many cases stage models fail to explain adequately processes of innovation which are found to be complex, iterative, and circuitous, being both contextually embedded and socially shaped (Clark, 1987; Fleck, 1994). Thus, most often, the innovation process 'cannot be understood without careful attention to the personal, organisational, technological and environmental contexts within which it takes place' (Wolfe, 1994: 406). The outcomes of the innovation process are often unpredictable and emergent (Clark, 1987; Newell *et al.*, 1997; Slack and Hinings, 1995). This is particularly likely when the innovation process concerns the development of information technologies which, by definition, concern the interpretation and use of information by social actors in addition to physical or technical artefacts (Coombes et al., 1992). Typically IT innovations are not easily definable, not easily imitable, inter-subjective (depending on tacit as well as formalised knowledge), and heavily context-dependent. These characteristics apply equally to process innovations such as BPR.

Further, approaches such as BPR, which alter established technical and organisational practices, typically need to be appropriated by adopting organisations rather than simply being imitated (Clark, 1987[6]). Appropriation refers to the unpacking of supplied innovations and their reconfiguration to match the specific demands of the user's organisational and national context.[7] Case studies of innovation diffusion provide strong evidence that users introduce pivotal modifications that reshape the innovation as presented by the supply side (Clark, 1987; Fleck, 1987; Clark and Newell, 1993). Recent developments in process research in the organisational and sociological literature have therefore included the development of frameworks that allow a better understanding of complex innovation 'episodes' (rather than 'stages'), as they emerge and unfold over time (Wolfe, 1994). This research has been predicated on social constructivist theories and is aimed at understanding and identifying the social, cognitive, and political processes that mediate the articulation, construction, and outcomes of innovation episodes (e.g. Swan and Clark, 1992).

---

[6] Clark's distinction between altering and entrenching innovation processes has parallels with Zuboff's (1988) automating and informating technologies.

[7] cf. Kwon and Zmud's (1987) adaptation phase.

The notion that socio-cognitive processes, political interests, and conflict will inhibit successful IS implementation has been relatively uncommon in the IS literature (notable exceptions being Knights and Murray, 1992; Markus, 1983; Markus and Pfeffer, 1983), despite receiving considerable attention elsewhere (for example, in psychology and organisational behaviour—Swan and Clark, 1992; Hosking and Morley, 1992; Scarbrough and Corbett, 1992). In their case study research in a large financial transactions company, though, Levine and Rossmoore (1994) do investigate the power and politics associated with the implementation of a major IS. This study examined the power vacuum left by a senior executive in abrogating his authority and failing to delegate. This led to competition and confusion, wasted effort, and lack of progress. A key conclusion was that the privately held views and cognitive beliefs of key stakeholders are more salient and powerful than the publicly espoused goals of an organisation. The *prescriptive* element in this research was the implication that political considerations *must* be part of the diagnosis when considering the introduction of an IS.

Political processes also feature in Cooper's (1994) research on change inhibitors in IS projects. Specifically, resistance to IS implementation is seen to arise as a result of any realignment of status, power, and working habits, or any violation of a group's shared values and meanings. Citing Hirschheim and Newman (1988), Cooper identifies the following factors as contributors to failed implementation efforts: uncertainty over jobs and skills; lack of felt need for the IS; (perceived) redistribution of power and/or resources; lack of organisational validity; and lack of senior executive support (1994: 18). He concludes that competing values need to be taken into account when designing and implementing IS. In doing so, he points out that different cultures often require different information (Tricker, 1988)[8] and may well process information differently (Thompson and Wildavsky, 1986).

Much of this process stream of IS implementation research draws on the work of such organisational behaviourists as Lewin (1952), Kolb (Kolb and Frohman, 1970), and Schein (1961). In addition the IS literature itself provides some useful insights. For example, Ginzberg (1979, 1981) stresses the need for commitment to change, commitment to the implementation effort itself, and extensive project definition and planning as key components of the implementation process. Clearly, 'such findings are not inconsistent with those from the factors and mutual understanding research streams [but] suggest a more complete, though still quite sparse view of IS implementation' (Kwon and Zmud, 1987: 229).

Two further points could usefully be made regarding the implementation process, and both bring with them still more complexity. First, in

---

[8] This is particularly important in the context of inter-organisational systems and global information systems.

investigating the dynamics of the implementation process, it is reported that there are divergent impacts on various implementation 'phases' (cf. Apple and Zmud, 1984; Ginzberg, 1979; Zand and Sorenson, 1975)—a point which often appears to have been lost on many a BPR advocate. Second, we are increasingly concerned with the development and implementation of IS among and between organisations (Swanson, 1994), as well as across functions. The contextual, cultural, and political issues highlighted in the preceding analysis require particular attention in such circumstances.

We shall now draw the chapter to a close by attempting to identify a number of convergent streams arising from this analysis of the innovation and implementation literatures in order to draw key lessons for BPR, and for the role of IS in strategic change.

Lessons for BPR, and the Role of Information Systems in Strategic Change

We have seen that innovation does not stop at adoption; hence the need to consider implementation at the same time; the management of change dimension in IS/IT developments is therefore key. We have also noted that innovation is context specific and socially shaped. Notions of 'best practice', while understandable from a best interest perspective, are therefore called into question: while suppliers are interested in adoption, users are much more interested in implementation! We have noted too that, with best practice, it is the process of managing the strategic change (with the emphasis on the verb rather than the noun) which requires particular attention, but that the mechanistic application of methodology is unlikely to be effective. Innovation research has suggested that while the process may be viewed as a series of 'stages', or better, 'episodes', concerned with invention; diffusion; adoption; adaptation; and implementation, it may well be preferable to consider the process as a whole rather than a series of discrete stages, with innovation being viewed as a complex, iterative, and continuous process. Further complexity is added when one considers alternative stakeholder perspectives and inter-organisational change, and the varying impacts at different stages (*sic*) of the process.

The IS implementation (and failures) literature echoes much of the above; with entreaties to prepare for change by gaining commitment while understanding alternative perspectives and the undoubted resultant power shifts—the political dimension is highlighted in other words. In addition, greater attention is given to questions of design (the 'hows' in addition to the 'what(s)'), of the analyst–user relationship, and of the user–IS interface. While such entreaties may be seen to be little more than platitudes in some quarters (e.g. Hirschheim and Newman, 1988), the raising of issues associated with these aspects of the process, and concern for implementation *per se*, herald the greater likelihood of IS success, however measured.

Increasing attention has also been paid to the implementation of inter-
organisational IS in addition, with the added complexity that this brings
to the process

BPR, on the other hand, has often been touted as *the* simple solution to
complex organisational problems. Davenport and Short (1990) propose a
five-step approach which is typical of the genre:

1. Develop business vision and process objectives.
2. Identify processes to be redesigned.
3. Understand and measure existing processes.
4. Identify IT levers.
5. Design and build prototype of new process(es).

A single, agreed organisational objective is required: alternative viewpoints or visions of the future are not allowed, since these would be seen
in terms of dissension. The rhetoric of BPR is almost missionary in its zeal,
full of certainty in the appropriateness of the proposed radical change,
and the role of IT in it. There is a certain masculinity in the rhetoric: it
is prescriptive and brooks no questioning. The emphasis is on the 'what'
of organisational change, while the 'how' is relegated to something of an
afterthought: a mere matter of re-engineering processes. When issues associated with implementation warrant a mention, they are often couched in
tones bordering on surprise: 'Maybe more time could have been spent preparing the people involved for the change' (Baxter and Lisburn, 1994: 15).
Lessons have been learnt, of course, and the 'people' dimension is increasingly discussed—even by one of BPR's founding fathers (Davenport, 1996).
Perhaps surprisingly, given the increasing attention being paid to inter-
organisational and global IS, and to electronic commerce, BPR's focus has
tended to be on internal, albeit cross-functional, processes.

Viewing BPR from this perspective then, we might characterise it as
a complex, incompatible, altering innovation, with considerable inherent
risks. Indeed, we are led to believe that successful BPR projects are very
much in the minority. Why then has this particular technology been so
readily and so rapidly diffused? We have argued that its purported simplicity and the sheer dimensions of the purported business gains are likely
to have had some bearing on the rate of its adoption, particularly in Anglo-
American societies. In addition, the powerful symbolism of the three-
letter acronym and the role played by those who have a vested interested
in its promotion should not be underestimated either.

What then are the lessons we might draw from this analysis for the role
of IS in strategic change? Our intention here has not been to throw out
the BPR baby with the bathwater. There is clearly a great deal of common
sense associated with a technology that does not fall into the trap of computerising 'what is', when 'what is' is, in some way or another, inadequate.

The focus on simplifying processes (with echoes of TQM), and doing so with business imperatives in mind (cf. Checkland's soft systems methodology), and on IS and organisational alignment (cf. Ein Dor and Segev's, 1981, concept of 'fit'), is difficult to argue against. What we have attempted to do is to highlight the more facile and misleading aspects of the BPR message. In much the same way as IS academics have, albeit latterly, re-assessed our notions of IS for competitive advantage and IS strategy,[9] we have in this chapter attempted to utilise the hard-won lessons from relevant literatures to provide a critical review of BPR. All too often, in IS at least, we have been prone to adopting the latest fad, with little thought being given to existing knowledge—a view expressed by Keen (1981) when bemoaning the lack of cumulative IS research in the first twenty years or so of its existence.

While we have acknowledged that fads have their place (Abrahamson, 1991), it is incumbent on us as academics to add a note of caution and to provide a critical review, when and where necessary. We argue that BPR is a case in point. The role of IS in strategic change is far too important a topic to be treated in the superficial manner to which it has been subject for the most part. IS and strategic change is no more IT-enabled process innovation than it is IT-enabled competitive advantage. Having said that, we have also attempted to demonstrate that new knowledge may emerge from a trans-disciplinary treatment of a topic (cf. Gibbons, 1995). It is for the reader to judge whether we have been successful in achieving this objective.

References

Abrahamson, E. (1991), 'Managerial Fads and Fashions: The Diffusion and Rejection of Innovations', *Academy of Management Review*, 16: 586–612.

—— (1996), 'Management Fashion', *Academy of Management Review*, 21: 254–85.

Aldrich, H. E. (1979), *Organisations and Environments* (Englewood Cliffs, NJ: Prentice Hall).

Alter, C., and Hage, J. (1993), *Organisations Working Together* (Newbury Park, Calif.: Sage).

Alter, S., and Ginzberg, M. J. (1978), 'Managing Uncertainty in MIS Implementation', *Sloan Management Review*, 20, 1: 23–31.

Anderson, P., and Tushman, M. (1990), 'Technological Discontinuities and Dominant Designs: A Cyclical Model of Technological Change', *Administrative Science Quarterly*, 35: 604–33.

Apple, L. E., and Zmud, E. W. (1984), 'A Pharmacokinetics Approach to Technology Transfer: Implications for OR/MS/MIS Implementation', in R. L. Schultz

---

[9] See for example Ciborra's (1994) treatment of IS strategy.

and M. J. Ginzberg (eds.), *Management Science Implementation* (Norwich, Conn.: JAI Press).

Baker, B. (1995), 'The Role of Feedback in Assessing Information Systems Planning Effectiveness', *Journal of Strategic Information Systems*, 4, 1, Mar.: 61–80.

Baxter, S., and Lisburn, D. (1994). *Re-engineering Information Technology: Success through Empowerment* (New York: Prentice Hall).

Becker, M. H. (1970), 'Sociometric Location and Innovativeness: Reformulation and Extension of the Diffusion Model', *American Sociological Review*, 35: 267–82.

Benbasat, I., Dexter, A., Drury, D., and Goldstein, R. (1984), 'A Critique of the Stage Hypothesis: Theory and Empirical Evidence', *Communications of the ACM*, 27, 5: 476–85.

Blandin, J. S., and Brown, W. B. (1977), 'Uncertainty and Management's Search for Information', *IEEE Transactions on Engineering Management*, 24, 4: 114–19.

Boland, R. J., Jr. (1978), 'The Process and Product of System Design', *Management Science*, 24, 9: 887–98.

—— and Hirschheim, R. A. (1987) (eds.), *Critical Issues in Information Systems Research* (Chichester: Wiley).

Brancheau, J. C., Janz, B. C., and Wetherbe, J. C. (1996), 'Key Issues in Information Systems Management: 1994–1995 SIM Delphi Results', *MIS Quarterly*, 20, 2, June: 225–42.

Burke, G., and Peppard, J. (1995) (eds.), *Examining Business Process Re-engineering: Current Perspectives and Future Directions* (London: Kogan Page).

Churchman, C. W., and Schainblatt, A. (1965), 'The Researcher and Manager: A Dialectic of Implementation', *Management Science*, 11: B69–B87.

Ciborra, C. (1994), 'The Grassroots of IT and Strategy', in C. Ciborra and T. Jelassi (eds.), *Strategic Information Systems: A European Perspective* (Chichester: Wiley).

Clark, P. (1987), *Anglo-American Innovation* (Berlin: De Gruyter).

—— and Newell, S. (1993), 'Societal Embedding of Production and Inventory Control Systems: American and Japanese Influences on Adaptive Implementation in Britain', *International Journal of Human Factors in Manufacturing*, 3: 69–80.

—— and Staunton, N. (1989), *Innovation in Technology and Organisation* (London: Routledge).

Coombes, R., Knights, D., and Willmott, H. C. (1992), 'Culture, Control and Competition: Towards a Conceptual Framework for the Study of Information Technology in Organisations', *Organisation Studies*, 13, 1: 51–72.

Cooper, R. B. (1994), 'The Inertial Impact of Culture on IT Implementation', *Information and Management*, 27: 17–31.

Craig, J., and Yetton, P. W. (1997), 'The Real Event of Re-engineering', in Sauer, Yetton, and Associates (1997).

Culnan, M. J. (1983), 'Chauffeured versus End User Access to Commercial Databases: The Effects of Task and Individual Differences', *MIS Quarterly*, 7, 1: 55–67.

Damanpour, F. (1987), 'The Adoption of Technological, Administrative and Ancillary Innovations: Impact of Organizational Factors', *Journal of Management*, 13: 675–88.

Davenport, T. H. (1993), *Process Innovation: Re-engineering Work through Information Technology* (Boston: Harvard Business School Press).

—— (1996), 'Why Re-engineering Failed: The Fad that Forgot People', *Fast Company*, Premier Issue: 70–4.

—— and Short, J. E. (1990), 'The New Industrial Engineering: Information Technology and Business Process Redesign', *Sloan Management Review*, 31, 4, Summer: 11–27. Reproduced under the title 'Information Technology and Business Process Redesign', in Galliers and Baker (1994).

Di Maggio, P., and Powell, W. (1990), 'The Iron Cage Revisited: Industrial Isomorphism and Collective Rationality in Organisational Fields, *American Sociological Review*, 48: 147–60.

Drazin, R. (1990), 'Professionals and Innovation: Structural-Functional Versus Radical-Structural Perspectives', *Journal of Management Studies*, 27, 3: 245–63.

Earl, M. J. (1994), 'The New and the Old of Business Process Redesign', *Journal of Strategic Information Systems*, 3, 1, Mar.: 5–22.

—— and Skyrme, D. (1992), 'Hybrid Managers: What do we Know about Them?', *Journal of Information Systems*, 2(3), July: 169–87.

Egan, C. (1995), *Creating Organizational Advantage* (Oxford: Butterworth-Heinemann).

Ein-Dor, P., and Segev, E. (1981), *A Paradigm for Management Information Systems* (New York: Praeger).

Ettlie, J. (1980), 'Adequacy of Stage Models for Decisions on Adoption of Innovation', *Psychological Reports*, 46: 991–5.

—— and Bridges, W. P. (1987), 'Technology Policy and Innovation in Organisations', in J. M. Pennings and A. Buitendam, *New Technology as Organisational Innovation*, 117–37 (Cambridge, MA: Ballinger).

Fleck, J. (1994), 'Learning by Trying: The Implementation of Configurational Technology', *Research Policy*, 23: 637–52.

Galliers, R. D. (1987) (ed.), *Information Analysis: Selected Readings* (Sydney: Addison-Wesley).

—— (1992), 'Information Technology: Management's Boon or Bane?', *Journal of Strategic Information Systems*, 1, 2, Mar.: 50–6.

—— (1995), 'IT and Organisational Change: Where does BPR Fit in?', in Burke and Peppard (1995).

—— (1997), 'Against Obliteration: Reducing the Risks in Business Process Change', in Sauer, Yetton, and Associates (1997).

—— and Baker, B. S. H. (1994) (eds.), *Strategic Information Management: Challenges and Strategies in Managing Information Systems* (Oxford: Butterworth-Heinemann).

—— Merali, Y., and Spearing, L. (1994), 'Coping with Information Technology? How British Executives Perceive the Key Information Systems Management Issues in the Mid-1990s', *Journal of Information Technology*, 9(3), Sept.: 223–38.

—— and Sutherland, A. R. (1991), 'Information Systems Management and Strategy Formulation: The "Stages of Growth" Model Revisited', *Journal of Information Systems*, 1, 2: 89–114.

Gibbons, M. (1994), *The New Production of Knowledge: The Dynamics of Science and Research in Contemporary Society* (London: Sage).

Gibson, C., and Nolan, R. L. (1974), 'Managing the Four Stages of EDP Growth', *Harvard Business Review*, 52, 1, Jan.–Feb.

Ginzberg, M. J. (1979), 'A Study of the Implementation Process', *TIMS Studies in the Management Sciences*, 13: 85–102.

—— (1981), 'Early Diagnosis of MIS Implementation Failure: Promising Results and Unanswered Questions', *Management Science*, 27, 4: 459–78.

Granovetter, M. S. (1973), 'The Strength of Weak Ties', *American Journal of Sociology*, 78: 1360–80.

Grey, C., and Mitev, N. (1994), 'Reengineering Organizations: Towards a Critical Appraisal', working paper for *British Academy of Management Conference*, Lancaster, United Kingdom.

Hammer, M. (1990), 'Don't Automate, Obliterate', *Harvard Business Review*, July–Aug., 68, 4: 104–12.

—— and Champy, J. (1993), *Re-engineering the Corporation: A Manifesto for Business Revolution* (London: Nicholas Brealey).

Hirschheim, R. A., and Newman, M. (1988), 'Information Systems and User Resistance: Theory and Practice', *Computer Journal*, 31, 5: 398–408.

—— —— (1991), 'Symbolism and Information Systems Development: Myth, Metaphor and Magic', *Information Systems Research*, 2: 29–62.

Holland, C. P., Lockett, A. G., Richard, J. M., and Blackman, I. D. (1992), 'Planning for Electronic Data Interchange', *Strategic Management Journal*, 13: 125–43.

—— —— —— —— (1994), 'The Evolution of a Global Cash Management System: The Case of Motorola and Citibank', *Sloan Management Review*, 36, 1: 37–47.

Hosking, D. M., and Morley, I. E. (1992), *A Social Psychology of Organizing: People, Processes and Contexts* (London: Harvester-Wheatsheaf).

Ives, B., and Learmonth, G. P. (1984), 'The Information System as a Competitive Weapon', *Communications of the ACM*, 27, 12: 1193–201.

—— and Olson, M. H. (1984), 'User Involvement in MIS Success: A Review of Research', *Management Science*, 30: 586–603.

Jackson, M. C. (1995), 'Beyond the Fads: Systems Thinking for Managers', *Systems Research*, 12, 1: 25–42.

Keen, P. G. W. (1981), 'Information Systems and Organisational Change', *Communications of the ACM*, 24: 24–33.

—— Scott Morton, M. S. (1978), *Decision Support Systems: An Organisational Perspective* (Reading, Mass.: Addison-Wesley).

Kettinger, W. J., Teng, J. T. C., and Guha, S. (1997), 'Business Process Change: A Study of Methodologies, Techniques and Tools', *MIS Quarterly*, 21, 1, Mar.: 55–80.

Kimberley, J. R., and Evanisko, M. J. (1988), 'Organisational Innovation: The Influence of Individual, Organisational and Contextual Factors on Horizontal Adoption of Technological and Administrative Innovation', *Academy of Management Journal*, 24, 4: 689–713.

King, J., and Kraemer, K. (1984), 'Evolution and Organisational Information Systems: An Assessment of Nolan's Stage Model', *Communications of the ACM*, 27, 5, May.

Knights, D., and Murray, F. (1994), *Managers Divided* (Chichester: Wiley).

Kolb, D. A., and Frohman, A. L. (1970), 'An Organisational Development Approach to Consulting', *Sloan Management Review*, 12, 1: 51–65.

Kramer, K. L. (1981), 'The Politics of Model Implementation', *Systems, Objectives, Solutions*, 1, 4: 161–78.

Kwon, T. H., and Zmud, R. W. (1987), 'Unifying the Fragmented Models of Information Systems Implementation', in Boland and Hirschheim (1987).

Lacity, M., and Hirschheim, R. (1993), *Information Systems Outsourcing: Myths, Metaphors and Realities* (Chichester: Wiley).

Land, F. (1996), 'The New Alchemist: Or How to Transmute Base Organisations into Corporations of Gleaming Gold', *Journal of Strategic Information Systems*, 5, 1, Mar.: 5–17.

Levine, H. G., and Rossmoore, D. (1994), 'Politics and the Function of Power in a Case Study of IT Implementation', *Journal of Management Information Systems*, 11, 3, Winter: 115–33.

Lewin, K. (1952), 'Group Decision and Social Change', in Newcombe, S. and Hartley, J., *Readings in Social Psychology* (New York: Henry Holt).

Lucas, H. C., Jr. (1975), *Why Information Systems Fail* (New York: Columbia University Press).

—— (1981), *Implementation: The Key to Successful Information Systems* (New York: Columbia University Press).

Lyytinen, K., and Hirschheim, R. (1987), 'Information Systems Failures—A Survey and Classification of the Empirical Literature', *Oxford Surveys in Information Technology*, 4: 257–309.

McFarlan, F. W. (1981), 'Portfolio Approach to Information Systems', *Harvard Business Review*, 59, 5, Sept.–Oct.: 142–50.

—— (1984), 'Information Technology Changes the Way you Compete', *Harvard Business Review*, 62, 3, May–June: 98–102.

McGaughey, R. E., Jr., Snyder, C. A., and Carr, H. H. (1994), 'Implementing Information Technology for Competitive Advantage: Risk Management Issues', *Information and Management*, 26: 273–80.

March, J. G., and Simon, H. A. (1958), *Organisations* (New York: Wiley).

Markus, M. L. (1983), 'Power, Politics and MIS Implementation', *Communications of the ACM*, 26, 6, June: 430–44. Also in Galliers and Baker (1994).

—— and Pfeffer, J. (1983), 'Power and the Design and Implementation of Accounting and Control Systems', *Accounting, Organisations and Society*, 8, 2/3: 205–18.

Martin, J. (1982), *Strategic Data-Planning Methodologies* (Englewood Cliffs, NJ: Prentice-Hall).

Mukhopadhyay, T., Kekre, S., and Kalathur, S. (1995), 'Business Value of Information Technology: A Study of Electronic Data Interchange', *MIS Quarterly*, 19, 2, June: 137–56.

Mumford, E. (1994), 'New Treatments or Old Remedies: Is Business Process Redesign Really Socio-technical Design?', *Journal of Strategic Information Systems*, 3, 4, Dec.: 313–26.

—— (1996), 'Restructuring: Values, Visions, Viability', *Financial Times*, Friday, 19 Apr.: 12.

Myers, M. D. (1994), 'A Disaster for Everyone to See: An Interpretive Analysis of a Failed IS Project', *Accounting, Management and Information Technologies*, 4, 4, Oct.–Dec.: 185–201.

Newell, S., Swan, J., and Clark, P. (1993), 'The Importance of User Design in the Adoption of New Information Technologies: The Example of Production and Inventory Control Systems', *International Journal of Operations and Production Management*, 13: 4–22.

—— —— and Robertson, M. (1997), 'Exploring the Diffusion of BPR in Manufacturing Firms in Europe', *Proceedings of 5th European Conference on Information Systems*, III: 1155–62.

Nolan, R. L. (1979), 'Managing the Crises in Data Processing', *Harvard Business Review*, 57, 2, Mar.–Apr.

Nystrom, P. C., and Starbuck, W. H. (1981), *Handbook of Organizational Design*, vols. 1 and 2 (Oxford: Oxford University Press).

Oliver, I., and Langford, H. (1987), 'Myths of Demons and Users: Evidence and Analysis of Negative Perceptions of Users', in Galliers (1987).

Oz, E. (1992), 'Selection and Implementation of an Information System: A General Motors Case', *OMEGA International Journal of Management Science*, 20, 3: 283–93.

Passmore, W. (1994), *Creating Strategic Change: Designing the Flexible High-Performance Organization* (New York: Wiley).

Pettigrew, A. M. (1972), 'Information Control as a Power Resource', *Sociology*, 6: 187–204.

Porter, M. E., and Millar, V. E. (1984), 'How Information Gives you Competitive Advantage', *Harvard Business Review*, 63, 4, July–Aug.: 149–60.

Poulymenakou, A., and Holmes, A. (1996), 'A Contingency Framework for the Investigation of Information Systems Failure', *European Journal of Information Systems*, 5: 34–46.

Rainer, R. K., Jr., Snyder, C. A., and Carr, H. H. (1991), 'Risk Analysis for Information Technology', *Journal of Management Information Systems*, 8, 1, Summer: 129–48.

Robertson, M., Swan, J. A., and Newell, S. (1996), 'The Role of Networks in the Diffusion of Technological Innovation', *Journal of Management Studies*, 33: 335–61.

Rockart, J. F. (1979), 'Chief Executives Define their Own Data Needs', *Harvard Business Review*, 57, 2, Mar.–Apr. Also in Galliers (1987).

—— (1983), *Diffusion of Innovations* (New York: Free Press).

Rogers, Y. (1992), 'Mental Models and Complex Tasks', in Y. Rogers, A. Rutherford, and P. A. Bibby, *Models in the Mind* (London: Academic Press).

—— and Shemaker, F. (1971), *Communication of Innovations: A Cross-cultural Approach*. New York: Free Press.

Sauer, C. (1993), *Why Information Systems Fail: A Case Study Approach* (Henley-on-Thames: Alfred Waller).

—— Yetton, P. W., and Associates (1997), *Steps to the Future: Fresh Thinking on the Management of IT-Based Organisational Transformation* (San Francisco: Jossey-Bass).

Scarbrough, H., and Corbett, J. M. (1992), *Technology and Organization: Power, Meaning and Design* (London: Routledge).

Schein, E. H. (1961), 'Management Development as a Process of Influence', *Industrial Management Review*, 2, 2.

Scott, W. R. (1981), *Organisations: Rational, Natural and Open Systems* (Englewood Cliffs, NJ: Prentice-Hall).

Slack, T., and Hinings, B. (1995), 'Institutional Pressures and Isomporphic Change: An Empirical Test', *Organisation Studies*.

Slappendel, C. (1996), 'Perspectives on Innovation in Organisations', *Organisation Studies*, 17, 1: 107–29.

Steers, R. M. (1977), *Organisational Effectiveness* (Santa Monica, Calif.: Goodyear).

Swan, J. A., and Clark, P. A. (1992), 'Organisation Decision-Making in the Appropriation of Technological Innovation: Cognitive and Political Dimensions', *European Work and Organisational Psychologist*, 2, 2: 103–27.

—— Newell, S., and Robertson, M. (1996), 'The Illusion of "Best Practice" in Information Systems for Production Management', *Proceedings of the European Conference on Information Systems* (Lisbon: Lisbon School of Business).

Swanson, E. B. (1994), 'Information Systems Innovation among Organisations', *Management Science*, 40, 9, Sept.: 1069–92.

Synott, W. R. (1987), 'The Emerging Chief Information Officer', *Information Management Review*, 3, 1, Mar.: 21–35.

Tate, P. (1988), 'Risk! The Third Factor', *Datamation*, 15, Apr.: 58–64.

Thompson, J. D. (1967), *Organisations in Action* (New York: McGraw-Hill).

Thompson, M., and Wildavsky, A. (1986), 'A Cultural Theory of Information Bias in Organisations', *Journal of Management Studies*, 23: 273–86.

Tichy, N. M. (1981), 'Networks in Organisations', in P. C. Nystrom and W. H. Starbuck (eds.), *Handbook of Organisational Design*, vol. ii (London: Oxford University Press).

Tornatzky, L. G., and Fleisher, M. (1990), *The Processes of Technological Innovation* (Lexington, Mass.: Lexington Books).

—— and Klein, L. (1982), 'Innovation Characteristics and Innovation Implementation: A Meta-analysis of Findings', *IEEE Transactions on Engineering Management*, 29, 1: 28–45.

Tricker, R. I. (1988), 'Information Resources Management: Cultural Perspectives', *Information and Management*, 15: 37–46.

Tushman, M. L., and Nadler, D. A. (1978), 'Information Processing as an Integrating Concept in Organisational Design', *Academy of Management Review*, 3: 613–24.

Van de Ven, A. H. (1986), 'Central Problems in Management of Innovation', *Management Science*, 32, 5: 590–607.

—— and Ferry, D. (1980), *Organisational Assessment* (New York: Wiley Interscience).

Watson, R. T., Kelly, G. G., Galliers, R. D., and Wetherbe, J. C. (1997), 'Key Issues in Information Systems Management: An International Perspective', *Journal of Management Information Systems*, 13, 4: 91–115.

Watts, J. (1993), 'The Future of BPR', *Business Change and Re-engineering: Journal of Corporate Transformation*, 1, 3, Winter: 4–5.

Weick, K. E. (1969), *The Social Psychology of Organizing* (Reading, Mass.: Addison-Wesley).

—— (1990), 'Technology as an Equivoque: Sensemaking in New Technologies', in P. Goodman and L. Sproull (eds.), *Technology and Organisations* (San Francisco, Calif.: Jossey-Bass).

Wilson, F., Desmond, J., and Roberts, H. (1994), 'Success and Failure of MRPII Implementation', *British Journal of Management*, 5: 221–40.

Wolfe, R. A. (1994), 'Organisational Innovation: Review, Critique and Suggested Research Directions', *Journal of Management Studies*, 31, 3, May: 405–31.

Zaltman, D. E., Duncan, R. E., and Holbeck, J. (1973), *Innovations and Organisations* (New York: Wiley).

Zand, D. E., and Sorenson, R. E. (1975), 'Theory of Change and the Effective Use of Management Science, *Administrative Science Quarterly*, 20: 530–45.

Zuboff, S. (1988), *In the Age of the Smart Machine: The Future of Work and Power* (Oxford: Heinemann).

PART IV

Organisation and Management Issues

Introduction

A critical theme in the MIS literature concerns organisation and management issues. Within business and management schools internationally, a plethora of research has been published concerned broadly with the relationship between technology and organisation structures and cultures and its impact on managerial work.[1] Important debates have covered areas such as the interdependencies between organisation structure and technology, the social shaping and cultural dimension of technology, the role of knowledge workers in the information society, and the changing nature of managerial work, among many others. Whilst it is outside the scope of the present volume to cover all these fields of investigation, we present four chapters which explore some of the above themes. Clearly, organisation and management issues are not merely confined to this final section of the volume as they are implicit in many chapters throughout.

Bob Tricker's chapter on 'The Cultural Context of Information Management', explores how the subject has changed in recent years with the development of the Internet, electronic commerce, 3D application programming and groupware, etc. His chapter examines three empirical studies at three levels: the individual, corporate, and state. These studies support the thesis that, as information management becomes increasingly global, the cultural dimension is of fundamental importance at all these levels.

The chapter by Wendy Currie and Ian Glover considers the managerial and technical division of labour within organisations. It asserts that the concept of the 'hybrid manager', whilst offering a definition of a problem, is not a solution in itself. This is because the structural and cultural constraints which have historically precluded those with a technical (engineering) background from gaining entry into managerial hierarchies persist today. Indeed, one explanation of the continuing skills shortage in certain technical specialisms is because those with a technical background often

[1] B.-A. Vedin (1994) (ed.), *Management of Change and Innovation* (Aldershot: Dartmouth); M. Earl (1996) (ed.), *Information Management: The Organisational Dimension* (Oxford: Oxford University Press); T. J. Allen and M. S. Scott Morton (1994) (eds.), *Information Technology and the Corporation of the 1990s* (Oxford: Oxford University Press); R. D. Galliers and B. S. H. Baker (1994), *Strategic Information Management: Challenges and Strategies in Managing Information Systems* (Oxford: Butterworth-Heinemann). These volumes comprise a number of articles which discuss key debates broadly concerned with organisational and managerial issues of innovation and technology.

disregard this expertise in favour of becoming managers. Having chosen this path, their technical expertise and knowledge soon become out of date in the fast-changing information technology environment within which we work. A possible solution to the managerial-technical divide is to recognise that both sets of capabilities and skills should be well rewarded to allow an organisation to compete effectively. Moreover, technical people should not simply be perceived as part of the growing, non-core (support) element of the overall activities of an organisation.

The subject of capabilities and skills is further analysed by David Feeny and Leslie Willcocks. These authors identify nine core capabilities and skills for the information systems function. They suggest that whilst a single individual may be able to provide more than one of the nine capabilities, each one is logically distinct and implies a set of behaviours, skills, and motivations. As such, organisations must meet a series of challenges before they can successfully recruit and retain a cohort of high-calibre professionals able to create the 'high-performance IS' function.

The final chapter of this volume considers the management of knowledge workers. This is a controversial concept and one which continues to attract much interest in the academic and practitioner communities. In this chapter, Harry Scarbrough argues that there are three major reasons for analysing the concept of knowledge workers. The first is concerned with issues of labour-market mobility and management control. The second is related to the structural and bureaucratic changes in the IS function, particularly as a consequence of delayering and elimination of routine administrative roles. The third is linked to the political role and status of knowledge workers within organisations. As knowledge work becomes strategically important, the author explores how traditional power bases relying upon hierarchy and bureaucratic control may be replaced by knowledge-based networks.

The primary objective of Part IV is to examine some of the organisational and managerial issues relevant to the MIS field. Whilst it is outside the scope of the present volume to consider other relevant material, the central theme of these contributions is that behavioural aspects of managing change are critical to understanding policies, practices, and outcomes.

16

The Cultural Context of Information Management

ROBERT I. TRICKER

Introduction

In this chapter we consider some of the diverse fields and alternative perceptual viewpoints that are embraced by the notion of MIS and add the cultural dimension. Three principal arguments are advanced. First, that what is needed is not so much a unifying theory or framework for MIS, but answers to some fundamental questions. This is not the time for testable hypotheses and a pervasive scientific paradigm, it is argued, but for perceptual pluralism which can offer relevant insights, knowledge, and experience. Second, the study of management information systems has become the study of information management. The successful application of IT is less of a challenge than the effective use of information. Third, as information management has become global, the cultural dimension, though seldom articulated, has become fundamentally important at the levels of the individual, the enterprise, and the state. Empirical evidence to support this later thesis is drawn from three areas: a study of individuals' perceptions in strategic decision-making which contrasts Western and Asian managers' experience; joint research on IT infrastructure within corporate groups around the world; and case research on the development of state-wide EDI (electronic data interchange) in Singapore and Hong Kong. In the concluding discussion, some current issues in information management which have cross-cultural dimensions are used to support the principal arguments.

In Search of a Pervasive Paradigm

MIS (management information systems) has been studied for over thirty years. Yet the subject still lacks a coherent conceptual framework, a pervasive paradigm or even clear boundaries. But does that matter?

The diversity of topics within the field can readily be seen in the subjects suggested in three recent information system conferences—the 1996

Harvard University conference on the Internet and society; the 1996 Pacific Multimedia Information Systems Workshop; and the 1997 Pacific Asia conference on the confluence of information systems theory and practice:

- electronic commerce;
- marketing on the Internet;
- government information industry strategy;
- information security management;
- video on demand and home shopping;
- hypermedia design methodology;
- cultural imperialism on the net;
- democracy in the digital age;
- the government's role in the Internet;
- multi-paradigm visual information systems;
- global and long-term impact of ATM;
- security and encryption;
- new organisational forms;
- who owns the Internet?
- distributed multimedia data modelling;
- 3D application programming;
- information brokering;
- information literacy;
- groupware and work flow;
- cross-cultural studies in information systems.

The organisers of the 1996 Pacific Multimedia Information Systems Workshop further suggested that 'the development of National Information Infrastructure (NII) is under way in many countries. NII is a seamless web of communications networks, computers, databases and consumer electronics that will put a vast amount of information at users' fingertips [and] transform the way people live, work and interact with each other. Every kind of business will be changed as commerce, finance, government services, manufacturing of all kinds, education, entertainment and healthcare employ multimedia' (Lee, 1996).

Given such diversity of topic, where is the coherence in the subject? What is it about, other than, perhaps, that all the topics involve computer-assistance in some way or that all relate to the use of information? But can such diversity really be presented as part of a integrated whole? Can the boundaries, functions, and levels for such a subject be determined? Indeed, does a valid subject really exist?

From the outset the body of knowledge referred to as management information systems (MIS) has not lacked commentators. There has long been discussion about the scope, structure, and standing of the subject that is taught as MIS (to take some examples from the past decade—the

ACM/IEEE-CS Curriculum Task Force, 1991; Ang and Lo, 1991; Avison, 1994; Bacon, 1992; Boaden and Locket, 1991; Buckingham et al., 1987; Laribee, 1992; Probert, 1994; Swanson et al., 1991).

Others have offered or commented on the conceptual frameworks, theories, and academic paradigms underlying the study of MIS (Anthony, 1965; Backhouse et al., 1991; Bariff and Ginsberg, 1982; Banville and Landry, 1989; Bell, 1973; Bjorn-Andersen, 1985; Brehaut, 1991; Cavaye and Cragg, 1993; Cheon et al., 1993; Culnan and Swanson, 1986; Davies and Ledington, 1991; Gorla, 1989; Grimshaw, 1992; Keen, 1987; Landry and Banville, 1992; Lucas et al., 1974; Lyytinen, 1987; Reponen, 1993; Sabherwal and King, 1991; Stamper, 1985; Tricker, 1992; Van Gigch and Pipino, 1986; Weber, 1987; Zuboff, 1988).

Like spotlights casting beams onto a stage, some of these insights provide a penetrating but narrow light, illuminating part of the scene but casting the rest into shadow. Other viewpoints offer a broader but softer light. None is capable of giving an overall, balanced, and focused perspective. In the early days MIS was seen as a component of accounting. More recently, MIS has been treated as a subset of organisational theory, of strategic management theory, or of management and computer science. But is an agreed theory set, an accepted discipline base important?

The Significance of Western Thought in MIS Studies

Predominantly, contributions to our knowledge about MIS teaching and research have been based on Western scholarship—on an academic tradition rooted in the conventions of a classical philosophy of science, dominated by the English language, reflecting Western values influenced by Judaeo-Christian religious thinking, the Renaissance, and the Reformation: a scientific tradition that embraces typically unarticulated (and often unrecognised) beliefs in individualism, personal freedoms, and the common law. But this is not the only cultural milieu in which information and its management can be studied. In Japan, for example, the developments in science and technology that followed the Mediji restoration were not held back by English beliefs in the nobility of science and the need to intellectualise it.

Compounding the ethnocentric, Western domination of the process of discovery are the cultural and subject paradigms preserved by learned journals published in the West. Typically rooted in a single discipline, limited to specific theoretical constructs, often set in the concrete of inordinate conservatism, the boundaries and paradigms of subjects can be fanatically protected by editors, referees, and contributors alike, not least because all in this inner elite have a vested interest in maintaining the status quo of their shared perceptions.

The catch 22 of scientific method in the Western world is that anyone who seeks to challenge a conventional paradigm will not get published within it: yet not being published in the top journals is tantamount to the work being classed by other scholars as second rate and inferior. Such cultural imperialism denies the chance of changing or even challenging the paradigm.

In 'the structure of scientific revolutions', Thomas Kuhn argues that developments in scientific thinking do not progress smoothly from one rational step to the next, but lurch from one uncertainty to another in stages that are at best only partially rational. Significant contributions, he argues, occurred when basic concepts, or paradigms, were seen no longer to meet the anomalies that had been recognised—and a new theory needed to be developed. If the new thinking was accepted, a paradigm shift then occurred. Rational choice between the competing paradigms was not an alternative, Kuhn believed, because the different paradigms represented different ways of thinking about the underlying phenomena. People had to change their beliefs. The adoption by scholars of systems theory, or more recently of agency theory, provides examples. Do MIS studies need a new paradigm?

No subject has an automatic right to existence. The history of management-related scientific thought is replete with subjects which were once paraded as penetrating and pervasive insights into management issues, ultimate solutions to management problems—the behavioural theory of the firm, cybernetics, industrial dynamics, management control systems, operations research, general systems theory—only subsequently to become the preserve of small bands of specialists and enthusiasts. In the long term the standing and status of a subject comes from its contribution to understanding, and ultimately to practice; not from its publications and proclamation.

For thirty years the scope of MIS teaching has been decided by answers to the question: what do academics want to teach? For thirty years the content of MIS research has been determined by the topics that academics want to study and write about. For thirty years these have been the wrong questions. We have been talking to ourselves. More appropriate questions might have been:

- what do people need to know to live successful lives, build effective organisations, and create worthwhile societies? In other words, what information is needed to achieve such ends?
- what data needs to be managed and made available, to provide such information?
- what are the implications for individuals, organisations, and states?

Essentially, the study of management information systems has become the study of information management (an idea recognised by Earl and Hopwood in 1980). What is needed is not so much a unifying theory or framework for MIS, but answers to some fundamental questions. This is not the time for testable hypotheses and a pervasive paradigm, but for perceptual pluralism which offers relevant insights, knowledge, and experience to help change society.

This leads to the central tenet of this chapter that, as the effects of information and information management become global, the cultural dimension is not just an interesting attribute of information systems development, of occasional relevance when cultures conflict, but is of fundamental significance to effective information management.

The Cultural Dimensions of Information Management

In reviewing the theoretical background to this field, the definition of culture becomes crucial. Many attempts have been made, drawing from the concepts of anthropology, social psychology, organisation theory, and other fields. Deal and Kennedy (1982) suggest that culture can be thought of as: 'the integrated pattern of human behaviour that includes thought, speech, action and artefacts and depends on mass capacity for learning and transmitting knowledge to succeeding generations'. Notice the emphasis on learning and the conveyance of knowledge between people and over time: an essential function, some might argue, of information systems.

An insight into organisational culture is offered by Hucznyski and Buchanan (1985):

the pattern of values, beliefs, norms and rituals which define the essential character of the company. Just as the social group may socialise its members, so too will the organisation socialise its new recruits to accept the status and power distribution, language, reward and punishment system and its ideology and philosophy.

For this chapter we will simply consider culture as the systems of beliefs, values, and perceptions that influence what people think, expect, and do, systems which are reflected in their language and routines, myths and rituals, records and artefacts.

In essence, culture is reflected in the information that is utilised by individuals, organisations, and states. People perceive situations in the light of information available to them, take decisions in response, and implement them in their cultural context. Organisations develop a corporate culture, richly reflected in its information processes, that affects the expectations, behaviours, and decisions of all the players involved. Likewise, the information processes of states, nations, and ethnic groups influence and shape their cultural contexts. Differences between them are presented as cross-cultural issues.

Yet none of the major MIS texts that have been used in the past decade have offered a cross-cultural perspective on the subject. Indeed, culture has seldom been offered as a relevant concept, except at the organisational level, where the corporate culture has been seen to influence the development of information systems. Conversely, other studies have shown that organisational culture can be influenced by information system developments (Ahituv and Neumann, 1990; Cash et al., 1988; Davis and Olsen, 1985; Dickson and Wetherbe, 1985; Earl, 1989; Jackson, 1986; McNurlin and Sprague, 1989; Martin et al., 1994; Parker and Case, 1993; Robson, 1994; Ward et al., 1990).

In their paper 'Knowing *Wu Li*, Sensing *Shi-Li*, Caring *Ren-Li*: The Methodology of the WSR Approach' (1996), Jifa Gu of the Institute of Systems Science at the Chinese Academy of Sciences in Beijing and Zhichang Zhu of the Centre for Systems Studies at the University of Hull in England outline a systems methodology derived from the philosophies of Taoism, Buddhism, and neo-Confucianism. Their study is also related to the work of Sawaragi et al. (1988) at the Japanese Koran University and the development of the Shiayaka systems methodology.

Emphasising the potential for cross-cultural learning in systems developments, the authors recognise limitations in both Western 'hard systems' concepts developed in operations analysis and formal systems analysis methodologies and 'soft system' concepts involving more value-related, participative, social systems analysis and design. Power relationships are involved in all systems development, they argue, and it can be difficult, given an existing political context, to have an open dialogue between the various stakeholders involved in and affected by a new system. Modelling the 'real' world inevitably draws on the culture of those involved: the training, knowledge, experience, values systems, and beliefs of the modeller affect their expectations and what they perceive.

The alternative approach, derived from the Chinese insights, accepts the need for subjective modelling. Other players, they argue, inevitably (and perhaps desirably) identify different models, which can be as valid as any others. An optimal solution cannot be derived analytically or mathematically; nor can one philosophically 'best' or organisationally most desirable design be created. Successful solutions depend on the perspectives of the participants. Contrast this view with the paradigm-dependence anticipated by many Western thinkers, as discussed earlier. Rather, the Chinese writers argue, convergence towards a mutually acceptable solution can best be achieved by adopting the concepts of mutual understanding or knowing (*Wu Li*), sensing (*Shi-Li*), and caring (*Ren-Li*). The concept *Li* in each of the underlying philosophies is concerned with laws and patterns in the way things are and emphasises harmony in both nature and human affairs. Research on organisation-cultural and cross-cultural aspects of information systems in the Western literature to date has been quite limited. We now consider a few representative examples.

Cooper (1994) argued that when IT implementation conflicts with an organisation's culture, the analysis and design process may be undermined, the implementation process sabotaged, and the system under-utilised in practice. The author drew on the organisational literature on culture and conflict resolution to develop a methodology for evaluating the likelihood of cultural conflict in MIS analysis, design, and development, which identified competing value systems and offered the means to move towards a resolution.

Gover et al. (1994) compared information technology utilisation and projects that were seen to be successful in the USA, France, and Korea. Similarities in the use of IT resources were found across the varying cultures. However, very distinct differences in IT practice were observed, including the role of IT, integration of strategic and IT planning, and the extent of risk taking in the different IS projects'. South Korean entities, the authors argued, 'seemed to view IT in a more traditional, operational vein with little tolerance for risk taking'. The study concluded that cultural differences, at the national or ethnic level, need to be recognised and their potential influence on IT policy and use appreciated.

Robey and Rodriguez-Dias (1989) drew on case research into the efforts of an American-centred multinational corporation to implement computer-based systems in their Latin America operations. They concluded that the local culture impeded implementation efforts because of the different perceptions of the meaning and likely effects of the system between the different players. For better results, compatibility between local and international managers and workers was essential.

But, overall, the significance of cultural and cross-cultural aspects in the study of MIS has tended to be peripheral to mainstream concerns. We now turn to some empirical evidence to support the thesis that, as information management becomes global, the cultural dimension, though seldom articulated, is of fundamental importance, at the levels of the individual, the enterprise, and the state.

Three Empirical Studies

The empirical studies cited in this chapter draw on three pieces of research: at the level of the individual, a study of decision-making perceptions in a major company in Asia-Pacific; at the level of the corporate organisation, a research project on IT infrastructure within companies in Australia, Asia-Pacific, Europe, and North America; and at the level of the state, case research on the development of state-wide EDI (electronic data interchange) systems in Singapore and Hong Kong.

A study of the use of information in strategic decision-making

The top management team of a major company in Asia-Pacific consisted of the chief executive (who was also chairman of the board of directors) and seven other senior executives each responsible for one of the main functions in the organisation, such as finance director, personnel director, and company secretary. Recognising the need for succession planning, the executive board wanted to identify the potential among the next level of executives for the appointment to executive directorships, perhaps after further job experience and management development. They drew an important distinction between managerial competencies as general managers and corporate governance competencies as directors.

A study was made of the core competencies required of executive directors in that company and an assessment centre was developed to assess the potential of the participants. These were thirty-four senior executives, each reporting to a member of the company's executive board. They came from a range of professional and academic backgrounds, had diverse functional and business experiences and included both Asian- and Western-born and educated members. Various exercises and psychometric instruments were employed in the assessment centre. (For a detailed case-study description and discussion of the project see Tricker and Lee, 1996.)

One of the exercises was a test of the strategic-thinking capability of each individual, which took the form of a three-hour written analysis of a case, undertaken without prior preparation or discussion, in examination conditions. Participants were asked to write a brief for the chairman of their company in reaction to merger proposals which the case explained had just been received between their company and another in the same industry.

Each participant was given an identical set of papers, containing historical, operational, financial, organisational, and governance information about both companies involved in the proposed merger. Each participant had the identical remit in the form of a simulated memo from the chairman explaining that:

I have an initial meeting with the other party in three hours. Please write a briefing paper for me to be able to make an initial response to the proposal. I appreciate that you do not have nearly enough time for a comprehensive strategic review, but give me an outline of the key issues. Let me know what other information we shall need to be able to make a considered response in due course.

However, despite having identical data, the executives tended to perceive the strategic issue at quite different levels of abstraction. The resultant written briefs could be readily grouped into four sets.

Level 1 respondents took a viewpoint in which they were, effectively, inside their own company looking out. They wrote about the anticipated effect of the proposed merger on their own organisation. Their comments were frequently negative. For example: 'a merger would result in a conflict of cultures. They do things quite differently from us. They have a more bureaucratic, authoritarian style of management; whereas we give managers more discretion'

Level 2 respondents had both companies in their reference frame. They articulated the pros and cons of the potential merger. Positively they saw potential benefits from a combined organisation, such as scale benefits, cost savings, and other synergies. Negatively they identified problems that might arise on such an integration, such as adverse effects in the market place, a lowering of employee morale, concerns about the share price, and so on.

Level 3 respondents took an industry-wide perspective. They felt the need to have present and potential customers, competitors, and strategic allies in their frame of reference. Their strategic review was wider, incorporating the interests of many more stakeholders. Consequently, their strategic conclusions and recommendations were necessarily more politically sensitive. They also felt the need for much more and varied information.

Level 4 respondents set their brief to the chairman in a competitive industry-wide setting but added a broader political, economic, social, and technological context. Their perceptions were the most truly strategic, taking into account many, if not most, of the significant strategic variables in the simulated merger situation. In effect, they looked at the strategies being pursued by the other company as well as their own. They were capable of seeing the world through the eyes of the other company's directors. 'What do they want to achieve from this merger?' they asked; and in the process utilised information in a significantly different way.

Although the form of the exercise did not permit rigorous relationships to be identified between the outcomes and the various personal characteristics of the respondents, the results demonstrated conclusively that respondents who came from diverse cultural backgrounds perceived the issue over a range of different levels of abstraction and perception and, consequently, produced strikingly different strategic insights.

In other words, despite being in receipt of identical information, the cultural background of each subject—their expectations, beliefs, and values which had inevitably been influenced by family, education, business experiences, and other cultural determinants—significantly affected the interpretation of that information and the resultant outcome.

A study of IT infrastructure

The second piece of work involved an international study of the provision of IT infrastructure within groups of companies and was undertaken by scholars in the Business Schools of the Universities of Melbourne, Boston, London, and Hong Kong. The assumption underlying this research was that all corporate groups had a strategic option in the extent to which

IT infrastructure (defined as the availability of networks, access to data, and the provision of systems support) was provided centrally to all subsidiary companies in the group or was the individual responsibility of each subsidiary.

IT provision and IT investment, it was argued, can be categorised into four elements—transactional, informational, strategic, and infrastructure. Infrastructure investment is often more difficult to justify economically because the benefits are shared across the organisation. The analogy used was the development of road or other utility networks within countries, where the benefits are shared by a wide variety of users. Notice that the underlying paradigm reflects Western organisational assumptions and experience.

However, the Hong Kong experience did not appear to fit the model (Whitman et al., 1995). The organisational approaches to IT in two important trading houses (Jardine Matheson and Hutchison Whampoa) and a major bank (the Bank of East Asia) were studied initially. Two problems became apparent.

First, unlike the Australian, American, and British respondent companies, none of the Hong Kong companies was prepared to disclose any financial or commercial quantitative data. This precluded any benchmark or other comparative analysis. One explanation could be the business culture among 'overseas' Chinese-managed companies. On the one hand, these are typically family businesses in which high interpersonal trust between members, rather than legal contract, exists. On the other hand, this is a low-trust society in which commercial information has to be jealously guarded.

Secondly, the companies' approach to the provision of IT within their corporate groups did not seem to map onto the model underlying the research—that in large and complex organisations IT infrastructure will be provided at the level of both the corporate and the individual strategic business unit. IT seemed to be provided solely business by business. In the trading companies particularly there was seldom a central IT strategy or provision of IT infrastructure. Where there were central IT staff, they only offered consultancy support to strategic business units on request. However, given the conglomerate nature of these companies, with activities ranging from import/export agencies, bottling, transport, retailing, property, as well as businesses in China and other countries in the region, this may not be so surprising. The strategic synergy in such corporate groups lies less in the core competencies of a well-focused industry and market presence, but in group-wide entrepreneurial, financial, and managerial competencies. Consequently, there was less call for the provision of group-wide IT services than in the Western companies.

These findings were supported by a related piece of research which explored the use of IT in Hong Kong, focusing on some of the major IT users. In every case subsidiary companies were expected to develop their own independent IT strategies and IT infrastructures. No attempt was made by a central function to impose or even offer infrastructural support, and there was no evidence that anyone expected it. It was also observed that, by international comparison, each of these companies was highly profitable (reflecting economic growth rates in Asia-Pacific).

In essence, this research demonstrated that Western organisational and business paradigms do not necessarily map onto Asia-Pacific approaches to doing business. Business strategies, organisational structures, indeed many aspects and assumptions about the way business is done, differ across the corporate cultures. So, too, must approaches to MIS.

In the Western-influenced companies, the provision of corporate IT infrastructure was consistent with the strategic thinking at group and strategic business unit (SBU) levels—strategic thinking influenced by concepts of 'core competencies', 'sticking to the knitting', and an aversion to conglomerates, with the strategic advantage, even the strategic necessity in some industries, of a group-wide IT strategy being well recognised.

In the firms influenced by overseas Chinese experience, by contrast, business is more often seen as trading, with companies themselves being treated as commodities. The family, rather than the corporate group, is the central focus of business strategy, with the dominant head using personal power to affect strategic decisions which tend to be more flexible, more emergent, and far more hidden than their Western counterparts. The provision of IT is seen as a support to the operations of each individual business and, consequently, is more significant at the business, rather than the group, level.

Two different interpretations can be advanced for this dichotomy. One is that the overseas Chinese approach reflects business cultures that are still developing and that, with the next generation of business leaders, the context and the concept of business will converge towards Anglo-American practices both operationally and strategically. The other is that Asia-Pacific overseas Chinese success reflects an alternative way of doing business, involving dynamic relationships in changing business networks, which owes little to and will be uninfluenced by Western experience.

Indeed, some might argue that this experience offers a model of the strategy, structure, and style of business for the coming millennium—more flexible and evolutionary, relying on shifting strategic alliances (sometimes between competitors as well as allies) rather than the nineteenth-century concepts of the bounded joint-stock, limited-liability company.

A further finding of the Hong Kong research was that, although firms had not invested in IT infrastructure *within* corporate groups, there had been significant IT system developments *between* companies not connected through ownership, but through their added-value chains and networks —what the researchers termed the development of IT 'superstructure'.

Such strategies for information systems reflected the companies' business strategies, which frequently involved strategic alliances, joint ventures, and outsourcing. Consequently, the effect of strategic developments between firms might, in information system terms, be the advent of systems at the industry-wide meta-level, linking together enterprises throughout the added-value network or chain with the ultimate users, rather than group- or firm-specific information systems.

Even though it may appear that the application of information techno-logy is converging around the world, the actual need for management information, the practical development of information systems to support business strategies, and the real use to which information technology is being put can have significantly different dimensions because of the cultural influences and expectations.

Comparative case study research of the development of state-wide EDI

The third piece of research involved information management at the state level and contrasted the experiences in building state-wide EDI (electronic data interchange) systems in Hong Kong and Singapore. The sources for this work included contract research involvement with the Hong Kong EDI project since 1990, an MBA dissertation on the Hong Kong experience (Griffith, 1995), Harvard Business School case studies on the Singapore experience (Harvard Business School, 1993) and a case study on the Hong Kong experience (Western Business School, 1994).

Singapore is an island of 625 square kilometres at the southern end of the Malaysian peninsular, with a population of 2.65 million. Under the direc-tion of President Lee Kwan Yue, the country sustained remarkable economic growth over more than twenty years. Significant government involvement in the economic life of the country, including public housing and owner-ship of telecommunications, airport, port, airline, and government busi-ness enterprises, was funded significantly from the mandatory employee retirement savings scheme.

Typical of the Singaporean government's involvement in the economic direction of the state was the IT2000 project. In April 1992, the govern-ment announced an information technology vision and plan for the next fifteen years, with 95 per cent of homes and all offices cabled for Internet and interactive TV and cable services. This, said the report, would turn Singapore into an 'intelligent island', providing an Asia-Pacific centre for expertise, goods, services, and information. At the heart of this plan was a national information infrastructure that would capitalise on information as a key factor of production and an important ingredient for enhancing the quality of life of its people (Soh et al., 1993).

The development of a state-wide EDI system, called TradeNet, was already well developed, having been launched in 1989. Today TradeNet facilitates the electronic exchange of all inter-company trade transactions, in a standard format, for Singapore's traders, including freight forwarders, agents, and carriers; shippers and freight receivers; banks, finance houses, and insurance companies; the Changi Airport; the Port of Jurong; and government agencies such as customs and excise, statistics, and the Trade Development Board.

Increasingly, TradeNet is being used to connect Singapore's business community to their counterparts around the world. The underpinning IT system runs on IBM equipment linked by dial-up or leased telephone lines to all members of the trading community, each of whom uses appropriate terminals to access the system. TradeNet has adopted the United Nations EDIFACT international message standards. It is now possible, for example, for a container ship en route to Singapore to connect via satellite to the Singaporean EDI system to arrange docking, unloading, customs clearance, and the notification of all other parties involved, including the shipping agents, the freight forwarders, banks, insurance companies, and the customers to make the necessary trans-shipment, transportation, or storage of cargo before the ship even arrives.

All trade transactions in Singapore now go through TradeNet, not least because the government no longer accepts anything other than electronic information for customs, excise, and trade-reporting purposes. Cost savings and other benefits have been reported by some of the business users; moreover government departments have been able to cope with increasing volumes of transactions with greater speed and accuracy than would otherwise have been the case with manual paperwork systems.

The Hong Kong experience of EDI, however, has been very different. Hong Kong has a population of some 6.2 million and has also been economically highly successful in recent years. The early initiative to develop EDI in Hong Kong pre-dated Singapore's. But unlike Singapore, this was led by a consortium of businesses, including leading banks, shippers, airline and shipping companies, and the Hong Kong Telephone Company. The government did not lead in the project, but contributed 10 per cent of the initial consultancy costs, with the other nine consortium members contributing the balance.

The initial consultancy proposal suggested that the provision of a business community-wide EDI system, catering for the needs of over 10,000 small businesses (five times more than Singapore), coping with trade documents in Chinese (the Singaporean system demands that all transactions be reported in English), and developing the system and educating user firms, would not be commercially viable in a free competitive market like Hong Kong. The consultants felt that a state-led initiative was not consistent with the *laissez-faire*, minimal government policies of Hong Kong. Consequently, they proposed that the provision of EDI services be left to the private sector to provide on a piecemeal basis, as and when commercially viable.

Nevertheless, in 1990 the consortium members, now called Tradelink, and including the government as a minority partner, decided to explore the possibilities of a territory-wide EDI utility further, funding a development study under the name SPEEDI. In 1991 Tradelink commenced discussions to implement the proposals. The Executive Council of the government (Hong Kong was then a British colony with a governor appointed in London) agreed that Tradelink be given an exclusive franchise to generate a secure revenue stream that could be used to fund the uncommercial community activities, and a seven-year right to offer EDI services for government trade transactions (such as import/export documentation) was given the following year.

Tenders for the provision of the hardware and software were received in 1992 and 1993 and IBM was announced as the lead systems integrator. Subsequently, IBM withdrew and was replaced by Hewlett Packard. Systems development and testing was expected to be carried out in the following two years. However, in 1996 an emergency meeting of the Legislative Council was called on to make an allocation of funds to enable the project to proceed. Although trials were continuing, the system had not accepted responsibility, at that time, for carrying any live transactions. In 1997 the sovereignty of Hong Kong reverted to the People's Republic of China (PRC) with the British governor being replaced by a chief executive chosen by an electoral college nominated by the PRC and a new Executive Council, again appointed by the PRC authorities.

What might be concluded by comparing the Singaporean and the Hong Kong experiences in providing state-wide EDI? The Singapore TradeNet was successfully implemented quite quickly and is now carrying all trade transactions in the territory. This was achieved by strong government strategic leadership, government funding (both directly and through subsidised support from government agencies and enterprises), and government edicts to business that required them to use the EDI system. Singapore now has centralised EDI, facilitating and recording all trade transactions in the country, under government control.

By contrast, the Hong Kong Tradelink system lacked a government sponsor: indeed, some government departments appeared less than enthusiastic to the idea. Similarly, there was no major government funding in the earlier years.

But, by the same token, Hong Kong does not have centrally addressable files that record all trade transactions in the territory in detail: files which are potentially available to government departments and others in power seen to have a legitimate 'need to know' about prices, trading details, market shares, or whatever. Both case studies will provide ongoing evidence of the importance of political and cultural issues in information system developments.

Discussion

Each of these three studies shows the significance of the cultural dimension in understanding the management of information. In the first study, individuals drew fundamentally different conclusions for a strategic decision even though they were in receipt of identical information. Their perception of the nature of the issue was at differing levels of abstraction: some saw only the operational implications in their own narrow confine, whilst at the other extreme, some were able to ride the conceptual helicopter seeing the situation from on high and through the eyes of the other players.

Consequently, we can conclude that, in analysing needs for management information and designing appropriate support systems, an understanding of the cultural context of the individual players is vital. Such an appreciation of culture needs to go far beyond national, regional, or ethnic cultural differences (the cross-cultural differences which are typically associated with the concept of culture) to embrace differences of belief, knowledge, and expectation.

The second study, which looked at differences in the provision of IT infrastructural support within corporate groups around the world, found that some (predominantly Western) assumptions about the way business was done and enterprises were organised did not map onto the experience of successful groups of companies run by overseas Chinese entrepreneurs.

This work emphasises the importance of an appreciation of corporate or organisational culture in the development of IT and information system support. Again, whilst the cultural differences may be influenced by national, regional, or ethnic cultures, the appreciation of culture needs to go deeper to incorporate differences in corporate and organisational cultures, which may be influenced by the history of the firm (the significant learning experiences of its opinion-formers to date), the personality of its leaders, how power is exercised, its industry, its scale, its ownership, indeed any experience that has created its values, beliefs, and expectations.

The third study introduced issues in the management of IT and information at the level of the state. In contrasting the experiences of Singapore and Hong Kong in the development of state-wide EDI, we saw the importance of the culture at the national level, with its political, social, and economic implications. Again an understanding of the development of effective IT and information management support at this level calls for an appreciation of the cultural context.

The three pieces of research support the original thesis that culture influences the use of information (and consequently the development of information systems and the successful application of IT) at the levels of the individual, the enterprise, and the state. Consequently, it is argued, culture needs to be an inherent component in all studies of information management, management information systems, and the application of information technology. It is not an optional extra.

Furthermore, it is now apparent that, as information management becomes increasingly global, the cultural dimension, though seldom articulated to date, has become fundamentally important. This is again true at the levels of the individual, the enterprise, and the state.

Finally, we can conclude that the study of management information systems has become the study of information management. The successful application of IT is much less of a challenge than the effective use of information. That needs an understanding of the cultural context.

Conclusion

In conclusion, we can now consider some of the outstanding issues in the appreciation of the cultural context of MIS studies; issues that need to be addressed by scholars and practitioners of the subject at the level of the individual, the enterprise, and the state.

State involvement in information management

The ideological underpinnings of information management have typically been ignored in IS studies to date. The mainly Western-oriented literature frequently makes sweeping and unarticulated ideological assumptions: for example that individual freedom is to be preferred to state controls, that private ownership is preferable to state ownership, and that open-market competition is preferable to state planning. But totalitarian, centralist, and authoritarian regimes do not necessarily share such perspectives. Yet they may develop information systems for management decision-making that are highly successful.

As George Ayittey, president of the Free Africa Foundation, wrote in *The Economist* on 15 June 1996, 'an efficient and competent authoritarian state, pursuing the right policies, can lift its people out of poverty. People may be willing to give up some of their liberties and cede massive resources to the state to improve their economic lives (Chile); to combat an external communist threat (the Asian tigers); or to redeem nationalistic pride (Japan after 1945).'

Issues of free speech, civil liberties, state security, and control are all involved. An unanswered question is whether free access to economic information underpins long-term economic success. Regulation and enforcement of many aspects of information management can fall to the state, including the ownership and control of information, rights of access to information, and the privacy and security of information. This area promises to be an important field in future MIS studies—and a fascinating one because, ultimately, it is about the use of power.

The ownership and control of information

Issues currently being faced by countries in Asia-Pacific demonstrate dramatically some of the issues that need to be part of MIS studies. In China, with a population of over 1.2 billion people, all Internet users must be registered with the Ministry of Posts and Telecommunications (MPT). All networks are supposed to be controlled by the MPT, using regulated portals that the ministry provides. CHINANET, the national Internet backbone joint venture between the MPT and the Ministry of Communications, may well become the world's largest wide-area network. However, the 'spreading of information that would "hinder public order" is forbidden'. Xinhua, the official news agency, which is under the authority of the Central Committee of the Communist Party, is one of China's principal propaganda organs. It also has exclusive authority to regulate the distribution of economic information in China.

Foreign wire services including Reuters have been blamed for destabilising the financial markets, the Chinese authorities complaining of 'aggressive reporting' of problems in their stock markets. 'Approved foreign economic information providers will be punished . . . if their information to Chinese users contains anything forbidden by Chinese laws and regulations, or slanders or jeopardises the national interests of China.'

Essentially, China needs to control the dissemination of information, to uphold Communist orthodoxy, and prevent opposition, particularly campaigning by exiled dissidents. Investigative journalism is not allowed. To quote Li Kehan, vice-director of the Ministry of Radio, Film, and Television, 'radio and television at all levels in China should be the tongue and throat of the Communist Party and the people of China'. To reinforce their commercial advantage, the Australian News Corporation's Star TV satellite broadcasts to China withdrew the BBC World Service in 1995 and entered a joint venture with the state-owned China Central Television.

By contrast, Hong Kong with 6 million people has more Internet service providers than any Asia-Pacific country except Japan. With the change of sovereignty in 1997, from a British colony to a reunification with China, the availability and access to the Internet, and the uses to which it is put, may prove to be the economic and political battlefield on which the contrasting ideologies of Hong Kong and China, and the reality of 'one country, two systems', are fought out.

Meanwhile the overseas Chinese businesses in other countries throughout the Asia-Pacific region continue to enhance their increasingly global power by international information access, using IT networks to reinforce their 'guanxi' relationships, which tend to be based on mutual respect and trust, rather than relying on contract and law.

Singapore (which has 100,000 Internet accounts for its 2.6 million people) also exercises tight controls over broadcast and print media, prohibiting anti-government comment. A government minister has said that 'the information highway that passes through Singapore must be clean: Internet providers down to cybercafes must register with the Broadcasting Authority . . . the influx of objectionable materials via the new electronic media, if left unchecked, will undermine our values and traditions' (George Yeo, Minister of Information and the Arts, *Singapore Times*, 6 Mar. 1996).

Thailand has a high-quality Internet based on its universities and technical institutions, with many Internet-literate people. Fidel Ramos, President of the Philippines, has his own WWW page; but so does the military junta that runs Burma Myanmar. Vietnam prohibits access to the WWW, permitting only email.

Rights of access to information

But there is the other side of the argument on the ownership and control of information described above. The Communications Decency Act passed by the US Congress in February 1996, as part of a telecommunications control bill, which attempted to ban offensive material from any net or on-line site that could be accessed by a minor, was ruled unconstitutional by a Philadelphia court in June because it conflicted with the US constitution's guarantee of free speech. Free speech and civil liberties groups had already mounted a worldwide protest campaign on the Internet opposing the anti-pornography measures in the act. The importance of appreciating cultural (in this case the cross-cultural) differences in applying IT and developing MIS is apparent.

Privacy and security of information

The right of access by individuals to files containing personal data has been enshrined in the statutes of many Western countries. It is far from being a universal right. Freedom of information laws, which enable individuals and organisations to access government information, are available in some but certainly not all Western countries. What is the appropriate answer to questions about privacy versus freedom of access to information, what is 'right' in a given context, is another issue determined by culture.

Meanwhile a degree of global convergence in information systems can be seen, for example, in the mutually agreed access to share price movements between members of IOSCO, the international organisation of securities trading commissions, which includes the regulators of over 80 per cent of the world's traded stock market capitalisation. The global convergence of securities trading, forex trading, and other aspects of financial markets further reflects this trend. The growing recognition of international accounting standards, auditing standards, and IT standards (such as the UNEDI standards) also illustrates this trend. Yet differentiation because of cultural differences remains significant.

The future structure and style of organisations

The implications for the structure and style of organisations as a result of professional information management are legion. Indeed, an alternative way to perceive an organisation is as an information network linked through its information processes. In addition to corporate-wide information systems, bounded by ownership, information networks mirroring the organisational relationships linking suppliers, manufacturers, distributors, merchants, customers, finance houses, and other elements in industrial and commercial added-value networks have become significant.

At the level of the firm, it is well known that organisational changes can be facilitated by the development of management information systems. Organisations can be 'flattened', power drawn towards the centre or distributed towards the periphery, individuals can be given the opportunity to search for information relevant to their decision-making needs. Indeed, in many industries these days, the professional application of IT is a commercial necessity as well as providing a strategic opportunity (retail banking ATM networks, airline reservations and operations, procurement and distribution systems in manufacturing and retailing, to name but a few).

Nor have the organisational implications of such IT applications yet been fully reached. Over 2 million copies of the program Lotus Notes Groupware were sold in the early 1990s, to facilitate the information and communication processes prevailing in the conventional organisational wisdom of that time: team management, flattened bureaucracy, empowered workers, and open communications. In 1995 IBM bought Lotus for $3.5bn —a record for the software industry (*The Economist,* 13 Jan. 1996). But now such facilities are being replaced by intranets—networks internal to companies, replicating the Internet at the corporate level, running on private networks with similar network equipment and software, web server, browser, and email software for employees' own PCs, user-friendly with multi-media access—linking parts of an organisation round the world, fenced off from the rest of the Internet by 'firewalls', allowing employees to access corporate files and communicate with each other and, in the process, significantly influencing organisational structures and styles. Such developments are inevitably affecting the cultures of organisations. The importance of an awareness of the cultural context of the application of IT and the management of information is self-evident.

Yet the underlying theoretical paradigms in the practice of information systems management and the theory-building of MIS research, to date, have tended to be economic and managerial, sociological and organisational, overlaid on a basis of operational information technology and computer science. Contingency theory, organisational theories, agency theory, and transactional analysis, plus the systems and expectations approaches, have each provided relevant theoretical structures. In this chapter it has been argued that it is now essential to add a cultural and cross-cultural element, not as an optional extra, but as a fundamental foundation of the subject.

The management of information systems (and the teaching of MIS) can be approached from two quite different perspectives:

- the application of information technology to organisational processes;
- the satisfaction of individuals', organisations', and states' information needs.

If MIS is perceived as being essentially about the application of IT to organisational processes, then the research, writing, and teaching will be about IT hardware and software, system analysis and design methodologies, and data management techniques. Decision-makers' information needs can be predetermined. They can be treated as a required output. Cultural aspects will be 'outside' the system under focus.

On the other hand, if MIS is perceived as meeting the information needs of individuals, enterprises, and states, then the research, writing, and teaching has to be about objectives, strategy formulation, decision-making, and the processes of control and accountability. IT becomes the means to the end, not the end in itself. The cultural context becomes a primary concern. Those with such a cultural orientation will see that decision-makers in different cultural contexts think and act differently and, therefore, need access to different information. Both perspectives are entirely legitimate. Each is necessary. But they are fundamentally different in their scope, focus, and content.

Of course, information technology needs to be managed professionally. The level of IT investment in many organisations is now immense. But in managing information, information technology is seldom the issue that determines overall success. For many years information technology has been far ahead of the ability of top management to appreciate the strategic opportunities and threats of that technology and of operational management to perceive the organisational implications. Information is a crucial resource for individual, enterprise, and state. Data, even information, may be culture free but knowledge is culturally determined. And at the end of the day it is knowledge that determines the ultimate effectiveness and success of individuals, of enterprises, and of nation-states.

Discussion Questions

1. What might the successful organisation of the twenty-first century look like? Which companies will succeed, which fail—and why?
2. What might the consequences of the information explosion in networked communication be for the nation-state?
3. Can we better the odds that individuals of different ages, languages, experiences, and cultures will be able to assimilate and use the knowledge to which they now have shared access?

(Inspired by a talk reported in the *Washington Post*, 16 January 1996, by Dr Charles M. Vest, president, Massachusetts Institute of Technology.)

References

ACM/IEEE-CS Curriculum Task Force (1991), 'Computing Curricula', *Communications of the ACM*, 33, 3, June.

Ahituv, N., and Neumann, S. (1990), *Principles of Information Systems for Management*, 3rd edn. (Dubuque, Ia.: William Brown).

Ang, A. Y., and Lo, B. W. N. (1991), 'Changing Emphases in Information Systems Curriculum: An Australian Perspective', *Second Annual Conference on Information Systems and Database Special Interest Group, University of New South Wales, Australia, February.*

Anthony, R. N. (1965), *Planning and Control Systems: A Framework for Analysis* (Cambridge, Mass.: Harvard University Press).

Avison, D. (1994), 'What is IS?', Inaugural Lecture, University of Southampton, November.

Backhouse, J., Liebenau, J., and Land, F. F. (1991), 'The Discipline of Information Systems', *Journal of Information Systems*, 1, 1.

Bacon, C. J. (1992), 'A Model for Teaching the Management of IST', *12th World Computer Congress of IFIP, Madrid, Aug.*

Banville, C., and Landry, M. (1989), 'Can the Field of MIS be Disciplined?', *Communications of the ACM*, 32, 1, Jan.

Bariff, M., and Ginsberg, M. (1982), 'MIS and the Behavioural Sciences: Research Patterns and Prescriptions', *Data Base*, 14, 1.

Bell, D. (1973), *The Coming of Post-industrial Society* (New York: Basic Books).

Bjorn-Andersen, N. (1985), 'IS—a Doubtful Science? Research Methods in Information Systems', in E. Mumford, R. Hirschheim, G. Fitzgerald, and A. Wood-Harper (eds.), *A Participative Approach to the Design of Computer Systems* (Elsevier: North-Holland).

Boaden, R., and Locket, G. (1991), 'Information Technology, Information Systems and Information Management: Definition and Development', *European Journal of Information Systems*, 1, 1.

Brehaut, S. (1991), 'Teaching Information Systems: A Useable Concept of Information', *Interface*, 12, 4, Winter.

Buckingham, R. A., Hirschheim, R. A., Land, F. F., and Tully, C. J. (1987), 'Information Systems Curriculum: A Basis for Design', in R. A. Buckingham et al. (eds.), *Information Systems Education: Recommendations and Implications* (London: Cambridge University Press).

Cash, J. I., Jr., McFarlan, H. W., and McKenney, J. I., and Vitale, M. R. (1988), *Corporate Information Systems: Text and Cases*, 3rd edn. Homewood, Ill.: Irwin).

Cavaye, A. L. M., and Cragg, P. B. (1993), 'Strategic Information Systems Research: A Review and Research Framework', *Journal of Strategic Information Systems*, 2, 2, June.

Cheon, M. J., Grover, V., and Sabherwal, R. (1993), 'The Evolution of Empirical Research in IS: A Study in IS Maturity', *Information and Management*, 24, 3.

Cooper, R. B. (1994), 'The Inertial Impact of Culture on IT Implementation', *Information and Management*, 27, 1: 17–31.

Culnan, M., and Swanson, E. (1986), 'Research in Management Information Systems, 1980–1984: Points of Reference', *MIS Quarterly*, Sept.

Davies, L., and Ledington, P. (1991), *Information in Action: Soft Systems Methodology* (Basingstoke: Macmillan).

Davis, G. B., and Olsen, M. H. (1985), *Management Information Systems: Conceptual Foundations, Methods and Development*, 2nd edn. (New York: McGraw Hill).

Deal, T., and Kennedy, A. (1982), *Corporate Culture: The Rites and Rituals of Corporate Life* (London: Addison Wesley).

Dickson, G. W., and Wetherbe, J. C. (1985), *The Management of Information Systems* (New York: McGraw Hill).

Earl, M. J. (1989), *Management Strategies for Information Technology* (Englewood Cliffs, NJ: Prentice Hall).

—— and Hopwood, A. G. (1980), 'From Management Information to Information Management', in H. Lucas, F. Land, T. Lincoln, and S. Supper (eds.), *The Information Systems Environment* (Amsterdam: North-Holland).

Gorla, Narasimhalah (1989), 'Identifying MIS Research Issues Using a Research Framework', *Information and Management*, 17, 3.

Gover, V., Segars, A. H., and Durand, D. (1994), 'Organisational Practice, Information Resource Deployment and Systems Success: A Cross Cultural Survey', *Journal of Strategic Information Systems*, 3, 2, June.

Griffith, E. K. (1995), 'Electronic Data Interchange in Hong Kong: Barriers to Implementation in the International Trading Community', unpublished MBA dissertation for Brunel University, Henley-on-Thames.

Grimshaw, D. J. (1992), 'Towards a Taxonomy of Information Systems', *Journal of Information Technology*, 7, 1, Mar.

Gu, J., and Zhu, Z. (1996), 'Knowing *Wu Li*, Sensing *Shi-Li*, Caring *Ren-Li*: The Methodology of the WSR Approach', working paper, Institute of Systems Science, Chinese Academy of Sciences, Beijing, and the Centre for Systems Studies, University of Hull, Hull.

Harvard Business School (1993), 'Singapore TradeNet: A Tale of One City', case study 9-191-009 and 9-191-025. Cases prepared by John King and Benn Konsynski, Harvard Business School, Boston.

Harvard Conference on the Internet and Society (1996), Harvard University, Cambridge, Mass., May.

Hucznyski, A., and Buchanan, D. (1985), *Organisational Behavior* (Englewood Cliffs, NJ: Prentice Hall).

Jackson, I. F. (1986), *Corporate Information Management* (Englewood Cliffs, NJ: Prentice Hall).

Keen, P. G. W. (1987), 'MIS Research: Current Status, Trends and Needs', in R. A. Buckingham et al. (eds.), *Information Systems Education: Recommendations and Implementation* (London: Cambridge University Press).

Landry, M., and Banville, C. (1992), 'A Disciplined Methodological Pluralism for MIS Research', *Accounting, Management and Information Technologies*, 2, 2.

Laribee, J. F. (1992), 'Building a Stronger IRM Curriculum', *Information Systems Management*, 9, 2, Spring.

Lee, W. (1996) (programme coordinator), Pacific Multimedia Information Systems Workshop, University of Science and Technology, Hong Kong, 25–8 June.

Lucas, H. C., Clowes, K. W., and Kaplan, R. B. (1974), 'A Framework for Information Systems', *INFOR*, 12.

Lyytinen, K. (1987), 'Different Perspectives on Information Systems: Problems and Solutions', *ACM Computing Surveys*, 19, 1, Mar.

McNurlin, B. C., and Sprague, R. H., Jr. (1989), *Information Systems Management in Practice* (Englewood Cliffs, NJ: Prentice Hall).

Martin, E. W., deHayes, D. W., Hoffer, J. A., and Perkins, W. C. (1994), *Managing Information Technology: What Managers Need to Know*, 2nd edn. (London: Macmillan).

Pacific Asia Conference on Information Systems (1997), programme committee co-chaired by Professor Guy Gable and Ron Weber.

Pacific Multimedia Information Systems Workshop (1996), programme co-ordinator Winnie Lee, University of Science and Technology, Hong Kong, 25–8 June.

Parker, C. S., and Case, T. (1993), *Management Information Systems: Strategy and Action* (New York: McGraw Hill).

Probert, S. K. (1994), 'Teaching and Research in Information Systems: Three Basic Issues', *Systemist*, 16, 1, Feb.

Reponen, T. (1993), 'Strategic Information Systems: A Conceptual Analysis', *Journal of Strategic Information Systems*, 2, 2, June.

Robey, D., and Rodriguez-Dias, A. (1989), 'The Organisational and Cultural Context of Systems Implementation: Case Experience from Latin America', *Information and Management*, 17, 4.

Robson, W. (1994), *Strategic Management and Information Systems: An Integrated Approach* (London: Pitman).

Sabherwal, R., and King, W. R. (1991), 'Towards a Theory of Strategic Use of Information Resources: An Inductive Approach', *Information and Management*, 20, 3.

Sawaragi, Y., Nakayama, Y., and Nakamuri, Y. (1988), 'An Introduction to a New Systems Engineering Approach: Shiayaka Systems Approach', *OHM* (in Japanese).

Soh, C., Siong Neo, B., and Markus, L. (1993), 'IT2000: A Critical Appraisal of Singapore's State-Wide Strategic Planning Process for Information Technology', *Journal of Strategic Information Systems*, 2, 4, Dec.

Stamper, R. K. (1985), 'Towards a Theory of Information: Information—Mystical Fluid or the Subject of Scientific Enquiry?', *Computer Journal*, 28, 3.

Swanson, E. B., Land, F. F., and Targett, D. (1991), 'Information Systems as a Field of Study: Its Place in the Graduate Business School', *Journal of the Graduate Management Admissions Council* (Los Angeles), Spring.

Tricker, R. I. (1977) (ed.), *The Individual, the Enterprise & the State* (London: Associated Business Programmes).

—— (1992), 'The Management of Organisational Knowledge', in R. D. Galliers (ed.), *Information Systems Research: Issues, Methods and Practical Guidelines* (Oxford: Blackwell).

—— and Lee, K. (1996), 'Assessing Directors' Core Competencies: The Case of the Mass Transit Railway Corporation, Hong Kong', *Corporate Governance: An International Review*, 5, 2.

Van Gigch, J. P., and Pipino, L. L. (1986), 'In Search of a Paradigm for the Discipline of Information Systems', *Future Computer Systems*, 1, 1.

Ward, J., Griffiths, L. L., and Whitmore, P. (1990), *Strategic Planning for Information Systems* (Chichester: John Wiley).

Weber, R. (1987), 'Towards a Theory of Artifacts: A Paradigmatic Base for Information Systems Research', *Journal of Information Systems*, Spring.

Western Business School (1994), 'Hong Kong's Tradelink: An EDI Vision', unnumbered, case prepared by Lisa Surmon under the supervision of Sid L. Huff, University of Western Ontario, London.

Whitman, John, Farhoomand, A., and Tricker, R. (1995), 'How Hong Kong Firms View Information Technology', an unpublished report for the joint Information Technology Infrastructure Study of the Universities of Melbourne, Boston, London, and Hong Kong sponsored by IBM (Hong Kong: University of Hong Kong School of Business).

Zuboff, S. (1988), *In the Age of the Smart Machine: The Future of Work and Power* (New York: Basic Books).

17

Hybrid Managers
An Example of Tunnel Vision and Regression in Management Research

WENDY L. CURRIE AND IAN A. GLOVER

Introduction

The notion of the hybrid manager[1] as someone to be put in charge of information technology (IT) and other technical operations has prevailed in UK management research in recent years, especially in the last two decades. In this chapter, writings on the hybrid manager are evaluated against a background of twentieth-century discussion of management, managers, and technical and scientific professionals in the UK. The discussion is divided into five sections. First, we consider literature on managers and professionals in the UK from a historical perspective. Second, we review work on engineers and scientists and their entry into British management and compare their experiences with their counterparts in continental Europe. The third section considers the concept of generalisable core competencies in organisations and asks whether it is possible or even practical and efficient to differentiate between what is 'core' and 'peripheral' to economic activity. The fourth section moves on to discuss the literature on hybrid managers in the context of how managerial and technical work is perceived in different countries. Finally, the fifth section offers a critique of the hybrid manager concept by suggesting that divisions between managerial and technical work essentially construct a false dichotomy, often referred to in the wider business and management literature as 'a culture gap'. This serves to reinforce the division of labour between what is perceived as managerial and technical work respectively. The chapter concludes by arguing that as opposed to constructing a barrier between the two areas by offering 'the hybrid manager' in the form of *the solution*, we should instead seek to integrate managerial and technical work by re-evaluating the role and

[1] A range of definitions of the hybrid manager exist. However, within an IS context, one of the most cited definitions is offered by Earl (1989) who contends that hybrid managers are 'people with strong technical skills and adequate business knowledge, or vice versa . . . people with technical skills able to work in user areas doing a line functional job, but adept at developing and implementing IT application areas'.

nature of work in the new information society. To this end, the concept of hybrid manager becomes redundant.

Managers and Professionals in the UK

To understand why the notion of the hybrid manager has arisen along with its problems and prospects, it is necessary to explore and understand the general character of UK management and managerial work, if not over the last 100 years, then at least over the last few decades. As many studies have shown, definitions of management and managerial work differ across continents and between and possibly within countries (Granick, 1962; HMSO, 1987; Currie, 1994, 1995). The terms 'technocrat', 'custodian', and 'professional' have been used to identify and compare different kinds of management-level job-holder in industrial countries (Glover and Hughes, 1996). Technocrats, who in western and north-western Europe combine the qualities of both generalists and specialists, are high-powered, broadly educated experts who are qualified to about master's degree level. Custodians are generally products of the English-speaking countries, are usually graduates in liberal arts and pure science subjects, and tend to be employed in government, in very senior posts in the civil service and elsewhere. Terms like 'talented-amateur', 'generalist', and 'philosopher-king' have been used for them, and they were expected to be guardians of the UK's imperial and other governing traditions. Integrity, intelligence, objectivity, and cultivation are among their best qualities. But they have been criticised for their technical ignorance, personal eccentricity, disdain for industry and 'trade', and intellectual narrowness.

Professionals, in the UK and in slightly different ways in other English-speaking countries, have filled, from the nineteenth century onwards, something of a historic vacuum in the education and training of expert specialists and middle managers for most kinds of employing organisation. Professional occupations tended to have provincial origins in the UK. They grew from the original professions of law, medicine, and the clergy through civil engineering and surveying and other tasks concerned with land and the environment, through university teaching, other kinds of engineering, accounting, into the late nineteenth and twentieth century with the proliferation of professions, commercial, communications, educational, health, industrial, social welfare, and so on. However the assumption in relatively individualistic English-speaking countries that elite forms of post-school education were for government, academic, and the most senior professions, and that commerce and industry were slightly inferior activities not needing the most prestigious forms of education, was associated with the professionals who filled most expert specialist positions and middle management in commerce, industry, and local government, effectively being the second eleven in management. This situation contrasted with that in Germany, much of Scandinavia, and elsewhere on the Continent and in the Far East, where more technocratic and state-directed approaches prevailed. To help explain such differences, Sorge (1979) distinguished between state school, individualist, and association approaches to the role of the state, of public non-state bodies like professional associations and trade unions (and the medieval guilds), and of individual employers and employees in education and training. In brief, the British had chosen the individualist and, to a lesser extent, the association approach; the French had followed the state school one; and the Germans had used the state school approach at the management level and the association approach at the skilled worker level respectively.

In another paper, Sorge (1978) explained how Germany had steadfastly refused to copy American approaches to management education after the Second World War (see also Locke, 1966a). In the USA, management courses and the identity of managers had helped to unify people from diverse ethnic, occupational, social, and geographical backgrounds. In the UK they had later helped graduates with 'non-relevant' degrees to learn about business and to identify with it, and professionals and holders of vocational degrees to round themselves out and to become eligible for promotion (see also Fores and Sorge, 1981).

The traditional division in the UK between 'generalist' holders of non-relevant degrees from the older universities and holders of relevant ones from less socially favoured institutions has long been reflected in two major ways of organising and employing units in the UK. The custodian-dominated 'metropolitan one' is associated with London, large prestigious employers, Oxford and Cambridge universities, and central government. Top jobs were staffed by graduates in traditional academic subjects who, it is felt, irrespective of their lack of specialist knowledge, are able to rise above problems and see the wood for the trees. They were supported by professional specialists and other vocationally qualified people in middle management. The other is a provincial approach, associated with smaller and medium-sized companies, public corporations and nationalised industries, professional practices, and local government. Here the professionals tend to be *on top* as well as *on tap*. This approach is in part a reaction against the metropolitan one.

The two models have tended to converge since the 1950s as university-level education was established and became more vocational. Professionals and vocational graduates, and the more traditional kind of graduate with a vocational postgraduate or professional qualification, have multiplied considerably. An increasingly broad, varied, and mixed range of relevant and often innovative courses has been, and continues to be, developed in the UK. This is slowly taking the UK and its education system and managers in a broadly technocratic direction. Yet whilst specialist graduates and

professionals have increasingly had to learn about other specialities, qualifications remain either generalist or specialist in orientation. This is evident when we consider the generalist nature of the MBA degree compared
with the more specialist M.Sc.s or MAs in such areas as technology management or information systems. Certainly, it is indeed the case that many
graduates with a specialist degree in engineering, maths, and economics,
to name but a few, wish to broaden their education with a more general
master's level qualification. They perceive this strategy as more appropriate for entry into managerial work (and hence better-paid jobs) later on.

The more general aspects of Anglo-continental differences in approaches
to management, employment, work, and related educational and training
matters were summarised by Glover and Hughes (1996: 5), as follows. The
western and north-western European *Technik* approach 'tends to emphasise
the value of production, process, the long-term, management *in* specialist
activities and the more positive side of the state's role in economic life',
whereas the Anglo-Saxon one 'stresses consumption, outcome, management
of specialist activity, and the more negative side of the state's role'. This
distinction is very important for our purposes here.

Writing in 1961 in a book entitled *The European Executive*, Granick considered cross-national comparisons of management. In the case of Britain,
unlike France and Germany, he stressed that 'character building' was more
important than developing intellectual or practical skills. The promotion
of *narrow* specialists into managerial work was not encouraged since the
'talented amateur' was believed to be the appropriate role model for management: in other words, a person with a good education who possessed the
rather vague and impenetrable qualities of leadership, flair, and decision-
making ability. Being able to 'fit in' was important, as was being a 'good
team-player'. Notwithstanding the different interpretations of management
throughout Europe and North America, many writers have attempted to
delineate the key activities of management common to all organisational
settings.

The traditional models of management promulgated by Fayol (1949)
and Taylor (1911) have been examined by a number of writers. Kotter
(1982), Mintzberg (1973), and Stewart (1961), for example, focused on
behavioural aspects of managerial work and revealed that management
was not simply about rational, systematic, and reflective planning based upon
the evaluation of hard information reminiscent of economic models of
man (Carley, 1981). Rather it was characterised by responsive and intuitive
decision-making processes. Here, complex tasks and decisions were initiated through political and informal processes where 'soft' information was
considered vitally important. Unlike the former, more clinical approach
to management advocated by Fayol (1949) and Taylor (1911), managerial
decisions were taken at a hectic pace, and were constrained rather than
innovative. To complicate the picture, Smith (1985) found that managerial

jobs change over time, and posited a number of stages or cycles which they commonly pass through. As Mumford (1987) suggests, these studies seem to lie much closer to the reality of managerial experience both in the private and public sectors.

Table 17.1 contrasts earlier work on the key aspects of management with later writers. What is noticeable about this lexicon of key managerial activities is the similarity between the traditional and more recent definitions. For example, Fayol's five-point schema of planning, organising, commanding, co-ordinating, and controlling is, in part, reproduced in the lists of Kotter (1982) and Luthans et al. (1988). Hill (1992) produces a rather long list of attributes, none of which focuses upon technical skill or even awareness. This is interesting in the light of such a list being prepared in the so-called information society. Based upon the relative similarity of the five lists covering more than a forty-year period, are we therefore to assume that management and managerial work remains constant in spite of the significant changes in economic activity characterised by international competition and revolutionary technical changes such as electronic commerce, the Internet, networking, and advances in telecommunications?

Some fairly recent research, which reviewed twenty-nine studies of what managers do, included only two from the public sector (of necessity because of the relative paucity of such studies). The research revealed a wide diversity of behaviour, practice, and job content in managerial work, thus posing difficulties for identifying commonalities across sectors and between organisations belonging to the same sector (Hales, 1986). Such findings at best contradict the *catch-all* interpretations of management outlined in Table 17.1, or at worst render these studies too general to provide a meaningful interpretation of what managers actually do in the workplace. Key problems emerge in examining many of the traditional studies on management, since they rarely comment on whether their sample organisations share a common conceptualisation of management, or share categories for meaningful analysis. Crucially they tend to ignore important contextual and structural factors such as institutional sector; market position; technological capability; power relations between managers and non-managers (e.g. technical specialists); and internal and external social and economic factors which help explain managerial behaviour. Nor do they examine the extent to which tasks done by those called managers were not labelled managerial in other settings (e.g. the public sector), or the degree to which management tasks were assigned to and accomplished by those who did not hold the title of manager (e.g. technical specialists with responsibilities for supervising others). As such, they tend to perceive management as an homogeneous group rather than a heterogeneous one comprised of individuals with competing and conflicting interests, unequal status and power, and different career trajectories and motives (Knights and Murray, 1994).

TABLE 17.1. *Key activities of management*

Fayol (1949)	Mintzberg (1973)	Kotter (1982)	Luthans et al. (1988)	Hill (1992)
Planning	Figurehead	Setting goals and strategies	Exchanging information	Team leader
Organising	Leader	Allocating resources	Handling paperwork	Sales leader
Command	Liaison	Monitoring activities	Decision-making	Boss
Co-ordination	Monitor	Getting information, co-operation, and support from superiors	Controlling	Supervisor
Control	Disseminator	Getting co-operation from other groups	Interacting with outsiders	Organiser
	Spokesperson	Motivating, controlling, and managing conflict	Socialising	Liaison
	Entrepreneur		Managing conflict	Politician
	Disturbance Handler			People manager
	Resource Allocator			Negotiator
	Negotiatior			

What emerges as significant here is the degree to which management is a social construction within organisations. A key example is found in public services, where the lack of people with the title *manager* has too often and too easily been taken for a corresponding dearth of relevant management activity. But simply to accept the labelling of organisational members as either managers or non-managers without questioning the nature of their roles and responsibilities and their approximation to common definitions of management is problematic and likely to create distortions in interpreting reality.

In fact, many people, including technical specialists, undertake activities which approximate to those which are labelled *management*, yet are not given the title of manager. Some even undertake specialist activities, even though they have the title of *manager*! Given this is the case, it follows that we should treat the whole concept of management as rather ill defined and in some respects *meaningless*. Or rather, we may wish to redefine our understanding of management and what constitutes managerial work, and include all those activities which have not been hitherto incorporated into the concept, while at the same time eliminating some activities which seem to be common across all organisational roles. This is of course to recognise the politically contentious nature of undertaking such a task.

The above attempts to contextualise more closely the socially constructed demarcation between generalists and specialists, managerial and non-managerial work, which is characteristic of UK management theory and practice. This helps to explain the concept of the *hybrid manager* which we discuss in more detail below. Such a concept has prospered in a climate of immense change in private and public sector organisations over the last few decades. Intensifying international competition has fuelled the delayering and downsizing of numerous British and overseas companies, especially from the mid-1970s onwards. The manufacturing sector has faced growing competition from the emerging markets of Asia, and the financial services sector has been progressively deregulated creating new entrants from a variety of sectors now offering financial products (i.e. retailing). New technologies in the form of electronic commerce, the Internet, telecommunications and networking, etc., have forced companies to re-evaluate the way they compete, control, and conduct their business operations both nationally and internationally. Similarly in the public sector, we have witnessed unprecedented changes from 1979 onwards. The UK Conservative government administered unpalatable medicine to the public sector by way of legislation on market testing, compulsory competitive tendering (CCT), and contracting out of activities and services. This meant that central and local government departments were coerced to seek partnerships with the private sector to discern the most cost-effective way of administering services to citizens and communities. So, over the last two decades, public services IT departments have been progressively contracted out or *outsourced* to private sector IT providers (Currie, 1996). For example, an ITNet survey found that central government remains the largest IT outsourcing customer in the UK, accounting for £324m of the £1,393m total value of contracts. Central government spent approximately £311.1m in 1996 with one of the major contracts between the Inland Revenue and EDS which is worth as estimated £1.6bn (Currie and Willcocks, 1997).

Clearly, the widespread changes which have taken place in private and public sector organisations have fuelled a debate about managerial capabilities and skills and the relationship between managerial and non-managerial work. Questions which have been posed in the business and management literature have asked: 'What new capabilities and skills are needed for the manager of the 21st century?'; 'How will the information society or age change managerial work and roles?'; 'Will managers need to have a combination of managerial and technical expertise?'; 'How can managers control the activities of knowledge workers?' Although these questions are commonplace in the management literature, they are problematic in themselves since they are derived more from rhetoric than reality. Few of those who seek to pose questions of this nature first define terms such as *information society*, *managerial work*, *managerial* and *technical expertise*; and *knowledge workers*. What is apparent is that, as technological change has revolutionised the world of work, particularly in manufacturing and financial services sectors, commentators have identified a problem which concerns the relationship between managerial and non-managerial work. In other words, how can managers plan, organise, co-ordinate, and control the activities of non-managers? A reading of previous works on this issue shows that this problem is not new and has been the subject of much discussion by academics and practitioners since the industrial revolution. Indeed, the thesis by Berle and Means (1932) considered the separation between ownership and control of industrial organisations, thus placing the nature of managerial work at centre stage! The role of engineers and scientists in management has also been the subject of much research, though often overlooked in much of the recent business and management literature.

Engineers and Scientists in Management

One now fairly well-known strand of thought concerning the positions of technical and scientific experts and expertise in different societies concerns the ways in which subjects for study are classified and regarded. The English language groups subjects into the more precise 'sciences', *pure* and *applied*, and the more discursive 'arts', whereas Continentals have long separated engineering and science (*Technik* and *Wissenschaft* in German), both linguistically and institutionally. Engineering is not 'mere' applied science, but a separate and largely different field of endeavour from science. It synthesises, science analyses. It makes things, and science studies them. It generally attracts more, not less, able school leavers than science, as was long the case in the UK. It does not try to shelter under the wing of science by describing itself with words ending in '-ology'. Those who practise it are both generalists and specialists and tend to dominate organisational hierarchies (cf. Fores and Rey, 1979; Lawrence, 1980).

Another area of research enquiry concerns the place of engineers in management in the UK (cf. Glover and Kelly, 1987; Gospel, 1991; Lee and Smith, 1992). The data and arguments in these books broadly reinforce points made above about engineers and other technical specialists in the UK lacking power and influence in most if not all sectors, for the kinds of reasons already described above. Of perhaps more interest as far as IT specialists are concerned is the literature on scientists (science graduates), and related technical professionals in industry. This has tended to be separate from writings on engineers, because whereas the latter are more straightforwardly interested in why so centrally important an occupation or profession as engineering can be so weak in the sectors in which one might expect it to be dominant, scientists are seen as something of a different case, because they have been assumed to have rather different motives from engineers and the commercial employers in industry. The love of truth, of the pursuit of it both for its own sake and for the reputation which a successful scientist can gain, was seen as being in conflict with the motives of the businessmen and bureaucrats who employed increasing populations of science graduates after the Second World War. Another work in this genre was *Scientists in Industry* (Kornhauser, 1982): the arguments of this American book were questioned in the UK by Cotgrove and Box (1970), who showed how the science graduates who entered industrial employment tended to be motivated more by interest or the content of complex scientific technical work and opportunities for advancement into management than academic scientists, who were genuinely concerned with truth and reputation. Well-known works with diverse relevance both to this literature and to the much more recent one on hybrid managers include Prandy (1965), on the attitudes to professional associations and trade unions and the social class affiliations of scientists and engineers; Schön (1983), on how professionals (not IT ones or scientists in this case) develop their knowledge and skills through their work and their thoughts about their work; and Pettigrew (1985), on the evolution of ICI, a major UK employer of scientists and engineers and other technical specialists, over two decades.

There are also burgeoning literatures on technology manpower and R&D management (Ackroyd, 1995; Demirag, 1996; Thomas, 1996), gender and information technology employees (Baroudi and Igbaria, 1995), knowledge workers (Blackler, 1995), and IT and the effect of its use on middle managers (Dopson and Stewart, 1993). Some links, but precious few systematically spelt-out ones, can be perceived between these writings and those on hybrid managers.

All these literatures are relevant (in varying degrees) to the nature of management; managerial work; the relationship between managers and non-managers in organisations; and the concept of the 'hybrid manager' as a solution to the so-called 'culture gap' between generalists and specialists within organisations. The literature on scientists and engineers in management in the UK, however, offers some interesting insights into Anglo-Saxon approaches to management and managerial work. Certainly, the separation between managerial and technical activities in the UK, unlike West Germany and Japan (Currie, 1994) yet in common with the USA, has fuelled the problem which now faces many industrial and commercial organisations, that is, 'How can generalist and specialist knowledge and expertise be more closely interlinked to enhance efficiency and profit maximisation?' Paradoxically, much of what we have witnessed in management research and practice over the last two decades at least has reinforced rather than eliminated the division of labour between managers and specialists. For example, one the most influential theoretical contributions in recent years has suggested that organisations should retain what is core to their business operations, e.g. their core competencies, and outsource their non-core activities to a third party (Prahalad and Hamel, 1990; Hamel and Heene, 1994; Hamel and Prahalad, 1994). By so doing, senior management will be able to concentrate their attention on achieving value-added results for their organisation rather than waste their time on peripheral activities and services which can be provided more efficiently by a supplier.

Generalizable 'Core' Competencies

To this end, it is worth considering the issue of generalizable *core* competencies and skills in more detail in a UK context. From the mid-1980s at least three influential reports pointed to the inadequacies of British private sector management practice. Somewhat surprisingly, Handy (HMSO, 1987) and Mangham and Silver (1986) remained largely silent about the competencies and skills needed by British managers to enable them to compete with their international rivals. But what do we mean by *core competencies*? By 1988 a series of research projects was launched with the purpose of identifying core competencies relevant to all forms of managerial work. The Chartered Management Initiative had been launched under the aegis of the British Institute of Management, the Confederation of British Industry, and the Foundation for Management Education to devise a professional structure for management in Britain, based on the gradual attainment of those skills defined as core competencies.

Given that managerial work embraces a wide variety of activities where skills, expertise, and knowledge are inextricably linked by a complex web of external and internal conditions, the pursuit of generalizable core competencies becomes problematic. Hirsh and Bevan (1988) for example, found that even where large companies used the same terms to describe specific management competencies, such as leadership or communication, each assigned a different meaning to them. Thus, 'If we ask "Is there a shared language for management skills?" the answer seems to be "yes" at the level of expression, but "no" at the level of meaning.'

Similarly, a European-wide survey by the Ashridge Management Research Group attempted to identify the competencies and skills required for the manager of the future. This report found a mismatch between the competencies and skills advocated by the classical management writers and those put forward by the sample organisations. The main difference was the emphasis by the sample organisations that competencies and skills should become organisation specific. Managers of the future would need to learn about the specific business sector in which they are employed, in addition to acquiring in-depth knowledge about their organisation and technical capabilities (Currie, 1999).

In a more recent report on European and US practices of IT outsourcing, Currie and Willcocks (1997) found that much confusion and disagreement exists between managers both across and within different sectors about the meaning and scope of core competencies. Whereas some managers believed that outsourcing was a by-product of retaining core competencies by contracting out non-core activities and services, others argued that it was not possible for any business reasonably to differentiate between what is *core* and *non-core* respectively. As one IT director at an insurance company opined, 'What is core today is probably non-core tomorrow and vice versa. It's a risky business to outsource any service that may be part of the intellectual capital of the business.'

The Literature on Hybrid Managers

By contextualising our discussion of the hybrid manager using historical, cross-national, labour-market, and organisational data and insights, it is not surprising that such a concept has found a place within management research. The literature on hybrid managers is an important component of a wider and, in recent years, burgeoning one on the management of innovation, technology, and technical work in the UK. A central issue in these writings (whether explicit or implicit) is the relationship between generalists and specialists, or managers and technical staff. In the late 1970s to mid-1980s, fears about deskilling through the use of IT were commonplace, with the publication of alarmist literature on 'the collapse of work' and the 'leisure shock'. But during the mid-1980s to the present time, the notion of widespread deskilling and unemployment as a consequence of technical change has given way to more considered discussion on how to develop appropriate mixes of capabilities and skills in managers and technical specialists. Indeed, the worrying notion of job degradation and elimination from technology has been reduced somewhat in the light of the many information systems disasters over the years. For example, one could argue that the mismanagement of many IS projects has actually contributed to job creation! This is because many new IS projects have often been commissioned from previous disasters (most notably the Crest system following the demise of the Taurus system in the city of London, see Currie, 1994).

In advocating the concept of the hybrid manager, it is believed that a blend of managerial awareness and technical skills will develop people who will counter the deficiencies of those with only generalist *or* technical capabilities. The corollary of this thinking is the hybrid manager. So in a 1990 British Computer Society (BCS) report, UK companies were exhorted to train *circa* 10,000 people to become hybrid managers by 1995. This report suggested that at least 30 per cent of all British managers will need to be 'hybrids' by the year 2000 (Palmer and Ottley, 1990). Such people would conceive and operate information systems to help their organisations compete on a global scale. In 1989, Earl defined hybrid managers as 'people with strong technical skills and adequate business knowledge or vice versa'. They would be 'able to work in user areas doing a line functional job, but adapt at developing and implementing IT application ideas'. The notion of the hybrid manager has been discussed, according to Earl and Skyrme (1992), in writings on IT, IS, and project, finance, R&D, and general management, and on management roles and career development. Earl and Skyrme found that organisations which claimed to possess hybrid managers said they were usually business managers with IT experience rather than the other way around. Skyrme (1996) put forward four essential attributes for the hybrid manager:

1. business knowledge (detailed working knowledge);
2. IT knowledge (capabilities rather than detailed technical knowledge);
3. organisational knowledge (how to get things done);
4. management qualities ('soft skills', e.g. interpersonal and negotiating skills).

Whilst the concept of the hybrid manager has been discussed at some length by Earl and Skyrme (1992) and Skyrme (1996), these writers claim that such a concept represents ' a capacity for a role'. One writer who was involved with the CBI IT skills agency (ITSA) on the future demand of IT professionals suggested that hybrid managers should be responsible for 'Defining and determining the information needs of the business function in which he/she is specialised, for example, accounting, personnel, marketing, engineering, IT services; integrating IT into the function strategy; and assessing and evaluating IT performance within the business' (Judd, 1993).

In summary, the central theme within the literature on hybrid managers is that contemporary managers need to blend business knowledge with technical awareness. Whilst this may not be the case for *all* managers, the assumption is that many organisations would be able to compete more effectively if they developed a cohort of their managers with *dual* skills. In reviewing the literature, it seems that the accent is more on the business than on technology. As such, hybrid managers are not expected to be *experts* in technology, but at least to understand how technology can be applied to support and improve the business. We shall now evaluate the literature on hybrid managers in the light of the wider business and management work discussed earlier.

A Critique of the Hybrid Manager Concept

Whilst the concept of the hybrid manager is intended to offer a solution to the so-called 'culture gap' between generalist and specialist activities within organisations, it is apparent that such a solution is inherently Anglo-Saxon in design, scope, and orientation. For unlike the situation in west Germany where there is not such a fixed demarcation between managerial and technical roles; and in Japan where manufacturing success in the 1980s is attributed, at least in part, to the effective use and deployment of technical capabilities and skills (Currie, 1994), UK and US managers alike continue to distinguish business activities from technical work. This is witnessed in several ways and, as we shall argue, sometimes to the detriment of the organisation. In the following discussion, we consider four critical elements which need to be addressed by those who espouse the virtues of the hybrid manager concept. They concern organisational hierarchy; the debate about core competencies (including outsourcing); the technical (IT) labour market, especially the role of IT contractors; and education and training policies and the management of IT projects and staff. In considering these factors, new questions and concerns are raised about the usefulness of the hybrid manager concept.

First, we consider the issue of organisational hierarchy. In the post-war period, possibly up to the late 1970s, a dual career path has existed for managers and technical specialists. Graduate career paths tended to take one of two distinct forms, managerial or technical. In the former case, individuals gained experience across the non-technical functions of accounting, finance, human resources, marketing, and sales. This was common for graduate management trainees, particularly in Anglo-American companies.

In the latter case, especially in regard to the IT function, individuals progressed from basic programming, systems analysis, into project management (Friedman, 1994). It was very unlikely that anyone in the former group would move across into programming, or to any other *hands-on* kind of technical work, in order to develop their careers. Yet movement in the opposite direction was commonplace and even encouraged by management.

So the British notion of *general management* (cf. Lawrence, 1996) involves access to senior management through a pre-defined career path which emphasises the traditional skills of organising, co-ordinating, budgeting, and planning, rather than broadly defined technical competencies (Boynton et al., 1992; Morone, 1993). While accountants are (in spite of popular misconceptions to the contrary) much less numerous at senior and top management levels of UK companies than is commonly supposed (*Professional Engineering*, 1995), their influence on the character of the strategic decision-making of companies has been stronger than that of their counterparts in other countries, notably west Germany and Japan (e.g. HMSO, 1987). Indeed, this influence is demonstrated in research conducted by the Chartered Institute of Management Accountants which considers the financial and non-financial evaluation of new technology. To this end, the research shows that, in UK and US companies, unlike west Germany and Japan, financial considerations far outweigh other, non-financial justifications such as *time-to-market, quality, reliability,* and *flexibility* (Currie, 1994).

One consequence of the distinction between the business and technical functions has been to create a barrier between these areas. Whilst some organisations have introduced more radical human resources strategies in recent years to eliminate this barrier, the language of many senior managers suggests they continue to perceive technical work as playing a supporting role to the *core* business units. The corollary of this is for management to restrict promotion opportunities of technical specialists, preferring instead to advance the careers of people with business and management skills. In fact, research has shown that senior managers tend to be relatively unsympathetic to arguments which elevate the position of technical specialists equal to, or over and above, those of people with business awareness. There is also a view which holds that technical expertise is, in fact, a disqualification for entry into managerial work (Currie, 1994; Currie and Glover, 1995).

The danger for technical people who relinquish their technical skills for managerial work is pointed out by Earl and Skyrme (1992), who claim they could run the risk of losing their technical edge without even being seen as 'real business people'. This is more likely to occur in countries such as Britain and the USA where people tend to value first degrees in business and management and postgraduate degrees such as the MBA and to devalue technical qualifications (Ackroyd, 1996). Yet failure to relinquish their technical background for a management role could leave them in a career cul-de-sac as far as promotion opportunities, pay, and conditions are concerned.

Whilst the concept of the hybrid manager offers a 'capacity for a role' (Earl, 1989) it must be addressed in the context of organisation hierarchy in conjunction with issues of power, politics, and control. What is evident is that managerial and technical work continues to carry with it an unequal status in the minds of many senior managers and technologists alike. As such, those who wish to progress in their careers are unlikely to do so by developing capabilities and skills which they perceive are unmarketable in the wider labour market.

Second, it is important to consider the hybrid manager concept in relation to some of the significant developments in business and management theory and practice in recent years. Here we shall consider the debate about core competencies and outsourcing. In regard to the issue of core competencies, the IT function is usually perceived as peripheral to the core business functions or units within commercial organisations. This view has been widely promoted by Hemel and Prahalad (1994). Put simply, an organisation may seek to differentiate between what it believes to be its core competencies. This may be in the form of intellectual property (patents, trade marks, brand names, etc.) as well as other activities which cannot easily be done by a third party (vendor/supplier).

As a result of this thinking, all those activities which may be provided by a third party more cost effectively and efficiently should be outsourced. This logic is found to be behind many of the large- and small-scale outsourcing deals in the USA and Europe (Currie and Willcocks, 1997). In fact, the prolific rate at which technical work (equipment and staff) has been outsourced in recent years is indicative that senior management do not perceive this activity to be part of the core competencies portfolio of their organisation. Large-scale outsourcing (more than 70–80 per cent of the IT activities) will remove much of the technical capability and skill of the organisation since it will be transferred to a third party.[2] In turn, a high proportion of UK and US organisations categorise IT departments as cost centres and service providers to the core businesses, thus making IT staff vulnerable when cost-cutting exercises are implemented (Currie, 1995).

Given moves to outsource the IT function, the concept of the hybrid manager becomes problematic. Indeed, IT staff will be given a straightforward message from outsourcing initiatives that technical capabilities and skills are not part of the complement of core competencies of the organisation. This is likely to deter people from developing technical expertise within

---

[2] Large-scale outsourcing deals usually involve a third party taking over much of the IT resource (equipment, software licences, maintenance contracts, etc.). IT staff are also transferred, taking with them their technical knowledge, expertise, and skill.

their existing organisations, and even from entering technical work in the first place. Whilst advocates of the hybrid manager concept will no doubt argue that it is important to retain people with a combination of business and technical awareness, the very act of outsourcing is likely to encourage people to overplay their business awareness whilst at the same time underplaying their technical know-how. It is also not easy to determine how people can become hybrid managers in a situation where IT is progressively stripped out of their organisation and put into the hands of a third party. To this end, IT people are more likely to find more lucrative career opportunities by either joining a company specialising in providing technical solutions or by entering the IT contracting labour market. What seems certain is that the hybrid manager concept sits uncomfortably in an environment of progressive IT outsourcing.

Third, and related to the previous two issues, the hybrid manager concept needs to be examined in the context of the labour market for IT professionals which has expanded considerably over the last two decades. Here, we are more concerned with the peripheral labour market[3] where many IT professionals now work as *freelance contractors* or consultants on employment contracts ranging from three months to a year. Indeed, many *contractors* remain 'employed' with a client organisation for periods in excess of a year (sometimes as many as six years!) even though they do not enjoy the same conditions of employment as permanent members of staff (i.e. holidays, pension, sick pay, training, etc.). Given the growth of this important peripheral IT labour market, any discussion of the hybrid manager concept must surely take into account differences in employment conditions across organisations. It should also seek to reveal how IT professionals perceive their employment and career opportunities in a dynamic and changing labour market.

To some extent, the rapid pace of technical change has fuelled the IT skill shortage which now adversely affects many organisations. Equally, the problems of the managerial-technical divide and of constantly changing skills requirements have not been resolved. In fact, the rhetoric in favour of hybrid managers has, arguably, not helped the IT skills shortage problem, particularly where IT specialists have actively relinquished their technical capabilities and skills to become *more rounded* business managers. Whereas an awareness of the latest technologies was seen by some as sufficient to qualify business managers for the role of hybrid manager, these people have also come under criticism by IT professionals for possessing what they describe as 'over hyped and phoney technical knowledge'.

---

[3] A distinction can be made between the peripheral IT labour market where people work on short-term, temporary employment contracts and the permanent IT labour market where people work as IT professionals on a permanent basis. In recent years, the growth of the former, peripheral IT labour market, has been significant, with many IT professionals now wishing to work on lucrative short-term, freelance contracts.

Moreover, the hype surrounding new technology has shown that managers[4] with little direct technical experience (i.e. programming, systems analysis, networking, testing, etc.) may resort to bluff in an attempt to retain their legitimacy in managing an IT project. One analyst/programmer at a UK bank summed up this situation well by stressing that,

A lot of so-called 'hybrid managers' know very little about IT, particularly the latest client server systems. Many of them have programmed in COBOL and have knowledge of legacy systems, but not the latest IT such as client server, networking and databases. Although some of them have read the 'idiots guide to IT', they come unstuck when they have to advise senior management about the intricacies of IT work. Having said that, they know all the buzz-words and can bluff their way out of a problem. But I am not surprised that a lot of poor decisions get taken about IT. If you don't understand what you are managing, I can not see how you can know whether or not your technical decisions are sound. It is no use criticising IT people for speaking a language you don't understand. You should try to understand the language. That's what happens in the medical profession!

Although much of the work on innovation and technical change over the last two decades has claimed that IT has a strategic role in achieving competitive advantage, with Kantrow (1980) writing about the *strategy–technology connection,* and Porter extolling the virtues of using technology for competitive advantage and market leadership (Porter, 1985), IT professionals to some extent continue to suffer from a poor commercial image. IT people are often stigmatised and sometimes perceived as being narrow, introverted, and lacking social skills, and are therefore unsuitable for managerial positions. Some companies even employ graduates with non-technical degrees because they feel that these people are better at communicating across functions than computer graduate counterparts. The dubious separation between managerial and technical work characteristic of a high population of UK and US organisations, with 'line positions depleted of technical tasks' in the words of Sorge and Warner (1986), seemingly continues.

A fourth issue therefore broadly concerns education and training policy. Mirroring the views and practices of many organisations, business and management courses in UK universities tend to be built partly on an assumption that technical skills are not part of managerial work. Business schools have increasingly excluded production and operations and other technology management subjects from the *core* management subjects of finance, strategy, human resources, and marketing (Armstrong, 1996). Companies have spent increasing amounts on IT since the 1970s and IT

---

[4] There has been a tendency to put non-IT literate managers in charge of IT projects and staff. Whilst this may work in some capacities, evidence shows that IT professionals often disparage the lack of technical awareness demonstrated by some managers, sometimes to the detriment of the project.

is now widely perceived by many writers as a strategic device which may enhance competitive position and market leadership. However, the management of IT is often excluded from the business of top management because of the assumption just described. The often very different educational and occupational backgrounds of managers and IT professionals have fuelled many of the problems in managing IT-enabled projects and, to this end, a closer examination of the business–technical divide becomes important. So one of the most central issues now concerns what sort of people should be in control of technical work (IT project, professionals, and related resources)—people with technical or non-technical backgrounds, or those who can combine business and technical skills?

Commercial pressures to ignore product quality, to reduce time-to-market, and to globalize operations have increased pressures on line managers to manage interdependencies within and external to their companies. Boynton et al. (1992: 32) suggested that in the UK, since the early 1980s, IT management responsibilities had increasingly been given to general managers other than information systems line managers. But while IT managers possess important technical and systems know-how, IT applications are best led by line managers who thoroughly understand the business situation. Many researchers have recorded the change that took place in the 1980s, when IT and other business activities became inextricable.

Many have also argued that senior executives align IT strategies with business strategies so as to manage in co-ordinated and holistic ways. Adler et al. (1992: 19) argued that technical functions like MIS, R&D, manfacturing, and so on were too often left 'out of the business strategy process and [exempted] from senior management's expectation that all functions manage their operations strategically'. The issue of whether IT should be managed centrally by one IS department or function, or decentralised to business units, is part of the debates produced by those changes. Increasingly, line managers try to use IT resources, although many organisations persist in retaining a central IS function, particularly when IT is cross-functional in orientation because it is used across departments, functions, and business units. In this situation the management responsibility for and control of IT is typically problematic, largely because of the gaps in knowledge which exist between technologists and business managers.

So one approach has been to try to make a virtue out of necessity by creating hybrid managers, people with both technical and business skills in varying combinations. These are rarely employed in contradiction to the prevailing belief that IT is best implemented and evaluated under the guidance and control of non-technical managers. Their employment, and even credibility, faces all kinds of difficulty because of the very rapid pace of technical change with IT, which means that skill shortages at all levels are endemic and costly both to cope with and to try to remedy. Staff often possess few relevant IT skills, or ones which are redundant. Managers often do not comprehend the capabilities of new systems or their relevance to their units' work. In-house IT or IS departments may consist of people with mainframe skills even though the latest developments involve increasing use of PCs. Inadequate training can lead to ad hoc, uncoordinated, and technically inappropriate IT strategies and solutions being adopted. Also, and most seriously of all, while managing the evaluation, implementation, use, and development of technologies clearly demands at least some technical knowledge, and certainly a sophisticated understanding of what IT can do, traditional careers continue to be followed, with non-technical general managers being promoted over technical specialists. In such a context the hybrid manager solution seems obvious and commonsensical to some people, as it certainly does attempt to fuse business and technical expertise.

But there is a significant sense, as suggested in previous sections of the chapter, in which such thinking demonstrates a staggering *naïveté* about education, training, the requirements of tasks, and the division of managerial and technical labour within organisations. This is not however surprising given the origins of the hybrid manager idea in the mid-1980s. It drew on the development of a number of approaches to project management in construction, shipbuilding, and other sectors in which teams of people are regularly brought together for the duration of contracts, projects, and/or tasks. Project management has often been used to make patterns of working more flexible in times of rapid technical change, heightened competition, and when operations are geographically diverse.

Yet much of the literature on hybrid managers shows a profound failure to address the centrally important organisation-specific and sector-specific details and requirements critical to project management. When IT contractors have deep technical understanding and significant experience, e.g. five years, in the same sector (financial services, manufacturing, etc.) they are likely to make useful contributions. However when they are MBA-style hybrids who flit from contract to contract, or from job to job, the issue is often not so much one of trained incapacity, but one of incapacity, period. The idea that the person with technical skills and some business knowledge (e.g. the new MBA holder who has had technical education and experience) is capable of contributing both breadth and depth to the work of any sector is often taken completely for granted by advocates of the hybrid manager. Business knowledge is thought of, by such people, as MBA-type knowledge of functional specialisms, not sector-specific business specialisms. An example of a effective hybrid manager in the eyes of such people would be an accountant with an MBA and no sector-specific knowledge outside the practice of accountancy. Such a person is, however, seriously deficient in experience of the details and peculiarities of *all* functions when employed in or contracted to a particular sector.

The study of comparative management suggests (cf. Glover and Hughes, 1996; Locke, 1996*a*) that superior competence is a product of breadth of education and practical understanding (neither of which are completely and necessarily best gained in formal education) and deep knowledge of the affairs and peculiarities of particular employment sectors. The job-hopping Anglo-Saxon with a first degree of varied and uncertain relevance topped up with a generalist MBA and its promise of upward social and economic mobility will normally fail to satisfy all or enough of these requirements. Our main point here, however, is that self-styled hybrid managers who have some relevant skills and some practical knowledge but who lack deep experience of their sector of employment are likely to find themselves at a serious disadvantage.[5]

A typical example of such a person in IT would have started his career, possibly after graduation, by working in programming for say, two to three years, then becoming a data processing (DP) or, the more common term nowadays, an IT manager. Having achieved this position, he then discovers that there is no higher position within the IT function, and therefore realises he is caught in a career cul-de-sac. The only alternative for attaining promotion is to move *up* into business management. So he obtains an MBA. Then he changes job, or moves in his original organisation into the management of IT projects, or simply leaves IT altogether and gets another 'general management job' in the same organisation or in a similar capacity working for another organisation, possibly in a different sector.

What is certain from the above is that education and training policies differ widely for managerial and technical personnel respectively. To the extent that some twenty-three UK institutions offer an undergraduate degree in business information technology (BIT) (see *UCAS Handbook*, 1996), which intends to combine business awareness with practical technical training, the wider labour market, and businesses in general, continue to draw a distinction between business and technical activities. In doing so, they tend to reinforce the distinction between these two activities and, in turn, create a false dichotomy. Indeed, if we consider the activities of many commercial enterprises, particularly the financial services sector, it is evident that technology in the form of mainframe computers, personal computers (PCs), other communications, and networking technologies, etc., is now embedded into the entire business activities of the enterprise. So to remove the IT infrastructure and staff within a bank or insurance company would surely render the business unable to provide any services whatsoever.

Recent research into IT outsourcing (Currie and Willcocks, 1997) found that much confusion existed over what managers perceive to be the core

---

[5] This may become more apparent over time as businesses reorganise themselves into geographically dispersed networks.

competencies of their organisation, and what is peripheral. One IT manager said, 'What is core competence today, may be a service activity tomorrow. If you outsource all your IT facility, you may end up losing your key assets. It is certainly a risky thing to do in the medium to long term.'

Conclusion

This chapter began by considering the nature of management and managerial work in the UK, with some examples of US, Japanese, and west German practice. Key differences were identified between British and overseas approaches to management education, training, and development. These differences were further reinforced in the interrelated sets of writings about engineers, scientists and other technical specialists, and so-called *knowledge workers*. Contextualising the hybrid manager concept in this wider literature raised a number of important questions, particularly about the viability and usefulness of such a concept. One of the central observations was the British and US tendency to separate business and technical activities, thus creating a barrier (problem) in search of a solution (the hybrid manager). Indeed, to distinguish business activities from technical work is a central theme of much of the literature on hybrid managers, which often expresses the problem in over-simple terms in the form of a 'culture gap' between managers who act in the interests of the business and technical (usually IT) staff who focus purely on technical matters. But such a simple view is shown to overlook important historical developments in management, managerial work, and the relationship between managers and technical specialists. To this end, empirical research implies that, as technology becomes deeply embedded into core and services business activities (most notably in banking, insurance, and other information-intensive sectors), those without a knowledge of how new technologies can be developed and exploited for commercial gain are likely to find themselves at a competitive disadvantage in the labour market. This is not to argue for the supremacy of the technologist, but to suggest that, in an economic climate which perceives international competitiveness as synonymous with developing intellectual property, the strategy–technology connection, (Kantrow, 1980) the exploitation of a global information infrastructure, knowledge workers, the information society, and a whole host of other essentially technologically driven business changes, it is difficult to see how writers can argue with convincing logic that a separation exists between *business* and *technology*. Consequently, if we start by using a faulty premise by creating a false dichotomy of this kind, we are likely to end up pursuing an over-simple, if not sterile debate.

Whilst we may concede that the hybrid manager literature opens up a debate about the problems of exploiting business and technical capabilities and skills, it is deficient in its lack of regard for historical literature within management research. Moreover, it tends to ignore important issues such as the configuration of organisational hierarchies; the core competency thesis; the proliferation of IT outsourcing; the emerging *peripheral* IT labour market; and education and training provision within the wider society (higher and further education institutions, etc.) and within companies (HRM/training departments). As we saw above, the hybrid manager concept sits uncomfortably with some of the past, present, and even future developments within organisations. Indeed, many writing on the hybrid manager justify the concept on the basis of a list of companies which claim to *use* hybrid managers, yet fail to specify why these people are any different from any other technologist who wishes to become a manager for reasons of *self-development*. Such logic produces a circular argument which is inherently faulty.

As Child (1972), Pettigrew (1973), and Willmott (1984), and many others, have now long argued, management is an essentially political, as well as a practical, activity. The literature on hybrid managers, however, tends to overlook this in its somewhat naive assertion that people will readily opt to become *hybrid managers* even though contemporary management thinking perceives technical qualifications to be outside common definitions of *managerial work*. As such, self-styled hybrid managers may find themselves neither fish nor fowl. In other words, they are quasi-managers with a smattering of technical know-how. Yet such an appeal to create the generalist only serves to eclipse the role of the specialist which, as history reminds us, has been critical in the development of organisations since the industrial revolution.[6]

History shows that management research has expanded and proliferated at great speed since the 1960s and it is inevitable that some new phenomena will be conceptualised in an empiricist, sometimes crassly empiricist, way at times. Writings on the hybrid manager appear to belong to this category. To some extent, the hybrid manager concept offers a soft target for the more discerning management researcher in view of its inherent contradictions, unanswered questions, and conceptual own-goals. Yet there is a worrying sort of affinity between the lack of attention to history and the seemingly popular managerialist appeal of the hybrid manager concept (to generalists and specialists alike).

[6] The terms generalist and specialist are widely misused in the debate about hybrid managers. Whilst a significant proportion of management research has exaggerated the qualities of the generalist (i.e. the general manager) it has done so by overlooking the important nature of specialist expertise. For example, a university department is more likely to make its reputation on the strength of expertise (specialist knowledge) in a particular (narrow) field of research than it is by claiming to be 'administratively competent'. Whilst this is not to disparage managerial or administrative competence, it is to remind us of the criticality of the role of the specialist. However, with outsourcing and other initiatives, organisations run the risk of stripping out specialist knowledge from their organisations. This will become more apparent over time and may see the decline of some business organisations (banking) as new entrants appear in the market place.

In summary, this chapter has sought to deepen our understanding, not especially about the hybrid manager (with all its imperfections) but about the false dichotomy between managerial and technical work which is peddled within business and management schools and also in contemporary organisations. Historically, it would seem that organisations are continuing to undergo a transformation with technology being a major player. Yet instead of recognising the importance of technology within commercial (and many non-commercial) organisations, many writers continue to treat technology as merely an adjunct to other *core* activities. In so doing, they further reinforce the so-called culture gap between the business and technology through activities such as outsourcing the IT function. Perhaps a more logical approach would be to begin to treat the business and technology as two sides of the same coin so that solutions are not offered to organisations without first understanding the cause of the problem.

References

Ackroyd, S. (1995), 'On the Structure and Dynamics of Some Small, UK-Based Information Technology Firms', *Journal of Management Studies*, 32, 2.

—— (1996), 'Organisation Contra Organisations: Professions and Organisational Change in the United Kingdom', *Organisation Studies*, 17, 4: 599–621.

Adler, P. S., McDonald, D. W., and MacDonald, F. (1992), 'Strategic Management of Technical Functions', *Sloan Management Review*, Winter: 19–37.

Armstrong, P. (1996), 'The Expunction of Process Expertise from British Management Teaching Syllabi: An Historical Analysis', in Glover and Hughes (1996).

Baroudi, J., and Igbaria, M. (1995), 'An Examination of Gender Effects on Career Success of Information Systems Employees', *Journal of Management Information Systems*, 11, 3: 181–201.

Berle, A., and Means, G. (1932), *The Modern Corporation and Private Property* (New York: Macmillan).

Blackler, F. (1995), 'Knowledge, Knowledge Work and Organisations: An Overview and Interpretation', *Organisation Studies*, 16, 6: 1021–46.

Boynton, A. C., Jacobs, G. C., and Zmud, R. W. (1992), 'Whose Responsibility is IT Management?', *Sloan Management Review*, Summer: 32–8.

Carley, M. (1981), 'Analytic Rationality', in A. G. McGrew and M. J. Wilson (eds.), *Decision Making* (Manchester: Manchester University Press).

Causer, G., and Jones, C. (1996*a*), 'Management and the Control of Technical Labour', *Work, Employment and Society*, 10, 1: 105–23.

—— —— (1996*b*), 'One of Them or One of Us? The Ambiguities of the Professional as Manager', in R. Fincham (ed.), *New Relationships in the Organized Professions* (Aldershot: Avebury).

Child, J. (1972), 'Organisational Structure, Environment and Performance: The Role of Strategic Choice', *Sociology*, 6: 1–22.

Coldstream, P. (1996), 'Looking Back from the Future', *Times Higher Educational Supplement*, 30 Aug.: 9.

Cotgrove, S., and Box, S. (1970), *Science, Industry and Society* (London: Allen & Unwin).

Crompton, R. (1993), *Class and Stratification* (Oxford: Blackwell).

Currie, W. (1994), *The Strategic Management of Advanced Manufacturing Technology in the US, UK, Japan and West Germany* (London: CIMA).

—— (1995), *Management Strategy for IT: An International Perspective* (London: Pitman).

—— (1996), 'Outsourcing in the Private and Public Sectors: An Unpredictable IT Strategy', *European Journal of Information Systems*, 16, 1: 51–64.

—— (1999), *The Global Information Society* (Chichester: Wiley).

—— and Glover, I. (1995), 'General Managers, Technical Specialists and the Mis-management of IT: An Anglo-American Phenomenon?', *Conference on Professions and Management, University of Stirling*.

—— and Willcocks, L. (1997), *New Strategies in Information Technology Outsourcing: A Study Guide to Current Trends and Best Practices in Europe and the USA* (London: Business Intelligence).

Dawson, S. (1994), 'Changes in the Distance: Professionals Reappraise the Meaning of Management', *Journal of General Management*, 20, 1: 1–21.

Demirag, I. (1996), 'The Impact of Managers' Short-Term Perceptions on Technology Management and R&D in UK Companies', *Technology Analysis and Strategic Management*, 8, 1: 21–32.

Dezalay, Y. (1995), ' "Turf Battles" or "Class Struggles": The Internationalization of the Market for Expertise in the "Professional Society" ', *Accounting, Organisations and Society*, 20, 5: 331–44.

Dopson, S., and Stewart, R. (1993), 'Information Technology, Organisational Restructuring and the Future of Middle Management', *New Technology, Work and Employment*, 8, 1: 10–20.

Earl, M. (1989), *Management Strategies for Information Technology* (London: Prentice Hall).

—— (1996), 'The Risks of Outsourcing IT', *Sloan Management Review*, Spring: 13–25.

—— and Feeny, D. (1994), 'Is your CIO Adding Value?', *Sloan Management Review*, Spring, 35, 3: 11–20.

—— and Skyrme, D. J. (1992), 'Hybrid Managers: What do we Know about Them?', *Journal of Information Systems*, 2: 169–87.

Fayol, H. (1949), *General and Industrial Management*, trans. C. Storrs (London: Pitman).

Fores, M., and Glover, I. A. (1978) (eds.), *Manufacturing and Management* (London: HMSO).

—— and Rey, L. (1979), 'Technik: The Relevance of a Missing Concept', *Higher Education Review*, 11, 2: 43–57.

—— and Sorge, A. (1981), 'The Decline of the Management Ethic', *Journal of General Management*, 6, 3.

Friedman, A. (1994), 'The Stages Model and the Phases of the IS Field', *Journal of Information Technology*, 9: 137–48.

—— and Cornford, D. (1992), *Organisations in Society* (London: Macmillan).

Glover, I. A. (1978*a*), 'Executive Career Patterns: Britain, France, Germany and Sweden', in Fores and Glover (1978).

—— (1978*b*), 'Professionalism and Manufacturing Industry', in Fores and Glover (1978).

—— and Hughes, M. (1996) (eds.), *The Professional-Managerial Class: Contemporary British Management in the Pursuer Mode* (Aldershot: Avebury).

—— —— (1997), *Professions at Bay: Control and Encouragement of Ingenuity in British Management* (Aldershot: Avebury).

—— and Kelly, M. P. (1987), *Engineers in Britain* (London: Allen & Unwin).

Gospel, H. E. (1991) (ed.), *Industrial Training and Technological Innovation: A Comparative and Historical Study* (London: Routledge).

Granick, D. (1962), *The European Executive* (London: Weidenfeld & Nicolson).

Green, A. (1992), *Education and State Formation* (Basingstoke: Macmillan).

Gunz, H. (1989), *Career and Corporate Cultures: Managerial Mobility in Large Corporations* (Oxford: Blackwell).

Hales, C. (1986), 'What Do Managers Do? A Critical Review of the Evidence', *Journal of Management Studies*, 23, 1: 88–113.

Hemel, G., and Heene, A. (1994) (eds.), *Competence-Based Competition* (Chichester: John Wiley & Son).

—— and Prahalad, C. (1994), *Competing for the Future* (Boston: Harvard Business Press).

Hill, L. A. (1992), *Becoming a Manager* (Cambridge, Mass.: Harvard Business School Press).

Hirsh, W., and Bevan, S. (1988), *What Makes a Manager?*, Institute of Manpower Studies, Report No. 144 (Brighton: Institute of Manpower Studies).

HMSO (1987), *The Making of Managers* (London: HMSO).

Jackall, R. (1988), *Moral Mazes: Inside the World of Corporate Managers* (Oxford: Oxford University Press).

Judd, S. (1993), 'Hybrid Managers in Information Technology', in R. Ennals and P. Molyneux (eds.), *Managing with Information Technology* (Berlin: Springer-Verlag).

Kantrow, A. M. (1980), 'The Strategy–Technology Connection', *Harvard Business Review*, May/June: 1–7.

Knights, D., and Murray, F. (1994), *Managers Divided: Organisation Politics and Information Technology Management* (Chichester: John Wiley).

Kornhauser, W. (1982), *Scientists in Industry: Conflict and Accommodation* (Berkeley and Los Angeles: University of California Press).

Kotter, J. (1982), *The General Managers* (New York: Free Press).

Lacity, M., Willcocks, L., and Feeny, D. (1996), 'The Value of Selective IT Sourcing', *Sloan Management Review*, Spring: 13–25.

Lane, C. (1995), *Industry and Society in Europe: Stability and Change in Britain, Germany and France* (Aldershot: Edward Elgar).

Lawrence, P. (1980), *Managers and Management in West Germany* (London: Croom Helm).

—— (1996), 'Through a Glass Darkly: Towards a Characterization of British Management', in Glover and Hughes (1996).

Lee, G., and Smith, C. (1992), *Engineers in Management: International Comparisons* (London: Routledge).

Locke, R. R. (1996*a*), *The Collapse of the American Management Mystique* (Oxford: Oxford University Press).

Locke, R. R. (1996*b*), 'The Limits of America's *Pax Oeconomica*: Germany and Japan after World War II', in Glover and Hughes (1996).

Luthans, F., Hodgetts, M., and Rosenkrantz, S. A. (1988), *Real Managers* (Cambridge, Mass: Ballinger).

Macdonald, S. (1995), 'Engineering or Metal-Bashing? Changing the Image', *Long Range Planning*, 28, 6.

Mace, J. (1977), 'The "Shortage" of Engineers', *Higher Education Review*, 10, 1: 23–41.

Mangham, I., and Silver, M. (1986), *Management Training: Context and Practices* (Bath: School of Management, University of Bath).

Millman, T. (1997), 'Restructuring and Repositioning of the UK Engineering Profession', in Glover and Hughes (1997).

Mintzberg, H. (1973), *The Nature of Managerial Work* (New York: Harper & Row).

Morone, J. G. (1993), 'Technology and Competitive Advantage: The Role of General Management', *Research Technology Management*: 6–25.

Mumford, E. (1972), *Job Satisfaction: A Study of Computer Specialists* (London: Longman).

—— (1987), 'Using Reality in Management Development', *Management Education and Development*, 18, 3: 223–43.

Palmer, C., and Ottley, S. (1990), *From Potential to Reality: Hybrids—a Critical Force in the Application of Information Technology in the 1990s* (London: British Computer Society).

Pettigrew, A. (1973), *The Politics of Organisational Decision-Making* (London: Tavistock).

—— (1985), *The Awakening Giant: Continuity and Change in ICI* (Oxford: Blackwell).

Porter, M. (1985), *Competitive Advantage: Creating and Sustaining Superior Performance* (New York: Free Press).

Prahalad, C., and Hamel, G. (1990), 'The Core Competence of the Corporation', *Harvard Business Review*, 68, 3: 79–91.

Prandy, K. (1965), *Professional Employees: A Study of Scientists and Engineers* (London: Faber & Faber).

Professional Engineering (1995), 'Tipped for Failure at the Top', 1 Nov.

Quinn, J. B., Anderson, P., and Finkelstein, S. (1996), 'Managing Professional Intellect: Making the Most of the Best', *Harvard Business Review*, Mar.–Apr.: 71–80.

Schön, D. (1983), *The Reflective Practitioner* (New York: Basic Books).

Simonds, A. P. (1978), *Karl Mannheim's Sociology of Knowledge* (Oxford: Clarendon Press).

Skyrme, D. (1996), 'The Hybrid Manager', in M. Earl (ed.), *Information Management* (Oxford: Oxford University Press).

Smith, P. (1985), 'The Stages in a Manager's Job', in V. Hammond (ed.), *Current Research in Management* (London: Pinter).

Sofer, C. (1970), *Men in Mid-career: A Study of British Managers and Technical Specialists* (Cambridge: Cambridge University Press).

Sorge, A. (1978), 'The Management Tradition: A Continental View', in Fores and Glover (1978).

—— (1979), 'Engineers in Management: A Study of the British, German and French Traditions', *Journal of General Management*, 5, 1: 46–57.

—— (1994), 'The Reform of Technical Education and Training in Great Britain: A Comparison of Institutional Learning in Europe', *European Journal of Vocational Training*, 3: 58–68.

—— and Warner, M. (1986), *Comparative Factory Management: An Anglo-German Comparison of Manufacturing, Management and Manpower* (Aldershot: Gower).

Stewart, R. (1961), *The Reality of Management* (London: Pan Management).

—— Barsoux, J., Kieser, A., Ganter, H., and Walgenbach, P. (1994), *Managing in Britain and Germany* (London: Macmillan; New York: St Martin's Press).

Taylor, F. W. (1911), *Principles of Scientific Management* (New York: Harper).

Thomas, P. (1996), 'The Devil Is in the Detail: Revealing the Social and Political Processes of Technology Management', *Technology Analysis and Strategic Management*, 8, 1: 71–84.

Tylecote, A. (1995), 'Technological and Economic Long Waves and their Implications for Employment', *New Technology, Work and Employment*, 10, 1: 3–18.

Whitley, R. (1974) (ed.), *Social Processes of Scientific Development* (London: Routledge & Kegan Paul).

Willmott, H. (1984), 'Shaping Managerial Work: A Critique and Proposal', *Journal of Management Studies*, 24, 3.

18

Rethinking Capabilities and Skills in the Information Systems Function

DAVID F. FEENY AND LESLIE P. WILLCOCKS

Abstract

Despite wide recognition of the usefulness of resource-based approaches to organisational survival and competitiveness, these have rarely been applied in detail to the question of how the IS function in contemporary organisations can be configured. Against several trends—most notably outsourcing and that towards business ownership of IS—that for some commentators imply the steady demise or 'withering away' of the IS function, our own empirical work has led us to posit the emergence in practice of the 'high-performance' IS function. This has four 'faces', or fundamental tasks. We advance a portfolio of nine core capabilities, several new to the IS function, which are required to deliver high performance in this context. The relative importance of each capability will vary according to the nature of the business and its dependence over time on IS/IT. While a single individual may be able to provide more than one of the nine capabilities, the nine are logically distinct and each implies a distinct set of behaviours, skills, and motivations. We detail the significant challenges to be met before any organisation can successfully identify, recruit, and retain a small group of high-calibre professionals to deliver the 'high-performance IS' concept. Finally, the chapter suggests that sourcing IS/IT capability needs a more fundamental analysis than many organisations are willing to make. Apart from 'outsourcing' there are real opportunities to 'insource', and such 'insourcing' options will probably be important in any successful delivery of the 'high-performance IS' concept.

Introduction

From the early 1980s configuring the information systems (IS) function has presented a perennial, often intractable set of issues for researchers and practitioners alike. Essentially the importance and intractability relate to dynamic changes in the wider global and national economies, increased competitive pressures in most sectors together with cost containment drives, mergers and acquisitions, rapid developments in information-based technologies, and regular reorganisations and organisational changes to anticipate or react to fluctuating markets and financial results.

In the face of these pressures, one important concern has been to restructure IS. The degree of centralisation has been a prime subject of debate, and, in search of balance, many IS functions have regularly been moved up and down the centralisation–decentralisation continuum to reflect specific contingencies (George and King, 1991; Strassmann, 1995). IS has also become variously a corporate service, an internal bureau, a business venture, and latterly also the subject of various degrees of outsourcing (Willcocks et al., 1996). In large complex organisations we found the federal structure the major trend in configuration in the early 1990s (Earl et al., 1997). An important finding by Hodgkinson (1996) was the need for the structure of the IS function to reflect, and not be in tension with, that of the wider organisation.

Another ongoing concern from the 1980s has been with the difficult task of aligning business and IT/IS strategies (Broadbent and Weill, 1993; Henderson and Venkatraman, 1993). However, even where achieved, such alignment has seemed to have little effect on the catalogue of implementation problems revealed in a range of studies. One research-based explanation suggested by Walton (1989) and Willcocks and Mark (1989) has been the frequent lack of follow-through on alignment from strategy through the development and implementation stages into routine operations. Other reasons cited for implementation difficulties include poor project management, slow systems development methods, and lack of line management involvement in the implementation process (Willcocks and Griffiths, 1994; Taylor-Cummings, 1997).

A further piece in the jigsaw of explanation has been referred to as the 'culture gap' between IS and the business (Grindley, 1995; Willcocks, 1991). Closing the gap means working on bringing both the business closer to IS, and IS closer to the business. Particular areas of study here have been the central role played by CEO/CIO relationships; the advantages gained from bridge-building mechanisms, user–IS collocation, and joint working processes; and the need to reshape skill mixes, including the development and role of hybrid managers (see for example Feeny et al., 1994; Feeny et al., 1992; Taylor-Cummings, 1997; Skyrme, 1992).

In rethinking these several research strands, it becomes clear that restructuring, strategic alignment, improving project management expertise, providing better development tools and methodologies, and making line managers/users more responsible for IS, and more IT literate—these are necessary but not sufficient conditions for successful IS. In particular we note two further points. First, the focus of attention has shifted from structuring the IS function towards issues of IS–user relationships, processes, and skills. Secondly, a particularly neglected area is that of capabilities, and skills within information systems functions themselves. Our research over the last three years has focused on these missing, critical, and essentially human resource elements in the equation—the capabilities and skills required to run a business value-adding IS function.

A focus on key capabilities and skills reflects a resource-based approach to how organisations can survive, pursue stakeholder objectives, and compete. Early exponents of the theme of competitive advantage/strategic necessity through IT tended to adopt positioning frameworks for locating the role of IT; by implication the supportive role of the IS function was to deliver the systems required (McFarlan, 1984; Porter and Millar, 1985). Latterly we have seen more resource-based theories applied to how effective IT can be developed and sustained (for example Ciborra, 1993; Feeny and Ives, 1997). This fits with moves in the broader strategy and organisation literature toward resource-based theories and notions of core competence (see for example Grant, 1995; Hamel and Prahalad, 1994). In practice top management are seen to be debating whether IS is core or non-core/peripheral to the future of their business; and what arrangements for IS best reflect their analysis. However, an uneasy juxtaposition of concepts bedevils this debate. For example, large IS outsourcing deals are signed but regularly labelled 'strategic partnerships', recognising that IT exploitation remains a 'critical', but somehow 'non-core', element in the future of the business. Here we argue that resource-based theory needs to be unequivocally applied not just to the organisation but also to the IS function itself. In doing this a key, but neglected question is produced, namely: which IS capabilities are core to the business's future capacity to exploit IT successfully?

This chapter addresses this issue. First, we detail the major contextual pressures shaping IS in the 1990s. Then, in the light of these pressures and research findings, we develop a revised perspective on the emerging shape of the IS function. This is detailed in terms of key capabilities and skills. Here IS capability will refer to an assembly of skills, techniques, and know-how developed over time that enable an organisation to acquire, deploy, and leverage IT investments in pursuit of business strategies. The challenges and implications of developing and applying these capabilities and skills will be discussed, then related finally to the issue of sourcing IT/IS capability.

Pressures on the IS Function

Before examining these core capabilities and skills, it is important to understand in more detail the key forces that are shaping their development. There are four main pressures. The first is the increasing business reliance on information technologies that are subject to rapid change. In some industries the IT infrastructure is becoming almost synonymous with the organisation structure. As one CIO at a major bank commented: 'If the bank was without its major IT systems for 24 hours we would go out of business.'

As IT penetrates to the core of operations, so its reliability, the speed with which IT solutions can be delivered, and understanding of new technologies and their potential application, become business critical. The growth of business process re-engineering has also concentrated minds. Research, by ourselves and others, shows IT regarded as a key enabler of the process-based organisation. Within these trends, IT delivery and support become key performance indicators for the IS function.

Secondly, successive recessions, allied with intensive competition across sectors, have led to pressures for cost containment and headcount reductions together with ever more concern for IS to demonstrate the business value it represents.

Thirdly, there is evidence of a long-term shift in the way organisations are configured and managed. In pursuit of 'core competence' strategies, an increasing number of firms look to apply the principles embedded in a core–periphery model of functioning (Prahalad and Hamel, 1990; Quinn, 1992; Quinn et al., 1990). An organisation, it is argued, can only be effective at a few core activities, and should concentrate on developing these to world class. Anything else should be eliminated, minimised, or outsourced. This raises important questions about whether the whole or parts of the IS function itself are perceived as core or support. On applying the core competence concept to the IS function at oil major BP Exploration, an IT manager commented: 'It's a method of rebuilding the focus of your organisation so that you focus on what is important to the company, and not what's important to the traditional IT world.'

A related fourth trend has been the growing number, size, and maturity of external IT services providers. Senior executives have been attracted by the outsourcing potential for IT driven by supplier promises of up to 40 per cent IT cost reductions, the 'bandwagon' effect, disappointment with in-house performance, and/or the desire to focus on core activities in difficult economic and competitive climates (Loh and Venkatraman, 1992; Moad, 1993; Willcocks et al., 1997*b*). In practice, recent research has shown that selective IT outsourcing in particular can realise a range of financial, business, and technical advantages for organisations, provided it is carefully entered into and managed (Lacity et al., 1995; Willcocks and Fitzgerald, 1994).

These trends raise key related issues of performance, business value, relevance, and alternative sourcing that provide considerable challenges for more traditional IS functions. In an earlier paper, based on studies of information systems leaders in sixty organisations, one of the authors

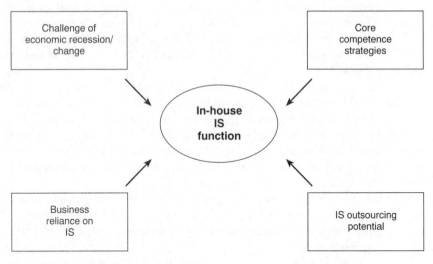

Fɪɢ. 18.1. *Forces shaping the future IS function*

suggested how CIOs should think of their work as adding value in certain key areas (Earl and Feeny, 1994).

This chapter provides a more extensive review of our thinking on the multiple capabilities and mix of skills organisations will need to successfully manage over time the supply and demand for IS/IT services. Our research leads us to conclude that, in the face of the trends and challenges outlined above, a critical emerging need is for the development of what later we call the 'high-performance' IS function.

Research Base and Emergent Model

In this section we detail the research base and the model of the IS function emerging from a reconsideration of the implications of our combined findings. The view presented here of core IS capabilities and the 'high-performance' IS function has been developed from three strands of research carried out in the 1992–5 period. Further details of the research methodologies adopted can be gained from the references provided.

1. The first strand concentrated on the role, person, and experiences of the CIO. Three parallel studies used a variety of techniques, including face-to-face interviews and psychometric tests, to provide rich data on IS leadership in sixty-one organisations (Earl and Feeny, 1994; Feeny, 1997; Feeny et al., 1992). The research programme also provided insights into the capabilities which leading CIOs believed to be crucial to the IS function.

2. In the second strand, Feeny et al. (1996) investigated four of the capabilities which were consistently highlighted by CIOs. Twelve participating organisations identified fifty-three individuals who were considered to demonstrate outstanding ability in one of the target areas. Data on these individuals was captured using personal background and perceived ability questionnaires, critical event interviews, and a variety of psychometric testing instruments. The research provided insights into both the way target capabilities were delivered, and the profile of individuals who delivered them.

3. An extensive third strand has involved research into IT/IS outsourcing experience. Data from 142 organisations has been collected by questionnaire, and face-to-face interviews have been conducted with multiple stakeholders in 30 case study organisations. An overview of the findings was reported in Willcocks and Fitzgerald (1994). Significantly for our purposes here, many of the case study organisations were found to be addressing the question of what they often referred to as the scope of the 'residual' IS in-house function (Willcocks and Fitzgerald, 1996).

In reviewing this research, organisations seemed to be converging on core capabilities concepts from two different directions. Some organisations we can characterise as starting with the principle that IS/IT is to be outsourced, and the main question was: what if any capability should be retained in-house? These organisations tended to have particular insights into the various capabilities required to contract for and manage externally provided IS/IT services. By contrast, other organisations had worked from the premiss that IS/IT represents an important strategic resource, and focused their analysis on what must exist to ensure their continuing ability to exploit it. These latter organisations tended to have sharper insights into the capabilities required to understand and articulate business-driven IS/IT needs, and those which relate to developing the appropriate technical platform. They were often less sophisticated in their definition of supply management capabilities even though they often accepted that much IS/IT service will become externally sourced in the fullness of time. By synthesising the learning that was being achieved from these two different start points, we can provide a rich picture of the core capabilities required in IS functions in contemporary organisations.

The first step in the synthesis is represented by Fig. 18.2. Here we present the four faces of the target, or emergent, IS function. We will present this model followed by the nine key research-derived capabilities that populate it before then discussing the implications and challenges this form of IS function represents. Some points on terminology are in order. Throughout this chapter we employ a working definition of the information systems function as the set of activities, personnel, and IT assets set up to define and ensure delivery of the information systems requirements of the business. We have already seen that such a function will be variously

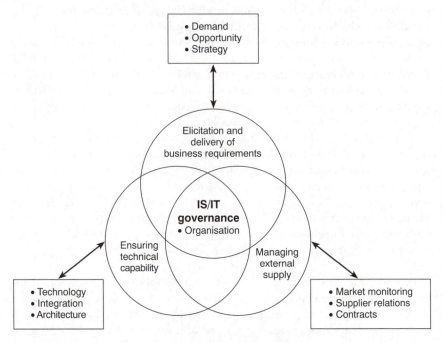

F IG. 18.2. *Four 'faces' or tasks of the emerging IS function*

structured, physically located, and staffed within different organisations. Fig. 18.2 represents a development from existing terminology in the IS literature. Following Earl (1996), and in a continuation from previous work where the conceptual clarification proved consistently useful, we distinguish between information management (IM), information systems (IS), and information technology (IT) (Willcocks et al., 1997a; Willcocks, 1994). Additionally, the growth in IT/IS outsourcing in the 1990s, together with a maturing and expanding IT/IS service market, leads us to make explicit the need for IT/IS sourcing strategy and supportive capabilities within the contemporary organisation. Some brief description of these four faces, or tasks, is now provided.

- The business 'face' is concerned with the elicitation and delivery of business requirements. The domain of *information systems strategy*, capabilities here are business focused, demand led, and concerned with defining the systems to be provided, their relationship to business needs, and where relevant the interrelationships and interdependencies with other systems. A further focus here is a strategy for delivery, together with actual IS implementation.
- The technical 'face' is concerned with ensuring that the business has access to the technical capability it needs—taking into account such issues as current price/performance, future directions, and integration

potential. This is the domain of *information technology strategy* that is defining the blueprint or architecture of the technical platform that will be used over time to support the target systems. IT presents the set of allowable options from which the technical implementation of each system must be selected. A further concern is to provide technical support for delivery of the IT strategy.

- The 'governance' face is concerned with *information management strategy*, which defines the governance and co-ordination of the organisation's IT/IS activity. It elaborates such issues as:
  - the role/mission of IS/IT within the business;
  - the respective responsibilities of IS/IT and business staff in achieving that role;
  - the people and processes involved in creation of the information systems strategy to support the business;
  - the people and processes involved in achieving the chosen approach to systems implementation;
  - the principles which should guide the development of information technology strategy;
  - the processes which will be used to evaluate any proposals for IS/IT investment or services;
  - the purpose and scope of any standards which should apply to IS/IT activity.

- The supply 'face' encompasses understanding and use of the external IS/IT services market; its activity is driven by decisions about the sourcing of activity. As such it is the domain of *IT/IS market sourcing strategy*. Particularly critical here are decisions on what to outsource and insource, on which external suppliers to use and how. A further concern is ensuring appropriate delivery of external services contracted for.

Requisite Capability in the Emerging IS Function

In this section we further develop the model of the future IS function by detailing nine capabilities required to render it dynamic and fully operational. These capabilities, expressed as roles, are shown in Fig. 18.3. It should be noted that the nine capabilities populate seven spaces. As will emerge, these spaces are not accidentally arrived at. Three are essentially business, technology, or service facing. One is a linchpin governance position covered by two capabilities (see Fig. 18.3—CIO and Informed Buyer). Finally there are three spaces that represent various interfaces between the three faces. The capabilities that populate these spaces are crucial for facilitating the integration of effort across the three faces. We now move to detailing each of the nine capabilities.

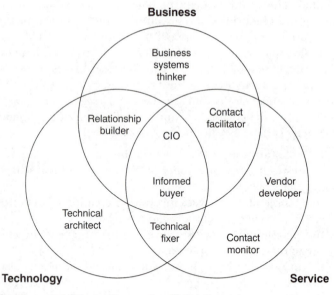

FIG. 18.3. *Nine capabilities in the emerging IS function*

Capability 1: IS/IT governance

'*Integrating IS/IT effort with business purpose and activity.*' At the heart of Fig. 18.3, in the overlapped space of the three faces, is the need for effective IS/IT governance. The central task is to devise organisational arrangements—structures, processes, and staffing—to manage the inter-dependencies successfully. Information systems strategy requires that knowledge of the business and its external context is brought together with knowledge of the technology and its directions. Operational service requires that the information system is integrated into a wider business process whose owners have understood how that process can best be enhanced by technology. And so on. Provision of IS/IT governance capability is the traditional role of the IS/IT manager or director, the chief information officer or 'CIO' of the local business.

Capability 2: business systems thinking

'*Envisioning the business process which technology makes possible.*' We are frequently told that business thinking should precede consideration of technology, that processes must be redesigned before being automated. The truth is more complicated. Business processes should be redesigned in the light of technology potential. Within the exclusive space of the business face (presented in Fig. 18.3), the key capability needed is the business systems thinking which brings together ideas of business strategy and technology application. In best practice organisations, business systems thinkers from the IS/IT function are important contributors to teams charged with business problem-solving, process re-engineering, and strategic development. The information systems strategy emerges from these teams' recommendations, which have already identified the technology components of solutions to business issues.

Capability 3: relationship-building

'*Getting the business constructively engaged in IS/IT issues.*' The need for relationship building is symbolised by the overlap between business and technical faces in Fig. 18.3. While the business systems thinker is the individual embodiment of integrated business/IS/IT thinking, the relationship-builder facilitates the wider dialogue. Extensive research has confirmed the popular folklore, that 'techies' have particular characteristics which inhibit their ability to communicate with the business. Relationship-builders are comfortable in both business and technology domains, and are able to help bridge the culture gap to achieve the understanding and commitment of all parties.

Capability 4: designing technical architecture

'*Creating the coherent blueprint for a technical platform which responds to present and future business needs.*' Designing technical architecture, or information technology strategy, is the main task within the technical face. The principal challenge to the architect is to anticipate technology trends so that the organisation is consistently able to operate from an effective and efficient platform—without major investment in energy-sapping migration efforts. Anticipating future business change would be even more challenging. In practice, technical architects try to build in flexibility rather than to foresee the unforeseeable.

Capability 5: making technology work

'*Rapidly achieving technical progress—by one means or another.*' Operating the overlap between the technical and supply faces of Fig. 18.3 is the technical fixer. The fixer requires much of the insight found in the technical architect role, allied to a pragmatic nature and short-term orientation. In today's environment of high complex/networked/multi-supplier systems, the technical fixer makes two critical contributions: rapidly to troubleshoot problems which are being disowned by others across the technical supply chain; and to identify how to address business needs which cannot be properly satisfied by standard technical approaches. The need to retain technical 'doing' capability is recognised even amongst organisations that have 'total' outsourced IT. As a senior manager in an oil company commented: 'We have retained in-house some significant technical consulting expertise, we regard it as important. It's not so much a doing organisation now, but it's one which is capable of debating technical development routes with our outsourcing partners.'

Capability 6: informed buying

'*Managing the IS/IT sourcing strategy which meets the interests of the business.*' In the intercept between supply and governance faces of Fig. 18.3 we can position the capability of informed buying. It involves analysis of the external market for IS/IT services; selection of a sourcing strategy to meet business needs and technology issues; leadership of the tendering, contracting, and service management processes. In an organisation which has decided to outsource most IS/IT service, the Informed Buyer is the most prominent role behind that of the CIO. One respondent described the role in this way: 'If you are a senior manager in the company and you want something done, you come to me and I will . . . go outside, select the vendor and draw up the contract with the outsourcer, and if anything goes wrong it's my butt that gets kicked by you.' By 1994 Philips Electronics had totally outsourced its IT. One development has been to push Informed Buyers, with IT, management, and contract skills, into the businesses: 'Philips have got control of their IT through business based IT managers who are absolutely critical . . . they are now responsible for buying IT products and services from our two preferred suppliers.'

Capability 7: contract facilitation

'*Ensuring the success of existing contracts for IS/IT services.*' Most IS/IT outsourcing situations involve considerable complexity. Typically a large population of users within the business are receiving a variety of services from multiple suppliers (or supply points) under a set of detailed and lengthy contracts. The Contract Facilitator operates in the overlap between the business and supply faces (presented in Fig. 18.3), trying to ensure that problems and conflicts are seen to be resolved fairly within what are usually long-term relationships. In our experience, both users and vendors place high value on effective contract facilitators. The role arises for a variety of reasons:

- it provides one-stop shopping for the business user;
- the vendor or user demands it;
- multiple vendors need co-ordinating;
- it enables easier monitoring of usage and service;
- users may demand too much and incur excessive charges.

One contract facilitator noted: 'They [users] have been bitten a few times when they have dealt directly with suppliers, and it's a service we can provide, so now we do.'

Capability 8: contract monitoring

'*Protecting the business's contractual position, current and future.*' Another consequence of IS/IT outsourcing complexity is the need for a Contract Monitor. While the Contract Facilitator is working to 'make things happen' on a day-to-day basis, the Contract Monitor is ensuring that the business position is at all times protected. Located in the exclusive space of the supply face, the role involves holding suppliers to account against both existing service contracts and the developing performance standards of the services market. Following a major 1994 outsourcing deal in the defence industry, an IT manager in the company commented: 'We need a significant number of people in-house to monitor vendor service performance. In one business unit alone we have 16 people working on contracts, six exclusively on the monitoring side. Admittedly we are still in the settling-in period, but I can't see the work declining that much.'

Capability 9: vendor development

'*Identifying the potential added value of IS/IT service suppliers.*' The single most threatening aspect of IS/IT outsourcing is the presence of substantial switching costs. To outsource successfully in the first place requires considerable organisational effort over an extended period of time. Subsequently to change suppliers may well require an equivalent effort. Hence it is in the business interest to maximise the contribution of existing suppliers, which is the role of vendor development. Anchored in the supply face of our Fig. 18.3 model, the Vendor Developer is concerned with the long-term potential for suppliers to add value, creating the 'win–win' situations in which the supplier increases its revenues by providing services which increase business benefits. A major retail multinational has a number of ways of achieving this, including an annual formal meeting: 'It's in both our interests to keep these things going and we formally, with our biggest suppliers, have a meeting once a year and these are done at very senior levels in both organisations, and that works very well.'

Capabilities, High Performance, and Contingencies

We have asserted from a synthesis of three research strands that there are nine capabilities that can be identified for any effective future in-house

IS function. We have briefly described the nine with reference to their roles in delivering the four overlapping tasks of Fig. 18.2. But are there contingencies that make different capabilities more, or less, important? Earlier we flagged that the emerging IS function would also seem to need to be a high-performance function. High performance would seem to be a function mainly of who is recruited and their ability to work together as a team (see below). But one initial finding is also that the high-performance IS concept properly embraces all nine capabilities. What has been interesting in the research is the degree to which when a particular capability is missing or is stretched across too few people, pressure arises, pushing towards the full complement of capabilities and skills. For example, a common tendency when outsourcing is initially to appoint a contract manager, conceived as some mix of the informed buying and contract monitoring roles. However in one major US bank:

I am not physically managing anyone in the data centre environment . . . but a lot of my time is being taken up as being not contract management but service relationship management . . . dealing with senior managers in the bank who are coming to me to explain service issues on a day to day basis. We are having to do lots of work we thought we had outsourced.

In fact the contract manager was being stretched across four of the 'service face' capabilities, and the vendor development capability did not exist.

The underestimation of capability and skills required came through several times in the research on companies that had outsourced: 'I was managing central systems, EDI and telecommunications. Only the latter had been outsourced but it took up 70 per cent of my time . . . luckily we kept on someone who happened to know about telecommunications . . . it's what saved us in the end' (IT manager, retail company). Clearly the manager was being spread across technical, business, and service faces, and little thought had been given to requisite capability and skills in a selectively outsourced IT/IS environment. In an electronics company where major outsourcing had taken place in the early 1990s, a senior IT manager commented: 'The IT people we put into the business end became isolated, their IT skills were not wide ranging enough for their new roles that also needed a lot more contract management skills than they possessed.' Here again the company was not only conflating several capabilities—in this case informed buyer, technical fixer, and relationship-builder—into a one-person role, but also only learning by experience the type of skills needed to support each capability.

However, while we argue that all nine capabilities are needed, it is clear that their relative importance can vary. To date we have identified five factors which differentiate: three are aspects of the business context (concerned with structure, mission, and nature of activity); two are functions of the IS/IT context (the maturity of IS/IT exploitation, and the experience of IS/IT outsourcing). Each factor and its general consequences are briefly discussed in turn.

In terms of *structure*, here consideration needs to be given to the degree to which the business or unit is physically and/or logically dispersed. Multiple locations increase the need for relationship-building capability. Our research experience is that relationship-builders need physically and emotionally to locate within the relevant part of the business; they cannot operate well across multiple locations or logical units (Willcocks and Fitzgerald, 1994). Secondly, if the business is physically dispersed but logically centralised, the technical architect role increases in importance —whether or not IS/IT service is outsourced.

In terms of *mission*, the distinction is between a business or unit with a stable/well-defined/bounded role, and one which is more externally oriented. The more the focus is on a changing external world—linking to other departments, or third party organisations, for example—the more important will be the chief information officer and business systems thinkers, followed by technical fixers to ensure delivery of IS/IT commitments.

In terms of business *activity*, we are thinking of the relative emphasis between policy development and operational service. Policy-oriented units will benefit primarily from relationship-building capability and technical fixers. Operations-oriented units should be more concerned with the chief information officer, business systems thinker, and technical architect roles.

Businesses with limited experience of *IS/IT exploitation* have particular need for relationship-building capability. As experience increases, so does the need for business systems thinkers, informed buyers, and technical fixers (Feeny et al., 1994).

Finally the need, or more precisely the recognition of need, for various supply-oriented roles develops with *experience of IS/IT outsourcing*. Every organisation needs the information-buying capability; as its use of external IS/IT services grows, so does its reliance on contract monitoring. Although there are real and immediate benefits from contract facilitation, many organisations do not seem to recognise the role until they have had painful experience in its absence. And it is our research experience that very few have so far understood the importance of vendor development (Lacity et al., 1996).

These points also lead us to stress that the model in Fig. 18.3 cannot be taken as static. A specific organisation will need different emphases on different capabilities at different points in its history. As yet we can give little overall guidance on how organisational context can be translated into staffing requirements for high-performance IS. We strongly recommend that all nine capabilities be represented at some level. But further research is needed to establish, for example, the extent to which 'less important' capabilities can be combined within 'small' IS/IT groups, though some suggestions are made on this point in the next section. We now consider the profiles of those who deliver the nine capabilities.

The Capability–Skills Matrix

Each of the nine capabilities/roles required to deliver the 'high-performance IS' concept implies a set of people behaviours, characteristics, and skills. Table 18.1 profiles what our research shows to be the critical attributes for high performance in each role.

In contrast to the more traditional skills found in IS functions (Scarbrough, 1995; Willcocks, 1991) our work suggests four key human resource developments:

1. There needs to be a much greater emphasis on business skills and business orientation in nearly all roles, the exceptions being the 'technical fixer', and to some extent the 'technical architect' roles;

2. There is a significantly increased requirement for 'soft' skills across all roles, the exception being the 'contract monitor' role;

3. The nine roles all demand high performers. The major shift we are observing in organisations with some experience at developing the IS function along the lines suggested in this chapter is toward fewer personnel, but of very high quality.

4. Each role requires a specific set of skills, attributes, and drivers. Through possessing one set, a person will be potentially disabled from high performance in the other roles. Our experience to date is that one person could deliver high performance in no more than two or three roles at any single point in their career path. This has considerable implications for staffing, and personal and career development.

We now consider these propositions in more detail.

Business skills and orientation

The generic requirement for these in the 'high-performance IS' model should not disguise the fact that a distinctive set of business skills are needed in each role. Reference back to Fig. 18.3 and the location of roles within business or supply faces helps to illustrate this. The business skills required by a CIO will relate to developing business vision and strategy, identifying business opportunities for IT, and the business potential of new technologies. The business systems thinker will be even more concerned with these issues, and from a more holistic business rather than technical perspective. The informed buyer has high-business skills but these are focused on extracting value from suppliers, through monitoring the market and specific

TABLE 18.1. *The capability-skills matrix*

Capability	Exhibited behaviours in role	Skills			Drivers
		Technical	Business	Interpersonal	
1. IS/IT Governance	• Establishes and maintains executive relationships • Strives to achieve shared and challenging vision of role of IT in the business • Develops the culture and orientation of the IT/IS function • Searches for and promotes best practice in information management	Medium	High	High	• Adding value to the business • High concern for acceptance and exploitation of IT • Continuous business and personal development
2. Business systems thinking	• Contributes to development of business strategy and operation • Identifies/communicates current patterns of organisation and activity • Envisions potential new patterns • Identifies connections and interdependencies	Low/medium	High	Medium/high	• Adding value to the business • Holistic understanding • Innovation/creativity
3. Business–IT relationship building	• Develops user understanding of potential of IT • Helps users and IT specialists to communicate and work together • Ensures user ownership and satisfaction	Medium/high	Medium	High	• Adding value to the business • Curiosity about individual personalities and motivations • Concern to achieve progress
4. Designing technical architecture	• Analyses trends in development of a range of technologies • Develops vision of integrated technical platform • Formulates policies to ensure necessary integration and flexibility of IT services	High	Low/medium	Medium	• Fascinated by new technologies • Holistic thinking and design • Acceptance as technology thought leader
5. Making technology work	• Focused on action and problem-solving	High	Low	Medium	• Hobby as work • Getting the right result

TABLE 18.1. (*cont'd*)

Capability	Exhibited behaviours in role	Skills			Drivers
		Technical	Business	Interpersonal	
6. Informed buying of IT service	• Understands internal design of IT systems • Delivers very high programming productivity • Comfortable with wide range of technical regimes • Monitors available services of external suppliers • Analyses nature of service requirements for immediate and longer term • Structures tendering process • Oversees contract negotiations	Medium	High	High	• Recognition for professional prowess • Freedom to perform • Understanding bargaining structures • Involvement in negotiating • Achieving hard but fair results
7. Contract facilitation	• Facilitate/manage people relationships • Devise/pursue processes for conflict resolution • Interpret business and technical issues within established contract framework	Medium	Medium	High	• Achieving day-to-day progress • Building and sustaining partnerships • Protecting business interests
8. Contract monitoring	• Monitoring results against goals • Benchmarking existing contracts against developing market capability • Negotiating detailed amendments • Identifying/protecting against potential precedents	Medium	Medium	Low/ medium	• Delight in detail • Focus on hard measures • Professional standards and networking
9. Vendor development	• Analyses emerging structure of services market • Assess specific vendors—goals and capabilities • Explores potential for new vendor services • Identifies opportunities for added value to business and vendor	Medium	High	Medium	• Innovation • Potential from partnership • Industry analysis orientation

suppliers, negotiation and supply management. The relationship-builder is highly concerned to add value to the business but the business skills are more operational in their focus, as is the case with the contract facilitator and contract monitor. With the other roles in place, business skills are of lesser importance for performance of the more technically focused 'architect' and 'fixer' roles.

The 'soft' Skills

The importance of interpersonal skills in seven of the roles reflects the greater external 'face' the modern IS function requires as IT becomes pervasive in organisations, and also the increasing dependence on external IS/IT provision. In the 'high-performance' model there are also fewer retained staff resulting in greater contact with business users/managers; team-working within the group also becomes critical. Type of interpersonal skills will vary across the roles. Again, reference back to Fig. 18.3 is helpful here. Many of the roles are defined within the overlap between two or more faces. Bridge-building is critical in these roles. Leadership skills are prominent in the CIO, informed buyer, and to a lesser extent in the systems thinker role. Communication, team-building, and facilitation skills are highest in the CIO, relationship-builder, contract facilitator, and informed buyer roles. Negotiation skills are a prime requirement for informed buying, relationship-building, and contract facilitation.

The 'high-performance' team

The nine roles form a team in two senses: the roles are complementary and interdependent; secondly, the role-holders need to be able to work together interpersonally. The roles require high performers, that is people who outperform others by a considerable margin. Subject to the qualifications made above, our research shows some evidence for these high performers sharing three characteristics. First, they are achievers with a projects/results orientation. They tend to set high standards for themselves, are decisive and tough-minded, with good communication/influencing skills. Secondly, they have a learning orientation. They are motivated by change, have a high learning capability, are imaginative, and enjoy experimenting. Finally, they are adaptable with flexibility in their management style profile, and a networking/partnership orientation (Feeny et al., 1996).

Given that these high performers have distinctive styles and motivations, there is a potential threat to the teamwork in the high performance IS function. However, mutual respect for ability, together with the network orientation of most role-holders, does allows creative rather than destructive tension.

Distinctive sets of skills and drivers

A further point illustrated by Table 18.1 is that while high performers may share many characteristics, in specific roles they will also require different assemblies of skills and motivations. We have already argued that it is a mistake to assume that the same business and interpersonal skills are required for carrying out each role. For these reasons we envisage the high performer being adaptable and capable enough to fulfil two or three adjacent roles only—business systems thinker and relationship-builder is an example combination from our experience so far. When the high-performance requirement is removed, then it becomes more possible for people to move around the different roles. However, the attractions of this approach are outweighed by considerable disadvantages. Within the context of a small residual IS group, individual capability is very visible. And one observation we can make is that neither users nor IS colleagues seem to have much patience with an unconvincing colleague (Feeny et al., 1996).

A final point needs to be made on technical skills. In some cases we have seen the high-performance IS concept founded primarily on a mix of business and interpersonal skills. The downplay of technical skills is particularly inherent in the notion of outsourcing IT supply. Technical know-how is spread thinly through all the roles and retained to the degree that a watching rather than a doing technical brief can be delivered. In this scenario the technical fixer role is discarded, the architect role retained, but with less technical skill. Alternatively, it too is combined with another role, typically that of CIO. In our view this approach is seriously mistaken. Significant technical expertise and building capability must always be retained to enable the organisation to maintain a degree of control over its IT destiny. This should apply even, or perhaps especially, in total outsourcing deals, as several pieces of research demonstrate—to guard against risks and irreversibility of contract (Lacity and Hirschheim, 1993). As one example, in 1990 First Fidelity bank outsourced all data centre operations and systems conversions to EDS on a $450m ten-year contract (Moad, 1993). Though EDS had hire/fire power over the systems developers throughout systems conversions, 250 systems developers remained on the bank's payroll during and after the conversion projects. This was to protect the bank's ability to maintain new systems in the future.

Human Resource and Organisational Implications

We have argued for a larger function—in terms of capabilities and roles—than seems generally expected amongst organisations as they increasingly look for supply from the external IS/IT services market. Nevertheless, we are talking about a small group of people, particularly when a contrast is made with the size of the in-house IS/IT functions of the 1980s. This section points to some major challenges in getting and retaining such staff. Furthermore we highlight some contextual features that influence the degree to which a high-performance IS function can be effective in larger organisational terms.

Human resource challenges

The chapter has argued for a small group of high performers, each more able than is normally found in in-house IS functions. The argument for high performers wins strong support from the experiences of respondents in over thirty organisations where IS/IT was seen as a strategic resource; and in the thirty selective and total outsourcing histories we studied in the 1991–5 period. As two total outsourcing examples, one respondent manager from a multinational oil company commented: 'You've got to be able to upskill your organisation and to have a human resource policy which provides such training to people in your organisation.' On a similar theme the logistics manager of a major retail company said: 'To be honest, we had to recruit a few people.'

In practice, recruitment and retention of a small high-quality group is a major challenge in human resource management terms. The people being targeted here would look more familiar as senior professionals within a major management consulting firm. Even though they are largely self-driven, and job satisfaction oriented, how can an organisation:

- pay them at a level which is 'within striking distance' of that provided by alternative employers?
- provide them consistently with the level of challenge they look for in the job?
- provide them with a career path despite the very small numbers?

These are major challenges in the IS functions of private and public sector organisations alike. In several respondent organisations, and across sectors, we have witnessed a reactive rather than anticipatory approach to human resource issues in IS. Many firms have some sense of operating a core–periphery model, the notion being that core workers have superior working terms and conditions, employment security, training and development opportunities, and long-term career paths within the firm. Core workers give stability in key areas together with functional flexibility. Meanwhile non-core workers on more limited contracts offer financial and numerical flexibility (Atkinson and Meager, 1986). In reality, in a volatile labour market with many IT/IS-based skills in short supply, we find full-time IT/IS staff frequently on disadvantageous contract terms, and inflexible reward and promotion systems, a high use of contract staff on high pay rates, and the more marketable in-house staff induced away by offers of significant pay increases (Willcocks, 1991; for an example in a major bank see Willcocks and Currie, 1995). Clearly in such organisations, the erosion or absence of the 'core worker' concept in the IS function would need radical re-examination and action if the proposals in this chapter are to be taken seriously.

We have observed an additional disadvantage accruing in organisations where there is lack of any understanding of IS/IT contribution demonstrated by senior executives. This threatens the availability of any of the 'transformational' excitement which high performers hold most dear (Feeny et al., 1992). One conclusion is to consider carefully the career management/ownership—and therefore deployment over time—of individuals who fulfil the roles comprising the high-performance IS function. The highest value of such individuals is usually the availability of a stream of learning and change opportunities. This is much more easily delivered through centrally co-ordinated career management. A second possibility, discussed below, is that a richer model of IS/IT sourcing may point to other ways of staffing at least some of the roles.

A further human resource challenge rests with what one respondent termed 'the legacy people' problem. In other words, what about existing IS staff that the high-performance model specifically excludes? Some approaches we have observed in various combinations are: early retirement, redundancy packages, making people redundant as the in-house legacy systems become redundant, and relocation and retraining. In outsourcing situations one common response has been to transfer such staff to vendors. Thus Willcocks and Fitzgerald (1994) found staff reductions occurring in 58 per cent of cases, with the average reduction in these cases being 44 per cent, most staff being transferred to the vendor. One difficulty is that vendors, understandably, prefer to take only the better-motivated and skilled staff; sometimes the result has been that the staff that remain are not sufficiently motivated, or capable of delivering on the in-house high-performance requirement (Willcocks and Fitzgerald, 1996).

A final point made to us by some respondents is the role of suppliers in supporting the high-performance concept. In specific projects or services, they need to have complementary rather than competing or duplicating capabilities and skills. Furthermore it is important to develop mutual co-operation and understanding between the in-house and supplier groups. In some cases, however, different terms and conditions have been a source of friction and resentment; suppliers may turn lack of in-house skills to their own opportunistic advantage; and in-house employees may stand back and let vendor staff take all responsibility (Lacity and Hirschheim, 1993; Willcocks and Fitzgerald, 1994). Some of the ways in which firms sought a more constructive relationship are indicated by the following:

We put people in the vendors' organisations for months, even years, to help them understand our needs. They [the in-house staff] changed from a systems delivery group to a consulting group which would question the need to have a system to begin with . . . it took massive reskilling.' (principal consultant, oil company)

They [the vendor staff] are part of my team, they sit with my team, so for all intents and purposes they could be working for me. We have brought them into the organisation almost, because they are running a very important production system for us . . . they also deal directly with the business users of the system . . . it's worked well because they actually get a sense of responsibility for the service like the internal people.' (IT manager, UK retailing company)

Organisational Issues

The 'high-performance team' concept in IS provides additional challenges for the wider organisation, and assumes for its operationalisation a supportive environment that was not always prevalent in respondent organisations.

Human resource policy

Outdatedness, mismatching, and inflexibility in the human resource policy of the wider organisation often disadvantage the in-house IS function against the external labour market. This echoes Rajan and Fryatt's (1988) findings in their 1987–92 study of City institutions, in what later work showed to be the key UK human resource/IT planning issues in microcosm, namely short-termism, reliance on buying in staff, lack of training, development, and career paths, and considerable neglect of human resource strategy generally (Willcocks, 1991).

Project management

There is no explicit mention in Fig. 18.3 of project management capability. In dynamic business environments, the emphasis has shifted from hierarchical, functionally based organisations toward task- and project-based ways of operating. The assumption here is that project management skills will be spread throughout such organisations and not be the preserve of one function or department. Whatever the IT component in a project, in practice its project manager can come from anywhere in the business, the main primary criterion being his or her credibility, which in turn relates to proven successful project experience (Earl, 1996; Willcocks et al., 1997a). Without this in a pharmaceuticals company we saw a project manager, appointed from the business to implement a MRP2 system, fail through lack of technical credibility. In a bank and insurance company several projects managed by IT personnel failed to deliver effective business systems through a narrow, technical view of the requirement.

In terms of Fig. 18.3, depending on how user driven the project needs to be, candidates for project management would most likely be found in the relationship-builder and technical fixer roles. In connection with projects two other roles are usually mentioned in addition to project manager, namely project sponsor and project champion (Beath, 1996; Edwards, 1996). Depending on the technical content of the project, and its importance, these roles are most likely to be held by senior business managers, though from Fig.18.3 the CIO may be a candidate.

Location

The issue of physical location of the nine key capabilities in the organisation structure can be largely answered by referring to the findings and prescriptions from work already referred to (see Earl et al., 1997; Hodgkinson, 1996). A vital requirement is that a person fulfilling a key IS capability can be in easy and regular contact with his or her salient senior management, user, and IS function constituency. Thus a relationship-builder is more likely to be located and spend time within business units; a technical architect may be located centrally in a planning unit; a contract facilitator needs to be located close to both users generating requirements and vendor staff; but for all these much depends upon the specific contingencies, problems, and projects of the day.

Sourcing IT/IS: The Core–Periphery Model Revisited

So far we have outlined the emerging nine key capabilities required for any future high-performance IS function. We have also discussed issues around how such a function can be operationalised. This final section returns to the notion of core capabilities and relates it more explicitly to the growing use of the external market for IT services. This yields further insight into sourcing strategy, and the capability needed to support it.

Over many years organisations have consistently used the external market to some degree to source their IS/IT whether in the form of technology, services, or human resources. However, in the 1990s, as a response to the four pressures described earlier we have increasingly seen advanced a view of the in-house IS function as having primarily what has been variously described as a 'strategic', 'residual', 'governance', or 'intelligent customer' role. Essentially this definition emphasises full in-house involvement in 'upstream' activities—particularly IM and the continuing development of IS strategy to meet business needs—followed by a 'procure and manage' role related to 'downstream' activities such as systems development, operational service, and support. This perspective incorporates much of the thinking that underpins how major, or even total, outsourcing of IT/IS

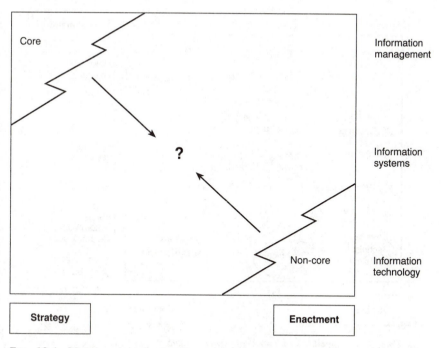

FIG. 18.4. *Mapping choice in sourcing activity*

services may be supported by a demand-led, strategy-focused residual IS function. One unfortunate consequence of such thinking we have observed in several case studies is where 'residual' becomes all too accurate a phrase for the human resource capabilities and skills remaining to plan for future needs, administer outsourcing contracts, and look after the organisation's IT/IS destiny (Willcocks and Fitzgerald, 1996).

The dilemma is illustrated in Fig. 18.4. As discussed earlier, every organisation must somehow ensure that it has in place the information management, information systems, and information technology components of overall information strategy. For each element there is a spectrum of activities required, represented by the horizontal axis of Fig. 18.4. Some of the activities are necessary enablers of the strategy process, such as relationship-building and information-gathering. Then there is the strategy creation process itself, involving analysis, brainstorming, evaluation, and so on. At all three levels there is the requirement to enable/create/build/operate/improve, with at least some level of activity in each phase of the process all of the time. Sourcing decisions need to be made along the Demand–Supply and the Strategy–Enactment axes.

A key question arises: how do resource-based concepts of core capabilities/distinctive competencies relate to this model of IS/IT activity in the light of the developing external market for IT/IS services? The minimalist

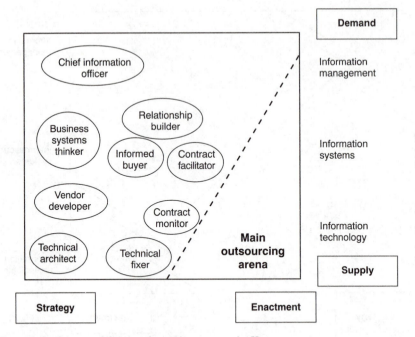

FIG. 18.5. *Core capabilities and sourcing strategy in IS*

view—which some organisations have taken—is that core capability occupies a small space in the top left corner of the map. The information
management strategy—to outsource—is owned by the business, and the
rest of the space is occupied by a vendor who is a 'strategic partner' responsible for creating and implementing the IS and IT strategies, as well
as implementing IM. Our experience strongly and consistently challenges
this view. No organisation can remain informed of its demand-side needs
and in control of its IS/IT investment without a richer definition of core
capability in the IS function. But where should the line be drawn? Fig. 18.5
suggests how the concept—together with its IM, IS, and IT dimensions—
needs to be populated by the nine capabilities that describe the high-
performance IS function. Fig. 18.5 seeks to illustrate what our research
evidence shows strongly—that IS core capabilities cannot be different
from, but must be virtually synonymous with, what we have defined as
the high-performance IS function.

It is worth considering this proposition in a little more detail. The terms
core competence/distinctive competence were coined to distinguish those
things an organisation does particularly well relative to its competitors, and
that are fundamental to a firm's performance and strategy (Hamel and
Heene, 1994; Quinn, 1992; Selznick, 1957). Our research reveals nine key
capabilities that need to be developed to enable an organisation to acquire,

deploy, and leverage IT investments over time as a basis for sustainable survival and competitive success. Clearly, much depends upon the quality of these capabilities, and the degree to which they are supported by the wider organisation, relative to competitors. Feeny and Ives (1997) describe three bases for sustainable competitive advantage through IT: generic lead-time, competitive asymmetry, and pre-emption potential. They note that projects that rely solely on generic lead-time for advantage are at risk. Sustainability is much more likely where the prime mover in the sector earns a decided advantage by going first, or where competitive asymmetry makes it difficult or impossible for a competitor to respond. Core IS capabilities contribute by providing the organisational and knowledge sources from which competitive asymmetry can be developed. But they also provide the capability both to identify the prime moves that can be made, and to ensure that pre-emption is not immutable.

In researching sixteen companies Runge and Earl (1988) found competitive advantage from IT developing from 'marginal' managers operating on the edge of the organisation and close to external customers, with strong business sponsorship, outside formal procedures and the IT department, together with strong internal marketing. Three points arise. First, they found that competitive edge systems mostly developed incrementally over time, and outside planning systems. Secondly, processes, power, and relationships were an important source of getting the IT investment off the ground. Thirdly, the organisations and their IT departments were configured mainly on functional and hierarchical lines. On the first two points the high-performance model offers the capability to match the requirement closely. In particular research in respondent organisations suggests that the relationship, roles, and how they are fulfilled bridge real gaps in previous organisational arrangements, facilitating a flow of information and ideas and creating support mechanisms for leveraging IT investments. Moreover business systems thinking that spans organisational and IT-based systems represents a significant development for the capability of developing business-based systems (see Fig. 18.5). On the third point, the model of the emergent IS function also offers, on our evidence, much-needed ways of reconfiguring some major barriers to leveraging IT effectively.

However we have said little so far about IT/IS market sourcing strategy and its relationship to organisational performance. Fig. 18.5 delineates four critical capabilities for dealing with external suppliers. A richer picture of the sourcing options needs to be supplied to show how optimal decisions can be arrived at and delivered on. This will also help to indicate how some, at least, of the human resource challenges presented by the high-performance IS function may be met.

All too often the trade press, and some academic studies, tend to present IS/IT sourcing decisions as binary choices: in-house or outsourced. We have consistently promoted a more complex model (Feeny et al., 1993;

Lacity et al., 1996). A key distinction can be made between contracts that specify a service and result which the market is to provide (outsourcing); and contracts which call for the market to provide resources to be deployed under the buyer's management and control (insourcing). The purchasing style can either be consistently open tender (i.e. competition for each market transaction); or relationship oriented (i.e. single tender to a preferred vendor provided certain conditions are met). This analysis suggests five different sourcing options. Three of them—buy in, preferred supplier, and in-house—we refer to as 'insourcing'. Two others—contract out and preferred supplier—are 'outsourcing'. In practice these multiple options offer more opportunities for gaining leverage from external and internal IT/IS services, but also provide more potential pitfalls. We are also finding many large organisations moving to a complex set of sourcing arrangements where all five options are taken up to some degree simultaneously. The high-performance model specifically provides the capability in-house to make choices in this complex arena, and also enforce those choices.

Finally, insourcing options may also be used to address some of the human resource challenges presented by the high performance model. The chief information officer, informed buyer, business systems thinker, relationship-builder, and contract facilitator all fall within the 'business' face of Fig. 18.3. These are the priorities for in-house resourcing, which provides the best opportunity for ongoing business orientation. But four other roles—technical architect, technical fixer, contract monitor, vendor developer—lie outside the business face. If these roles are 'insourced' to a preferred supplier, they may successfully provide a check and balance on the contractors to whom service provision has been 'outsourced'. Better, surely, to insource on this basis than to deprive the high-performance IS function of some of its facilities.

Conclusion

This chapter has sought to provide fresh thinking on the key capabilities required in the IS function in contemporary organisations. Three research strands showed the importance of capabilities and skills—essentially human resource based—in identifying, delivering, and operating IT for organisational advantage. In particular respondent organisations seemed to be making in some instances incremental, in others planned, moves toward an emergent model of the IS function. Our analysis has distilled these moves into nine key capabilities and posited the need, if the promise of IT is to be fully exploited, for a high-performance IS function.

At the same time as developing, from research, the notion of the high-performance IS function, we have been deeply aware of the challenges it poses for organisations. Historically, in both IT and the wider organisation, human resource issues have been neglected, and are still rarely the subject of anticipatory, let alone strategic, action. Resource-based approaches and notions of building long-term core capabilities also appear more regularly in the academic literature, and in a few high-profile cases of success, than in actual organisational practices. However, there have been encouraging signs in the organisations we have studied. Moreover, there are many indications that, if most organisations fail to move in the direction of the high-performance model, then those that do would gain even more sustainable advantage than might otherwise be the case.

References

Atkins, M., and Galliers, R. (1992), 'Human Resource Development for I.S. Executives', *Proceedings of the SIGCPR Conference, Cincinnati, Ohio, 3–7th. April.*

Atkinson, J., and Meager, N. (1986), *Changing Working Patterns: How Companies Achieve Flexibility to Meet New Needs* (London: National Economic Development Office).

Beath, C. (1996), 'The Project Champion', in Earl (1996).

Broadbent, M., and Weill, P. (1993), 'Improving Business and Information Strategy Alignment: Learning from the Banking Industry', *IBM Systems Journal,* 32, 1: 162–79.

Ciborra, C. (1993), *Teams, Markets and Systems* (Cambridge: Cambridge University Press).

Couger, D. (1996), 'The Changing Environment for IS Professionals: Human Resource Implications', in Earl (1996).

Earl, M. (1996) (ed.), *Information Management: The Organisational Dimension* (Oxford: Oxford University Press).

—— Edwards, B., and Feeny, D. (1997), 'Configuring the IS Function in Complex Organisations', in Willcocks et al. (1997*a*).

—— and Feeny, D. (1994), 'Is your CIO Adding Value?', *Sloan Management Review,* 35, 3: 11–20.

Edwards, B. (1996), 'The Project Sponsor', in Earl (1996).

Feeny, D. (1997), 'The Five Year Learning of Ten IT Directors', in Willcocks et al. (1997*a*).

—— Abl, V., Millie, E., Minter, A., Selby, C., and Williams, J. (1996), 'Defining New IS Skills and Competencies', OXIIM/KPMG Research and Discussion Paper (Oxford: Templeton College).

—— Earl, M., and Edwards, B. (1994), 'Organisational Arrangements for IS: The Role of Users and IS Specialists', OXIIM Research and Discussion Paper RDP94/6 (Oxford: Templeton College).

—— Edwards, B., and Simpson, K. (1992), 'Understanding the CEO/CIO Relationship', *MIS Quarterly,* 16: 435–48.

—— and Ives, B. (1997), 'Information Technology as a Basis for Sustainable Competitive Advantage', in Willcocks et al. (1997*a*).

Feeny, D., Willcocks, L., and Fitzgerald, G. (1993), 'Strategies for IT Management: When Outsourcing Equals Rightsourcing', in S. Rock (ed.), *Directors' Guide to Outsourcing* (London: Institute of Directors).

George, J., and King, J. (1991), 'Examining the Computing and Centralisation Debate', *Communications of the ACM*, 34, 7: 63–72.

Grant, R. (1995), *Contemporary Strategy Analysis* (Oxford: Blackwell).

Grindley, K. (1995), *Managing IT at Board Level* (London: Price Waterhouse).

Hamel, G., and Heene, A. (1994) (eds.), *Competence-Based Competition* (Chichester: John Wiley & Son).

—— and Prahalad, C. (1994), *Competing for the Future* (Boston: Harvard Business Press).

Henderson, J., and Venkatraman, N. (1993), 'Strategic Alignment: Leveraging Information Technology for Transforming Organisations', *IBM Systems Journal*, 32, 1: 4–17.

Hodgkinson, S. (1996), 'The Role of the Corporate IT Function in the Federal IT Organisation', in Earl (1996).

Lacity, M., and Hirschheim, R. (1993), 'The Information Systems Outsourcing Bandwagon', *Sloan Management Review*, Fall: 73–93.

—— Willcocks, L., and Feeny, D. (1995), 'IT Outsourcing: Maximising Flexibility and Control', *Harvard Business Review*, May–June: 84–93.

—— —— —— (1996), 'The Value of Selective IT Sourcing', *Sloan Management Review*, 37, 3: 13–25.

Loh, L., and Venkatraman, N. (1992), 'Determinants of Information Technology Outsourcing: A Cross Sectional Analysis', *Journal of Management Information Systems*, 9, 1: 7–24.

McFarlan, W. (1984), 'Information Technology Changes the Way you Compete', *Harvard Business Review*, May–June: 98–103.

—— and Nolan, R. (1995), 'How to Manage an IT Outsourcing Alliance', *Sloan Management Review*, 36, Winter: 9–23.

Moad, J. (1993), 'Inside an Outsourcing Deal', *Datamation*, 15 Feb: 20–7.

Porter, M., and Millar, V. (1985), 'How Information Gives you Competitive Advantage', *Harvard Business Review*, 63, 4: 149–60.

Prahalad, C., and Hamel, G. (1990), 'The Core Competence of the Corporation', *Harvard Business Review*, 68, 3: 79–91.

Quinn, J. (1992), 'The Intelligent Enterprise: A New Paradigm', *Academy of Management Executive*, 6, 4: 44–63.

—— Doorley, T., and Paquette, P. (1990), 'Technology in Services: Rethinking Strategic Focus', *Sloan Management Review*, 31, 2: 79–87.

Rajan, A., and Fryatt, S. (1988), *Create or Abdicate: The City's Human Resource for the 1980s* (London: Witherby & Co.).

Runge, D., and Earl, M. (1988), 'Gaining Competitive Advantage from Telecommunications', in M. Earl (ed.), *Information Management: The Strategic Dimension* (Oxford: Clarendon Press).

Scarbrough, H. (1995), 'Blackboxes, Hostages and Prisoners', *Organisation Studies*, 16, 6: 991–1021.

—— (1996), 'Commodifying Professional Expertise: IT in Financial Services', in H. Scarbrough (ed.), *The Management of Expertise* (Basingstoke: Macmillan).

Selznick, P. (1957), *Leadership in Administration: A Sociological Interpretation* (New York: Harper & Row).

Skyrme, D. (1992), 'From Hybrids to Bridge-Building', OXIIM Research and Discussion Paper RDP 92/1 (Oxford: Templeton College).

Smits, S., Mclean, E., and Tanner, J. (1993), 'Managing High Achieving Information Systems Professionals', *Journal of Management Information Systems*, 9, 4: 103–20.

Strassmann, P. (1995), *The Politics of Information Management* (New Canaan, Conn.: Information Economics Press).

Taylor-Cummings, A. (1997), 'Bridging the User–IS Gap: Successful Integration Arrangements for Systems Involving Significant Organisational Change', in Willcocks et al. (1997*a*).

Walton, R. E. (1989), *Up and Running: Integrating Information Technology and the Organisation* (Boston: Harvard Business School Press).

—— (1994) (ed.), *Information Management: Evaluation of Information Systems Investments* (London: Chapman & Hall).

Willcocks, L. (1991), 'Information Technology and Human Resource Issues into the 1990s: Integration through Culture', *Proceedings of the Fifth Annual Conference of the British Academy of Management—Business: Advancing the Horizons, Bath University 22–24th. September.*

—— and Currie, W. (1995), 'Does Radical Reengineering Really Work? A Cross-sectoral Study of Strategic Projects', OXIIM Research and Discussion Paper 95/10 (Oxford: Templeton College).

—— Feeny, D., and Islei, G. (1997*a*) (eds.), *Managing Information Technology as a Strategic Resource* (Maidenhead: McGraw Hill).

—— and Fitzgerald, G. (1994), *A Business Guide to Outsourcing IT: A Study of European Best Practice in the Selection, Management and Use of External IT Services* (London: Business Intelligence).

—— —— (1996), 'The Changing Shape of the Information Systems Function', in Earl (1996).

—— —— and Feeny, D. (1995), 'IT Outsourcing: The Strategic Implications', *Long Range Planning*, 28, 5: 59–70.

—— —— and Lacity, M. (1996), 'To Outsource IT or Not? Recent Evidence on Economics and Evaluation Practice', in Willcocks et al. (1997*a*).

—— and Griffiths, C. (1994), 'Predicting Risk of Failure in Large-Scale Information Technology Projects', *Technological Forecasting and Social Change*, 47, 1: 205–28.

—— Lacity, M., and Fitzgerald, G. (1997*b*), 'IT Outsourcing in Europe and the USA: Assessment Issues', in Willcocks et al. (1997*a*).

—— and Mark, A. (1989), 'IT Systems Implementation: Research Findings from the Public Sector', *Journal of Information Technology*, 4, 2: 92–103.

19

The Management of Knowledge Workers

HARRY SCARBROUGH

Introduction

The relevance of this chapter on knowledge workers to a book on information systems needs to be touched on only briefly. There are (at least) three major reasons why students and practitioners of IS should be concerned with the management of this particular group. For one, as possessors of specialist expertise many IS staff fall into the knowledge worker category. Their job mobility and the problems of controlling their work are the kind of management problems we see with other knowledge workers. Secondly, IS functions are increasingly finding that they have to tailor their services to user groups whose work is knowledge based. By removing routine and bureaucratic roles, the delayering of organisations has tended to expose (and sometimes undermine) the underlying knowledge-base of the firm. Thus, information systems which were originally concerned with the processing of data and later the processing of information are beginning to be applied to knowledge support activities. Thirdly, information systems are closely implicated in the wider patterns of organisational change that endow a strategic status on knowledge work. Power and practices within organisations increasingly derive from knowledge and networks rather than from hierarchy (Scarbrough, 1996).

Despite widespread agreement on the growing importance of knowledge work and workers, the implications for organisations and IS are less clear. This is largely because many writers have treated the knowledge worker as a kind of 'New Age' concept; a figure shrouded in mystery and only dimly revealed through their crystal-ball gazing. Instead of treating the knowledge worker as a New Age icon, this chapter aims to develop a more empirically grounded and critical perspective which highlights the problems and dilemmas which this emerging group poses for management. In contrast to the uncritical gloss offered by some management gurus, I will present an account which is conflict based, centring on the tensions that knowledge work and workers create for conventionally hierarchical organisations. This will involve unpacking the concept and locating the management of knowledge workers within the wider social context for the production and exploitation of knowledge.

Unpacking the Concept

In this chapter, I want to argue that the concept of the knowledge worker usefully characterises some powerful patterns in industrial and occupational change. However, before it can become usefully applied the concept needs to be rescued from some of its more enthusiastic advocates. In the first instance, this involves tackling the problem of definition—what is knowledge work and who are the knowledge workers?

Peter Drucker (1969) claims the credit for coining the notion of 'knowledge work', which he contrasts with service work and manual work. Although the term has been developed and refined by other writers subsequently, the main themes of Drucker's analysis have continued to influence the debate. Thus, knowledge workers are presented as a new type of occupation which is qualitatively different from the occupational groups of the old industrial economy. Their growing importance is associated with the emergence of a globalized, post-industrial economy in which knowledge displaces capital as the motor of competitive performance. Subsequently, numerous writers have seized on these ideas to advocate fundamental changes in the way firms view and manage themselves. Thus, to summarise the drift of their argument, since firms increasingly compete through their know-how or 'core competencies' (Hemel and Prahalad, 1994) as much as through specific products, they are correspondingly dependent on the workers who supply such know-how (Reich, 1991). Further, successful exploitation of this know-how requires changes in the structure, culture, and management style employed within organisations. The traditional command and control structure will have to be jettisoned in favour of team- and project-based management approaches.

Although these kinds of argument represent the received wisdom on knowledge workers, their far-reaching proposals for management are usually supported by only the sketchiest evidence as to the real extent and character of this occupational group. Thus, at one level, the idea of the knowledge worker is a portmanteau term which has been applied to the growing number of occupations that defy conventional categories but which seem to be principally concerned with the production and transmission of knowledge. In this context, the typical characteristics of 'knowledge work' have been described as follows:

- variety and uncertainty in inputs and outputs;
- unstructured and individualised work rules and routines;
- lack of separation among process, outputs, and inputs;

- lack of measures;
- worker autonomy;
- high variability in performance across individuals and time (Davenport et al., 1996).

The problem with this kind of definition is that distinguishing knowledge work from routinised or Taylorised jobs does not differentiate either amongst different kinds of knowledge work or between the latter and jobs which simply defy programming (for example, managerial jobs). Machlup's original 1962 study (reprinted 1990) sowed the seeds for much of this confusion by adopting a definition so broad that even striptease dancers were classified as knowledge workers.

Many writers have sought to avoid this ambiguity by differentiating further between data workers or information workers and knowledge workers (Tjaden, 1996). Thus, information workers carry out routine information-processing tasks, whereas knowledge workers apply high levels of abstract and specialised knowledge to the interpretation of information and the production of goods and services. On this basis, a number of different groups have been labelled 'knowledge workers'. For example, Reich (1991) classifies knowledge workers (or in his terms 'symbolic analysts') as 'problem solvers' such as R&D experts and designers, 'problem identifiers' (marketers, advertisers), and 'brokers' (financiers, contractors). Another recent study applied the label to groups as diverse as auditors, HRM managers, credit controllers, R&D, and IS staff. These groups were identified as knowledge workers because their roles involved acting on knowledge in some way; finding, creating, packaging, applying, or reusing knowledge (Davenport et al., 1996). However, these broad-brush definitions of knowledge work are symptomatic not so much of strict occupational analysis as of a general mood that prevails in the debate around knowledge workers—a mood which is pretty well evoked in the following comment from Argyris:

The fact is more and more jobs—no matter what the title—are taking on the contours of 'knowledge work'. People at all levels of the organisation must combine the mastery of some highly specialised technical expertise with the ability to work effectively in teams, form productive relationships with clients, and critically reflect on and then change their own organisational practices. And the nuts and bolts of management . . . increasingly consists of guiding and integrating the autonomous but interconnected work of highly skilled people. (Argyris, 1991: 36)

To critics of the knowledge worker idea, this kind of argument represents a sprawling mass of generalisations which is open to attack on several different fronts. One obvious source of criticism, for example, is the tendency to lump a variety of occupational groups under the heading of knowledge workers. This tendency reflects the slippery qualities of knowledge

TABLE 19.1. *A comparison between industrial and post-industrial societies*

	Industrialism	Post-industrialism
Major relationship	Against nature	Between organisations
Dominant industrial sector	Secondary	Tertiary, quaternary
Key resource	Energy	Information
Dominant social group	Semi-skilled worker	Professional/technical Scientists
Key mechanisms	Machinery	Knowledge
Key institutional form	Business firm	Research institute

Source: Bell (1973).

itself. Knowledge is arguably an 'anthropological constant' (Stehr, 1994: 184) in all human societies. This not only makes it extremely difficult to discriminate between different forms of work or occupation, but taking the term literally might lead us to see all workers as knowledge workers. And if we do not apply it literally, we might be accused of giving respectability to a socially elitist distinction (Knights et al., 1993), or, worse, of masking the political influence of technocrats in the guise of disinterested knowledge (Fischer, 1990).

The most frontal attacks, however, focus on the model of the post-industrial society which has coloured much of the debate around knowledge workers. In this model, abstract knowledge is presented as the 'axial principle' of a massive societal change in which primary and secondary industries give way to tertiary and service industries and their associated social and cultural connotations (Bell, 1973). This model promotes a 'rupturist' analysis of social change (Lakatos, 1974). In other words, it can be characterised in terms of a 'before and after' portrait of society as summarised in Table 19.1.

Now, this analysis has been extensively criticised for overstating the extent of occupational and industrial change. Some authors (e.g. Kumar, 1997, 1995) have suggested that social change is much more layered or stratified in its effects than the rupturist view would suggest. Traditional manufacturing industries and established institutions persist as important elements in the social and economic fabric of nations. Thus we find that moves towards a service-based economy are countered by the trend for domestic services to be supplied through manufactured product (entertainment and information being supplied via the TV, hi-fi, personal computer, etc. (Gershuny, 1978)). Again the impact of change is much more ambiguous than the most upbeat post-industrial commentaries propose. The loss of manufacturing jobs is not directly compensated for by service jobs which are in any case often low-skill and low-paid—the so-called 'McJobs' (Ritzer, 1993).

A more specific criticism has to do with the futurology which is implicit in much of the debate. Because 'knowledge workers' are presented as an emerging force in society, accounts are often based as much on projections of the future as they are upon the actual (and inconveniently complicated) realities facing these groups. In the post-industrial vision, the 'knowledge worker' serves the same kind of function that the industrial proletariat did for Karl Marx—at once a living symbol of industrial change and a prototype of things to come. Indeed, Charles Handy makes the connection explicit when he argues that 'in ten years time . . . the workers will truly own the "means of production" because those means will be in their own heads and at their fingertips' (*Financial Times*, 29 Dec. 1993). 'In ten years time' is a telling phrase. Extrapolating madly from current trends leads to a predicted pattern of change which is both uniform and inexorable, glossing over the contested and contradictory aspects of change.

This point leads on to a third set of criticisms of the knowledge worker idea which focus on the role of IT in promoting knowledge work. Again, assumptions that IT will always operate in a benign way are open to question. Take, for instance, the claim that 'Knowledge plays a new role in an information age business. It is the most important asset to be managed by such businesses, replacing labour and financial capital' (Tjaden, 1996). Yet, IT systems may be used to convert specialised expertise into a portable commodity—a package or a system—allowing the reproduction of knowledge at minimal cost. If anything, this arguably has the potential to overturn the benign predictions of writers like Handy and Tjaden by finally liberating capital from labour. Certainly, this potential has been eagerly seized on by those financial service firms who have transferred their 'back office' operations to low-wage or underdeveloped countries (Davis and Stack, 1992). The rosy picture for knowledge workers is further undermined by other studies which have found IT being used for surveillance and monitoring (Sewell and Wilkinson, 1992). As a result, the same trends which are said to be spawning knowledge-based jobs also contain the potential to eliminate or deskill such roles. Some knowledge workers may thus enjoy privileged positions within organisations, while others are subject to the pressures of outsourcing and de-skilling (Knights et al., 1993).

It is also worth noting that it is entirely possible to see knowledge as central to firms' competitive success without implying a special status for knowledge workers. Much of the knowledge of an organisation is embedded in routines and procedures or encoded in systems. In some firms, the specialist knowledge of individuals may be much less important than the know-how built into structure, culture, and practices (Blackler, 1995). Indeed, some writers would argue that individual expertise can never serve as an enduring competitive advantage simply because it is not an organisational asset—outstanding individuals usually being highly mobile between firms (Grant, 1991).

Rescuing the Concept

Accepting these criticisms does not mean that talk of knowledge workers has to be abandoned altogether. As long as we view it with caution and reject the futuristic and deterministic overtones, this is a powerful way of characterising some important changes in the way people work; changes which, though, broadly based, are not nearly as uniform in their effects as many commentators suggest.

One step in rescuing the knowledge worker concept is to see it as a relative rather than an absolute attribution. That is to say, rather than denoting fixed occupational roles or tasks, it can be seen as signalling points of relative difference amongst or change within such roles. In particular, it draws our attention to change in those organisational roles which are broadly concerned with the production and communication of knowledge. In this context, the rise of the knowledge worker seems to be very largely a consequence of, first, the codification of knowledge, and second, its commodification. These are processes in which knowledge is translated into symbolic form (computer programs being the most obvious example) and consequently becomes more readily marketable as a commodity. Now, many societal institutions have a bearing upon these processes. In the UK, for example, the deregulation and privatisation of the 1980s together with the growth of internal markets in the public sector helped to codify and commodify the expertise of a wide range of professional groupings, ranging from actuaries in the insurance industry through to groups such as R&D workers and NHS doctors who found their disciplines increasingly subjected to market pressures (Scarbrough, 1996). However, it is also true to say that IT and communication technologies have played a significant role in this process—actuarial expertise, for instance, was turned into a marketable commodity through the pioneering developments of complex policy databases at the Direct Line company. As a recent OECD report notes: 'ICTs (information and communication technologies) allow for increased codification of knowledge, that is its transformation into "information" that can easily be transmitted . . . through codification knowledge takes on more and more the properties of a commodity' (OECD, 1996: 13).

The impact of IT on the commodification of knowledge occurs at three major levels. First, tacit and embodied knowledge is encoded through IT into symbolic forms which can be transmitted or incorporated in artefacts. Second, the encoding of knowledge means that it can be manipulated more easily—it is no longer opaque but can be objectively deployed and combined with other packaged forms of knowledge. Third, IT has an impact on the range of organisational forms through which knowledge can be managed. Advances in information and communications technologies have encouraged the emergence of looser and more spatially distributed organisational forms. The traditional modes of knowledge management —essentially, the professional institutions and/or specialist functions within business hierarchies—give way to networking and market-style arrangements (Whittington, 1991).

The overall effect of the commodification process is not only to expand the market for knowledge but also to create new occupational roles for both the providers and users of knowledge. Under the traditional model of the professions typified by medicine and the law, knowledge was acquired through education and socialisation within highly demarcated social groups. Expertise was jealously guarded and subject to professional norms and controls. Although such knowledge was predominantly abstract (compared to say the manual skills of a craft worker), it could only be accessed through the expertise of the professionals themselves.

Historically, we find that as large business organisations began to draw on scientific and professional expertise, they tended to internalise the professional model within their hierarchies. They adopted the 'black box' approach to managing professionals (Quinn et al., 1996). So-called 'organisational professionals' such as R&D scientists, IT specialists, and accountants emerged to be managed through a watered-down version of professionalism. These groups lacked the formal powers of the classic professions in that their professional bodies were weak or non-existent and exercised much less control over their work. On the other hand, they did display certain attributes of the professional model. For example; they usually enjoyed a degree of autonomy compared to other work groups; they were committed to professional standards; and their work practices were dependent on specialised learning and abstract knowledge. Enclaves of organisational professionals, such as central R&D or IT functions, were more or less autonomous from top management.

Although the 'organisational professional' is still an influential model for the management of expertise, recent developments in IT have prompted a further shift in management strategies. Information systems have expanded the distribution of specialist knowledge and made its deployment more transparent. This has advanced organisational innovations which seek in their different ways to bring about a radical shift in the way such knowledge is managed. Thus, business process re-engineering exploits greater organisational transparency to attack the functional distribution of expertise, while outsourcing trades on the commodification of expertise to promote the use of market controls. Clearly, these innovations are far from being panaceas for the management of expertise—a point which will be addressed later in this chapter. However, their widespread adoption is at least symptomatic of the decline of the organisational professionals and their replacement by this disparate grouping of occupations which can only be called 'knowledge workers'. As a result of these wider technological and

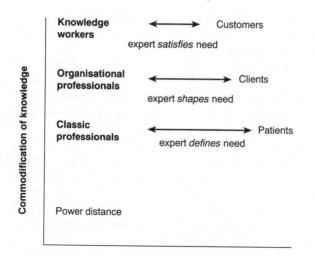

FIG. 19.1. *Changing relationships between experts and users*

organisational changes, knowledge workers operate much closer to the market than their professional forebears. This is reflected not only in their structural position within and outside organisations, but also culturally in the relationships between experts and users. Where professionals dealt with clients, knowledge workers have to satisfy customers. As summarised in Fig. 19.1, we can say that the power distance between expert and user roles has declined both across time and as between old and new expert groupings.

Clearly, knowledge work is regulated much more by the economic forces of supply and demand, as reflected in product and labour markets, than by professional norms and standards (McGovern, 1995). Insofar as knowledge workers display some of the outward features of the classic professional—for instance, retaining some autonomy and self-management in their working practices—this is to do with their labour-market position and the opaque and unpredictable nature of the work they do rather than the institutional power of the profession (Friedman and Cornford, 1989).

The Challenge to Management

There are many ways of characterising the managerial challenges posed by knowledge workers. Drucker (1988), for example, focuses on management style. He likens the knowledge-based organisation to an orchestra, arguing that managers will need to abandon traditional styles and act more like conductors. Handy (1995) prefers to focus on structure and argues that firms are moving towards the 'shamrock' organisation, involving more decentralised forms of control. However, in contrast to both these positions, I want to argue that focusing on issues of either style or structure is actually glossing over some of the most important and long-term implications of managing knowledge workers. The framework which I will develop for addressing these issues is based not on symptomatic changes in style and structure but on the analysis of different kinds of *conflict* embedded in the knowledge worker role.

In talking about conflict, I should make it clear that I am not concerned with outright antagonism between different groups and individuals. Rather, conflict here refers to the tensions between the different imperatives or 'logics of action' (Karpik, 1978) created by the multi-level contexts for knowledge work. Insofar as these tensions share a common theme it derives from the contradictions between the *social processes* involved in the production of knowledge and the *exchange processes* which create economic value. Thus, the production of knowledge requires the kind of openness and tight-knit social groupings that characterise the workings of the science laboratory or the development team. Economic exchange, however, is characterised by the guarded attitudes and transactional closure that we associate with the buyer–seller relationship (Scarbrough, 1995).

Identifying a conflict between these two fundamental features of knowledge work is not to say that they are ultimately incompatible. In fact, every day managers find ways of marrying knowledge production to the economic goals of profitability. However, this analysis suggests that their success in doing so depends primarily on achieving a trade-off between the respective logics of knowledge production and economic exchange. In short, the challenge of managing knowledge workers can be usefully characterised as the 'quasi-resolution of conflict' (Cyert and March, 1963): that is, of uniting, however temporarily, two divergent sets of social practices. And if this suggests that the management process is simply a matter of 'satisficing' competing goals or placating the odd prima donna—which it undoubtedly sometimes is—it is also important to remember that firms which succeed in managing this conflict also benefit from the creative tensions that it produces. The management of innovation centres precisely on this quasi-resolution of conflict within organisational processes and structures (Feldman, 1989)—making innovation management one of the most sought after but also maddeningly inimitable competencies of the organisation.

The impact of these conflicts can be briefly outlined in terms of three major levels of analysis (see Fig 19.2). In this model, conflict at the institutional level derives from the fundamental tensions between the economic institutions of firms and markets and the knowledge-producing institutions of science, education, and the professions. It finds further echoes at the organisational level in the contradictory coupling of the open, 'organic'

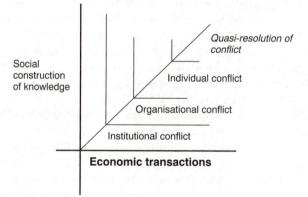

F IG. 19.2. *Levels of conflict in the management of knowledge workers*
Source: Adapted from Burrell (1996).

settings required for knowledge work (Burns and Stalker, 1961) and the tightly controlled actions required for business efficiency. Finally, at the individual level, the employment relationship enshrines important potential conflicts of interest between individual knowledge workers and their employer.

Analysing the management of knowledge workers in these broad terms has a number of advantages. For one it should make us sceptical about the usefulness of simplistic recipes that focus on the management process without addressing the context for that process. Advice to locate knowledge workers in teams, for instance, or alternatively to link their pay to individual performance may be perfectly valid ideas but they depend on the context (trying to do both at the same time, though, is probably wrong regardless of context). In addition, it highlights the deep-rooted and multi-causal character of the managerial problems posed by knowledge work. This effectively casts doubt on the notion that these problems can be resolved by changes in structure alone, or style, or culture, or even all three together. In place of one-dimensional solutions, this analysis highlights the need to adopt multiple perspectives in managing knowledge workers—to be able to see knowledge work in terms of institutional constraints as well as in terms of structural or even psychological concerns.

Institutional conflict

My analysis of knowledge workers begins not within the organisation but outside it. To understand the limits on management's ability to control and deploy knowledge workers we have to look to the institutional environment within which firms operate. And this is not simply the immediate economic environment composed of competitors, suppliers, and customers. Firms' strategic responses are also conditioned by surrounding social and political institutions, including labour markets, government, the professions, higher education, and science (Whittington, 1993). These institutions are important to this particular debate because they exert a powerful influence on the way knowledge is colonised by knowledge-based occupations within different societies (Abbott, 1988).

A particular feature of the institutional environment in Britain and North America, for instance, is the importance of the professional model as the preferred means of organising specialist knowledge (Freidson, 1986). These professional groups tend to promote an 'occupational principle' for the division of labour which cuts across the 'administrative principle' based on hierarchical authority which is favoured by organisations (Freidson, 1994). As we will see later, this particular institutional conflict often translates into various forms of organisational conflict.

At the same time, though, we need to be chary of generalising the Anglo-American experience to the rest of the world. There is an obvious contrast with Japan where firms have developed a much more organisation-centred approach to the acquisition of knowledge, downplaying occupational specialization in favour of generalist skills and rotation between functional departments. As Friedman (1987) notes, this generalist approach has led to a much wider spread of IT skills within Japanese firms but has also inhibited the deepening of such skills.

Finally, we should not forget the institutional influences on management itself. Management in the UK is generally held to be accountancy dominated with relatively little technical expertise to be found at the highest levels of management (Armstrong, 1992). This managerial bias reflects wider institutional factors, in this case the links between the City and industry, and certainly tends to exacerbate tensions between top management and technical professionals. By way of contrast, German firms draw many of their top managers from the ranks of technologists and engineers, thus spreading the culture of *Technik* throughout the management structure (Lee and Smith, 1992).

A further institutional constraint on the management of knowledge workers comes from the operation of labour markets. Where labour markets are deregulated and there is high job mobility, it becomes more difficult for employees to secure a reasonable return on any investments they make in training their knowledge workers. Once these workers have acquired high-level skills, they become a more marketable proposition and are liable to be poached by competing employers. This poaching of skills represents a major disincentive to invest in anything but the most company-specific training—the resulting skills shortages which periodically affect the job market (for IS workers in particular, it has to be said) further aggravate the problem.

But as well as inhibiting the *volume* of skills training, labour markets can also influence the *content* of the skills and knowledge which knowledge workers acquire. A case in point here is the long-standing demand for greater managerial and business skills on the part of IS workers. In the UK, this demand has crystallised into the notion of the 'hybrid manager'. With the growing importance of user relations and the spread of fourth generation languages, there have been calls—notably, from the British Computer Society—for a reorientation in the skills of IS managers. Anxious to overcome the rift between business objectives and the concerns of technically oriented IS managers, writers have argued for the creation of a new type of 'hybrid manager' who would possess both business knowledge and IT skills. Yet, despite the powerful arguments advanced for this new role —and despite the British Computer Society appeal for the development of 10,000 hybrids by 1995—companies employing hybrid managers remain 'the exception rather than the norm' (Skyrme, 1996: 449). (See Chapter 17.)

On the face of it, this lack of response may seem surprising—if organisations really do need hybrids why have they been so slow to produce them? The explanation, however, seems not to be a matter of the BCS and others misreading organisational needs, but rather of their neglecting labour-market influences on IS careers. The undoubted pressures for change in IS roles and skills are countered by the relative inertia of occupational and labour-market factors. There is evidence, for instance, that employers recruiting from external labour markets do not see any major need for change in IS skills. The personnel requirements specified in job ads have changed little, if at all, over a twenty-year period. A recent study of IS job ads in the USA over the 1970–90 period found remarkable stability in role requirements for different IS groups (Todd et al., 1995) . For example, in relation to programmers, researchers found that: 'little has changed in the composition of these ads over time. The ads indicate that technical knowledge remains paramount . . . with business knowledge . . . slightly lower than systems knowledge' (p. 5). And, in fact, with systems analysts, ads showed an increasing emphasis on technical skills: 'In 1970 about 35 per cent of the ads referenced the need for technical skills. By 1990, about 75 per cent of the ads contained such references' (p. 6).

Nor were IS managers immune from this tendency to look for greater technical expertise. While ads for such positions showed consistent demand for business and systems skills, there was also an increasing reference to technical knowledge. Calls for the incorporation of business and management skills into the IS role have been no less vociferous in the USA than the UK, yet this analysis of job ads suggests that technical skills are no less important now than before, and may even be becoming more important. Reasons for this have to do with the increasing diversity of technologies encompassed by IS, and with the way labour markets work

—technical skills are more easily specified and identified when recruiting externally than, say, people skills.

Organisational conflict

Many of the organisational conflicts surrounding the management of knowledge workers reflect the importation of the wider institutional tensions noted above. Whereas the individual firm is a site of knowledge application, the creation and diffusion of specialist knowledge involves a much broader constituency of organisations and groups. Thus as well as their inward-facing commitments to their employing firm, knowledge workers will also be facing outwards to external networks of technology suppliers, peer communities, and professional associations. In the case of IS staff, these broader 'knowledge communities' (Spender, 1992) comprise the networks linking IS practitioners to each other and to hardware and software suppliers and consultants (Friedman and Cornford, 1989). Barley (1996) even goes so far as to argue that computer workers: 'operate largely independently of an organisation's hierarchy . . . They function as "brokers" who mediate between a firm's users and the larger technical community that creates the hardware and software for a firm's computational infrastructure' (p. 36).

These external networks and communities reinforce the occupational principle and underline the knowledge worker's role as an intermediary between business organisations and technology suppliers.

It follows from this that the more dependent a firm is on external sources of technology and innovation the more that the management of knowledge worker groups will reflect the wider conflict between occupational and administrative principles of control. This conflict is internalised but not resolved by the organisation's division of labour. It resurfaces as the structural and cultural barriers that bedevil relationships between line managers and in-house professional groups. Thus, in developing and applying their occupational knowledge-base, professionals pursue norms and standards which may clash with the business goals of line managers. This is the so-called 'clash of cultures' addressed by Raelin (1991: 1) who comments: 'The inherent conflict between managers and professionals results basically from a clash of cultures: the corporate culture, which captures the commitment of managers, and the professional culture which socialises professionals.'

These cultural divisions are linked to a number of factors, but ultimately derive from the contrasting institutional roles played by managers and expert groups. Managers enjoy delegated authority from the owners of capital, whereas the power of experts comes from their control of valued knowledge. The differentiated roles, career structures, and affiliations of the two groups inevitably create conflicting orientations towards organisational goals.

Individual conflict

Some writers have made a great deal of the tensions between management and knowledge workers (Scarbrough, 1993). Certainly, it is a recurring theme in the information systems literature and crops up very often in the context of poor communications or culture clashes between managers and IS workers. Explanations for the perceived rift often focus on the individual characteristics of IS specialists. These behavioural and attitudinal traits are said to differentiate IS experts from the rest of the organisation and particularly from management. One study, for instance, found that 'the majority of people attracted to the IS profession have some extreme differences from the general corporation population' (Couger, 1996: 432). In comparison with other occupational groups, IS personnel were said to be characterised by: a high growth need for challenge and learning; the lowest need for social interaction; and a high need for feedback.

Studies of this kind suggest that managing knowledge workers is largely to do with reconciling the distinctive personal needs of knowledge workers with the goals of the organisation. In this perspective, creating the right work context for individual knowledge workers can help to adapt them to changing organisational goals. Couger (1996), for instance, claims that managers can adapt their IS personnel to shifting roles by convincing them that 'future advancement is based on an ability to communicate well, and to be successful at interpersonal activities' (p. 434). He is optimistic that 'these personnel can successfully make the transition to the new environments if their managers understand their unique characteristics and plan transition activities to prepare IS professionals properly for their new environments' (p. 434).

Although much can be done to achieve the kind of psychological integration advocated in these studies, focusing exclusively on the individual level of conflict runs the risk of downplaying the important institutional and structural issues described above. Managing knowledge workers on the basis of their personal characteristics glosses over the contextual factors that favour certain characteristics over others. The traits of IS personnel, for example, may be the result of self-selection into certain kinds of work, but they can only persist in a competitive market environment because they also represent a functional adaptation to the demands of such work. Certainly, psychological traits alone could not explain the occupational influences on IS work noted earlier. IS careers are not only structured vertically by the individual organisation but horizontally by occupational grouping (Ginzberg and Baroudi, 1988). In other words, many IS personnel pursue inter-organisational careers that allow them to accumulate specialised skills in a particular technology or method. Whereas the job-hopping of unskilled workers underlines their lack of employment security, for IS workers it frequently represents a rational career strategy that gives them a degree of independence from particular employers. Indeed, it is this labour-market power which ensures that managers go on tolerating the irksome demands and inflated salaries of knowledge work groups such as IS staff.

At the same time, this dependence on the labour market also reminds us that knowledge workers are still workers—in other words, they are still subject to the vagaries of the employment relationship. This relationship fosters both co-operation and conflict between individual and employer; co-operation in the work process yet also potential conflict between their respective goals and interests. Even some of the more upbeat assessments of knowledge work acknowledge this potential conflict. Handy's (1995) argument about the need for knowledge workers to pursue 'portfolio careers', for example, is not only a piece of career advice but also a judgement on the decreasing levels of job security offered by employers.

Handy's advice suggests, though not in so many words, that firms are seeking to *externalise* many of the conflicts created by knowledge work, passing them on to the workforce and to the wider society. Many of the problems created by accelerating industrial change, including the problems of redundant skills and technological unemployment, can be partially absorbed by weakening the ties between employer and employee. The conflict between long-run skills development and short-term efficiency is simply handed on to employees. Knowledge workers are given responsibility for their own skills development and are hired for narrowly defined projects rather than broadly defined jobs. The organisation is able to hire expertise on the basis of immediate need and the individual carries more of the risks of skills development. The result is much greater levels of individual conflict (reflected in psychological stress levels) as knowledge workers have to balance the demands of work and family, and the pressures of the short-term job against the longer-term career.

The quasi-resolution of conflict

I have attempted to show that the managerial problems posed by knowledge workers are not the result of psychological differences or even cultural divisions, though these certainly play a part, but that they reflect a deep-seated conflict between different logics of action, variously embodied in occupational versus administrative principles, professional versus managerial norms, and long-run innovation versus short-term efficiency. In short, this conflict-based account suggests that we need to be wary about supposed 'best practice' in the management of knowledge workers.

Rather, the key to understanding the management process here is to view it as a constant drive towards the quasi-resolution of conflict.

This conflict-based analysis finds a good deal of support from empirical evidence on the management of knowledge workers (e.g. Alvesson, 1993; Kunda, 1992; Starbuck, 1992). Certainly, we find no uniform recipe or single solution, and no style or structure that is able to endure for very long. Instead, we see managers making trade-offs between the different logics of action embodied in, say, organic and mechanistic structures or between managerial efficiency and technological capability.

This is not to say that the management of knowledge workers is in a constant state of flux, with no significant change in the methods and approaches applied. Changes in the wider ecology of knowledge production outlined earlier, not least the impact of IT, have encouraged a move from bureaucratic towards what have been termed 'adhocratic' approaches for managing knowledge work.

The bureaucratic response to managing organisational professionals involved the creation of specialist centralised functions. These usually operated in a fairly uneasy relationship with administrators or line management. They did have the advantage, however, of quasi-resolving organisational conflict by carefully differentiating between the goals and norms of the two different groups. In theory, this separation of functions offered a way of reconciling managerial goals with professional autonomy. Bailyn (1988), for instance, claims that organisational professionals' demands for autonomy can generally be satisfied by the granting of 'operational autonomy'—essentially, the choice of work methods—leaving management the 'strategic autonomy' to determine organisational goals.

This kind of vertical differentiation between management and expert groups was complicated, however, by the need for managers to understand the work processes of such groups. In consequence, organisations often relied on so-called 'player managers' to fulfil this function (Whalley, 1986). Managers with specialist expertise were inserted into the chain of command to provide the necessary blend of technical know-how and managerial authority. This had the added bonus of providing a separate, if truncated, career ladder into management for the expert groups concerned.

But despite its widespread adoption, by and large the bureaucratic solution failed to inspire enthusiastic support. It may have represented the least worst alternative but too often it deferred to vested interests rather than organisational goals. The problems of functional barriers and of a perceived detachment from business aims left the professional bureaucracy highly vulnerable to attack by other groups. Peters (1992) was one of many writers who highlighted the flaws of this approach. He claimed that the experts of the professional bureaucracy resisted learning, cloaked their expertise in unnecessary mystique, and generally became bureaucratic policemen rather than innovators. They were also overrated, because some kinds of expertise (in quality control, for instance) could be readily devolved to line management or employees.

These and similar criticisms of centralised expert functions led many organisations to develop 'bridging mechanisms' that aimed to bridge the gap between line management and specialist groups. Skyrme (1996) outlines a number of 'ways of building bridges between IS and business' (p. 449). These include structural devices such as IS strategy committees, decentralised structures, and IT director roles, as well as processes such as joint business planning and systems development methods.

These bridging mechanisms aim to alleviate some of the worst problems of functional specialisation through organisational means. A further step towards integrating knowledge workers into the organisation involves addressing the individual conflicts outlined above. In its most radical form, this approach leads to the replacement of centralised expert functions with volunteer-driven learning and a 'vestigial structure' to develop and offer consultancy in specialised expertise (Peters, 1992). The aim is to make knowledge more manageable by decentralising it to the problem-solving parts of the organisation. The uneasy relationships between line and support functions are smoothed away through an integrated team-working approach. Equally importantly, specialist knowledge is thus problem driven not discipline driven.

Mintzberg coined the term 'operating adhocracy', to describe this kind of organisation. He contrasts it with professional bureaucracy in the following way:

Faced with a client problem, the operating adhocracy encourages a creative effort to find a novel solution; the professional bureaucracy pigeonholes it into a known contingency to which it can apply a standard program. One engages in divergent thinking aimed at innovation; the other in convergent thinking aimed at perfection. (Mintzberg, 1983: 257)

There is ample evidence of organisations attempting to move in the direction sketched out by Peters and Mintzberg, using project teams and other adhocratic forms to manage their knowledge workers. This is partly a reflection of their unhappiness with traditional bureaucratic approaches, but also seems to reflect the longer-term erosion of many of the institutional causes of organisational conflict (Gibbons et al., 1994). This erosion has been produced by the increasing reach of market forces and the consequent blurring of distinctions between the economic domain of business and the cultural and intellectual domains of professionals and scientists. Professional and semi-professional groups ranging from medical practitioners to R&D scientists are increasingly subject to the disciplines of market forces and control by a management hierarchy (Whittington, 1991: Whittington et al., 1994). The influence of professional institutions has been weakened both by deregulation and globalization, and by IT systems that threaten professional autonomy with surveillance and remote control.

Implications for IS

The management of knowledge workers has a number of important implications for the IS field. The most obvious implication is to do with the tools and support systems provided by IS functions. As the role of IS evolves from the processing of data to the support of knowledge-based work, there will be a need to integrate the technical system of the firm not only with the social system, but also by extension with the firm's 'knowledge system'. In the first instance, such integration will certainly involve developing new tools and infrastructures for the knowledge worker including data-mining from data warehouses, decision support systems, groupware, and conceptual mapping tools. However, addressing the knowledge system means more than fitting IS tools to the needs of a new-style workforce. It also means addressing 'knowledge management' in its widest sense.

According to Earl (1996), knowledge management involves developing an 'ethos of knowledge as strategy' (p. 48). By this, he seems to mean the creation of the right motivational environment: 'If organisation members are to share knowledge, collaborate and be willing to learn continuously, the incentive and support must be present' (p. 48). However, the earlier conflict-based analysis of knowledge work suggests that this is more easily said than done. Management are frequently tempted to adopt what might be termed 'absolutist' solutions to their organisational problems. Business process re-engineering and outsourcing, for example, both promise in their different ways to 'obliterate' the kinds of conflict described above (Hammer and Champy, 1993). My analysis makes enough points about the deep-rooted nature of the conflicts surrounding knowledge workers to warrant some scepticism about such organisation-centred recipes. These absolutist approaches place the emphasis on externalising conflict, either by removing functional conflicts or by empowering the customer. However, this involves an assumption that knowledge can be treated as either a commodity or an organisational asset—an assumption which seems to be challenged by the unhappy experience of many firms adopting these strategies (Lacity et al., 1994; Grint, 1995).

An alternative approach to knowledge management involves rejecting *absolutist* solutions in favour of a more *pluralist* approach. Instead of externalising the conflicts surrounding knowledge workers, this involves developing the organisation so that it is pluralistic enough to accommodate them. Different cultures and logics of action could be allowed to thrive alongside each other without subordinating one to the other.

Some advocates of pluralism argue their case on strictly pragmatic grounds. Ginzberg and Baroudi (1988), for example, view the issue in terms of the motivation and retention of technical expertise in a competitive labour market. Arguing from the occupational affinities of IS experts, they suggest that 'the organisation must determine what the occupational community values, and make these options available internally' (p. 592). Spender (1992) extends the argument further by highlighting the links between corporate innovation and external 'knowledge communities' and networks. 'In due course', he says, 'the management of the technologically-intensive firm is forced towards a pluralistic form of organisation in which the organisation itself becomes a community of communities' (1992: 412).

Pluralism in this context also means accepting paradox—in short, the ability to work with two contradictory logics simultaneously. The example of the so-called 'skunkworks' at 3M where innovators were able to 'boot-leg' as much as 15 per cent of their budget to apply to their own pet projects is one of the best-known examples of this kind of pluralism (Peters, 1988). Another example is the paradox that we see in the informal knowledge networks which proliferate in R&D environments. One recent study of R&D scientists and academic specialists (Kreiner and Schultz, 1993) found management turning a blind eye to informal networking so that industry–university relationships could be developed. Achieving the firm's long-term goals of innovation meant selectively setting aside the pursuit of control and efficiency.

The problems of tapping the knowledge of distributed networks of knowledge workers apply both inside and outside organisations. Boland and Tenkasi (1995), for example, argue that even within a firm knowledge is distributed and embedded in different social communities. It follows that 'the problem of integration of knowledge in knowledge-intensive firms is not a problem of simply combining, sharing or making data commonly available. It is a problem of perspective taking in which the unique thought worlds of different communities of knowing are made visible and accessible to others' (p. 359). Again this leads to a paradox: 'In order to integrate knowledge through perspective taking, communication systems must first support diversity of knowledge through the differentiation provided by perspective making within communities of knowing' (p. 359).

The adoption of a pluralist approach to managing knowledge workers is based on a recognition that suppressing diversity and conflict means suppressing creativity and innovation. More than that, though, it also leads to a redefinition of the problem itself. Pluralist writers tend to see the fundamental problems in managing knowledge as deriving not from the workforce, but from the habits and preoccupations of management. Put simply, one of the major obstacles to the pluralist approach is management itself (Scarbrough and Burrell, 1996). Whether it be the self-interest of middle management or the entrenched roles that they occupy, managers find it difficult to accept anything that involves the relaxation of their ability to command and control. Indeed, the very idea of a more pluralist organisation offends both managerial theory and managerial instincts. As Barley comments:

Neither managerial theory nor managerial culture currently offers administrators viable models of how to co-ordinate fragmenting expertise. Partly as a result, even when firms earnestly wish to adopt more collaborative methods, hierarchical practices and ideologies frequently re-establish themselves. (Barley, 1996: 46)

Given these deeply ingrained instincts and assumptions, the pluralist organisation is less in need of 're-engineering' than the 'imagineering' advocated by Morgan (1986). Only by imaginatively addressing the conflicts, ambiguities, and paradoxes posed by knowledge work will management succeed in harnessing it to business goals. And—paradoxically—the first step in achieving that may be to question the pursuit of business goals as the sole criterion of knowledge and value for the organisation.

References

Abbott, A. (1988), *The System of Professions* (London: University of Chicago Press).

Alvesson, M. (1995), *Management of Knowledge-Intensive Companies* (Berlin: Walter de Gruyter).

Argyris, C. (1991), 'Teaching Smart People How to Learn', *Harvard Business Review*, May–June.

Armstrong, P. (1992), 'The Engineering Dimension and the Management Education Movement', in Lee and Smith (1992).

Bailyn, L. (1988), 'Autonomy in the Industrial R&D Lab', in R. Katz (ed.), *Managing Professionals in Innovative Organisations* (New York: Ballinger Publishing Co.).

Barley, S. R. (1996), *The New World of Work* (London: British-North American Committee).

Bell, D. (1973), *The Coming of Post-industrial Society* (New York: Basic Books).

Blackler, F. (1995), 'Knowledge, Knowledge Work and Organisations: An Overview and Interpretation', *Organisation Studies*, 16, 6: 1021–46.

Boland, R. J., and Tenkasi, R. V. (1995), 'Perspective Making and Perspective Taking in Communities of Knowing', *Organisation Science*, 6, 4: 350–72.

Burns, T., and Stalker, G. M. (1961), *The Management of Innovation* (London: Tavistock Publications).

Burrell, G. (1996), 'Hard Times for the Salariat?', in Scarbrough (1996).

Couger, D. (1996), 'The Changing Environment for IS Professionals: Human Resource Implications', in Earl (1996).

Cyert, R. M., and March, J. G. (1963), *A Behavioral Theory of the Firm* (Englewood Cliffs, NJ: Prentice Hall).

Davenport, T. H., Jarvenpaa, S. L., and Beers, M. C. (1996), 'Improving Knowledge Work Processes', *Sloan Management Review*, Summer: 53–65.

Davis, J., and Stack, M. (1992), 'Knowledge in Production', *Race & Class*, 34, 3: 111–14.

Drucker, P. F. (1969), *The Age of Discontinuity: Guidelines for our Changing Society* (New York: Harper & Row).

—— (1988), 'The Coming of the New Organisation', *Harvard Business Review*, Jan.–Feb.: 45–53.

Earl, M. J. (1996) (ed.), *Information Management: The Organisational Dimension* (Oxford: Oxford University Press).

Feldman, S. P. (1989), 'The Broken Wheel: The Inseparability of Autonomy and Control in Innovation within Organisations', *Journal of Management Studies*, 26, 2: 83–102.

Fischer, F. (1990), *Technocracy and the Politics of Expertise* (London: Sage).

Freidson, E. (1986), *Professional Powers* (Chicago: University of Chicago Press).

—— (1994), *Professionalism Reborn: Theory, Prophecy and Policy* (Cambridge: Polity Press).

Friedman, A. (1987), 'Specialist Labour in Japan and the Subcontracting System: The Case of Computer Specialists', *British Journal of Industrial Relations*, 25: 353–69.

—— with Cornford, S. D. (1989), *Computer Systems Development: History, Organisation and Implementation* (Chichester: Wiley & Sons).

Gershuny, J. (1978), *After Industrial Society? The Emerging Self-Service Economy* (London: Macmillan).

Gibbons, M. (1994), *The New Production of Knowledge: The Dynamics of Science and Research in Contemporary Society* (London: Sage).

Ginzberg, M. J., and Baroudi, J. J. (1988), 'MIS Careers: A Theoretical Perspective', *Communications of the ACM*, 31, 5: 586–94.

Grant, R. M. (1991), 'The Resource-Based Theory of Competitive Advantage: Implications for Strategy Formulation', *California Management Review*, 34, Spring: 114–35.

Grint, K. (1995), 'Utopian Reengineering', in G. Burke and J. Peppard (eds.), *Examining BPR: Current Perspectives and Research Directions* (London: Kogan Page).

Hammer, M., and Champy, J. (1993), *Reengineering the Corporation: A Manifesto for Business Revolution* (New York: Harper Collins).

Handy, C. (1995), *Beyond Certainty: The Changing World of Organisations* (London: Hutchinson).

Hemel, G., and Prahalad, C. K. (1994), *Competing for the Future* (Boston: Harvard Business School Press).

Karpik, L. (1978) (ed.), *Organisation and Environment: Theory, Issues and Reality* (London: Sage).

Knights, D., Murray, F., and Willmott, H. (1993), 'Networking as Knowledge Work: A Study of Interorganisational Development in the Financial Services Sector', *Journal of Management Studies*, 30: 975–96.

Kreiner, K., and Schultz, M. (1993), 'Informal Collaboration in R&D: The Formation of Networks across Organisations', *Organisation Studies*, 14, 2: 189–209.

Kumar, K. (1978), *Prophecy and Progress: The Sociology of Industrial and Post-industrial Society* (London: Allen Lane).

—— (1995), *From Post-industrial to Post-modern Society: New Theories of the Contemporary World* (Oxford: Blackwell).

Kunda, G. (1992), *Engineering Culture: Control and Commitment in a High-Tech Corporation* (Philadelphia: Temple University Press).

Lacity, M. C., Hirschheim, R., and Willcocks, L. (1994), 'Realizing Outsourcing Expectations: Incredible Expectations, Credible Outcomes', *Information Systems Management*, Fall: 7–18.

Lakatos, I. (1974), 'Time and Theory in Sociology', in J. Rex (ed.), *Sociology* (London: Routledge).

Lee, G. L., and Smith, C. (1992), *Engineers and Management: International Comparisons* (London: Routledge).

McGovern, P. (1995), 'To Retain or not to Retain: Multinational Firms and Technical Labour', *Human Resource Management Journal*, 5, 4: 7–23.

Machlup, F. (1990), *Knowledge: Its Creation, Distribution and Economic Significance*, vol. i (Princeton: Princeton University Press).

Mintzberg, H. (1983), *Structure in Fives: Designing Effective Organisations* (Englewood Cliffs, NJ: Prentice-Hall).

Morgan, G. (1986), *Images of Organisations* (Beverly Hills, Calif.: Sage).

OECD (1996), *Technology, Productivity and Job Creation*, i: *Highlights* (Paris: OECD).

Peters, T. J. (1988), 'A Skunkworks Tale', in R. Katz (ed.), *Managing Professionals in Innovative Organisations* (New York: Ballinger Publishing Co.).

—— (1992), *Liberation Management: Necessary Disorganisation for Nanosecond Nineties* (London: Macmillan).

Quinn, J. B., Anderson, P., and Finkelstein, S. (1996), 'Managing Professional Intellect: Making the Most of the Best', *Harvard Business Review*, 74, Mar.–Apr.: 71–80.

Raelin, J. A. (1991), The Clash of Cultures: Managers Managing Professionals (Boston: Harvard Business School Press).

Reich, R. (1991), *The Wealth of Nations: Preparing Ourselves for 21st Century Capitalism* (London: Simon & Schuster).

Ritzer, G. (1993), *The McDonaldization of Society* (London: Pine Forge Press).

Scarbrough, H. (1993), 'Problem-Solutions in the Management of Information Systems Expertise', *Journal of Management Studies*, 30, 6: 939–55.

—— (1995), 'Blackboxes, Hostages and Prisoners', *Organisation Studies*, 16, 6: 991–1021.

—— (1996) (ed.), *The Management of Expertise* (London: Macmillan).

—— and Burrell, G. (1996), 'The Axeman Cometh: The Changing Roles and Knowledges of Middle Managers', in S. Clegg and G. Palmer (eds.), *The Politics of Management Knowledge* (London: Sage).

Sewell, G., and Wilkinson, B. (1992), 'Someone to Watch over me: Surveillance, Discipline and the Just-in-Time Labour Process', *Sociology*, 26, 2: 271–90.

Skyrme, D. J. (1996), 'The Hybrid Manager', in Earl (1996).

Spender, J. C. (1992), 'Knowledge Management: Putting your Technology Strategy on Track', in T. Khalil and B. A. Bakravtar (eds.), *Management of Technology*, (Norcross, Ga.: Institute of Industrial Engineers): iii. 1011–29.

Starbuck, W. H. (1992), 'Learning by Knowledge Intensive Firms', *Journal of Management Studies*, 29, 6, Nov.: 713–40.

Stehr, N. (1994), *Knowledge Societies* (London: Sage).

Tjaden, G. S. (1996), 'Measuring the Information Age Business', *Technology Analysis and Strategic Management*, 8, 3: 233–45.

Todd, P. A., McKeen, J. D., and Gallupe, R. B. (1995), 'The Evolution of IS Job Skills: A Content Analysis of IS Job Advertisements from 1970 to 1990', *MIS Quarterly*, 19, 1: 1–28.

Whalley, P. (1986), *The Social Production of Technical Work* (London: Macmillan).
Whittington, R. (1991), 'Changing Control Strategies in Industrial R&D', *R&D Management*, 21: 43–53.
—— (1993), *What is Strategy—and Does it Matter?* (London: Routledge).
Whittington, R., McNulty, T., and Whipp, R. (1994), 'Market-Driven Change in Professional Services: Problems and Processes', *Journal of Management Studies*, 31, 6: 829–46.

Postscript

The central message of this volume on 'Rethinking Management Information Systems: An Interdisciplinary Perspective' is to encourage a broader intellectual and interdisciplinary approach to the subject of MIS, broadly conceived. Whilst it is not our intention to argue the case for establishing MIS as a discipline in its own right, we nonetheless contend that its status should at least be equal to other quasi-disciplines within business and management education.[1] In common with these subject areas, MIS suffers from a lack of theoretical coherence and methodological rigour. Yet this diversity has enabled MIS to amass a vast body of knowledge on a variety of topics, many of which are discussed in this volume.

To a large extent, MIS is an emerging and dynamic field, offering a fertile ground for research work. But like other subject areas, it must not succumb to the pitfalls of building theoretical and methodological barriers which ultimately serve to create intellectual tunnel vision. For, as we have seen in the pages of this volume, MIS is more fruitfully served when researchers seek to broaden their intellectual horizons by venturing into other disciplinary territories. Indeed, many of the more enduring theoretical contributions like socio-technical theory, systems thinking, and structuration theory, to name only three, have influenced and informed current thinking on MIS. These ideas, along with others (past and present), have helped to define what we now think of as MIS. Put another way, MIS has its theoretical, empirical, and methodological antecedents in the so-called reference disciplines.[2]

As we approach the twenty-first century, the golden anniversary of MIS will be marked by new thinking on themes and perspectives which are currently emerging. For example, the Internet and electronic commerce[3] offer much scope for future projects within MIS, and the wider business and management domain. Conversely, ideas like business process re-engineering, total quality management, activity based costing, and just-in-

---

[1] These disciplines are notably HRM, corporate strategy, marketing, and accounting and finance.

[2] Reference disciplines are sociology, history, philosophy, psychology, economics (see also Chapter 1 by Alan Lee).

[3] It is likely that the Internet and electronic commerce will have significant implications for business organisations in four key areas: supply chain management and logistics; the role of suppliers as intermediaries or 'cybermediaries'; standardisation and customisation of technology; and payment and security systems. All these areas will generate new research interests within the field of MIS.

time, though still topical, may cease to be of much interest to academic and practitioner communities over time. This is not to suggest that we adopt a sell-by-date perspective on ideas, but merely to recognise that MIS is a changing and dynamic field of investigation, and one which is not conducive to 'quick-fix' management panaceas. As we have attempted to show in this volume, the influence of past ideas on present forms of thinking within MIS is critical for understanding and even speculating on possible future trends and outcomes. We therefore suggest that we should become increasingly eclectic about the contributions we use to inform our research enquiries. Whilst this may avoid reinventing the wheel with new management fads every few years, it may also broaden international research agendas by encouraging deeper and more rigorous intellectual analysis. Such an approach may mean that progress in thinking and re-thinking MIS may take the form of a few small steps at a time. But at least this will avoid the 'big bang' approach of new fads and solutions which have, in practice, not served the MIS community well over the years.

INDEX